Cement-based Composites: Materials, Mechanical Properties and Performance

Other books on Concrete Materials and Structures from E & FN Spon

Alternative Materials for the Reinforcement and Prestressing of Concrete
Edited by J.L. Clarke

Autoclaved Aerated Concrete – Properties, Testing and Design
RILEM

Building the Future: Innovation in Design, Materials and Construction
Edited by F.K. Garas, G.S.T. Armer and J.L. Clarke

Concrete 2000: Economic and durable concrete construction through excellence
Edited by R.K. Dhir and M.R. Jones

Concrete in Hot Environments
I. Soroka

Construction Materials – Their Nature and Behaviour
Edited by J.M. Illston

Creep and Shrinkage of Concrete
Edited by Z.P. Bažant and I. Carol

Durability of Building Materials and Components 6
Edited by S. Nagataki, T. Nireki and F. Tomosawa

Fibre Reinforced Cement and Concrete
Edited by R.N. Swamy

Fibre Reinforced Cementitious Composites
A. Bentur and S. Mindess

Fly Ash in Concrete: Properties and Performance
Edited by K. Wesche

Fracture and Damage of Concrete and Rock – FDCR-2
Edited by H.P. Rossmanith

High Performance Concrete: From Material to Structure
Edited by Y. Malier

High Performance Fiber-Reinforced Cement Composites
Edited by H.W. Reinhardt and A.E. Naaman

Hydration and Setting of Cements
Edited by A. Nonat and J.-C. Mutin

Interfaces in Cementitious Composites
Edited by J.C. Maso

Polymer Composites for Civil and Structural Engineering
L. Hollaway

Special Concretes: Workability and Mixing
Edited by P.J.M. Bartos

Structural Grouts
Edited by P.L.J. Domone and S.A. Jefferis

Structural Lightweight Aggregate Concrete
Edited by J.L. Clarke

Cement-based Composites: Materials, Mechanical Properties and Performance

A.M. BRANDT

Institute of Fundamental Technological Research
Polish Academy of Sciences
Poland

E & FN SPON
An Imprint of Chapman & Hall
London · Glasgow · Weinheim · New York · Tokyo · Melbourne · Madras

Published by E & FN Spon, an imprint of Chapman & Hall, 2–6 Boundary Row, London SE1 8HN, UK

Chapman & Hall, 2–6 Boundary Row, London SE1 8HN, UK

Blackie Academic & Professional, Wester Cleddens Road, Bishopbriggs, Glasgow G64 2NZ, UK

Chapman & Hall GmbH, Pappelallee 3, 69469 Weinheim, Germany

Chapman & Hall USA, One Penn Plaza, 41st Floor, New York NY10119, USA

Chapman & Hall Japan, ITP-Japan, Kyowa Building, 3F, 2-2-1 Hirakawacho, Chiyoda-ku, Tokyo 102, Japan

Chapman & Hall Australia, Thomas Nelson Australia, 102 Dodds Street, South Melbourne, Victoria 3205, Australia

Chapman & Hall India, R. Seshadri, 32 Second Main Road, CIT East, Madras 600 035, India

First edition 1995

Typeset in 10/12 pts Times by Thomson Press (India) Ltd, New Delhi
Printed in Great Britain by St Edmundsbury Press, Bury St Edmunds, Suffolk

ISBN 0 419 19110 0

A catalogue record for this book is available from the British Library

∞ Printed on acid-free text paper, manufactured in accordance with ANSI/NISO Z39.48–1992 (Permanence of Paper).

Contents

Preface

This book is the result of the author's studies and research during the last few years. In that time not only has research activity created a basis of some general and particular opinions, but also it was possible to gather remarks and comments of many outstanding scientists and professional engineers encountered on different occasions: internal seminars at the Institute in Warsaw, national and international workshops and conferences, visits to universities in several countries, etc. It is impossible to mention here all those who at many of these occasions and in various forms agreed to share with the author their research results, comments, doubts and opinions. Without all the friendly contacts with numerous outstanding personalities the book could never have appeared and very kind thoughts are addressed to them.

In the rapid development of the science in the last few decades, a book covering in a limited volume a relatively large scope of knowledge cannot attempt to encapsulate all the problems or develop them in a homogeneous way and with equal competence. Unavoidably, several advanced readers will find ommissions, mistakes and imprecisions. Certain chapters are written in more detail than others. With certain problems the author had less personal experience than in others. All these weaknesses of the book are due to the author's subjective viewpoint and to his incompetence. All fruits of human activity are imperfect and that is the case with this book. It is the author's hope that the most dissatisfied readers will decide to write something better in the near future.

It is the author's pleasure and obligation to present thanks and acknowledgements to several individuals who accepted to help him in preparation of the book.

The thanks are addressed to my closest co-workers·in the Department of Strain Fields of the Institute of Fundamental Technological Research (IFTR), Polish Academy of Sciences in Warsaw, namely to Professor J. Kasperkiewicz, Dr A. Burakiewicz, Dr M.A. Glinicki, Dr M. Marks, and Dr J. Potrzebowski. Without their cooperation in all tests and studies and their helpful discussions it would have been impossible to prepare this book. Thanks are due to Mr M. Sobczak, who prepared the majority of drawings and participated at certain tests. Among other members of the staff of IFTR special thanks are addressed to Professor W. Marks who agreed to participate in research which completed Chapter 13. Results mentioned in Sections 10.4 and 10.5 were based on experiments carried out by Professor G. Prokopski at the Czestochowa Technical University with competence and courage.

Particularly warm thanks are due to Professor L. Kucharska from the Wroclaw Technical University who kindly agreed to read most of the chapters and who made many useful comments and criticisms.

Partial financial support in completing Chapter 13 was provided by the National Committee for Research in Poland (Grant No. 700409101) which is gratefully acknowledged.

The book was written while the author was a staff member of the IFTR, Centre of Mechanics, and all support from colleagues and administration is kindly acknowledged.

Kind cooperation and patience exhibited by the staff of Chapman & Hall in London and particularly by Ms Susan Hodgson and Mr Nick Clarke is acknowledged with pleasure.

Warsaw, November 1993

1 Introduction

The term 'cement-based composites' requires some explanations. Why not simply 'cements and concretes'? The proposed term covers in fact a larger group of materials and is justified by various reasons.

Cement mortars and concretes have been used extensively in their present form since the beginning of our century. There is no need to set out here their history or to describe their properties and applied technologies, because nearly every year several excellent books are published on these subjects. However, there is perhaps at present a new phase of development of Portland cement-based materials, stimulated by the following circumstances:

1. New types of these materials appear and are available for professional engineers. They satisfy new performance demands but also require research and testing. In certain materials, traditional components disappear, e.g. Portland cement in polymer concretes.
2. New theoretical and experimental methods are available taken from various technical fields but mainly from high strength advanced composites.
3. Concrete-like materials behaviour is more correctly understood and these materials are better used in practice when a similar modern approach is applied to them as to the composite materials.

New concrete-like materials are developed to satisfy particular requirements in present day building and civil engineering works. Corrosive environments and decreased material durability, impact and thermal actions imposed on industrial structures and building facades, degradation due to freezing and thawing of modern highways and runways, the necessity to abandon asbestos fibres – these are only examples of situations which are common in many industrialized countries. Traditional concretes cannot satisfy new requirements and concrete structures do not behave satisfactorily in all circumstances: it is sufficient to mention that in all countries many concrete structures require considerable effort and money to restore and maintain their serviceability because they have failed to fulfil their planned purpose.

Durability is one of the most important aspects considered in the book. It is the author's strong belief that using present knowledge and without any great increase in unit cost it will be possible in the near future to avoid the necessity of restoring and rehabilitating the thousands of civil engineering and building structures which after only a few years are nearly in an unserviceable state.

Cement-based materials correspond well to the definition of composites. Their behaviour and properties may be better understood, designed and predicted using a modern approach than was possible on the basis of traditional concrete technology. These materials belong to a larger group of brittle matrix composites which among others also contains ceramics. This approach is consequently followed throughout the book.

Advanced composite materials used in vehicles and aircraft are designed and manufactured using the results of extensive studies. Non-classical phenomena like cracking, fracture, plastic deformations and fatigue are considered to assure adequate fracture toughness and reliability in various situations. These methods are now available also for cement-based composites and are considered in detail in the book because their direct application is not possible: if the basic notions and methods are similar, other features and all quantitative relations are completely different. That is the reason why the mechanics of concrete-like composites requires a new set of rules, methods and research results which should bridge the gap between material scientists and civil engineers. This book is a modest attempt to collect together the available knowledge in this field.

There is another special aspect of cement-based materials, mainly in comparison with high strength composites: they are used in large quantities and therefore they cannot be too expensive or their technologies too sophisticated. Local component materials should be used and relatively simple manufacturing methods should be adopted. Consequently, the design and testing methods should account for all these circumstances.

In the book, information on classical cement-based composites, their properties and technology, is limited to a strict minimum. On the other hand, new composite materials with special internal structures are examined in more detail and traditional materials are also studied using the composite approach. Material structure and composition, crack propagation and control, the influence of interfacial zones and of debonding processes are described using theoretical studies, experimental results and practical examples.

One of the features of composites is the importance of their internal structure. It is well known that the same volume of the main components, but arranged differently in space, may produce completely different materials. That observation leads to material design and optimization also in cement-based materials. The rational composition of layers, pores, fibres and particles may respond perfectly and in the cheapest way to particular requirements of exploitation or to production technology. That way of thinking may help to tailor-make concrete and to improve concrete structures' design and execution.

To keep the length of the book within acceptable limits many problems which are usually included in lectures for students at technical universities are here omitted or presented very briefly. For many questions which are perhaps peripheral to the book's scope, the reader is referred to selected references where basic data may be found. Also, concrete-like composites without cement, such as polymer concretes (PC) and bitumen concretes, are only briefly mentioned. For similar reasons the scope of the book is limited to materials, and the problems of structures are not considered. Mechanical properties—strength, deformability, fracture toughness, etc. – are more closely examined than other physical properties of cement-based composites. The reader is also referred to many original papers and reports where detailed data are given and opinions are explained at full length.

The book is not a traditional collection of detailed information about one material after another. It would be perhaps inappropriate to present in such a way this field of materials science in which progress has been so fast in the last decades: new materials and technologies appear nearly every year. Such a presentation could become obsolete soon after its publication.

The aim of this book is to analyse, together with the reader, how to examine material properties and behaviour in relation to material structure and composition. That understanding is then applied to particular problems which arise in material design, execution, testing and prediction of properties.

In the first three chapters the basic notions are introduced and the main groups of materials are presented. The next four chapters concern different components or phases, their properties and distribution which form a material structure. The following chapters deal with the main mechanical properties of the materials considered and describe their characteristic features in various loading and environmental conditions. In the closing chapters problems related to design and optimization are considered, together with some remarks about the economics of these materials. The chapters consider the main problems and questions which should be solved by an engineer attempting to apply non-classical cement-based materials or to understand better the behaviour of classical ones. These chapters are also addressed to the researcher who wants to be familiar with the modern approach to the mechanics of cement-based materials. This kind of presentation should help to deal also with new materials which will appear or will find their application in the next few years.

The future will bring many new solutions to the present problems in design, testing and exploitation of cement-based composites, but, as in all other fields of human knowledge, without any doubt there will appear more questions than answers.

2 Composites and multiphase materials

2.1 Properties and requirements

A multiphase material is usually defined as a heterogeneous medium composed of two or more materials or phases which occupy separate regions in space. If the term 'multiphase materials' is understood to include the larger group containing natural and man-made materials, the term 'composites' is more often reserved for man-made ones.

The properties of a composite or multiphase material derive not only from those of its constituents but there are also synergetic properties. This means that some properties may be derived from the properties of constituents and their volume fractions using the rule of mixtures. Others, however, are different and new and are caused by interactions between the constituents. These interactions are called synergetic effects and are important for understanding the behaviour of composites, cf. Section 2.5.

Two conclusions are obvious from these definitions.

1. Between separate regions occupied by component materials there are boundaries in which mutual interactions are transferred; this is a clear difference between composites and alloys.
2. Unlike in mixtures, certain properties of composite materials cannot be simply deduced from their composition and must be specially determined, in most cases by experiments.

In the above definitions, a phase is understood as a region of a material that has uniform physical and chemical properties. This means that, not only are cement paste and rock aggregate grains or voids different phases in concrete when it is considered as a composite material, but, for example, so also are any water or ice which fills these voids.

In various books and manuals the above definitions are formulated in slightly different ways but the differences have rather formal character and do not deserve much attention here.

Multiphase natural materials like bone, timber and rock have been encountered and used by humans since the beginning of their existence. Composites have also been known for several thousands of years. The first reference to mud bricks reinforced by straw is to be found in Exodus, the second book of the Old Testament. Layers of mud with chopped straw or horse hair were used for roads in Babylon and in China. The Babylonians and Assyrians bonded stone and semi-baked bricks together with natural bitumens. Plaited straw with mud or clay was used to build walls independently by civilizations in different parts of the world. Gypsum and lime mortars are found in Egyptian pyramids. In the ancient Roman Empire the use of natural pozzolanic binders with sand and crushed stone helped to build the magnificent structures which are still admired in present times.

The use of composites was not limited to building materials. Medieval armour and swords in China and Japan .were constructed with wrought iron and steel forged together. In Central Asia, bows were built of animal tendons, timber lamellae and silk threads with adhesives as binding agents. The resulting laminated composites had ductility and hardness from their constituents but toughness was one of the synergetic effects of their behaviour.

The continuity of application of composites is reflected in modern languages and certain words in materials science have common Latin origins. For example, the word *caementum* meant finely crushed ceramics with binding properties. The word *betunium* was used to designate a mixture of stone and crushed bricks with lime or pozzolanic mortar. Also, the word *pozzolana* was taken from the locality of Pozzuoli near Naples where volcanic tuffs were found in abundance. *Concretus* meant something which had grown together.

The evolution of materials engineering over the centuries was perhaps less spectacular than the evolution of structures but certainly more important for human civilization. In archaeology some periods are named after the mastery or universality of particular materials used for weapons, tools and jewelry: the Neolithic periods – the last part of the Stone Age – was followed by the Bronze Age and the Iron Age.

In modern times there are several examples when an advance in new forms of construction was not possible until an appropriate material was available. The prestressing of concrete structures was attempted in the years 1938–44 in Germany with negative results. The reason was very simple: ordinary low quality steel was used for the prestressing wires. The relaxation of the steel and creep of the concrete quickly reduced the designed prestressing force to zero. But in 1945 the series of successful tests by G. Magnel in Belgium and E. Freyssinet in France were based on high strength steel with a yield point over 1000 MPa, where losses due to both the above-mentioned effects were equal only to a small percentage of the imposed prestressing force.

As another example, titanium-based alloys may be mentioned. Their application in the aircraft industry permitted the barrier imposed by elevated temperature at high speed to be overcome, which had previously ruled out the use of aluminium and magnesium alloys, and new generations of airplanes were built with great success.

In recent times the application of composite materials is growing rapidly. It is difficult to find a field of technical activity or objects produced for everyday life where composites are not used. The materials science dealing with composites has become an independent branch of science in itself and not just a part of metallurgy as it was before. Faculties at universities, research institutes and international organizations are concerned with materials science and technology. Many types of production of advanced composites are considered as symbols and proof of technical development in most advanced countries.

The recent progress in composite materials is connected to new requirements imposed on modern equipment in industry, building, transportation and other fields. These requirements cannot be satisfied either by natural materials or by metallic alloys. Composite materials are therefore indispensable with their tailored properties, obtained by optimum material design and appropriate technology. These properties are of various characters: starting from high strength and low deformability through low weight and excellent insulation properties, up to enhanced toughness and temperature resistance. Limiting the considerations to mechanical properties only, it may be concluded that in composite materials two main goals are achieved: high strength or hardness simultaneously with appropriate ductility or toughness.

There is a special group of requirements imposed on composite materials which concern the cost and production conditions. In several fields of application of composites for very expensive equipment only small volumes of material are needed for the safety or reliability of the entire systems. For example, thin layers of high temperature resistant materials used for shields of space craft and for cutting edges of tools are made of particularly hard composites. In these cases the unit price of an appropriate composite may be of lesser importance in view of the high overall cost of the equipment and the enhanced performance. The performance viewpoint is vital, among others, in aircraft construction: if certain metallic parts can be replaced by composite ones with lower weight, this saving may be used to increase payload or range or both, and in that way the overall performance of that aircraft may be completely changed, largely covering the extra cost of the composite material used. An interesting review of this question for commercial and military airplanes produced in the USA is given in [2.1].

The situation is completely different for composite materials applied in building and civil engineering. Their unit price must be well adapted for the large volumes of material used, to ensure the right proportions between the cost of all parts of the work, as was mentioned in Chapter 1. But here, also, there are particular regions where a small amount of a high quality material can considerably improve the performance of the entire structure, cf. Chapter 14.

Similar differences exist in manufacturing methods. High strength composites are produced in specialized factories or laboratories with sophisticated equipment and in precisely controlled conditions. Cement-based materials are often manufactured *in situ* or in field factories where only simple technologies are possible and where quite large variations in composition and component properties are unavoidable.

All these questions are developed in more detail in the next chapters.

It may be concluded from the above, that composites are strongly heterogeneous and anisotropic materials, with random and irregular or regular internal arrangement of different phases. Their properties and behaviour result from their constituents' composition, distribution in space (structure) and also from their interaction (synergetic properties). Their behaviour is conditioned also by local effects at interfaces between matrix and inclusions.

Composites may be characterized according to the kind of their anisotropy. The structural anisotropy created by appropriate distribution of fibres or inclusions should be distinguished from anisotropy of crystals or natural organic materials like bone or wood. The anisotropy of composites is generated more or less purposefully, according to design and adequate technology. At various scales composites with random, unidirectional, bi-directional (laminates) and multidirectional anisotropy are produced.

2.2 Components of composite materials

The components of composite materials may be presented in a somewhat simplified way in three main groups: binders, fillers and reinforcements. That classification is based on functions fulfilled by the components, but all three groups are not always represented by different materials. Sometimes the roles of particular components are more complicated, for example, in polymer concretes the polymers play both roles of binder and reinforcement for the aggregate grain skeleton.

In another classification of composite components attention is paid to their characteristic form. The continuous phase (matrix) is embedding the dispersed phase (inclusions). The inclusions may have the form of more or less regular particles and grains, fibres and pores or voids separated or interconnected. The terms matrix and inclusions may be used at different levels: the matrix itself may be composed of inclusions embedded in a binder.

Between matrix and inclusions there is an intermediary region called the interface. Stresses are transmitted from matrix to inclusions (particles, grains or fibres), and vice versa, through that interface. Local failures occurring there in the form of plastic yielding or cracks modify considerably the behaviour of the composite material under external actions.

Binders are the materials which by their binding properties and bond to other components assure the transmission of stresses. The chemical or mechanical bond (friction) may play a more important role according to the constituent properties and situation. The binders are used as matrices or they form matrices together with other constituents, e.g. smaller inclusions.

A few large groups of matrices may be mentioned: polymers, cement-based materials, metals, bitumens and ceramics. In Table 2.1 the examples of binders are listed with their mechanical characteristics. The data given in that table, as well as in the others in the book, should be considered only as general information not suitable for particular calculations, because the variety of materials used all over the world and the new kinds appearing each year on the market do not allow the preparation of comprehensive listings.

Table 2.1 Examples of binders and matrices of composite materials

Type of material	Density γ $\times 10^3$(kg/m^3)	Strength compr. f_c (MPa)	Strength tensile f_t (MPa)	Modulus of elast. E (GPa)	f_t/γ $\times 10^6$(mm)	E/γ $\times 10^6$(mm)
Hydraulic binders:						
Lime paste	1.0	1–10	0.2		0.02	
Gypsum paste	1.2	10–12	3.0		0.25	
Portland cement paste	2.0–2.2	10–25	2.0–9.0	10–20	0.10–0.41	500–900
Portland cement mortar	2.1–2.3	10–40	1–7	10–30	0.05–0.30	480–1 300
Resins hardened by polymerization:						
Polyesters	1.05–1.3	90–250	30–90	1.5–6.0	2.9–7.0	140–460
Epoxies	1.1–1.2	90–200	35–100	1.5–7.0	3.2–8.3	136–580
Acrylics	0.95–1.25	50–150	40–120	3.0–6.0	4.2–9.6	316–480
Polyurethanes	1.1–1.2		20–70	1.5–2.5	1.8–5.8	136–210
Styrenes	1.0–1.1	70–150	45–90	2.0–5.0	4.5–8.2	200–450
Resins hardened by polycondensation:						
Furanics	1.1–1.2	80–150	9–15	1.0–14	0.8–1.25	90–1 200
Phenolics	1.15–1.2	25–70	8.5	1.0–9.0	0.7	90–750
Urethanes	1.25	22–50		1.0		80
Bitumens:						
Asphalts and tars	1.2–1.4					
Metals:						
Aluminium	2.7		70	70	2.6	2 600
Aluminium alloys 4–14% Cu			110–220			1 200–1 400
4–23% Si			150–230			
4–12% Mg			150–280			
Copper and alloys	8.95		100–300	107–125	1.1–3.4	

Table 2.2 Examples of fibres as reinforcement of composite materials

Type of material, characteristic dimension of cross-section d, characteristic length l	Density $\gamma \times 10^3$(kg/m^3)	Tensile strength f_t (MPa)	Modulus of elasticity E (GPa)	$f_t/\gamma \times 10^6$(mm)	$E/\gamma \times 10^6$(mm)
Steel $d = 0.1–1$ mm	7.85	280–4 200	210.0	3.6–54	2 680
Aluminium	2.71	29	70.0	1.1	2 580
Tungsten $d = 10$ µm	19.20	2 700	400.0	14	2 080
Alkalic glass A	2.45	3 200	72.5	130	3 000
Low alkali glass B, E	2.54	3 700	77.5	150	3 050
Corrosion resistant glass C	2.54	3 150	70.0	124	2 750
High modulus glass M	2.89	3 500	110.0	120	3 800
High strength glass S	2.45	4 300	88.0	175	3 600
Alkali resistant glass CemFIL		2 500	80.0		
Polycrystalline oxides	2–6	1 000–2 000	400–500	30–50	8 300–20 000
Al_2O_3, SiO_2, TiO_2					
Boron with tungsten	2.60	3 000–4 000	420	120–150	16 000
Substitute $d = 100$ µm					
Silicon carbon SiC	3.50	1 000–4 000	400–450	30–115	11 400–12 900
Boron carbon B4C	2.70	2 400	580	90	21 500
Carbon graphitized fibres	1.6–2.2	1 500–4 000	200–450	95–180	12 500–20 500
'Thornel' 16	1.33	1 150	96	86	7 200
25	1.42	1 240	186	87	13 100
40	1.56	1 730	276	110	17 700
50	1.67	2 180	392	130	23 500
75	1.82	2 640	544	145	29 900
100	1.85		688		
VSB–32 P55	2.02	2 070	380	102	18 800
VSC–32 P75	2.06	2 070	517	100	25 000
VS–0054 P100	2.10	2 070	688	99	32 800
Low modulus carbon	1.63	600–900	38.6	0.5	2 370
Fibres from pitch					
$d = 14,5$ µm $l = 3–10$ mm					
Asbestos fibres:					
Chrysotile (white) $d = 0,02$ µm	2.4–2.6	3 100	60–80	80–120	2 700

Crocidolite (blue) $d = 0, 1\ \mu m$	3.2–3.4	3 500	180–200	100–110	5 800
Amorphous metal					
(metal–glass)					
Thickness 20–30 μm					
Width 1–2 mm, length 15–60 mm	7.52	3 500	156	46	2 100
Natural organic fibres:					
Cotton 12–30 μm	1.5	300–600	6–10	20–40	400–700
Flax 20–35 μm		440–700			
Wool 12–37 μm	1.3	130–200		10–15	
Coconut coir $d = 0.1–0.3$ mm	1.12–1.15	40–200	1.9	3–18	165
$l = 1800–2800$ mm				24–35	
Jute $d = 0.1–0.4$ mm	1.02–1.04	250–350			
$l = 50–350$ mm					
Indian hemp 15 μm		750–850			
Sisal 125–500 μm	1.45	850	45	60	3 100
Cellulose 13–24 μm	1.2	300–500	10	25–42	830
Horse hair 50–400 μm	1.3	160		12	
Polymeric fibres:					
Polyethylene $d = 0.25–1.3$ mm	0.9	400–650	5–8	45–72	560–90
Polypropylene		400–600	4–8	45–65	450–900
$d = 10 \times 100–30 \times 200\ \mu m$					
Nylon	1.1	870	4	80	360
Polyester	1.4	1 030	1.1	74	80
Vinyl polymers	1.7	180–420		10–25	
Polyamides		420–700			
Acrylic fibres		800	17		
Whiskers SiC $d = 0.5–5–10\ \mu m$	3.2	21 000	490–880	656	15 300–27 500
Al_2O_3 $d = 0.5\ \mu m$	4.0	43 000	490	1 075	12 250
Whiskers of various materials		6 900–34 500	1 260–2 300		
High modulus organic fibres:					
Kevlar: PRD 49 $d = 10\ \mu m$	1.45	2 900–4 000	133	200–275	9 170
$l = 6–65$ mm					
PRD 29 $d = 12\ \mu m$	1.44	3 000	69	200	4 790
Basalt fibres		480–750	70–120		

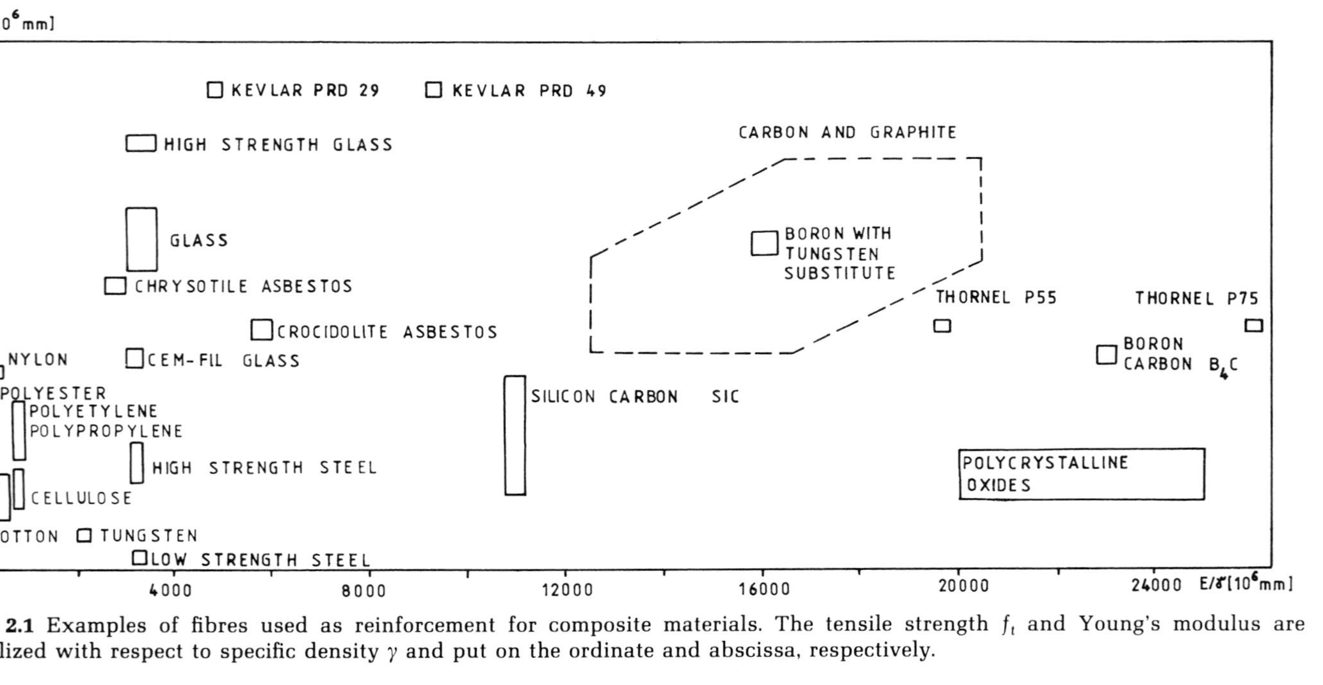

Figure 2.1 Examples of fibres used as reinforcement for composite materials. The tensile strength f_t and Young's modulus are normalized with respect to specific density γ and put on the ordinate and abscissa, respectively.

The fillers or inclusions are used as particles or grains of various shapes and dimensions. They are introduced into the matrix for different reasons: to improve the mechanical properties by hard particles in sufficient volume fraction, to control crack propagation or, in the case of small particles, to control the movement of dislocations. Sometimes cheap and porous inclusions are introduced to decrease the material cost or to improve the thermal insulation properties. The inclusions may be made of superhard particles, crushed stones, sand, voids filled with air or specially produced gas, etc. In laminar composites, internal layers are often made of cheap and lightweight materials only to maintain the distance between external rigid and hard layers and thus to increase the overall stiffness.

The reinforcement may have also various forms: stiff and tough layers, fibres and fabrics, and grains of hard materials are also used as reinforcement.

In certain cases hybrid reinforcement is used; this means that the reinforcement is composed of two or more types of fibres, layers or grains, carefully designed for their separate purposes.

In brittle matrices the reinforcement may be either in the form of ductile fibres to increase toughness or of deformable particles and pores to block the propagation of cracks. Stiff fibres or hard particles are introduced into ductile matrices to increase their strength. Short, chopped fibres are used in many cases, but also long continuous fibres and different types of nets and fabrics. The polymer structure introduced to a porous stiff matrix of hardened concrete may be also considered as its reinforcement.

In Table 2.2, examples of fibres used as reinforcement for composite materials are presented. In Figure 2.1, examples of fibre properties are plotted in such a way that their relative tensile strength f_t/γ [10^6 mm] and relative Young's modulus E/γ [10^6 mm] are ordinate and abscissa, respectively, of a rectangular system of coordinates. The points and regions in the diagram show how strong and stiff the fibres are, both properties being related to their density.

There is a large variety of materials which are used as composite constituents. Their selection is based on their properties with respect to the final goal, their availability and cost, and also to the applied technology. It is important that, before the composite constituents are selected, possible synergetic properties and local effects at stress transmission regions are also thoroughly analysed.

2.3 General description of composite materials

2.3.1 CLASSIFICATIONS

Composite materials may be classified according to various criteria. The most important from the physical viewpoint relates to the type of discontinuities created in the material structure. Systems of discontinuities may be introduced on the levels of micro-, meso- or macro-structure. The structural elements are

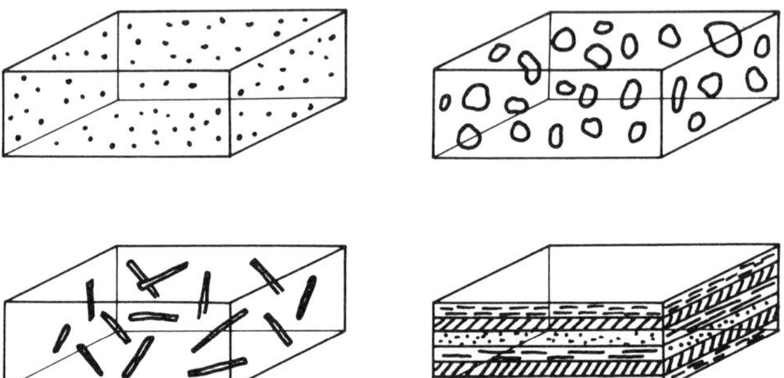

Figure 2.2 Schematic representation of four groups of composites.

distributed at random or regularly, using many different techniques, which are described in specialized books and manuals. Different elements may fulfil various conditions: blocking and controlling crack propagation, improving strength, increasing porosity, improving thermal isolation, modifying the transfer of fluids and gases across the material, and so on. Four main groups of composite materials with different types of discontinuities are shown schematically in Figure 2.2:

1. dispersion strengthening, e.g. metals with fine dispersed particles of hard material which restrain the motion of dislocations;
2. grain strengthening, e.g. Portland cement-based matrices with sand and aggregate grains randomly distributed;
3. fibre-reinforced, e.g. cement paste with asbestos fibres or polymer matrices with glass fibres;
4. laminated composites, e.g timber plywood or laminated plastics.

The distinction between composite materials and composite structures is not sharp and laminated composites form a group which may logically be considered for different purposes either as materials or as structures. Composite materials are used to build up composite structures, but homogeneous ones may also be used. It is usual to consider concrete or fibre-reinforced concrete as composite materials. A concrete beam reinforced with steel bars or a set of steel beams connected together with a steel-reinforced concrete slab to create a bridge deck are examples of composite structures. The distinction has only a formal character and limited importance.

Other proposals worth consideration for classifying composite materials have also been published, [2.2] and [2.3].

2.3.2 COMPOSITES WITH DISPERSION STRENGTHENING

In this type of composite material the main load-bearing constituent is the matrix. Small hard particles are distributed evenly in the matrix to block dislocations. The mechanism of the strengthening is described by several authors, [2.4] and [2.5]. The matrices are made of metals or polymers. The particles are of different origin: silica powder or fine sand are used for polymer matrices and for metallic matrices – second phase precipitates and particles made of oxides, nitrides, carbides and borides. Precipitates are small particles which crystallize from impurities dissolved in metal alloys. The crystallization during the cooling process results in very small and hard particles, closely distributed in the metal matrix. When ceramic particles are used the resulting composites are called cermets. The size of this type of particle varies from that of atoms to micrometres for ceramic ones and their volume fraction from 1% to 15%.

When particles are bigger than 1 μm and their volume increases, for example exceeding 15%, then both the matrix and the particles share the load-bearing function in appreciable proportions and the materials obtained may be considered as belonging to the next group of the above proposed classification. These composites maintain several properties from the matrix as their continuous phase: its ductility and toughness, heat and electric conductivity, etc.

If a uniform distribution of particles may be assumed, then the material structure is described by two values, (cf. [2.6]): d – particle diameter or its other characteristic dimension for irregular shapes, V_d – volume fraction of particles in the composite.

Using d and V_d, the mean distance L between particles may be calculated, which determines the mechanism of reinforcement and the preventing of plastic flow, explained schematically in Figure 2.3. The driving force which pushes the

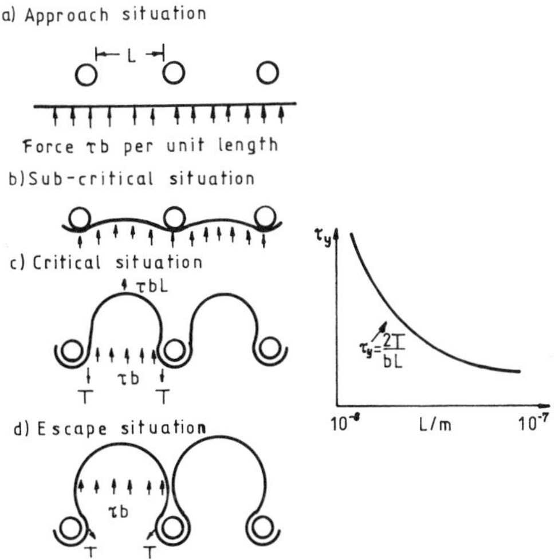

Figure 2.3 Schematic explanation of the dislocation motion across a system of small particles dispersed in a matrix. (Reprinted from Ashby, M.F. and Jones, D.R.H., *Engineering Materials*, (1980), Figure 10.2, p. 99, with permission from Pergamon Press, Ltd., Headington Hill Hall, Oxford OX3 OBW, UK.) [2.6]

dislocations is provided by the stress t_y. The force acting on one segment of the row of particles is equal to $t_y bL$, where b is the perpendicular dimension. That force is balanced by the line tension T in the following manner, $t_y bL = 2T$.

The dislocations move when the equilibrium is exceeded by the growing stress t_y.

The reinforcement effect increases with d and V_d and as a result a higher energy of external load is required to assure the motion of dislocations.

The boundary between dispersion-strengthened and grain-reinforced composites is based on the particle size and dimension level of the processes: the grains control the crack propagation and not that of dislocations.

Composites with dispersed particles are not only used as load-bearing materials. Rocket propellants in which aluminium powder or other particles are dispersed to obtain a steady burning, and paints with silver or aluminium flakes to assure electrical conductivity or excellent surface covering, are examples.

2.3.3 GRAIN-REINFORCED (PARTICULATE) COMPOSITES

In this group, different concrete-like materials are included. They are composed of a matrix in which grains of apparent diameter from 1 μm up to 100 mm (or even more) are embedded. The volume fraction of these inclusions usually exceeds 15%.

Hard grains strengthen the matrix in ordinary concretes and in other structural composites. In materials used as insulation layers on building walls or for various non-structural purposes the lightweight and porous grains are applied or systems of pores are created.

In the range of elastic deformations hard grains reduce the matrix deformability. After crack opening, the grains control the crack propagation because each deviation of a crack to contour a hard grain requires additional input of external energy. Soft grains, beside improvement of insulation properties, also block the cracks which are passing through these grains.

The matrices are usually brittle, based in most cases on Portland cement, but also on other kinds of cement or gypsum. In the group of concrete-like materials ductile matrices are also used. These are polymers and bitumens which behave as brittle at least in certain conditions, but in others, they flow plastically.

The strength and deformations of grain-reinforced composites may be designed and forecast using various theoretical models. In the following chapters these questions are described in more detail.

2.3.4 FIBRE-REINFORCED COMPOSITES

This is perhaps the most important group of modern materials applied since the 1940s in various fields: from aircraft and spacecraft structures, through housings for electronic equipment up to concrete layers on runways and highways.

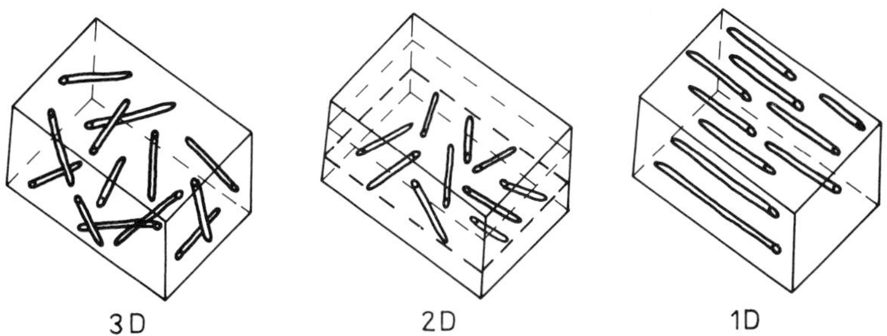

Figure 2.4 Idealized orientation of short fibres in a matrix.

The fibre reinforcement causes a high degree of anisotropy and heterogeneity of the composites. Two cases may be distinguished: in ductile matrices, hard and stiff fibres are introduced to increase the overall stiffness and strength, and in brittle matrices, ductile fibres control the crack opening and propagation.

The volume fraction of fibres and their distribution determine the way in which the fibres influence the behaviour of composite materials. All situations occur in practice as the fibre content may be as low as 0.5% in certain types of polypropylene or steel fibre-reinforced cements and may be higher than 60% in advanced composites used in construction of aircraft.

The role of fibres depends also on their form, i.e. whether they are used as short chopped fibres (Figure 2.4), continuous single fibres or used in rovings, mats or fabrics, distributed at random in the matrix or arranged in a more regular way (Figure 2.5). The quality of bond between the fibres and the matrix is another decisive element. In some advanced composites, but also in glass-fibre-reinforced cements, the chemical interaction between these two constituents may be destructive for the composite integrity. The fibre–matrix bond is assured by different processes: by adhesion, mechanical anchorage and by friction, depending on the chemical and mechanical properties of both phases. The quality of bond may vary with the intensity of load and its duration.

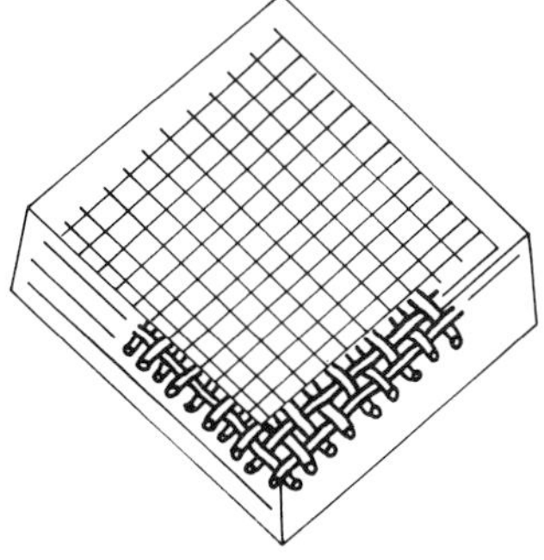

Figure 2.5 Composite material reinforced by a woven fabric.

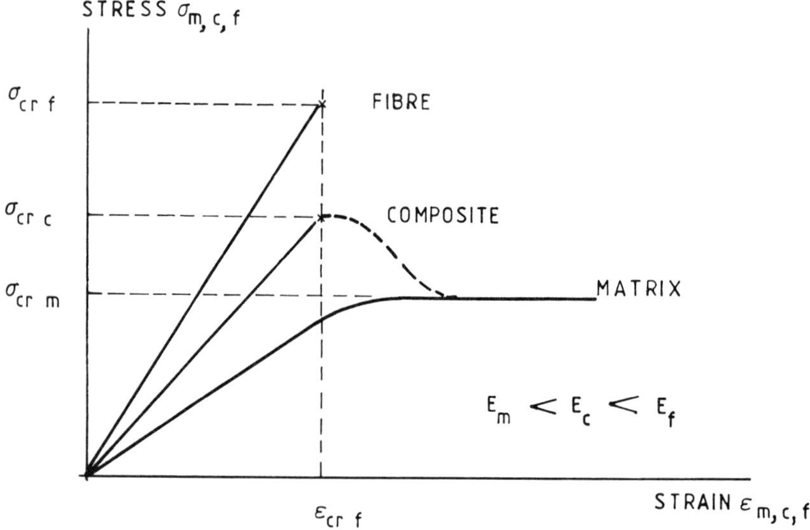

Figure 2.6 Typical stress–strain diagram for fibre, matrix and composite material.

A typical stress–strain diagram for a composite material, in which strong and brittle fibres are reinforcing a ductile matrix is shown in Figure 2.6 together with separate diagrams for fibres and matrix, cf. also Figures 10.6 and 10.18. The failure of the composite material occurs shortly after the failure of fibres and the post-failure behaviour of the matrix is highly nonlinear.

A detailed description of mechanical problems arising in fibre-reinforced composites exceeds the scope of this chapter. Below, only a few groups of problems are briefly described, and the questions relevant for brittle matrix composites are considered in detail in the next chapters. The interested reader may find further information concerning high strength fibre composites in specialized manuals such as [2.5] and [2.7].

Polymer resins reinforced with glassfibres (GFRP – glass fibre reinforced plastics) were the first high strength composites. For example, using a woven fabric of glassfibres of volume fraction $V_f = 40\%$ and polyester matrix the tensile strength of the composite was about $f_t = 300$ MPa and its Young's modulus was in the range of $E_c = 5$–10 GPa, (cf. [2.8]).

GFRP did not satisfy the growing requirements for stiffness in load-bearing elements of aircraft. New types of composite were introduced with resin matrices reinforced with high modulus boron or carbon fibres (CFRP). As an example, the Polyamid 66 matrix reinforced with carbon fibres with $V_f = 20\%$ may be quoted from [2.9]. The composite properties were: $f_t = 100$–130 MPa and $E_c = 20$–25 GPa.

The next generation of fibre-reinforced materials were the metal matrix composites (MMC) of ductile alloys reinforced with hard carbon or ceramic fibres and whiskers. MMC offer serious advantages over other types of composite, mainly in the following aspects:

1. better temperature capability;
2. improved wetting of fibres and better load transfer by strong matrix–fibre bond;
3. higher strength and stiffness;
4. better machinability.

For example, the properties of a tested composite [2.10] were the following: $E_c = 380\,\mathrm{GPa}$ and $f_t = 1400–2000\,\mathrm{MPa}$ for an Al alloy reinforced with fibres FP α–A1203 with $V_f = 50–60\%$.

A particular type of fibre-reinforced composites are the directionally solidified eutectics in which matrix and reinforcement are made in one single process from one or two different materials. The reinforcement usually has the form of plates or rods and their orientation may be designed and controlled in the solidification process. Only the volume fraction of the reinforcement cannot be designed arbitrarily and is determined by the applied technological processes.

Eutectic composites have excellent mechanical properties at normal and elevated temperatures: high strength and Young's modulus may be maintained after exposure during hundreds of hours at temperatures over 1200 °C. In several applications these properties are necessary to assure the fulfilment of service conditions by the composite material.

2.3.5 LAMINATED COMPOSITES

Laminated composites are built of at least two different layers connected together, but more often the number of layers is higher. To bond together laminae of different materials or of the same material but differently oriented is the most effective and economical way to achieve a material which satisfies simultaneously several different requirements, some of them conflicting like high strength and reduced weight, or abrasion resistance and thermal insulation. This is possible by applying different layers which have particular roles in the final laminate composite.

The layers are built of homogeneous or composite materials. Metal sheets and polymers are used as well as timber and lightweight foams. The layers are flat or curved, e.g. pipes of different kinds.

As examples of laminated composites produced in large volumes the following may be mentioned:

- Two external layers made of stiff and hard material are bonded to an internal layer of a lightweight core which maintain their distance and flexural rigidity of the composite, so-called sandwich plates, (Figure 2.7a).
- Two or more layers are bonded together to satisfy conflicting requirements, like corrosion or thermal resistance of the outer skin and strength of the next lamina, necessary for the global bearing capacity, (Figure 2.7b).

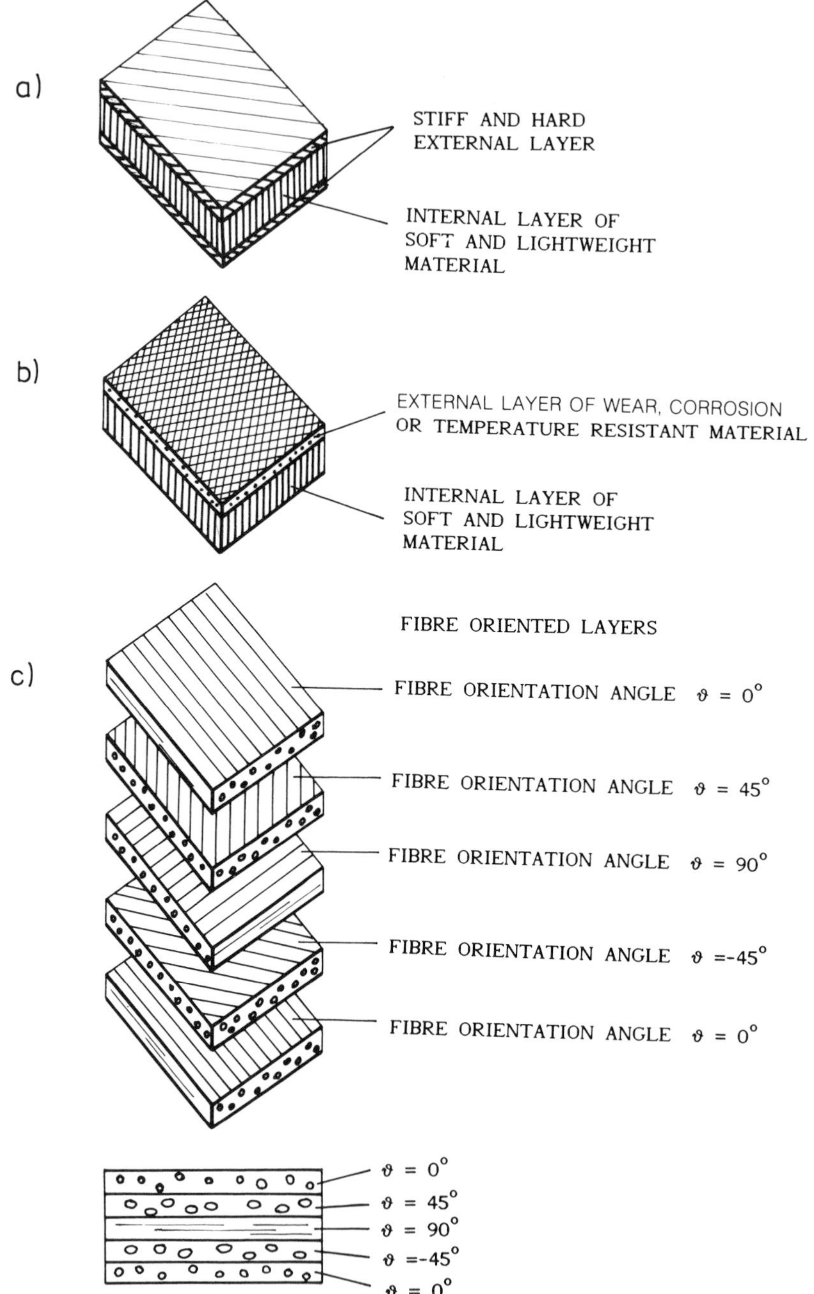

Figure 2.7 Examples of laminated composites. a) sandwich panel composed of two thin strong sheets with a thick core of light and less resistant material; b) composition of an external layer assuring corrosion or thermal resistance with a hard internal lamina giving global bearing capacity; c) composition of five fibre-reinforced layers with different fibre orientation angle.

- Several layers of orthotropic composites, e.g. reinforced with parallel systems of fibres, are combined together in such a way that adjacent laminae are oriented in different directions and thus the strength and stiffness of the composite plate may be tailored to the specific design requirements, (Figure 2.7c).

The mechanical behaviour of laminated composites under external load and other actions is very complicated. The global properties should be designed and tested together with those of each single lamina. In addition, the conditions of their bonding should be verified because destruction may occur by different processes:

1. failure of external resistant layer by tension, compression or buckling;
2. failure of internal layers by shearing;
3. shearing along interfaces between layers (delamination);
4. local failures and damage of various types;
5. global buckling or rupture.

The forms of failure depend on the loading and supporting conditions but also on local properties of the constituents and their bond properties.

The mechanical properties of laminated composites as well as their fracture behaviour have been considered in many books and papers. Interested readers are referred to the classical book on anisotropic plates [2.11], to a review of basic mechanical problems [2.12], to design and optimization methods [2.13] and to handbooks [2.14], [2.15] and many others.

2.4 Structure of composite materials

The material structure of a composite consists of its elements (grains, particles, fibres, voids), of their volume fractions, shapes and orientations, and of their distribution in space.

A complete description of the material structure should contain characteristic properties of the constituents. Depending on the precision required, that information should indicate:

1. type of matrix and reinforcement with their volume or mass fractions;
2. forms and dimensions of the elements of the discontinuous phase, with the statistical distribution of these data, if needed;
3. arrangement of all these elements in space;
4. orientation of the elements, for instance, the direction of fibres;
5. types and dimensions of the interfacial zones between the constituents.

In particular cases other data may also be useful.

Only the physical and chemical description of the constituents are given separately and are not usually included in the notion of the structure.

The material structure may be considered on various levels, both by theoretical and experimental methods. These levels are defined conventionally in many ways by different authors. For the purpose of the next chapters, the following levels are distinguished:

1. molecular level, in which atomic bonds are considered and observations are made by various indirect methods; the characteristic dimensions are of the order of $1\,\text{Å} = 10^{-10}\,\text{m} = 0.1\,\text{nm}$;
2. structural level or micro-level, in which crystals and dislocations are observed with different types of electronic microscope; the characteristic dimension is of the order of $1\,\mu\text{m} = 10^{-6}\,\text{m}$;
3. meso-level, in which the main objects which measure about $1\,\text{mm} = 10^{-3}\,\text{m}$ may be observed using optical microscopes, this means that the mortar situated between the biggest grains of aggregate is studied with grains of sand and pores;
4. macro-level, of large grains or that of structural elements made of composites, where the smallest characteristic dimension is 10^{-2}–$10^{-1}\,\text{m}$.

In investigations of composite materials, usually the micro- and meso-levels are particularly considered and the macro-level is characteristic for composite structures. In [2.7] a more diversified system of levels has been proposed, also characterized by dimensions of observed objects.

The selection of an appropriate level for consideration and observation of the structure of a given composite is important for the results and depends considerably on the aims of the investigation. At every level, different objects appear and different processes may be observed while the others are neglected. For example, if the macro-level is considered in Portland cement composites, then they may be treated as homogeneous materials and all processes which are developing in lower levels remain unknown. Moreover, it may appear that, without entering to these lower levels, certain phenomena cannot be understood. That is the case with several properties of cement-based composites: important factors and agents act at the lower levels and results appear in the forms of cracks or spalling on the macro-level or on that of structural elements.

At the meso-level, the stresses and strains in the fibres and in the matrix are considered separately, and at the macro-level average values characterize the overall composite material behaviour.

The material structure may be described qualitatively and quantitatively and represented in various ways: on radiograms and photograms without any magnification or obtained through all kinds of optical, electronic and acoustic microscopes. Other types of specialized equipment may indicate chemical composition of particular structural elements together with their various physical properties. The precision of all these indications varies with the requirements and methods. Local data concerning certain points, i.e. sufficiently small regions of composite constituents, but also global information, are needed.

For instance, the porosity may be given by one number indicating the volume fraction of voids or may be obtained with full details of the dimensions of pores, distance to the nearest neighbour and their statistical distribution. For some overall material characteristics, like frost resistance of concretes, global information on the porosity is imprecise and nearly useless and much more data are needed. Material structure is also often represented on schematic images.

For the numerical description of the material structure and its quantitative analysis, special computerized equipment has been used since the 1970s. At the beginning, they were known under the commercial name Quantimet. Later, several other firms started to produce such equipment, e.g. Joyce–Loebl, Morphopericolor, and its performance is quickly developing together with application in various fields of material science. Image analysis is used in biology, petrography and metallurgy but also for treatment of satellite or aerial photographs, which explains the rapid development of that technique.

Images of material structures may be analysed at full scale as obtained from polished faces or cross-sections of specimens. Also, images obtained by means of all types of microscopes may be analysed. The main objective of the analysis is the quantification of images. This means that, in an observed field, particular objects like grains, fibre cross-sections, cracks and voids are distinguished and quantified as to their area fraction, shape, perimeters, distribution, etc.

The observed fields should be prepared by different technical means to improve the visibility of the objects of interest and illuminated in an appropriate way. The image is recorded by a video camera, transformed into electronic signals and stored in a computer. With special programs the stored images are analysed according to the aim of research. The output is obtained in a graphical and numerical form, ready for further treatment. Using known stereological methods, image analysis gives ample information on the three-dimensional structure of the examined materials.

Moreover, thanks to the large memories and high speed of operations of modern microcomputers, analysis and comparison of great numbers of images are possible within relatively short times. In this way, the results of various processes may be found out (e.g. ageing or corrosion progress), influence of different technologies and the quantified results are obtained for further analysis.

Image analysis methods are described in many books, among others in [2.16], cf. also Chapter 6.

In the micro-mechanics of material structures, the notion of the Representative Volume Element (RVE) is important. It is the smallest region of material in which all structural elements are represented in appropriate proportions. Therefore, over the RVE the stress and strain distribution may be considered as macroscopically uniform. This means that statistical homogeneity is assumed in the RVE determination and it implies that material averages and RVE averages are the same. It is often assumed that the minimum linear dimension of the RVE is equal to four times the maximum linear dimension of an

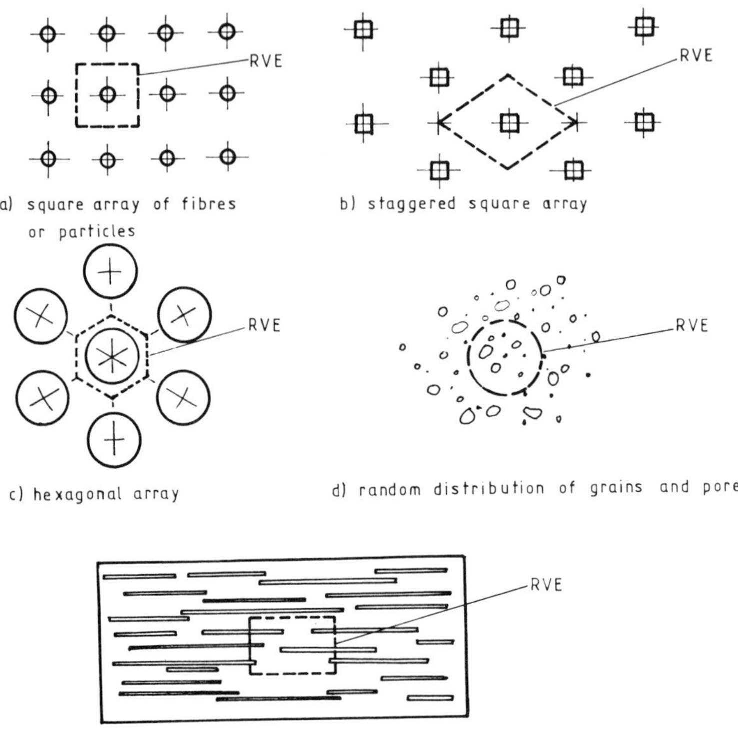

Figure 2.8 Examples of the Representative Volume Elements in composite materials with various material structures.

inhomogeneity like a grain, pore or crack. For further discussion of the RVE the reader is referred to [2.17] and papers [2.18] and [2.19]. Examples of RVE for different material structures are shown in Figure 2.8.

In the determination of RVE dimensions for a material structure with randomly distributed elements, e.g. short fibres, the probability should be established that the material is correctly represented by its RVE. When the required probability is increased then the RVE dimensions are also increased.

The dimensions of the RVE are not constant for a material structure, i.e. they may vary with the loading and with development of the crack pattern, if the RVE is selected to represent the cracked material in its actual state. Also the RVE may be different for different material characteristics: if the interest of material representation is reduced only to one group of its characteristics, then the RVE does not take into account the others. In that sense two different groups of material properties are distinguished: structure-sensitive and structure-insensitive ones.

The structure-sensitive or constitutive properties of a considered material, like strength, stiffness or water permeability, are, in a more or less direct way, related to the distribution and orientation of the structure elements and to their reciprocal interaction. Other properties, called structure-insensitive or additive, depend only on the material composition, on the volume (or mass) fractions of all its constituents, and on their properties. There are few structure-insensitive properties of composite materials, and, as an example, specific weight may be quoted.

Because the most important material properties of the composites are structure-sensitive, design and optimization of the material structure are believed to be the main approach in the material science. The material structure is closely connected to the material technology and they should be designed together if an optimal structure of a composite material has to be obtained as a result of an industrial production.

2.5 Models and theories

When a composite material is designed for a particular application and its behaviour under load and various other actions should fulfil certain given requirements, a natural attitude of the designer is to imagine a theoretical model of the material. A model represents a system of more or less simple rules and formulae which describe material behaviour. That description should comprise the following elements:

1. all coefficients for stress–strain relations in linear elastic deformations and for a given system of coordinates;
2. rules for non-linear, viscous and inelastic behaviour;
3. behaviour over time, i.e. under long-term loads and imposed deformations, including the influence of the rate of loading;
4. strength criteria under various stress states and types of fracture process.

In this way a system of constitutive equations is established, giving complete stress–strain relations, together with a description of the mode of fracture.

Other parts of the material behaviour description should consider the variation of the material properties with position. These variations are related to initial material structure or to local discontinuities and damages due to load and other actions. In composite materials the assumption of homogeneity may be justified with several restrictions only: for limited regions, under small loads and for considerations with well-defined degrees of approximation. If the relations for homogeneous media are applied, then special methods of homogenization are used, e.g. RVE. This means that effective variable properties are replaced in well-defined regions by calculated constant values. Instead of a real heterogeneous material with properties varying from one point to another, a fictitious material is considered in which homogeneous regions have calculated properties, (cf. Section 2.4).

In general, it is difficult or even impossible to express completely material behaviour by theoretical considerations. The attempts are aimed at approximate information, usually submitted to experimental verification. The simpler the model used, the easier it is to get information. However, very simple models cannot describe effective properties of a real material.

The basic approach to material behaviour of composites is derived from the Hooke's law in its generalized form, which in fact concerns only linear elastic and homogeneous media. Then additional mechanisms are used to account for the complexity of the material behaviour. For composite materials, a few simple models are used which were initially proposed in general solid mechanics.

The Hookean model (Figure 2.9a) has the form of a spring, which represents a linear stress–strain relation. In a three-dimensional orthogonal system of coordinates, it is represented by the following relations:

$$\sigma^{ij} = C^{ijkl}\varepsilon_{kl}, \quad i, j, k, l = 1, 2, 3 \tag{2.1}$$

where σ^{ij}–stress tensor, ε_{kl}–strain tensor and C^{ijkl} is the tensor of elastic constraints. Taking into account the symmetry of indices, 21 independent elastic constants determine an anisotropic material. For materials with particular symmetry with respect to certain planes or axes, the number of constants is reduced, and for an isotropic material only two constants are needed, e.g. coefficient of elasticity E and Poisson ratio ν. Further development of that approach may be found for example in [2.13].

In the Hookean model all supplied energy is stored and the displacement appears immediately after application of load.

The above-mentioned concept of an isotropic material described by two constants is practically never encountered when real materials are studied, and it is only used for:

1. very rough approximations of examined materials;
2. school exercises and training examples;
3. particular cases where, at the macroscopic level, it may be admitted that in certain conditions the microscopic grains, particles or fibres are distributed at random in space and randomly oriented.

Therefore, in all other cases the composite materials are considered as having different properties in different directions. This is characteristic for most fibrous and all laminated materials where certain directions are intentionally reinforced.

When a composite is treated as an anisotropic elastic material, the stress–strain relations are based on a general approach (cf. [2.5]), which is valid in a region of small deformations. These theoretical relations were developed for application in high strength composites which, under service loads, should remain elastic. That part of composite materials theory is not examined here because there are many excellent handbooks covering the subject which may be considered as a classical one. Moreover, for brittle composites the zone of elastic deformation is very limited. These materials are characterized by early appearance of

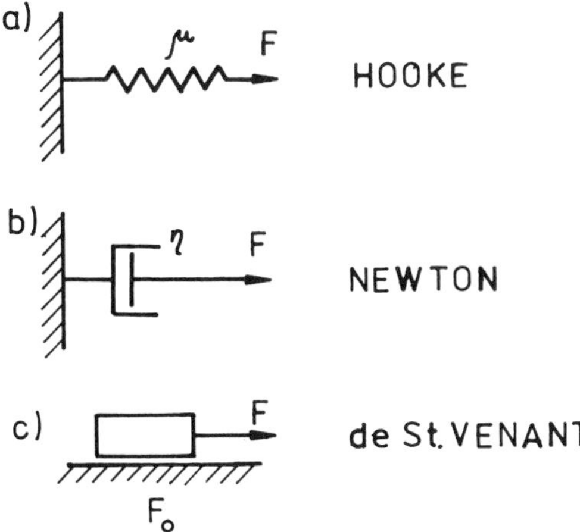

Figure 2.9 Simple theoretical models.

nonelastic behaviour in the form of microcracks of various kinds. They obey Hooke's law only when subjected to small loads, and under higher loads develop more or less plastic, quasi-plastic and non-linear deformations. To express the material behaviour close to fracture as well as the inherent plasticity and viscosity of many materials the Hookean model is completed by other simple models shown in Figure 2.9.

In the Newtonian model (Figure 2.9b), the displacement is proportional to load P and to time t, but here all energy is dissipated. The model has the form of a piston in a cylinder filled with fluid (a dashpot). The displacement is inversely proportional to a coefficient of viscosity η which characterizes the motion of the piston in the cylinder.

In the de St. Venant model (Figure 2.9c), a block starts to slide when the load P reaches a certain value P_o. Below that value there is no motion in the model.

Even for approximate calculations, these simple models are used in combination. Examples of such combinations are presented in Figure 2.10. Further details of rheological models may be found in various handbooks on solid mechanics, e.g. [2.20].

The calculations of composite materials properties require the application of rather complicated models, composed of several simple elements. The validity of results depends on the type of composite material and its heterogeneity and also on the load and intensity of other actions. The theoretical model may express small deformations of materials having regular structure much better, for example, laminates composed of orthogonal layers, than assuring satisfactory representation of a randomly reinforced and strongly heterogeneous material under intensive load, producing local plastic deformations and cracks. In that last case, a satisfactory model probably does not exist.

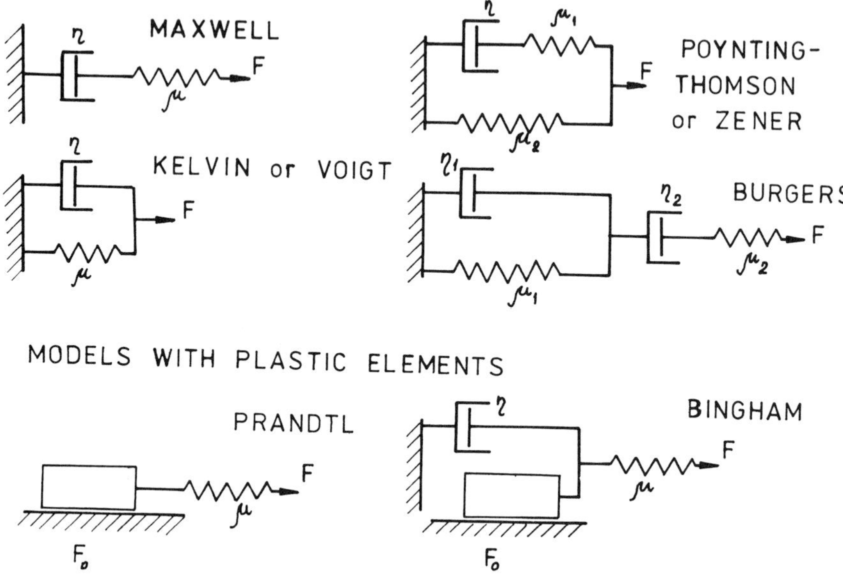

Figure 2.10 Models of viscoelastic materials.

An example of the application of theoretical models is the calculation of Young's modulus of a two-phase composite. Both phases behave as linear elastic and homogeneous materials according to Hooke's model, but having different Young's moduli E_1 and E_2. They are randomly distributed in the space with respective volume contents V_1 and V_2, where $V_1 + V_2 = 1$. To obtain upper and lower bounds for the Young's modulus of the composite material under compression, two extreme possibilities of internal structure are considered, as shown in Figure 2.11. In a parallel system, both phases are subjected to equal strain, and in a series system, to equal stress.

It may be derived that, for the parallel model, the following formula gives

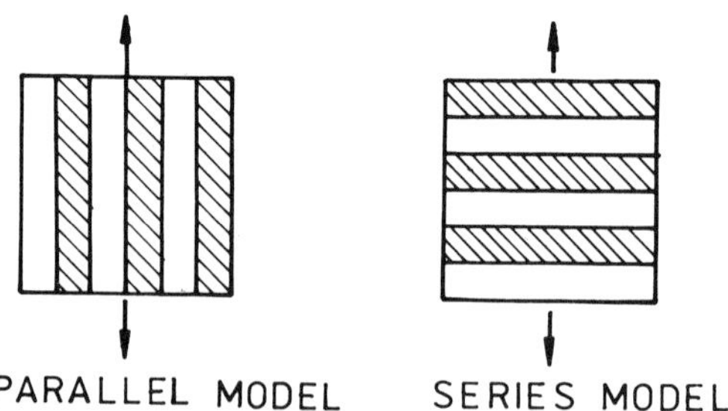

Figure 2.11 Two extreme possibilities of structure of two-phase materials.

the Young's modulus of the composite:

$$E_c = E_1V_1 + E_2V_2 = E_1V_1 + E_2(1 - V_1), \tag{2.2}$$

which is a simple application of the rule of mixtures.

For the series model, it is:

$$E_c = \left[\frac{V_1}{E_1} + \frac{V_2}{E_2}\right]^{-1}. \tag{2.3}$$

These expressions for E_c are the upper and lower bounds for all possible phase arrangements, and may be used for approximate calculations, providing that they give close numerical results – if the difference is too large, the obtained answer is practically useless.

As an example, a two-phase composite material is considered, of unknown phase arrangement with equal contents $V_1 = V_2$. Two cases of Young's moduli of both phases are considered:

1. $E_1 = 2E_2$;
2. $E_1 = 100E_2$.

Using these values of elastic constants the upper and lower bounds may be calculated from equation 2.2 and equation 2.3:

1. $E_c = 1.5E_2$ and $E_c = 1.33E_2$;
2. $E_c = 50.5E_2$ and $E_c = 1.98E_2$.

In the first case both formulae give close values which may be used for approximate calculations. However, in the second case the obtained values are so different that they cannot give any useful approximation of the range of volume fractions. These two examples are shown in Figure 2.12. Further proposals are therefore aimed at constructing a more sophisticated model (cf. [2.6]) in which the two previous ones are combined. The phase arrangements in the models shown in Figure 2.13 are built up to obtain better results for heterogeneous bodies.

The Young's modulus represented by Hirsch's model is expressed by the following relation:

$$E_c = \left[\frac{x}{V_1E_1 + V_2E_2} + (1 - x)\left(\frac{V_1}{E_1} + \frac{V_2}{E_2}\right)\right]^{-1}, \tag{2.4}$$

where $x \in (0; 1)$ and is equal to the relative fraction corresponding to the parallel model.

A similar relation for Counto's model has the following form:

$$E_c = \left[\frac{1 - \sqrt{V_2}}{E_1} + \frac{1}{[(1 - \sqrt{V_2})/\sqrt{V_2}]E_1 + E_2}\right]^{-1}, \tag{2.5}$$

The curves obtained from the above formulae as functions of V_1 with $x = 0.5$

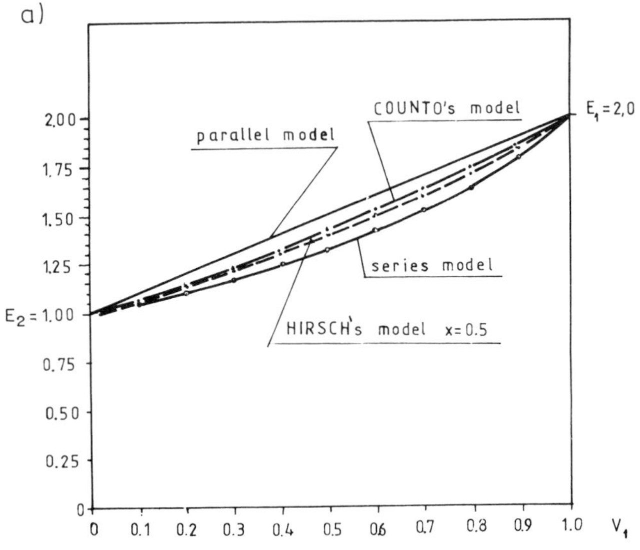

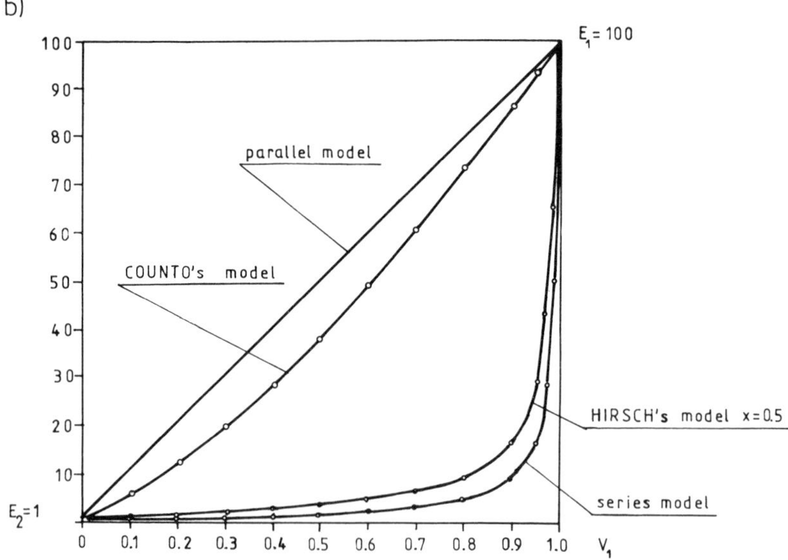

Figure 2.12 Examples of relations between the modulus of elasticity of two-phase ($V = V_1 + V_2$) composites and the volume fraction V_1 for four different theoretical models. a) for a weakly heterogeneous material with $E_1 = 2E_2$; b) for a strongly heterogeneous material with $E_1 = 100E_2$.

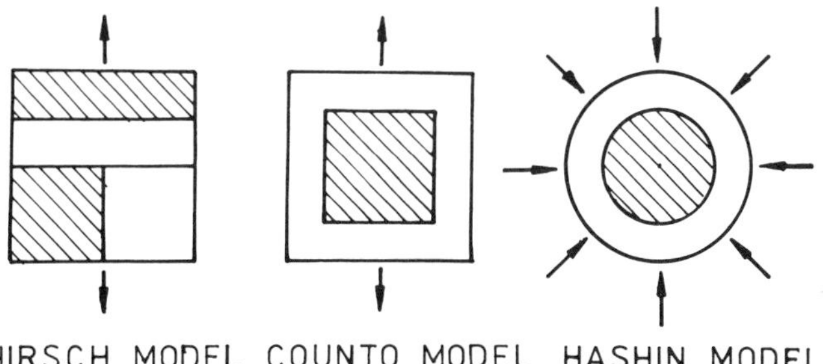

Figure 2.13 Models for heterogeneous materials.

are also shown in Figure 2.12. The conclusion is that even more complicated models do not furnish bounds which may be practically useful for strongly heterogeneous materials. Problems which concern these kinds of materials are also examined in Sections 10.5 and 11.7.

The phenomenon of the fracture of composites is not included in the theoretical description given by the above-mentioned models and is much more difficult than the prediction of elastic properties of the materials. Fracture may have different forms and is itself preceded by different effects which should be represented by other models. There are, for example:

- brittle fracture with small or even quite negligible plastic deformations;
- ductile fracture with extensive deformations;
- rupture when a tensile element shows necking up to the complete disappearance of its cross-sectional area.

Under increasing load or other external actions (imposed deformations, temperature) in an element built of composite material, various forms of local failure appear: cracks in the matrix, fractures of the fibres, failures of bonds between phases, plastic deformations, etc. All these effects develop in the fracture processes under the influence of increasing external actions and also with ageing, corrosion, shrinkage, fatigue. To study the failure process, not only single phenomena should be considered separately, but also their interactions. In many cases, the homogenization and superposition of effects are not valid or should be used with caution within well defined limits.

In very complicated processes of fracture all theoretical approaches and models are aimed at qualitative explanation of basic features. Quantitative predictions should be completed by extensive experimental data.

In a group of similar composites, different types of fracture may be observed in various conditions, e.g. materials considered as ductile behave as brittle at low temperature or under high rates of loading. Therefore, if a group of materials like glasses and ceramics are named brittle without particular explanations, it means that it concerns their behaviour in normal conditions. The notions of brittleness and ductility have only relative meaning and do not include any quantification. It depends on various circumstances what plastic deformation accompanying the fracture is considered as small. However, brittle fracture is perhaps more often studied because its appearance in any structure without plastic deformations as prior warning is particularly dangerous. In the next chapters, brittle fracture is considered in more detail as characteristic for brittle matrix composites: fracture in such materials is initiated by pre-existing cracks which propagate due to load or other imposed actions. Plastic or quasi-plastic deformations are usually restricted to small regions around the tip of the propagating crack. In many cases the existence of plastic deformations may be therefore neglected to simplify the relations.

Fracture mechanics for brittle materials is basically derived from the theory presented in [2.21]. Initially it was proposed for an elliptical crack in an infinite elastic and homogeneous medium subjected to distant tensile forces and the conditions for crack propagation were formulated for that case. Later, brittle fracture mechanics was developed for various situations in real structural elements, with non-negligible plastic deformations and with several complications necessary to account for heterogeneity of materials, time effects, etc. In that approach, the crack's appearance and propagation is considered as a basic effect of loading and as a phenomenon directly related to final failure.

In all the above considerations a consistent deterministic approach has been applied. It means that all variables (material properties, phase distribution, local discontinuities and their interaction) were treated as having well determined values, positions, directions, etc. In reality, all these parameters are subjected to random variations and detailed data on their statistical distributions are usually not available. To simplify the considerations, the notion of the representative volume element (RVE) has been proposed. As explained in Section 2.4, the RVE is selected in such a way that different phases are correctly represented. It means that all statistical moments calculated for an RVE are the same for the entire considered heterogeneous body. The notion of the RVE is often applied even without its detailed definition, simply using certain statistical moments like average values or variance to characterize the composite material.

In conclusion, the three following observations may be formulated:

1. For high strength composites, the theoretical models are based on the generalized Hooke's law, with all necessary complements for local effects, time and temperature influences, nonhomogeneity, etc.
2. For brittle matrix composites, in which cracks and various types of internal discontinuities are also considered in normal conditions and under service loads, the formulae for prediction of behaviour should be derived from fracture mechanics or should at least account for fracture phenomena. The analytical representation of fracture processes is, however, not fully available because of their complexity and heterogeneity.
3. All values which characterize any composite material should be considered as random variables. If a detailed statistical analysis is impossible because

of the complexity of the problem or incomplete data, appropriate approximate procedures should be chosen, completed by experimental results.

For composite materials, due to the complexity of their structure and variability of their properties in both deterministic and probabilistic approaches, experimental results are of particular importance. They are necessary not only for verification of all theoretical calculations but also they should supply numerical data for factors, coefficients and distributions which are used in the formulae.

Another aspect has to be considered here to conclude this general information on the composites. The synergistic effects mentioned above are of special importance and are introduced into the definition of a composite material: its properties and behaviour are not only determined by the properties and contents of the components, but also certain new features appear due to the joint action of different components and external agents. Synergism is defined according to Aristotle by the sentence: the whole is something more than just the sum of the parts. It may be expressed as follows:

$$F(A, B) = \underbrace{F(A) + F(B)}_{\substack{\text{additive} \\ \text{mechanism}}} + \underbrace{F(A)^{*}F(B)}_{\substack{\text{synergetic} \\ \text{effects}}} \tag{2.6}$$

for a material composed of two components. Here F is a property as a function of contents A and B, [2.22].

Synergetic effects may be positive or negative, which means that they may act along with our needs and may be stimulated by the designer, or on the contrary may go in an opposite direction. Examples are the strength and toughness of a composite material which are increased by the joint influence of the components. Negative synergetic effects appear when an external load and a corrosive agent produce larger or faster damage than their additive effects.

The design of composite materials and structures is based on an appropriate application of positive synergetic effects.

References

2.1. Vinson, J.R. (1981) On the state of technology and trends in composite materials in the United States, in Proc. Japan–US Conf. *Composite Materials; Mechanics, Properties and Fabrication*, (eds K. Kawata and T. Akasaka), Appl. Sc. Publ. 353–361.

2.2. Tsai, S.W. and Hahn, H.T. (1980) *Introduction to Composite Materials*, Techn. Publ. Co., Westport, US.

2.3. Hull, D. (1981) *An Introduction to Composite Materials*, Cambridge Univ. Press, Cambridge.

2.4. Kelly, A. (1964) *The strengthening of metals by dispersed particles*, Proc. Roy. Soc., A282, 63, London.

2.5. Vinson, J.R. and Chou, T.W. (1975) *Composite Materials and their Use in Structures*, App. Sc. Publ. London.

2.6. Ashby, M.F. and Jones, D.R.H. (1980) *Engineering Materials*, Pergamon Press, Oxford.

2.7. Ashby, M.F. and Jones, D.R.H. (1986) *Engineering Materials 2*, Pergamon Press, Oxford.

2.8. Kawata, K. *et al.* (1981) Dynamic behavior analysis of composite materials, as [2.1], 2–11.

2.9. Taya, M. and Chou, T.W. (1981) Prediction of the first and second stages of stress–strain curves of unidirectional short fiber reinforced thermoplastics, as [2.1], 119–30.

2.10. Dhingra, A.K. (1981) Inorganic alumina fibers for reinforcement of metal castings, as [2.1], 239–44.

2.11. Lekhnitskiy, S. (1968) *Anisotropic Plates*, trans. from Russian, 2nd ed., Gordon and Breach, New York.

2.12. Tsai, S.W., Halpin, J. and Pagano, J. (1968) *Composite Material Workshop*, Technomic Publ. Co., Westport, USA.

2.13. Nicholls, R. (1976) *Composite Construction Material Handbook*, Prentice-Hall Inc., New Jersey.

2.14. Schwartz, M.M. (1984) *Composite Materials Handbook*, McGraw-Hill, New York.

2.15. Holmes, M. and Just, D.J. (1983) *GRP in Structural Engineering*, Elsevier Appl. Sc. Publ., London.

2.16. Joyce-Loebl (1985) *Image Analysis. Principles and Practice.* Gateshead, England.

2.17. Jones, R.M. (1975) *Mechanics of Composite Materials*, McGraw-Hill Book Co., NewYork.

2.18. Hashin, Z. (1983) Analysis of composite materials, *J. of Applied Mechanics.* **50**, Sept., 481–505.

2.19. Valliappan, S. and Curiskis, J.I. (1984) Constitutive relationships for composite materials through micromechanics, in *Mechanics of Engineering Materials*, (eds C.S. Desai and R.H. Gallagher), John Wiley and Sons Ltd, Chichester, 611–32.

2.20. Fung, Y.C. (1965) *Foundations of Solid Mechanics.* Prentice-Hall, Englewood Cliffs, New Jersey.

2.21. Griffith, A.A. (1920) The phenomena of rupture and flow in solids. *Phil. Trans. Roy. Soc.*, A 221, 163–98.

2.22. Czarnecki, L. and Weiss, V. (1985) Meaning of synergy effects in composite materials and structures, in Proc. Int. Symp. *Brittle Matrix Composites 1*, (eds A.M. Brandt and I.H. Marshall), Elsevier Applied Science, 311–21.

3 Concrete-like composites – main kinds

3.1 Definitions and classifications

The definitions and classifications of cement and concrete-like composite materials presented below are used consequently in the next chapters. Various authors have put forward slightly different definitions and classifications and these can be found in [3.1], [3.2], [3.3], [3.4] and others. The variety is not suprising, because concrete-like composites are produced in the largest mass and volume among other building materials in the world. They are applied in different structural and non-structural elements and are made with various constituents, used in different combinations. The term concrete-like composites is somewhat wider than cement-based composites. In fact, in this chapter a few materials are mentioned which do not contain any kind of cement and other binders are applied.

Throughout the book the terms taken from classic concrete technology are used, together with those from the field of advanced composite materials. This is one of the results of consequent application of the composite materials science to the cement-based materials.

The main mechanical properties: bending strength, toughness and stiffness for a few cement composites can be compared with plastics, alumina, aluminium and steel, cf. [3.5].

Concrete-like composites are the composite materials built in an analogous way, as the concretes are. It means that they are composed of a binder and a filler, and possibly also a system of reinforcement. This group of materials is by definition larger than the scope of this book which is defined as cement-based composites.

In the ordinary concretes the Portland cement combined with sand and water is used as the binder. The filler is composed of coarse aggregate made of natural stones with specially selected grain fractions. The role of a reinforcement is played partly by the aggregate grains.

Under the term concrete-like composites a large group of materials is understood in which, with respect to ordinary concretes, all constituents may be replaced by the others. Not only Portland cements are used as binders but also other types of hydraulic cements, gypsum, bitumens, polymers and resins. The natural stone grains are replaced by various kinds of artificial lightweight aggregate, organic fillers and also by systems of separated or interconnected voids. The natural sand as the matrix component is also replaced by other fine grain fillers.

The short and long fibres and polymers which impregnate the voids systems may be used as reinforcement. Also, hard grains of any dimension play a role of reinforcement for the matrix. If the reinforcement has the form of regularly distributed steel bars and tendons, then according to the classification proposed in Section 2.3 it is a composite structure rather than a material.

Cement-based materials are limited to the composites with cements as binders. This means Portland cements as well as all other kinds of cements.

Binders can include many kinds of adhesives which provide a good bond to other constituents. Their role is to bind together fine and coarse aggregate grains and even fibres.

The word binder is used in two meanings: it may denote the Portland cement which when mixed with water binds together the sand grains; but it is also applied to cement mortar which is a binder for the coarse aggregate grains.

In most cases when a cement is mentioned, it is Portland cement that is being considered. However, the word cement also denotes other inorganic binders. When a doubt arises, the name Portland cement is used, but in other cases the word cement is sufficient for the same meaning.

In concrete-like composites two groups of organic binders are used: synthetic polymers and bitumens. The ordinary Portland cement is used together with organic binders or may be replaced entirely.

For some types of binders, like polymers or bitumens, water is not used in preparation of the mixes.

Concrete admixtures are special chemical compounds, minerals and other substances which are added in relatively small volume to the concrete or mortar batch before or during mixing, with a view to improving certain particular properties of the composite material in its fresh or hardened state. Some authors use the term admixtures to also cover substances added at the cement manufacturing stage. These substances are more often termed *additives*.

Aggregate is a system of grains of various materials, forms and dimensions. The boundary between dimensions of, so called, coarse and fine aggregates is defined conventionally at different dimensions, e.g. the maximum dimensions of a sand is 4.75 mm according to ASTM, 9.52 mm according to BSI and 2 mm according to the Polish Standards, cf. Section 4.2. That definition has certain importance when different methods of mix design are examined.

The coarse aggregate is treated as a discontinuous phase of a composite. Each particular grain is an inclusion in the matrix – the discontinuities and stress concentrations caused by the grains are often the origins of cracking.

The grains of the fine aggregate are made of natural sand in most kinds of concrete-like materials and are considered as a matrix when mixed with cement and water. On a lower level, they may also be considered as inclusions causing micro-cracks in cement paste.

The fine grain fraction may also be composed of other materials, like nonhydrated cement particles, fly ash, etc.

Different kinds of solid waste materials are used as concrete aggregate. These are slag from blast furnaces or metallurgical plants, crushed concrete and bricks, rubber particles and even municipal wastes.

The word filler is applied in most cases to those kinds of aggregate which have low strength and are used to fill a certain volume with a cheap and lightweight material.

Voids between aggregate grains are packed with a matrix in which a system of pores exists filled with air or other gases, and sometimes, temporarily, by water. Pores in the matrix appear in a natural way during the mixing processes of concrete-like materials but may be also specially induced to increase the insulation properties, to decrease the weight or to improve resistance against freezing. The pores may be separated or interconnected by channels or micro-cracks in the matrix and the overall pore fraction is an important material characteristic. However, more precise information, covering pore diameters and average distance between pores, is often required to evaluate the material frost resistance cf. 6.5.

Aggregate grains also contain pores.

Reinforcement is the component in cement-based materials which should increase their toughness and control the crack propagation. Its impact on particular kinds of strength depends on its nature and volume.

Classic reinforcement for concretes is used in the form of steel bars, wires or prestressing cables and tendons. In composite materials thin fibres are applied, either short or continuous, randomly dispersed or regularly distributed, and also in the form of mesh or fabrics, called dispersed reinforcement.

When a system of interconnected pores in a hardened concrete matrix is filled with a polymer during the impregnation process, then another type of reinforcement is created.

Ordinary concrete is a composite material made of Portland cement, sand, coarse aggregate and water. The specific weight of ordinary concrete is usually within the limits of 1800 and 2500 kg/m^3.

High performance and high strength concretes have a composition similar to ordinary concretes but are modified in such a way that high strength and other features are achieved.

Lightweight concrete is a modification of concrete in which special lightweight aggregate or admixtures, producing pore systems, are used to lower its specific weight below 1800 kg/m^3.

Heavyweight concrete is a kind of concrete obtained by using special heavy aggregate to increase its specific weight over 2400 kg/m^3.

Portland cement mortar is a mixture of Portland cement, sand and water.

Portland cement paste is a mixture of Portland cement and water.

These last four terms are mentioned only briefly, because all necessary information may be found in any handbook for concrete technology or building materials and also in the following chapters.

The examples of classification of concrete-like composites given below were selected according to the importance of the classification criteria. The main groups of materials are described in next chapters.

For the sake of brevity it is assumed here that concrete-like composites are built of three groups of components:

1. continuous phase, i.e. cement matrix;
2. discontinuous phase, i.e. grains and pores;
3. micro-reinforcement, i.e. fibres or polymer systems.

All three groups may be represented in a 3-dimensional system of coordinates

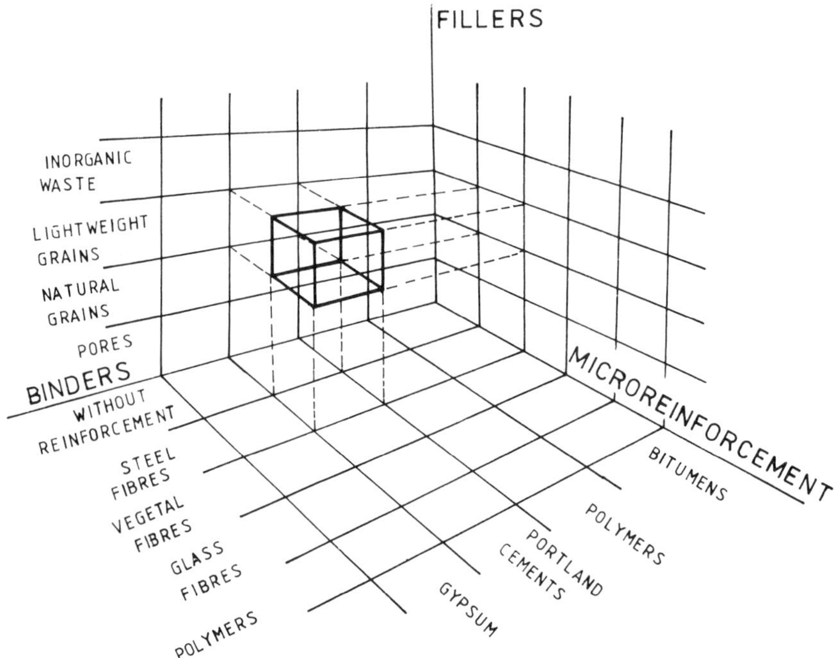

Figure 3.1 Concrete-like composites presented in a system of rectangular coordinates. (Reproduced from Brandt *et al.*, *Bases for application of concrete-like composites*; published by Center for Building Information, Warsaw, 1983.) [3.6]

in Figure 3.1. Not all regions in this space diagram are related to real materials, but all materials may be shown in particular regions. For instance, in Figure 3.1 a region is indicated which corresponds to steel-fibre reinforced concrete (SFRC) with lightweight aggregate.

The proposed classification does not cover all kinds of composite materials because only three variables are used. Therefore, several kinds of materials obtained with various types of admixtures and using different technologies may be represented only in a multi-dimension space.

In Figure 3.2 the main constituents of concrete-like materials are shown with their relations to the material structure. According to that scheme, fine aggregate grains have a double role in composite materials: together with a binder they form a continuous phase around inclusions and reinforcement, but also these grains should be considered as inclusions with respect to cement paste. Also, single fibres should be treated as inclusions when the stress concentrations are examined, for instance around the fibre ends.

The composites with brittle and ductile matrices are distinguished with respect to the matrix behaviour. The Portland cement-based materials belong to the group of brittle matrix composites, as well as ceramics. Also, resin concretes which behave in a ductile manner may show signs of brittleness in particular conditions: in low temperatures or when subjected to high rate loadings.

The brittleness of the material does not have an objective measure and usually it is determined in a relative way. This question is also considered in Chapters 9 and 10.

The concrete-like composites may be also classified according to their

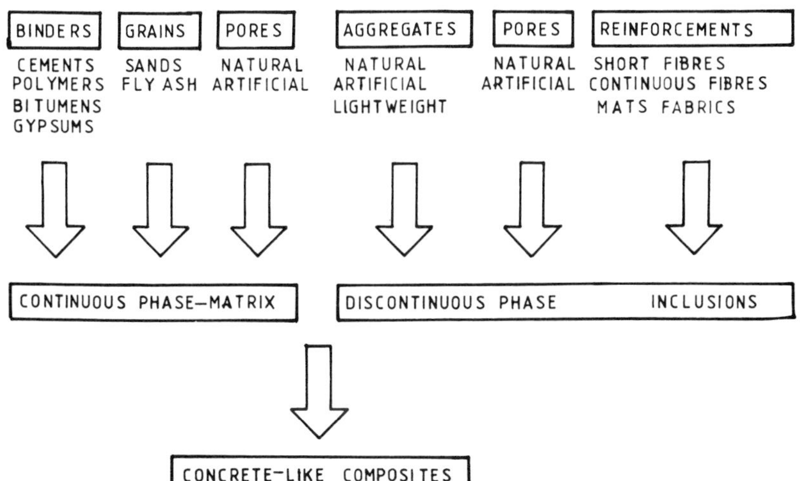

Figure 3.2 Constituents of concrete-like composites. (Reproduced from Brandt *et al.*, *Bases for application of concrete-like composites*; published by Center for Building Information, Warsaw, 1983.) [3.6]

application in construction. In such a way it is possible to distinguish the structural and nonstructural materials, the latter being used for insulation, decoration, etc. In this book the main emphasis is on structural materials whose strength and toughness are considered to be important.

3.2 Main kinds of concrete-like composites

(a) Ordinary concretes

Ordinary plain concrete is a composite material and its constituents are Portland cement mixed with water, fine aggregate (sand) and coarse aggregate which is available in the form of natural gravel or crushed stones, cf. Section 4.2.

The matrix called cement mortar is composed of cement paste with fine aggregate and the coarse aggregate grains are embedded in the matrix. Spaces between grains are filled with a matrix which cements them together. There are voids between the grains and in the matrix itself. The voids may be considered also as inclusions in a continuous matrix, causing stress concentration and crack initiation.

The ordinary concrete is used as a structural material for non-reinforced elements subjected to more or less uniform compression. Because of its low tensile strength and brittleness the main use of concrete is with passive or active reinforcement. The concrete elements reinforced with steel bars or grids are used for various types of structures thanks to the ability of concrete to be cast in any shape in a prepared framework. Tensile forces are supported by steel which starts to bear the load after a crack opens. In prestressed structures the active forces, imposed by an intermediary of steel cables or tendons, counterbalance the tensile stresses.

The concrete's strength is characterized by the results of standard compression tests which are traditionally executed 28 days after mixing and all other kinds of strength at that time, or at other ages, are related to these results. At present, one-parameter characterization of concretes is considered as insufficient and the compressive strength is believed to be somewhat inadequate. These problems are also considered in Chapter 8.

Starting from the ordinary concrete, several modifications may be obtained with different kinds of aggregate, by the introduction of a special pore structure of appropriate parameters, by the variation of quality and quantity of cement and also by application of a large variety of available admixtures and reinforcements. The application of various technologies also contributes to enlarging the field of materials based on ordinary concrete. High performance and high strength concretes are described in Section 14.5.

(b) Fibre-reinforced cement matrices

This group of materials also called fibre-reinforced concretes contains concretes and mortars reinforced with short fibres, distributed at random or linearized in a certain way as mats and fabrics. The fibres are of different materials: steel, glass, polypropylene, asbestos, etc. There are also natural organic fibres, which are used as reinforcement, (cf. Chapter 5).

The volume of fibres is usually limited by technological reasons, because with increasing fibre content the correct mixing becomes difficult or even impossible. Also the cost and efficiency of fibres are arguments put forward to reduce fibre volume to the lowest limit necessary.

The influence of fibres on the composite behaviour of elements subjected to loading is complex. In the limits of elastic deformation the fibres are not active and their role may be derived from the law of mixtures. When the micro-cracks are open, the fibres act as crack-arrestors and control their propagation. The total strength is increased thanks to fibre contribution. The load corresponding to the first crack appearance is the same or is increased when a specially high volume of fibres is added. The main fibre effect is a considerable increase in deformability and in the amount of energy of the external load which may be accumulated before the rupture occurs. The load-displacement diagram is completely different and quasi-ductility of the material behaviour is observed. The fibre-reinforced concretes and mortars offer increased toughness and that advantage is decisive for their applications.

Fibre-reinforced composites are considered in several subsequent chapters.

(c) Ferrocements

If long and thin steel wires in the form of nets and grids are introduced into the cement-based matrix the composite material obtained is called ferrocement. The nets are welded in the nodes, woven or plaited; usually they are plane but 3-dimensional are also possible. The wires are thicker than for fibre-reinforced concretes and diameters from 2 to 10 mm are used.

The application of nets has a somewhat similar influence to that of dispersed fibres, but the technology is quite different. Structural elements of various forms may be obtained at a low cost, without complete formwork, because the mortar may be placed directly on to steel nets by various procedures. Curvilinear shells, thin-walled pipes and plates are produced with ferrocement, as well as boat hulls, using only simple equipment and relatively unskilled workers.

The nodes in nets are origin-of-stress concentrations and the regular distribution of wires often corresponds to the crack pattern. There are several techniques to improve ferrocement properties by addition of thin fibres, impregnation, etc., cf. Section 14.2.2.

(d) Polymer and resin concretes

The modification of cement concretes and mortars by polymers and resins is aimed at improvement of their mechanical properties: compressive and tensile strengths, matrix-reinforcement bond, impermeability, corrosion resistance, etc.

By appropriate composition and technology a large variety of different materials may be obtained. For that purpose several kinds of monomers may be used: it means that low viscosity liquid organic materials can be formed from simple molecules which are capable of being combined chemically into polymers, composed of very large molecules.

Three kinds of concretes with polymers and resins may be distinguished:

1. Polymer Cement Concrete (PCC) in which, during mixing, monomers are added to concrete or mortar composition. The added monomers polymerize after this mixing simultaneously with the hardening of the cement or are used in the form of latexes.
2. Polymer Impregnated Concrete (PIC) obtained with hardened ordinary concretes which are permeated with monomers of sufficient viscosity. The polymerization is obtained by chemical means, by heat or radiation.
3. Polymer Concretes (PC) composed of polymers and fillers or aggregate, in which Portland cement is completely eliminated. The particulate constituent is added to pure monomer and the polymerization takes place after mixing.

Polymers and resins used in these kinds of modified concretes are presented in Section 4.1. Two groups of polymer concretes: PCC and PIC are examined in more detail in Section 14.3.

(e) Asbestos cements

Asbestos cements may be considered as the oldest man-made fibre-reinforced material. They are often considered separately because they have been produced since 1900 when other fibre-reinforced materials were not known. Natural inorganic asbestos fibres are used only with neat cement paste and a composite material is obtained with high, tensile and flexural strength and several other excellent mechanical properties.

Asbestos cements were extensively applied in building construction, mostly in the form of tiles and plates for roofs and thin-walled pipes.

Since, over the last few years evidence has emerged of a serious hazard to the health of workers in the asbestos fibres industry, the application of asbestos cements in building construction has decreased considerably. In many countries these fibres are excluded from all buildings by administrative regulations. Polypropylene fibres are used mostly as replacements [3.7].

Asbestos cements are considered in more detail in Section 14.2.1.

(f) Bitumen concretes

In bitumen concretes two kinds of organic binders are used: asphalts and tars, their properties are described in Section 4.1.

Bituminous mixes are obtained by mixing asphalt or tar with stone aggregate; also, sometimes up to 5% of rubber admixture may be added. Strong and tough coarse aggregate is required with angular grains for better interlocking. The aggregate fraction may vary considerably from 5% up to 85% of total volume. The grains should not exceed 25 mm in diameter, with sufficient volume of fine grains and dense grading to avoid segregation during preparation and placing. Because the bituminous mixes are used mostly on roads and runways a good skid resistance is required as well as resistance to freeze–thaw cycles. Angular grains are preferable, because interlocking of grains and internal friction in aggregate structures are increased and the stability of the road surface under heavy traffic and temperature variation is better assured. For the same reason, natural fine aggregate may be replaced by industrial ash. These measures also prevent the segregation, during handling, of aggregate and ravelling caused by rolling of separate layers.

Three main types of aggregate structures may be distinguished:

1. Dense graded structures with low total volume of voids and increased number of intergranular contacts are appropriate when a hot-mix with bituminous matrix is prepared.
2. Open-graded structures which do not contain the lowest sizes are used for cold mixes.
3. One-size structures (cf. Figure 6.6a) are appropriate when the spraying with bituminous matrix is executed after spreading and compacting the layer of the aggregate [3.3].

The structure of aggregate is designed usually in such a way that upper layers are formed with small grain sizes only, mostly with fine sand and stone flour as a filler, lower layers – with continuous grading, and bottom layers – with increased volume of bigger grain sizes.

Two aspects should be respected when aggregate structure is designed for bituminous mixes.

The total volume of voids filled with bitumen should be maintained as low as possible, because with the excess of the matrix the viscous deformations enhanced by long-term loading and higher temperature in the summer season may compromise the stability of the aggregate structure leading to its segregation.

Long-term properties should also be checked: low creep deformations and adequate durability of the matrix–aggregate bond are needed. Another group of practical requirements concerns the fresh-mix workability.

The volume fraction of a bitumen matrix may vary widely from 0.05 up to 0.85. To improve tensile strength, fibre reinforcement is used for road and runway overlays, utilizing various kinds of fibres: polystyrene, nylon, glass or asbestos, [3.8].

More information on bitumen concretes may be found in publications on composites and on materials for road construction, e.g. [3.3] and [3.9]. Bitumen concretes are outside the scope of this book.

(g) Fibre-reinforced gypsum

Gypsum is used in buildings for plasters, decorations, claddings and partition walls. It is considered as a non-water-resistant material and brittle if nonreinforced. There are two main types of gypsum: β-hemihydrate, called also plaster of Paris, and α-hemihydrate. The latter requires lower water content and higher strength of hardened product may be obtained.

Since the 1970s gypsum is extensively applied as a matrix with glassfibres as reinforcement. Ordinary E-glass fibres are used and the composite obtained is suitable for various indoor applications, having excellent fire resistance thanks to water combined with gypsum and to crack control by fibres.

Ordinary E-glass fibres are particularly suitable as reinforcement because of their low price. In the gypsum matrices the glassfibres do not corrode as they do in all kinds of Portland cement matrices and the main reason for introducing glassfibres gypsum in this chapter is that these products may replace in several applications the glassfibre cements, which in spite of many attempts have more or less limited durability, cf. Section 5.3. Two examples of stress–strain curves for glassfibre reinforced gypsum are shown in Figure 3.3. Specimens were cut out of sheets of a thickness of 10–13 mm produced by spraying. Plaster slurry of water/plaster ratio between 0.4 and 0.6 was reinforced with glassfibres of 50 mm. Fibres were distributed by a chopper mounted on a spray gun and the excess

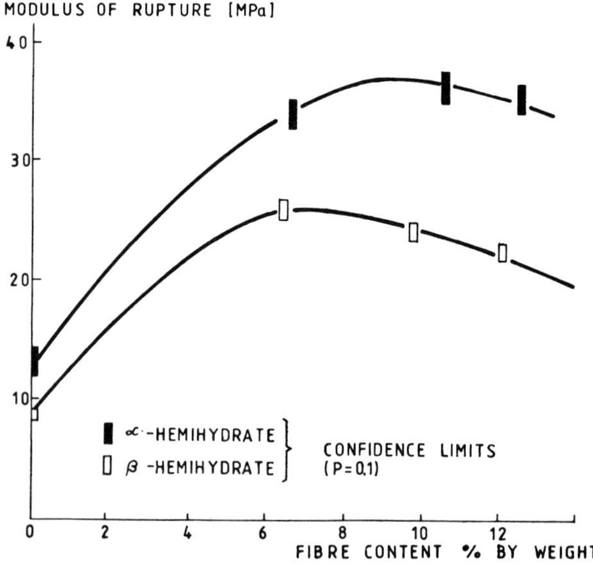

Figure 3.3 Modulus of rupture for glassfibre reinforced gypsum specimens as a function of fibre content, specimens 50 × 150 mm, thickness 10 mm. (Reproduced with permission from Ali, M.A. and Grimer, F.J., Mechanical properties of glassfibre reinforced gypsum; *J. of Materials Science*, **4**(5), pp. 389–95, published by Chapman & Hall, 1969.) [3.10]

Table 3.1 Glassfibre reinforced gypsum compositions

Components	Plain gypsum (GRG) (% mass)	Polymer modified gypsum (PGRG) (% mass)
α-hemihydrate gypsum	73.70	54.50
Polymer emulsion	–	19.00
Melamine resin	–	5.40
Total water	26.50	19.50
Antifoaming agent	–	1.20
Catalyst	–	0.27
Retarder	0.01	0.01
Glass fibres	13.00	13.00

Source: Bijen, J. and van den Plas, C., Polymer modified glassfibre reinforced gypsum; published by Chapman & Hall/Spon, 1992. [3.11]

water was extracted by suction, [3.10]. Different strength and optimum fibre contents for two matrices may be observed in Figure 3.3.

Tested specimens of glassfibre gypsum [3.11], with and without the addition of polymer emulsion and their compositions, are presented in Table 3.1. The test results produced better mechanical properties of these composites than did Portland cement matrices reinforced with glassfibres (GRC). Also, the durability of composites with polymer admixture when tested according to various accelerated procedures proved to be quite good, in high moisture, corresponding to outdoor applications and no decrease of strength and durability was observed.

Gypsum-based composites are not considered in further detail in this book.

References

3.1. Venuat, M. (1984) *Adjuvants et traitements*, published by the author, Paris.

3.2. Mindess, S. and Young, J.F. (1981) *Concrete*, Prentice-Hall, Englewood Cliffs, N. Jersey.

3.3. Nicholls, R. (1976) *Composite Construction Materials Handbook*, Prentice-Hall, Englewood Cliffs, N. Jersey.

3.4. Hannant, D.J. (1978) *Fibre Cements and Fibre Concretes*, J. Wiley, Chichester.

3.5. Birchall, J.D. and Kelly, A. (1983) *Scientific American*, **248**, 104–10.

3.6. Brandt, A.M., Czarnecki, L., Kajfasz, S. and Kasperkiewicz, J. (1983) *Bases for application of concrete-like composites*, (in Polish), Center for Building Information, Warsaw.

3.7. Krenchel, H. and Hejgaard, O. (1975) Can asbestos be completely replaced one day? in Proc. RILEM Symp., *Fibre-reinforced Cement and Concrete*, Sheffield, 335–46.

3.8. Kalabińska, M. and Piłat, J. (1985) *Technology of materials and road pavements* (in Polish), PWN, Warsaw.

3.9. Saal, R.N.J. (1966) Asphalts systems, in *Composite Materials*, (ed. L. Holliday), Elsevier Publishing Co., Amsterdam, 453–74.
3.10. Ali, M.A., and Grimer, F.J. (1969) Mechanical properties of glass-fibre reinforced gypsum. *J. of Materials Science*, **4**, no. 5, 389–95.
3.11. Bijen, J. and van den Plas, C. (1992) Polymer modified glass-fibre reinforced gypsum, in Proc. Int. Workshop RILEM/ACI, (eds H.W. Reinhardt and A.E. Naaman), June 23–26, 1991, Mainz, Chapman and Hall/Spon, London, 100–15.

4 Components of cement-based matrices

4.1 Cements and other binders

Binders and cements by their compatibility with other composite constituents bind them together and assure transmission of forces and displacements. The following are the main groups of inorganic binders:

1. hydraulic cements (pozzolans, slag cements, natural cements, high alumina cement and Portland cements);
2. non-hydraulic cements (gypsum, lime, magnesium cement);
3. hydrothermal cements;
4. sulphur cement.

The adjective hydraulic means that the product when hardened is water-resistant. Non-hydraulic materials are those that decompose when subjected to water and cannot harden under water. Among non-hydraulic cements lime may be quoted as an exception because its hardening is caused by carbon dioxide from atmospheric air; however formed $CaCO_3$ is water-resistant [4.1].

Pozzolans were obtained initially from volcanic rocks and ashes in Italy. After grinding, a kind of cement was produced. In present times that production has only local importance but 'pozzolanic' admixtures are obtained also from fly ash or burnt clays and shales. These admixtures are added to Portland cements as a less active binder which partly plays the role of a fine aggregate of low cost. As waste materials the fly ashes accumulate in industrial zones and their utilization is beneficial for ecological reasons. Silica fume also exhibits pozzolanic properties, cf. Section 4.3.9.

Slag cements are obtained from rapidly cooled blast furnace slag which is then subjected to processes of grinding and mixing with lime and Portland cement in different proportions. Besides being at a lower cost than Portland cement, the addition of slag cement improves resistance against sulphate corrosion of mortars and concretes. The form used as an admixture or additive in concrete composition is usually called Ground Granulated Blastfurnace Slag (GGBS).

Natural cements are produced from the same raw materials as Portland cements but in natural composition, therefore they are less homogeneous, cheaper, but offer lower strength.

High alumina cements are obtained from bauxite Al_2O_3 fused together with limestone at a temperature of 1600 °C to form clinker which is then ground into powder. The chemical composition of high alumina cement is given below, after [4.1], [4.2] and [4.3]:

Lime	CaO	35–44%	Magnesia	MgO	1%
Alumina	Al_2O_3	33–44%	Titanium dioxide	TiO_2	1%
Ferric oxide	Fe_2O_3	4–12%	Sulphur trioxide	SO_3	0.5%
Silica	SiO_2	3–11%	Alkalia	$K_2O + Na_2O$	0.5%
Ferrous oxide	FeO	0–10%			

High alumina cement is about three times more expensive than Portland cement, mainly because of the high energy consumption involved in grinding the hard clinkers.

Hydration of high alumina cement requires more water and mixes of better workability are obtained. The hydration process starts later, after mixing with water, but occurs more quickly with high rates of liberated heat. Also, hardening is quick and usually within 24 hours about 80% of final resistance is obtained. The hardened cement has both lower porosity and permeability.

Mortars and concretes made with high alumina cement are resistant against sulphate attack and also resist better CO_2 from ordinary drinking or mineral water. In comparison, the resistance against alkalis is lower than that of Portland cements.

High alumina cement is used in mortars for refractory brick walls and in refractory concretes when mixed with special aggregate, like corundum or fire clays.

As a result of exposure to humidity and even slightly elevated temperature a conversion reaction may start in hardened cement paste. It develops in the calcium aluminate hydrates where hexagonal crystals are transformed into cubic ones which have a smaller volume. This causes an increase of porosity and considerable decrease of strength. It has been proved that even a temperature of +38 °C can initiate the reaction, [4.4], for which the remaining amount of mixing water may be sufficient.

The conversion reaction may occur at any time during the life of a structure without prior warning, when favourable conditions appear, namely when temperature and humidity increase. This was the origin of serious failures of roofing structures in Great Britain. At present the application of high alumina cement is limited to refractory structures where there is no risk of high humidity, and to non-structural elements. Other applications are in repair work where rapid hardening is required.

Portland cements are by far the most important binder for concrete-like composites. They are obtained by grinding and mixing raw materials which contain argills and lime: clays, shales and slates together with limestones and marls. The ground materials are fused in temperature of about 1400 °C into

Table 4.1 Mineralogical composition of Portland cements

Chemical name	Abbreviated name	Chemical notation	Abbreviated notation	Mass contents (%)
Tricalcium silicate	Alite	$3CaO \cdot SiO_2$	C_3S	38–60
Dicalcium silicate	Belite	$2CaO \cdot SiO_2$	C_2S	15–38
Tricalcium aluminate		$3CaO \cdot Al_2O_3$	C_3A	7–15
Tetracalcium aluminoferite	Celite	$4CaO \cdot Al_2O_3 \cdot Fe_2O_3$	C_4AF	10–18
Pentacalcium trialuminate		$5CaO \cdot 3Al_2O_3$	C_5A_3	1–2
Calcium sulphate dihydrate	Gypsum	$CaSO_4 \cdot 2H_2O$	$C\bar{S}H_2$	2–5

clinker which is ground again into powder of particles below 100 μm and gypsum is added. The product obtained is completed by different additions to obtain the final composition which therefore may be well adapted to designed properties: strength after hardening, hydration and hardening time, colour, resistance against chemical agents, etc.

Raw materials to produce various types of Portland cement are situated and exploited in nearly all regions of the world and this is perhaps one of the reasons for its universal importance. In Tables 4.1 and 4.2 mineralogical and chemical compositions of Portland cement are shown after data published by several authors. A slightly different way of presentation of the major constituents of the Portland cements is proposed in [4.5]. The details of cement technology are beyond the scope of this book and the reader is referred to special manuals on the subject.

Not only composition but also fineness of cement has a considerable influence on the hydration process and properties of the hardened product. The fineness is expressed as a ratio between surface and mass of the grains and is usually

Table 4.2 Chemical composition of Portland cements

Chemical name	Abbreviated name	Chemical notation	Abbreviated notation	Mass contents (%)
Calcium oxide	Lime	CaO	C	58–66
Silicon dioxide	Silica	SiO_2	S	18–26
Aluminium oxide	Alumina	Al_2O_3	A	4–12
Ferric oxides	Iron	Fe_2O_3+FeO	F	1–6
Magnesium oxide	Magnesia	MgO	M	1–3
Sulphur trioxide	Sulphuric anhydrite	SO_3	$\bar{S}$	0.5–2.5
Alkaline oxides	Alkalis	K_2O and Na_2O	K+N	$\leqslant 1.0$

kept within limits from 200 to 900 m^2/kg. The fine cements offer a higher hydration rate and higher final strength. On the other hand, the higher water requirement of fine cement increases its shrinkage.

The main kinds of Portland cement are:

1. standard for ordinary concrete structures without special features;
2. rapid setting and high early strength for winter concreting and repair work;
3. low hydration heat, for massive structures like dams, large foundations, etc.;
4. high strength for high performance concretes in outstanding structures, prestressing, etc.;
5. sulphate-resistant for elements exposed to organic sewage;
6. Portland slag cements with a substantial proportion (25–85%) of ground blast-furnace slag which increases resistance against chemical corrosion but may decrease durability when exposed in outdoor conditions (blended cements).

In various countries several types of Portland cements are produced; obtained by different composition of the basic raw materials, different fineness and also by different additives. In the book [4.2] 11 main kinds of Portland cement are mentioned. Interesting data on the subject are also given in other handbooks, e.g. [4.3], [4.6] and [4.7]. The variety of cements is developing quickly and interested readers should consult recent editions of national guidelines and information published by cement producers. The chemical composition of several kinds of cement, as well as their required physical properties, are defined by those types of documents.

Further development in the variety of Portland cements is focused on the production of special kinds, like:

1. very low-heat cements for massive structures;
2. cements with spherical particles for high strength and for flowing concretes;
3. cements with grains of small and very small dimensions for high strength and improved tightness;
4. rapid set and rapid hardening cements for repair works, etc.

Expansive cements are special kinds of Portland cements which contain particular constituents that increase their volume during hydration and hardening. By appropriate composition, the shrinkage of Portland cement may be entirely compensated for, or even a final increase of total volume may be obtained, [4.5]. The expansive cements are used for special purposes, e.g. for repairs of old concrete or for structures in which shrinkage cracking should be excluded.

Gypsum is a kind of non-hydraulic cement obtained from mineral of the same name, composed mainly of $CaSO_4 . 2H_2O$ and certain amounts of different impurities. The production is based on crushing the raw material and heating it to temperatures between +130 and +170 °C for dehydration. If burnt in higher temperatures, a gypsum of higher strength is obtained. The last stage of production is the grinding into a fine powder and mixing with additives which delay and control the setting time to enable effective mixing with water and easy placing in forms.

Gypsum is used as a paste for indoor decorations and plasters for walls and ceilings. When mixed with sand and lime, various kinds of mortar are obtained for non-structural and even structural elements. The compressive strength varies within large limits from 1.0 to 7.0 MPa for the type called plaster of Paris and from 12 to 15 MPa for α-hemihydrated gypsum, [4.8]. Gypsum based composites are outside the scope of the book and only a basic description is given in Section 3.2.

Lime as quicklime CaO is obtained from natural limestone or dolomite burnt at temperatures between 950 and 1100 °C. The slaked lime obtained in the form of porous grains is mixed with water using about 2–3 m^3 of water for 1000 kgs of lime. The dense paste should be stored in conditions preventing drying and the influence of atmospheric factors, e.g. in a hole in the ground and covered by a layer of soil. The duration of maturing is decisive for the product quality: from 3 weeks up to 6 months, or even longer. The density of lime paste is about 1400 kg/m^3.

The hardening of the lime is a slow process called carbonation, which is based on the absorption of CO_2 from the atmosphere. The lime is then transformed again into limestone $CaCO_3$ and free water is evaporated. In thick brick walls the joints filled with lime mortar harden over several years.

The lime mortar is obtained by mixing lime with sand in proportions from 1:2 up to 1:4.5, adding water according to the required consistency. Also Portland cement is added to increase strength.

The strength of lime mortar specimens tested on cubes of 70 mm after 28 days was $f_c = 0.6$ MPa, and tensile strength $f_t = 0.2 - 0.3$ MPa, [4.9].

Magnesium oxychloride is obtained from magnesium oxide MgO (Sorel cement) produced by burning of magnesite $MgCO_3$ at temperatures between 600 and 800 °C. The MgO is mixed with magnesium chloride $MgCl_2$ and not with water. The hardening process is quick and already after 28 days a compressive strength of about 100 MPa may be reached. The application of magnesium oxychloride is limited to the interiors of buildings because its durability when exposed to moisture is insufficient. The main use is as a binder for sawdust to produce a composite material for floors, [4.3].

Hygrothermal cements are produced from finely ground lime and silicates mixed together and cured in high-pressure steam (autoclaving). The material obtained is used mostly in brick production. As silicates, the fly ash may be used, but its addition increases the hydration time, [4.10].

Sulphur cement has been used as a molten bonding agent for centuries. At present, sulphur cement is applied when modified with carbon and hydrogen in various proportions (not less than 80% of sulphur). For mixing with aggregate a temperature between 132 and 141 °C is required. The gradation of aggregate should ensure the appropriate volume of voids and minimum cement consumption, usually between 10 and 20% per weight.

Sulphur cement concrete offers over 70% of its final strength after 24 hours when cooled at 20 °C. The hardened concrete has considerable resistance against the highly corrosive influence of acids and salts, [4.11].

Sulphur cement requires special care and equipment *in situ*. The disadvantages of sulphur cement are the brittleness of hardened elements, low frost resistance and low melting point of +119°C and these limit larger applications.

Supersulphated cement is obtained from blast furnace slag (80–85%), calcium sulphate (10–15%) and lime or Portland cement klinker (appr. 5%). After hardening, the strength comparable to that of ordinary Portland cement may be obtained with considerably lower heat of hydration, [4.2], [4.5].

Supersulphated cement may be used in various concrete structures but is particularly useful in situations where action of acid fluids, sea water and oils should be foreseen, e.g. for foundations and harbour structures. Mixing with Portland cements and special treatment like accelerated hardening are not possible.

Bitumens are composed of two groups: asphalts and tars. These are hydrocarbons with small fractions of sulphur, oxygen, nitrogen and traces of metals. The typical composition is given by various authors; [4.1], [4.12] and [4.13]:

Carbon	80–87%
Hydrogen	9–15%
Oxygen	2–8%
Nitrogen	0.1–1%
Sulphur	0.2–7%
Metals: iron, nickel, vanadium, calcium	0–0.5%

Asphalts are obtained mostly by different refining procedures after distillation of crude oil. Also natural asphalts are exploited from surface deposits (Trinidad, Syria) or from pores filled by asphalt in sandstones and limestones where asphalt content may reach 25% of total volume of the rock. Natural asphalts are added to those obtained from oil to increase their hardness.

Asphalts may be modified to improve their properties by additions of natural or synthetic rubber or polyethylene. In modified asphalts the bonding with stone aggregate is increased as well as their resistance against atmospheric agents.

Tars are by-products from distillation of coal, brown coal, timber and peat.

Synthetic resins are used as additives in order to modify the properties of tars for application as matrix for road overlays.

The principal differences between asphalts and tars relate to temperature sensitivity and wetting ability for aggregate grains. Physical properties of tars are more dependent than asphalts on temperature influences: they become softer in high temperatures and brittle in lower ones and such effects may be observed on road pavements in summer and winter. On the other hand, tars offer higher skid resistance and wet better the aggregate grains. Good bonding is less related to the quality of grain surface: its cleanness and roughness. Ageing processes accelerated by the influence of oxygen from the atmosphere and by sunlight are quicker in tars and they lead to increased brittleness, [4.13].

Mechanical behaviour of bitumens is basically viscoelastic. Under high loading rates they are elastic and brittle. When the load is imposed over a long time their deformability is similar to viscous materials. With respect to temperature variations, tars behave as thermoplastics; this means that with increasing temperature they are transformed gradually from brittleness to fluidity, with a simultaneous decrease of material adhesion and cohesion when softening temperature is attained. That transformation is entirely reversible within a certain range of temperature.

To characterize a bitumen several physical values should be measured, e.g.:

1. dynamic viscosity, expressed in Pa.s;
2. softening point which is the temperature in °C mentioned above;
3. penetration grade as the distance expressed in 0.1 mm units that a standard needle penetrates in 5 seconds under 100 g load and at a temperature of 20 °C;
4. ductility expressed by the distance in 10 mm units to which a 10 mm square cross-section briquet can be deformed by tensile load applied at 20 °C and with displacement rate equal to 50 mm/min.

These are examples of standard tests of the main properties, but in different countries other testing procedures are required.

Bitumens are used as insulation layers and coatings, but their use as binders in mixes with natural stone aggregate for road and runway pavements is the main application. Addition of sulphur (up to 50%) improves the penetration index and matrix–aggregate bond. In special cases, like pavement repair, asphalts may also be used in the form of emulsions and cutbacks. Tars are usually more expensive than asphalts and their application for road pavements may be considered as non-rational.

Organic cements is the general name covering: bitumens, synthetic polymers and resins. These materials are briefly described below with more emphasis placed on their properties as composite constituents, i.e. as mortars and pastes than on their application as, for instance, insulation layers. Details of technological processes and chemical composition are described only briefly here and

Table 4.3 Properties of resins for polymer concretes

Types of materials	Density ρ (kg/m^3)	Viscosity in 20 °C η (Pa.s)	Strength compr. f_c (MPa)	Strength tens. f_t (MPa)	Modulus of elasticity E (GPa)	Hardness H_B (MPa)
Hardened by polymerization:						
Polyesters	1050–1300	0.2–2.0	90–250	30–90	1.5–6.0	100–200
Epoxies	1100–1200	2–80	90–200	30–90	1.5–7.0	100–300
Acrylics	940–1250	0.0006–0.0015	50–150	40–120	3.0–6.0	160–200
Polyurethanes	1100–1200	0.3–3.0		20–70	1.5–2.5	
Styrenes	1000–1070	0.0008–0.002	70–150	45–90	2.0–5.0	140–300
Hardened by polycondensation:						
Furanics	1090–1200	0.5–3.0	80–150	9–15	1.0–14.0	100
Phenolics	1140–1200	0.5–3.0	25–75	8.5	1.0–9.0	200
Urethanes	1250–1260	0.05–3.0	22–50			

(Source: Czarnecki, L., *Resin Concretes*; published by Arkady, 1982.) [4.14]

further information should be sought in specialized handbooks on building materials, e.g. [4.1].

Synthetic polymers and resins considered here are those which are used for concrete-like materials. Polymers are applied for modification of the properties of concrete and three main groups of these modifications may be distinguished: as binders for aggregate systems together with Portland cement, as the sole binder or as impregnants for hardened concretes and mortars.

The synthetic materials may be classified into two groups:

1. Thermoplastics become ductile when heated but within a certain range of temperatures there are no permanent chemical transformations. Here polyvinyls, acrylics, polyamides, polymethyl methacrylates and polystyrenes may be mentioned as examples.
2. Thermosets are stiff and rigid in normal temperatures, but when heated the irreversible modifications appear. Here there are polyepoxies, polyesters, aminoplastics, polyurethanes, silicons, etc.

The resins may be also considered according to the methods of their confection and that viewpoint is represented in Table 4.3 where examples of resins used for PC and PCC are listed with their mechanical properties.

The examples of monomers which are used for PIC are shown in Table 4.4. The low viscosity of monomers is essential to obtain required depth of impregnation within reasonable time of a few hours. The monomers should also have capability of quick polymerization by heating or radiation, or preferably by chemical means without additional expenditure of energy. Hardened polymers increase

Table 4.4 Properties of polymers for PIC

Types of materials	Density ρ (kg/m^3)	Viscosity in 20 °C η (Pa.s)	Strength compr. f_c (MPa)	Strength tens. f_t (MPa)	Modulus of elasticity E (GPa)
Monomers:					
Methyl methacrylate MMA	945	0.00085	80–130	40–80	3.0
Styrene S	906	0.00076	80–110	35–80	2.8–3.5
Trimethylolpropane trimethacrylate TMPTMA		0.00058			
Butyl acrylate BA		0.0009			
Prepolymers:					
Polyester styrene PE/S	1050–1300	0.2–2.0	90–200	30–90	1.5–6.0
Epoxies E	1160	0.4–12	130–140	50–80	4.0–4.5

(Source: Brandt, A.M., Czarnecki, L., Kajfasz, S. and Kasperkiewicz, J., published by COIB, Warsaw 1983) [4.15]

considerably the strength, toughness and durability of final products. Moreover, the composite properties may be tailored by selection of monomer composition and by appropriate technology.

A basic description of PCC and PIC composites is given in Section 14.3.

4.2 Aggregates and fillers

4.2.1 KINDS OF AGGREGATES

The amount of aggregate or filler is usually between 60 and 85% of volume fraction in all kinds of concrete-like composites. Therefore their influence on mechanical and other properties is important. Also the unit cost of composite material is closely related to the kind of aggregate used.

Aggregates may be classified according to their density into the following categories:

1. heavyweight aggregate of density above 3000 kg/m^3;
2. structural aggregate of density between 2000 and 3000 kg/m^3;
3. lightweight aggregate of density below 2000 kg/m^3.

Here the density is understood as absolute density; it relates to solid material excluding voids between grains. However, in this meaning of density the inherent porosity of the material is taken into account which varies from a few percent for hard rocks to much larger values for porous natural or artificial aggregates.

Table 4.5 Examples of aggregates and fillers for concrete-like composites

Types of materials	Characteristic dimension (mm)	Density ρ (10^3kg/m^3)	Compressive strength f_c (MPa)	Modulus of elasticity E (GPa)
Natural aggregates:				
Pit and river sand	0.05–2.0	2.6–3.0	150–350	40–90
Gravel and crushed aggregates:				
Basalt, gabbro	2–300	2.9–3.0	200–400	80–160
Granite	2–300	2.5–3.0	160–330	40–50
Sandstone	2–300	2.4–2.7	50–250	60–80
Limestone	2–300	1.7–2.8	100–240	60–80
Porphyrite	2–300	2.8	160–270	
Quartz	2–300	2.6		50–60
Shiste	2–300	1.5–3.2	60–170	
Natural lightweight aggregates:				
Pumice, scoria, tuff				
Volcanic cinders	5–80	0.5–1.0	8–12	
Sawdust, wood chips		0.3–0.8		
Cork		0.065–0.12		
Lightweight porous limestones		1.2–1.6		
Artificial lightweight aggregates:				
Burnt porous clays and shales	3–25	0.6–1.8		
Burnt porous shistes	3–25	0.8–1.9		5–15
Perlite, vermiculite		0.03–0.40	0.8–1.2	
Polystyrene beads	2–5	0.01–0.05		
Glass beads	0.5–5.0	2.1–3.0	50–120	40–80
Glass bubbles	10–30			
Blast-furnace slag (light wt.)	5–30	1.0–1.1	80–100	
blast-furnace slag (heavy wt.)	5–30	2.7–2.9	120–240	
Expanded blast furnace slag		0.65–0.9		
Crushed bricks	2–120	1.6–1.8	5–35	10–30
Crushed concrete	10–120	1.9–2.3		
Sintered fly ash		1.3–2.1		
Heavyweight natural aggregates:				
Barites and iron ore	2–300	3.4–6.3	50–80	
Heavyweight artificial aggregates:				
Iron beads, scrap iron	2–20	7.8	300–400	210

In concrete-like composites natural stone aggregate is used in the form of gravel or crushed rock and sand.

Aggregates are obtained from all kinds of rocks as a result of the natural processes of abrasion and weathering. Natural aggregates are also produced in quarries where rock is crushed into applicable sizes. The main types of rocks are: basalts, granites, sandstones and limestones, but other rocks are also used according to their availability in proximity to application. For ordinary applications it is usually meaningless to distinguish other types of rocks according to their origin and mineralogical composition. Only for high performance concretes or when danger of alkali–aggregate reaction exists is there a need for deep petrographical and mineralogical studies, cf. Sections 4.2.2 and 14.5.

Artificial aggregate may be obtained from various kinds of slags, fly ashes, burnt clays and shales, crushed bricks and concrete, etc. Also mineral and organic wastes are used as fillers for concrete.

As a special heavy-weight aggregate, barite $BaSO_4$, and other heavy-weight minerals as well as iron ores or scrap iron are used for concrete shields against radiation and for other structures where increased weight is needed. Barite together with coarse marble aggregate is used for industrial anti-static floors.

Examples of aggregates and fillers are listed in Table 4.5.

4.2.2 PROPERTIES OF AGGREGATES

The most important characteristics of aggregate grains are:

1. shape and texture;
2. compressive strength;
3. other mechanical properties;
4. distribution of grain sizes.

Other properties of aggregate which should also be considered are: cleanness, humidity, thermal expansion coefficient, chemical relation to Portland cement, etc.

According to their shape, rounded grains of natural gravel and sand are distinguished from angular grains obtained from crushed rocks. The grains may be more or less similar to spheres and cubes or very elongated, needle-like, which are considered as inadequate for good concretes.

In concrete-like composites the aggregate grains participate in load bearing together with the cement matrix, relative to the stiffness of both these phases. The necessary condition is, however, a sufficient bond strength along the aggregate–matrix interface. The bond depends not only on the roughness of the grain surface but also on its cleanness, lack of very fine clay particles and other impurities. In some cases also, a chemical bond between grains and cement paste appears, but the aggregate–matrix bond is mostly of a mechanical character. The bond is never ideal and continuous: local effects and discontinuities are always detected.

The grain surface texture is very important. For instance, the surface of basalt grains is much less developed than that of limestone ones. That is one of the reasons why the basalt grain–matrix bond is usually weak and cracks are more susceptible to develop and propagate in the interface. Another reason is the chemical affinity. The properties of that interface are different for limestone grains. The problems related to aggregate–matrix bonding are presented in detail in Section 7.2.

Hard and strong aggregate is a necessary constituent of a high quality structural concrete. Less strong kinds of aggregate are more suitable when lower concrete strength is required. However, the relation between the strength of aggregate and that of hardened composite is not linear, mostly because of the influence of the interface, mentioned above. When strong aggregate is used, then the matrix is weaker and cracks are propagated across the matrix. In contrast, in concretes with lightweight aggregate the matrix is stronger and cracks cross the aggregate grains, cf. Section 9.2. It is, however, generally admitted that for high performance concretes both characteristics: grain strength and aggregate–matrix bond, should be considered.

The shock and abrasion resistance of aggregate may be important for structures where actions of that kind are to be foreseen. The porosity of grains, even as it increases their bond, may cause excessive variability of moisture content. The porosity of aggregate grains adversely influences the frost resistance of the composite. In many regulations and standards concerning concretes the aggregate properties and percentage of weak grains, impurities etc. are limited.

In several countries the deposits of hard natural rocks or gravels, which may be used for concretes, are already exploited or are distant from regions of mass concrete production. Therefore, lower quality aggregates are used which often implies serious difficulties in maintaining the concrete quality. Lower concrete strength and inadequate durability, lower workability or higher cement consumption, poor aspect after a few years and other negative outcomes are observed as resulting from the use of low quality aggregate.

The chemical properties of aggregate were previously often neglected in concrete composition. It was believed that the aggregate behaved as though inert in the cement paste and that any kind of aggregate may be used to produce a good concrete, provided that the physical properties of grains are taken into account and that adequate grading is designed. However, it is known at present that certain kinds of rocks are susceptible to react with moisture and highly alkaline Portland cement paste where pH is equal to around 13.5.

The main type of alkali–aggregate reaction (AAR) is observed when aggregates with a special reactive form of silica is used, like opal, chalcedony and tridymite. Other types of alkali reactions occur when the decomposition of dolomites takes place, also due to alkalis present in Portland cement or introduced with de-icing agents. In 1940 it was shown [4.16] for the first time that chemical reactions may develop, between certain kinds of aggregate and the alkaline environment of Portland cement paste, which induce swelling due to reaction products. As a result Féret's thesis about the inert character of aggregate in concrete has been contradicted and abolished.

In all cases, the products of reaction $nNa_2O.mSiO_2.pH_2O$, in the form of gels, increase their volume and swell, which may have disastrous consequences on the integrity of the hardened concrete. Even after several years large cracks appear on external faces of concrete elements and serious repairs are necessary.

In many countries and regions the types of rocks mentioned above are encountered relatively seldom and are avoided without serious difficulties. In other countries, like Japan, where volcanic rocks are prevailing, their use can be made possible with Portland cements blended with fly ash or silica fume to decrease their alkalinity, [4.17]. Silica fume binds alkalis from the Portland cement into stable and non-expansive products, thus decreasing alkalinity approximately from a pH of 13.6 to 12.5. There also exist possibilities for use of these rocks with other binders, for instance in bitumen concretes. The methods of checking the aggregate for that kind of risk are long, expensive and not perfectly reliable and for important works the use of aggregate tested by previous experience is advised. It is not clear why in many structures made with potentially reactive aggregate no deleterious results were observed, while in other cases large cracks and even disasters occurred. These different behaviours are probably related to different moisture conditions and temperature: reaction is quickest when temperature is close to +40 °C.

In the last few years tests also prove that in countries apparently free from any volcanic activity, certain categories of post-glacial aggregates may produce dangerous effects of AAR, encountered for example in concrete structures of buildings in Poland, [4.18].

The principal measures aimed at preventing destructions due to AAR may be summarized as:

1. use of low alkali Portland cements, i.e. below 0.6% of equivalent of Na_2;
2. limitation of the Portland cement content to keep alkali content below $3\,kg/m^3$;
3. blending the reactive aggregate with non-reactive ones;
4. application of mineral admixtures and fillers like condensed silica fume, fly ash, stone powder, which may replace up to 20% of Portland cement.

The influence of fly ash was experimentally examined in [4.19]. High amounts of fly ash were used with potentially reactive aggregate and proved its efficiency in inhibiting expansion due to AAR products.

All these measures should be considered when for economical reasons total elimination of reactive aggregate is not possible.

Extensive research results on AAR are reported in [4.20]. For further details on aggregate properties the reader is also referred to handbooks on concrete technology [4.5] or to a few special works on that subject like chapters in [4.21] and [4.22].

4.2.3 LIGHTWEIGHT AGGREGATES

Natural lightweight aggregates are mostly obtained from volcanic rocks and their application is of local character.

Artificial aggregates are produced in several countries for three main reasons:

1. to satisfy the increasing demand for aggregate, if possible, close to concrete production;
2. to exploit large volumes of industrial wastes, accumulated in the neighbourhood of metallurgical and other plants;
3. to obtain various kinds of lightweight concrete for non-structural elements and insulation layers.

The production of artificial aggregates requires several procedures, according to particular conditions and requirements.

Blast-furnace slags are crushed into grains.

Clays and shales are burnt in temperatures between 1000 and 1200 °C to generate gases and to obtain porous structure of final material after cooling and crushing.

Expanded slag is produced by cooling molten slag with water to entrap steam and to obtain porous material.

Expanded glass and polystyrene beads are of lowest density and they create a system of pores in the structure of hardened concrete or mortar.

The bulk density of lightweight aggregate may vary between 30 and 1800 kg/m^3, as is shown in Table 4.5. Much information on lightweight aggregate may be found in [4.22].

4.2.4 FILLERS

This term is used for those kinds of aggregates which because of very low Young's modulus do not participate at the load bearing. Their strength is low or quite negligible and the role of fillers is:

- to improve the insulation properties of concretes;
- to decrease the weight of these concrete elements and layers, where high strength is not needed;
- to fill a part of volume with relatively lightweight and inexpensive material;
- to decrease the amount of cement, which is expensive and is a source of shrinkage.

As fillers, different kinds of materials are used: sawdust and timber chips, cork, rubber waste and various other types of wastes.

The most important kind of fillers are pores produced in a fresh mix by different procedures and admixtures, producing foam in cement paste.

Systems of pores are specially created in the matrix to increase the freeze–thaw resistance. Air-entrained mixes also behave better during handling and placing in forms. In so-called cellular concrete a perfect control of final material density is achieved by selection of pore volume and dimensions. The structures formed with pores are described in more detail in Section 6.5.

The following are used as micro-fillers:

- calcareous powders with specific area around $0.6\,m^2/g$;
- fly ashes, which are not always improving the material properties and sometimes are considered as decreasing the durability of outdoor structures;
- silica fumes which are particularly widely used in recent years.

Intergranular spaces and micro-pores may be partly blocked by micro-fillers acting as inert components. This effect is enhanced by intrinsic pozzolanic activity of the majority of micro-fillers (cf. Section 4.3.9).

4.2.5 AGGREGATE GRADING

The grain size distribution of aggregate should be carefully designed and checked if concrete of good quality is to be prepared. The grading is established after sieve analysis using sieves in accordance with local standards; usually separate sieve systems are used for coarse and fine aggregates.

The aggregate grading selection for application in concrete structures is restricted by national standards and international recommendations, e.g. [4.23]. Examples of grading curves showing the limits of admissible grading variation are given in Figure 4.1. According to the Polish Standard, 2.0 mm diameter

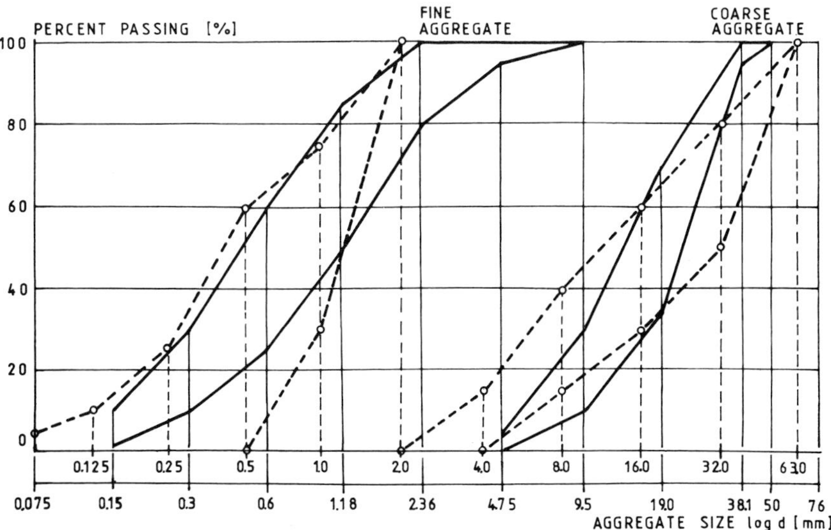

Figure 4.1 Examples of limit grading curves for fine and coarse aggregates, according to ASTM C33 (continuous line) and to Polish Standard for Ordinary Concrete PN-1989/B-06250 [4.24] (broken line). Admissible regions are situated between the respective curves.

grain has been accepted as a boundary between coarse and fine aggregate. It is based on an observation that the voids between tightly packed grains of diameter equal to approximately 2.4 mm, form an effective boundary between qualitatively different absorption abilities of the capillary water, [4.25]. The phenomenon of water retention in sand has been accepted as a physical basis to distinguish between coarse and fine aggregate. In other national regulations that limit is different, e.g. in the USA according to ASTM it is 4.75 mm (No. 4 sieve). Several examples of sieve limit curves are shown in [4.5].

The aggregate grading may be represented not only by sieve curves, but also by triangular diagrams. An example of such a diagram is shown in Figure 4.2 in which sieve limit curves from Figure 4.1 as indicated by the Polish Standard are reproduced. In that representation only three aggregate components are taken into account and the corresponding admissible region is determined.

In the design of grading several factors should be taken into account and it is generally assumed that there is no 'ideal' grading suitable for all occasions. For concretes of controlled quality it is usually necessary to separate available aggregate into sizes and to recombine it according to desired proportions.

In continuous grading all grain sizes are represented and theoretically the volume is best packed by grains. The highest strength may be then expected but the workability of such a mix is unsatisfactory, therefore the maxing and

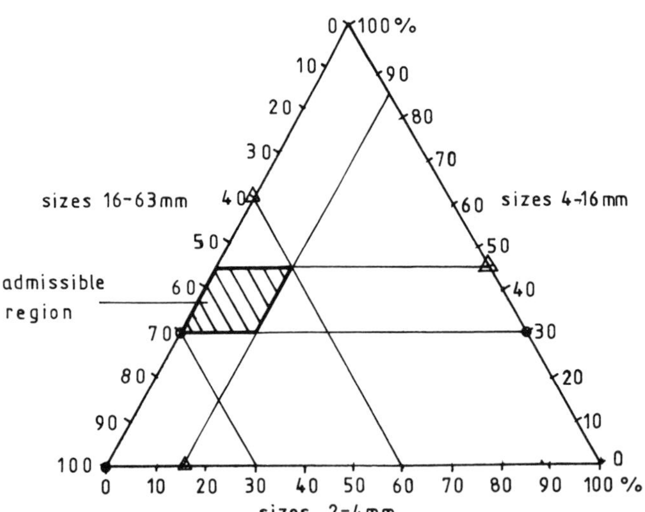

Figure 4.2 Limit curves from Polish Standard as indicated in Figure 4.1 represented in the form of a triangular diagram.

placing in forms may be expensive and ineffective. For such a mix an additional amount of cement paste is necessary.

When the grading is discontinuous, called gap grading, it means that when certain segments of a corresponding curve obtained after sieve separation are horizontal, even if that curve is situated within the prescribed limits, some grain sizes are absent. In that case usually less sand and cement may be used to achieve the same concrete strength, but the danger of segregation arises during transport and handling of the fresh mix.

A very careful design of grading is difficult to achieve, because probably such aggregate is not readily available and the collection or transportation at long distance requires additional expense. Therefore, final design of aggregate is a compromise between a solution obtained from theoretical considerations and the economic situation.

The aggregate grading may be described not only graphically but also in a numerical way. In the latter case, the description is less detailed and limited to one or two numbers. The advantages of numerical description are obvious for example in application to simple optimization problems. Among the numerical characterizations of aggregate the fineness modulus and the specific surface may be mentioned. Pertinent details can be found in handbooks, e.g. [4.5].

The design of concrete composition, including the selection of optimum aggregate grading, considering both mechanical and economical factors, is a typical problem for mathematical optimization, cf. [4.26], Section 12.4 and Chapter 13. In any case, every designed grading of aggregate should be checked by a trial mix to determine its effective workability, eventual segregation or other negative effects.

For further information concerning selection and properties of aggregate the reader is referred to the above mentioned sources and other text books for concrete technology, e.g. [4.1], [4.6] and [4.27].

4.3 Concrete admixtures

4.3.1 KINDS OF ADMIXTURES

According to the definition in Section 3.1 the admixtures are added to the batch before or during mixing. The objective of admixtures is to modify and to improve certain properties of the fresh mix or of the hardened composite. It is important to mention that a well designed and correctly executed concrete already may have these properties in a larger or smaller degree.

There are many different kinds of admixtures and it would exceed the scope of this section to describe them all in detail. The main groups of admixtures are:

1. accelerators or retarders which influence the processes of cement hydration to help in application of special technologies;
2. plasticizers and superplasticizers which increase the fluidity of the fresh mix or reduce the volume of mixing water for the same fluidity;

3. air-entraining agents which introduce a system of well-sized and distributed pores to the matrix;
4. other admixtures which improve resistance against certain external actions, reduce the hydration heat of Portland cement, decrease the permeability, modify the colour of hardened concrete, etc.

The admixtures are manufactured by various specialized firms as ready-to-use products with guaranteed properties. In most countries every year several new admixtures appear. Their producers are obliged to give all technical data together with detailed instructions for use. Also, the main and additional effects of admixtures should be clearly stated. It is, however, advisable to verify every admixture in local conditions before serious application on a larger scale.

New generations of admixtures present very advanced properties, e.g. enabling considerable water reduction, up to 30%, to be obtained together with air-entrainment.

The admixtures are presented in full detail in [4.10] and also, in a shorter way, in several handbooks for concrete technology, e.g. [4.3], [4.5], [4.6], [4.27] and [4.28]. Recent products are introduced permanently onto the market and users should follow the producers' recommendations, always controlling the results obtained, possible side effects and compatibility with other components of the mix.

4.3.2 ACCELERATORS

The acceleration of hydration and hardening is needed for different purposes, e.g. concreting in low temperatures, repair works, etc. The most commonly used accelerator is calcium chloride $CaCl_2$; its amount is limited to up to 2% of the

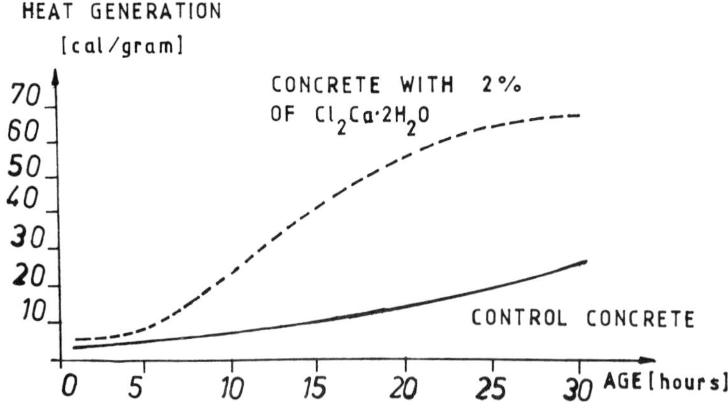

Figure 4.3 Heat generated during cement hydration – influence of an accelerating admixture. (Reproduced with permission from Venuat, M., (*Adjuvants et traitements*; published by the author, 1984.) [4.10]

cement mass. By accelerating the hydration of Portland cement, the rate of heat is increased which helps to maintain an acceptable temperature in cold weather. The temperature should not fall lower than a few degrees below 0 °C. The amount of heat liberated with and without the admixture for concreting at a temperature of +5 °C is shown in Figure 4.3, after [4.10]. For higher temperature the admixture is less effective.

It is considered as inadmissible to increase the amount of $CaCl_2$ because several negative effects may be expected: increase of drying shrinkage, lower resistance against frost and sulphate aggression and higher risk of aggregate–alkali reaction. The most important effect, however, is an increased risk of corrosion of reinforcement and that is why the application of $CaCl_2$ is decreasing.

There are accelerating admixtures based on other compounds, but these are more expensive, e.g. $Ca(NO_3)_2$.

Another kind of admixture is used when an acceleration of normal processes of cement hydration is not needed, but a very rapid set in a few minutes is necessary to execute particular technological operations, like repair or shotcrete of wet surfaces, [4.27]. In such a case the following are used: aluminium chloride, potassium carbonate, ferric salts and others.

4.3.3 SET-RETARDERS

These admixtures to slow down the cement hydration are used in hot climates to decrease the rate of heat liberation. A similar effect is needed in the execution of external surfaces which are finished by special procedures, like exposing coarse aggregates. In other cases these admixtures are used when more time is needed for casting fresh concrete before cement hydration takes place.

Various compounds are used as set-retarders based on sugar, lignosulphonic or hydroxy-carboxylic acids and salts, also inorganic salts, [4.6]. For example, sugar added as 0.05% of cement mass may delay the set by four hours approximately.

The long-term concrete strength is not modified by set-retarders.

4.3.4 PLASTICIZERS

Plasticizers are applied for the following reasons:

1. to obtain higher strength of hardened concrete by decreasing the water/cement ratio with the same workability of the fresh mix;
2. to obtain the same workability with smaller cement content and reduced generation of internal heat during cement hydration;
3. to increase the workability and to reduce risk of segregation, which results in cheaper and more effective handling of fresh mix;
4. to improve impermeability and frost resistance together with other properties related to reduced water/cement ratio.

Certain plasticizers may also accelerate or delay the hydration processes.

The action of plasticizers consists of increasing the mobility of cement particles by reduction of the interfacial tension and increase of electrokinetic potential. In this way the flocculation tendency of cement particles, and also of other fine particles in the fresh mix, is considerably reduced and a thin water cover appears around these particles.

The reduction of water by 5 to 10% is normally achieved by use of plasticizers.

Because the active surface of cement is increased, a higher initial and final strength of concrete is obtained of better durability.

The plasticizers are produced on the basis of several organic compounds: lignosulphonic and hydroxylated carboxylic acids and salts, polyols and others. Usually between 0.2 and 0.5% of cement mass is added in an appropriate way, more often directly to the mixing water. The increased amount of a plasticizer may cause retardation effects and a longer setting time.

4.3.5 SUPERPLASTICIZERS

Superplasticizers are used at present in three situations for different aims:

1. to produce flowing concrete without considerable modification of the initial mix composition and without a large loss of strength;
2. to obtain the concrete with required strength using small amounts of Portland cement;
3. to achieve high strength concretes thanks to considerable reduction of amount of water and water/cement ratio but maintaining the required workability.

The effects are more important than with plasticizers, for example, water may be reduced by 15–30%. Such results cannot normally be obtained by increasing the amount of a plasticizer without a risk of large side effects: considerable slow down of the rate of cement hydration or excessive porosity.

The result of a superplasticizer is shown schematically in Figure 4.4 in the form of a relationship between the water/cement ratio and workability. By using superplasticizers all modifications indicated by arrows 1, 2 and 3 are possible. The plasticizers act principally as water reducers for constant workability, which is indicated by arrow 3 in Figure 4.4.

The improvement of workability is limited to a short time and usually after 30–45 minutes it returns to normal. Therefore, the handling of concrete and placing it in forms should be appropriately scheduled.

Different compounds are used as superplasticizers, e.g.:

1. sulphonated melamine formaldehyde condensates;
2. sulphonated naphthalene formaldehyde condensates.

The hydration and hardening processes in concrete are not modified by superplasticizers, only a slight increase of porosity is sometimes observed. If

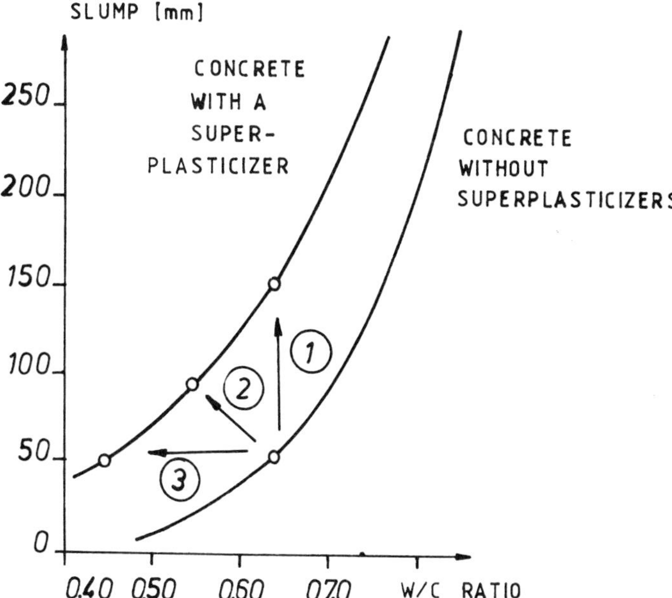

Figure 4.4 Influence of a superplasticizer on the workability and w/c ratio of concrete; 1) increase of workability; 2) increase of workability together with decrease of w/c; 3) decrease of w/c ratio. (Reproduced with permission from Venuat, M., *Adjuvants et traitements*; published by the author, 1984.) [4.10]

the water/cement ratio is decreased, then a considerable increase of strength may be expected, even by 50%, Figure 4.5. Additional increase of strength occurs due to better packing of particles in the fresh mix. Various kinds of high strength and high performance concretes are designed and executed with low and very low values of w/c, which is possible by appropriate application of superplasticizers. On the other side there are flowing concretes which may be pumped without difficulties.

The application of superplasticizers may also facilitate obtaining good workability with a composition of aggregate grains which is far from perfect. In such a case, while avoiding improvements of aggregate, considerable economies may be obtained.

New generations of superplasticizers containing reactive polymeric dispersants allow workability to be maintained over a 60 minute period which helps considerably in all on-site operations.

4.3.6 AIR-ENTRAINERS

The purpose of air-entrainment in cement mortar and concrete is to improve their frost resistance. Only uniformly distributed air pores of appropriate

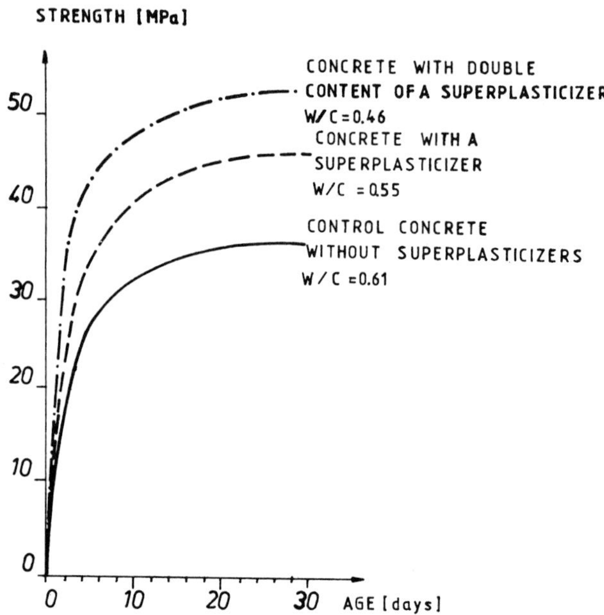

Figure 4.5 Increase of concrete strength as a function of age for various superplasticizer content with constant workability. (Reproduced with permission from Venuat, M., *Adjuvants et traitements*, published by the author, 1984.) [4.10]

dimensions increase the resistance against freeze–thaw cycles. Concrete structures exposed directly to natural weather conditions in regions of cold and moderate climate are in danger of surface destructions of various kinds (cf. Section 6.5). In many countries application of air-entrainers for such structures is imposed by standards. Other kinds of large pores and air voids caused by an excess of water and incomplete compaction of the fresh mix have no effect on that property, which is very important for durability of outdoor structures. The necessary amount of air-entraining agent is determined as a function of the volume of water in the capillary pores where it might be transformed into ice. In very high performance concretes with low water/cement ratios the air-entraining agents are not needed, cf. Section 14.5.

An effective system of air pores may be obtained by special admixtures. The conditions imposed on them are:

1. volume of entrained air should be controlled and it remains usually between 3 and 4%, only rarely may reach 10%;
2. average spacing between nearest air pores should be about 0.18 mm for concretes and 0.30 mm in mortars.

The volume of entrained air is treated as additional with respect to unavoidable

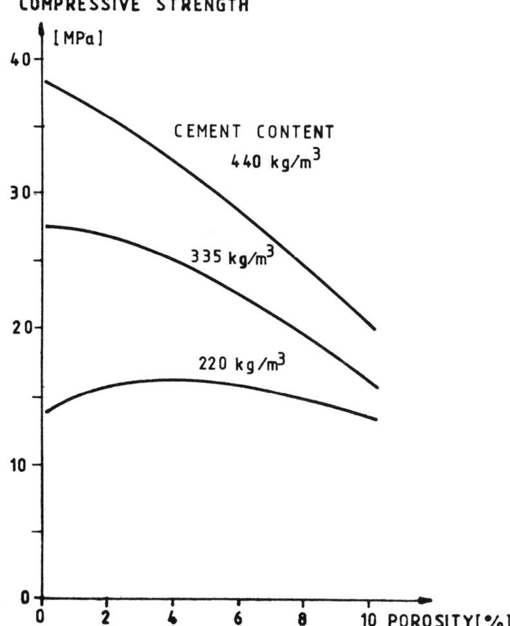

Figure 4.6 Influence of volume of closed pores on the compressive concrete strength for different cement contents and constant workability (slump 80–110 mm). (Reproduced with permission from Venuat, M., *Adjuvants et traitements*; published by the author, 1984.) [4.10]

air pores and voids entrapped during mixing. The pores decrease the concrete strength and that effect should be considered in material design and strength prediction, cf. Figure 4.6.

Air-entrainers are manufactured from:

1. salts of wood resins, sulphonated lignins and petroleum acids;
2. synthetic detergents; or
3. other compounds, producing in the cement-based matrix a foam of dense air bubbles which can survive the handling and mixing operations.

The application of air-entrainers also has other results: the workability of the fresh mix is increased and impermeability is improved, therefore better resistance against de-icing agents is achieved.

There exist, also, air-detraining admixtures, e.g. silanes in an emulsified mineral oil base or tributyl phosphate, [4.29].

4.3.7 WATER REPELLENTS

These admixtures decrease water penetration across a hardened porous cement matrix, but cannot be used to eliminate water migration and the term 'dampproofing' is not correctly applied. They are used on concrete surfaces against rain and ground water penetration. The water repellents are produced on the bases of silicones, acrylic resins or petroleum products.

4.3.8 ADMIXTURES DECREASING PERMEABILITY

They are composed of fine mineral particles (bentonites, ground limestone, rock dust) and chemical compounds (e.g. sulphonates) in order to limit water migration. These admixtures are added as 1–2% of mass of Portland cement. Other effects are the workability improvement and decrease of mixing water by 5–10%.

4.3.9 POZZOLANS AND INERT MINERAL ADMIXTURES

Several kinds of finely ground materials are added to cement mix in order:

1. to increase concrete density, impermeability and strength;
2. to improve workability without increasing cement content;
3. to decrease risk of segregation during transport and handling;
4. to decrease cement content for lower heat generation and cost.

Silica fume (SF) was considered initially as a waste material, obtained in the production of ferrosilicon and silicon metal. Already, in the early 1970s in Scandinavian countries and in USA, SF was used as a valuable admixture for high strength cement composites. It has a form of very small particles of average diameter between 0.1 and 0.3 μm which fill capillary pores in cement paste, increasing in this way the concrete density and impermeability. Because of the high content of amorphous SiO_2 (usually above 80% and sometimes up to 96% by mass) its reaction with lime liberated from cement hydration develops appreciable pozzolanic effects and increases the strength of hardened cement paste. Influence of SF on the compressive strength of concrete is shown in Figure 4.7 and is partly attributed to a reduction of the aggregate–matrix transition zone thickness. That reduction from about 50 μm to less than 8 μm has been observed [4.31]. Reinforcing that zone by both reaction products of silica fume with Portland cement and the presence of hard silica particles is suggested in [4.32].

Silica fume acts also as a superplasticizer and the desired workability of fresh mix is obtained with lower water volume. It is, however, always used together with a superplasticizer because of its high water demand. Mixing time is increased to allow a good distribution of silica fume with all the other components of the mix. For that reason, as well as to decrease the dispersion of silica fume in the air, it is delivered not only as a powder but also in the form of a slurry or in a compacted form with over twice the density.

The content of SF is usually limited to 30% of cement mass as addition or replacement and in most cases 10–20% is sufficient. Higher amounts may

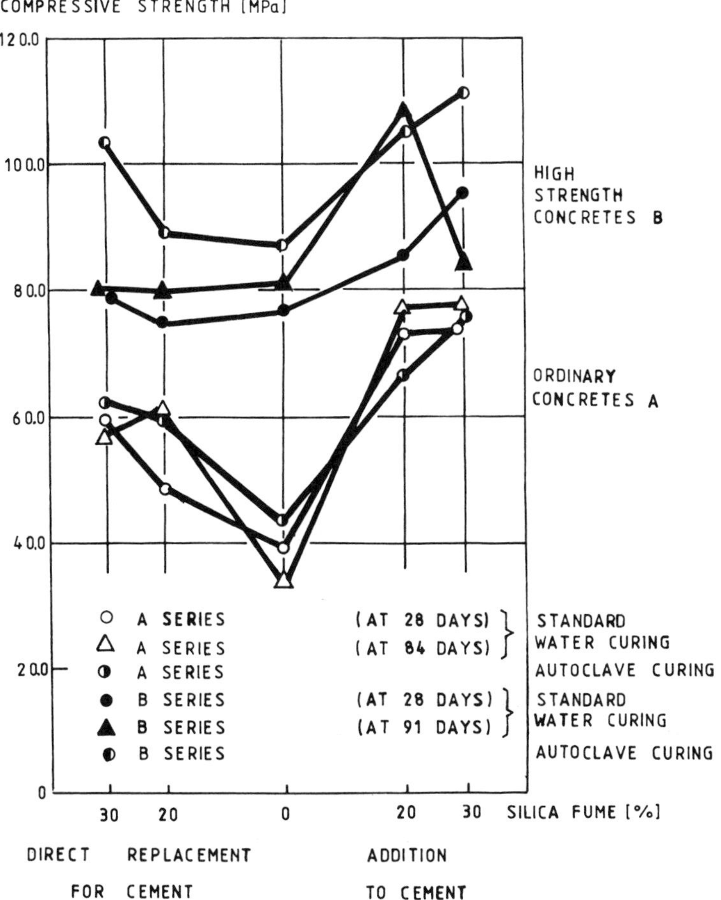

Figure 4.7 Influence of silica fume on compressive strength of concrete. (Reproduced with permission from Takagi, N. and Akashi, T. Properties of concrete containing silica fume; published by Japan Concrete Institute, 1984.) [4.30]

adversely decrease the hydrated cement paste alkalinity below the normal value of pH = 12.5 which is considered to be necessary for protection against corrosion of steel reinforcement.

The influence of the alkali content of the silica fume on its pozzolanic properties has been studied [4.33] using 20 different SF compositions and kinds of cements and plasticizers. The authors of [4.33] have proposed certain empirical relations to forecast the compressive strength of very high performance mortars and concretes.

Examples of SF properties are given in Table 4.6 from [4.34]. With its increasing application, SF is not considered any more to be a waste material

Table 4.6 Chemical composition and physical properties of silica fume

a)

ig. loss[1]	SiO	AlO	FeO	CaO	MgO	NaO	KO	Total
3.0	90.6	1.2	1.1	0.3	0.8	0.45	1.97	99.4

b)

Specific gravity (20 °C)	Average particle dimension (μm)	Specific surface area (m^2/g)
2.2	0.1–0.3	28.32

[1] Loss on ignition – loss of a sample after heating to 1000 °C
(Source: Ohama, Y. *et al.*, Properties of polymer-modified mortars containing silica fume; published by Elsevier Applied Science, 1989.) [4.34]

but rather as a necessary admixture for high quality concrete. Its price equals approximately three times that of Portland cement.

Addition of SF has also had a positive influence on wet mix shotcrete by improving the following characteristics [4.35] and [4.36]:

1. extremely low rebound <5%;
2. high early and final strength;
3. high resistance against chemical attack;
4. improved density thanks to additional formation of CSH during hardening of cement paste;
5. reduced carbonation due to increased density.

Pulverized fly-ash (PFA) is an inexpensive waste material obtained from the gases exhausted by furnaces of coal power stations and is trapped by special electric devices which are installed to reduce air pollution. PFA does not require grinding and its particles are spherical and of comparable dimensions to the cement grains. It is a kind of artificial pozzolan which is used with Portland cement as an additive or partial replacement. The main reasons for its application are:

1. PFA is cheaper than cement and its utilization has positive effects on ecology problems in industrialized regions;
2. addition of PFA improves workability of fresh mix;
3. partial replacement of cement decelerates the hydration processes and reduces the hydration heat;
4. addition of about 25% of fly-ash with respect to cement mass decreases risk of alkali aggregate reaction;
5. increase resistance against chemical attack, e.g. sulphates;
6. improvement of permeability of hardened composite by inclusion of fine grains in the mix.

PFA is composed of silica, alumina and ferric oxides (at least 70%), a small amount of MgO, SO_3 and Na_2O. The quality of PFA depends on its fineness and high silica content and on reduced carbon volume. Usually the percentage of PFA in blended cement is limited to 30%. Other pozzolans are:

1. natural volcanic ash;
2. ground blast furnace slag;
3. clays and shales calcinated at 650–1000 °C.

Application of pozzolan admixtures or silica fume is considered to be indispensable for high strength concrete. Pozzolan is defined as siliceous and aluminous material which having only little cementitious properties may react with lime (calcium hydroxide, CH) if finely ground and mixed with water. Reaction with lime from Portland cement hydration gives cementitious products: calcium silicate hydrates, CSH.

The initial strength of concretes blended with pozzolans is lower at 28 days and later recovery of strength depends on the intensity of pozzolanic reaction. Strength increase due to active fly-ashes may be expected after 90 days.

Inert admixtures are applied to low or medium strength concretes. Even though they are basically inert, finely ground mineral materials have some bonding effect and contribute to strength by pozzolanic reaction.

Rock dust and ground dolomite or lime are used as mineral admixtures and also finely ground blast furnace slag and natural pozzolanic materials of volcanic origin. In the blended cements, which are cheaper than pure Portland cement, the amount of ground slag may reach 90% and should be clearly indicated in delivery. These kinds of cements have increased resistance against chemical corrosion, particularly against sulphate attack.

4.3.10 OTHER ADMIXTURES

There are other admixtures not described here, which improve some particular properties of concrete composites. These are for example:

- admixtures to obtain volume expansion during hydration and hardening in order to compensate natural drying shrinkage of Portland cement, used in repair works or in grouting of prestressing reinforcement ducts;
- gas-forming admixtures to produce lightweight concretes;
- admixtures increasing bonding, usually polymer emulsions (latexes), in most cases used in repair works when fresh concrete is placed on old; also concrete bonding to steel reinforcement is increased;
- colouring admixtures for decoration elements of buildings.

References

4.1. Nicholls, R. (1976) *Composite Construction Material Handbook*, Prentice-Hall Inc., New Jersey.

4.2. Neville, A.M. (1965) *Properties of Concrete*, 2nd ed., Pitman, London.

4.3. Bukowski, B. (1963) *Concrete Technology*, part 1 and 2, (in Polish), Arkady, Warsaw.

4.4. Robson, T.D. (1962) *High-Alumina Cements and Concretes. Constructors Record*, Wiley, London, New York.

4.5. Popovics, S. (1979) *Concrete-Making Materials*, Hemisphere Publ. Co., New York.

4.6. Mindess, S. and Young, J.F. (1981) *Concrete*, Prentice-Hall, Englewood Cliffs, New York.

4.7. Ashby, M.F. and Jones, D.R.H. (1986) *Engineering Materials 2*, Pergamon Press, Oxford.

4.8. Hannant, D.J. (1978) *Fibre Cements and Fibre Concretes*, J. Wiley, London.

4.9. Żenczykowski, W. (1938) Mortars for building, in *Calendar of Building Review* (in Polish), (ed. I. Luft), SZPRP, Warsaw, 80–94.

4.10. Venuat, M. (1984) *Adjuvants et traitements*, published by the author, Paris.

4.11. American Concrete Institute (1988) Guide for mixing and placing sulphur concrete in construction. Report of the ACI Committee 548.

4.12. Saal, R.N.J. (1966) Asphalts systems, in *Composite Materials*, (ed. L. Holliday), Elsevier Publishing Co., Amsterdam, 453–74.

4.13. Kalabińska, M. and Piłat, J. (1985) *Technology of materials and road pavements* (in Polish), PWN, Warsaw.

4.14. Czarnecki, L. (1982) *Resin Concretes* (in Polish), Arkady, Warsaw.

4.15. Brandt, A.M., Czarnecki, L., Kajfasz, S. and Kasperkiewicz, J. (1983) *Bases for application of concrete-like composites* (in Polish), COIB, Warsaw.

4.16. Stanton, T.F. (1940) Expansion of concrete through reaction between cement and aggregate. *Proc. Amer. Soc. of Civ. Engrs.*, **66**, 1781–95.

4.17. Kawamura, M., Koike, M. and Nakano, K. (1989) Release of alkalis from reactive andesitic aggregates and fly ashes into pore solution in mortars, in [4.19], 271–7.

4.18. Kaczkowska, D. and Tabak, R. (1989) Akali reactivity of aggregate used in concrete industry (in Polish), *Cement-Wapno-Gips*, **56**(5), 88–97.

4.19. Alsali, M.M. and Malhotra, V.M. (1991) Role of concrete incorporating high volumes of fly ash in controlling expansion due to alkali-aggregate reaction. *American Concrete Institute Materials Journal*, **88**(2), March–April, 159–63.

4.20. Okada, K., Nishibayashi, S. and Kawamura, M. (eds) (1989) Proc. 8th Int. Conference *'Alkali-Aggregate Reaction'*, Kyoto, July, Elsevier Appl. Sc., London.

4.21. Hobbs, D.W. (1988) *Alkali–Silica Reaction in Concrete*, Thomas Telford, London.

4.22. CEB/FIP (1977) *Lightweight Aggregate Concrete. Design and Technology*. CEB/FIP Manual, The Construction Press, Lancaster, England.

4.23. American Concrete Institute (1984) *Guide for use of normal weight aggregates in concrete*, ACI Committee 221, ACI Journal, March/April, 115–39.

4.24. *Ordinary Concrete* (in Polish), Standard PN-1989/B-06250.

4.25. Paszkowski, W. (1933) *Physical properties of fine aggregate for concrete* (in Polish), *Cement*, **48**, 131–5.

4.26. Popovics, S. (1982) Production schedule of concrete for maximum profit. *Materials and Structures*, RILEM, **15**(87), May–June, 199–204.

4.27. Neville, A.M. and Brooks, J.F. (1987) *Concrete Technology*, Longman Scientific & Technical, London.

4.28. American Concrete Institute (1989) Chemical admixture for concrete, Comm. Rep., ACI *Materials Journal*, **86** (3), May–June, 297–327.

4.29. Manning, D.G. and Northwood, R.P. (1980) The rehabilitation of structures on an urban freeway. A case study. Proc. Conf. *Bridge Maintenance and Rehabilitation*, IABSE and ASCE, West Virginia, August 12–16, 644–68.

4.30. Takagi, N. and Akashi, T. (1984) Properties of concrete containing silica fume. *Trans. of the Japan Concrete Institute*, **6**, 47–54.

4.31. Mehta, P.K. and Monteiro, P.J.M. (1988) Effect of aggregate, cement and mineral admixtures on the microstructure of the transition zone, Proc. Int. Symp. *Bonding in Cementitious Composites*, (eds S. Mindess and S.P. Shah), 2–4 December 1987, Boston, Materials Research Soc., Pittsburgh, Pn., 65–75.

4.32. Bentur, A., Goldman, A. and Cohen, M.D. (1988) The contribution of the transition zone to the strength of high quality silica fume concretes, as [4.30], 97–103.

4.33. de Larrard, F., Gorse, J.F., and Puch, C. (1990) Efficacités comparées de diverses fumées de silice comme additif dans les bétons à hautes performances. Bull. de Liaison des Laboratoires des Ponts et Chaussées, No. 168, 97–105.

4.34. Ohama, Y., Demura, K., Morikawa, M., and Ogi, T. (1989) Properties of polymer-modified mortars containing silica fume, in Proc. Int. Symp. *Brittle Matrix Composites 2*, Sept. 20–22, 1988, Cedzyna, (eds A.M. Brandt and I.H. Marshall), Elsevier Applied Science, London.

4.35. Hillemeier, B. (1989) New methods in the rehabilitation of prestressed concrete structures, Proc. IABSE Symp. *Durability of Structures*, Sept. 6–8, Lisbon, **1**, 311–16.

4.36. Fédération Internationale de la Précantrainte (1988) Condensed silica fume in concrete. State of art report. FIP, Thomas Telford, London, 37pp.

5 Reinforcement of cement-based composites

5.1 General remarks

The purpose of reinforcement in cement-based composites is to increase their fracture toughness. The aim is to improve resistance against crack propagation by a control of crack opening and propagation. The reinforcement increases the composite material tensile strength which is an average value developed by a composite material. The tensile strength of the matrix itself is low, for instance that of Portland cement mortars and concretes is approximately equal to 10–12% of their compressive strength. Much higher composite tensile strength is obtained thanks to various systems of reinforcement.

Traditional reinforcement of concrete elements in the form of steel bars and prestressing cables is not considered here as it is mentioned in Section 3.1. Here, dispersed reinforcement in the form of fibres is considered. Macro-fibres are usually of 10–60 mm in length and 0.1–1.0 mm of the least dimension. Micro-fibres are of 10–30 μm of diameter and length below 10 mm. In subsequent chapters both these two categories of fibres are considered.

5.2 Asbestos fibres

Asbestos fibres are extracted from natural deposits in several regions in the world. The best known are in Quebec province in Canada, near Sverdlovsk in Russia, in Cyprus, near Turin in Italy, in Zimbabwe and in the Republic of South Africa. The rock containing asbestos is crushed to separate fibres by mechanical methods.

The following are the main kinds of asbestos fibres:

Chrysotile asbestos	93.5% of world production;
Crocidolite (blue)	4.0% of world production;
Amosite	2.2% of world production;
Anthophyllite	0.3% of world production.

Other kinds have no industrial importance.

The most frequently available chrysotile asbestos is the fibrous form of serpentine $3MgO.2SiO_2.2HO_2$ – hydrated magnesium silicate. The fibres are thin, their diameter varies from 0.012 up to 0.03 μm. The fibre length is normally 5 mm, rarely reaching 40 or even 100 mm. There is an empty channel in the middle of a fibre, [5.1]. Asbestos fibres are considered as micro-fibres. Some kinds of polypropylene, mica, wollastonite and xonotlite fibres are also included in that category.

The tensile strength of asbestos fibres is assumed within the limits of 550 and 750 MPa. However, single fibres may have much higher strength: up to 1000 MPa for chrysotile asbestos and to 3500 MPa for crocidolite asbestos. The fibres are lightweight and have a high resistance against most of the chemical agents and maintain strength in high temperatures. The bond is excellent due to affinity to cement paste. The strong fibre/matrix interface does not contain increased amounts of CH which is formed around other kinds of fibres. Because of those outstanding properties the asbestos fibres have been used extensively since the beginning of the century as reinforcement for thin plates and pipes made of neat cement paste. Usually the fibre content reaches 10–15% of the cement mass. The commercially available asbestos fibres are considered too short to reinforce cement mortar and concrete.

Over the last 10 or 15 years it has been proved that asbestos dust which is produced at all stages of asbestos fibre extraction and handling is very dangerous for human health. The risk for occupants of the buildings is considered to be negligible and may occur only when careless repair work or demolition is carried out. In several countries the use of asbestos fibres in building and civil engineering is forbidden, e.g. in Great Britain and Scandinavian countries. In others it is strongly limited.

The imposed restrictions on application of the asbestos fibres in buildings, as reinforcement for cement-based composites, stimulated extensive research directed at other kinds of fibres. Because of its excellent mechanical properties, good durability and relatively low cost the appropriate replacement is difficult. The research concerned mainly cellulose, polypropylene and carbon fibres and positive results have been achieved, [5.2], [5.3] and [5.4]. The mechanical behaviour of asbestos cements is described in Section 14.2.1.

5.3 Glassfibres

There are several kinds of glass used to produce fibres and the main ones are presented in Table 5.1. The fibres are available in various forms:

- single fibres, continuous or chopped, of circular cross-section and diameter 5–10 μm; there are also tubular and rectangular cross-section fibres (USA);
- rovings, which means 1–60 bunches of single fibres; rovings may be coated with various materials;
- yarn of single fibres, continuous or discontinuous, also remnant shorter fibres may be used;
- woven fabrics, made of continuous or discontinuous fibres, also of rovings;
- non-woven mats of fibres, bound together mechanically or by gluing.

Table 5.1 Main components of glass for glassfibres

Types of glass	Components							
	SiO_2	Al_2O_3	B_2O	CaO	Mg_2O	K_2O	Na_2O	ZrO_2
High alkali A glass, used for thermal and acoustic insulation in the form of wool, $d = 15$–$30\,\mu m$	72.0	1.3	–	10.0	2.5		14.2	–
Low alkaline glass, used for filtration layers, as fibre reinforcement for plastics and in textiles, $d = 5$–$10\,\mu m$	65.0	4.0	5.5	14.0	3.0	8.0	0.5	–
Nonalkaline E glass, used as electric insulation, as fibre reinforcement for plastics	54.5–58.0	14.0–14.5	6.5–8.0	17.5–21.0	4.5	0.5		–
Zirkonian G 20 glass, obtained by Majumdar *et al.* in Build. Research Establ. in 1968	70.27	0.24	–	0.04	0.04	11.84	0.04	16.05
CemFIL glass, Pilkington, UK, 1970	63.0	0.56	–	5.2	–	–	14.2	16.5
CemFIL 2 glass, Pilkington, UK, 1979	60.0	0.7	–	4.7	–	–	14.5	18.0
NEG, Nippon Electric Glass	61.6	0.2	–	0.4	–	2.3	15.8	19.1

As reinforcement for concrete-like composites the short fibres of about 25 mm in length, chopped from rovings, are mostly used.

In matrices based on Portland cement the glassfibres are subjected to strongly alkaline aggression and the main problem consists of identifying appropriate ways of preventing the corrosion. These ways are:

- modification of matrix by decreasing its alkalinity;
- covering the fibres with various kinds of protective coatings;
- increasing the fibre resistance against alkaline corrosion.

Sometimes different measures are used simultaneously.

First applications of glassfibres in concrete-like composites were published where tests were carried out on elements with high alumina cement [5.5]. The paste made with that cement is characterized by pH ranging from 11.8 up to 12.05, with total amounts of alkalis only from 0.15 to 0.20% and during hydration calcium hydroxide does not appear. In the Portland cement paste pH is higher and ranging from 12.5 to 13.0 with large amounts of crystallized calcium hydroxide. These are the reasons why the glassfibres are not subjected to corrosion in high alumina cement paste. But the elements made of that kind of cement are exposed to dangerous conversion when in humid conditions and higher temperatures (cf. Section 4.1) and as a result they may lose a considerable part of their bearing capacity at any time during exploitation.

According to tests published in [5.5] the composite elements made with a mixture of high alumina cement, granulated blast furnace slag and gypsum and reinforced with ordinary glassfibres had invariable strength over a few years. These results were not confirmed [5.6], where a decrease of strength in similar elements with fibres made of E-glass was observed. That decrease was more important the more humid were the storage conditions for tested elements.

The apparent divergences in these two series of tests can be attributed to possible substantial differences in properties of fibres and matrices, and also in other conditions of testing.

According to a general conclusion proposed in [5.1] the application of E-glassfibres is not advised in elements made of high alumina cement if they may be exposed to high humidity. That condition does not concern non-structural elements whose strength is needed during transportation and construction only, e.g. lost forms incorporated into structural element and cladding plates.

After numerous tests [5.7], [5.8] and other authors, it has been shown that fibres made of ordinary E-glass are subjected to corrosion in Portland cement matrix within the first few weeks, particularly when stored in high humidity. In similar elements stored in dry air no appreciable decrease of strength was observed even after a few years.

Fibres made of alkali-resistant glass (cf. Table 5.1) also show slow corrosion when elements are stored in water or in natural outdoor conditions, [5.9].

It was expected that a considerable improvement could be obtained by the introduction of special alkali resistant fibres called CemFIL. The fibres are produced through a large addition of zircon oxide by Pilkington Brothers in the United Kingdom after a concept published in [5.10]. These fibres are chopped from roving into lengths of about 40 mm and their diameters vary from 12 to 14 μm, [5.11].

The test results of elements reinforced with CemFIL fibres did not fully confirm the expectations. Thin mortar plates were stored in different conditions over 10 years and it appeared that with access to humidity, already, after 6 months, their strength decreased considerably. At the end of the 10 years period the strength of the reinforced plates was already equal to that of non-reinforced mortar, which was attributed to advanced corrosion of fibres, (Figures 5.1 to 5.4).

The mechanism of corrosion of fibres and its influence on composite strength are not completely known and explained. There are two factors acting in opposite directions: alkali-resistance of fibres and their bond to the matrix. Low alkali-resistance and high environmental humidity increase bonding but also accelerate the corrosion of fibres. When fibres are more alkali-resistant and elements are stored in dry air, then a risk of poor bond strength appears and the elements may behave as a brittle non-reinforced matrix.

Furthermore, there are two different processes developing with time: corrosion of glassfibres and embrittlement of the matrix in zones around and between single glassfibres, [5.12]. Both these processes gradually decrease the strength and fracture toughness of composite elements. The rate of these processes is a function of environmental conditions: humidity and temperature.

The quality of bonding was determined in the above mentioned tests [5.10] not only indirectly with regard to composite strength, but also the surface of fibres taken out of elements was closely examined using SEM.

Research led by Pilkington Brothers was directed at providing an additional coating of alkali-resistant glassfibres and at the beginning of the 1980s new kinds of fibres called CemFIL 2 appeared. An extensive programme of tests in various storage conditions was undertaken to verify their durability in long periods.

The attempts continued to decrease the alkalinity of cement matrices by various admixtures. Among others the fly ash decreases the 28 days' strength of mortar and concrete because of lower filtration of water in the pore system in the matrix, but in longer periods that difference is gradually disappearing. The admixtures of polymer dispersions were not helpful in that respect, because their influence was weak in high humidity when alkali corrosion of fibres is most dangerous.

Tests reported in [5.11] were executed on specimens with blend cement composed of 80–85% of granulated blast-furnace slag, 10–15% of gypsum and a small amount of lime or Portland cement. That kind of cement assured high resistance against most chemical agents and lower alkalinity which enabled the application of glassfibres as reinforcement, but the mechanical strength at an age of 28 days was significantly lower than that of Portland cement specimens. Final results of the long-term tests with this cement are not available. In the

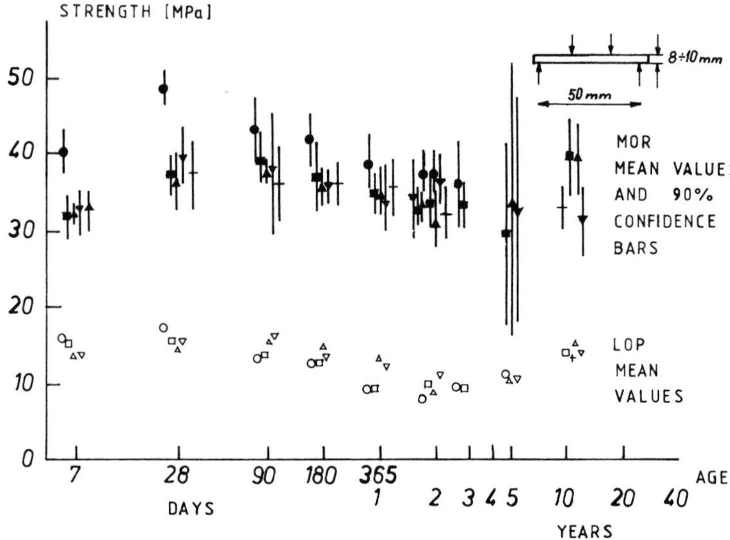

Figure 5.1 Modulus of rupture (MOR) and limit of proportionality (LOP) in bending for CemFIL glassfibre-reinforced mortar elements, stored in air at 18–20 °C and 40% RH. Different symbols indicate results of various series of specimens. (Reproduced with permission from Majumdar, A.J., Properties of GRC; Symp. '*Concrete International 80, Fibrous Concrete*', The Construction Press, Elsevier Science Publishers, 1980.) [5.11]

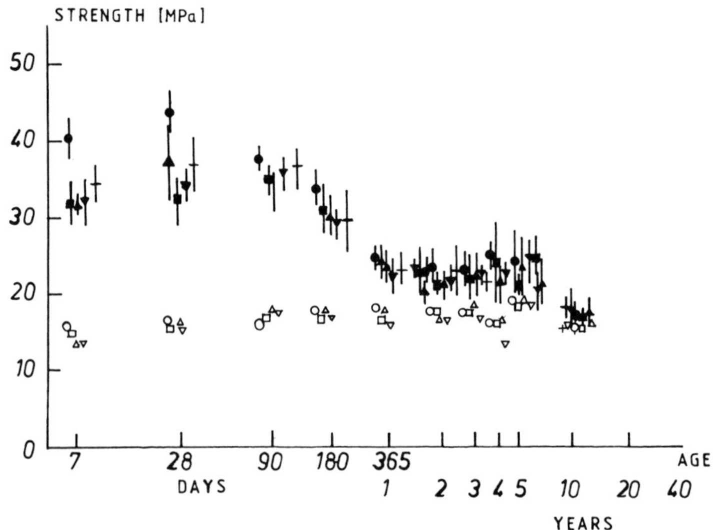

Figure 5.2 Modulus of rupture (MOR) and limit of proportionality (LOP) in bending for CemFIL glassfibre-reinforced mortar elements, stored in water at 18–20 °C. (Reproduced with permission from Majumdar, A.J., Properties of GRC; Symp. '*Concrete International 80, Fibrous Concrete*', The Construction Press, Elsevier Science Publishers, 1980.) [5.11]

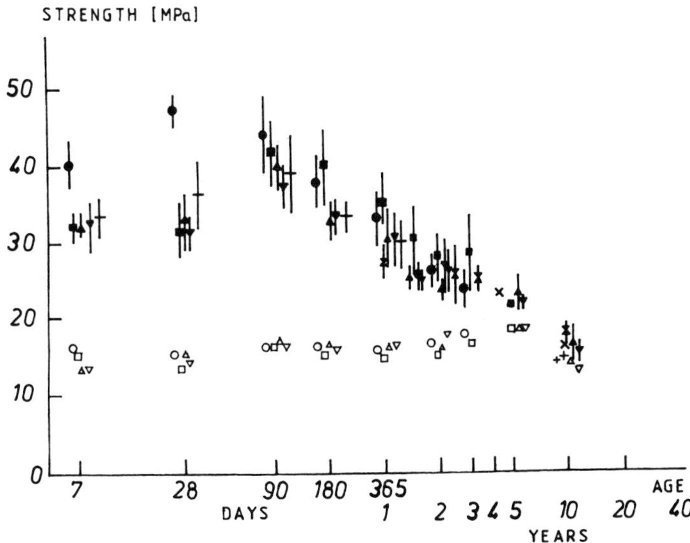

Figure 5.3 Modulus of rupture (MOR) and limit of proportionality (LOP) in bending for CemFIL glassfibre-reinforced mortar elements, stored in natural weather conditions in the UK. (Reproduced with permission from Majumdar, A.J., Properties of GRC; Symp. '*Concrete International 80, Fibrous Concrete*', The Construction Press, Elsevier Science Publishers, 1980.) [5.11]

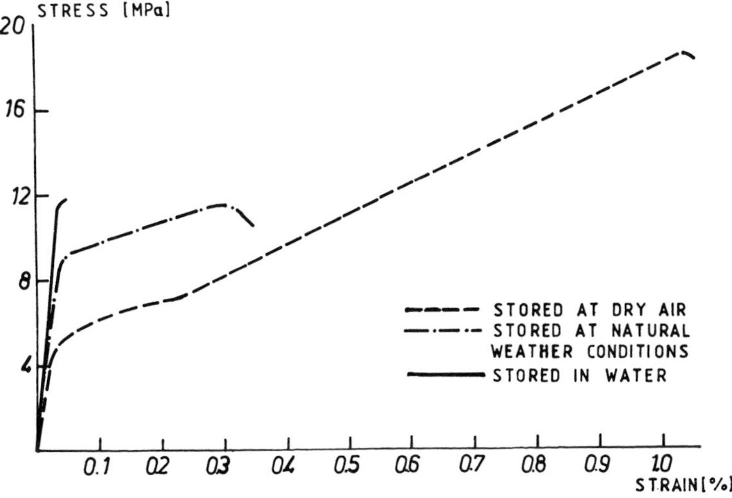

Figure 5.4 Tensile stress–strain curves for CemFIL glassfibre-reinforced mortar elements stored for five years at different conditions. Fibre length 40 mm, 8.2% vol. (Reproduced with permission from Majumdar, A.J., Properties of GRC; Symp. '*Concrete International 80, Fibrous Concrete*', The Construction Press, Elsevier Science Publishers, 1980.) [5.11]

laboratories of the Centre de Recherches de Pont-à-Mousson (France) successful attempts have been made to decrease considerably the detrimental influence of Portland cement paste on the durability of glassfibre reinforced composites. Using metakaolinite as an admixture to the matrix and alkali-resistant fibres in a composite material called 'Cemfilstar', both the above mentioned processes were considerably slowed or even stopped, [5.13], [5.14]. Tests performed on specimens made of 'Cemfilstar' and subjected to accelerated ageing have shown that long-term performance may be expected [5.15].

The E-glassfibres in gypsum matrices are not subjected to alkaline corrosion and are applied in partition walls, internal cladding, etc., cf. Section 15.2.

The conclusion which summarizes the present state of knowledge and technology is that probably only combinations of alkali-resistant glassfibres with special modifications of Portland cement matrices should be used for composites if their long-term serviceability is required. The use of ordinary glassfibres is therefore limited to the elements where reinforcement is needed only during the first few months of their exploitation. The application of glassfibres of various kinds in concrete-like composites is very large and is still developing in all non-structural elements and with matrices other than Portland cement.

5.4 Steel fibres

Steel fibre-reinforced concretes (SFRC) were originally developed in the USA, invented by J.P. Romualdi as US Patent 3 429 094 in 1969 and produced initially by the Batelle Development Corporation of Columbus, Ohio, followed by a few other producers of chopped steel fibres.

There are now different forms of short steel fibres used as reinforcement for concrete-like composites. The main types are presented in Table 5.2 and a few examples are shown in Figure 5.5.

The fibres are produced by various methods, e.g.:

- chopped from cold drawn wire of circular cross-section, mostly indented (Duoform), waved (Johnson and Nephew), with hooks (Bekaert) or enlargements at the ends (Tibo);
- cut out from strips of thin plates, of square or rectangular cross-sections, often twisted along their longitudinal axes during cutting, some kinds also with enlargements at the ends (EE);
- machined, of rough surface and varied cross-section related to the technology of machining (Harex);
- obtained from molten metal, with a rough surface (Johnson and Nephew).

Fibres of type 1 were applied since the beginning of Steel Fibre-Reinforced Cement (SFRC), but their unit cost is relatively high due to the complicated technology of cold drawing and cutting. Additional operations are required to increase their bonding by surface indentation or wavings. Plain, straight fibres are rarely used because of their low efficiency due to poor bonding.

Table 5.2 Types of steel-fibres

No.	Description production	Dimensions (mm) diameter	Dimensions (mm) length	Tensile strength (MPa)
1.	Straight, plain, round IFTR Poland	0.40	40	600–700
2.	Straight, plain, round Type 3 Trefil-Arbed Type 2	0.30 0.38	25 25	960
3.	Straight, plain, round stainless steel National Standard (USA) 0.25 × 13 0.25 × 25 0.25 × 60 0.38 × 13 0.30 × 25 0.38 × 60 0.64 × 13 0.38 × 25 0.64 × 60 0.40 × 25 0.64 × 25	0.25–0.64	13–60	
4.	Straight, plain, round Svabet kamma Scanovator A/B Sweden	0.25–0.50 0.60	25 60	780
5.	Straight, plain fibres glued together in bundles Dramix OL Bekaert (Belgium)	0.25–0.50	6–30	
6.	Straight, plain, square or rectangular cross-section Sumitomo Metal Ind. (Japan)	0.80	30	
7.	Straight, indented in two perpendicular planes Duoform National Standard (USA) 0.25 × 13 0.25 × 25 0.25 × 30 0.38 × 13 0.38 × 25 0.38 × 60 0.64 × 13 0.64 × 25 0.64 × 60	0.25–0.64	13–60	1000
8.	Straight, plain, with enlarged ends EE Australian Wire Ind.		18	
9.	Straight, plain, with enlarged ends Tibo	0.80	50	1150
10.	Waved, made with plain wire Johnson and Nephew UK	0.40–0.60	20–40	
11.	Waved on the ends Trefil-Arbed (7 + 11 + 7) = 25 mm	0.25–0.50	25	
12.	Plain with hooks at the ends, glued together in bundles Dramix ZL Bekaert Wire Corp. Belgium	0.35 0.40 0.50 0.60	30 40 50 60	1400
13.	Melt extracted fibres also stainless steel irregular shape Battelle Corp. Ohio (USA)	0.3 × 1.0[1] 0.40[2] 0.58[2]	10–50 35 38	
14.	Melt overflow stainless fibres Microtex $E = 150\,000$ MPa $\varepsilon_u = 0.15$, Fibre Technology Ltd, UK	0.025 × 0.150[2]	10–50	1500–2000
15.	Straight, rough, machined, irregular, Harex Japan and FRD	0.8 × 2.0[1] 0.15 × 4.0[1]	16–32	1630–2100
16.	FIBERCON	0.25 × 0.56	60	

[1] Here are given only the smallest and the biggest dimensions of a series of fibres produced.
[2] Characteristic dimensions of irregular cross-sections.

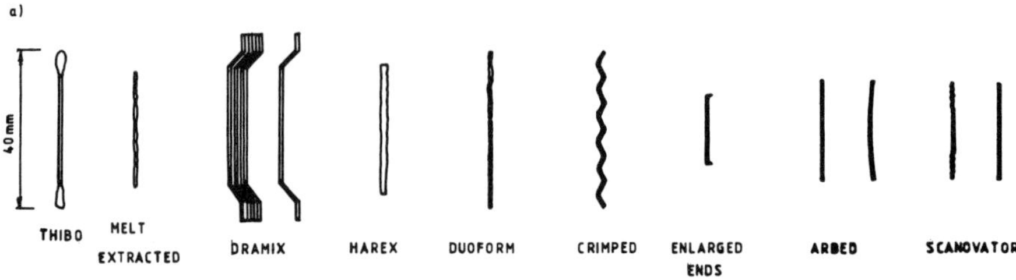

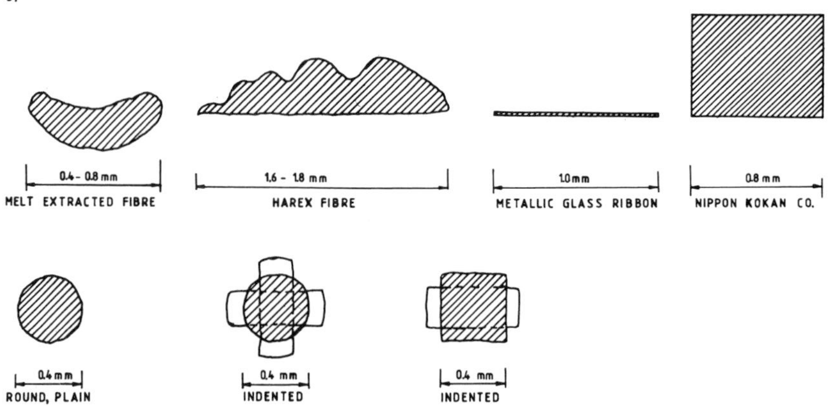

Figure 5.5 Examples of a few kinds of short steel fibres a) shapes b) cross-sections.

Fibres of type 2 are less expensive and have better bond strength without special operations.

Fibres of type 3 were introduced later and their application is quickly developing. They are less expensive than fibres chopped from wires and their uniform distribution in the fresh matrix is easier. Their shape ensures better adherence to the matrix.

Fibres of type 4 are also inexpensive and have increased bond strength. There are, however, few results available from tests or practical applications of these fibres.

In comparison to short fibres, fibres of 100–200 mm long are rarely used. A few experimental applications are known together with the technology called SIFCON, cf. Section 14.2.4.

The surface of steel fibres may be covered by a thin coating of other metals like copper or of epoxy resin in order to increase their resistance against corrosion.

The main characteristics of fibres which decide upon their efficiency as reinforcement for brittle matrices are:

- aspect ratio, it means length to diameter ratio l/d,
- quality of surface and eventual anchorages at the ends,
- mechanical properties of the material, it means tensile strength and ductility.

The efficiency of fibre reinforcement is dependent also upon distribution and orientation of fibres in the matrix. The fibres form an internal structure and the various kinds of such structures are described in Section 6.6.

The anchorage of steel fibres in the matrix is indispensable for their efficiency. Because of weak chemical adherence, the load is transferred from matrix to fibres mostly by mechanical bond. The shape of the fibre surface and its cleanness as well as the shape of a fibre itself and the quality of the matrix are decisive. The fibre–matrix bond was tested by many authors (e.g. [5.16], [5.17], [5.18], [5.19], [5.20], [5.21] and [5.22].

If the bond along a fibre is not sufficient, and usually for plain, straight fibres a correct anchorage would require longer fibres than it is possible to produce, then hooks or enlarged ends are necessary. The length of a fibre should satisfy a condition $l/d \leqslant 100$, otherwise the distribution of fibres in a fresh mix is difficult. The fibres with improved bond may be much shorter and their appropriate distribution is easier.

The unit price of steel fibres is an important factor deciding upon their application, because they are in most cases the most expensive component of the mix. That is why many producers are looking for new kinds of cheaper fibres and melt extract or machined fibres are quickly developing.

The fibres are produced of various kinds of steel, but usually they are of low carbon and low strength steel. Their tensile strength is equal to about 500 MPa and only rarely is higher strength steel up to 2400 MPa used. For refractory elements, like walls in blast furnaces, fibres made of stainless steel assure better durability. Young's modulus of all kinds of steel is close to 210 GPa and good ductility is an advantage.

The forces appearing in a fibre under load are low because of their short length and relatively weak bond to Portland cement paste. As a result, the fibres are never ruptured when cracks are propagating and elements are subjected to failure. The fibres which cross a crack are pulled out of the matrix controlling in this way how the crack opens. Therefore, the use of high strength steel for fibres is usually not justified. The situation may be different in polymer-modified cement-based composites or in other kinds of matrices where bonding is considerably improved.

The total amount of fibres in a composite material is defined as a fraction of its volume rather than mass. It is believed that the upper limit for fibre fraction is 3% for the normal technology of ordinary steel fibre cements. Generally, the applied volumes vary between 0.5 and 2.0% and these limits are based on the following arguments:

- The workability of fresh mix decreases rapidly when higher fractions of fibres are added and the porosity due to entrapped air voids is increased.

Even with intensive vibration it is difficult to place and to compact correctly the fresh mix into forms when too many fibres are added.

- The fibres have a tendency to form balls and with a higher fraction it is very difficult to distribute them properly.
- The total price of composite increases considerably with high fibre fractions.
- The optimal efficiency of fibres depends on several factors, but in most cases it corresponds to volumes between 1 and 2%.

Special technologies were tested to introduce much more fibres, even up to 20% by volume. Fibres were put into the form and next soaked with fluid cement slurry. That technology called SIFCON (Slurry Infiltrated Concrete) was applied in the repair works of concrete structures, [5.19], [5.24] and [5.21], cf. Section 14.2.4.

Steel-wool mats composed of thin continuous wires are used as cement paste reinforcement. Wires with irregular and high aspect ratios up to 500 are produced by shaving, or slitting and shredding, from thin sheets or foils of low carbon steel. Mats about 6 mm thick of variable density from 0.85 to 1.75 kg/m^2 are used, keeping the volume content of fibres below 4%. Composite plates are produced by infiltration of these mats with cement slurry and then hardening under constant pressure. Composite plates obtained have high toughness and strength, comparable to those of asbestos cement products, [5.26].

5.5 Metallic glass ribbons

A new type of reinforcement for concrete-like composites was proposed in 1986 in France in the form of thin ribbons made of metallic glass. The ribbons are produced by rapid quenching of a liquid alloy which is a composition, namely, $Fe_{75}Cr_5P_8C_{10}Si_2$. The ribbons are 20–30 μm thick, 1–2 mm wide and they are produced of variable length from 15 to 60 mm. Under direct tension a ribbon behaves as a nearly linear elastic material without plastic deformations.

Because of the amorphous structure of the material the ribbons have excellent corrosion resistance. The pull-out tests proved their good adhesion to cement-based matrices. When crossing a crack, the ribbons are gradually pulled out like ordinary metal fibres. The tests of composite elements reinforced with ribbons have shown their high efficiency with relatively low volume fraction required.

Interesting details of tests performed with amorphous ribbons are published in [5.27], [5.28], [5.29] and [5.30].

5.6 Polymeric fibres

Polypropylene fibres have been produced since 1954 and since 1960 have been applied as concrete reinforcement, [5.31]. Initially, the plain and straight polypropylene fibres were used but their bond to a cement matrix was insufficient because mechanical interlocking was weak or the chemical bond did not exist at all. These fibres of low Young's modulus do not represent a valuable reinforcement in comparison with steel and glassfibres with regard to the increase of composite strength.

Considerable progress had been achieved and large research programmes were started in the 1970s, directed at replacement of asbestos fibres, [5.32] and [5.33]. New types of fibres called 'Krenit' invented by H. Krenchel were produced by splitting extruded tapes, which were pre-stretched and heat treated. The Young's modulus of these fibres is equal $E = 18$ GPa and tensile strength $f_t = 600$ MPa, [5.2]. Ultimate elongation at rupture may reach 5–8%. The bond strength to cement matrix is increased by special electrical surface treatment and thanks to fine fibrils protruding from fibre edges after cutting. The fibres have rectangular cross-section 20 × 100 μm and 30 × 200 μm and are chopped into lengths from 3 to 20 mm or longer. The cement mortar reinforced with these fibres may reach maximum elongation equal to $0.4\% = 4000.10^{-6}$ as compared to approximately $0.02\% = 200.10^{-6}$ for plain mortar. Other types of polypropylene fibres known as 'Crackstop' and 'Cemfiber' are as thin as 18 μm in diameter and 18 mm long. When distributed evenly in the bulk of the matrix they control the cracking process very well due to shrinkage or thermal actions in constrained elements. It has been proved by several applications that even quite low percentages of 0.067% per volume had such an effective result that potential large cracks were replaced by tiny microcracks which are neither visible without magnification nor detrimental for durability of the composite element. Fibres of that kind are also used as a reinforcement for elements exposed to impact loading.

Also, at present, twisted polypropylene fibres and 3-dimensional fabric are available with the mechanical bond considerably increased, [5.30].

Polypropylene fibrillated fibres chopped to lengths 25–75 mm are used to reinforce mortar and concrete. They are traditionally mixed with fresh mortar and used for various thin walled, precast elements for building and other purposes (flower boxes, tanks, boats, etc.). These fibres are also used in shotcrete, mainly for repair works, and their different applications are quickly increasing.

Under the patented name 'Dolanit' polyacrynitrile fibres of diameter 13–100 μm with lengths 2–60 mm are used up to 3.5% vol with the best results attained for 30–35 kg/m^3. Fibre–matrix bonding is good and is estimated to be approximately equal to 4 N/mm^2. Reinforcement with 'Dolanit' fibres reduces shrinkage cracking, increases ductility of the matrix and 'Modulus of Rupture' (MOR) for elements subjected to bending. Applications range from non-structural elements like tunnel and building cladding, to the main reinforcement for edge beams of bridge decks and secondary reinforcement of industrial floors, [5.35].

Polypropylene fibres have a low melting point and lose strength in higher temperatures. Nevertheless, their application is developing in those situations where these disadvantages are not serious.

5.7 Carbon fibres

Carbon fibres are obtained from different organic fibres (precursors) by pyrolysis which consists of decomposition into smaller molecules at high temperatures. Carbon fibres may also be produced from crude oil deposits like pitches or asphalts. Three main groups of carbon fibres are considered as composite materials reinforcement:

1. Graphite fibres with 99% of carbon content after additional treatment, with high strength $f_t = 2300–3000$ MPa and $E = 400–700$ GPa, e.g. Thornel produced by Union Carbide and PAN fibres, produced from precursors of polyacrylonitryle.
2. Carbon fibres produced with the same precursors but without complete graphitization; their properties are $f_t = 900–1000$ MPa, $E = 30–50$ GPa.
3. Carbon fibres produced from less expensive materials like pitch with much lower properties: $f_t = 6–10$ MPa, $E = 30–50$ GPa, (cf. Table 2.2).

The last group of carbon fibres has been considered for the past few years as a possible reinforcement for cement-based composites for general application because of their reasonable price, [5.36]. More expensive carbon fibres are used for particular purposes, like reinforcement in very corrosive environments or in structures in which the application of any metallic elements is excluded. Because of their dimensions they are considered as micro-fibres.

Carbon fibres have high chemical resistance and may be applied in elements exposed to increased temperature and mechanical wear. They are used together with other kinds of fibres as, so called, hybrid reinforcement. Their small dimensions and relatively high stiffness enable the control of early microcracking, as was shown in [5.37]. Where acoustic emission records were used to distinguish the influence of carbon and ordinary steel fibres: the first, reduced microcracking at the initial stage of deformation and the second, controlled larger cracks and increased overall strength of composite elements subjected to bending. Because of low density, the correct distribution of carbon fibres in a fresh cement matrix requires special attention, e.g. the application of silica fume and superplasticizers, [5.38].

5.8 Natural vegetable fibres

The classification of organic fibres was proposed in [5.35] as is shown in Figure 5.6. Here only the natural vegetable fibres are considered in more detail because of their importance and application as reinforcement for brittle matrices.

Wood fibres are produced in the form of chips, usually it is a waste material in the wood industry. Wood chips mixed with cement paste were used since the 1920s for the production of plates applied for thermal insulation in housing.

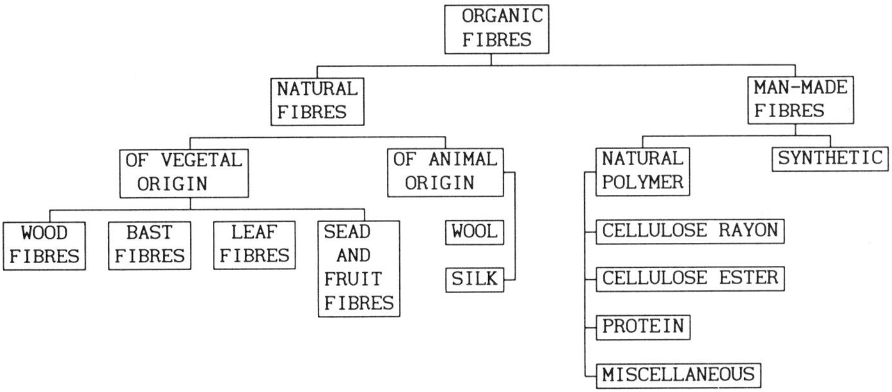

Figure 5.6 Classification of organic fibres. (Reproduced with permission from Gram H.E. *et al.*, *Natural Fibre Concrete*; Swedish Agency for Research Cooperation with Developing Countries, 1984.) [5.39]

The chips are subjected to chemical pre-treatment to avoid any cement hydration disturbed by organic acids. Recently, the application of wood-origin fibres as a reinforcement for structural elements has also been developing.

Bast fibres are obtained from a few kinds of plants, e.g. bamboo, hemp, flax, jute and ramie. The fibres are stronger and stiffer than other vegetable fibres. Jute fibres, for example, may be 3.0 m in length. For reinforcement of brittle matrices the jute fibres are chopped into sections of 12–50 mm. Bamboo fibres have low Young's modulus and tend to be used in the form of woven meshes.

Leaf fibres are mainly obtained from agave plants and are called sizal. Sizal is planted on an industrial scale in a few countries – the most important producers are Indonesia, Tanzania and Haiti. Sizal fibres are chopped or used as continuous fibres in lengths up to 1.5 m for making nonwoven mats. Their maximum strain is 2–4%. Sizal fibres are also used as twine and spun with short chopped fibres and a small amount of steel fibres. Such a hybrid reinforcement has proved to be cheap and efficient, [5.40].

Seed and fruit fibres are limited mostly to coconut coir if it concerns application as reinforcement. Fibres are usually considered as a waste product in the production of copra from the coconuts. The fibres are extracted from the space between the external shell and the seed inside. The maximum length of fibres is about 300 mm; maximum strain around 30%. The fibres are used also to produce ropes and mats.

Other plants with fibres suitable for reinforcement are: sugarcane bagasse, akwara, elephant grass, water reed, plantain and musamba, [5.41]. In Nordic countries with large timber industries the exploitation of cellulose fibres may prove interesting in order to reinforce cement mortar or paste matrices, [5.42], and [5.43].

Cellulose fibres are obtained from softwood and hardwood. Softwood fibres are 30–45 μm in diameter and 3–7 mm long. Hardwood fibres are thinner (10–20 μm) and shorter (1–2 mm). Their tensile strength is significantly greater than that of the wood, e.g. lumber wood without macro-defects may have a tensile strength equal to 70 MPa, but a single fibre – 700 MPa. The fibres are extracted from wood pulp by different chemical and mechanical processes.

Cellulose fibres are used in the production of flat and corrugated thin cement sheets, pipes and other elements. The fibre volume content varies between 6 and 10%. Production is similar to the classic Hatschek process developed for asbestos fibre cement elements. The final properties of the product depend upon composition and production techniques. At a fibre content of about 8% by volume, maximum flexural strength was obtained [5.40], but up to 14% was required for maximum flexural toughness. The addition of fly ash and silica fume increases the flexural strength.

The sheet elements reinforced with cellulose fibres exhibit considerably increased strength with respect to a non-reinforced matrix and great flexural toughness. Flexural behaviour is compared with other composites in Figure 5.7.

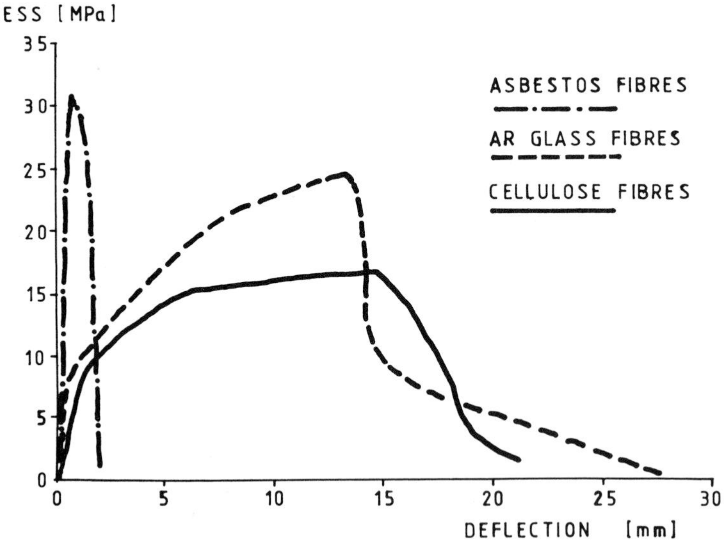

Figure 5.7 Comparison of flexural behaviour of cellulose fibre cements with glassfibre cements and asbestos cements. (Reproduced with permission from Soroushian, P. and Marikunte, S., High performance cellulose fibre reinforced cement composites; in Proc. Int. ACI-RILEM Workshop '*High Performance Fiber Reinforced Cement Composites*', Mainz, 1991, Spon/Chapman & Hall, 1992.) [5.44]

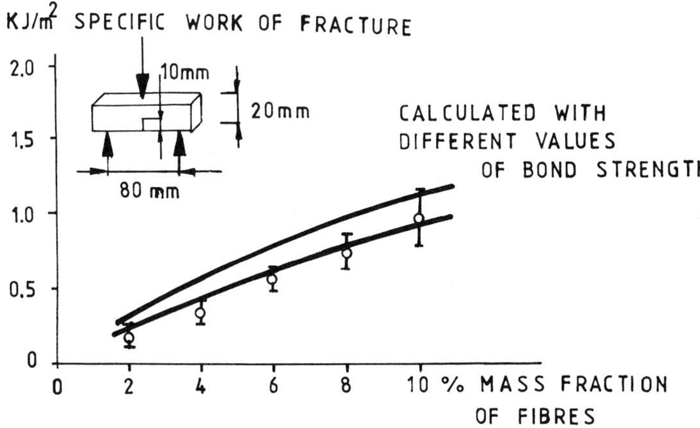

Figure 5.8 Variation of specific work of fracture with cellulose fibre mass fraction in composite elements subjected to bending. (Reproduced with permission from Andonian, R. *et al.*, Strength and fracture properties of cellulose fibre-reinforced cement composites; *International Journal of Cement Composites*, **1**(4), pp. 151–8, Elsevier Science Publishers, 1979.) [5.45]

After tests carried out in Australia, it has been found that when composites fracture under tension the cellulose fibres are both pulled-out and broken and the relationship between the specific act of fracturing and fibre content has been established, Figure 5.8.

Beside their low cost and availability for local applications, natural fibres are also efficient as reinforcement. Elements produced show increased tensile strength and post-cracking resistance, sufficient fatigue strength and energy absorption at fracture. Examples of stress–strain relation are shown in Figure 5.9; in Figure 5.10 the influence of volume fraction on composite strength is presented.

Unskilled labour and simple equipment may be used to produce the various elements required for roofing low-cost houses and building non-structural elements.

Several problems arise connected to the fibre corrosion in a highly alkaline cement matrix and to the influence of high outdoor humidity. The durability of the fibres and of composite materials is also endangered by biological attack (bacteria, fungus). The fibres' instability appears in high humidity and flow of moisture. All these factors are particularly dangerous in tropical climates. Because of the alternations of wet and dry periods in tropical and subtropical conditions, cracking of elements may cause rapid degradation by corrosion. The process of embrittlement due to fibre corrosion is dangerous for the strength of elements. A short review of the application of vegetable fibres in cement composites is also given in [5.43]. The main countermeasures against poor durability are impregnation of fibres by various chemical agents, resin coatings of fibres, reduction of the matrix alkalinity and improvement of impermeability

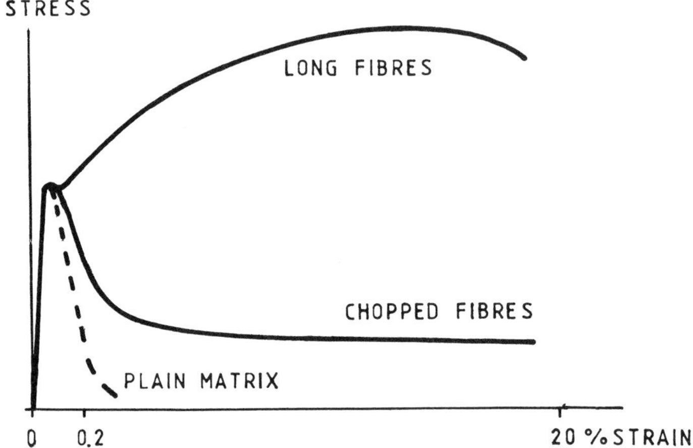

Figure 5.9 Examples of stress–strain curves for plain mortar elements and reinforced with sizal fibres. (Reproduced with permission from Gram, H.E. *et al.*, *Natural Fibre Concrete*; Swedish Agency for Research Cooperation with Developing Countries, 1984.) [5.39]

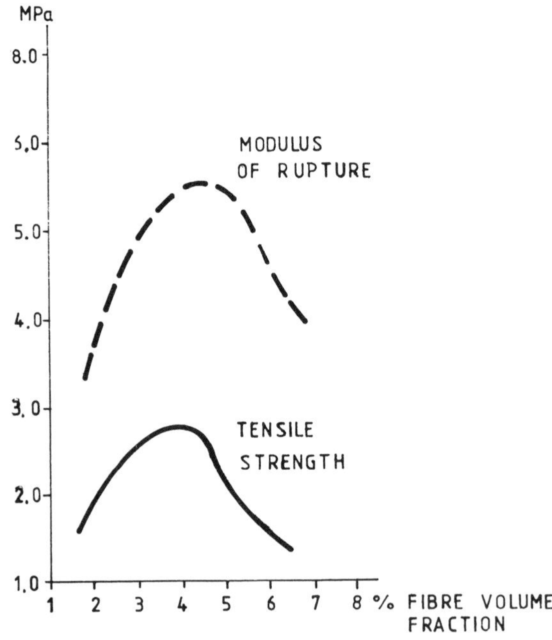

Figure 5.10 Effect of fibre content on tensile strength and modulus of rupture of composite elements. (Reprinted from *Housing Science*, **2**(5), Das Gupta, N.C. *et al.*, Mechanical properties of coir reinforced cement paste composites, pp. 91–406, 1978, with permission from Pergamon Press Ltd, Headington Hill Hall, Oxford OX3 OBW, UK. [5.46]

by sealing the internal pore system in the matrix. Efficient impregnation agents are mentioned in [5.35]: photochemicals and calcium stearate, boric acid and polyvinyl dichloride, sodium nitrite and chromium stearate. Formine and stearic acid are considered to be the best pore blocking and water repellent agents. The alkalinity of environment may be reduced by replacing 30–50% of Portland cement by fly ash or other pozzolan, [5.44]. All these measures may be used conjointly and considerable research effort is spent to ensure that elements reinforced with vegetable fibres are durable in local conditions.

Another problem is the fibre–matrix bond which is based mostly on mechanical interlocking. For example, the surface of bamboo fibres should be subjected to special treatment like sand blow to increase its roughness.

The amount of fibres in a cement matrix may vary from 0.1 to 0.9% of mass of cement [5.49] and [5.50]. The dispersion of fibre properties is usually rather large because of natural variations in the plant population and simple production techniques also increase the variability of composite material properties.

Vegetable fibres are also used to replace asbestos fibres, which are expensive and dangerous for health. The coconut fibres were tested for that aim and their strength and deformability, as well as thermal and acoustic properties, were determined and proved comparable with those of asbestos fibres, [5.51]. Similar tests on specimens reinforced with flax fibres from New Zealand and Australia showed their ability to replace asbestos in thin cement sheets, [5.52].

Vegetable fibres are used mostly in developing subtropical and tropical countries in Africa and South-East Asia as reinforcement for concrete elements for housing. The application of cheap and locally available fibres may help considerably in building low-cost houses, [5.53].

5.9 Textile reinforcement

Textile reinforcement is not defined in an unambiguous way, but it is usually admitted that all non-metallic fibres, fabrics and mats are considered as such. General classification of textile fibres is shown in Figure 5.11; some of them are used for cement-based materials. Several kinds of textile fibres, short chopped or long continuous ones, are described in more detail in other chapters and only their common features are considered here.

Besides fibres, the reinforcement of textiles can take the form of platelets, mats and woven or non-woven fabrics. Interesting data on textile reinforcement and its application may be found out in [5.55] and [5.56].

The main mechanical problems in brittle matrix composites with textile reinforcement relate to the bond between cement paste and fibres and durability of the fibres [5.57]. Both these problems are interrelated. If the alkalinity of the cement paste is not corrosive for the material of the fibres, then the chemical bond does not exist and adherence should be ensured in other ways, for example by:

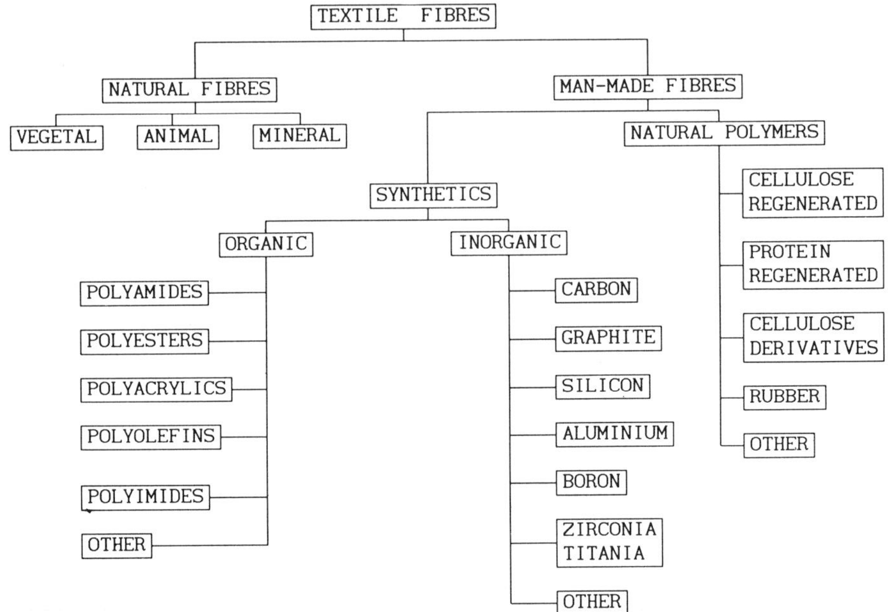

Figure 5.11 Classification of fibres used in textiles. (Reprinted from Kelly, A. (ed.), Fibres and Textiles: An overview, in *Concise Encyclopedia of Composite Materials*, 1989, pp. 92–8, with permission from Pergamon Press Ltd, Headington Hill Hall, Oxford, OX3 OBW, UK.) [5.54]

- increasing the length of a single fibre;
- using the fabrics, mats or meshes, where purely mechanical bonding is concentrated at the nodes and enhanced by entanglements;
- using fibres with additional hairs (fibrillated fibres).

The nodes provide not only better bonding but also may induce appreciable stress concentrations and act as crack initiators. It is sometimes observed that the crack pattern reflects the distribution of fibres.

Textile reinforcement with natural vegetable fibres or with glassfibres is particularly exposed to alkaline corrosion. These questions are described in Sections 5.3 and 5.9.

Textile fibres are useful as hybrid reinforcement; it means that two kinds of fibres, e.g. steel and polymeric ones when mixed together can control cracking at different stages: hardening with early shrinkage, shrinkage during drying, excessive strain due to external loading, etc.

The design of composite materials with textile reinforcement is executed mostly by a method of trial and error and by using previous experience or test results.

Sound and reliable methods for design and optimization are not available, partly because of highly nonlinear behaviour.

Textile reinforcement can be applied for several types of cement mortar or concrete products, [5.58]:

- shingles for roofing with cement blended with fly ash, characterized by good durability when exposed to climatic actions;
- inflated shell roofs or entire buildings;
- folded core sandwich panels, sometimes of complicated shapes, used for roofing;
- liners for lightweight precast concrete elements or thin plates for building facades.

The cost of composite materials with textile reinforcement depends not only on the cost of reinforcement itself but to a large measure on the selection of adequate technology. Overall cost should be calculated taking into account the durability of the product during exploitation. Some textile reinforcements, like mineral wool, are particularly cheap and are used to reinforce structural elements for low-cost buildings. However, even in such a case, the cost of reinforcement is comparable with that of the matrix. The production costs depend upon whether the reinforcement is carefully positioned in the forms or situated in a random way without much care. In the former case considerable gains can be obtained by optimum positioning and orientation of reinforcement. The latter case is more appropriate for the simple production of building elements by non-trained workers and without the use of expensive equipment.

Textile reinforcements called geotextiles are used extensively in earth constructions: walls, footings, road and runway foundations, etc. Also asphalt matrices are reinforced with polymer fabrics.

References

5.1. Hannant, D.L. (1978) *Fibre Cements and Fibre Concretes*, J. Wiley, Chichester.

5.2. Krenchel, H. and Shah, S.P. (1985) Applications of polypropylene fibres in Scandinavia. *Concrete International*, **7**(3), 32–4.

5.3. Krenchel, H. and Hejgaard, O. (1975) Can asbestos be completely replaced one day? in Proc. RILEM Symp. *Fibre-reinforced Cement and Concrete*, Sheffield, 335–46.

5.4. Mai, Y.W. (1979) Strength and fracture properties of asbestos–cement mortar composites. *J. of Mat. Sciences*, **14**, 2091–102.

5.5. Biryukovich, K.L., Biryukovich, Yu.L. and Biryukovich, D.L. (1965) *Glass-fibre-reinforced cement*. Budivelnik, Kiev 1964, CERA Translation, no. 12, November 1965.

5.6. Majumdar, A.J. and Nurse, R.W. (1975) *Glass-fibre-reinforced cement*, Building Research Establishment Current Papers, CP 65/75, July.

5.7. Majumdar, A.J. (1975) The role of the interface in glass-fibre-reinforced cement. *Composites*, January, 7–16.

5.8. Cohen, E.B. and Diamond, S. (1975) Validity of flexural strength reduction as an indication of alkali attack on glass in fibre-reinforced cement composites, Proc. RILEM Symp. *Fibre-reinforced Cement and Concrete*, Sheffield, 315–25.

5.9. Majumdar, A.J., West, J.M. and Larner, L.J. (1977) Properties of glassfibres in cement environment. *J. of Materials Science*, **12**, 927–36.

5.10. Majumdar, A.J. and Ryder, J.R. (1968) Glassfibre reinforcement of cement products. *Glass Technology*, **9**(3), 78–84.

5.11. Majumdar, A.J. (1980) Properties of GRC, Symp. *Concrete International 80, Fibrous Concrete*, April, The Construction Press, London, 48–68.

5.12. Bentur, A. and Mindess, S. (1990) *Fibre Reinforced Cementitious Composites*, Elsevier Applied Science, London and New York.

5.13. Thiery, J., Vautrin, A. and Francois-Brazier, J. (1991) High durability glassfiber reinforced concrete, in *Fiber Reinforced Cementitious Materials*, (eds S. Mindess and J. Skalny), *Mat. Res. Soc. Symp. Proc.*, **211**, 79–91 Mat. Res. Soc., Pittsburg.

5.14. Francois-Brazier, J., Soukatchoff, P., Thiery, J. and Vautrin, A. (1991) Comparative study of the mechanical damage and durability of glass cement composites, in *Proc. Int. Symp. Brittle Matrix Composites 3*, Warsaw, Sept. 1991, (eds A.M. Brandt and I.H. Marshall), Elsevier Applied Science, London and New York, 278–89.

5.15. Glinicki, M.A., Vautrin, A., Soukatchoff, P., Francois-Brazier, J. (1993) Impact performance of glass fibre reinforced cement plates subjected to accelerated ageing, in *Proc. of 9th Biennial Congress of The Glassfibre Reinforced Cement Association*, Copenhagen 1993, 1/1/I-1/1/X.

5.16. Maage, M. (1977) Interaction between steel fibres and cement based matrices, *Materials and Structures* RILEM, **10**(59) Sept.–Oct., 297–301.

5.17. Pinchin, D.J. and Tabor, D.J. (1978) Interfacial contact pressure and frictional stress transfer in steel fibre cement, in Proc. RILEM Symp. *Testing and Test Methods of Fibre Cement Composites*, (ed. R.N. Swamy), Sheffield, The Constr. Press, Lancaster 337–44.

5.18. Burakiewicz, A. (1979) Fibre to matrix bond in SFRC (in Polish), IFTR Report 42, Warsaw.

5.19. Burakiewicz, A. (1978) Testing of fibre bond strength in cement matrix, as [5.17], 355–65.

5.20. Potrzebowski, J. (1986) Behaviour of the fibre/matrix interface in SFRC during loading, in Proc. Int. Symp. *Brittle Matrix Composites 1*, (eds A.M. Brandt, I.H. Marshall), Jabłonna, Sept. 1985, Elsevier Applied Science, London.

5.21. Baggott, R., and Abdel-Monem, A.E.S. (1992) Aspects of bond in high volume fraction steel fibre reinforced calcium silicates, in Proc. RILEM Int. Workshop *High Performance Fiber Reinforced Cement Composites*, (eds H.W. Reinhardt and A.E. Naaman), Mainz, 23–26 June 1991, Spon/Chapman and Hall, London, 288–99.

5.22. Banthia, N., Trottier, J.F., Pigeon, M. and Krishnadev, M.R. (1992) Deformed steel fiber pull-out: material characteristics and metallurgical processes, as [5.21], 456–66.

5.23. Lankard, D.R. (1985) Preparation, properties and application of cement-based composites containing 5 to 20% steel fibres, in *Steel Fiber Concrete*, US–Sweden Joint Seminar, (eds S.P. Shah and Å. Skarendahl), CBI, Stockholm, 189–217.

5.24. Naaman, A.E. and Homrich, J.R. (1989) Tensile stress–strain properties of SIFCON. *Amer. Concr. Inst., Materials Journal*, **86**(3), May–June, 244–51.

5.25. Reinhardt, H.W. and Fritz, C. (1989) Optimization of SIFCON mix. Proc. Int.

Symp. *Fibre Reinforced Cements and Concretes. Recent Developments*, Cardiff, 18–20 September 1989, (eds R.N. Swamy and B. Barr), Elsevier Applied Science, London.
5.26. Bentur, A. (1989) Properties and reinforcing mechanisms in steel wool reinforced cement, Int. Symp. *Fibre Reinforced Cements and Concretes. Recent Developments*, Cardiff, 18–20 September 1989, (eds R.N. Swamy and B. Barr), Elsevier Applied Science, London.
5.27. de Guillebon, B. and Sohm, J.M. (1986) Metallic glass ribbons – a new fibre for concrete reinforcement, Proc. RILEM Symp. *Developments in Fibre Reinforced Cement and Concrete*, Univ. of Sheffield, Sheffield.
5.28. Rossi, P., Harrouche, N. and de Larrard, F. (1989) Method for optimizing the composition of metal-fibre-reinforced concretes, Proc. Int. Symp. *Fibre Reinforced Cements and Concretes. Recent Developments*, Cardiff, 18–20 September 1989, (eds R.N. Swamy and B. Barr). Elsevier Applied Science, London, 1–10.
5.29. Kasperkiewicz, J. and Skarendahl, Å. (1986) Fracture resistance evaluation of steel fibre concrete, as [5.20], 619–28.
5.30. Rossi, P., Harrouche, N. and Le Maou, F. (1989) Comportement mécanique des bétons de fibres métalliques utilisés dans les structures en béton armé et précontraint. Ann. de l'ITBTP, 479bis, sér. Mat. 73, Paris, December 1989, 167–82.
5.31. Venuat, M. (1984) *Adjuvants et traitements*, published by the author, Paris.
5.32. Krenchel, H. and Jensen, H.W. (1980) Organic reinforcing fibres for cement and concrete, Proc. Symp. *Fibrous Concrete CI 80*, The Construction Press Ltd, Lancaster, 87–94.
5.33. Naaman, A.E., Shah, S.P. and Throne, J.L. (1984) Some developments in polypropylene fibers for concrete. Int. Symp. *Fibre Reinforced Concrete*, SP–81, ACI, Detroit, 375–96.
5.34. Ramakrishnan, V. (1987) Materials and properties of fibre reinforced concrete, Proc. Int. Symp. *Fibre Reinforced Concrete*, December 16–19, Madras, Oxford and IBH Publ. Co., New Delhi, 2.3–2.23.
5.35. Wörner, J.D. and Müller, M. (1992) Behaviour, design and application of polyacrylonitrile fibre concrete, as [5.21], 115–26.
5.36. Ohama, Y., Amano, M. and Endo, M. (1985) Properties of carbon fibre reinforced cement with silica fume. *Concrete International*, **7**(3), March, 58–62.
5.37. Brandt, A.M. and Glinicki, M.A. (1992) Flexural behaviour of concrete elements reinforced with carbon fibres, as [5.21], 288–99.
5.38. Katz, A. and Bentur, A. (1992) High performance fibres in high strength cementitious matrices, as [5.17], 237–47.
5.39. Gram, H.E., Persson, H. and Skarendahl, Å. (1984) *Natural fibre concrete*. Swedish Agency for Research Cooperation with Developing Countries, Stockholm.
5.40. Mwamila, B.L.M. (1985) Natural twines as main reinforcement in concrete beams. *Int. Journ. of Cement Composites and Lightweight Concrete*, **7**(1), 11–19.
5.41. Aziz, M.A., Paramasiwam, P. and Lee, S.L. (1981) Prospects for natural fibre reinforced concrete in construction. *Int. Journ. of Cement Composites and Lightweight Concrete*, **3**(2), 123–32.
5.42. Mindess, S. and Bentur, A. (1982) The fracture of wood fibre reinforced cement. *Int. Journ. of Cement Composites and Lightweight Concrete*, **4**(2), 245–9.
5.43. Fordos, Z. and Tram, B. (1986) Natural fibres as reinforcement of cement-based composites. Proc. of RILEM Symp. *Developments of fibre reinforced cement and concrete*, Univ. of Sheffield, Sheffield.

5.44. Soroushian, P. and Marikunte, S. (1992) High performance cellulose fiber reinforced cement composites, in Proc. ACI-RILEM Int. Workshop *High Performance Fiber Reinforced Cement Composites*, Mainz, 23–26 June, Chapman & Hall, London, 84–99.

5.45. Andonian, R., Mai, Y.W. and Cotterell, B. (1979) Strength and fracture properties of cellulose fibre reinforced cement composites. *Int. Journ. of Cement Composites*, **1**(4), 151–8.

5.46. Das Gupta, N.C., Paramasivam, P. and Lee, S.L. (1978) Mechanical properties of coir reinforced cement paste composites. *Housing Science*, **2**(5) Pergamon Press, London, 91–406.

5.47. Brandt, A.M. (1987) Present trends in the mechanics of cement-based fibre reinforced composites. *Construction & Building Materials*, **1**(1), 28–39.

5.48. Bergstrom, S.B. and Gram, H.E. (1984) Durability of alkali-sensitive fibres in concrete. *Int. Journ. of Cement Composites and Lightweight Concrete*, **6**(2), 75–80.

5.49. Rafiqul Islam, M.D. and Khorshed Alam, A.K.M. (1987) Study of fibre reinforced concrete with natural fibres, Proc. of the *Int. Symp. on Fibre Reinforced Cement*, Madras, Oxford & IBH Publ. Co., New Delhi, December 16–19, 3.41–3.53.

5.50. Singh, R.N. (1987) Flexure behaviour of notched coir reinforced concrete beams under cycle loading, Proc. of the *Int. Symp. on Fibre Reinforced Cement*, Madras, December 16–19, Oxford & IBH Publ. Co., New Delhi, 3.55–3.66.

5.51. Paramasivam, P., Nathan, G.K. and Das Gupta, N.C. (1984) Coconut fibre reinforced corrugated slabs. *Int. Journ. of Cement Composites and Lightweight Concrete*, **6**(1), 151–8.

5.52. Coutts, R.S.P. (1983) Flax fibres as a reinforcement in cement mortars. *Int. Journ. of Cement Composites and Lightweight Concrete*, **5**(4), 257–62.

5.53. Nilsson, L. (1975) Reinforcement of concrete with sisal and other vegetal fibres, Swedish Council for Building Research, Doc. D14, Stockholm.

5.54. Kelly, A. (ed.) (1989) Fibres and Textiles: An overview, in *Concise Encyclopedia of Composite Materials*, Pergamon Press, Oxford 92–8.

5.55. Hamelin, P. and Verchery, G. (eds) (1990) *Textile Composites in Building Construction*, Proc. Int. Symp. in Lyon, 16–18 July 1990, Editions Pluralis.

5.56. Hamelin, P. and Verchery, G. (eds) (1992) *Textile Composites in Building Construction*, Proc. of 2nd Int. Symp. in Lyon, 23–25 June 1992, Editions Pluralis.

5.57. Brandt, A.M. (1990) Cement based composite materials with textile reinforcement, in [5.55], part 1, 37–43.

5.58. Nicholls, R. (1990) Composite materials for construction, in [5.55], part 1, 5–14.

6 Structure of cement composites

6.1 Elements and types of structure

Cement-based composites are highly heterogeneous and their structures are composed of different elements:

- grains of fine and coarse aggregate;
- non-hydrated cement grains;
- hardened binder (cement paste, bitumens, etc.) with its own internal structures;
- voids of various kinds, like pores, cracks;
- reinforcement (fibres, steel meshes or bars, polymer films and particles);
- water and air or other gases, which partly fill up voids and pores.

Several parameters are used to describe the structure: ratio of matrix to inclusion stiffness, type of aggregate, maximum and minimum dimension of aggregate grains, their size distribution, texture and roughness of the surface of aggregate grains etc.

The grains and eventual reinforcement are bonded together in a more or less continuous way by a binding material, which fills up the inter-granular voids and also covers the grain surface with a thin film. The mechanical adhesion of the binders to surfaces of all kinds of structural elements and the chemical reactions with binders are the main factors ensuring bonding, each of them of differing importance in each case. It is assumed, however, on the basis of experimental evidence, that the mechanical roughness of aggregate grains and of reinforcement surfaces decides the quality of bonding. In the case of Portland cement paste, its shrinkage plays an important role in increasing mechanical adhesion.

On the faces of aggregate grains and fibres which are in contact with cement paste another element of the material's structure appears: the interface which is understood as the region of direct contact between the two adjacent materials or material phases. The properties of interfaces are related mainly to the roughness of material surfaces, to their purity, to the ability for wetting one material by the other and to particular conditions in which thin layers of binders are hardening. The interface also appears in composites with other kinds of binders. Further remarks on the interface types and properties in concrete-like materials are given in Chapter 7 and interesting general information may be found in paper [6.1].

The structure of concrete-like materials may be considered at different levels (cf. Section 2.4). The lowest level, where the required resolution of observation is of the order of a few Angstroms, is used mostly for examination of the micro-structure of cement paste. The main interest is concentrated between so-called micro- and macro-levels; meaning between the size of Portland cement grains or those of small pores of few micrometres in diameter, up to tens of millimetres for maximum grains of coarse aggregate and the diameters of steel bars.

The material's structure is changing with time, mainly because during the hydration and hardening processes the fresh cement paste is becoming a hard and brittle material. This strong time-dependency is perhaps one of the characteristic features of concrete-like composites and their structures.

The structure is composed of randomly distributed and disorientated elements, but certain elements may be ordered. For research purposes artificial materials may be constructed with regularly distributed ([6.2] and [6.3]) or with selected one-size grains of aggregate, [6.4]. Also in real materials, reinforcing fibres may be aligned ([6.5] and [6.6]). Reinforcing steel bars and meshes built of continuous wires are also regularly distributed. The general characteristics of the material structures of concrete-like composites are related, however, to their randomness and high heterogeneity on all levels of observation. That is the reason for the considerable difficulties in providing any quantitative description.

The principal mechanical and other properties of concrete-like composites are related to the material's structure and very few are structure-independent and related only to the material's composition (cf. Section 2.4). That obvious conclusion leads to a modern approach in material design: it is not sufficient to determine the proportions of the main constituents, but it also becomes necessary to select appropriate grain fractions and their distribution in space, to find out the optimal fibre orientation and to create an efficient system of pores, as well as to decide upon several other parameters for obtaining the best structure of the material for fulfilling imposed requirements.

The importance of appropriate technologies grows in line with any complications of designed material structure, because only by adequate methods of execution can the designed parameters be obtained.

For theoretical studies the structure composed of aggregate grains is simulated using various structural models. In recent years, the finite elements method (FEM) was often applied, e.g. [6.7]. This type of approach is discussed in more detail in Section 2.5.

6.2 Methods of observation and representation of materials structures

A materials structure is observed on polished cross-sections or lateral faces of elements and specimens. Thin layers sawn out of specimens may be subjected to x-ray analysis and very thin layers are transparent enough to enable observation and structural analysis. The volume fractions of particular constituents, their spatial distribution and orientation, may be deduced from two-dimensional images using stereological methods.

In most cases observations are made on photograms and therefore the specific characteristics of that technique determine the quality of obtained images, like possible colour modifications and the influence of photographic material sensitivity or resolution. On the other hand, the photograms are easy to handle, relatively cheap and give the possibility of large magnification.

Observations with the naked eye, possibly assisted by a magnifying glass or the application of low power microscopes are usually sufficient for the analysis of the structure in macro-level. At that level the main elements of the material structure are clearly visible – the grain of fine aggregate, fibres, large pores and cracks. The observed surface should be well polished and correctly illuminated. The observations are often executed during testing and several photograms are made in order to follow the modification of observed structures under load or during ageing processes. Without any magnification objects of a diameter equal to 0.5 mm may be identified.

The observation is more difficult when certain elements are not clearly differentiated from others. On the images of the concrete fractured surface shown in Figure 6.1 the varying intensity of the grey colour of different phases allows them to be distinguished without having any great experience. In other cases, additional procedures are necessary – special illumination in which a particular phase will reflect the light, selective colouration, etc.

Several methods were suggested for enhancing the visibility of crack patterns

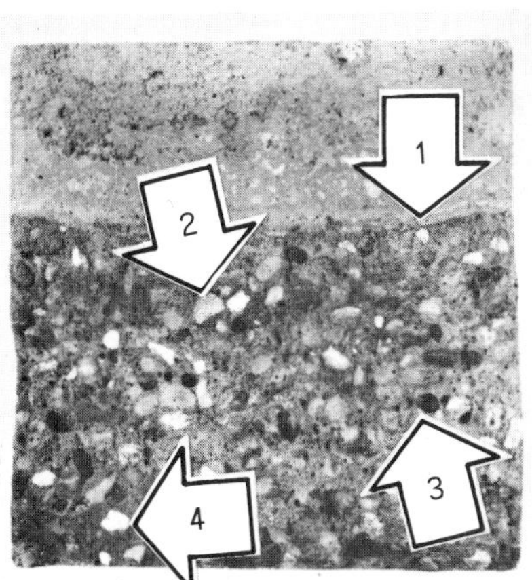

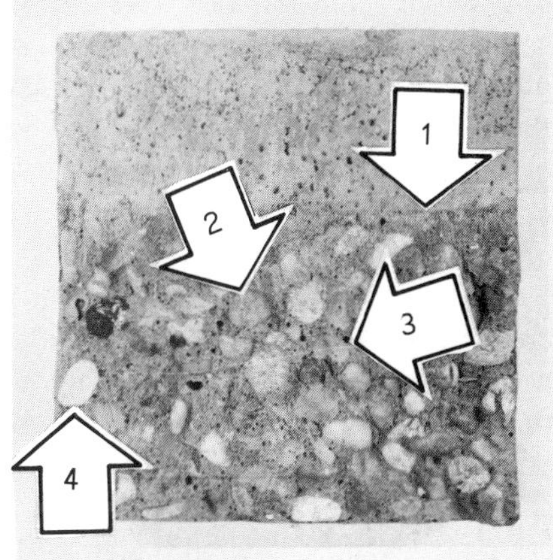

Figure 6.1 Views of fractured surface of concrete elements after Mode II fracture. a) max. grains of 2 mm; b) max. grains of 10 mm; 1) front of the initial sawn out notch, 2) fractured aggregated grain, 3) micropores in the matrix, 4) imprints of grains pulled-out from the matrix. (From tests by Professor G. Prokopski, 1989.)

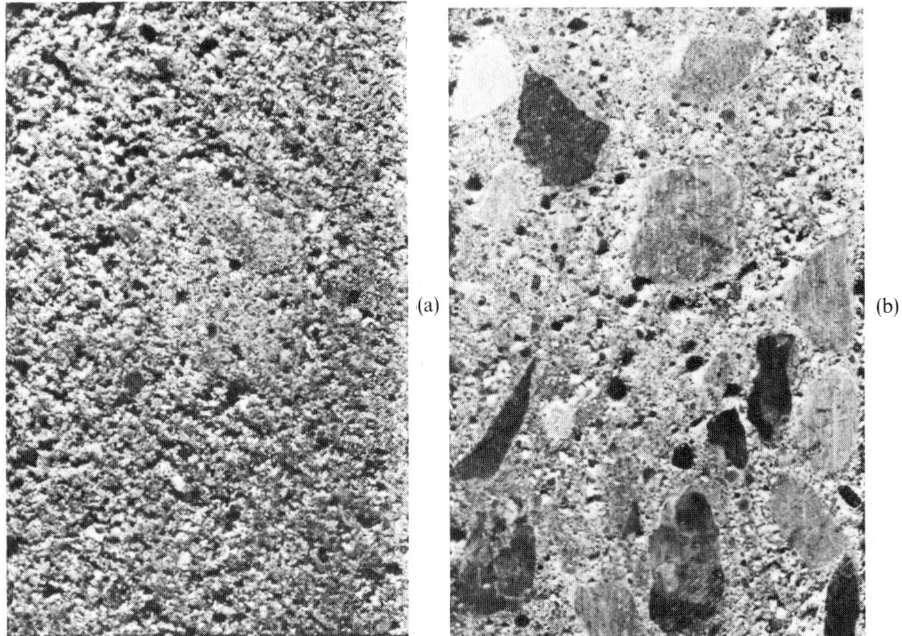

Figure 6.2 Examples of structure of Portland cement mortar and concrete. Unpolished surfaces of sawn out specimens. Pores up to 3 mm. a) mortar with sand grains <2.0 mm; b) concrete with natural crushed aggregate grains 8–12 mm. (From tests by Dr M.A. Glinicki, 1989.)

in concretes and mortars, [6.8]. Cracks are more visible when soaked with a coloured ink (penetrant) [6.9] or with a water solution of citron acid and potassium permanganate [6.10]. Fluorescent ink 'Cermor' was sprayed on to the surface of a specimen to facilitate the observation of narrow cracks in UV light, [6.4]. The ink is a dispersion of a light petroleum oil consisting of line organo-metallic particles which form a deposit on the crack edges and fluoresce under UV light.

In Figure 6.2 examples of images with the structure of mortar and concrete are shown. The images are obtained at life size with a slight magnification made possible by the reproduction of photograms. The calculation of pore area and their analysis is impossible on images as shown in Figure 6.2a and further polishing and enhancement of pores is needed. The structure of large aggregate grains of crushed stone, as well as numerous pores of diameter up to 3.0 mm, are clearly visible in Figure 6.2b.

In Figure 6.3 the randomly distributed polystyrene beads may be clearly identified in cement mortar on the sawn face of a specimen without any additional treatment. The beads were added to obtain the characteristic structure of pores of known diameter (2–4 mm) and volume of 10% in the cement-based matrix, cf. Section 11.2.2.

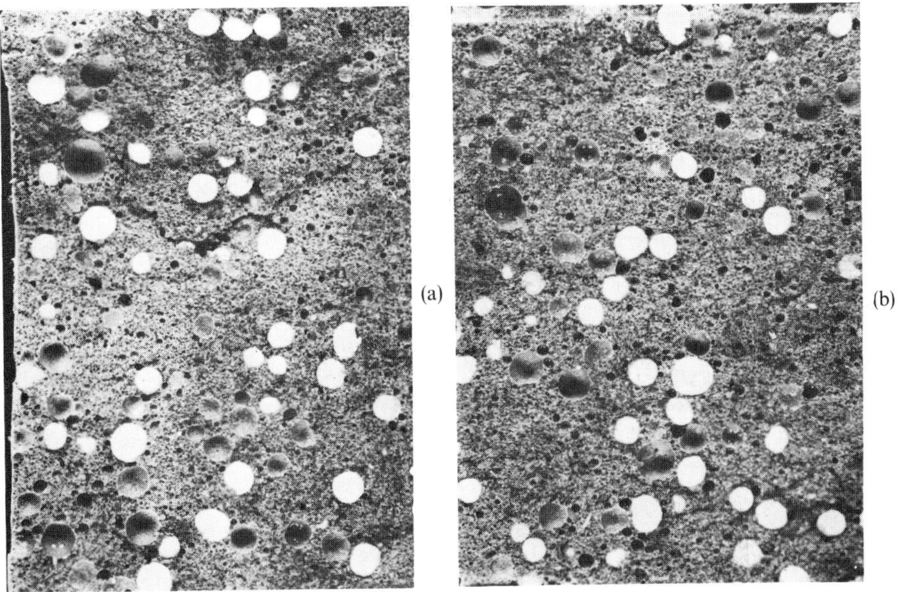

Figure 6.3 Examples of structure of Portland cement mortar with 10% vol of polystyrene beads of 0.4–4 mm in diameter. Sand grains <2.0 mm. Random distribution of components with slightly different volume fraction of beads: 18.2% (left) and 14.6% (right). Overall porosity of composite 28%. (From tests by Dr M.A. Glinicki, 1989.)

Larger magnifications are required for the micro-level where the average size of objects is approximately 1.0 micrometer. At that level for example the distribution of small pores induced to increase frost resistance may be observed and microcracks may be detected in the specimens cut out from the neighbourhood of a crack tip.

As example, the SEM images showing various forms in cement paste are given in Figure 6.4.

The observations are executed using various types of visible light or electron microscopes. The technical side of these methods of observation is omitted here because several specialized handbooks are available in that field, e.g. [6.11], [6.12] and [6.13].

X-radiography is extensively used to obtain images of internal structural features, like cracks and steel-fibres, but also other elements – aggregate grains and voids. An excellent review of possibilities and methods in relation to that technique is given by [6.14]. The images of fibre structures are discussed in Section 6.6.

Every image obtained by any method in a micro- or macro-scale may be subjected to computerized image analysis providing quantitative results, if particular elements in that image can be distinguished from the others. Several systems are known (e.g. Quantimet, Joyce–Loebl, Morphopericolor) which

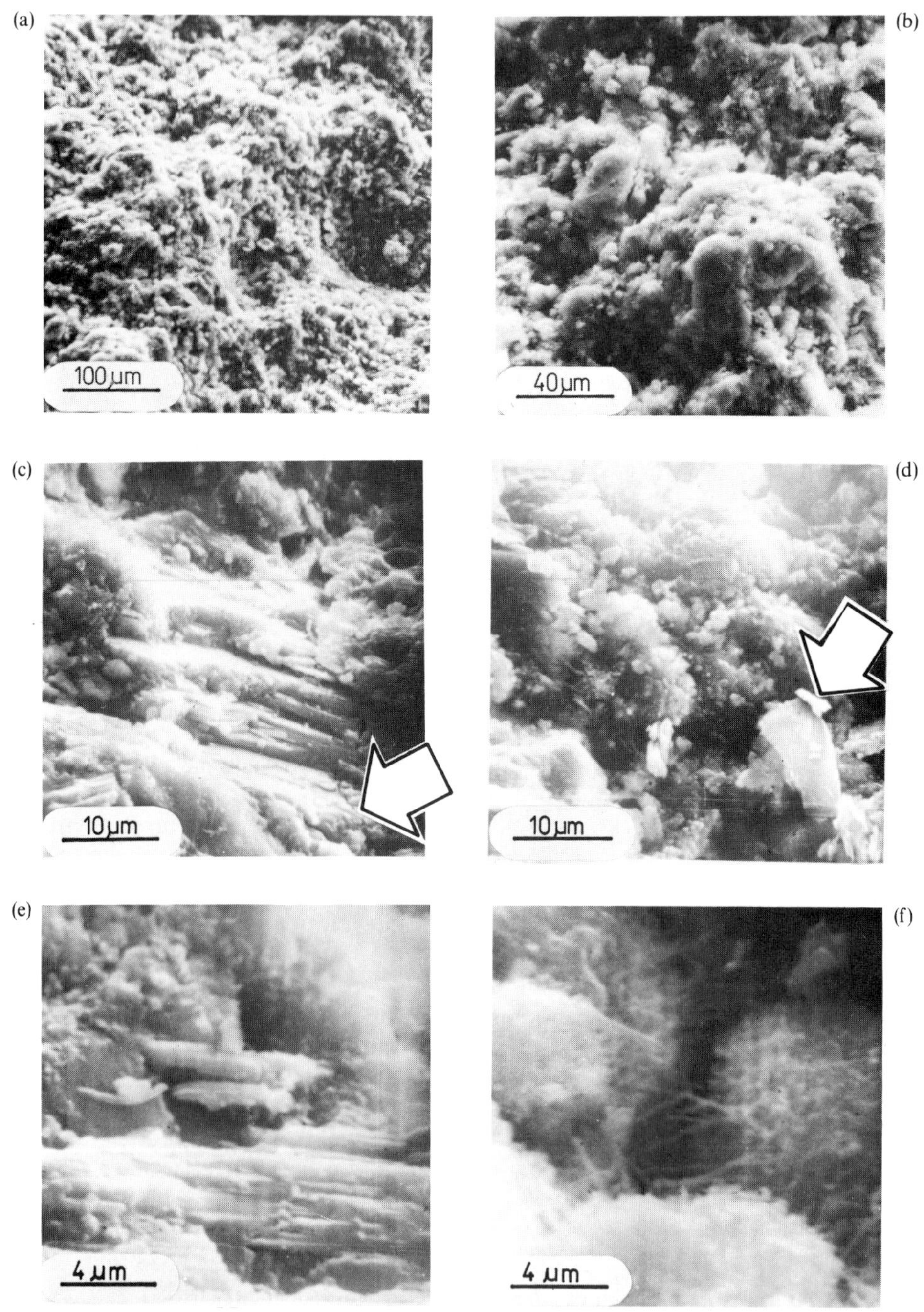
(a)
100 µm
(b)
40 µm
(c)
10 µm
(d)
10 µm
(e)
4 µm
(f)
4 µm

allows us to record and calculate different features of selected elements in an image – area and perimeter, distribution, shape, etc. The possibilities of such a system depend not only upon the technical performance, but mainly on available software which allows more or less advanced quantitative analysis, cf. also Section 6.6.2.

Beside the above mentioned direct methods, in which material structure and its elements may be observed, various indirect methods are applied, also giving information on material structure, e.g.:

- overall porosity and pore-size distribution of pore structure (suction porosimetry, [6.15], mercury intrusion porosimetry, physical adsorption of gases);
- extent of cracking or of other cavities and irregularities of the material structure (ultrasonic pulse velocity across examined elements, Eddy current method).

Acoustic emission events under loads and other actions are calculated and recorded and may be analysed as a result of cracking, debonding and other fracture phenomena. Simple counting of events gives information on overall material behaviour, from which conclusions on material structure may be drawn in an indirect way. The intensity of cracking in a brittle matrix varies with the loading and may indicate different phases of the fracture processes, cf. Section 9.4. The more advanced level of application of the acoustic emission method is based on signal transformation into various parameters extracted from the time and frequency domains. Pattern recognition techniques and statistical analysis allow the identification of microfailures and enable their origin to be deduced – cracks in the matrix, fibre damages, delaminations, debondings, etc., [6.16] and [6.17].

A short description of all the methods of structural observation is given by [6.18] and a few important groups of experimental observation methods are shown in Table 6.1 as proposed by [6.19] and [6.20].

The observation of images of composites may lead to qualitative conclusions only, but it does mean that the existence of certain objects and their reciprocal relations may be confirmed. For quantitative analysis on the basis of these images computer image analysis and different stereological methods are applied, in which the results of counting the objects in plane images are generalized to

◄

Figure 6.4 SEM images of structure of Portland cement paste. a) Cement paste, w/c = 0.6, magnification × 200; b) Cement paste, w/c = 0.6, magnification × 500; c) Cement paste in gravel concrete. Transcrystalline crack across layers of crystals $Ca(OH)_2$, w/c = 0.7, magnification × 2000; d) Large crystal $Ca(OH)_2$ is visible and several pores, w/c = 0.5, magnification × 2000; e) Crystalline platelets of $Ca(OH)_2$, w/c = 0.4, magnification × 5000; f) Very thin fibre crystals of CSH (calcium silicates) are formed in pores, w/c = 0.6, magnification × 5000. (From tests by Professor G. Prokopski, 1989.)

Table 6.1 Methods for identification of the microstructure of hydrated cement paste

Type	Microstructure	Methods
Indirect	Porosity	Mercury intrusion, porosimetry (MIP), gaseous adsorption (BET)
	Pore size distribution	Differential scanning calorimetry (DSC)
	Free and bound water, degree of hydration	Thermogravimetric analysis (TGA), differential thermal analysis (DTA), x-ray diffraction (XRD)
	Surface analysis	Secondary ions mass spectroscopy (SIMS)
Direct	Porosity	Back scatter electron imaging (BSE), energy dispersive x-ray analysis (EDXA)
	Morphology, intergrowth	Scanning electron microscopy (SEM)
	Inner structure, phase distribution	High voltage electron microscopy (HVEM), scanning transmission electron microscopy (STEM)
	Hydration characteristic morphology	SIMS, NMR spectroscopy
	Cement type, admixtures, water/cement ratio, compaction, alcali–silica reaction	High resolution scanning acoustic microscopy (SAM)

(Source: Pratt, P.L., Physical methods for identification of microstructures; *Materials and Structures*, **21**(122), pp. 106–17, RILEM, 1988. [6.19] and Jennings, H.M., Towards establishing a relationship between microstructure and properties of cement-based materials, in *Ceramic Trans.*, **16**, Advances in Cementitious Materials, ed. S. Mindess, 1991, 289–317 [6.20])

obtain volume fractions and distribution. A concise presentation of stereological methods, with examples of their application, may be found in [6.4].

In diffractive methods, electrons and x-rays, which better penetrate the specimens, are scattered as an effect of collisions with electrons in the material. The diffraction pattern obtained is recorded and compared with reference ones. The specimens are prepared as powders of 10 μm being the maximum grain size.

For spectrograph methods infra-red spectrography is used to identify organic materials, minerals and their molecular structures. These methods are based on the analysis of interaction between tested material and electromagnetic radiation. The spectrum of the amount of radiation absorbed for variable wavelengths is matched with a reference sample.

Differential thermal analysis (DTA) is based on heat transfer between matter (absorption or liberation of heat) and the environment. The heat transfer is measured at various temperatures with respect to an inert material, e.g. calcined alumina. The thermographs obtained are compared with model ones of known materials and processes such as dehydration, decarbonation, oxidation, crystalline transition, decomposition or lattice destruction.

6.3 Micro-structure of cement paste

Hydrated and hardened cement paste is that element of concrete-like composites which fills the voids between fine aggregate grains and binds all elements of the material structure together. To obtain images of cement paste with its constituents, the maximum possible magnification is necessary. The micro-structure is built of three main elements:

1. Calcium silicate hydrate $C_3S_2H_3$, designed also as CSH, has the form of very small and weakly crystallized particles which by their dimensions and irregularity resemble clay. CSH covers from 50 up to 70% of total volume of the cement paste and its properties and behaviour are complicated because they depend on several interrelated processes. Its representation by models and theoretical relations is not yet completely satisfactory.
2. Calcium hydroxide CH is strongly crystallized in the form of hexagonal prisms and covers 20–25% of the total volume. Its large crystals measure from 0.01 to 1.0 mm.
3. Calcium sulphoaluminate $C_5AS_3H_{32}$ is called ettringite and has the form of long needles or plates and strips, its volume corresponds to 10–15%.

Other components of the cement paste structure are magnesium hydroxide MgH which may occupy up to 5% of total volume and capillary pores with volume depending mainly on the water/cement (w/c) ratio.

In each of these three groups of constituents different compounds exist, but their chemical formulae are not used and discussed in detail here. Interested readers are referred to handbooks on concrete technology, e.g. [6.21].

The dimensions of the above mentioned constituents are from 0.1 μm for single crystal depth up to 100 μm for crystal needle length. These constituents are mixed together, forming a dense and very irregular structure, partly crystallized and interlocked, also containing non-hydrated cement grains and water in different forms. In Figure 6.5 the micro-structure of hardened cement paste is shown schematically in successive phases of hydration.

In the initial stage, (Figure 6.5a), thin concentric layers of crystallized needles and plates are developed around unhydrated cement grains. These crystal forms are becoming thicker because additional hydration products are growing, (Figure 6.5b). The products of hydration are called cement gel, i.e. an aggregation of colloidal material. After progression of hydration, the neighbouring grains are in contact and a dense gel structure fills available spaces. This leaves thin gel pores in the gel structure and capillary pores between the gel layers, (Figure 6.5c). Unhydrated parts of cement grains remain embedded in gel and their further hydration proceeds slowly, provided that two conditions are satisfied–water is available for chemical processes and there is enough space for hydration products.

Chemical processes involved in the hydration of cement depend on several factors for their development. The constituents' composition and proportions,

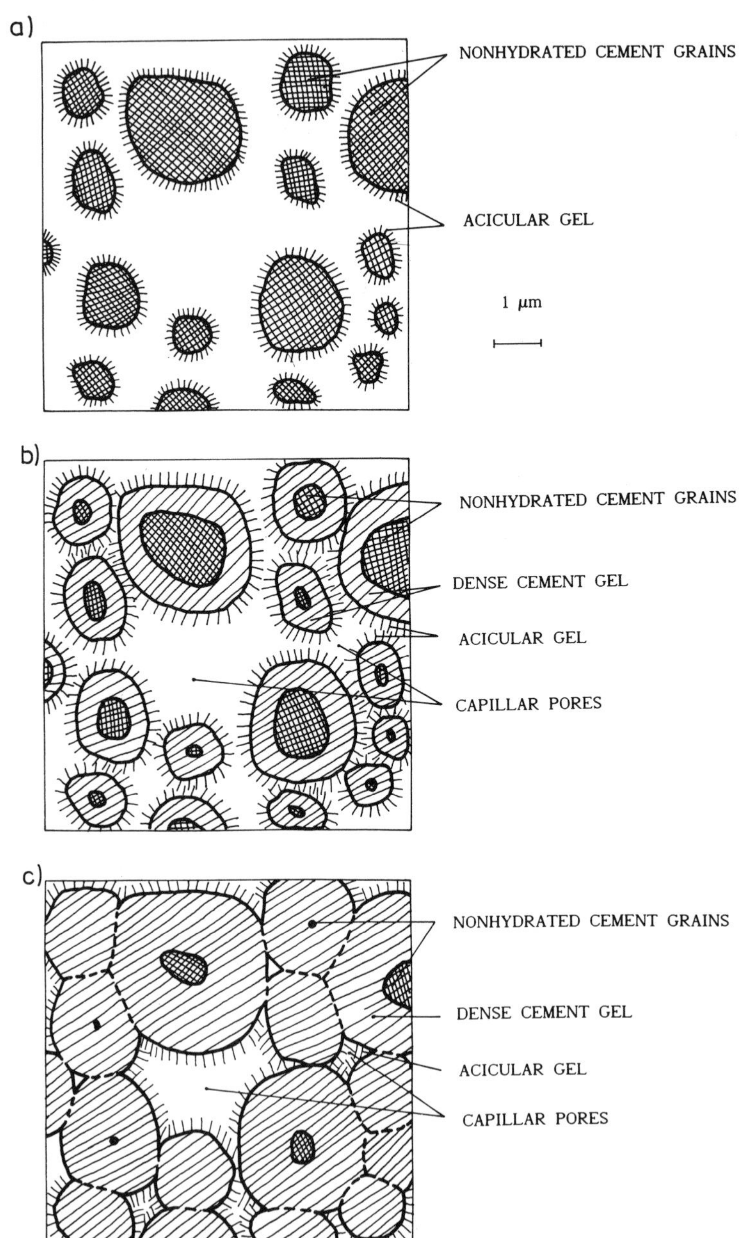

Figure 6.5 Schematic representation of cement paste structure: sequence of hydration in time.

the amount of water available for hydration and ambient temperature may be quoted.

The rate of hydration depends on the properties of cement and on admixtures. Usually, the admixture of gypsum is necessary to decrease the early hydration rate and to adapt it to the technology for handling and placing the fresh mix. The rate of hydration is indicated in regulations for different kinds of cement and conventionally it is accepted that hydration is achieved after 6 hours. In that period only about 15% of cement volume is effectively hydrated and these processes develop further by different mechanisms and at a rate decreasing with time during the next period of hardening. The deceleration of hardening is explained by the fact, that the amount of available water is decreasing and also its access is reduced by the hydration products which double the initial volume of cement and gradually fill up all accessible voids and channels. It is usually admitted that for cement hydration only 22% of water by cement mass is required. The hydration processes are described in several books, e.g. [6.22], [6.23], [6.24], [6.25] and many others. Interesting remarks are also published in [6.26].

Finally, the cement paste becomes a hard and brittle material. Its deformability is characterized by linear elasticity and brittle fracture under short time load and by its shrinkage and creep under varying humidity and long-term loading. The behaviour of cement paste is very brittle, i.e., failure under load takes the form of a rapid progression of internal microcracks, accompanied by only small deformation. The crack propagation is controlled to some extent by inclusions – aggregate grains, pores and eventual reinforcement. These questions are dealt with in Chapters 9 and 10.

Porosity is considered usually at the meso- and macro-level and is described in Section 6.5.

6.4 Structure built of aggregate grains

The aggregate grains are often called the 'concrete skeleton'. In fact, in all ordinary concretes with hard stone grains they form a kind of rigid skeleton, where voids are filled with mortar and cement paste. A variety of lightweight grains are used in lightweight concretes. Examples of different structures built of aggregate are shown in Figure 6.6 and are discussed below.

The grains of similar size and in contact with each other are shown in Figure 6.6a. The voids are of large volume fraction and can only be partly filled with matrix. This structure is rarely applied for cement concretes, and is more often used for granular insulation materials or for bitumen concretes used as structural layers in road pavements.

A similar structure but without direct contact between the grains is obtained with additional amounts of matrix. The structure as in Figure 6.6b may be

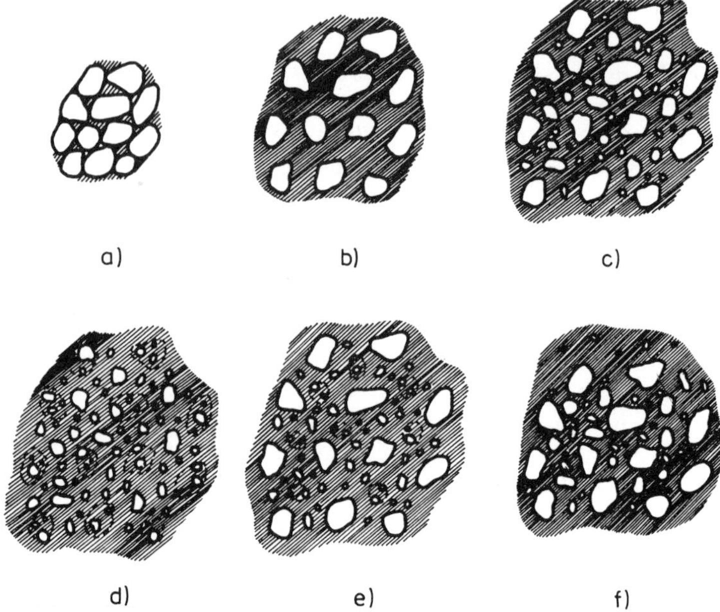

Figure 6.6 Examples of the aggregate grain structures in concrete.

obtained by mixing in an ordinary concrete mixer. However, because of the equal size of grains, a large volume of the matrix is needed.

In Figure 6.6c, a continuous structure of grains is schematically represented in which a large range of sizes is applied and minimum volume may be obtained. If in such a structure the biggest grains are replaced by smaller ones, then the matrix volume will obviously increase (Figure 6.6d).

In Figure 6.6e the grain structure is composed of big and small grains, the intermediary ones being removed. Gap-grading is particularly sensitive for segregation during transportation and handling. An unfavourable example is shown in Figure 6.6f – the grains are segregated and the upper part of the element looks rather like a mortar.

The examples of grain structures are discussed in [6.21], [6.23], [6.24] and [6.25].

The design of aggregate structure should begin by determining the maximum grain size, according to the density of reinforcement and characteristic dimensions of the element to be cast. In several countries, for different structural elements, the maximum grain diameter is limited by prescriptions to 20, 40 and 80 mm, the last value corresponding to large foundations and concrete dams.

A lower limit for the grains size is imposed in cement paste having in mind their negative influence on crystallization processes. They may also increase shrinkage, reduce the entrained air content and diminish durability. However, it has been proved that lowest sizes of inert aggregate grains, called stone flour, improve the workability of the fresh mix, reduce bleeding and increase considerably the impermeability of hardened composite. Fine grains of silica fume are used for high quality concrete, cf. Section 4.3. The volume fraction of particles smaller than 75 μm should be limited and their influence controlled in every case, because it is closely related to the particle nature (clay, silt or harsh stone dust) and form (free particles, lumps or coating on larger grains of aggregate); the kind of concrete is also important, [6.25].

For a general control of the grading one can use an approximate formula giving appropriate percentage p of material passing a given sieve of opening d which is proposed in the following form, $p = 100(d/D)^h$, where D is the maximum grain diameter and h is a coefficient which should be close to 0.5. When h is smaller, then more fine grading is obtained and more coarse when h is greater, cf. Figure 6.7. Examples of sieve diagrams are given in Section 4.2, where it is also mentioned that the choice of aggregate concerns not only its grading, but also the grain properties – their strength, porosity, surface roughness, etc.

The shape of single grains which build the aggregate structure is of certain importance. Flat or elongated grains require more matrix to fill the voids than spherical or cuboid ones. Detailed discussion on the grain shape is given in [6.21].

The structure of grains embedded in the mortar matrix may be quantitatively analysed on images obtained from cross-sections as shown in Figures 6.2 and 6.3 using the linear transverse method, [6.25]. It consists of superimposing a regular grid several times in a random way on the examined image and the

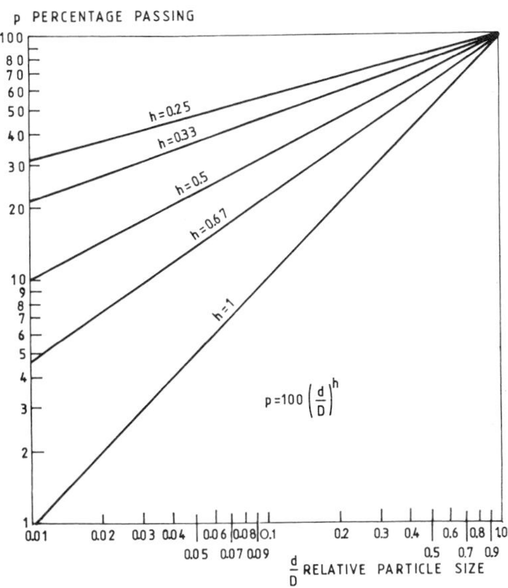

Figure 6.7 Fuller curves of various degrees. (Reproduced with permission from Popovics, S., *Concrete-Making Materials*; published by Hemisphere Publ. Co., 1979.) [6.25]

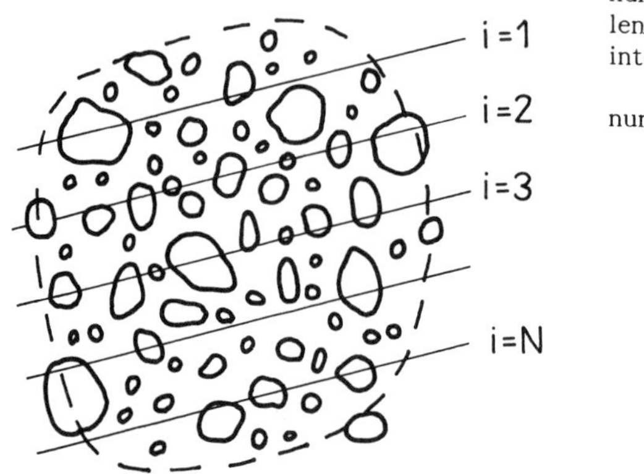

number of lines $i = 1, 2, \ldots, N$

length of mortar intercept on line i ℓ_i

number of lengths on line i n_i

$$\mathrm{AMI} = \frac{\sum_{1}^{N} \ell_i}{\sum_{i}^{N} n_i}$$

Figure 6.8 Example of application of the linear traverse method to calculate average mortar intercept.

length of lines between intercepts with aggregate grains are measured, summed and averaged. The number obtained is called the average mortar or grain intercept and its value may be considered as characteristic for the amount of that component in a given structure of the examined composite. The calculation procedure is explained in Figure 6.8 as being one of the simplest applications of the stereological methods for quantitative analysis of the structures of materials. The manual measurements and calculations are at present usually replaced by computerized equipment of the 'Quantimet' type, mentioned in Section 6.2.

According to several authors, the value of the average mortar intercept (AMI) should be equal to 3.5 mm for composites of continuous grading and manual compaction to ensure appropriate workability. When vibration of the fresh mix is applied which is common practice at present, that value may be lower. Similar modification of that limit value is needed when very fine sand is used. A larger value for the average mortar intercept may indicate that the composite structure is not correct – additional amount of coarse aggregate would probably improve it.

The increase of lower fractions will necessarily increase the amount of water and, consequently, of Portland cement. Inversely, carefully designed gap-grading may require less matrix. In that case, the workability of fresh mix is more dependent on precise proportioning and mixing to avoid segregation. Therefore, gap-graded aggregates are not recommended when segregation is possible and particular care in handling the fresh mix cannot be guaranteed.

In a gap-graded aggregate mix a phenomenon of excessive bleeding may appear in cement-based materials, i.e. a part of the mix water is not retained by small grains and is upward flowing. The upper layer of hardened material becomes weak and porous due to a local increase of the water/cement ratio, all with negative consequences for concrete durability. In the case of bleeding water, this also accumulates under larger aggregate grains, creating local cavities. That problem is discussed also in Section 9.2.

There are several aspects which should be considered when the structure composed of aggregate grains is designed. In general, the properties which have to be achieved are completely different in their nature and may be summarized as follows:

1. facility and efficiency of execution, low energy consumption, limitation of aggregate segregation, reduction of care during the hardening period;
2. high strength of hardened composite, low shrinkage, adequate fracture toughness and resistance to external actions which can be foreseen in that particular case;
3. adequate durability in local conditions, frost and corrosion resistance.

These properties are interrelated and often depend in a conflicting way on the composition and structure of the aggregate. The properties may be translated into unit cost, including cost of maintenance during service life, (cf. [6.27]). Correctly determining the cost of composite material is a complex problem which may be included as one of several criteria in a multicriteria optimization problem. Methods of the mix design are discussed in Chapter 12 and a general formulation is presented in Chapter 13 and only questions related to the aggregate structure are discussed in this section.

In order to achieve the minimum unit cost of final composite material the cement volume and energy consumption should be minimized. Both these parameters are closely related to the aggregate system.

The condition of minimum voids, which is often imposed for aggregate design, is derived from conditions of low permeability and high strength, connected to resistance against corrosion and frost destruction. Minimum voids are obtained in such an aggregate composition, in which voids between big grains are adequately filled by smaller ones. However, such a composition may be very expensive and thus practically impossible. A very elaborate grading requires much work and energy consumption, because local aggregate deposits are rarely correct and require careful segregation, completion and transportation of particular fractions over long distances. Certain compromise solutions are often necessary between high quality and low cost.

For good workability the matrix fraction should be increased which may have a negative effect on strength and durability.

For high freezing and thawing resistance a very dense structure of material is required with an appropriate system of pores obtained by application of air-entraining admixtures. Aggregate grains should also exhibit adequate frost resistance.

The choice between crushed stones and gravel as coarse aggregate has its effects on strength and workability. For Portland cement mixes, crushed aggregate requires more cement paste to fill the void and more energy for mixing and compacting, but higher strength may be obtained than with gravel thanks to better bonding to cement paste.

The behaviour of aggregate grains in the matrix under load depends on the ratio between their Young's moduli $n = E_m/E_a$. In structural concretes usually $n < 1$ and hard grains reinforce the matrix. The cracks propagate through the matrix and aggregate grains control that propagation. In the concretes with lightweight aggregate $n > 1$ and the grain resistance is lower than that of the cement matrix. Examples of crack patterns in composites characterized by both these relations are shown in Figure 9.2.

In all problems of material design the local conditions *in situ* should also be considered. A theoretical solution to such a problem should always be checked in the laboratory and then, in natural scale, with actual constituents and technologies, also taking into account the qualifications of personnel and severity of technical control required for high quality.

6.5 Structure of pores and voids

6.5.1 POROSITY OF CEMENT PASTE

The porosity of concrete-like composites is an important characteristic which determines to a large extent their mechanical properties. The pores are of different shapes and dimensions. Their classification is not strictly established and recognized. The pores of various dimensions, distributed at random, are contributing to the heterogeneity of the composite material.

High porosity is strongly detrimental to the strength and permeability of cement-based composite materials, particularly if the pores are of large diameter. The permeability to gases is much higher than to fluids across the pore structure because the viscosity of the former is about 100 times lower than that of the latter. Increased permeability adversely affects durability, mainly for materials in the structures exposed to outdoor conditions. The structure of the external layers of concretes and their porosity are different from the core of the elements. The cement hydration is less advanced due to quicker desiccation, the size distribution of aggregate grains is shifted to smaller diameters and higher porosity may be observed. Due to all these effects, the strength and resistance against corrosive factors of these parts of concrete elements are usually lower.

Porosity may be determined by one parameter, i.e. by the ratio of pore volume to total volume, but for most purposes it is necessary to consider separately pores of different kinds and dimensions in relation to the mechanical properties of composite materials. Using the definitions proposed by the International Union of Pure and Applied Chemistry (IUPAC) three groups are distinguished according to their characteristic dimension d, [6.27]:

1. micro-pores $d < 2$ nm,
2. meso-pores 2 nm $< d < 50$ nm,
3. macro-pores $d > 50$ nm.

The lower limit is not defined because it depends upon the method of pore detection and examination. The upper limit is related to capillary effects and usually is assumed to be equal to about 0.5–1.0 mm. Larger voids are not called pores but they also influence the material's strength and permeability.

As it concerns the connections between pores, there may be distinguished – interconnected pores, closed pores and pores closed at one end. The roles of these kinds of pores in the flow of fluids and gases across materials are different.

The porosity and pore systems in cement-based composites may be one example of the fractality which is characteristic of these materials. Fractal quantity depends on the scale used to measure it; for example the fracture area of a concrete element cannot be determined in an unambiguous way if the method and scale of its determination are not given, cf. Section 10.5. The classification and analysis of a pore system, and all quantitative results derived, depend among other things upon the method of observation and magnification of microscopic images, [6.29] and [6.30].

Other notions which are very important in a consideration of pore systems is percolation and percolation threshold. The permeability of the system composed of strongly disordered pores is non-linearly related to pore number and total volume and that relation may be characterized by a threshold – until a certain pore density is reached the system is impermeable. When the density becomes higher than that critical value, then permeability appears and increases rapidly, [6.31].

Four different types of pores in cement paste are proposed to be distinguished [6.15], [6.21], [6.25], [6.32] and others:

- Gel pores are of characteristic dimensions from 0.0005 μm up to 0.01 μm (0.5–10 nm).
- Capillary pores are of 0.01 to 10 μm, mostly between 0.02 and 0.03 μm of average diameter.
- Intentionally introduced pores of spherical shape and defined diameters during so-called air entrainment, usually between 0.05 and 1.25 mm.
- Air voids larger than capillary pores which are inevitably entrapped during mixing and compaction of fresh mix.

The pore distribution is schematically represented in Figure 6.9 where the main types mentioned above are shown and their reciprocal relations and possible overlap are visible.

The pore dimensions may be compared to other elements of the material structure:

- fine aggregate (sand) > 100 μm;
- unhydrated cement grains 1–100 μm;
- cement needle-like crystals length 1 μm, width 0.05 μm;
- silica fume particles 0.1–0.3 μm;

and it appears that pores are distributed at various levels of the structure.

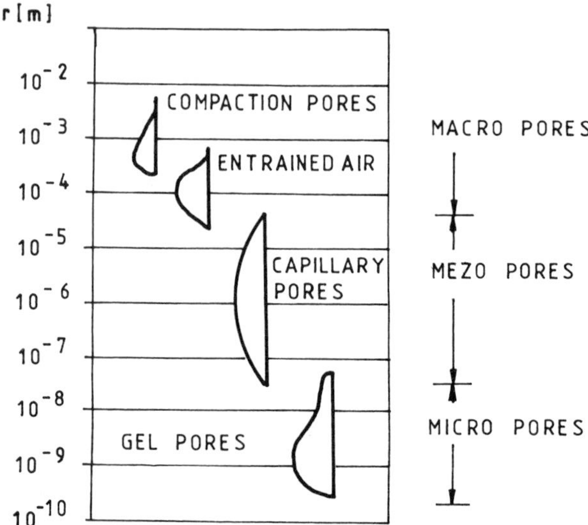

Figure 6.9 Pore-size distribution in Portland cement concrete. (Reproduced with permission from CEB (Comité Euro-International du Béton) Bulletin No. 182, *Durable Concrete Structures– CEB Design Guide*, 2nd edition, Lausanne, June 1989.) [6.33]

The gel pores form a part of CSH (calcium silicate hydrate), also called tobermorite gel and may be classified as micro- or meso-pores. The principal difference between gel and capillary pores is that the former are too small to be filled by the hydration products and for capillary effects it means that no menisci are formed. The gel pores occupy between 40 and 55% of total pore volume but they are not active in water permeating through cement paste and they also do not influence the composite strength. Water in the gel pores is physically bonded. It is believed that gel pores are directly related to the shrinkage and creep properties of the cement paste.

The capillary pores and air voids are partially or completely filled with water which depends on the environmental hygrometry and takes part in the continuous hydration of cement grains. The total volume of these two categories of pores is related to the decrease in strength of the hardened paste. The capillary pores are caused by that part of the mixing water which is not absorbed by cement grains during hydration. With the development of the hydration and hardening processes the capillary pores are filled with the hydration products and the possibility of water flow is gradually reduced. When the initial value of the w/c ratio > 0.5, there is an excess of water and then the capillary pores are large and probably cannot be filled completely. Otherwise, for a water/cement ratio < 0.5 only reduced water flow is possible.

The w/c ratio has to be equal to 0.35–0.40 in the cement paste in order to ensure full hydration of the cement [6.32]. Then there is enough water for hydration and also enough space for hydration products which swell during the process so that the capillary pores may have reduced permeability. These values are different for mortars and concretes and the same applies when special admixtures are added to modify the fluidity of the fresh mix. So called structural pores may be included in the same category. These appear when the volume of water is insufficient for hydration. The difference between the total volume of the fresh mix components and the final volume of this mix, (the latter is smaller due to the chemical reactions of hydration) if not filled up with hydration products, appears as voids called contraction pores.

Gel pores constitute approximately 28% of Portland cement paste and the capillary pores constitute between 0 and 40%, depending on w/c ratio and progress of the hydration processes. The voids of entrapped air should not exceed a small proportion – 1% of the total volume, otherwise the concrete must be considered as inadequately executed.

The duration and quality of cure of the fresh mix determine the progress of hydration and the volume of hydration products which may eventually fill the capillary pores and reduce their permeability. For decreased w/c ratio and prolonged cure the pore size distribution diagrams are shifted towards smaller sizes, with decreasing total volume. The saturation of capillary pores plays an important role in composite durability if the material is exposed to freeze–thaw cycles. Damage is more probable when the critical value of saturation is attained and the increasing volume of ice cannot be accommodated without additional

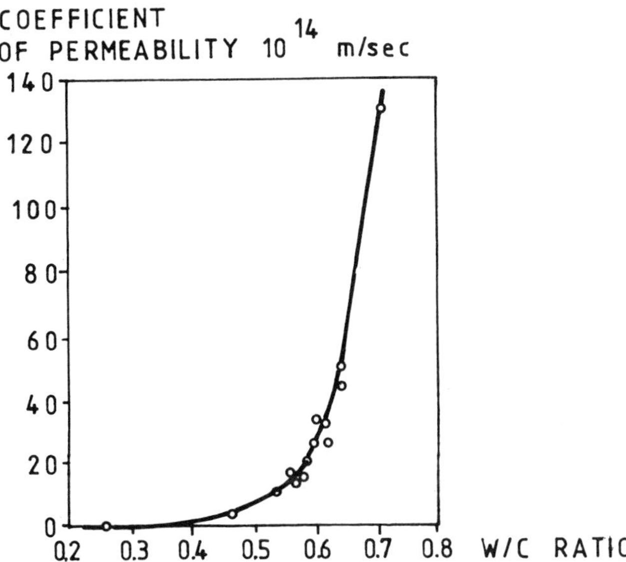

Figure 6.10 Experimental relation between permeability and w/c ratio for cement paste. (Reproduced with permission from Powers, T.C. *et al.*, Permeability of Portland cement paste, *J. of the American Concrete Institute*, **51**, pp. 285–98, ACI, 1954.) [6.34]

stresses. The density of the hardened paste is also important to ensure resistance against all other external attacks.

In Figure 6.10 it is shown how the permeability of cement paste increases with the w/c ratio. At first it increases slowly, then beyond w/c = 0.5 it increases very quickly. The permeability may therefore be regarded as an indirect and partial measure of porosity. Considering the components of cement-based composites it may be assumed that permeability is determined more by matrix properties than by aggregate ones. Particularly, the matrix–aggregate interface has the largest content of pores and microcracks which affect overall permeability, cf. Chapter 7.

There are three characteristics of the structure of air-entrained pores. The total porosity is usually between 3 and 10% of concrete volume, but these numbers do not give sufficient information about the size distribution of the pores and their anti-frost efficiency. The size distribution of pores determined by one of the known methods gives a deeper insight into the pore system and allows its influence in increasing the resistance of the concrete against freeze-and-thaw cycles to be assessed.

Another measure is the average space which constitutes the mean maximum distance of any point in the cement paste from the periphery of nearest air bubble. In Figure 6.11 a schematic diagram is given showing the relationship between spacing and the durability factor.

The mechanism for preventing damage to a concrete structure by air pores

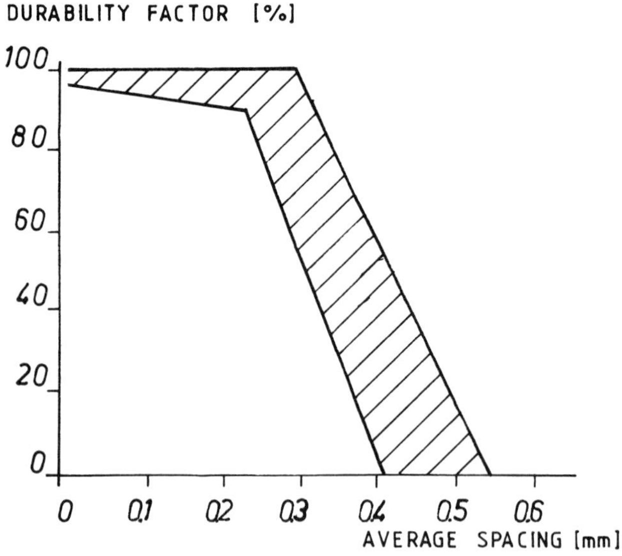

Figure 6.11 Relative durability of concrete as function of average spacing of air entrained pores. (Sidney Mindess and J. Francis Young, *Concrete*, 1981, p. 173. Reprinted by permission of Prentice-Hall, Englewood Cliffs, New Jersey.) [6.21]

was explained first in [6.35]. The conversion of water to ice causes an increase of volume of 9.03%. That increase produces hydraulic pressure of unfrozen water in capillary pores and additional tensile stress in concrete structures. The intensity of the hydraulic pressure is proportional to the length of the capillary pores. A densely distributed system of air bubbles reduces considerably the length of the capillary pores and the bubbles act in a similar manner to dilatation reservoirs in a central heating system. Therefore, the air voids are helpful only when they are sufficiently small and densely distributed. Spacing factor determined according to CEB [6.33] should not exceed 0.2 mm and that recommendation is based on results obtained by several authors who also published information on the pore diameter. For example, it is recommended [6.36] that for maximum aggregate grains of 63.5, 38, 19 and 9.5 mm the optimum spacing factor should be equal to 0.18, 0.20, 0.23 and 0.28 mm, respectively, for mortars spacing factor 0.30 mm is proposed. Consequently, the mean diameter of the air bubbles should be between 0.05 and 1.25 mm, [6.23].

Only the pores obtained by air-entrainment are of regular spherical shape and distribution; others are very irregular, as between interrelated needle- and plate-like crystals of hydrated cement.

The testing of specimens subjected to freeze–thaw cycles does not reflect very precisely the material's actual resistance in real structures. One of the reasons is that delays between particular cycles are of great importance and the possibility of the partial drying out of pores are different in a laboratory test than in natural conditions.

The formation of air bubbles depends upon many circumstances, primarily:

- the kind and amount of air-entraining agent;
- the composition of concrete, also eventual application of other admixtures;
- the technique of mixing and compaction of the fresh mix; also, temperature during these operations is of importance.

In particular, in many experimental verifications the total volume of entrained air rose with a decrease of cement and increase of fine aggregate content, with lower temperature and with an increased content of angular aggregate grains, [6.37].

A fourth category of air voids is caused by air entrapped during compaction. These voids are usually larger and have no beneficial influence on the freeze–thaw resistance. An excessive volume of entrapped air increases considerably the concrete permeability and decreases its strength.

The relationship between pore system characteristics, its capillarity and permeability can be presented schematically, [6.24] and in Figure 6.12. Because the pore structures are usually composed of pores of various dimensions, their capillarity and permeability reflect the pore size distribution and also existing interconnections between the pores. Therefore, the description of the pore structure solely as a system of spheres seems inadequate – it is assumed that pores have regular shape, cf. [6.38].

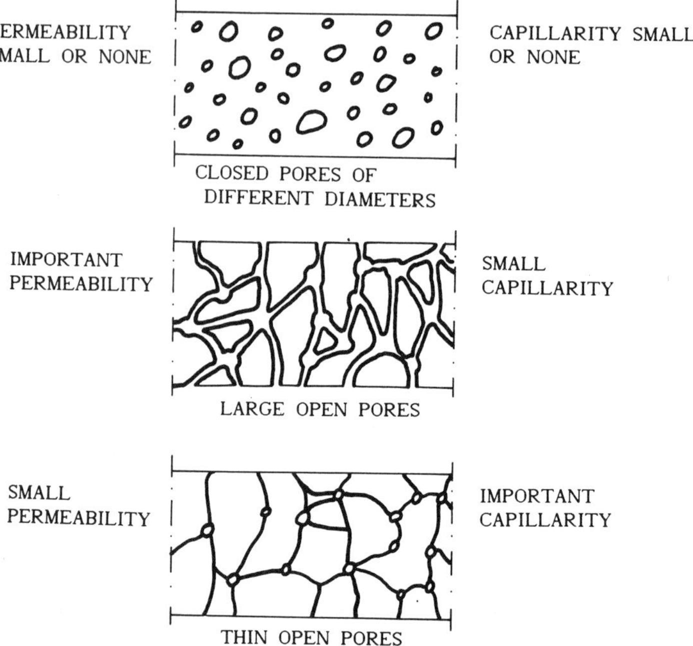

Figure 6.12 Example of pore systems, their permeability and capillarity. (Reproduced with permission from Venuat, M., *Adjuvants et traitements*; published by the author, 1984.) [6.24]

The determination of the pore structure in hardened cement-based materials is based on a direct and indirect approach.

In direct measurement methods the microscopic examination by optical or scanning electron microscopes is eventually completed by computer image analysis. Stereology formulae are used to deduce three-dimensional structures from plane images. However, the complex shapes of pores in cement paste do not facilitate this task.

In indirect methods other processes are applied and there are three main groups of methods for studying the micro-structure of hardened cement-based composites [6.39]:

1. bulk techniques like thermogravimetric analysis (TGA) and quantitative x-ray diffraction (QXRD) give information on the average volume fraction for particular phases, e.g. pores,
2. selective techniques provide data on the size distribution of certain components, e.g. pore size distribution, and there are mercury intrusion porosimetry (MIP), nitrogen adsorption and methanol adsorption techniques, low temperature calorimetry.

The results obtained from the indirect methods are often controversial, because the pore systems are actually not examined but rather the processes applied in these methods; the results reflect only the pore size distribution response. Any value established of pore diameter has only conventional meaning and may be different from diameters obtained from other methods. The indirect methods more or less influence the object of observation and measurements because the interventions disrupt the structure of the material, e.g. mercury intrusion may damage and alter the material's micro-structure. Furthermore, the intrusion of mercury into a pore is related to the orifice of the pore rather than to its real dimension.

The distribution of pore diameters in the cement paste, determined by the mercury porosimetry method, was partly confirmed for example by observations and counting the pores on images from SEM [6.40]. Other methods, like capillary condensation, give considerably different values. Interesting results concerning the pore diameter distribution have been published [6.41] and an example from this paper is shown in Figure 6.13. The pore size distribution for three different values of w/c ratio is given. It appears from these diagrams that observed maxima correspond well to two categories of pores: gel pores and capillary pores. These maxima move in the direction of larger or smaller diameters when the w/c ratio increases and decreases.

The distribution of pore diameter may be determined by a relation proposed

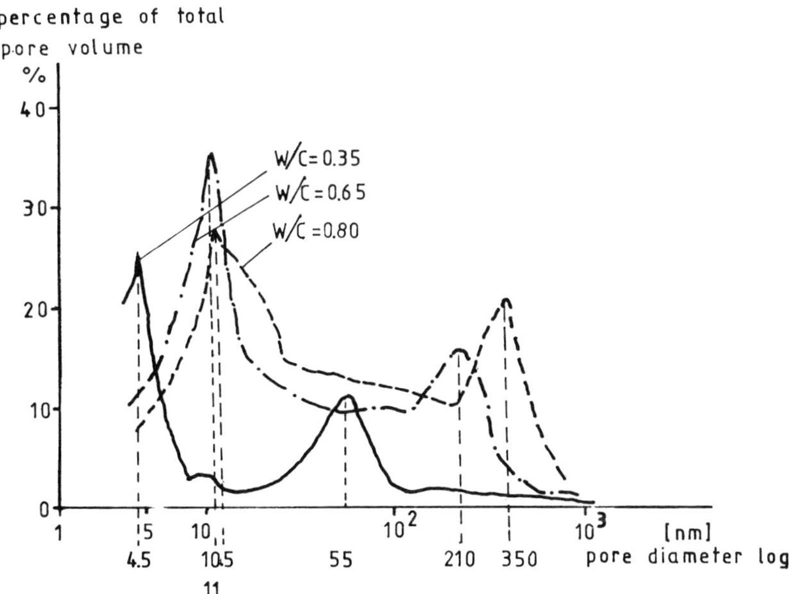

Figure 6.13 Pore-size distribution in a moist cured cement paste at an age of 11 years. (Reproduced with permission from Verbeck G.J. and Helmuth, R.H., Structures and physical properties of cement pastes; published by Japan Cement Ass., 1969.) [6.41]

in [6.42] between external pressure q, characteristic diameter d_p, contact angle ϕ and surface tension γ, [6.43]:

$$q = -4\gamma \cos\phi/d_p \tag{6.1}$$

here it is assumed that $\gamma = 484$ MN/m and the angle between solid surface and liquid surface depending also on the solid surface roughness is $\phi = 117°$, $\cos\phi \approx -0.45$.

6.5.2 POROSITY AND STRENGTH

The strength of composite material is reduced by the existence of a pore structure and that reduction depends upon the pore shape, distribution and the type of loading. In [6.44] a simple formula is proposed to relate porosity and strength, assuming that the compressive strength is proportional to the cross-sectional area of the solid material:

$$f_c = f_o(1 - 1.2P^{2/3}), \tag{6.2}$$

where f_c is the composite strength of a material with a system of pores, f_o is the strength of a solid material and P is the porosity. From simple application of the law of mixtures it would be:

$$f_c = f_o(1 - P). \tag{6.3}$$

In equation 6.2 the following factors are only approximately covered by numerical coefficients:

- the pores may act as stress concentrators, depending on the state of stress (compression, tension, shearing) and their shape;
- with increasing porosity P several phenomena may be expected which do not interfere when the porosity is low, e.g. rupture of walls between neighbouring pores, non-homogeneous distribution of internal stresses.

The formula in equation 6.3 may therefore be considered as the upper bound. The experimental data for cement-based materials are approximated by relationships in which the above mentioned factors are partly considered. For example two of them are quoted in [6.45], [6.46] and [6.47]:

$$f_c = f_o(1 - P)^C \tag{6.4}$$

$$f_c = f_o \exp(-C_1 P) \tag{6.5}$$

where C and C_1 are constants. Both these formulae were initially proposed for ceramics and in equation 6.5 the value of C_1 was estimated for tensile strength to be between four and seven. Their application to cement-based materials was associated with additional coefficients and modifications. It has been observed that for values of porosity P below a certain value P_o the formulae, equation 6.4 and equation 6.5, are in close agreement with experimental data. However, at higher porosities for $P > P_o$ it is advisable to introduce the notion of critical porosity P_{cr} corresponding to the strength f_c approaching zero and to use the following relations proposed in [6.48]:

$$f_c = f_o\left[1 - \left(\frac{P}{P_{cr}}\right)C_2\right], \quad \text{or} \tag{6.6}$$

$$f_c = C_3\, ln\frac{P_{cr}}{C_4} \tag{6.7}$$

here C_2, C_3, C_4 are empirical constants.

The porosity P_o which corresponds to a clear variation of a curve $f_c(P)$ may be considered as a kind of a percolation threshold proposed in [6.49], and shown in Figure 6.14. The experimental relationship between concrete strength and capillary porosity is shown in Figure 6.15 and it is confirmed by extensive experimental results which were published in [6.50]. Relations between the volume of capillary pores of different dimensions and the strength of cement

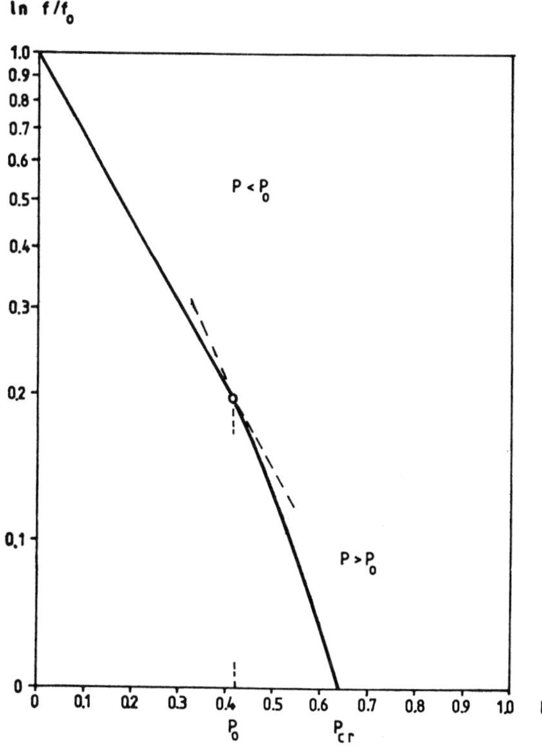

Figure 6.14 General relation between porosity and strength of porous materials. (Reproduced with permission from Fagerlund, G., Samband mellan porositet och materials mekaniska egenskpaper; published by Lund Inst. of Technology, 1979.) [6.49]

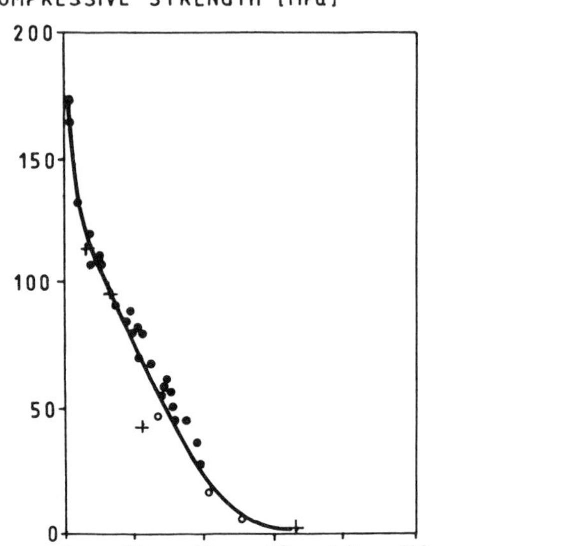

Figure 6.15 Experimental relation between capillary porosity and compressive strength of various concretes. (Reproduced with permission from Verbeck, G.J. and Helmuth, R.H., Structures and physical properties in cement pastes; published by Japan Cement Ass., 1969.) [6.41]

paste, mortar and concrete are presented in Figure 6.16. Large sections of the curves may be assumed as corresponding to linear relations.

The influence of porosity on the Young's modulus may be represented by similar empirical formulae, e.g. for hardened cement paste:

$$E = E_o(1 - P_o)^3, \tag{6.8}$$

where E_o is the value of Young's modulus for capillary porosity equal to zero $P = 0$. After tests outlined in [6.51] equation 6.8 has been confirmed for both compressive strength and Young's modulus.

All the above formulae should be considered as only approximate, because obviously the influence of porosity on the mechanical behaviour of a composite material cannot be reflected solely by one-parameter relations. The two- and multi-phase models mentioned in Section 2.5 may be also applied to composite materials in which a pore structure represents one phase. As is shown in Figure 2.12, the theoretical models are inadequate for pores which have no stiffness. In certain cases, spherical pores even represent obstacles for crack propagation. In the others, sharp pores in the material's structure stimulate crack opening and propagation.

Probably only large pores have an important detrimental influence on composite strength. Based on tests on high alumina cement specimens [6.52]

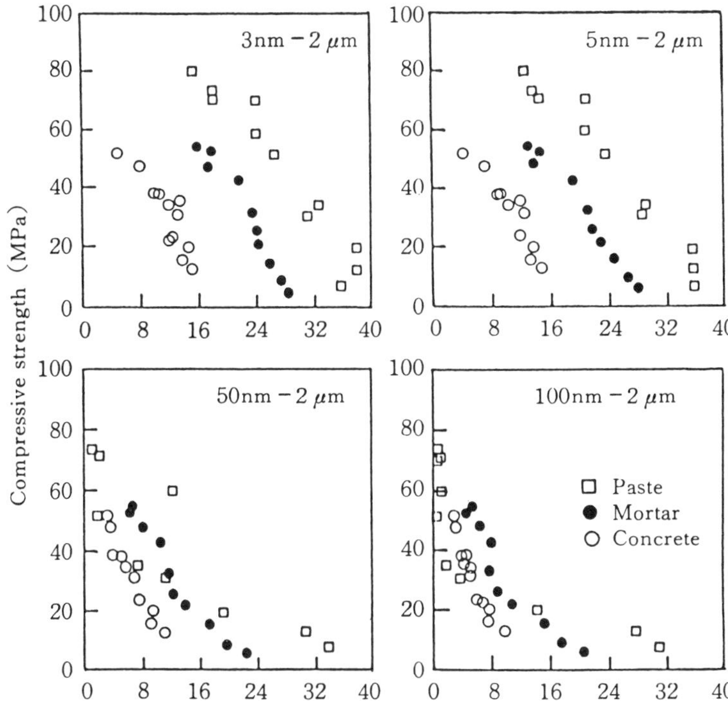

Figure 6.16 Relationships between volume of capillary pore space and compressive strength of hardened cement paste, mortar and concrete for different pore distributions. (Reproduced with permission from Uchikawa, H., Similarities and discrepancies of hardened cement paste, mortar and concrete from the standpoints of composition and structure; published by Onoda Cement Co. Ltd., 1988.) [6.50]

it has been shown that a clear correlation existed only when porosity with pores larger than 1 μm was taken into account.

The pores, and their influence on the material strength, were studied as randomly distributed structural imperfections [6.53].

The influence of pores should be analysed by considering the parameters of pore structure and of pore shape, or eventually the empirical formulae with approximately calibrated coefficients may be applied. Attempts have been made [6.54] to characterize pore structure by special parameters like mean distribution radius and a clear relation with compressive strength was obtained. A general model does not exist yet, but attempts to construct one taking into account various processes in hardened concrete-like materials have been published, [6.55].

The above experimental observations are reflected in [6.56] where it was proposed to distinguish clearly the influence of two populations of pores – small gel or colloidal pores entrapped between hydrated particles of about 2 nm in size and larger crack-type pores of a length equal to about 1 mm. The influence of the first group on the concrete strength is proportional to its total volume and is reflected by the law of mixtures or the classic Féret's equation where volume of air is taken into account, cf. Section 8.2.

The colloidal pores do not start cracks as their dimensions are extremely small and this fact is correctly represented by the Griffith's equation,

$$f_t = \sqrt{\frac{E\gamma}{\pi c}}$$

here f_t – tensile strength, E – Young's modulus, γ – fracture energy, c – characteristic dimension of a notch or a pore.

The theory formulated in [6.56] combines the influence on strength of both groups considered independently: the first one characterized by its total volume p but without long cracks, and the second one without appreciable volume but characterized by length c. The criterion for crack extension is,

$$f_t = \left[\frac{E_o\gamma_o(1-p)^3\exp(-\mathrm{k}p)}{\pi c}\right]^{1/2},$$

here E_o and γ_o correspond to non-porous body and k is a constant.

The relevant curves corresponding to experimental verification are shown in Section 14.4.2 and Figure 14.15.

Low porosity is necessary for high strength in concrete-like composites. To achieve that aim the material components must be carefully selected for best packing and a low w/c ratio. The optimum packing is obtained with appropriate composition of all aggregate fractions by application of superplasticizers acting as deflocculants, but also the fine voids between aggregate grains should be filled up with microfillers, e.g. silica fume, [6.57] and [6.58]. Low water content is possible when excellent compaction is assured by superplasticizers without excess of water – the w/c ratio may be as low as 0.3 without decreasing the workability of the fresh mix. For more detailed description of materials with low w/c ratios, cf. Section 14.5.2.

There exists a particular kind of concrete in which high permeability is required and regulated by specially created pore systems. It is used mainly for irrigation works and similar purposes, and is not considered here.

6.6 Structure of fibres

6.6.1 TYPES OF STRUCTURES

The structure composed of reinforcing fibres or wires in the matrix may be characterized by the following groups of parameters:

- material of fibres (steel, glass, polypropylene, etc.);
- shape of a fibre (short chopped or continuous, single fibres or mats, meshes, fabrics);

- distribution of fibres in the matrix (random, linearized, regular);
- amount of fibres in the matrix (volume or mass fraction).

The number of above listed parameters indicates how many different types of reinforcing fibre structures may be used in concrete-like composites.

The first two groups of parameters are considered by the designer who decides on the material's structure and composition. As described in Section 5.4, steel fibres are used as short chopped lengths, as continuous woven wires, non-woven or welded at the nodes (ferrocement) and as a kind of wool composed of thin and long entangled wires. Short fibres are in most cases randomly distributed but their alignment is also possible. Glass and other kinds of fibres may be also chopped or used in the form of mats and fabrics.

The reinforcement in the form of fibres or wires is by its nature subject to randomness, in comparison with classical reinforcement by bars or pre-stressing cables which are very precisely positioned in the reinforced elements. Fibres are described by their average volume fraction and average direction; usually the precise determination of these parameters is neither possible nor needed. However, these average values of characteristic parameters are used in both design and control because the required distribution and orientation is often disturbed by various factors related to execution techniques, wall and gravity effects during vibration, etc. When these influences act in a systematic way, the randomness of distribution, or its regularity, may be considerably modified.

The execution of operations aimed at the realization of designed fibre structure requires special care and control. In experimental testing effective fibre distribution and direction is determined after the analysis of images obtained on cross-sections or on radiograms.

6.6.2 STRUCTURES COMPOSED OF SHORT FIBRES

Three types of idealized structures of short chopped fibres may be distinguished:

1. linearized fibres (1D);
2. random distribution in parallel planes (2D);
3. random distribution in space (3D).

All real structures are subjected to more or less significant deviations; sometimes they are considered as combinations of the idealized ones. These deviations may be introduced voluntarily, e.g. the steel fibres may be distributed in the fresh cement by the vibration over a long time with variable density along the depth of the element. The correct execution of the designed distribution, and also a random one, requires special care and equipment. A more detailed description of execution methods is beyond the scope of this book. Interested readers are referred to [6.5] and to special recommendations in [6.59] and [6.60].

Examples of fibre distribution are shown in radiograms in Figure 6.17.

In any type of fibres distribution the balling of fibres and their agglomerations

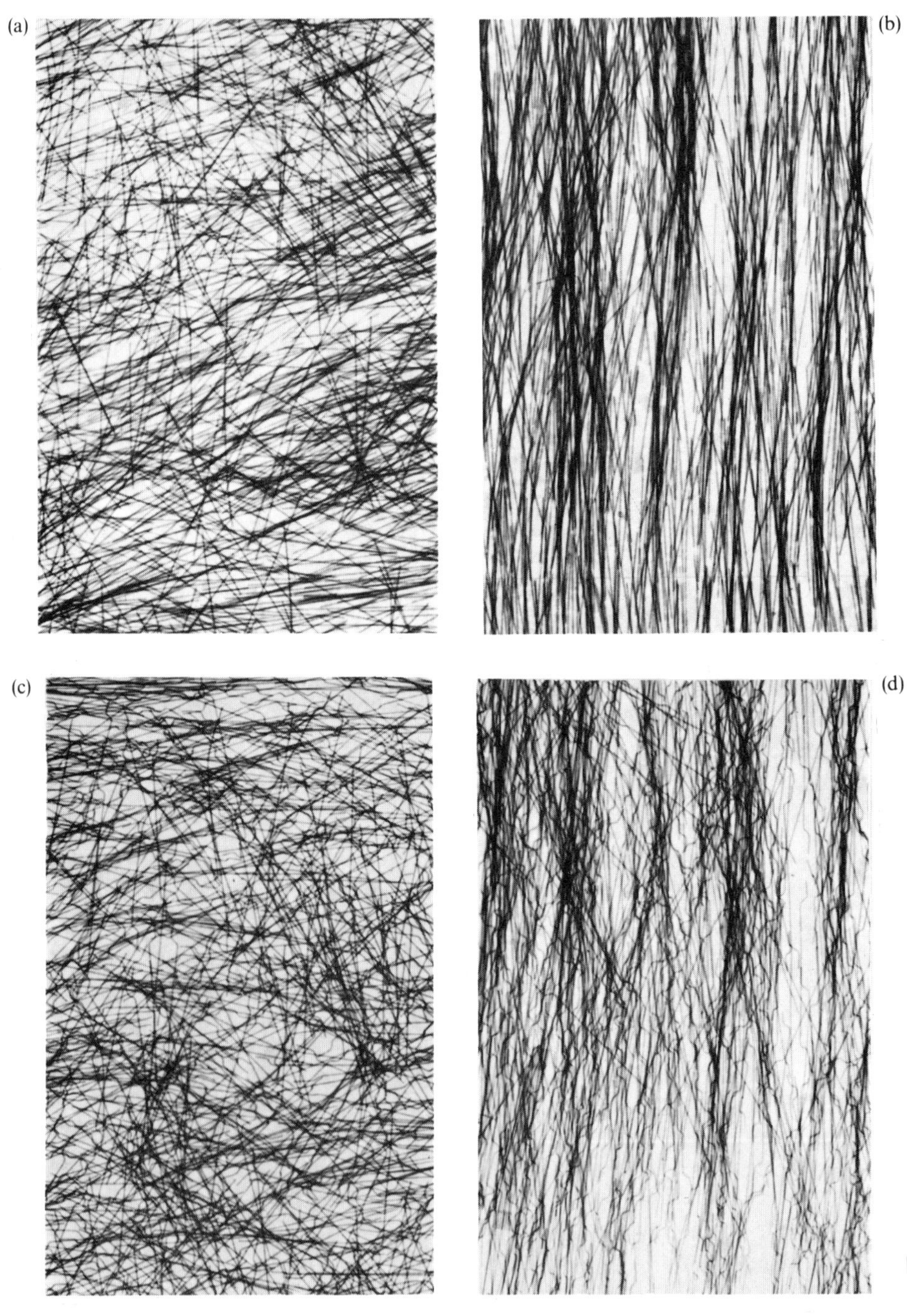
(a)
(b)
(c)
(d)

into clusters should be avoided, because the fibres interconnected with others are not efficient. Their bonding to the matrix is weak and reduced to local contacts and large air voids in the matrix may be created. When an appropriate technology is applied to a correctly designed mix (cf. Section 4.3 and Chapter 12), then the fibre clusters do not appear.

The description of idealized and real structures of fibres may be based on several different approaches. Already in 1964 a formula was proposed [6.61] in which the average distance between the centroids of the fibres called spacing s is related to diameter d and fibre volume fraction V_f by the following relation:

$$s = 1.38\, d\sqrt{1/V_f} \tag{6.9}$$

To derive that formula it was assumed that the fibres were uniformly oriented in space and that the average length of the fibres in a direction perpendicular to the crack opening was $0.41\,\ell$, where ℓ is the single fibre length. This reflects an assumption, that the directional efficiency is assumed equal to 0.41.

In that formulation the spacing s has no direct physical meaning and the proposed formula (equation 6.9), mentioned in many books, was strongly criticized. The fibre efficiency assumed here is based on a non-verifiable assumption and has not been generally accepted. Inaccuracies in experimental verifications of the relation 6.9 were indicated in [6.62] and it has been proved that the coefficient 1.38 is too high for all types of ideal fibre distribution [6.63].

The formulae proposed in [6.64] give the numbers of fibres for three ideal structures.

The number of aligned (1D) fibres crossing a plane of unit area and perpendicular to their direction is:

$$N^{1\mathrm{D}} = 4V_f/\pi d^2 \tag{6.10}$$

For fibres randomly oriented in a plane (2D), the corresponding relation is:

$$N^{2\mathrm{D}} = 8V_f/\pi^2 2d^2 \tag{6.11}$$

and for random distribution in three dimensions (3D):

$$N^{3\mathrm{D}} = 2V_f/\pi d^2 \tag{6.12}$$

Later these formulae were derived [6.6] and presented in the form of cross-sectional areas corresponding to a single fibre:

$$\alpha^{i\mathrm{D}} = 1/N^{i\mathrm{D}}, \quad i = 1, 2, 3. \tag{6.13}$$

Figure 6.17 Examples of X-radiograms of cement mortar plates reinforced with steel-fibres $V_f = 2\%$, plate depth 20 mm, direct exposition 15 min.; a) Plain straight fibres 0.38 × 25 mm, random distribution of fibres 2D; b) Plain straight fibres 0.38 × 25 mm, linearized 1D; c) Bekaert fibres with hooks 0.4 × 40 mm, random distribution 2D; d) Bekaert fibres with hooks 0.4 × 40 mm, linearized 1D.

So called effective fibre spacing has been proposed [6.65] in the form:

$$s_{\text{eff}} = \mathrm{A}\sqrt{d/\ell V_f} \tag{6.14}$$

where the constant A = 2.5 for ultimate state of loading and A = 2.7 for the first crack opening. Here the fibre distribution is not analysed and assumed as 3D.

On the basis of geometric probability theory, efficiency and spacing concepts (mean free spacing and average nearest neighbour distance) have been developed [6.66] for idealized fibre structures. Using the stereological approach, a method has been determined to assess, after a cross-section or a projection analysis, the deviations from idealized structures in the form of segregation and anisometry.

A coherent system of characteristics has been proposed for fibre structures with two interdependent parameters [6.6], [6.67], [6.68] and [6.69]. α^{iD} – the area corresponding in a cross-section to one fibre and given by equation 6.13 together with equation 6.10 – equation 6.12 and s_{app} – the apparent spacing between fibre intercepts on a basing measuring line l_b. Both these parameters are explained in Figure 6.18. On a fracture surface or on a cross-section the fibres may be counted to establish the value of α, i.e. the area corresponding to one single fibre.

Values of α^{iD} calculated on a few fracture or cross-sectional areas of examined elements may be compared with theoretical ones calculated from equations 6.10–6.13. Conclusions may be obtained as a result of such comparisons about the effective fibre structure and its relation to the idealized ones. In many cases

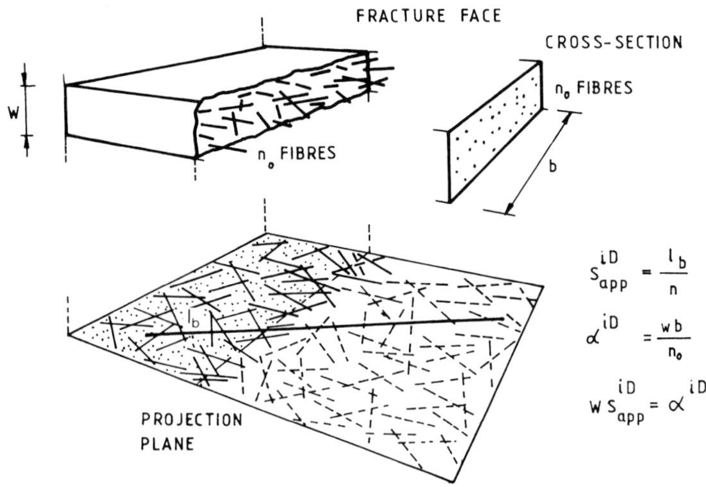

Figure 6.18 Parameters describing the fibres distribution. (Source: Kasperkiewicz, J. Internal structure and cracking processes in brittle matrix composites; published by IFTR, 1983.) [6.8]

the effective structures are situated somewhere in between the ideal ones and may be described as 1D–2D or 2D–3D.

Apparent spacing s_{app} is defined as a mean distance between intercepts of fibre projections on a basic line ℓ_b (Figure 6.18). If w denotes the depth of the examined layer, the following relation is valid:

$$w s_{\text{app}}^{i\text{D}} = \alpha^{i\text{D}}, \quad i = 1, 2, 3. \tag{6.15}$$

It may be observed that both parameters α and s_{app} do not depend on the fibre length ℓ, like spacing s proposed in [6.61].

In Figure 6.19 a few curves are shown representing $\alpha^{i\text{D}}$ plotted against fibre volume fraction V_f for two fibre diameters $d = 40$ mm and $d = 25$ mm and for three types of distribution. These curves may be used to determine the values of $\alpha^{i\text{D}}(V_f)$ or of $V_f(\alpha^{i\text{D}})$. For arbitrary values of volume fraction V_f introduced to the mix, the value of $\alpha^{i\text{D}}$ may be found, provided that the kind of distribution is assumed. Or, knowing the kind of distribution, values of α obtained from the

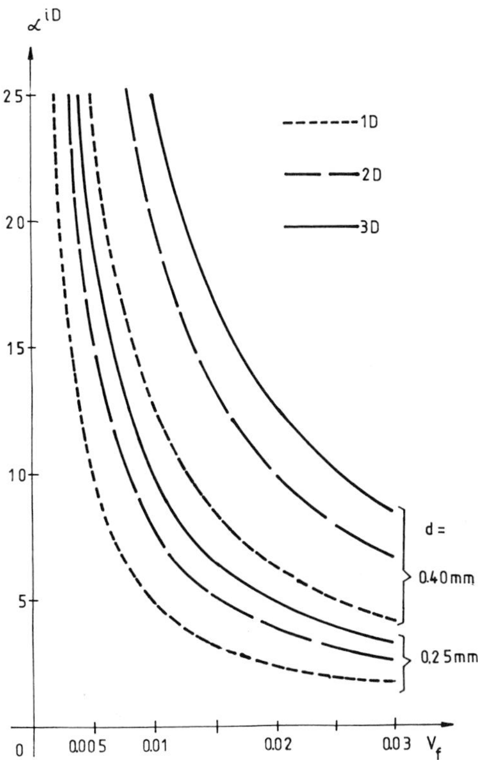

Figure 6.19 Parameters $\alpha^{iD}(i = 1, 2, 3)$ as functions of fibre content V_f for two fibre diameters d = 25 mm and 40 mm. (Source: Kasperkiewicz, J., Apparent spacing in fibre-reinforced composites; published by Bull. Acad. Pol. Sci., 1978.) [6.67]

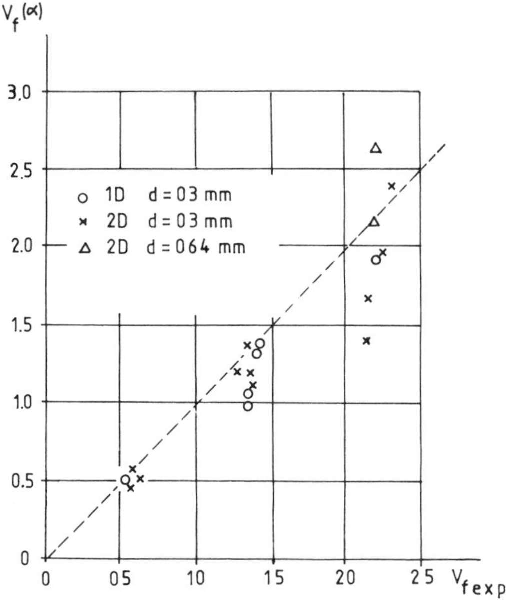

Figure 6.20 Verification of fibre content $V_f(\alpha)$ obtained analytically from radiogram and curves in Figure 6.18 and $V_{f\,\mathrm{exp}}$ obtained directly by counting fibres washed out from crushed elements. (Source: Kasperkiewicz, J., Apparent spacing in fibre-reinforced composites; published by Bull. Acad. Pol. Sci., 1978.) [6.67]

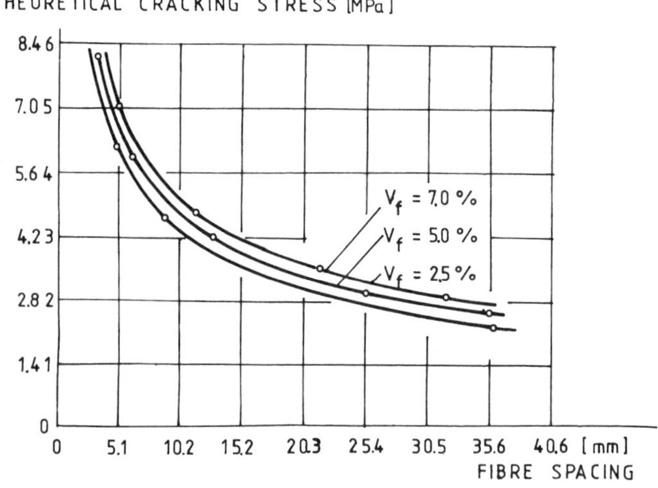

Figure 6.21 Cracking stress as a function of fibre spacing, assuming $G_c = 3.5$ N/m. (Reproduced with permission from Romualdi, J.P. and Batson, G.B., Mechanics of crack-arrest in concrete; published by American Society of Civil Engineers, 1963.) [6.70]

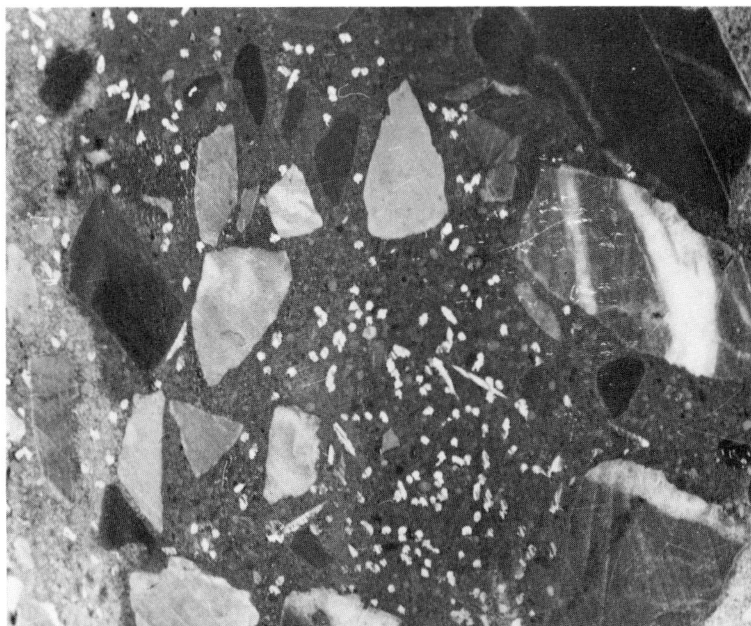

Figure 6.22 Cross-section of a steel fibre-reinforced element with visible structure of fibres.

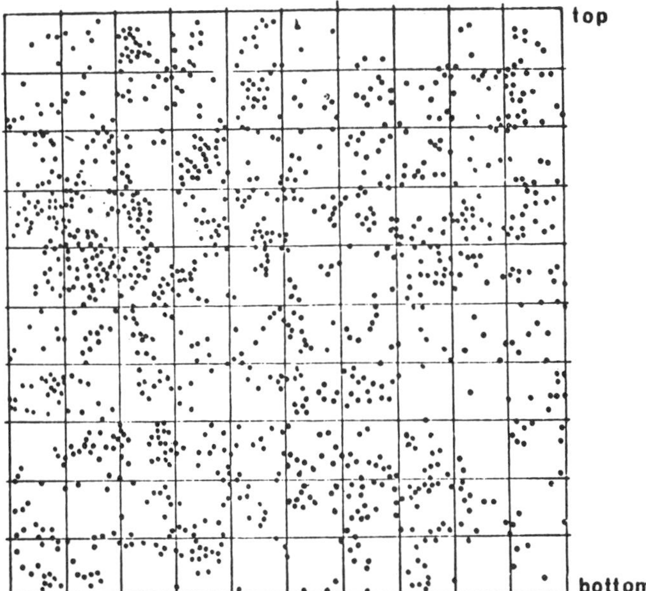

Figure 6.23 System of points representing traces of fibres in a cross-section, prepared for analysis in a computerized image analyser.

curves may be compared to those from experimental calculations. Proposed formulae were verified experimentally in [6.8] and [6.67] and a satisfactory agreement has been found. An example is shown in Figure 6.20 where $V_f(\alpha)$ is calculated from the radiograms and $V_{f\exp}$ is obtained after crushing the same specimen and washing out the fibres.

Theoretical calculations of the influence of efficiency of fibre reinforcement on cracking stress were proposed as early as 1963, [6.70] and examples of such curves are shown in Figure 6.21.

Experimentally the number of fibres in a cross-section is exposed by appropriate illumination and may be counted on an image as shown in Figure 6.22. Because of the random orientation of fibres their cross-sections have various forms from circular to prolonged ellipses. Between aggregate grains in natural rock the traces of steel-fibres are not always clearly visible and sometimes it is necessary for counting to replace a natural image by an equivalent system of points (Figure 6.23) which then is easily discerned by computerized image analyser. Counting fibres is a reliable way to check effective reinforcement in the elements produced, for instance to compare it with the assumed design volume of reinforcement or to evaluate the influence of different methods of casting.

References

6.1. Holliday, L. (1966) Geometrical considerations and phase relationships, in *Composite Materials*, (ed. L. Holliday), Elsevier Publ. Co., Amsterdam.

6.2. McGreath, D.R., Newman, J.B. and Newman, K. (1969) The influence of aggregate particles on the local strain distribution and fracture mechanism of cement paste during drying shrinkage and loading to failure. *Bull. RILEM*, **2**(7), 73–85.

6.3. Pigeon, M. (1969) The process of crack initiation and propagation in concrete, Ph.D. Thesis, Imperial College, London.

6.4. Stroeven, P. (1973) Some aspects of the micromechanics of concrete, Ph.D. Thesis, Stevin Laboratory, Technological University of Delft.

6.5. Hannant, D. (1978) *Fibre Cements and Fibre Concretes*, J. Wiley & Sons, Chichester.

6.6. Kasperkiewicz, J. (1979) Analysis of idealized distributions of short fibres in composite materials. *Bull. de l'Acad. Pol. Sci.*, Ser. Sci. Techn., **27**(7), 601–9.

6.7. Schorn, H. and Rode, U. (1989) Numerical simulation of 3D crack formation in concrete structures, in: *Brittle Matrix Composites 2*, (eds A.M. Brandt, I.H. Marshall), Elsevier Applied Science, Barking, 152–9.

6.8. Kasperkiewicz, J. (1983) Internal structure and cracking processes in brittle matrix composites, (in Polish), *IFTR Reports*, 39, Institute of Fundamental Technological Research, Warsaw.

6.9. Shah, S.P. and Slate, F.O. (1968) Internal microcracking, mortar-aggregate bond and the stress-strain curve for concrete, in *The Structure of Concrete and its Behaviour under Load*, (eds A.E. Brooks and K. Newman), Cem. and Concr. Ass., London 82–92.

6.10. Frolov, N. *et al.* (1965) *Ferrocement Structures*, (in Russian), Nauka i Tekhnika, Minsk.

6.11. Hartshorne, N.H. and Stuart, A. (1964) *Practical Optical Crystallography*, Edward Arnold and Co., London.

6.12. Murr, L.E. (1970) *Electron Optical Applications in Materials Science*, McGraw-Hill Book Co., New York.

6.13. Pluta, M. (1989) *Advanced Light Microscopy*, **1**, Principle and Basic Properties, PWN-Elsevier, Warsaw.

6.14. Slate, F.O. (1983) X-ray technique for studying cracks in concrete with emphasis on methods developed and used at Cornell University, in *Fracture Mechanics of Concrete*, (ed. F.H. Wittmann), Elsevier Science Publishers, Amsterdam, 85–93.

6.15. Fagerlund, G. (1973) *Methods of Characterisation of Pore Structure*. The Lund Inst. of Technology, Lund.

6.16. Maslouhi, A., Roy, C., and Piasta, Z. (1990) Digitized AE waveform processing and pattern recognition applied to microfailures identification in carbon fiber/metallic composites, in *Proc. Fifth Canadian Symp. on Aerosp. Struct. and Materials*, May, Toronto.

6.17. Roy, C., Allard, J., Maslouhi, A. and Piasta, Z. (1991) Pattern recognition characterization of microfailures in composites via analytical quantitative acoustic emission, in Proc. Int. Coll. *Durability of Polymer Based Composite Systems for Structural Applications*, August 1990, Brussels, (eds A.H. Cardon and G. Verchery), Elsevier Applied Science, London and New York, 312–24.

6.18. Broek, D. (1986) *Elementary Engineering Fracture Mechanics*, 4th ed., Martinus Nijhoff Publishers, The Hague.

6.19. Pratt, P.L. (1988) Physical methods for identification of microstructures. *Materials and Structures*, RILEM, **21**(122), 106–17.

6.20. Jennings, H.M. (1991) Towards establishing relationships between microstructure and properties of cement based materials in *Ceramic Trans.* **16**, Advances in cementitious materials (ed. S. Mindess), 289–317.

6.21. Mindess, S. and Young, J.F. (1981) *Concrete*, Prentice-Hall Inc. New Jersey.

6.22. Nicholls, R. (1976) *Composite Construction Material Handbook*, Prentice-Hall Inc., New Jersey.

6.23. Neville, A.M. and Brooks, J.F. (1987) *Concrete Technology*, Longman Scientific & Technical, Harlow.

6.24. Venuat, M. (1984) *Adjuvants et traitements*, published by the author, Paris.

6.25. Popovics, S. (1979) *Concrete-Making Materials*, Hemisphere Publ. Co., Washington DC.

6.26. Granju, J.L. and Maso, J.C. (1984) Hardened Portland cement pastes, modelisation of the micro-structure and evolution laws of mechanical properties, part I, Basic results, *Cement and Concrete Research*, **14**, 249–56.

6.27. Popovics, S. (1982) Production schedule of concrete for maximum profit. *Materials and Structure*, RILEM, **15**(87), May–June, 199–204.

6.28. Haynes, J.M. (1988) The influence of processing on the microstructure of materials. *Materials and Structures*, RILEM, **21**(122), 83–4.

6.29. Guyon, E. (1988) Matériaux fortement hétérogènes: effects d'échelle et lois de comportement. *Materials and Structures*, RILEM, **21**(122), 97–105.

6.30. Mandelbrot, B. (1982) *The Fractal Geometry of Nature*, Freeman, New York.

6.31. Stauffer, D. (1986) *Introduction to Percolation Theory*, Taylor and Francis, London.

6.32. Powers, T.C. (1964) The physical structure of Portland cement paste, in *The Chemistry of Cements*, (ed. H.F.W. Taylor), **1**, Acad. Press, London, 391–416.

6.33. CEB (1989) *Durable Concrete Structures. CEB Design Guide*, Comité Euro-International du Béton, Bulletin No. 182, 2nd ed., No. 183, Lausanne.

6.34. Powers, T.C., Copeland, L.E., Hayes, J.C. and Mann, H.M. (1954) Permeability of Portland cement paste. *Journal of the American Concrete Institute*, **51**, November, 285–98.

6.35. Powers, T.C. (1945) A working hypothesis for the further studies of frost resistance of concrete. *ACI Journal*, Proc. **41**, February, 245–72.

6.36. Klieger, P. (1978) *Significance of Tests and Properties of Concrete and Concrete-Making Materials*, ASTM STP 169B, Philadelphia, 787–803.

6.37. Mielenz, R.C., Wolkodoff, V.E., Backstrom, J.E., *et al.* (1958) Origin, evolution and effects of the air void system in concrete. *ACI Journal*, Proc. **55**, July–October, 95–122, 261–72, 359–76, 507–18.

6.38. Schneider, U. and Diederichs, U. (1983) Detection of cracks by mercury penetration measurements, *Fracture Mechanics of Concrete*, (ed. F.H. Wittmann), Elsevier Appl. Sc., Amsterdam, 207–22.

6.39. Scrivener, K.L. and Pratt, P.L. (1987) The characterisation and quantification of cement and concrete microstructures, *Proc. of 1st Congress of RILEM*, Versailles, September 1987, **1**, Chapman and Hall, London, 61–8.

6.40. Diamond, S. (1971) A critical comparison of mercury porosimetry and capillary condensation pore size distribution of Portland cement pastes. *Cement and Concrete Research*, **1**(5), 531–45.

6.41. Verbeck, G.J. and Helmuth, R.H. (1969) Structures and physical properties of cement pastes, in Proc. of the 5th Int. Symp. on the *Chemistry of Cement*, part III, Tokyo, 1–32.

6.42. Kayyali, O.A. (1987) Porosity of concrete in relation to the nature of the paste-aggregate interface. *Materials and Structures*, RILEM, **20**(115).

6.43. Washburn, E.W. (1921) Note on a method of determining the distribution of pore size in a porous material. *Proc. Nat. Acad. Sci.*, **7**, 115–16.

6.44. Hansen, T.C. (1966) Notes from a Seminar on structure and properties of concrete. *Stanford University, Civil Engineering Dept. Technical Report*, No. 71, Stanford University, Stanford, USA.

6.45. Fagerlund, G. (1973) Influence of pore structure on shrinkage, strength and elastic moduli, *Lund Inst. of Technology Rep. 44*, Div. Build. Mat., Lund.

6.46. Balshin, M.Y. (1949) Relation of mechanical properties of powder metals and their porosity and the ultimate properties of porous metal ceramic meterials. *Dokl. Akad. Nauk USSR*, **67**(5), 831–4.

6.47. Ryshkevitch, E. (1953) Compression strength of porous sintered aluminia and zirkonia. *Journ. of the Amer. Ceramic Soc.*, **36**, 65–8.

6.48. Schiller, K.K. (1958) Porosity and strength of brittle solids, in *Mechanical Properties of Non-Metallic Brittle Materials*, Butterworth, London, 35–49.

6.49. Fagerlund, G. (1979) Samband mellan porositet och materials mekaniska egensk-paper (in Swedish), *Lund Inst. of Technology Rep. 26*, Div. Build. Tech. Lund.

6.50. Uchikawa, H. (1988) Similarities and discrepancies of hardened cement paste, mortar and concrete from the standpoints of composition and structure. *J. of Res. of the Onoda Cem. Comp.*, **40**(19), 24pp.

6.51. Te'eni, M. (1971) Deformational modes and structural parameters in cemented granular systems, in *Structure, Solid Mechanics and Engineering Design*, (ed. M. Te'eni), Southampton 1969, Wiley Interscience, London, 621–42.

6.52. Murat, M. and Bachiorrini, A. (1987) Résistance mécanique et notion de porosité critique: Application aux composites à base de ciment alumineux, as [6.38], 203–9.

6.53. Carpinteri, A. (1987) Influence of defects and porosity on material strength, as [6.38], 183–90.

6.54. Atzeni, C., Massida, L. and Sanna, V. (1987) Effect of pore distribution on strength of hardened cement pastes, as [6.38], 195–202.

6.55. Parrot, L. (1985) Mathematical modelling of microstructure and properties of hydrated cement. *NATO ASI Series E: Applied Science*, No. 95, 213–28.

6.56. Kendall, K., Howard, A.J. and Birchall, J.D. (1983) The relation between porosity, microstructure and strength, and the approach to advanced cement-based materials. *Phil. Trans. Roy. Soc.* A310, 139–53.

6.57. Leodolff, G.F. (1987) Low porosity concrete, as [6.38], 1–8.

6.58. Takagi, N. and Akashi, T. (1984) Properties of concrete containing silica fume. *Trans. of the Japan Concrete Institute*, **6**, 47–54.

6.59. American Concrete Institute (1984) Guide for Specifying, Mixing, Placing and Finishing Steel Fiber Reinforced Concrete, ACI Comm. 544, 3R, 1–7.

6.60. RILEM (1984) Testing Methods for Fibre Reinforced Cement-based Composites, RILEM Tech. Comm. 49-TFR, Draft Recommendation, *Materials and Structures*, RILEM, **17**(102), 441–56.

6.61. Romualdi, J.P. and Mandel, J.A. (1964) Tensile strength of concrete affected by uniformly distributed and closely spaced short lengths of wire reinforcement. *J. of the American Concrete Institute*, June, 657–70.

6.62. Shah, S.P. and Rangan, B.V. (1971) Fibre reinforced concrete properties. *J. of the American Concrete Institute*, **68**(2), 126–37.

6.63. Krenchel, K. (1975) Fiber spacing and specific fiber surface, Proc. RILEM Symp. *Fibre Reinforced Cement and Concrete*, 14–17 September 1975, London, The Construction Press, 69–79.

6.64. Aveston, K. and Kelly, A. (1973) Theory of multiple fracture of fibrous composites. *J. of Materials Science*, **8**(3), 152–62.

6.65. Swamy, R.N. and Mangat, P.S. (1975) The onset of cracking and ductility of steel fiber concrete. *Cement and Concrete Research*, **5**, 37–53.

6.66. Stroeven, P. (1978), (1979) Morphometry of fibre-reinforced cementitious materials. *Materials and Structures*, RILEM, Part I, **11**(61), 1978, 31–8; Part II, **12**(67), 1979, 9–20.

6.67. Kasperkiewicz, J. (1978) Apparent spacing in fibre reinforced composites. *Bull. Acad. Pol. Sci.*, Ser Sc. Techn., **26**(1), 1–9.

6.68. Kasperkiewicz, J. (1978) Reinforcement parameter for fibre concrete. *Bull. Acad. Pol. Sci.*, Ser. Sc. Techn., **26**(1), 11–18.

6.69. Kasperkiewicz, J., Malmberg, B. and Skarendahl, A. (1978) Determination of fibre content, distribution and orientation in steel-fibre concrete by X-ray technique, in Proc. RILEM Symp. *Testing and Test Methods of Fibre Cement Composites*, (ed. R.N. Swamy), The Construction Press, Lancaster, 297–305.

6.70. Romualdi, J.P. and Batson, G.B. (1963) Mechanics of crack arrest in concrete. *J. Engng. Mech. Div.*, ASCE Proc., **89**, (EM3), 147–68.

7 Interfaces

7.1 Kinds of interfaces

The interface is a layer between two different phases of a composite material. In the concrete-like composites the stresses are transferred in the interface from one phase to another. Also, the flow of fluids and gases along and across an interface is more intensive than in other phases. The structure and composition of an interface depend on the nature of both neighbouring phases and also on the conditions of mixing, hydration and ageing of the material.

Several important test results and conclusions concerning the interfaces, their structure, properties and influence have been published [7.1].

There are different types of interface:

1. between small grains of aggregate and cement paste, i.e.: between matrix components;
2. between the matrix itself and larger grains of coarse aggregate of various nature;
3. between matrix and reinforcement (steel bars of fibres, other kinds of fibres, etc);
4. between the similar composite materials, but of different age or quality.

Without any doubt the transfer of forces between two adjacent phases is by far the most important factor for the mechanical behaviour of a composite material. The bond, in any of its forms ensured in the interface, is necessary to transform a mixture of various phases into a composite material. The bond itself is a combination of three phenomena which occur simultaneously but at different levels – mechanical interlocking of the cement paste and the surface of grains, bars or fibres, physical bonds between molecules and chemical reactions producing new compounds which are attached to both phases. Even as the nature of these phenomena is basically known, their proportions in each particular case are different and have not always been fully understood up to now.

The interface is formed partly by two neighbouring phases or predominantly by one of them, but in this region strong modifications with respect to both phases are observed. Its structure is often composed of several layers, with the inclusion of grains and pores. The structure of the interface may be very complex and in most cases it appears to be the weakest region of the composite material when exposed to the external actions and loads. Interfacial regions usually occupy only a small part of the volume of the material, but their properties influence considerably its behaviour and quality.

The interface layers have a lower density than the bulk matrix and are more penetrable by fluids and gases. Therefore, it is often the interface which determines the overall permeability of the material.

The interface problems between classic reinforcement in the form of steel bars and pre-stressing tendons are not considered here, because they exceed the scope of this book and are widely examined in the manuals on concrete technology and concrete structures.

7.2 Aggregate–cement paste interface

This interface was studied by many investigators who examined its morphology and nature. The present state of knowledge is far from complete but evidence has been obtained for the main characteristics of the interface. This transition zone is composed of a thin layer of 'duplex film' and a zone of acicular ettringite and larger portlandite crystals which passes continuously into the bulk cement paste. The 'duplex film' consists of two different layers – portlandite crystals and CSH phase, the latter not always being present or detectable, [7.2]. Duplex film is crystallized to a small extent only; its thickness is of order of 1 μm and is usually well adhered to the grain surface. In the zone next to the duplex film the orientation of crystals is to some extent influenced by the vicinity of the aggregate grain surface. The sequence of the processes in the interface layers at the beginning of cement hydration was considered by several authors without achieving conclusive results.

An example of the interface is shown schematically in Figure 7.1. In some cases the absence of the duplex film has been reported.

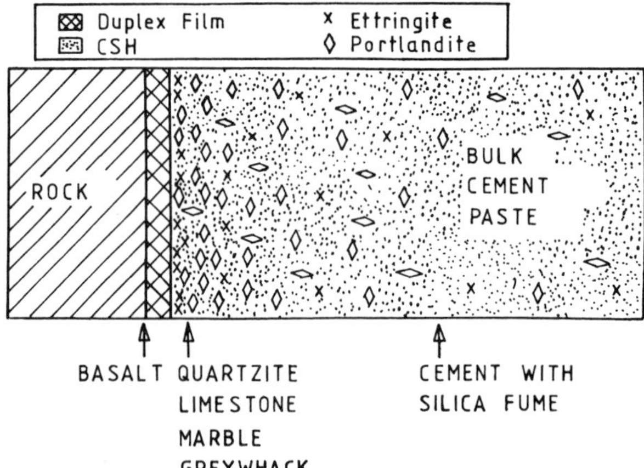

Figure 7.1 Scheme of aggregate–cement paste interface. Possible positions of debonding fracture in composites with different components are indicated. (Reproduced with permission from Odler, I. and Zurz, A., Structure and bond strength of cement–aggregate interface; published by Materials Research Society, 1988.) [7.2]

The structure of the interface varies as a function of the nature of aggregate and the grain surface texture. The quality of the cement paste and conditions of the hydration processes are also of great importance.

One possible measure of the quality of the interface presumably related to its strength is its micro-hardness. The results of published measurements [7.3] are shown in Figure 7.2. It appears from these tests that depending on various circumstances, weak and strong layers may be produced in both aggregate grains and cement matrix. These authors [7.3] proposed to distinguish two classes of interface according to the chemical affinity of the grains, the texture of their surface and the conditions of hydration processes in the cement matrix.

In class I aggregate grains obtained, for example, from basalt rocks are chemically inert and hydration products exhibit weak adhesion to their surface. In that case even a local increase of strength of the matrix close to the aggregate as shown in Figure 7.2a has no strengthening effect on the composite material, or only when it is under compression stress. That increase of the matrix strength

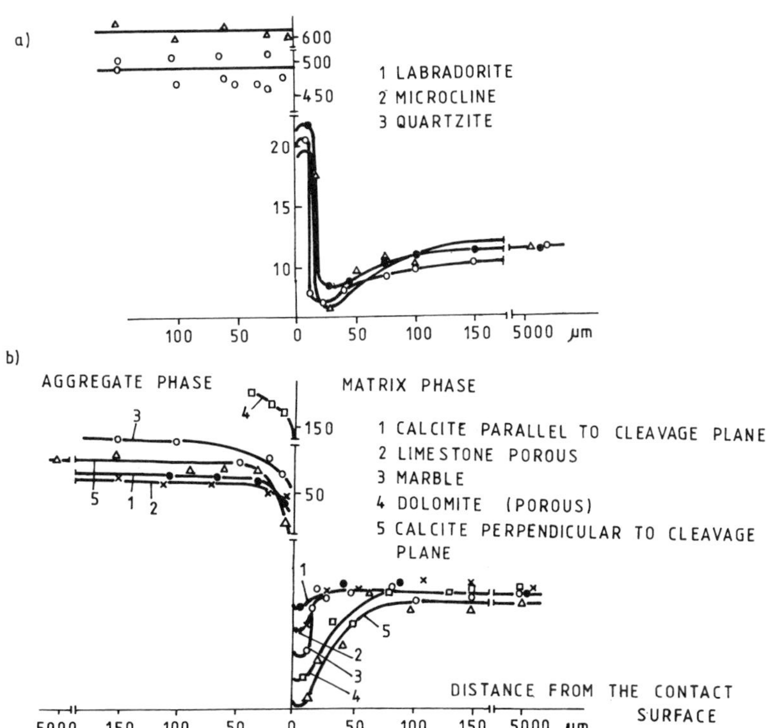

Figure 7.2 Variation of micro-hardness in the interface between aggregate grains and cement paste for various kinds of aggregate. (Reproduced from Lyubimova, T.Yu. and Pinus, E.R., Crystallization and structuration in the contact zone between aggregate and cement in concrete; *Colloidnyi Zhurnal*, **24**(5), pp. 578–87, 1962.) [7.3]

may be explained by different hydration conditions in the interface layer rather than in the bulk matrix.

The interface between ground quartzite sand grains and cement paste is classified to class IIa. A strong bond which is observed is partly of a chemical nature and the sand grains behave from the beginning of the hydration process as active elements in the material structure. In the case of the porous carbonate aggregate the bond is related to the highly developed surface of the grains. As a result, there is no clear distinction between grain and cement matrix, but the interface represents a kind of continuous passage from one to another. This type of interface is called class IIb. The strong interface of that class is not an origin of cracking, but on the contrary, it is a strengthening element of the composite's structure.

According to [7.3] the reaction zone extends, depending on their nature, from 0 to 100 μm in aggregate grains and from 25 to 200 μm in the hardened cement paste. Other authors have expressed opinions that the interface layer of higher porosity around aggregate grains may even be 1–2 mm thick. In concretes with the admixture of silica fume the difference between interface and bulk material is small or even non-existent. Where hard rock grains are used the strong contact zone in the matrix is observed, but a layer weaker than the rock is formed on the grain surface. In comparison, the grains of carbonate rocks have weaker zones on both sides of the contact face, and this is shown in Figure 7.2b. There are, however, some kinds of carbonate rocks which can develop a high bond strength to the cement paste and as a result a high strength concrete can be obtained. Similar effects were observed when blast furnace slag aggregate grains were used. The micro-hardness of the interfacial zone for aggregate grains made of different rocks – limestone, andesite and granite, was also tested [7.4]. The results, namely that the interactions between cement paste and aggregate do not seem to contribute to the bond strength, are not fully supported by other authors. However, the ease of crack propagation along the interface has been shown. These discrepancies in conclusions show the inadequate knowledge which exists of the role and importance of the interface in the fracture processes. In Figure 7.3 the diagrams show variations in the amount of unhydrated material and porosity across the interface in concrete with an aggregate/cement ratio equal to 4:1, water/cement ratio = 0.4, concrete age 28 days, [7.5]. From these measurements the thickness of the interface may be evaluated as 30 to 40 μm. The variation of observed properties was linear for the amount of anhydrous material and clearly non-linear for porosity. These properties of the interface explain why its micro-hardness and strength are also variable.

It can be concluded that there are two main factors determining the strength of the interface between aggregate and cement paste – chemical affinity and mechanical bond. Chemical reactions have been observed at the surface of siliceous grains and also on limestone ones, in both cases of different origin. Due to the reactions, an interface layer is created in most cases and its properties are different from neighbouring phases. Besides moderate chemical reactions

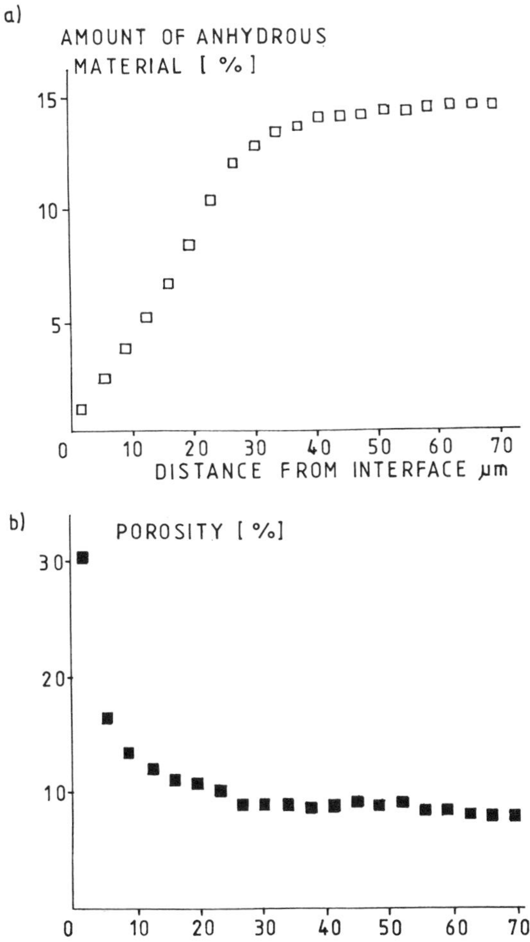

Figure 7.3 Microstructural gradients in the interfacial region of concrete; a) amount of anhydrous material; b) porosity. (Reproduced with permission of Scrivener, K. *et al.*, A study of the interfacial region between cement paste and aggregate in concrete; published by Materials Research Society, 1988.) [7.5]

which improve bonding and help increase the density of the interface, an alkali–aggregate reaction (AAR) may appear in certain conditions and in an extreme case it may ruin the material's structure. The nature and effects of AAR are described in Section 4.2.

A mechanical bond depends on the texture of the aggregate grains. There are different possibilities, from perfectly smooth grains which do not allow any appreciable mechanical bonding, up to porous rock grains in which the above mentioned transition zone is created. Epitaxial growth of calcium hydroxide was found on the grain surfaces by a few authors and thus mechanical interlocking is enhanced. The orientation of calcium hydroxide was measured [7.6] and [7.7] and it was observed to increase in the interface which helped explain the easier propagation of microcracks in this region. It has also been observed that ettringite was concentrated in the interface – probably another reason for its lower strength. Interesting comments on that subject are given in [7.8] and in [7.9].

It is clear from experience that for high strength concrete the material with good bonding should be always used. For example, the particularly weak bond of basalt grains is the reason for the opinion that a high strength concrete is rarely obtained with basalt aggregate. Without a proper bond even hard grains are only inert fillers and not strengthening inclusions. However, there is neither a universally adopted method to qualify the aggregate surface in this respect, nor is there a direct relationship established between the bond quality and the strength of these cement-based composites.

The low strength of the transition zone is attributed to higher porosity and to the orientation of large CH crystals which have weak intercrystalline bonds. It has been shown, [7.10] that hollow grains composed of Portland cement hydration products which increase porosity appear more often in the interface than in bulk cement paste. These grains are called Hadley grains [7.10]. The pores and voids may appear in the form of clusters which create critical flaws.

The technological reasons for the inadequate properties of the interfacial zone may vary – too high water/cement ratio, incorrect packing of grains in the mix due to wrong design of the aggregate size distribution, but also defective mixing in which a large amount of air is entrapped in the fresh mix. The influence of the interface porosity on the durability of the concrete seems obvious and was suggested in [7.11]. However, experimental evidence is still needed in this respect.

There are also microcracks in the interface prior to the application of any external load. They are initiated by bleeding and by shrinkage of the cement paste in regions close to aggregate grain faces, which play a restraining role and cause stresses which are bigger around larger grains of coarse aggregate than around the smaller sand grains. The bond to quartzite grains is also stronger than to most kinds of coarse aggregate grains. Therefore, the interface layers between the aggregate and cement matrix are the origin of microcracks. These microcracks and flaws propagate and form larger cracks under stresses and displacements caused by external loading, leading gradually to fracture. Experimental evidence of high local strain in the interface [7.12] is shown in Figure 7.4.

The composition and structure of the interface may be purposefully modified to improve the composite's mechanical properties, mainly by an increase of chemical affinity and mechanical interlocking of both phases. Examples of pre-treatment procedures applied to aggregate grains to improve the strength of the interfacial zone are described in [7.13] and [7.14]. The following may be mentioned as pre-treatment methods:

- coating of grains with high strength paste before mixing;

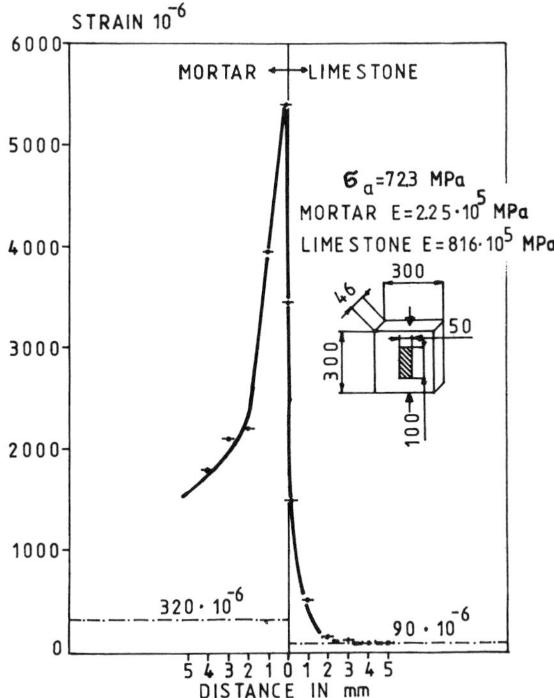

Figure 7.4 Results of the strain measurements at the border region between mortar and limestone inclusion. (Source: Lusche, M., The fracture mechanisms of ordinary and lightweight concrete under uniaxial compression; published by Ossolineum, 1974.) [7.12]

- coating with a mixture of water glass and $CaCl_2$;
- increasing density of cement paste by silica fume;
- increasing the specific area of Portland cement.

The pre-treatment is often necessary for lightweight aggregates.

The cement paste–aggregate grain zone was studied using computer simulation. A tri-dimensional micro-structural model representing the interfacial zone with mineral micro-fillers was applied [7.15]. The influence of different admixtures was simulated in a digital image-based model. A considerable improvement was observed in the integrity of the interface due to the pozzolanic reaction of admixtures.

The increase of the bond strength by improvement of the aggregate–matrix interface has also an unfavourable effect – the brittleness of the composite material may be increased. Consequently, in such a case, the fracture energy is diminished. It is necessary to select appropriate material properties in material design, not only compressive and tensile strength but also brittleness; all three being related to the quality of the aggregate–matrix interface. Other properties also to be taken into account are permeability, durability, resistance to abrasion, etc.

The mechanical role of the interface is visible in the overall behaviour of the cement-based composites. Both components – aggregate grains and hardened cement paste – behave as linear elastic and brittle bodies in a relatively large domain of applied stresses. However, these two components form a material with a non-linear and inelastic stress–strain relationship. This is caused by the microcracks which appear and develop under tension or bending mostly in the system of interfaces. This influence may be observed from almost the beginning of the stress–strain curve.

7.3 Fibre–cement paste interface

The fibre–cement paste interface has been studied by many authors, and for various kinds of fibres. Initially, attempts were made to use numerous results obtained for steel bars and cement mortar in reinforced concrete elements. It appeared, however, that because of the different scale and role of steel bars and thin fibres with respect to other elements of the material structure, like sand grains, pores, etc., only few similarities existed and this may help to explain the nature and properties of the interface in fibre-reinforced composites.

For steel fibres the chemical bond plays a relatively small role and the interfacial layer is mostly influenced by:

- the natural roughness of the fibre surface;
- the shape of the fibre and eventual special indentations and deformations;
- modification of the cement paste in the vicinity of the fibre surface, e.g. increased water/cement ratio, higher porosity due to restraints in packing, etc.

The transition zone around steel fibre is, as for the aggregate–cement paste

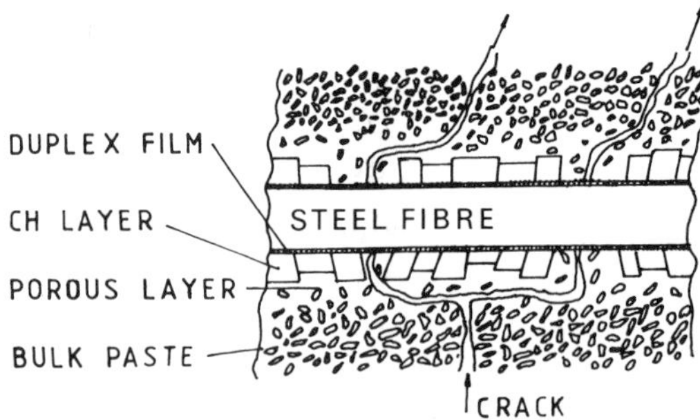

Figure 7.5 Scheme of steel–fibre–cement paste interface with a crack propagating in transversal direction. (Reprinted from *Cement and Concrete Research*, **15**(2), Bentur, A. *et al.* Cracking processes in steel-fibre reinforced cement paste, pp. 331–42, 1985, with permission from Pergamon Press Ltd, Headington Hill Hall, Oxford, OX3 OBW, UK.) [7.17]

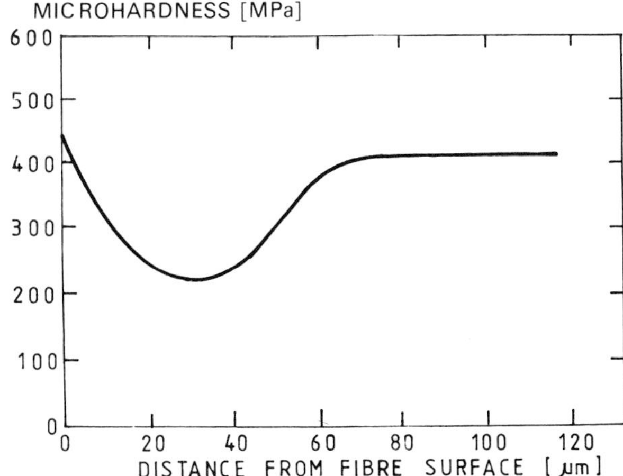

Figure 7.6 Microhardness of the cement paste measured from the steel fibre surface. (Reproduced with permission from Wei, S. *et al.*, Study of the interface strength in steel-fibre reinforced cement-based composites; published by American Concrete Institute, 1986.) [7.18]

interface, composed of a few different layers – duplex film, CH layer, porous layer of CSH and ettringite, [7.16]. This is shown schematically in Figure 7.5. The porous layer is characterized by lower micro-hardness and strength (Figure 7.6) and that is the weakest zone in which cracks between fibre and matrix are observed.

An example of the interface is shown in Figure 7.7. Upper part (black) is a steel fibre, lower part – cement mortar; in between there is a strongly heterogeneous transition zone. A schematic representation of the interface is shown in Figure 7.8.

The application of several methods to strengthen the interface around a 10 mm steel bar was reported in [7.19]. Improvement was obtained by an admixture of silica fume, by decreasing the water/cement ratio and by covering the surface of the bar with dry cement powder, using a special technique. The results were analysed by micro-hardness test, pore size distribution measurement, SEM observations and pull-out test. It has been concluded that:

- the improved interfacial layer was denser and harder than the bulk cement paste and a minimum level of micro-hardness across the interface thickness was not observed;
- the interface was composed of smaller crystals than in non-treated specimens;
- cement grains remained with a possibility of their later hydration, therefore further increase of strength and density may be expected;
- nearly 30% increase of pull-out force has been established with respect to non-treated specimens.

For fibres made of glass or polypropylene the main problems relate to the

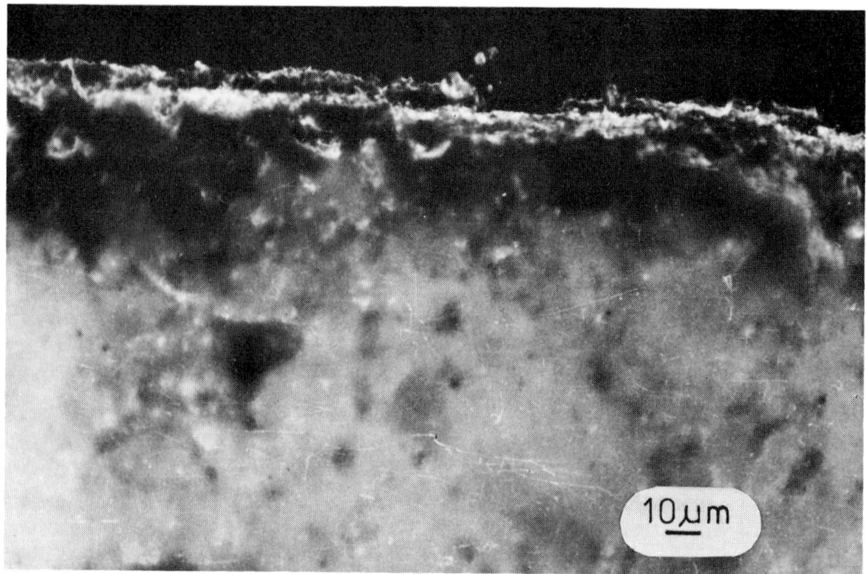

Figure 7.7 Example of steel fibre–cement mortar interface, image from optical microscope. (From the tests by Dr J. Potrzebowski in 1988.)

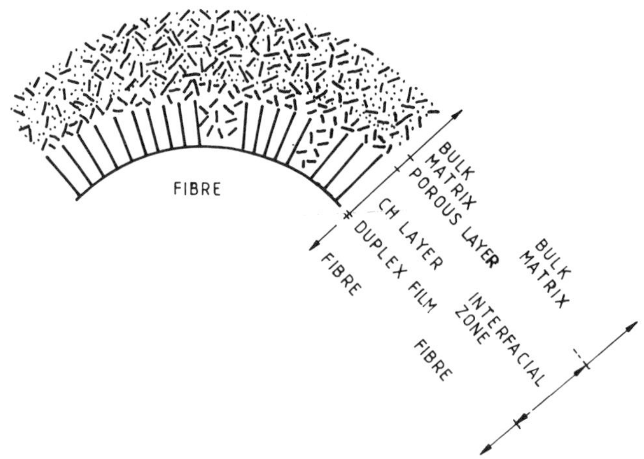

Figure 7.8 Scheme of the interfacial microstructure around a steel-fibre. (Reproduced with permission from Bentur, A., Interface in fibre-reinforced cements; published by Materials Research Society, 1988.) [7.16]

spaces between single fibres in a bundle. These spaces are only partly filled by hydration products and the transfer of stresses for internal fibres in a bundle is assured only by local contacts. The chemical bond is lower than for asbestos fibres and that is another reason for there being empty spaces around single fibres.

The fibre surface has a considerable influence on the composition of the transition zone. For highly corrosion resistant glassfibres with specially coated surfaces, like CemFIL2, this zone is very porous. This is in contrast to the strong interface formed around steel and asbestos fibres. In various composites with different kinds of fibres and matrices the transition zone is formed as a result of chemical affinity, quality of the fibre surface and the penetration of the cement paste into the bundles of fibres. The properties of the transition zone vary with time due to hydration of the cement grains, shrinkage and eventual corrosion processes, [7.20].

The effects of the weak zone around fibres are the mechanisms of crack arrest observed in many tests and described for example in [7.21]. In these mechanisms the interface fails ahead of the crack tip due to the tensile stress concentration which is shown schematically in Figure 7.9a. The following sequence of events is then supposed as is shown in Figure 7.9b:

1. crack approaches a weak interface;
2. interface fails ahead of the main crack;
3. crack stops in a T-shape or may be diverted (after [7.16]).

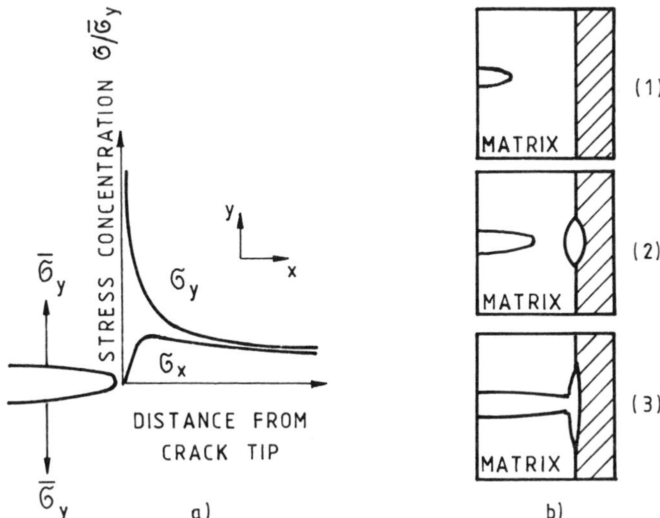

Figure 7.9 The Cook–Gordon arrest mechanisms of a crack. (Reproduced with permission from Bentur, A., Interface in fibre-reinforced cements; published by Materials Research Society, 1988.) [7.16]

The measurements of fibre–matrix displacements in the interface are briefly described in Section 8.5.

7.4 Interface between old and new composites

The strength of the interface between old and new materials is important in the repair of concrete structures. This mostly concerns structures of bridges, roads, dams, etc. which are exposed to the climatic actions of rain, frost, carbonation and various kinds of chemical agents. The problems related to repair are of increasing interest, because in many countries, every year, large amounts of public money and effort are spent on repair of existing structures, cf. Section 15.3. The quality of repair depends to a large measure upon the strength and durability of the interface. There are several reasons for that relationship.

The interface should ensure appropriate transmission of forces between the old and new material. These forces are caused by external loads when new layers are expected to contribute to load bearing and stiffness of the old structure. In structures subjected to traffic or to waves the external loads are of a dynamic character. Certain forces in the interface are induced, even without loading, by differential shrinkage and thermal deformations.

There is an unavoidable flow of moisture and heat across the interface, because the new material initially exhibits processes of hardening, and subsequently holds up external climatic actions which do not directly reach the deeper layers of old concrete.

The stresses between old and new materials vary with time and depend considerably upon the differences in their structure and composition. Even if both materials are specially matched in order to have similar properties, the difference in the age of the materials may prove to be the reason for stresses at the interface.

The interface should ensure high impermeability if exposed on external actions, otherwise diffusion of moisture may endanger its durability.

The reasons described above lead to a conclusion that the interface is probably the weakest element in the repair work. That is why there are many practical methods available to reinforce the interface and to ensure its high quality. Among several measures available, reinforcement with thin nets of steel or textile wires may be emphasized and also the need for careful preparation of the surface of old concrete. After cleaning and moistening, intermediary layers are created with increased Portland cement content, admixtures of polymeric materials or silica fume, etc. There are, however, few research studies reported, up to now, on the effects and behaviour of the interface between old and new materials. Brief details are given below on tests initiated in 1992 [7.22].

Specimens of old material were prepared a few years ago with two kinds of concrete using basalt and limestone aggregate, with a maximum aggregate grain size of 20 mm and compressive strength approximately $f_{28} = 25$ MPa. On these concrete slabs were cast layers of steel fibre-reinforced concrete (SFRC) after

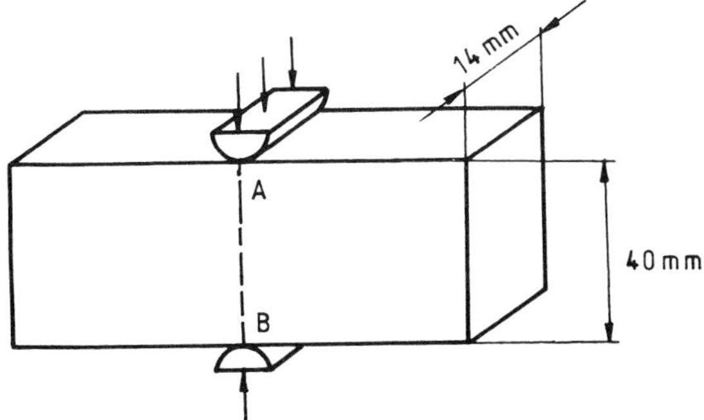

Figure 7.10 Specimen subjected to splitting test. (Source: Brandt, A.M. *et al.*, Application of concrete composites to repair of overlays, decks and structures of road bridges; unpublished report, 1992.) [7.22]

Table 7.1 Tensile strength from splitting tests

			Interface	
Concrete I basalt aggr. (MPa)	Concrete II limestone aggr. (MPa)	SFRC (MPa)	concr. I/SFRC (MPa)	concr. II/SFRC (MPa)
2.69	2.85	4.05	2.10	1.78

the old surfaces had been carefully cleaned and washed and their roughness has been artificially increased. The new material was reinforced with 1.5% of steel fibres of the Harex type (0.5 × 0.5 mm, l = 16 mm). After 7 days' curing in 100% RH the slabs were stored for 18 months in laboratory conditions. The specimens for testing were cut with diamond saws and fracture tests were executed under static loading as shown in Figure 7.10. Line A–B of tensile stress was situated in specimens of both old concretes, and just in the interface in SFRC. The mean values of obtained results are given in Table 7.1.

It may be concluded that even in laboratory conditions where specimens were thoroughly cleaned and wetted before casting the SFRC, the interface was the weakest point under tension. Further tests are needed on specimens with different kinds of interface and exposure to other types of loading. It may be expected that the influence of the scale of the specimens examined is of importance, particularly as it concerns stresses induced by differential shrinkage and thermal deformations.

References

7.1. Mindess, S. and Shah, S.P. (eds) (1988) *Bonding in Cementitious Composites*, Proc. Symp. in Boston, 2–4 December 1987, Materials Research Soc., Pittsburgh, Penn., 354 pp.

7.2. Odler, I. and Zurz, A. (1988) Structure and bond strength of cement–aggregate interface, in [7.1], 21–7.
7.3. Lyubimova, T.Yu. and Pinus, E.R. (1962) Crystallization and structuration in the contact zone between aggregate and cement in concrete (in Russian). *Colloidnyi Zhurnal*, **24**(5), 578–87.
7.4. Saito, M. and Kawamura, M. (1986) Resistance of the cement–aggregate interfacial zone to the propagation of cracks. *Cement and Concrete Research*, **16**, 653–61.
7.5. Scrivener, K.L., Crumble, A.K. and Pratt, P.L. (1988) A study of the interfacial region between cement paste and aggregate in concrete, in [7.1], 87–95.
7.6. Grandet, J. and Ollivier, J.P. (1980) Nouvelle méthode d'étude des interfaces ciment-granulats, in Proc. of the 7th Int. Congr. Chem. Cem., **III**, Paris VII85–VII89.
7.7. Grandet, J. and Ollivier, J.P. (1980) Orientation des hydrates au contact des granulats, as [7.6], VII63–VII68.
7.8. Struble, L. (1988) Microstructure and fracture at the cement paste–aggregate interface, in [7.1], 11–20.
7.9. Mindess, S. and Young, J.F. (1981) *Concrete*, Prentice-Hall, Englewood Cliffs, New Jersey.
7.10. Hadley, D.H. (1972) The nature of the paste–aggregate interface, PhD Thesis, Purdue University, pp. 173.
7.11. Valenta, O. (1969) Durability of concrete, Proc. of the 5th Int. Symp. on the Chemistry of Cement, Tokyo, **III**, 193–225.
7.12. Lusche, M. (1974) The fracture mechanisms of ordinary and lightweight concrete under uniaxial compression, in Proc. Conf. *Mechanical Properties and Structure of Composite Materials*, 18–23 November 1974, Jabłonna, (ed. A.M. Brandt), Ossolineum, 423–40.
7.13. Wu Xueqan, Li Dongxu, Wu Xiun and Tang Minshu (1988) Modification of the interfacial zone between aggregate and cement paste, in [7.1], 35–40.
7.14. Chen Zhi Yuan and Wang Jian Guo (1988) Effect of bond strength between aggregate and cement paste on the mechanical behaviour of concrete, in [7.1], 41–7.
7.15. Bentz, D.P. and Garboczi, E.J. (1991) Simulation studies of the effects of mineral admixtures on the cement paste–aggregate interfacial zone. *J. Amer. Concr. Inst. Materials*, **88**(5), 518–29.
7.16. Bentur, A. (1988) Interface in fibre reinforced cements, in [7.1], 133–44.
7.17. Bentur, A., Diamond, S. and Mindess, S. (1985) Cracking processes in steel fibre reinforced cement paste. *Cem. Concr. Res.*, **15**(2), 331–42.
7.18. Wei, S., Mandel, J.A. and Said, S. (1986) Study of the interface strength in steel fibre reinforced cement based composites. *J. Amer. Concr. Inst.*, **83**, 597–605.
7.19. Chen Zhi Yuan and Wang Nian Zhi (1989) Strengthening the interfacial zone between steel fibres and cement paste, in Proc. Int. Symp. *Brittle Matrix Composites 2*, 20–22 September 1988, Cedzyna, (eds A.M. Brandt and I.H. Marshall), Elsevier Applied Science, London 342–51.
7.20. Bentur, A. (1986) Mechanisms of potential embrittlement and strength loss of glass fibre reinforced cement composites, in Proc. Symp. *Durability of Glass Fiber Reinforced Concrete*, (ed. S. Diamond), PCInst. Chicago, 109–23.
7.21. Cook, J. and Gordon, J.E. (1964) A mechanism for the control of crack propagation in all brittle systems, *Proc. Roy. Soc.*, 282A, 508–20.
7.22. Brandt, A.M., Burakiewicz, A., Potrzebowski, J. and Skawiński, M. (1992) Application of concrete composites to repair of overlays, decks and structures of road bridges (in Polish), unpublished Report IFTR, Warsaw.

8 Strength and deformability under short-term static load

8.1 Models for unreinforced matrices

Analytical models of cement-based composite materials were initially based on the theory of elasticity with additional simplifying assumptions. The following notions were applied:

- Hooke's law not analytically related to the ultimate values of stress and strain which mean the rupture of a continuous body;
- mean stress and mean strain, in which homogeneity of the material was assumed;
- in most cases simplified formulae for stress calculations, based on so called technical theory of strength of materials;
- principles of superposition applied to composite materials.

That system is neither coherent nor experimentally verified, but it is simple enough for large application and safe enough when combined with an imposed system of safety coefficients. These coefficients help to keep structures and elements made of concrete-like composites away from extremes. Therefore, the inconsistencies of the system are only taken under consideration, when they become unacceptable for various reasons.

A compressive concrete strength may be examined as an example of such inconsistencies. The principal had been established since the beginning of the century on specimens of various shapes and dimensions but they were always subjected to axial compression. The resulting compressive strength is calculated assuming that stress is distributed uniformly over the cross-section and that its value corresponds to the failure of the specimen. The main discrepancies with reality are:

1. All cement-based composites are heterogeneous and the notion of a macroscopic stress has only very limited sense. Clear images of stress and strain variations in concrete were shown for the first time by Dantu [8.1]; they are presented in Figures 8.1 and 8.2.
2. Nobody ever has seen a specimen loaded by an axial compression where failure was caused by compression in its cross-section, because the distribution of other internal forces always produced different forms of failure, depending on conditions at the ends in other circumstances.

Another simple example is the direct tension test in which the load is again

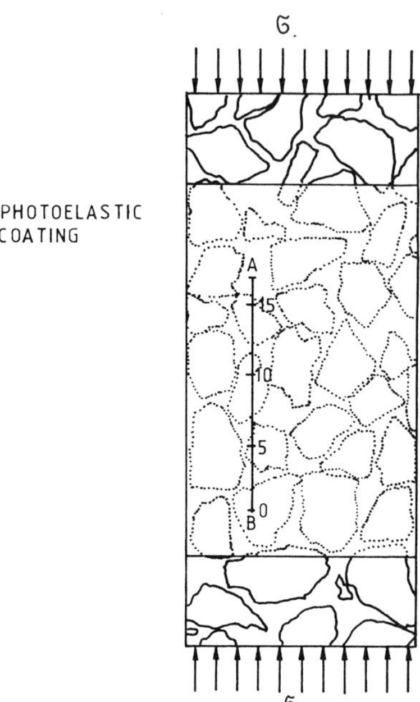

Figure 8.1 Concrete specimen subjected to axial compression $\sigma = 17\,\text{MPa}$ with one face covered with a photoelastic coating. (Reproduced from Dantu, P., Étude des contraintes dans le milieux hétérogènes. Applications au béton; published by the Institut Technique du Bâtiment et des Travaux Public, 1957.) [8.1]

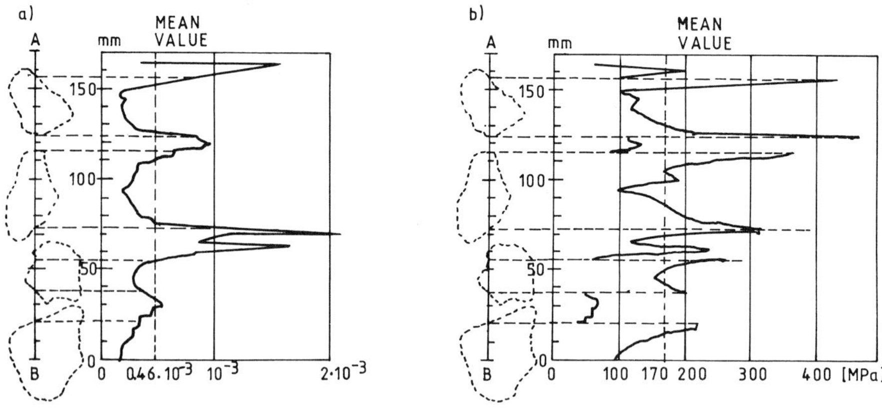

Figure 8.2 Diagrams obtained after measurement with a photoelastic coating on a lateral face of a compressed concrete element; a) Strain along AB line; b) Stress along AB line. (Reproduced from Dantu, P., Étude des contraint dans le milieux hétérogènes. Applications au béton; published by the Institut Technique du Bâtiment et des Travaux Public, 1957.) [8.1]

divided by the cross-sectional area, even though it is well known that a failure at tension is initiated at the weakest point, e.g. an initial crack or other defect.

The practical calculation of deformations and displacements of specimens and elements made of concrete-like composites is based on simple assumptions of Young's modulus and the Poisson ratio, corrected by experimental observations. In such an approach the strain–stress behaviour of concrete-like composites, as determined after the testing of specimens and elements, is considered in general as non-linear and non-elastic, as shown in Figure 8.3 for a case of bending or axial compression. Therefore, several different values of Young's modulus are distinguished, namely:

- E_i – initial modulus is determined after the slope of the tangent at the origin of the strain–stress curve;
- E_t – tangent modulus at any other point of the curve, which allows for the non-elastic strain component;
- E_c – secant modulus is determined at a conventionally accepted load level;
- E_d – dynamic modulus, determined after measurement of the fundamental frequency of longitudinal vibrations; it is assumed that $E_d = E_i$.

For any calculation of deformations or displacements the secant modulus E_c is usually considered. For plain concretes and mortars its value may be approximately determined after the material compressive strength $E_c(f_c)$ and respective formulae are given in standards and recommendations.

It is also assumed for practical calculations that within well-defined limits the assumptions of linearity and elasticity may be accepted however for cement-based materials and in that case the secant modulus E_c represents the approximate strain–stress behaviour of the material. Values of Young's modulus after the first, second, and n-th cycle vary and in Figure 8.3 their gradual increase is shown, which proves hardening of the material and decreasing creep in successive loading cycles. In such a case the behaviour at the n-th cycle may be considered as quasi-elastic and only slightly non-linear. It is the case for all concrete structures normally used, in which no accumulation of any damage is observed. A quite opposite process occurs when the level of load exceeds a certain limit and cracks appear. Then, the decrease of the Young's modulus over successive cycles is a measure of the progressing process of fracture, cf. Figure 9.5. The Poisson ratio v between transversal and longitudinal strain is assumed for concretes between 0.20 and 0.25.

Both coefficients E_c and v are approximations for much more complicated material behaviour. The relation between stress and strain varies with the load, as shown in Figure 8.3. The Poisson ratio depends upon the quality of the material, but it also varies with position and direction in a considered element and with the level of loading. This more complex image of the strain fields has been examined by many authors and has been demonstrated by precise measurements executed inside concrete elements. A special measuring device

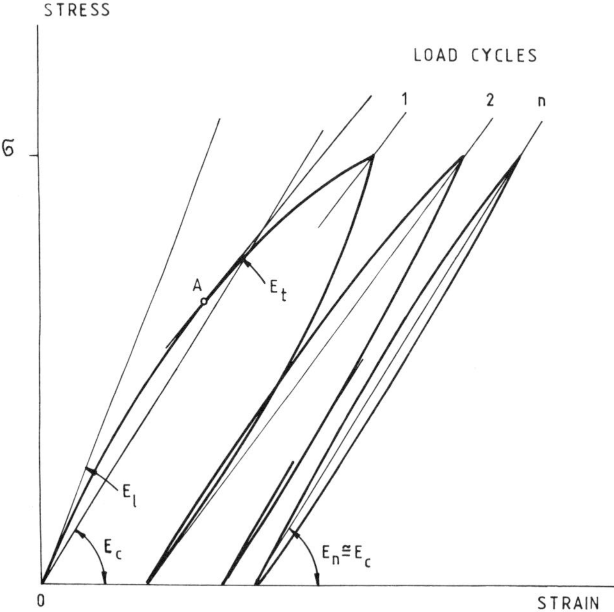

Figure 8.3 Example of a strain–stress curve for a cement based composite.

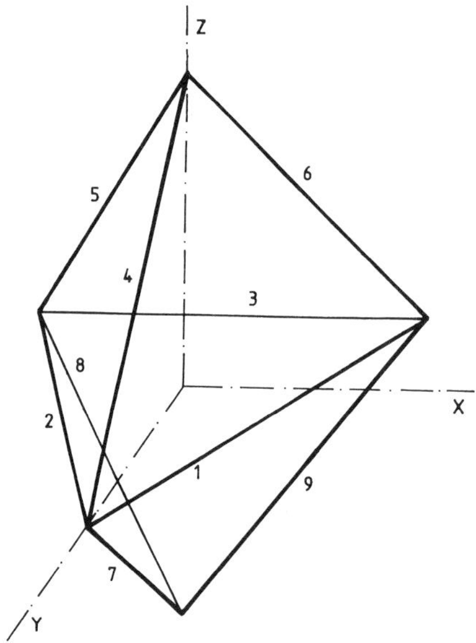

Figure 8.4 Spatial arrangement of gauges in the 9-gauges measuring device. (Source: Brandt, A.M., Nine-gauges device for strain measurements inside concrete; *Strain*, **9**(3), 1973.) [8.2]

with 9-gauges was used for this purpose (Figure 8.4), which furnished details on all six strain components together, and the possibility of evaluation of the scatter was ensured, thanks to the three additional gauges. Interested readers are referred to papers [8.2], [8.3] and [8.4].

The application of fracture mechanics to concretes which was proposed in the early 1960s by Kaplan was an important attempt to avoid the contradictions of homogeneity and continuity of cement-based composites, [8.5] and [8.6]. Further papers were published on this subject [8.7], [8.8], [8.9] and several others.

At the beginning, only linear elastic fracture mechanics (LEFM) was considered. The principal relations and formulae were taken from papers and regulations concerning metals, and their application to concrete-like composites was attempted. It appeared obvious that the most direct and natural representation for the behaviour of brittle matrix composites should be based on the examination of crack-opening and propagation processes.

The initial considerations concerned tensile and compressive strength and these were developed later into more complicated strength criteria. Their main objective was to analytically determine how the material fractured in various loading situations using different strain or stress tensor components. Because of the general conditions imposed on such criteria they should be expressed by tensor invariants, should satisfy conditions of symmetry, etc.

In the simplest criteria the material fracture was directly related to certain limits of the principal values of the stress or strain tensors. These criteria are connected to the great names of Galileo, Leibniz, Navier, Lamé, Clapeyron, Rankine and Clebsch for stress components and de Saint-Venant and Poncelet for strain components; but they have rather historical importance. The above mentioned notion of strength based on ultimate tensile or compressive stress may be considered as the simplest form of the general criteria which, by their simplicity and apparent relation to practical application in structural design, are still used.

In more complicated criteria, e.g. Huber-von Mises-Hencky, the energy of shearing strain is treated as representing the behaviour of the material and is expressed as combinations of the first invariants of the stress tensor. There are many other criteria which may be considered as more or less similar to those mentioned here. For a more detailed description of the strength criteria the reader is referred to [8.10], [8.11] and [8.12].

Only a few strength criteria were formulated with their application to brittle materials, such as natural rocks or concrete-like composites. They should take into account much lower tensile strength than compressive criteria, lack of effective plasticity which is replaced by microcracking, etc. Among these criteria the proposals made in [8.13], [8.14] and [8.15] should be mentioned.

The application of classical strength criteria to brittle matrix composites gives rather unsatisfactory results (cf. [8.16]) and at present it is reduced to two groups of considerations.

In the first of them the stress and strain distribution is calculated in the same manner as for homogeneous bodies and often only one stress or strain component is considered. Such calculations may only give valid results where homogenization is justified and the approximate values are acceptable for design or verification.

The second group of approaches which derives from the single strength criteria consists of various modifications of the law of mixtures. It is based on the so called parallel model (cf. Chapter 2) in which the Young's modulus of a two-phase (or more) composite is determined by the formula, $E_c = E_1V_1 + E_2V_2$; where the volumes of both phases V_1 and V_2 satisfy the condition, $V_1 + V_2 = 1$.

There are many proposals in the form of semi-empirical formulae based on the general concept of the law of mixtures and it is useful to review a few of them in more detail.

As applied to two-phase material, e.g. cement-based matrix and aggregate grains, the law of mixtures represents an upper bound. That formula and the others are discussed in Section 2.5.

8.2 Strength and destruction of brittle matrices

The destruction of a brittle matrix is based on the initiation and propagation of microcracks caused by local tensions. With increased load or imposed deformation the microcracks are transformed into a system of cracks. Then, one or two major cracks divide the element into separate parts and the continuity of the element disappears, in conjunction with a rapid decrease in bearing capacity. The progress of the fracture process requires an energy input, at least until a certain stage, e.g. in the form of an external increase in load. At different states of loading the destruction processes are influenced considerably by time, i.e. their duration, and also by the external constraints. The simplified description which follows is directly intended for elements subjected to axial tension, but it may be extended, with minor modifications, to other kinds of loading.

In cement-based matrices the internal microcracks exist from the very beginning and without any external load being involved (cf. Section 9.2). The cracks are concentrated in the interface layers between aggregate grains and cement paste, but intrinsic cracks also appear in the cement mortar itself. If a load is applied, then its distribution is uneven because of the high heterogeneity of the material. Certain regions are subjected to much higher stress and strain than others. Stress concentrations are the reason for crack development even under relatively low average stress and low values of total load. That initial, slow, crack growth explains two phenomena which are observed from almost the beginning of loading – limited acoustic emission (AE) and a small deviation from linearity of the stress–strain or load-displacement diagrams. The tests in which various phenomena of fracture progress were monitored during the initial loading stages were published as early as 1955, [8.17].

Under a load corresponding to about 30% of its maximum value the AE events are already numerous and the deviation from linearity starts to be visible. The stress level of 30% is mentioned here as an approximate value which varies within large limits, depending on material properties and the type of testing machine.

It is difficult to determine the maximum matrix strain ε_{mu} before cracks open because it may vary considerably. In a more developed material structure, composed of inclusions, pores, fibres, etc. the value of ε_{mu} is higher. The similar influence of biaxial or triaxial states of loading is observed in comparison with axial tension. The influence of the rate of loading and a weak or stiff testing machine is decisive.

In general, it is assumed that Portland cement paste offers a maximum tensile strain of about 100 to 200.10^{-6} but smaller values of 60.10^{-6} were also observed.

The determination of the maximum tensile strain is subjected to different factors like the sensitivity of measuring devices and the magnifying power of optical instruments used for crack detection. Also, the definition of matrix failure is not precise enough to exclude all ambiguity.

Another problem is related to high heterogeneity of the matrix, not only when the differences between hard inclusions, weaker paste and voids are considered but also in that the macroscopic regions have considerably different mechanical

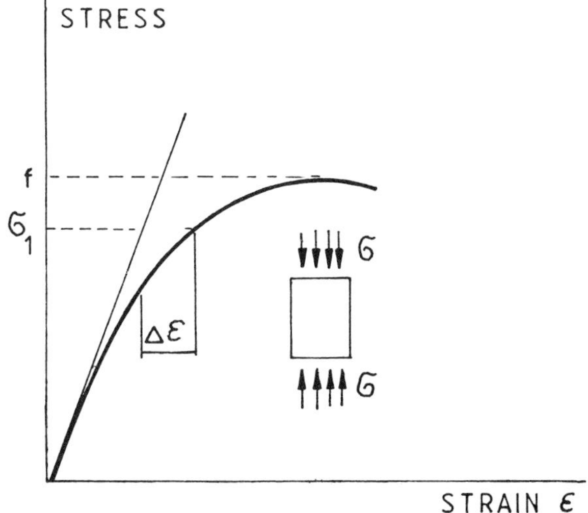

Figure 8.5 Stress–strain diagram for a compressed concrete element. By $\Delta\varepsilon$ apparent strain is denoted under stress σ_1 due to microcracks. (Source: Brandt, A. M., Application of experimental fracture mechanics to cement matrix composites; published by Ossolineum, 1983.) [8.19]

properties. The phenomenon called 'continuous heterogeneities' has been observed and described in [8.18].

When the load is further increased the cracks gradually propagate and interconnect. On the load-deformation or stress–strain diagram (Figure 8.5) deviation from a straight line is due to microcracking which may be observed under relatively low stress.

As the load is increased to about 70–80% of the maximum, there is an abrupt acceleration in cracking and all other phenomena related to progressive fracture. That level of stress is sometimes called the 'discontinuity point', because it corresponds to qualitative modification of several processes:

1. rapid progress of the AE counts due to multiple cracks which open and propagate;
2. inflexion of the transversal strain curve, caused by cracks which are measured as an apparent transversal deformation;
3. decrease of the ultrasonic pulse velocity, because ultrasonic waves cross cracks at lower velocity;
4. increase of the relative volume of material, in which voids start to be an important part of the apparent volume.

All these phenomena are explained by the crack formation and modification of the material structure. When the load is approaching its maximum value, the cracks cross the element, and this finally loses its bearing capacity in a more or less rapid way.

The above mentioned phenomena are presented schematically in Figure 8.6.

The onset of the destruction of the material may be observed on the diagrams, but its definition is somewhat conventional, depending upon assumed criteria. The shapes of particular curves shown in Figure 8.6 are related to properties of the components, to the material's structure, etc.

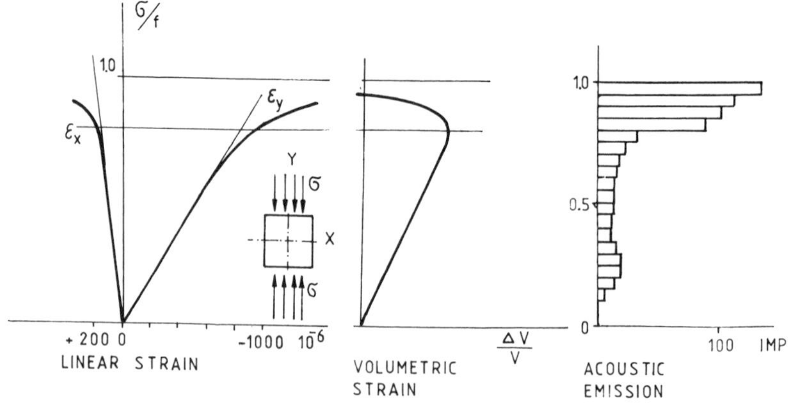

Figure 8.6 Diagrams representing the behaviour of brittle materials under load.

Non-controlled crack propagation beyond the discontinuity point is considered to be when the material destructs. The slow crack propagation before that level shows to what extent the behaviour of the real material is different from that of the brittle one. The external energy furnished by the load is dispersed on the gradual creation of new cracks in the surfaces which are stopped by inclusions of different kinds. The destruction is more abrupt in cement paste than in mortar and concrete, (Figure 8.7), where hard aggregate grains should be circled by cracks as additional energy is dispersed.

The form of the stress–strain or load-displacement curves depends not only upon the material properties but also on the way the load is applied. There are two criteria for classification of testing machines – load or displacement control and stiffness corresponding to capability of energy accumulation.

In machines with displacement control, the load is automatically adjusted to allow for the decreasing rigidity of the tested element. That system enables researchers to follow the gradual destruction of the element and to trace the actual descending branches of the load-displacement curve. In load-controlled machines such adjustment is practically impossible.

In 'soft' testing machines the energy accumulated in the loading system causes rapid fracture after initial cracking. The corresponding curve is modified by that effect and does not in fact reflect the material's properties. The behaviour of a soft machine may be compared to the action of a suspended weight placing a load directly onto a specimen in a tension test.

More often machines used in a research laboratories are displacement controlled. They are of sufficient stiffness and the actual post-cracking behaviour of brittle specimens may be represented thanks to an appropriate decrease of load which

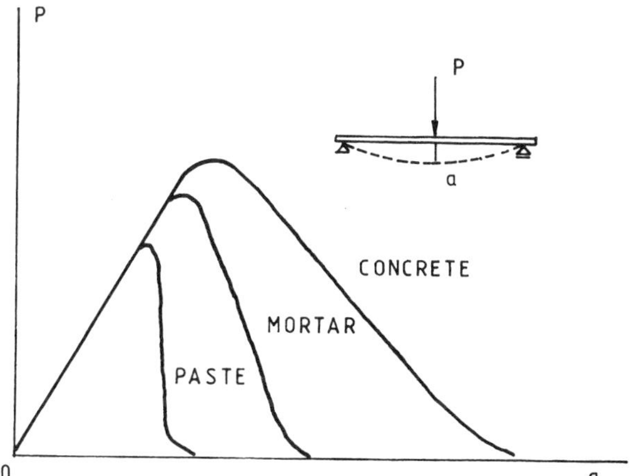

Figure 8.7 Load–deflection curves for materials more or less brittle. (Source: Brandt, A.M., Application of experimental fracture mechanics to cement matrix composites; published by Ossolineum, 1982.) [8.19]

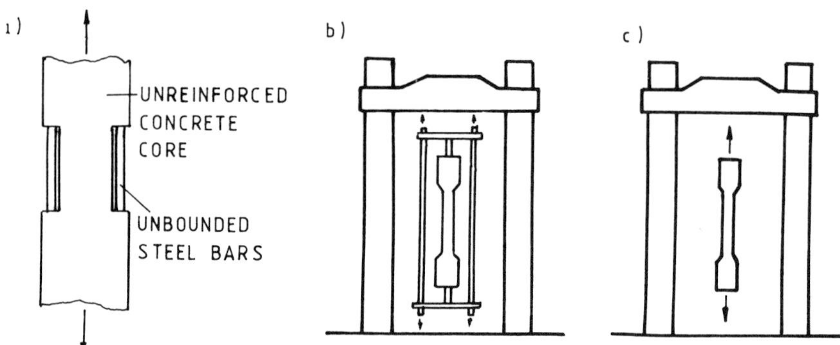

Figure 8.8 Schemes of types of loading equipment, a) non-reinforced concrete core stiffened by steel bars and subjected to tension. (Reproduced from; a) Balavadze, W. K., Influence of reinforcement on the properties of concrete subjected to tension; published in *Beton i Zhelezobeton*, 1959.) (8.20); b) testing with special stiffening frame, (Reproduced with permission from Evans, R.H. and Marathe, M.S., Microcracking and stress–strain curve for concrete in tension; published by RILEM, 1968.) [8.21]; c) ordinary testing of a specimen under tension.

follows the reduction of stiffness of the specimen. In a few cases special constructions were made to increase the stiffness of inadequate machines. Balavadze was probably the first to use special stiffening, in 1959, in the form of unbonded steel bars together with a non-reinforced concrete core which were subjected to axial tension [8.20] (Figure 8.8a). He obtained a maximum strain of about 1500.10^{-6} testing lightweight concrete specimens.

Steel frames were used [8.21] together with a specimen, which were deformed in order to control its deformations (Figure 8.8b). In such a frame, an explosive failure of the specimen such as would occur in an ordinary system where the specimen is placed under direct load is impossible (Figure 8.8c). Balavadze explained the high extensibility of his specimens by the more uniform distribution of internal stresses in the specimen, when failure cannot be caused by rapid crack propagation from the weakest region.

In the non-reinforced brittle matrix specimen subjected to tensile stresses in bending or direct tension testing the destruction is always initiated at the tip of an intrinsic crack which propagates across the specimen without obstruction. In the case of a single fracture only a small amount of energy is required and it is reflected by the small area below the stress–strain curve as compared with that of multiple-cracking. To increase the energy requirement for crack propagation reinforcement is necessary in the form of polymer impregnation, short or continuous fibres, traditional steel bars, etc.

The phenomenon of multiple-cracking occurs on such a material's structure where any crack caused by local stress $\sigma > \sigma_{mu}$ cannot propagate because its tips are blocked by regions of much higher ultimate strength due to any kind of reinforcement for which $\sigma_{fu} \gg \sigma_{mu}$. Increased loading and new external energy produce new cracks in neighbouring weak regions. In such a way a system of multiple cracks of reduced width appears in place of one wide crack. Instead of rapid failure a longer process is observed, in the form of a descending branch of the stress–strain curve. Such kinds of material behaviour are discussed in Section 9.4 and its dynamic character is analysed in [8.22].

It may be concluded that the main factor in the destruction of brittle materials is the propagation and development of cracks. That process is related to a material's structure and particularly to the distribution of weak and strong regions. It is therefore appropriate that fracture mechanics is proposed as the main approach for the explanation and modelling of fracture processes in brittle matrix composites.

In design considerations and for the practical prediction of compressive strength likely after 28 days, it is assumed that dependence is mainly on one parameter: this is the water/cement ratio. A few well known traditional formulae describe that relationship in the following forms –

Féret (1892): $f = \mathrm{A}\left[\frac{V_c}{V_c + V_w + V_a}\right]^2$, here V_c, V_w and V_a are volumes of cement, water and air, respectively; also, Abrams (1918): $f = \mathrm{A}_1 \exp(-\mathrm{B}w/c)$; here w and c are masses of water and cement, respectively; and Bolomey (1922): $f = \mathrm{A}_2(c/w - \mathrm{B}_1)$, here A, A_1, A_2, B and B_1 are empirical constants.

These formulae are used with the appropriate calibration of constants which allow for local conditions, specified properties of components, quality of curing, etc. On the basis of 28-days' compressive strength, other mechanical parameters like tensile strength or Young's modulus may be calculated from standardized formulae.

8.3 Fibres in an uncracked matrix

The application of the law of mixtures to fibre-reinforced composites, as shown in Section 2.5, is possible after several simplifications and assumptions have been made which transform the real behaviour of a highly heterogeneous material into that of an elastic and homogeneous one. Such an approach gives only approximate information which may, however, be useful as a general indication of the stress and strain values and their reciprocal relations.

For the simplest case of uniaxial tension or compression these assumptions are (cf. [8.23]):

- continuity of the matrix, i.e. there are no cracks and stress and strain are below cracking values $\sigma_m < f_m$, $\varepsilon_m < \varepsilon_{mu}$;
- perfect bond between matrix and fibres is maintained $\varepsilon_m = \varepsilon_f = \varepsilon$;
- only longitudinal stress and strain components are considered in the matrix as well as in the fibres σ_m, σ_f, ε_m, ε_f, without transverse components, i.e. the Poisson's coefficient is equal to zero.

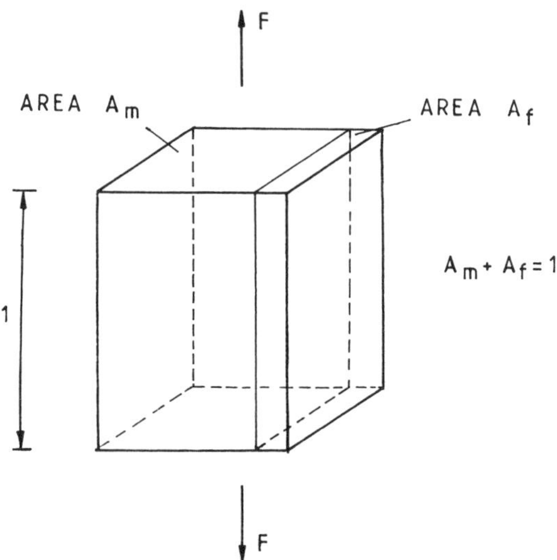

Figure 8.9 Two-phase composite material represented as a two-component model.

An element composed of brittle matrix and aligned continuous fibres may be considered as a two-component model subjected to uniform loading, as shown in Figure 8.9.

For unit total volume $V = V_m + V_f = 1$ and area $\mathrm{A} = \mathrm{A}_m + \mathrm{A}_f = 1$, the relations are simple, load $F = \sigma \mathrm{A} = \sigma_m \mathrm{A}_m + \sigma_f \mathrm{A}_f = (E_m \mathrm{A}_m + E_f \mathrm{A}_f)\varepsilon$,

$$\sigma = \frac{F}{\mathrm{A}_m + \mathrm{A}_f} = \sigma_m(1 - V_f) + \sigma_f V_f. \tag{8.1}$$

Because equal strain of both phases is assumed, therefore

$$\frac{\sigma}{E} = \frac{\sigma_f}{E_f} = \frac{\sigma_m}{E_m},$$

and

$$E = E_m(1 - V_f) + E_f V_f. \tag{8.2}$$

From equation 8.1 and equation 8.2 it is clear that for low fibre content the influence of fibres on stress or Young's modulus of composite is negligible.

Let us consider following numerical values:
$V_f = 0.02$, $E_m = 40\,\mathrm{GPa}$, $E_f = 210\,\mathrm{GPa}$, which represent a cement-based matrix reinforced with a rather high content of continuous steel fibres. Then

$$\sigma = \sigma_m(1 - V_f) + \sigma_m \frac{E_f}{E_m} V_f,$$

$$\frac{E}{E_m} = \frac{\sigma}{\sigma_m} = (1 - V_f) + \frac{E_f}{E_m} V_f = 1.085.$$

In the above example the quantitative influence of fibre-reinforcement on:

- average stress in a composite material corresponding to the cracking of the matrix, it means to strain ε_{mu}, and
- Young's modulus of the composite material is equal to 8.5%.

When, instead of continuous fibres, the short fibres or wires are used their efficiency should be accounted for by a coefficient $\eta_\ell \leqslant 1.0$.

Decreased efficiency is caused by the fact that the load is transferred from the matrix to the fibre by bond stress τ or friction on the fibre surface. Assuming that stress is uniformly distributed along the fibre length a concept of critical length l_{cr} was introduced [8.24] as a boundary between shorter fibres which are pulled out of the matrix and longer ones which break under tensile stress. That critical length may be derived from the equilibrium between the anchorage force acting on half of the fibre length on one side of the crack, and the tensile force:

$$\tfrac{1}{2} l_{cr} \pi d \tau = \tfrac{1}{4} \pi d^2 f_{tf}$$

$$l_{cr} = \tfrac{1}{2} d \frac{f_{tf}}{\tau} \tag{8.3}$$

where d – fibre diameter, τ – limit value of bond stress, f_{tf} – tensile strength of fibre.

The behaviour of the fibre in a tensioned element is presented in Figure 8.10 as a function of fibre length, assuming uniform distribution of the bond stress.

In these assumptions the efficiency coefficient was calculated as:

$$\text{for} \quad l \geqslant l_{cr} \quad \eta_l = 1 - \frac{l_{cr}}{2l} \tag{8.4}$$

$$\text{for} \quad l \leqslant l_{cr} \quad \eta_l = \frac{l}{2l_{cr}} \tag{8.5}$$

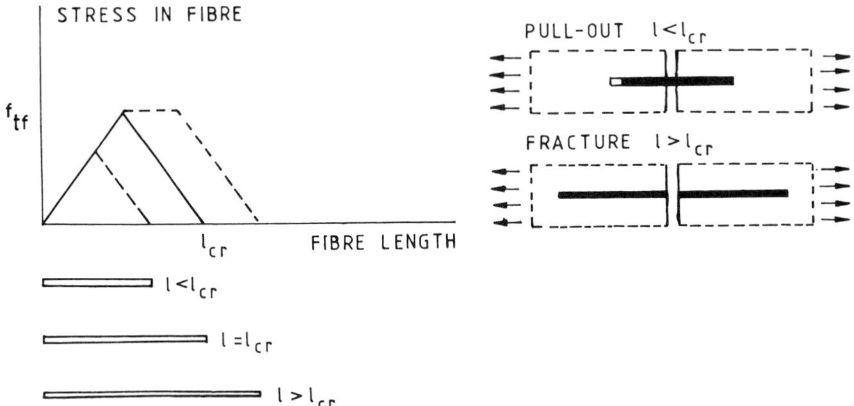

Figure 8.10 Behaviour of a fibre in an element subject to tension for different fibre length.

For brittle matrices the formulae (equation 8.4) and (equation 8.5) seem to be inadequate because the bond is not always perfect and cracking of the matrix modifies the phenomena completely. Several authors proposed different approaches, e.g. [8.25], [8.26] and [8.27].

Laws indicated that in the pre-cracking stage the composite strain around fibres should be accounted for [8.27] and the formula for the limit case when $\varepsilon_m = \varepsilon_{mu}$ was:

$$\eta_l = 1 - \frac{l_{cr}\varepsilon_{mu}}{2l\varepsilon_{fu}} \tag{8.6}$$

for long fibres with $l \geqslant l_{cr}$, where ε_{mu} and ε_{fu} are ultimate strain values for matrix and fibre, respectively.

For the post-cracking stage Laws proposed two formulae:
For long fibres with,

$$l > 2l'_{cr}\ \eta_l = \frac{l_{cr}}{2l}\left(2 - \frac{\tau_d}{\tau_s}\right); \tag{8.7}$$

for short fibres with,

$$l < 2l'_{cr}\ \eta_l = \frac{1}{2l_{cr}\left(2 - \dfrac{\tau_d}{\tau_s}\right)} \tag{8.8}$$

where $l'_{cr} = \frac{1}{2}l_{cr}(2 - \tau_d/\tau_s)$, τ_d is the static value of bond strength and τ_s is the friction during pull-out.

In the case of random distribution 2D or 3D, the fibres which are not parallel to the principal strain direction have considerably reduced efficiency. That reduction was determined experimentally and calculated using various geometrical and mechanical assumptions, by several authors, without reaching coherent results. The values proposed by different authors for directional coefficient η_ϑ are shown in Table 8.1.

Certain authors proposed to multiply the coefficients to obtain an overall efficiency coefficient $\eta = \eta_\vartheta \eta_l$, e.g. [8.28], but others suggested special combination of both, e.g. [8.27].

Table 8.1 Directional efficiency coefficient η_ϑ for short fibres

Year	Authors	2D	3D
1952	Cox [8.31]	0.333	0.167
1964	Romualdi, Mandel [8.8]	–	0.4053
1964	Krenchel [8.24]	0.375	0.200
1971	Parimi, Rao [8.32]	–	0.5–0.636
1972	Kar, Pal [8.33]	0.444	0.333
1973	Avestom, Kelly [8.34]	0.6366	0.500

These considerations above described have only limited importance for the design and forecasting of the mechanical properties of brittle matrix fibre-reinforced materials prior to cracking, because of the low fibre contents. Discussion of coefficients η_l and η_ϑ may be considered as interesting refinements, which are difficult to verify quantitatively as to their influence on the composite's behaviour. Furthermore, a greater significance of technological factors is to be expected – the introduction of fibres always creates additional difficulties in compaction of the fresh mix and its porosity is usually higher than that of plain matrix.

It may be also observed that when the strength or stiffness of the composite have to be increased before its cracking, that task may be made easier by modification of water/cement ratio than by the introduction of fibres.

For brittle matrix composites the influence of fibres on cracking stress and corresponding Young's modulus is negligible in the scope of the volumes of fibres usually applied. However, when the steel fibre volume fraction exceeds 2%, then the tensile strength of the matrix is enhanced. Further increase of reinforcement, together with applications of appropriate technology, may modify the behaviour of the composite considerably, improving its deformability, [8.29]. SIFCON is one of the examples of such a material, cf. Section 14.2.4.

Theoretical studies concerning the influence of fibres on the behaviour of composite material provided considerable knowledge which is used extensively for high strength composite materials where the fibre volume fraction is high and tends to be exploited mostly in an uncracked state. In brittle matrix composites the situation is somewhat different – the fibre volume fraction is usually low and its influence in an uncracked state is probably covered by a large scatter which is characteristic for these materials' properties. The fibres act on, and modify considerably, the brittle matrix behaviour only after cracking.

Considerations concerning behaviour in an uncracked stage are presented here in limited extent only and more information may be found out in [8.30].

8.4 Fibre-reinforced matrices as two-phase composites

The fibre-reinforced composites, namely asbestos cements and glassfibre-reinforced polymers were analysed as two-phase materials, [8.25]. Two different theories were proposed to calculate Young's modulus and Poisson's coefficient is also given in the second of these:

theory 1
$$E_c = E_m + V_f\left(\frac{3E_f}{8} - E_m\right) \tag{8.9}$$

theory 2
$$E_c = \mathrm{k}E_m + \frac{3V_fE_f}{8} - \frac{\left(\mathrm{k}\nu E + \frac{E_fV_f}{8}\right)^2}{\mathrm{k}E_m + \frac{3E_fV_f}{8}} \tag{8.10}$$

$$\nu_c = \frac{\mathrm{k}\nu E_m + \dfrac{E_f V_f}{8}}{\mathrm{k}E_m + \dfrac{3E_f V_f}{8}} \tag{8.11}$$

where $\mathrm{k} = \dfrac{1 - V_f}{1 - \nu^2}$ and Poisson's coefficient $\nu = \nu_m = \nu_f$.

Krenchel proposed to determine the tensile strength of the fibre reinforced composite from a formula:

$$f_{tc} = f_{tf}\eta V_f + \sigma'_m(1 - V_f), \tag{8.12}$$

where f_{tf} is the tensile strength of fibres, η is the overall coefficient of efficiency and σ'_m is the matrix stress corresponding to the ultimate deformation of the fibres. In the materials tested by Krenchel the ultimate strain of the fibres was always lower than that of the matrix. In other kinds of concrete-like composites reinforced with metallic, polymer or organic fibres that relation is the opposite.

The formulae proposed by Krenchel were partly verified experimentally [8.24]. Namely, agreement within a few percent has been found between calculated and observed values of Young's modulus and Poisson's coefficient. Also values of f_{tc} were only about 8% higher than the experimental ones. However, the experiments on other cement-based composites were not completed and asbestos cements were tested only under bending and shock. Other proposed formulae derived from the law of mixtures are described briefly below.

Kar and Pal proposed semi-empirical formulae for the ultimate tensile stress under bending (modulus of rupture) of fibre-reinforced concrete [8.33]:

$$\begin{aligned} f_{fc} &= f_{fm} 1.16 s_e^{-0.376} && \text{for } s_e \leq 1'', \\ f_{fc} &= f_{fm}(1.26 - 0.1 s_e) && \text{for } s_e > 1'', \end{aligned} \tag{8.13}$$

where s_e is effective fibre spacing expressed in inches, calculated from the following relation:

$$s_e = 9.545 \frac{d}{\sqrt{\dfrac{\eta v_f l}{d}\left(1 - \dfrac{l}{348d}\right)}}, \tag{8.14}$$

here l and d are length and diameter of a single fibre, η is the efficiency coefficient with values proposed by the authors for particular cases between 0.333 and 0.494. The formula in equation 8.14 was derived assuming that the bond stress is distributed along the fibre length equal to $58d$. That assumption has not been justified. Both values η and s_e have no geometrical meaning and cannot be directly verified.

Another group of semi-empirical formulae have also been derived, [8.35] and [8.36]. For the ultimate tensile stress and modulus of rupture of SFRC it was proposed:

$$f_{tc} = f_{tm}(1 - V_f) + 0.82\tau\frac{l}{d}V_f \qquad \text{(tension)} \tag{8.15}$$

$$f_{tc} = \frac{\beta'}{\alpha'}f_{fm}(1 - V_f) + 0.82\beta'\tau\frac{l}{d}V_f \qquad \text{(bending)} \tag{8.16}$$

where $\alpha' = \dfrac{f_{fm}}{f_{tm}}$, $\beta' = \dfrac{f_{fc}}{f_{tc}}$,

τ is the mean ultimate bond strength, f_{tm} and f_{fm} are tensile and flexural matrix strength, respectively. The numerical coefficient 0.82 is equal to the double value of the efficiency coefficient derived in [8.8]. The equation (equation 8.16) may concern both stages of the composite material behaviour – the first crack opening and ultimate strength, and in its general form the relation between composite strength f_c and matrix strength f_m is proposed as it follows:

$$f_c = Af_m(1 - V_f) + B\frac{l}{d}V_f. \tag{8.17}$$

The numerical values of A and B were determined after several series of tests of elements made of mortar and concrete and reinforced with short steel fibres – for first crack opening $A = 0.843$, $B = 2.93$; for ultimate strength $A = 0.97$, $B = 3.41$.

The form of these formulae is obviously related to the law of mixtures but other assumptions and coefficients are derived from tests of a given series of specimens. The general application of the formulae proposed would probably require an appropriate calibration of coefficients to examined elements, their dimensions and material properties.

Similar formulae have been proposed for axial compression [8.37] together with calibration of applied numerical coefficients for various shapes of specimens and other conditions.

Several other approaches to the behaviour of composite materials were based on the law of mixtures and for fibres-reinforced elements – on such characteristics as l/d, $l\tau/d_f$, $V_f\sqrt{(l/d)^3}$ and so on. In most cases satisfactory agreement was obtained with experimental results, provided that the numerical coefficients were well selected.

It may be concluded that the application of the law of mixtures may have only local importance, i.e. limited to accepted assumptions and introduced coefficients. There are two deficiencies of such an approach:

1. The fracture process is not considered and not included in proposed formulae which in fact represent other fictitious processes.
2. The material structure is considered in an approximate way.

The simplification of the structured materials, in general, may give unsatisfactory results for brittle matrix composites, because their internal structures are constructed just to increase composite strength and fracture toughness. Also, the existence and influence of weak points where rupture is initiated are neglected. Consequently, a material's structure should be taken into account in design procedures and strength verification.

From these various analytical approaches, confirmed by experimental data, several general observations have been proposed as to the influence of fibres on composite strength. On that basis, it was concluded [8.35] that the addition of 2% of steel-fibres with $l/d = 100$ to a concrete mix with cement/sand ratio 0.4, water/cement ratio 0.55 and 20% of coarse aggregate gives:

- approximately twice the flexural strength;
- increase of compressive strength by 10–25%.

Another analytical approach to flexural strength is based on the stress distribution analysis in a cross-section and on the application of equilibrium conditions in an analogous way as it is in classical theories of reinforced concrete elements. That approach has the advantage of using traditional methods and exploiting all available data concerning applied material components. Also, test results and measurement data may usefully be introduced to improve the precision of the calculations. Proposals along those lines have been published, [8.38], [8.39] and others. A comprehensive method for design and verification of fibre-reinforced elements for given limit states has also been published [8.40]. Its aim was to follow the basic procedure of a designer who should check bending moments in the main limit states. Here only two limit states are considered – crack opening limit state and ultimate limit state (fracture). A scheme of the procedure is given in Figure 8.11 and its main steps are as follows.

The 'designer' obtains from the 'experimentor' the values of bending moments in two considered states: M^f and M^u. Also, strain measurements on lower and upper faces of tested specimens are provided: $\varepsilon_{mc}, \varepsilon^u_{mc}, \varepsilon^u_{mt}$. These data are introduced to two equilibrium equations:
at the first crack opening,

$$\begin{aligned} D_m + D_f &= T_m + T_f \\ M^f &= (T_m + T_f)\tfrac{2}{3}h \end{aligned} \tag{8.18}$$

and at the maximum bending moment,

$$\begin{aligned} D_m + D_f &= T_m + T_f + NFz \\ M^u &= (T_m + T_f)\tfrac{2}{3}(h - z) + NFz(\tfrac{2}{3}h - \tfrac{1}{6}z). \end{aligned} \tag{8.19}$$

The following notations are used:

M^f and M^u – cracking and failure bending moments, respectively;
D_m and D_f – internal forces due to compression in matrix and fibres;
T^f and T^m – forces due to traction in matrix and fibres;
z – crack depth;

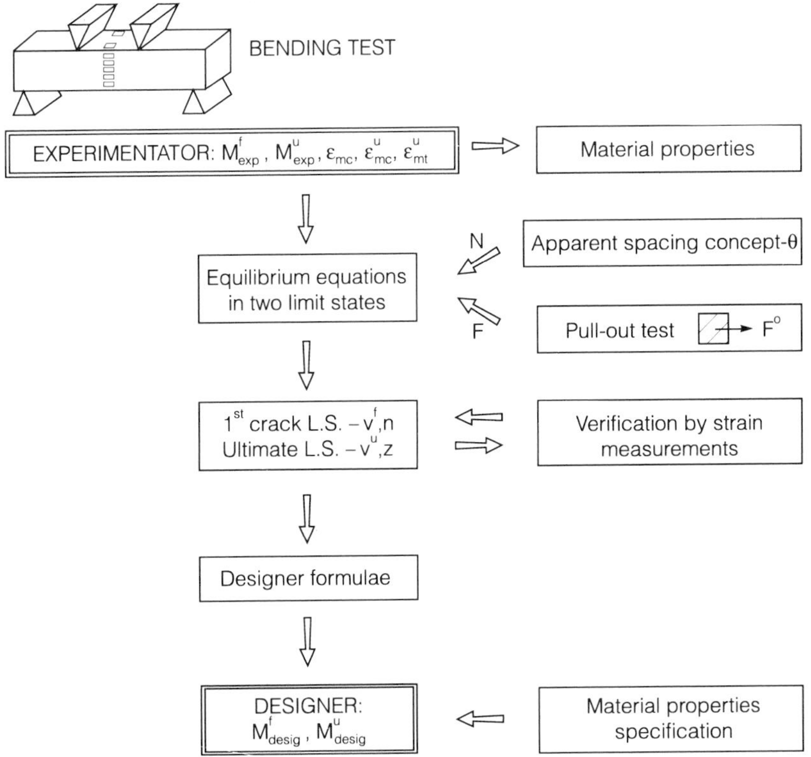

Figure 8.11 Scheme of the application of experimental data for a design procedure. (Source: Babut, R. and Brandt, A.M., The method of testing and analysing of steel fibre reinforced concrete elements in flexure; published by The Construction Press, 1978.) [8.40]

b and h – beam width and depth;
N – number of fibres which cross the crack of unit depth.

Equation 8.18 and equation 8.19 describe situations shown in Figure 8.12 concerning the central cross-section of the beam.

After the introduction of all necessary data, the equation 8.18 is transformed into the following:

$$\frac{\varepsilon_{mc}[1+(E/E_f)V_f\mathrm{k}]}{\varepsilon^u_{mt}[n+(E/E_f)V_f\mathrm{k}]}=\frac{v^f}{h-v^f}$$

$$m^f=\tfrac{1}{3}hbv^f\varepsilon^u_{mt}E_m[n+(E_f/E_m)V_f\mathrm{k}]. \tag{8.20}$$

Here V_f is the volume fraction of fibres, $\mathrm{k}=0.4$ is the efficiency coefficient for fibres distributed at random (3D), E_f and E_m are the Young's moduli of fibres and matrix, respectively, n is the ratio of the matrix of Young's moduli for tension and compression $n=E_{mt}/E_m$ and v^f is the position of the neutral axis in that limit state.

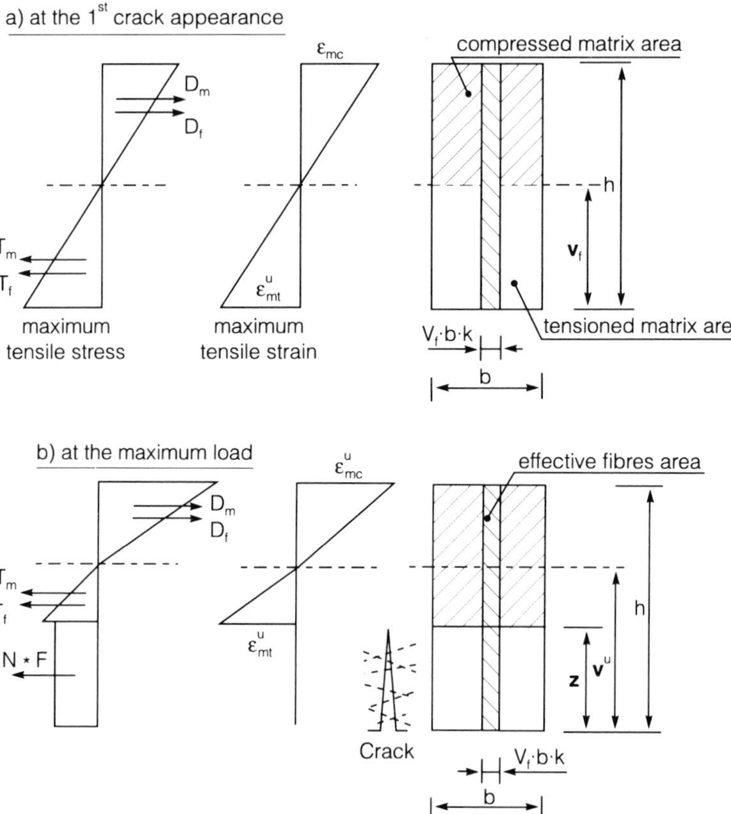

Figure 8.12 Strain and stress diagrams in the midspan cross-section of a beam in two limit states. (Source: after Babut, R. and Brandt, A.M., The method of testing and analyzing of steel-fibre-reinforced concrete elements in flexure; published by The Construction Press, 1978.) [8.40]

Similar transformation of equation 8.13 leads to the following:

$$\frac{\varepsilon^u_{mc}}{\varepsilon^u_{mt}} = \frac{v^u - z[n + (E_f/E_m)V_f k]}{h - v^u[1 + (E_f/E_m)V_f k]} + \frac{2NFz}{\varepsilon^u_{mt}(h - v^u)[1 + (E_f/E_m)V_f k]}$$

$$M^u = \tfrac{1}{3}b(v^u - z)(h - z)\varepsilon^u_{mt}E_m[n + (E_f/E_m)V_f k] + NFz(\tfrac{2}{3}h - \tfrac{1}{6}z). \qquad (8.21)$$

Here v^u indicates the position of the neutral axis at failure.

The number of fibres N is determined from the formulae given in Section 6.6, assuming the distribution of appropriate fibres. To calculate the force in a single fibre the data from the pull-out test are applied. Then, from equation 8.14 two unknown values are determined, namely, n and V_f.

In a similar way, the unknown values of z and v^u are calculated from equation 8.15.

The proposed procedure has been verified and confirmed by tests and measurements of strain distribution on the lateral faces of tested beams and a satisfactory agreement has been obtained. In the cases of designing or verification an appropriate selection of unknown values, designed values and average material characteristics are necessary to perform the calculations. For example, the only data known to the designer are – the required bending moments and materials' characteristics. For given dimensions of a beam, the strength parameters are to be verified in both limit states.

The procedure may be modified to suit various materials, limit states, beam dimensions, etc.

8.5 Pull-out of fibres from brittle matrices

8.5.1 GENERAL REMARKS

The problem of the fibre pull-out was studied by many authors because the transfer of load from the matrix to the fibres is particularly important for the efficiency of the fibre reinforcement. The partial or approximate solution to this problem is necessary for any rational design of the fibre-reinforced composite material.

There are at least two objectives to studying the fibre–matrix bond in all aspects of this process.

The first aim is to understand the nature of the bond and its relationship to the main material and technological parameters – quality of matrix, type of fibre surface and shape of a single fibre, chemical affinity of materials, influence of transversal compression due to matrix shrinkage and external load, etc. Similarly, the variation of the bond along the fibre length and its possible evolution with time are of interest. All these parameters may be considered as variables in a problem of material design or optimization and through their better understanding increased possibilities are opened up for purposeful material modifications. This is the justification for all the sophisticated tests and theoretical models proposed by various authors.

The second objective is to furnish the data necessary for material design in the form of characteristics of the bearing capacity of one single fibre. Usually two values are sufficient – maximum value P_{max} corresponding to the end of the elastic behaviour and P_f characterizing the friction region of the load–displacement curve after debonding. These values of forces are often replaced for the purposes of calculation by the values of apparent stresses τ_{max} and τ_f, respectively, assuming a uniform distribution of stress along an embedded section of the fibre.

The fibre–matrix bond is also mentioned in other chapters, for instance questions related to interface layers are examined in Section 7.3. The role of load transmission to fibres in cracking and fracture is studied in Chapters 9 and 10, respectively.

The fibre–matrix interaction is considered in more detail here in relation to short chopped steel-fibres. For other fibres the phenomena are different because they result from some other chemical affinity, shape of fibres, ratio of fibre and matrix or Young's moduli. Here, there are much less reliable experimental data and proposed theoretical models than for steel-fibres.

8.5.2 STEEL CHOPPED FIBRES

In an elastic and uncracked matrix the stress is transferred to short fibres by elastic bond stress. The fibres are considered as reinforcing inclusions. The situation of a single fibre in an imaginary cylinder cut out of the bulk matrix and subjected to tensile load in the direction parallel to the fibre was considered as shown in Figure 8.13. Several models were all based, more or less, on the shear lag theory proposed in [8.31] which derived that the load P in the fibre at distance x from one end may be represented by the following relation:

$$P(x) = EA\varepsilon\left[1 - \frac{\cosh\beta(l/2 - x)}{\cosh\beta(l/2)}\right] \tag{8.22}$$

where $\beta = \sqrt{H/EA}$ and $H = \dfrac{2\pi G}{\log(d/D)}$,

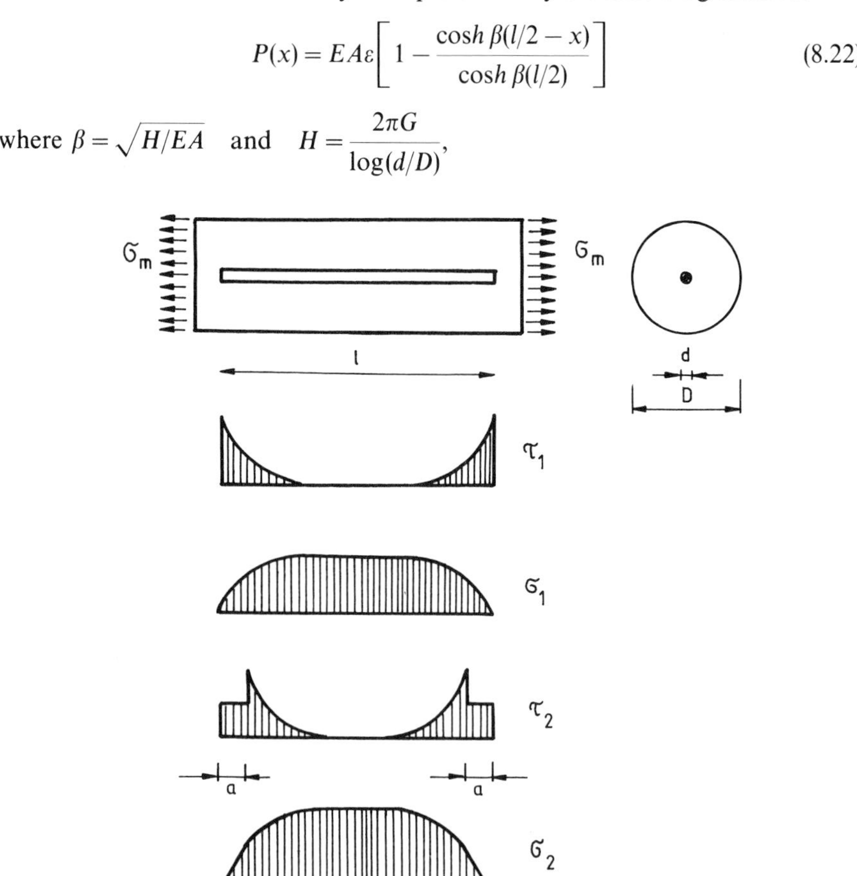

Figure 8.13 Behaviour of a steel-fibre in elastic matrix subjected to tension.

E and A are Young's modulus and cross-sectional area of the fibre, respectively, ε is the uniform matrix strain, and G is the shear modulus of the matrix.

Corresponding diagrams of bond stress τ and tensile stress σ in the fibre are shown in Figure 8.13. Values of the tensile stress $\sigma(x)$ in the fibre are obtained directly from equation 8.22.

Equation 8.22 and the diagrams in Figure 8.13 were discussed in view of their applicability to cement-based matrices. The solutions proposed in [8.31] and by other authors are based on several assumptions which are not satisfied in these materials.

The brittle matrices are characterized by low tensile strength, and the first cracks in the interface and fibre–matrix debonding occur under relatively a small load. The system of microcracks is present from the beginning, i.e. already before application of any external load. Diagrams for τ_1 and σ_1 in Figure 8.13 concern elastic behaviour and complete fibre–matrix bond. The values of the elastic bond strength τ_u are relatively low and after debonding along a certain distance a, the diagram of the bond stress takes the form as shown for τ_2 and σ_2. The values of tensile stress σ in a fibre are also low due to weak bond stress and consequently the tensile stress in the fibre represents only a small part of its strength. According to detailed calculations in [8.22] for a bond strength equal approximately to 15 MPa, the stress in the fibres does not exceed 200 MPa, which is a small part of the fibre strength. In most cases, the effective bond stress and consequently the fibre tensile stress are even lower.

An excellent review of theoretical studies and models based on shear lag theories is published in [8.30] and there is no value in repeating it here. Considerations given below concern the effective behaviour of steel-fibres in cracked cement matrix and are aimed at conclusions derived for the design of this kind of material.

The transfer of forces between the fibres and the matrix may be broken down for case of reasoning into a few mechanisms [8.41]:

1. Elastic shear bond is a stress in the interface when its bond strength is not exceeded, it is supposed that the elastic shear bond is uniformly distributed along the fibre.
2. Frictional shear bond occurs when the bond strength is exceeded and certain relative displacement (slip) occurs.
3. Mechanical anchorage is caused by indentation or irregularities on the fibre surface, or is due to the hooks on the fibre ends.

These mechanisms are in fact complicated by the interference of the neighbouring fibres and other inclusions, by variation of the matrix strength as a function of the distance from the fibre surface, and by radial tensile or compressive stress which may be exerted on the fibre, etc.

After debonding, the bond stress is gradually replaced by friction. The models for bond and friction combined were proposed in [8.42], [8.43] and others.

The role of fibres in a cracked matrix is usually studied on various kinds of

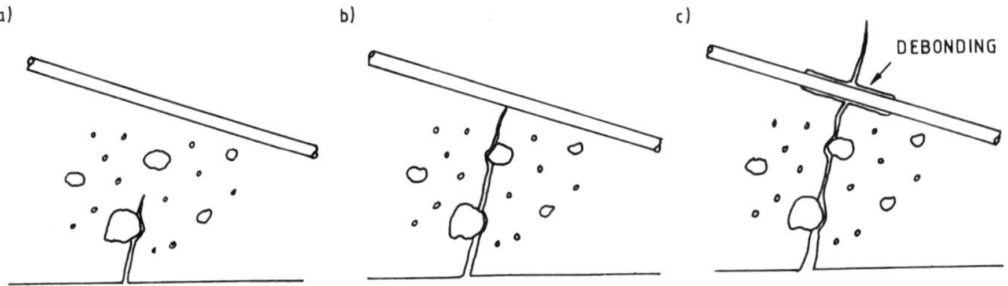

Figure 8.14 Successive stages of crack propagation across a steel fibre.

pull-out tests which simulate the situation of a fibre crossed by a crack as is shown schematically in Figure 8.14. After propagation across a non-reinforced matrix (a) a crack arrives at a fibre (b) and is stopped. Its further progress is conditioned by an additional energy input, e.g. by an increase of external load, producing tensile stress perpendicular to the crack plane. Then, the crack is crossing the fibre but a finite crack width at that point is possible only after partial debonding of the fibre and its elastic deformation (c). This phenomenon is a basis for the pull-out test in which a fibre is subjected to a force pulling out from the matrix.

The pull-out test was proposed by Greszczuk in 1969 [8.44] who derived and solved an equation relating external load to the interface shear stress. The verification of this solution was made by a pull-out test of aluminium rods with variable embedment length from the epoxy resin matrix.

Pull-out tests were executed by numerous authors and excellent reviews of methods and results are published in [8.45] and [8.30]. In Figure 8.15, two examples are given of the test arrangements for single fibres (a) and for groups of fibres (b) and corresponding load–displacement curves after [8.46] and [8.47]. The curves for single fibres show the difference between the pull-out process for plain and indented fibres. The main difference focuses on the area under the curve; this means that to pull-out an indented fibre a larger amount of energy is required than for a plain one. The influence of the neighbouring fibres in a group is shown by the curves in Figure 8.15b – it was the reinforcement of the matrix by neighbouring fibres which caused the increase of pull-out force for $V_f = 1.2\%$ than for $V_f = 0.8$ and 0.36%. The angle of direction of the fibres $\alpha = 30^\circ$ with respect to the direction of the pull-out force also modifies the load–displacement curve.

In pull-out tests several modifications may be applied to account for real conditions:

1. influence of other neighbouring fibres by testing simultaneously groups of fibres;
2. fibres which are situated in such a way that the angle other than 90° appears between the fibre and the crack;
3. load which is applied in a dynamic way, producing fatigue, etc.

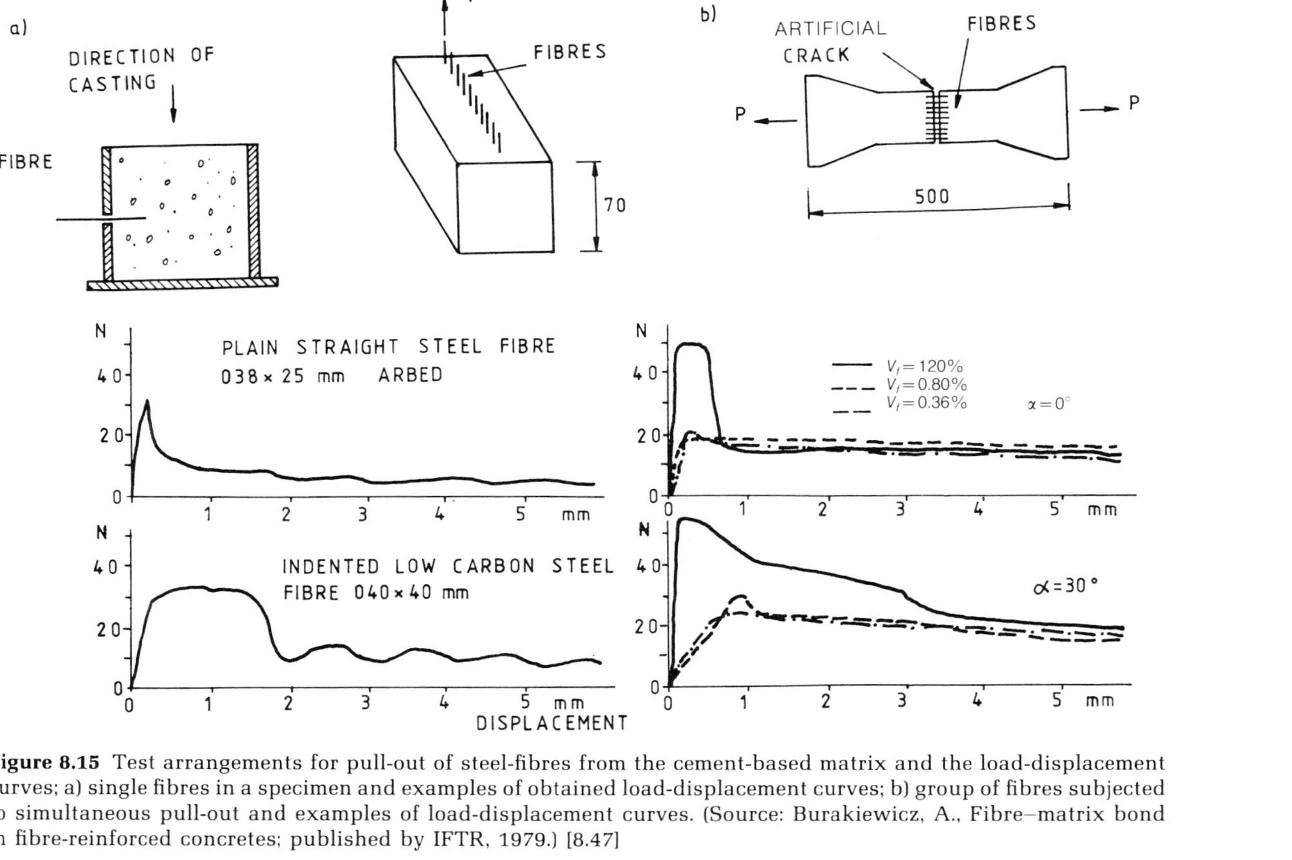

Figure 8.15 Test arrangements for pull-out of steel-fibres from the cement-based matrix and the load-displacement curves; a) single fibres in a specimen and examples of obtained load-displacement curves; b) group of fibres subjected to simultaneous pull-out and examples of load-displacement curves. (Source: Burakiewicz, A., Fibre–matrix bond in fibre-reinforced concretes; published by IFTR, 1979.) [8.47]

In pull-out tests not only the fibre properties may be tested but also those of the matrix, of the technology of casting, etc.

Tests of composite elements with specially prepared fibres to modify their bond in an artificial way are not considered in detail here. In an extreme case of fibres without any kind of adherence their role is limited to inclusions transmitting only compressive stresses. It is sufficient to mention that approximately 25% improvement in the efficiency of steel-fibres, in elements subjected to bending, has been obtained by chemical degreasing [8.48].

From a pull-out test, two values are usually considered as characteristic:

1. maximum load denoted P_{max} corresponding to the end of linear displacement and beginning of the debonding process;
2. load P_f corresponding approximately to the friction during the pull-out process itself.

Both these values, together with a characteristic value for elastic displacement v_o (Figure 8.16) may be used for attempts at calculating the bearing capacity and fracture energy of fibre-reinforced elements, cf. Section 10.3. For that aim, in many studies the values of average stress were calculated, assuming uniform distribution of stress along the embedment length l:

$$\tau_{av} = \frac{P}{\pi d l}, \tag{8.23}$$

where d is the fibre diameter.

Average interfacial shear stress τ_{av} has no physical meaning and is used only to compare the pull-out behaviour of fibres of different dimensions, as it is

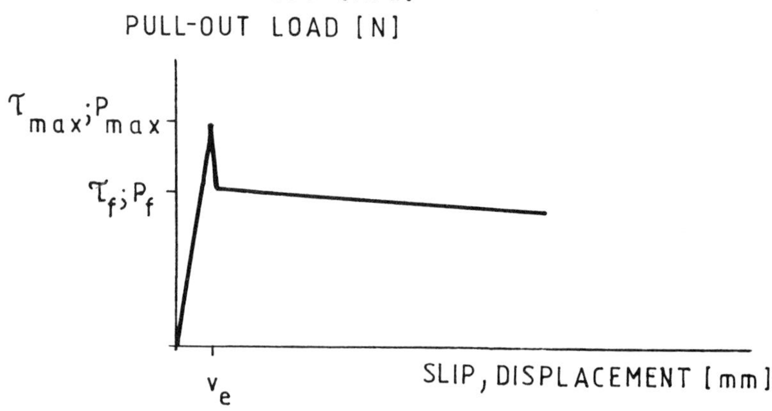

Figure 8.16 Typical diagram of pull-out load versus displacement, numbers denote points, when microscope observation were executed in tests reported by Potrzebowski. (Source: Potrzebowski, J., Processes of debonding and pull-out of steel-fibres from cement matrix; published by IFTR, 1991.) [8.53]

correctly indicated in [8.30]. The question of whether the stress is in fact uniformly distributed cannot be answered by simple pull-out tests only, because the measurements of load and displacement are executed outside the embedment zone.

All these tests lead to apparently justified conclusions that until P_{max} is reached the preceding linear part of the load–deflection curve corresponds to the elastic shear bond, and that the debonding processes start just at the maximum pull-out force. Such a simple image was completed by observations published in [8.49] which have shown that the crack appears along the pulled fibre at a certain distance of a few micrometers from its surface. These observations in the fibre–matrix interface after the pull-out test, corroborated well with measurements of micro-hardness of the interface, which have shown that the weakest layer was situated at some distance from the fibre surface (cf. Chapter 7).

The problem of how to observe the processes in the interface was solved in [8.50] where two series of combined tests were successfully realized. In the first one, precise observations were made of the fibre–matrix interface simultaneously with the pulling-out of the fibre from the matrix. For that purpose, special specimens were made in which the interface was partly exposed for external observation and measurements (Figure 8.17a). An example of the image given by an optical microscope is shown in Figure 8.17b, cf. also Figure 7.7. The load–deflection curve on which points corresponding to observations are indicated (Figure 8.17c), together with obtained images, proved that this crack had appeared already during the linear part of load – displacement curve.

By these observations it has also been confirmed that the crack was situated in the interface and not along the fibre surface.

In the next series of tests detailed in [8.51], [8.52] and [8.53] the relative displacements between fibre and matrix were measured in the interface by the method of laser interferometry. The results allowed the effective processes in the fibre–matrix interface to be represented in the following way. In Figure 8.17d three curves show the relative displacement between the points of the fibre and points situated on both sides of the matrix. The measurements by the speckle method were precise enough to easily distinguish parts of a micrometer. It was observed, as is shown on the examples in Figure 8.17d, that already an initial part of the pull-out curve (Figure 8.17c, points 1, 2 and 3) corresponded to measurable displacements between fibre and matrix.

After these results, the pull-out behaviour may be described in the following manner.

In the first stage, the elastic shear stress τ is transferred through the interface from the fibre to the matrix. This is reflected in the first part of the linear relation in Figure 8.16. In the next stage, the bond strength τ_u is reached at the beginning of the embedment zone and a crack starts to propagate in the interface along the fibre. The displacement between the fibre and the matrix, also called a slip, is observed and measured. The load is, however, transferred across the crack by friction and the existence of a crack is not visible on the bond–slip or

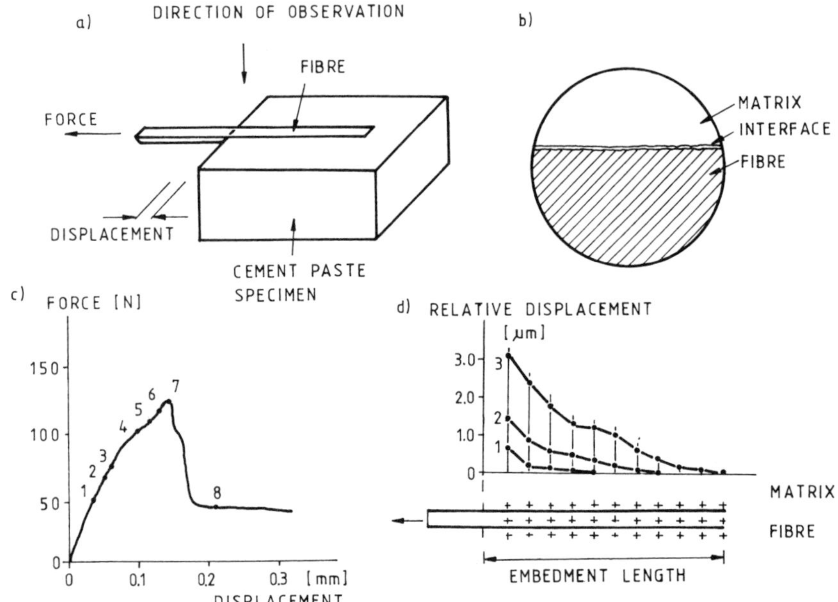

Figure 8.17 Load–slip curve combined with microscopic observations and measurements of the displacements in the interface; a) cement paste specimen with exposed fibre; b) scheme of microscopic image of the interface; c) force–displacement curve with points of observations and measurements; d) curves of relative displacements of the fibre with respect to the matrix, corresponding to points 1, 2 and 3 in the force–displacement curve. (Source: Potrzebowski, J., Processes of debonding and pull-out of steel-fibres from cement matrix; published by IFTR, 1991.) [8.53]

load–displacement diagram, which remains linear. Due to friction, the crack does not correspond to a decrease of the load until P_{max} is reached. At this stage, according to measurements and observations, not only has the crack reached the end of the embedment zone, but quite appreciable slip also occurs even at the end of that zone. The final stage corresponds to a gradual decrease of the load, accompanied by increasing pull-out of the fibre. The rate of the load decrease is closely related to the quality of the fibre surface or to the efficiency of end anchorages. This stage has not been subjected to close observations and measurements in the investigations published in [8.53].

The pull-out processes in brittle matrices were represented by different theoretical models. The linear model for the fibre–matrix bond was proposed in [8.54] in the form:

$$\tau = \mathrm{k}s \tag{8.24}$$

where k is a constant which characterizes the fibre and matrix properties in this process. This model was accepted and developed by several authors, including [8.46] and [8.47].

Such a simple relationship has not been confirmed by [8.53] where it has been proposed to consider the bond stress τ as a function of two variables:

$$\tau = f[s(x), x] \tag{8.25}$$

After the tests reported in [8.53] the model was proposed in the following form:

$$\tau(x) = \tau_{max} tgh\left[A\left(\frac{s}{s_u}\right)^{\beta}\right] e^{(-Bx/l_z)} \tag{8.26}$$

where τ_{max} is the maximum shear stress in the interface, of adherence or friction nature, s_u is the value of the slip at P_{max}, l_z is the length of the embedment zone, and A, B and β are coefficients which characterize the mechanical properties of fibres and matrix.

In the tests reported in [8.53] the coefficients were proposed as follows: $A = 3.5$, $B = 3.38$, $\beta = 0.92$ for $s_u = 40\,\mu\text{m}$ and $l_z = 21.3\,\text{mm}$. The relation given in equation 8.5 may be represented by a three-dimensional diagram shown in Figure 8.18. This image of the pull-out test is less simple than the previously accepted load–displacement curve, but it reflects the real process in which the relation $\tau = f(s)$ varies with the coordinate along the embedment zone.

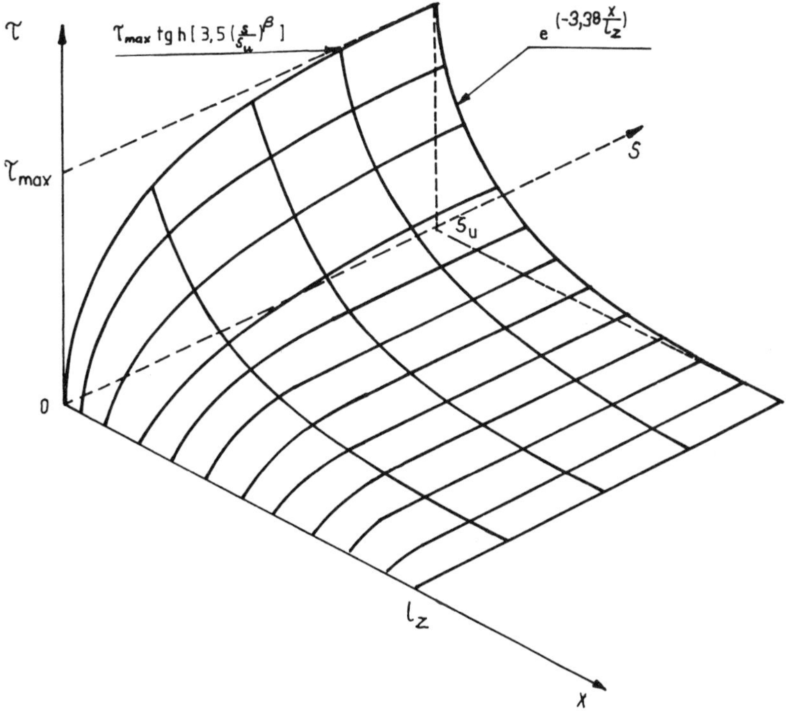

Figure 8.18 Three-dimensional diagram of relation $\tau = f(s, x)$ as in formula (equation 8.26). (Source: Potrzebowski, J., Processes of debonding and pull-out of steel-fibres from cement matrix; published by IFTR, 1991.) [8.53]

8.5.3 OTHER FIBRES

The bond between glassfibres and cement matrices depends mainly on chemical affinity and also on mechanical anchoring due to local surface irregularities and entanglement of single filaments in a strand.

Chemical affinity depends on the quality of the glass. The ordinary E-glass is subjected to accelerated corrosion in the highly alkali Portland cement environment and the corrosion processes increase the bond as a result of gradual destruction of fibre surface. For alkali resistant zirconian glassfibres and for fibres provided with protective coating, special measures should be taken to ensure bonding. The more alkali resistant fibres are characterized by a weaker bond to the cement matrix, cf. Section 5.3.

Glassfibres are used mostly in bundles and the load transfer is complicated by voids and spaces between each single filament which are not filled up with hydration products, [8.55] and [8.56]. The quality of the interface layer with respect to the pull-out resistance is also dependent on the hydration conditions of the cement paste – duration of cure in high humidity plays an important role in appropriately filling of the spaces around single filaments.

It has also been observed that the surface of the fibres influenced the intensity of the hydration product's deposition. The difference between alkali resistant glassfibres and CemFIL 2 fibres provided with a special coating has been observed, which resulted in different cementation of single filaments in a strand.

Tests are executed usually on glass strands composed of multiple single filaments, embedded in a cement matrix and subjected by an intermediary of special grips to pull-out load. Such tests were reported in [8.57] and [8.58]. The following conclusions may be derived from these studies.

There is considerable variability in the quantitative results due to different conditions in the interface which are difficult to define precisely. The maximum ultimate elastic shear flow recorded was $q_e = 62.9$ N/mm, where q_e was understood as a product of unknown stress τ and ill defined perimeter p: $q_e = \tau p$, and it corresponds to the pull-out force divided by the embedment length. After debonding, the maximum frictional shear flow recorded in these tests was $q_f = 4.44$ N/mm.

The length of embedment played a considerable role in the kind of failure – for short lengths pull-out occurred in most cases after complete debonding and longer strands are rather fractured.

In polymer modified cement matrices due to increased bonding no pull-out was observed bur rather the fracture of brittle fibres.

Another important parameter was the angle of the pulled-out strand with the crack simulated by the specimen edge. Because of the brittleness of the glass strands their sensibility to an angle other than 90° was higher than observed for steel-fibres, and fracture occurred, instead of plastic deformations, due to local bending. Characteristic load–displacement curves are shown in Figure

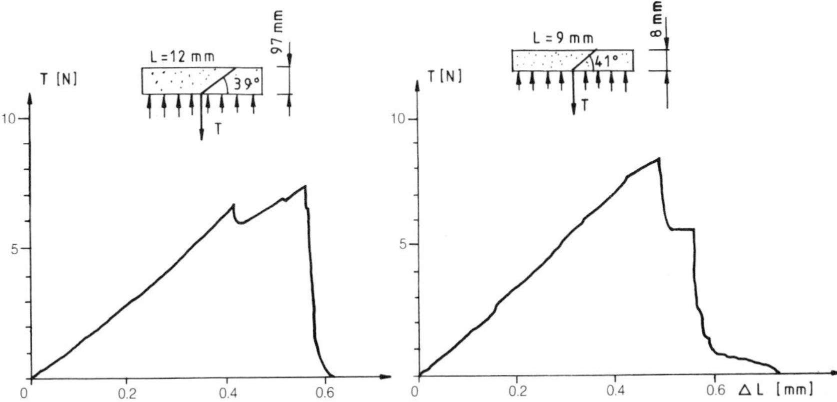

Figure 8.19 Characteristic load–displacement curves from the pull-out tests of glassfibre strands at an angle other than 90°. (Source: Bartos, P., Bond in glass reinforced cements; published by Applied Science Publishers, 1982.) [8.58]

8.19. The two consecutive peaks are related to the breaking off of the loaded matrix edge and to the fracture of the strand, respectively.

An excellent bond to cement paste for asbestos fibres is of chemical origin, and its result is the linear and brittle behaviour of asbestos–cement products and their quasi-homogeneity [8.59]. A strong interface is formed around the fibres. Very small dimensions of these fibres help in an efficient control of microcracking initially, provided that the bundles of fibres are dispersed and good distribution in the bulk mix is assured. Similarly, other kinds of thin dispersed fibres, e.g. cellulose and carbon fibres, have this ability to control crack nucleation and the initial stages of crack propagation.

Carbon fibres have been considered for several years to be the best reinforcement for cement matrices due to their durability in alkaline environments, good stability at variable temperatures and relatively high strength. Low modulus and low strength pitch-based carbon fibres are usually considered for these applications because they are cheaper than high modulus and high strength PAN fibres. The latter are used as reinforcement for polymer matrices in advanced, high strength, composite materials.

The problem of bonding is particularly important for carbon fibres, because their relatively high cost requires the maximum exploitation of their potential possibilities, but their hydrophobic nature and low affinity to cement paste make the transfer of load between fibres and matrix rather unreliable and discontinuous. Interesting tests of these questions are reported in [8.60]. The researchers used fibres 1.7 mm long and $18 \pm 4\,\mu m$ in diameter and the experimentally established, critical length was between 0.6 and 0.8 mm. The tests were arranged in such a way that fibres of different lengths were pulled out and the critical length l_{cr} was defined as corresponding to an equal percentage of fibres pulled-out and broken. The bond strength may be calculated therefore from the following relation:

$$\tau_{cr} = \frac{d\sigma_f}{4l_{cr}} \tag{8.27}$$

where d is the fibre diameter, σ_f is the tensile fibre strength. The bond strength calculated from this relation was between 2 and 4 MPa approximately, which was confirmed by tests. Neither the variation of the water/cement ratio with appropriate superplasticizer nor the addition of silica fume influenced the value of τ_{cr}. The increased bond was obtained with the styrene–butadiene latex admixture of 5–10%wt and by curing in hot water. It was observed, however, that increased bonding and related improved bending strength did not correspond to increased flexural toughness, because the higher was the bond strength, the more brittle was the composite behaviour.

For organic vegetable fibres, due to surface irregularities the bond is based mainly on local mechanical anchorages. No reliable test results have been published on this subject.

8.5.4 INFLUENCE OF THE FIBRE–MATRIX ON THE COMPOSITE'S BEHAVIOUR

The relation of the fibre–matrix bond, as determined in different pull-out tests, and the flexural or tensile behaviour of the composite elements is not completely established. In general, the better bond means higher first crack strength and ultimate strength as well. However, the relation between bond and composite strength is not linear. It has been observed for various fibres and matrices that a doubled bond resulted only in a slight improvement in the ultimate strength, [8.61]. There are probably at least two reasons for this:

1. The fibre reinforcement efficiency is dependent not only upon the fibre–matrix bond quality, but on several other factors.
2. The bond strength established after the pull-out tests does not fully reflect the behaviour of the fibres in the matrix when the element is subjected to external load, particularly in the cracking state.

8.6 Influence of fibre orientation on the cracking and fracture energy in brittle matrix composites

8.6.1 INTRODUCTION AND REVIEW OF PRESENT KNOWLEDGE

The orientation of fibres is an important factor in the design of a composite material structure. Strong anisotropic effects may be created by fibres and there have been several attempts both to determine the influence of fibre orientation on mechanical properties and to optimize it. The review given below and test results are based on [8.62].

Hill's yield criterion, to determine the filament orientation yielding maximum strength of transversally isotropic material subjected to normal and transversal stresses, is applied in [8.63]. This was developed for graphite/epoxy composites in [8.64]. Michell's theory [8.66] to find out the disposition of fibres of least weight for a specified loading system was applied in [8.65]. Several papers were devoted to the optimum orientation of fibres in advanced composite materials, e.g. [8.67], [8.68] and [8.69]. The variation of strength as a function of the fibre system orientation was studied in [8.70] and [8.71]. In the last mentioned paper the variation of composite strength, and also of the form of rupture with fibre orientation, has been shown, which was later mentioned by a number of authors.

All the above works concerned advanced composites with ductile matrices and the objective function for design or optimization was the composite's strength. In brittle matrix composites early cracking appears because the ultimate matrix strain is much lower than that of the fibres: $\varepsilon_{mu} \ll \varepsilon_{fu}$. For technological and economic reasons the volume fraction of fibres is low – only with special technologies can the fibre volume fraction be higher than about 3% for steel-fibres or 5% for other kinds of fibres. It is obvious then that fibres and their orientation play a completely different role in cement-based composites. Namely, the fibres control crack opening and propagation and substantially improve the material's toughness. The problem of the orientation of fibres in cement-based matrices was presented first in [8.72], where it was shown that the work of fracture may be considerably increased when fibres are not aligned with the direction of the principal tensile strain. These results have been based on previously published experimental works, [8.73], [8.74] and [8.75]. They have shown that the work of fracture, calculated as the amount of work of external load absorbed by the element, is the most important magnitude to be considered in the design of brittle matrix composites. This approach was developed by Brandt in proposed formulae for energy calculation, [8.76], and later in a simple optimization problem, [8.77] and [8.78]. An analytical solution was next compared with results of the experimental studies, [8.79] and [8.80].

The problem of the fibre orientation was recently examined in [8.81] which tested tensioned specimens, reinforced with unidirectional or bi-directional systems of polypropylene fibres. Because the polypropylene fibres behave differently in the cracked matrix than the steel ones, other fracture mechanisms were considered than those proposed in papers [8.77] and [8.78].

In this present chapter the influence of the orientation of steel-fibres on cracking characteristics has been examined based on experimental results.

8.6.2 OBJECTIVES OF REINFORCEMENT AND PRINCIPAL FRACTURE MECHANISMS

Fibres are introduced to brittle matrices neither to increase the initial cracking stress (first crack load) nor to improve the ultimate composite strength. The first cannot be reached with a low volume of fibres because it is limited by technological reasons and the high cost of fibres. Moreover, it is easy to improve the matrix by other ways, e.g. by decreasing the water/cement ratio. The increase of the ultimate strength of the composite is possible only by application of an efficient fibre-reinforcement of adequate volume and good fibre–matrix bond. That ultimate strength is, however, achieved after considerable cracking, provided that cracks are sufficiently thin and correctly distributed to satisfy other requirements, e.g. impermeability and durability.

The main reason for fibre-reinforcement is usually to control the cracking process. It seems, therefore, that this reason should be clearly taken into account in the design of the material. For that aim in papers [8.77] and [8.78] the fracture energy has been proposed as an objective function, formulated as a sum of a few components related to two main mechanisms:

1. debonding of the fibres; and
2. pulling-out the fibres from the matrix subjected to cracking.

These mechanisms may be specified in different ways and consequently presented in different analytical forms. The relations proposed in [8.78] were based on several simplifying assumptions, namely that:

1. all fracture energy involved in the rupture of the specimen is represented by the considered mechanisms;
2. the specified fracture mechanisms are not interrelated, cf. Section 10.3.1.

Among other simplifications, the multiple cracking was not taken into account. Moreover, the angle of the aligned fibre system with the direction of principal tensions was treated as the only variable.

The proposed relations may be improved by the introduction of more sophisticated mechanisms, without modifying the principle of the design method, based on the conviction that the best solution corresponds to the maximum area under the load–deflection or stress–strain curve. That maximum reflects the best crack control by the fibres.

8.6.3 COMPARISON OF THEORETICAL AND EXPERIMENTAL RESULTS FOR UNNOTCHED SPECIMENS

The approach developed in papers [8.77] and [8.78] was illustrated by examples of optimal solutions for an element subjected to tension and another – to bending. The fracture energy accumulated up to a specified limit state was selected as an objective function. The results calculated were obtained after derivation of proposed simplified expressions with respect to the only variable – the angle of fibre system orientation. Later, the tests of specimens with various fibre orientation were executed and appraised. All details of calculations and testing may be found in papers [8.79] and [8.82] and final results are summarized in Figures 8.20a and 8.20b. From these curves certain confirmation of theoretical

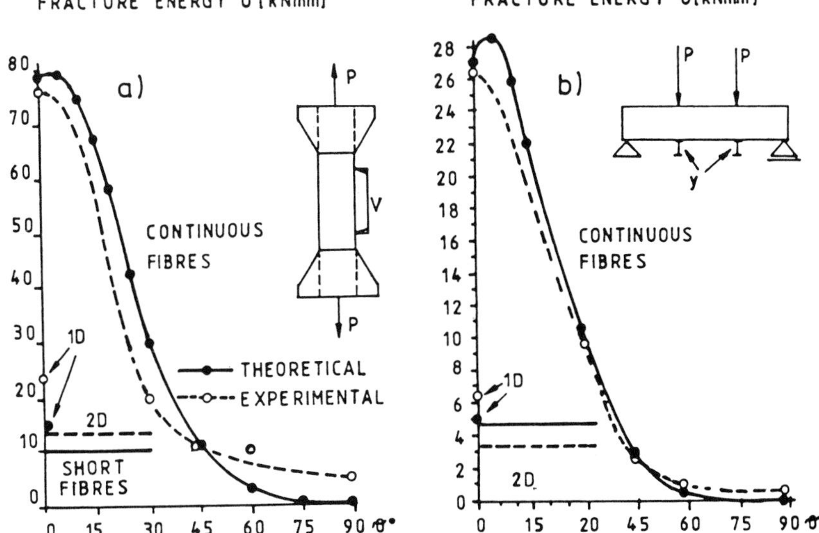

Figure 8.20 Variations of the fracture energy U with the angle ϑ, $V_f = 0.67\%$, results of calculations and tests; a) specimens subjected to axial tension; b) specimens subjected to bending. (Source: Brandt, A.M., [8.82]

results may be concluded, at least in the general shape of the curves and characteristic numerical values. However, there were no tests of elements with small values of angle $0° < \vartheta < 30°$ and the existence of an extremum for $\vartheta \neq 0°$ was neither confirmed nor denied.

8.6.4 TESTS OF NOTCHED SPECIMENS

The specimens were prepared with the same mix proportions and fibre distribution as described in [8.79]. The reinforcement was made with mild steel round and straight wire 0.4 mm in diameter, continuous or chopped into 40 mm fibres. The results reported here concern only one volume fraction of continuous or short fibres $V_f = 0.67\%$. The fibre orientation is shown in Figure 8.21, the angle ϑ being measured between aligned fibres and the longitudinal axis of the specimen. The continuous fibres were aligned in several layers in the forms before concreting, each successive layer of fibres with an angle $+\vartheta$ or $-\vartheta$ to avoid fracture of the matrix plane. The Portland cement mortar with 1.4 mm maximum aggregate grains was used as a matrix.

The specimens were sawn out of large slabs after hardening of the concrete and were stored in constant laboratory conditions of $+18° \pm 1°$C and $90\% \pm 2\%$ RH.

After a few years, the specimens were notched and subjected to four-point bending in an Instron testing machine with head displacement control. Load,

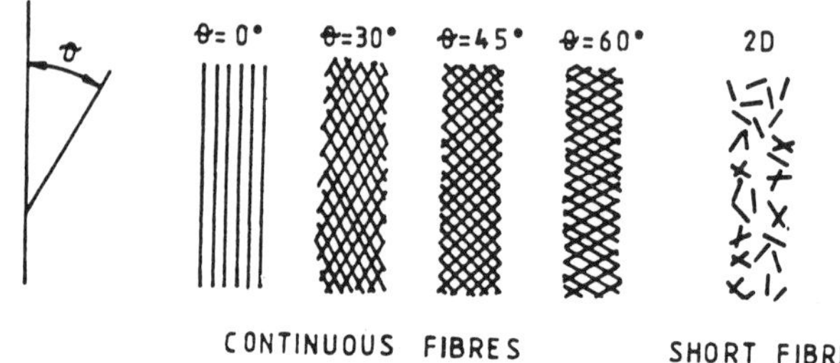

Figure 8.21 Fibre orientation systems in tested specimens. (Source: Brandt, A.M.) [8.82]

Table 8.2 Calculated and experimental values of characteristic parameters for notched specimens

Experimental values					Experimental values		Calculated values	
Angle	Load	Coeff.	Stress	Stress	Fracture		Energy	
ϑ	P_{cr}	K_{Ic}	σ_{app}	σ'_{app}	U'	U''	U'	U''
(°)	(kN)	($MNm^{-1.5}$)	(MPa)	(MPa)	(kNmm)	(kNmm)	(kNmm)	(kNmm)
Continuous fibres:								
0	3.26	1.165	9.2	16.6	3.73	5.82	2.73	4.02
30	2.36	0.850	6.8	11.2	2.32	3.10	2.62	3.03
45	1.72	0.591	4.6	7.0	1.16	1.76	1.92	2.70
60	0.85	0.327	2.6	3.9	0.66	1.19	1.01	1.39
90	0.42	0.198	2.1	3.6	0.08	0.10	0.00	0.00
Short fibres 2D:								
	1.66	0.815	7.3	9.3	0.88	2.82	0.49	2.69

(Source: Brandt, A.M., Influence of fibre orientation on the energy absorption at fracture of SFRC specimens; published by Elsevier Applied Science Publishers, 1986.) [8.79]

central deflection and crack opening displacement (COD) were measured to calculate the characteristics of the cracking process. The testing was monitored and recorded using a personal computer.

The values characterizing the cracking of specimens are reported in Table 8.2. All data are the mean values obtained from testing between four and six identical specimens.

The critical values of the stress intensity factor K_{Ic} were calculated from the classic formula of linear fracture mechanics (LEFM) for the initiation of crack propagation at the notch tip, and corresponding values of load P_{cr} were taken into account. The curves in Figure 8.22a show K_{Ic} and P_{cr} as functions of angle ϑ. For comparison, the values obtained for short fibres dispersed at random in horizontal planes (2D) are also given.

Values of the apparent stresses σ_{app} and σ'_{app} are calculated at the notch tip for two stages – crack opening and maximum load, respectively. These values have no physical meaning, as they are calculated assuming elastic behaviour

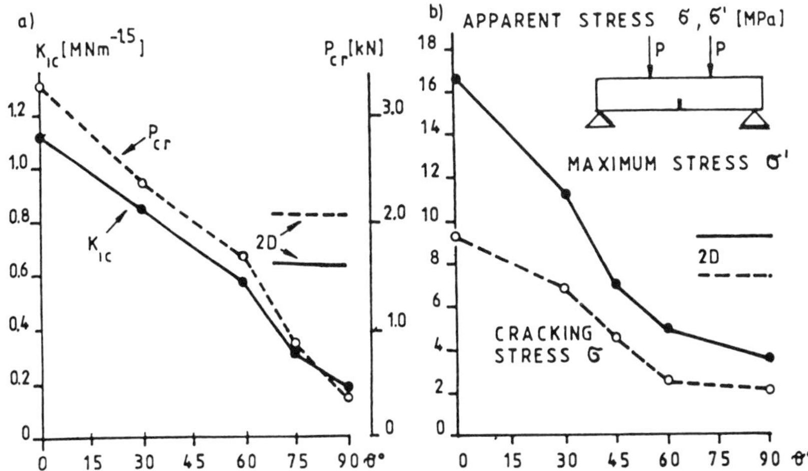

Figure 8.22 Variations of characteristic values with the angle ϑ; a) variation of P_{cr} – load corresponding to 1st crack opening and of K_{Ic}; b) variation of the apparent stresses σ_{app} and σ'_{app} corresponding to cracking initiation and to the minimum load, respectively. (Source: Brandt, A.M.) [8.82]

and neglecting the cracks. Therefore, they are used only to compare the specimens between themselves, thus eliminating the influence of different dimensions. Corresponding curves are shown in Figure 8.22b.

The fracture energy U' is calculated as the area under the curve load–deflection up to the maximum load. Specific fracture energy γ' is equal to U' divided by the area of fracture. That last magnitude was obtained in an approximate way by measuring the length of crack which propagated from the notch tip and was observed on both sides of each tested specimen. The area was calculated as a double product of the crack length and the beam width, without taking into account the roughness of fracture surface. It is obvious that more exact values could be obtained considering the roughness and waviness of the fracture surface which should be treated as a fractal object. However, it may be expected that the results obtained do have a certain significance because the same matrix was used for all specimens and the roughness of all fracture surfaces was similar. In the same way U'' and γ'' were determined for the final state of fracture. The values of U' and γ' for different angle ϑ are shown in Figure 8.23.

In last columns of Table 8.2, analytical and experimental values of fracture energies U' and U'' are listed up to the maximum load and to the final fracture, respectively.

The importance of the angle ϑ between aligned fibres and the direction of principal tension has been confirmed for various measures of fibre efficiency. The strength and cracking characteristics depend directly on that angle.

The shape of all the curves obtained is, however, essentially different from that shown for other kinds of composites, for example [8.81]. The difference is

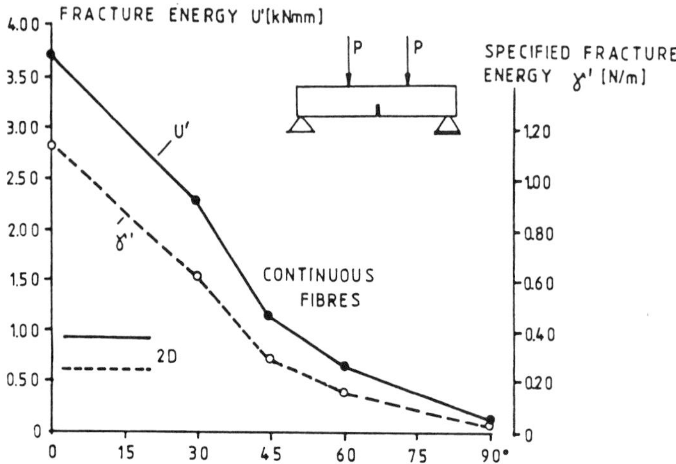

Figure 8.23 Variation of fracture energy U and specific fracture energy γ with the angle ϑ. (Source: Brandt, A.M.) [8.82]

probably related to such mechanisms as the pull-out of fibres and the passing of fibres across microcracks and cracks which appear differently in ductile and brittle materials.

The shape of the curves seems to indicate that the maximum efficiency is related to angle $\vartheta \neq 0°$, probably around 10°–15°. This situation was not observed because there were no specimens with such reinforcement, but it would be in agreement with theoretical considerations published in [8.77] and [8.78]. Perhaps future tests will give more information on that question.

In view of the influence of selected angle ϑ on the efficiency of the fibre reinforcement, it seems appropriate to consider this parameter in the design of materials for the fibre-reinforced cements and concretes. The execution of a system of short steel-fibres with arbitrary angle ϑ is possible using several methods – magnetic linearization of fibres in the fresh cement mix, casting of the mix through a kind of comb, shotcreting with appropriately designed parameters, etc.

In the case of any other kind of fibres or matrices it is also possible to determine adequate fracture mechanisms and to deduce analytical relations. Also the methods of execution should be adapted to properties of fibres and matrices.

The problems of fibre orientation examined here represent only a first step towards the optimization of the material structure of composites, cf. Chapter 13.

References

8.1. Dantu, P. (1958) Étude des contraintes dans le milieux hétérogènes. Applications au béton. *Annales de l'ITBTP*, **11**(121), 55–67.

8.2. Brandt, A.M. (1973) Nine-gauges device for strain measurements inside concrete. *Strain*, **9**(3), 122–4.
8.3. Brandt, A.M. (1971) Les déformations du béton d'après la mesure de six composantes. *Cahiers de la Recherche*, No. 29, Eyrolles, Paris.
8.4. Babut, R. and Brandt, A.M. (1977) Measurements of internal strains by nine-gauge devices. *Strain*, **13**(1), 18–21.
8.5. Kaplan, M.F. (1961) Crack propagation and the fracture of concrete. *J. of the American Concrete Institute*, **58**, 591–610.
8.6. Kaplan, M.F. (1968) The application of fracture mechanics to concrete. Proc. Conf. '*The Structure of Concrete and its Behaviour under Load*', (eds A.E. Brooks and K. Newman), Sept. 1965, London, Cement and Concrete Ass. 169–75.
8.7. Romualdi, J.P. and Batson, G.B. (1963) Mechanics of crack arrest in concrete. *J. of the Engineering Mechanics Div.*, ASCE, **89**, 147–68.
8.8. Romualdi, J.P. and Mandel, J.A. (1964) Tensile stress of concrete affected by uniformly distributed and closely spaced short lengths of wire reinforcement. *J. of the American Concrete Institute*, **61**, 657–70.
8.9. Shah, S.P. and McGarry, F.J. (1971) Griffith fracture criterion and concrete. Proc. ASCE, *J. Eng. Mech. Div.*, **47** (EM6), 1663–76.
8.10. Timoshenko, S.P. (1953) *History of Strength of Materials*, McGraw-Hill Book Co., New York.
8.11. Fung, Y.C. (1965) *Foundations of Solid Mechanics*, Prentice-Hall, Englewood Cliffs, New Jersey.
8.12. Stabilini, L. (1961) *La plasticita*, Libreria Editrice Politecnica Tamburini, Milan.
8.13. Mohr, O. (1906) Welche Umstände bedingen die Elastizitätsgrenze und den Bruch eines Materials? *Zeit. des VDI*, **44**.
8.14. Beltrami, E. (1920) Sulla condizione die resitenza dei corpi elastici, in *Opere matematiche di Beltrami Engenio*, vol. III, Hoepti, Milan, pp. 554.
8.15. Caquot, A. (1964) Commission d'études techniques, *Travaux*, No. 192 Courbon, J., Résistance des Matériaux, **1**, Dunod, Paris.
8.16. Voigt, W. (1883), (1915) *Ann. Physik*, **19**, 1883, p. 44; **46**, 191, p. 657.
8.17. L'Hermite, R. (1955) *Idées actuelles sur la technologie du béton.* La Documentation Technique du Bâtiment et des Travaux Publics, Paris.
8.18. Kasperkiewicz, J. (1983) Internal structure and fracture processes in brittle matrix composites in (Polish). *IFTR Reports*, **39**, IFTR, Warsaw.
8.19. Brandt, A.M. (1983) Application of experimental fracture mechanics to cement matrix composites (in Polish), in '*Mechanics of concrete-like composite materials*', Ossolineum, Warsaw.
8.20. Balavadze, W.K. (1959) Influence of reinforcement on the properties of concrete subjected to tension (in Russian), *Beton i Zhelezobeton*, nr. 10, 462–5.
8.21. Evans, R.H. and Marathe, M.S. (1968) Microcracking and stress–strain curve for concrete in tension. *Materials and Structures RILEM*, **1**(1), 61–4.
8.22. Mianowsk, K.M. (1986) Dynamic aspects in fracture mechanics, as [8.51], 81–91.
8.23. Hannant, D.J. (1978) *Fibre cements and fibre concretes*,. J. Wiley and Sons, Chichester.
8.24. Kelly, A. (1973) *Strong Solids*, 2nd ed., Clarendon Press, Oxford.
8.25. Krenchel, H. (1964) *Fibre Reinforcement*. Akademisk Forlag, Copenhagen.
8.26. Riley, V.R. (1968) Fibre/fibre interaction, *J. of Composite Materials*, **4**(2), 436–46.
8.27. Laws, V. (1971) The efficiency of fibrous reinforcement of brittle matrices. *J. of Physics D: Applied Physics*, **4**, 1737–46.

8.28. Chan, H.S. and Patterson, W.A. (1972) The theoretical prediction of the cracking stress of glassfibre reinforced inorganic cement. *J. of Materials Science*, **7**, 856–60.

8.29. Shah, S.P. (1991) Do fibers improve the tensile strength of concrete?, in Proc. *1st Canadian Univ.–Ind. Workshop on Fibre Reinforced Concrete* (ed. N. Banthia), Univ. Laval, Quebec, 10–30.

8.30. Bentur, A. and Mindess, S. (1990) *Fibre Reinforced Cementitious Composites*, Elsevier Applied Science, London, New York.

8.31. Cox, H.L. (1952) The elasticity and strength of paper and other fibrous materials. *British Journal of Applied Physics*, **3**, 72–9.

8.32. Parimi, S.R. and Rao, J.K.S. (1971) Effectiveness of random fibres in fibre-reinforced concrete. Proc. Int. Conf. '*Mechanical Behaviour of Materials*'. August 15–20, Kyoto, **5**, 176–86.

8.33. Kar, J.N. and Pal, A.K. (1972) Strength of fibre-reinforced concrete. *J. of Struct. Div.*, Proc. of ASCE, ST5, 1053–68.

8.34. Aveston, J. and Kelly, A. (1973) Theory of multiple fracture of fibrous composites. *J. of Materials Science*, **8**(3), 352–62.

8.35. Swamy, R.N. and Mangat, P.S. (1974) A theory of the flexural strength of steel-fibre reinforced concrete. *Cement and Concrete Research*, **4**, 313–25, 701–7.

8.36. Swamy, R.N. and Mangat, P.S. (1974) Influence of fibre-aggregate interaction on some properties of steel-fibre reinforced concrete. *Materials and Structures RILEM*, **7**(41), 307–14.

8.37. Tanigawa, Y., Hatanaka, S. and Mori, H. (1980) Stress–strain behaviour of steel-fiber reinforced concrete under compression. *Trans. of the Japan Concrete Institute*, **2**, 187–94.

8.38. Hughes, B.P. and Fattuhi, N.I. (1977) Predicting the flexural strength of steel and polypropylene fibre-reinforced cement-based beams. *Composites*, January, 57–64.

8.39. Dehousse, N.M. (1975) Méthodes d'essais et caractéristiques mécaniques des bétons armés des fibres métalliques, Proc. Int. Symp. RILEM '*Fibre Reinforced Cement and Concrete'*, The Construction Press, London.

8.40. Babut, R. and Brandt, A.M. (1978) The method of testing and analyzing of steel-fibre reinforced concrete elements in flexure, Proc. Int. Symp. RILEM '*Testing and Test Methods of Fibre Cement Composites*', (ed. R.N. Swamy), The Construction Press, Sheffield.

8.41. Bartos, P. (1981) Review paper: Bond in fibre-reinforced cements and concretes. *Int. Journal of Cement Comp. & Lightweight Concrete*, **3**(3), 159–7,7.

8.42. Lawrence, P. (1972) Some theoretical considerations of fibre pull-out from an elastic matrix. *J. of Mat. Science*, **7**, 1–6.

8.43. Gopalaratnam, V.P. and Shah, S.P. (1987) Tensile failure of steel-fiber reinforced mortar. *J. of Eng. Mech. Div.*, ASCE, 113, 635–52.

8.44. Greszczuk, L.B. (1968) Theoretical studies of the mechanics of the fibre–matrix interface in composites, in *Interfaces in Composites*, ASTM STP 452, Philadelphia, 42–58.

8.45. Gray, R.J. (1984) Analysis of the effect of embedded fibre length on fibre debonding and pull-out from an elastic matrix, Part 1: Review of theories. *J. of Materials Science*, **19**, 861–70; Part 2: Application to steel-fibre–cementitious matrix composite system. *J. of Materials Science*, **19**, 1680–91.

8.46. Burakiewicz, A. (1979) Testing of fibre bond strength in cement matrix, in Proc. RILEM Symp. in Sheffield 1978 '*Testing and Test Methods of Fibre Reinforced Cement Composites*', (ed. R.N. Swamy), The Construction Press, 312–27.

8.47. Burakiewicz, A. (1979) Fibre–matrix bond in fibre-reinforced concretes (in Polish), *IFTR Reports*, Nr 42.

8.48. Paillère, A.M. and Serrano, J.J. (1974) Vers un nouveau bétobn armé. *Bull. Liaison Labo.*, 72, June–July 1974, 18–24.

8.49. Pinchin, D.J. and Tabor, D. (1975) Mechanical properties of the steel/cement interface, some experimental results, in Proc. RILEM Symp. '*Fibre-Reinforced Cement and Concrete*', (ed. A.M. Neville), The Construction Press, 521–26.

8.50. Potrzebowski, J. (1982) Investigation of steel-fibres debonding processes in cement paste, in '*Bond in Concrete*', Proc. Int. Conf. in Paisley, June 1982, (ed. P. Bartos) Applied Science Publishers, London, 51–9.

8.51. Potrzebowski, J. (1986) Behaviour of the fibre/matrix interface in SFRC during loading, in Proc. Int. Symp. '*Brittle Matrix Composites 1*', Jabłonna 1985, (eds A.M. Brandt and I.H. Marshall), Elsevier Applied Science, London, 455–69.

8.52. Potrzebowski, J. (1989) Debonding processes between steel-fibre and cement matrix, in Proc. Int. Symp. '*Brittle Matrix Composites 2*', Cedzyna 1988, (eds A.M. Brandt and I.H. Marshall), Elsevier Applied Science, 352–61.

8.53. Potrzebowski, J. (1991) Processes of debonding and pull-out of steel-fibres from cement matrix (in Polish). *IFTR Reports*, 15, IFTR, Warsaw.

8.54. Nammur, G. Jr. and Naaman, E. (1989) Bond stress model for fiber-reinforced concrete based on bond-slip relationship. *J. of the Amer. Concr. Inst.*, **86**(1), 45–57.

8.55. Bentur, A. (1986) Microstructure and performance of glass-fibre-cement composites, in '*Research on the Manufacture and Use of Cements*', Proc. Eng. Found, Conf., (ed. G. Frohnsdorff), Engineering Foundation, 197–208.

8.56. Bentur, A. (1986) Mechanisms of potential embrittlement and strength loss of glass-fibre-reinforced cement composites, in Proc. Symp. '*Durability of Glass Fiber Reinforced Concrete*', (ed. S. Diamond), Prestressed Concrete Institute, Chicago, 109–23.

8.57. Oakley, D.R. and Proctor, B.A. (1985) Tensile stress-strain behaviour of glassfibre reinforced cement composites, in Proc. of RILEM Symp. on *Fibre Reinforced Cement and Concrete*, (ed. A.M. Neville), The Construction Press, 347–59.

8.58. Bartos, P. (1982) Bond in glass reinforced cements, in '*Bond in Concrete*', Proc. Int. Conf. in Paisley, June 1982, (ed. P. Bartos), Applied Science Publishers, London, 60–71.

8.59. Allen, H.G. (1971) Tensile properties of seven asbestos cements. *Composites*, **2**, June, 98–103.

8.60. Larson, B.K., Drzal, L.T. and Soroushian, P. (1990) Carbon fibre cement adhesion in carbon fibre cement composites. *Composites*, **21**(3), 205–15.

8.61. Gray, R.J. and Johnston, C.D. (1987) The influence of fibre–matrix interfacial bond strength on the mechanical properties of steel-fibre reinforced mortars. *Int. Journ. of Cement Comp. and Lightweight Concrete*, **9**(1), 43–55.

8.62. Brandt, A.M. (1985) On the optimization of fibre orientation in the brittle matrix composite materials. August, Rep. Stevin Lab., Delft Univ. of Techn.

8.63. Sandhu, R.S. (1969) Parametric study of Tsai's strength criteria for filamentary composites, AFFDL-TR-68-168, Wright Patterson AFB, Ohio, pp. 35.

8.64. Brandmaier, H.E. (1970) Optimum filament orientation criteria. *J. of Comp. Materials*, **4**, July, 422–5.

8.65. Cox, H.L. (1977) The general principles governing the stress analysis of composites, in Proc. Conf. '*Fibre Reinforced Materials: Design and Engineering Applications*', Instn. of Civil Engineers, Paper No. 2, London, 23–24 March, 9–13 and disc.

8.66. Michell, A.G.M. (1904) The limit of economy of material in frame structures. *Phil. Magazine*, **8**(47), 589–97.

8.67. Wright–Patterson AFB (1968) Structural Design Guide for Advanced Composite Applications, Air Force Base, Dayton, Ohio, USA.

8.68. Dow, N.F., Rosen, B.W., Shu, L., and Zweben, C.H. (1967) Design criteria and concepts for fibrous composite structures, Rep. NASA-CR-91728, Philadelphia, pp. 195.

8.69. Chamis, C.C. (1975) Design of composite structural components, in (eds Broutman, L.J. and Krock, R.H.), *Composite Materials*, **8**, Academic Press, New York.

8.70. Hayashi, I., Mori, K., Kaneko, S. and Mogi, F. (1978) Effect of fiber orientation on mechanical properties of short fiber reinforced composite materials, in Proc. of the *1st Japan Congr. on Mat. Research*, Kyoto, Society of Materials Science, 287–93.

8.71. Kelly, A. and Davies, G.J. (1965) The principles of the fibre reinforcement of metals. *Metallurgical Review*, **10**(37), 1–77.

8.72. Morton, J. (1979) The work of fracture of random fibre reinforced cement. *Materials and Structures*, RILEM, **12**(71), 393–6.

8.73. Hing, P. and Groves, G.W. (1972) The strength and fracture toughness of polycrystalline magnesium oxide containing metallic particles and fibres. *J. of Mat. Science*, **7**, 427–34.

8.74. Harris, B., Varlow, J. and Ellis, C.D. (1972) The fracture behaviour of fibre-reinforced concrete. *Cem. and Concr. Res.*, **2**, 447–61.

8.75. Morton, J. and Groves, G.W. (1974) The cracking of composites consisting of discontinuous ductile fibres in a brittle matrix – effect of fibre orientation. *J. of Mat. Science*, **9**, 1436–45.

8.76. Brandt, A.M. (1982) On the calculation of fracture energy in SFRC elements subjected to bending, in Proc. Conf. '*Bond in Concrete*', (ed. P. Bartos), Paisley 1982. Appl. Science Publishers, London, 73–81.

8.77. Brandt, A.M. (1984) On the optimization of the fiber orientation in cement-based composite materials, in Proc. Int. Symp. '*Fiber Reinforced Concrete*', Detroit 1982, (ed. G.C. Hoff), American Concrete Institute, SP81, Detroit, 267–85.

8.78. Brandt, A.M. (1985) On the optimal direction of short metal fibres in brittle matrix composites. *J. of Mat. Science*, **20**, 3831–41.

8.79. Brandt, A.M. (1986) Influence of the fibre orientation on the energy absorption at fracture of SFRC specimens, in Proc. of Int. Symp. '*Brittle Matrix Composites 1*', Jabłonna 1985, (eds A.M. Brandt and I.H. Marshall), 403–20, Elsevier Applied Science Publishers, London, 403–20.

8.80. Brandt, A.M. (1987) Influence of the fibre orientation on the mechanical properties of fibre-reinforced cement (FRC) specimens, in Proc. *1st RILEM Congress* in Versailles, **2**, Chapman and Hall, 651–8.

8.81. Mashima, M., Hannant, D.J. and Keer, J.G. (1990) Tensile properties of polypropylene reinforced cement with different fiber orientation. Amer. Concr. Inst. *Materials Journal*, **87**(2), 172–8.

8.82. Brandt, A.M. (1991) Influence of fibre orientation on the cracking and fracture energy in brittle matrix composites, in Proc. Euromech. Coll. 269 *Mechanical Identification of Composites*, (eds. A. Vautrin and H. Sol), Elsevier Applied Science, London, 327–34.

9 Cracking in cement matrices and propagation of cracks

9.1 Classification of cracks

One of the main phenomena studied in the mechanics of brittle matrix composites is cracking. The cracks may be classified according to various criteria, e.g.:

- origin – cracks due to shrinkage and temperature variations in restrained elements or due to load producing local tensions;
- position in the material structure – cracks in matrix, aggregates, interface (bond cracks);
- width and importance – microcracks, macrocracks, major cracks which lead to final rupture;
- shape and pattern – single and multiple cracks, branching cracks, etc.;
- exploitation of element – admissible or inadmissible cracks with respect to the safety, serviceability or durability requirements;
- mode of rupture and of crack propagation – Modes I, II and III as well as mixed modes may be distinguished (cf. Figure 10.3).

A flaw or a crack is defined in the mechanics of solids as a two-dimensional discontinuity in a plane with its two dimensions much larger than the third one. Certain authors reserve the first term for those discontinuities which are formed parallel to the smallest dimension without application of any tensile stress. In that convention the term crack covers all other discontinuities caused by stresses. In several manuals this distinction is not used and both kinds of discontinuities in solids are called cracks, e.g. [9.1]; this practice is also followed here.

Cracks may be characterized by their width, length and pattern. The opening of a crack is always related to the creation of new free surface in the material, where free means that the surface is not loaded by any stress. An amount of energy is required to create a unit area of a new free surface of a crack. It is considered to be an important material characteristic and is called 'specific fracture energy' which is difficult to measure directly but may be calculated in an approximate way when the amount of released energy and crack dimensions are estimated and considered as known.

The crack shape is usually irregular. The roughness or waviness of the crack surface is characteristic both for the material and for the origin of the crack. Because of this irregularity, the crack length and area of its surface may be considered as fractal objects. It means that they are depending on the scale of observation or on the unit of measurement, cf. Sections 9.3 and 10.5.

It is generally assumed that in brittle cement matrices that plastic phenomena, similar to those in metals, do not appear. In fact, when in specimens subjected to loading certain apparently plastic deformations are observed, i.e. an increase of deformation at a constant load, then this effect is caused by microcracks and therefore the term quasi-plasticity is used.

The cracks in reinforced and non-prestressed concrete elements subjected to tension are unavoidable due to differences in Young's moduli and in values of ultimate strain in concrete and steel. It is the task of the designer to select appropriate remedy for both serviceability and safety reasons by adequate reinforcement or prestressing. If perfect impermeability is required, then the cracks are inadmissible or their width is strongly limited. In that case, also, the pore system in concrete should be completely blocked by special admixtures. Another method is to provide protective coatings or tight layers of other materials.

In this chapter cracks are considered mostly in the context of the materials science and fracture mechanics. The cracking of reinforced concrete structural elements due to excessive loads or imposed deformations are not examined here as this subject is abundantly treated in relevant manuals and recommendations.

In principle the cracking, and particularly its advanced stage, is an irrecoverable process which is initiated after the discontinuity point, i.e. after the first variation of the slope of a stress–strain curve which is considered as the sign of first crack opening. Because in brittle matrix composites, due to their heterogeneity and hydration processes, the systems of fine cracks and other discontinuities are developed from the outset without any external load, the hypotheses of material continuity are no longer valid in an exact meaning of that notion and the stresses are applicable only with appropriate restrictions. These observations lead to the Kaplan's proposal in 1961 [9.2] to apply fracture mechanics to concretes, using its development in other fields of materials science. The Griffith's approach to cracks in perfectly brittle and homogeneous materials was extensively followed in numerous studies of cracking processes in cementitious materials. Then the question arose as to whether the cracks themselves, and which of them, were governed by the Griffith's approach. Later, however, it became clear that the situation in these materials is much more complex and requires a more diversified approach. The answer for the above question is therefore also more complex – the Griffith's approach is applicable to those materials but with several restrictions and complementary assumptions, together with the further development of new theories and proposals.

The 'healing' of microcracks under appropriate conditions can be observed and is primarily due to delayed hydration of the cement grains. This phenomenon is described briefly in Section 9.7.

9.2 Cracks in the matrix, in aggregate grains and in the interface

The cracking process develops when a system of stresses of any origin is applied to a solid and its tensile strength is exceeded or, in other words, when the ultimate tensile strain is exceeded. Theoretical strength may be calculated from molecular cohesion in the atomic structure, but the effective strength of materials is, by a few orders, lower. The reasons according to Griffith's theory are local defects, microcracks and flaws, with high stress concentrations at their tips. It is usually assumed that for ordinary Portland cement matrix the maximum tensile strain is equal $100–150.10^{-6}$ and may rarely attain 200.10^{-6}.

Also, an initial system of defects exists in all cement-based materials. These are cracks and microcracks, voids and pores, weaker are stronger regions, etc., which exist and may be recognized before the application of any load or imposed deformation. These defects cause concentrations of high stresses even under small external actions. The cracks propagate due to local exceedence of material tensile strength. Such systems of initial defects exist on a micro-, meso- and macro-level in all brittle materials.

The main causes of cracking in cement-based composites are:

- volume changes during hydration and hardening of matrices in the presence of restraints, e.g. shrinkage, temperature variation, chemical influence on particular material components like alkali–aggregate reaction or the swelling of reinforcing bar during their corrosion, these are intrinsic cracks;
- tensile stresses due to loads and deformations imposed during exploitation.

In the hardened cement gel which is a framework of crystals of different nature, the initial microcracks are formed between needle-shaped hydration products and also around sand grains. At the tips of these cracks only small amounts of energy are necessary to enhance further separation of the material. Gradually, if the input of external energy is assured, larger macrocracks open and transform into major cracks, which lead to the complete separation of different regions of what was considered a solid body.

Different types of intrinsic cracks, which appear during processes of hydration at the early age of a cement-based matrix, may be distinguished.

Plastic shrinkage cracks are considered to be caused by loss of water in a fresh mix because of evaporation to the air or suction by old, neighbouring concrete, cf. Section 11.4.

This phenomenon is the origin of the formation of microcracks in cement paste and was described, among others, in [9.3]. Contraction during the hydration process develops in the CSH gel but hard crystals $Ca(OH)_2$ are not subjected to volume changes related to wetting and drying. As the crystals are surrounded by a gel with low tensile strength, cracks appear which may be detected both by microscopical observation and by increased permeability of the paste. It is estimated that crack width varies between 0.125 and 1.0 μm. Plastic shrinkage can be controlled by keeping the concrete surface wet from the outset. As the direct cause is evaporation, the cracks may be reduced considerably if the loss of water can be limited during at least the first eight hours after casting.

A system of cracks also develops in concrete composites during exposure to thermal variations, because in these highly heterogeneous materials the thermal expansions of various components are slightly different, and produce a system of tensile and compressive stresses due to local restraints if the tensile strength is exceeded. The overall deformations of the elements also produce stresses and possible cracks if movements are restrained.

Cracks due to various forms of shrinkage and thermal expansion are the direct effect of restraint. The cement paste in which these processes actually develop is restrained at a local scale by grains of sand and most of all by coarse aggregate grains. There are several other causes of external restraints – reinforcing bars, neighbouring members and layers of old concrete or other rigid material, etc. As a result, in any kind of construction, the material has no possibility of free deformation. Restraint may cause compressive and tensile stresses and because of low tensile strength of concrete-like materials cracks appear, particularly at an early age.

Restrained shrinkage cracking was tested for fibre-reinforced concrete [9.4] and [9.5], and for cement mortars, [9.6]. The shrinkage deformations were restrained by some kinds of stiff inner rings and the cracks were observed on outer rings made of tested material. The progress of the cracks reflects the influence of material composition, structure and curing on resistance against cracking.

The intrinsic cracks and flaws are therefore dependent on material composition and ambient conditions – humidity, temperature and restraints, and are subjected to modifications in time together with these conditions. The opening of macrocracks and material fracture observed under load are closely connected to initial cracks and other defects.

The crack systems may be considered from various but interrelated viewpoints:

- as initiators and concentrators of cracks due to load during the working life of the material;
- as a reason for increasing permeability and lower durability;
- as phenomena inadmissible for structural serviceability for various reasons, e.g. external aspect, durability.

The structure of concrete composites is also macroscopically anisotropic in the direction of casting. The voids beneath aggregate grains are formed and partly filled with water. These voids create weak matrix–aggregate bonds in horizontal planes and are the origin of cracks when favourable stress fields are imposed due to external loading or other action, (Figure 9.1).

The cracks in the matrix open and propagate under excessive local stress. This means that because of a very non-uniform distribution of stresses in the

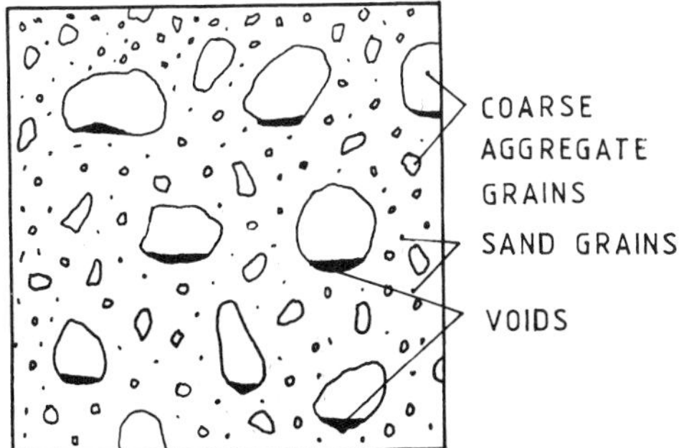

Figure 9.1 System of voids below aggregate grains in plain concrete.

material structure (cf. Figures 8.1 and 8.2), the local stresses produce local cracks even if in the macro-scale the load is relatively small and is considered to be causing an average stress below the limits of elastic behaviour. There are two characteristic points in the cracking process – crack initiation, i.e. opening of the first crack in the matrix, and the beginning of unstable cracking. After the first crack opening, also called the discontinuity point, stable crack propagation starts provided that additional energy is supplied, for instance by the increase in load. When the unstable cracking stage is reached, the cracks progress rapidly without any input of new energy and lead to a failure.

In ordinary and high strength materials, the matrix has lower strength than the aggregate grains. Under load the cracks are crossing the matrix and contouring the grains. In lightweight composites the situation is the opposite – the cracks propagate across the grains, (Figure 9.2). It should be remembered that what is macroscopically called a matrix also contains grains and inclusions of a lower level, i.e. the mortar which, with the aggregate grains, forms the ordinary concrete structure is itself composed of cement paste and grains of sand. Also, non-reacted grains of cement and micro-fillers like fly ash and silica fume are surrounded by interfacial layers.

The cracks initiate and propagate in the form of decohesions in the aggregate–matrix interface and these regions deserve more specific attention. The physical and chemical composition as well as the structure of the interface is essentially different from those of the bulk matrix. Cracks are often arrested just at the interface layer, a few micrometers before reaching an obstacle in the form of an aggregate grain or a fibre. The structure and properties of various kinds of interfaces are described in Chapter 7.

The increase in load corresponding to the first crack opening in elements subjected to bending or tension is an important objective in material design. It may be achieved by several methods – increase of the tensile strength of the matrix itself, improvement of bond strength to aggregate grains and reinforcement, transformation of major cracks to microcracks by adequate reinforcement, etc. If the first method improves resistance against crack opening, the others

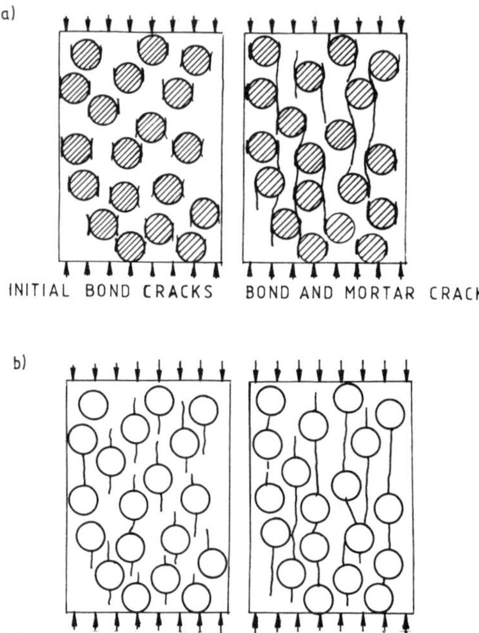

Figure 9.2 Cracking of concrete specimens with different ratio of strength of matrix to that of aggregate grains; a) ordinary concrete; b) lightweight aggregate concrete (Source: Lusche, M., The fracture mechanism of ordinary and lightweight concrete under uniaxial compression; published by Ossolineum, Wrocław, 1974.)[9.7]

tend to increase the fracture toughness of the composite material. The problem of how the fibre-reinforcement may enhance the tensile strength of the matrix is not, however, completely solved, cf. Section 8.3.

9.3 Dimensions and positions of cracks

The cracks may be characterized by their width, length and general pattern. All three parameters are strongly influenced by the sensitivity of observation and measurements.

The lower bound of the crack width cannot be specified without ambiguity, because very thin cracks and thin crack tips disappear in pores and cavities of the cement paste structure, (Figure 10.12). Ahead of the crack tip, a region of loosened material is observed, and determination of where the crack actually ends is rather conventional, cf. the excellent study on shape of cracks and on crack propagation in cement matrix, [9.8].

The measurement of the crack width is also difficult because of its irregular shape – it may vary within large limits depending on where it is measured. That

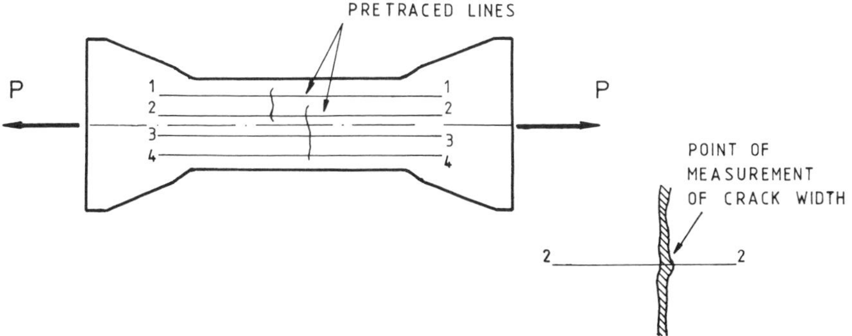

Figure 9.3 Measurement points of crack width at intersection with pre-traced system of lines.

is the reason why quite often only incremental measurements, made at arbitrarily selected points but at sequential stages of loading or at given time intervals, inform objectively about the progress of the cracking activity. Best practice is to have a system of more or less regular lines on the surface where cracking is expected and to record when, and under what conditions, cracks are crossing the lines. Then, the crack width at these intersections can be measured when it grows under load or other actions. An example of a system of lines for crack recording on an element subjected to axial tension is shown in Figure 9.3.

The determination of crack width, and to some extent of the crack length, is related to the method of observation and measurement. Therefore, for validity of results it is advisable to compare data only when it has been obtained with the same method and equipment and even by the same operator. If measurements are not realized in natural scale, then images of the same magnification should be used, because when magnification is increased not only quantitative but also qualitative modifications appear.

The opening of cracks and the importance of the crack system may be determined visually and also by various indirect methods, based on the overall behaviour of elements subjected to loads or other actions.

The appearance of the first crack is more or less clearly reflected on various curves which characterize the behaviour of specimens and elements under external load – load–deflection, stress–strain, etc. The first crack and its propagation and development are observed after the changes of slope of the respective curves, because simultaneously the element stiffness is decreased. This change of slope is not always sufficiently clear in the form of a 'knee' to indicate the load or the time of crack opening. In an element with a highly efficient system of reinforcement and subjected to bending, a very smooth load–deflection curve may be obtained as a result of well distributed microcracks, but without an offset indicating a certain threshold in the material's behaviour.

Other methods of crack detection are based on physical phenomena closely related to cracking – increase of apparent volume and Poisson ratio, abrupt increase of intensity of acoustic events, decrease of ultrasonic pulse velocity, etc. An acoustic emission is produced by cracking and the detailed analysis of the signals allows the location of crack tip advancing in the matrix to be determined and also the nature of the cracking to be deduced – debonding between two phases or fracture of one specific phase, cf. Section 6.2 and the paper [9.9].

The location of the crack may be also detected using photoelastic or brittle coatings on the external faces of tested specimens. Special techniques exist to make the cracks visible on the observed surfaces by increasing their contrast. This is achieved by filling the cracks with special dyes or by spraying the surface with fluorescent fluids. Brittle coatings belong to the same group of experimental techniques. Development of these methods has been very fast over recent years due to specialization and the improvement of technical equipment. The details of the indirect methods for detecting and following cracking processes are outside the main scope of this book and the reader is referred to specialized studies.

The surface of the crack depends on the properties of the material and on loading characteristics. The surface may be more or less rough and developed. It appears that the surface of the crack in cement-based materials has a fractal nature, which indicates that the effective determination of its area is related to the scale of magnification. General remarks about fractals and fractal dimension may be found out in [9.10] and particular precisions were given in [9.11]. The methods for characterizing the cracks and the fracture surfaces using the notion of fractal dimension are not established yet, but a few studies have been published on this subject (cf. Section 10.5).

Cracks as a reason for, and an element of, fracture processes are also considered in Chapter 10.

9.4 Single and multiple cracking

Cracks open or propagate under local stresses which furnish the amount of energy necessary for rupture of material bonds and for the creation of new surfaces. A replacement of a single crack by multiple cracks and microcracks may be beneficial for a number of reasons. The advantages are – increase of strength and stiffness, increase of fracture toughness, improvement of durability through increase of impermeability, better outward aspect, etc.

In composite materials crack propagation is blocked by inhomogeneities of various kinds – aggregate grains, pores and voids, fibres and other forms of inclusion. On the crack path the tensile strength of the matrix itself and its bond to inclusions must be overcome. The strength of the matrix against cracking is relatively low, and the above-mentioned inhomogeneities help to control cracks by increasing their length. A few examples of obstacles to crack propagation are shown in Figure 9.4. All these obstacles stop the cracks by

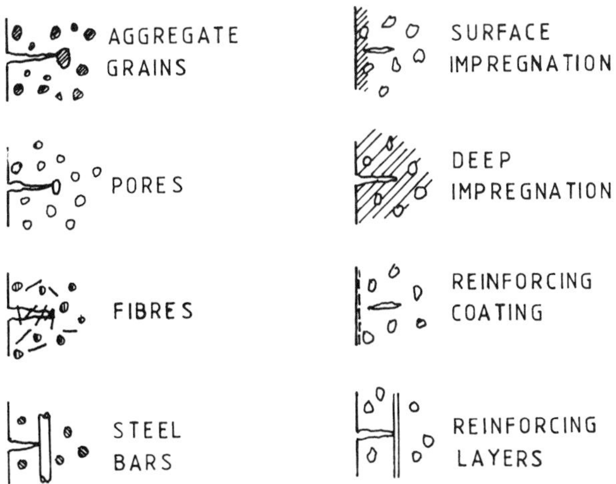

Figure 9.4 Example of obstacles against crack propagation.

arresting their propagating tips. These phenomena increase considerably the energy required for crack development and failure and are used in all methods of crack control.

When a crack meets one of the above-mentioned obstacles it is stopped and a new input of energy is required for its further propagation, for example by an increase of load. Then, the crack may pass across the obstacle or may contour it to follow another path along a weaker region or layer. A crack may then be divided into several finer cracks, i.e. crack branching is induced at an obstacle. Additional energy is also used for breaking the grain or for destroying the bond strength in the interface around it. All kinds of inhomogeneities which produce crack deviation, branching or multiplication increase the total area of fracture surface which becomes several times the area of the cross-section. The determination of effective fracture area is often impossible in an unambiguous way because it is a fractal object, depending on scale and unit of measurement.

The phenomenon of multiple cracking appears mostly in brittle matrices reinforced by efficient systems of bars or fibres. This means, for example, that enough fibres with good bonding may control the cracking process.

On the stress–strain curves the region corresponding to branching and multiplication of cracking is somewhat similar to the effects of plasticity of metallic materials – a smoothly curved line showing large deformation under constant or slowly increasing load. Multiple crack systems should be created of necessity, if large energy absorption and high toughness of the composite material is required. Therefore, in the design and composition of the material multiple cracking is one of the main objectives. In Figure 9.5 an example is shown where deflections after the first crack opening (point A) are related to multiple cracking in the central part of the steel-fibre-reinforced specimen sub-

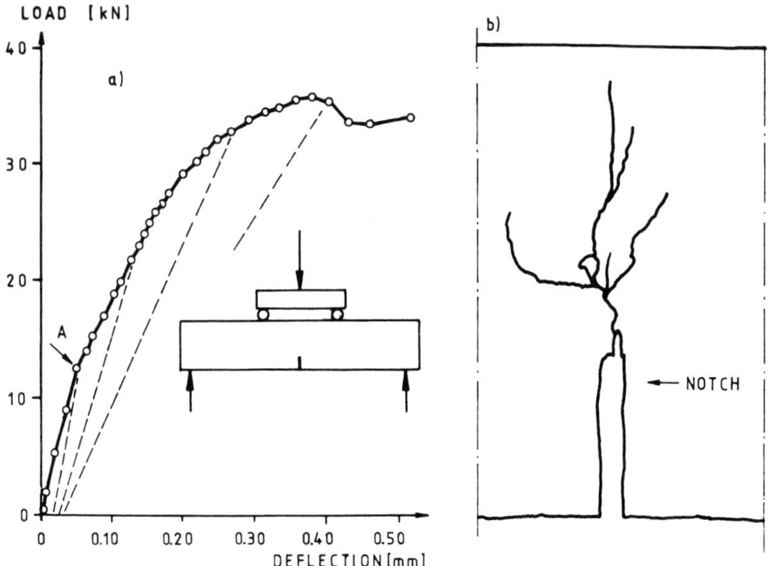

Figure 9.5 Multiple cracks; a) 'knee' at point A of the load–deflection curve; b) multiple cracks on lateral surface of a steel fibre-reinforced concrete beam. (Sources: Brandt, A.M. *et al.*, Fracture mechanics tests of reference concrete beams in pure bending: Tech. Univ. of Delft, 1989; Brandt, A.M. and Stroeven P., Fracture energy in notched steel fibre-reinforced concrete beams; Applied Science Publishers, 1991.) [9.12] and [9.13]

jected to bending. A full description of that test is given in [9.12] and [9.13]. Discontinuous lines show the gradual decrease of the Young's modulus of the tested beam due to development of the cracks, cf. Figure 8.3 where the opposite process of hardening with successive load cycles is presented.

Crack control by the fibres is also visible in those regions of the load–deflection curves where after the unloading–reloading cycle the elasticity of fibres bridging the cracks enables the recovery of the bearing capacity of the specimen before unloading.

The efficiency of fibres for crack control depends upon fibre dimension and stiffness. An interesting example of the diversified role of fibres has been revealed in [9.14]. Mortar specimens reinforced with various combinations of steel and carbon fibres were subjected to bending and acoustic emission (AE) was recorded. In Figure 9.6 diagrams are shown characterizing the behaviour of a specimen reinforced with 3.5% vol. of Kureha pitch carbon fibres (3 mm length, 14.5 μ diameter, 720 MPa tensile strength and 32 GPa Young's modulus). Similar diagrams shown in Figure 9.7 are obtained from a specimen reinforced with 7.5% vol. of steel Arbed fibres (0.25 × 25 mm) prepared with the SIFCON technique, cf. Section 14.2.4. On the left side of the diagrams in both figures the load and AE counts are shown as functions of time. On the right side of the diagrams the relative scale are used – all values are divided by those which

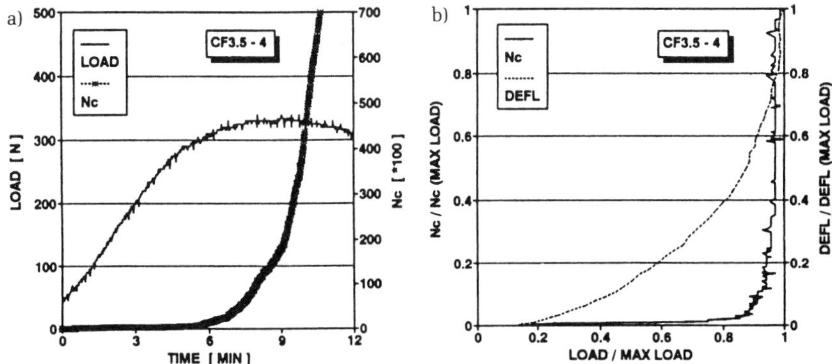

Figure 9.6 Comparison of curves for load and AE counts with relative deflections of a cement mortar specimen reinforced with 3.5% of carbon-fibres. (Source: Brandt, A.M. and Glinicki, M.A. Flexural behaviour of concrete elements reinforced with carbon fibres; published by Chapman & Hall/Spon, 1992.) [9.14]

correspond to maximum load. In the specimen reinforced with carbon fibres the number of counts is quite small until about 85–90% of the maximum load was reached. In fact, the acoustic emission was only initiated at that stage. The acoustic emission in the specimen reinforced with a high amount of steel-fibres (Figure 9.7) develops in a different way – the microcracks are recorded from virtually the beginning of loading, and at 30% of maximum load the total count is quite appreciable. For this specimen the ultimate strength is considerably increased by strong fibre reinforcement, but microcracks are not controlled at all. The carbon fibres in Figure 9.6 control microcracks and disperse them in such a way that they do not produce perceptible acoustic emissions, i.e. above

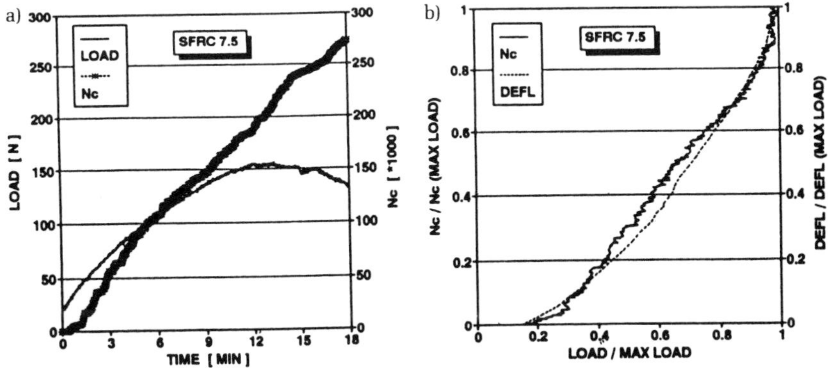

Figure 9.7 Comparison of curves for load and AE counts with relative deflections of a cement mortar specimen reinforced with 7.5% of Arbed fibres. (Source: Brandt, A.M. and Glinicki, M.A., Flexural behaviour of concrete elements reinforced with carbon fibres; published by Chapman & Hall/Spon, 1992.) [9.14]

the imposed discrimination level. However, the existence of microcracks is proved by the highly non-linear behaviour of the specimen.

The analytical approach to the problem of multiple cracking in fibre-reinforced brittle matrix composites was examined by many authors and some papers are particularly important, e.g. [9.15]. That approach called ACK theory is one of the best presented theories of fibrous composites. It was later described in several books, e.g. [9.16] and [9.17] and that is why it is only mentioned briefly in Section 10.2.2.

9.5 Modelling of cracking

Cracks, their opening and propagation in the structure of materials may be modelled and reproduced by computer experiments. Such simulations are based on different assumptions as to the behaviour of both matrix and inclusions. One of the first attempts in that direction was [9.18] which considered two-dimensional model structures with randomly distributed pores and inclusions in a cement matrix. A mainly linear behaviour is assumed, with some non-linear components. Cracks are induced by shrinkage and their propagation under external loads is modelled according to Modes I and II. Finally, cracks run across the matrix between hard aggregate grains and along interfaces between the grains and the matrix. In lightweight aggregate concrete models the cracks run across the grains as well. Computer simulations enabled the different relations between the strength of the matrix and the aggregate grains, influence of increasing load, quality of the matrix/aggregate bond, etc. to be investigated in a systematic way. Examples of crack patterns in various materials are shown in Figures 9.8, 9.9 and 9.10.

Computer analysis of crack propagation through finite element grids was developed by several authors. Cracks are represented by discontinuities of the finite element mesh and smeared crack models were also applied. Cement-based matrices were considered as linear elastic bodies up to the point where cracks open and later their behaviour becomes highly non-linear. Various methods were applied to represent non-linear and heterogeneous materials and to simulate their behaviour under load, cf. [9.19]. In discrete models cracks are represented as discontinuities in the finite element mesh. This is so when smeared crack models are introduced.

The computer experiments with modelled materials with inclusions, cracks, etc. enable researchers to check different situations against various sets of parameters. However, the results obtained are limited to a large measure by their authors' initiatives in the rational design of models reflecting the effective properties of materials and the shapes of structures. No new physical elements may be expected as the computer simulations cannot exhibit more information than was initially introduced by their authors and for this reason they cannot replace experiments. The facility for calculating various examples based on

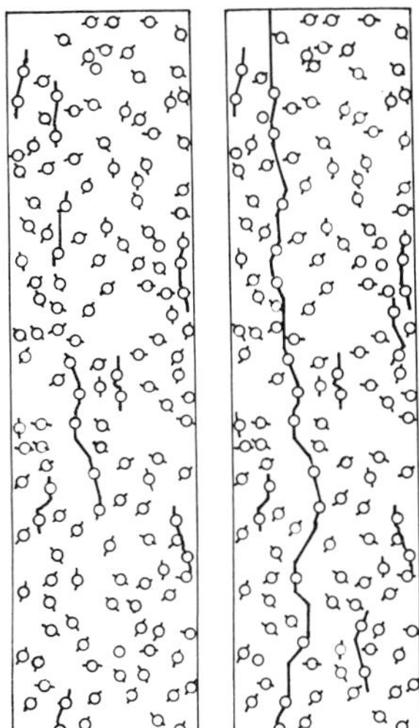

Figure 9.8 Crack patterns in hardened cement paste with randomly distributed initial pores and intrinsic cracks: initial load level and advanced load level. (Reproduced from Zaitsev, Y.V. and Wittmann, F.H., Simulation of crack propagation and failure of concrete; *Materials and Structures*, **14**(83), pp. 357–65, RILEM, 1981.) [9.18]

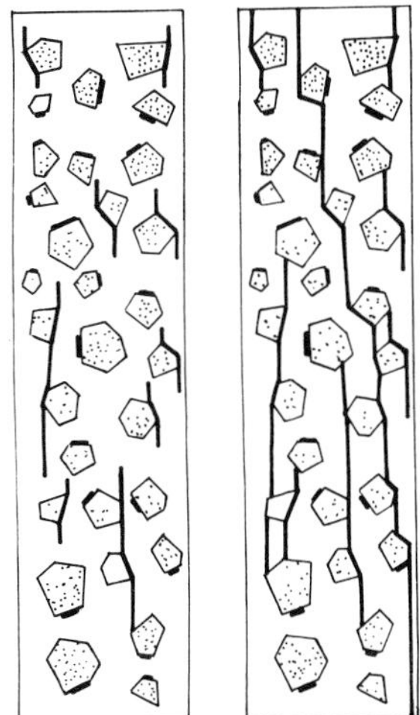

Figure 9.9 Crack patterns in normal concrete under two levels of load, cracks are running around the aggregate grains. (Reproduced from Zaitsev, Y.V. and Wittmann, F.H., Simulation of crack propagation and failure of concrete; *Materials and Structures*, **14**(83), pp. 357–65, RILEM, 1981.) [9.18]

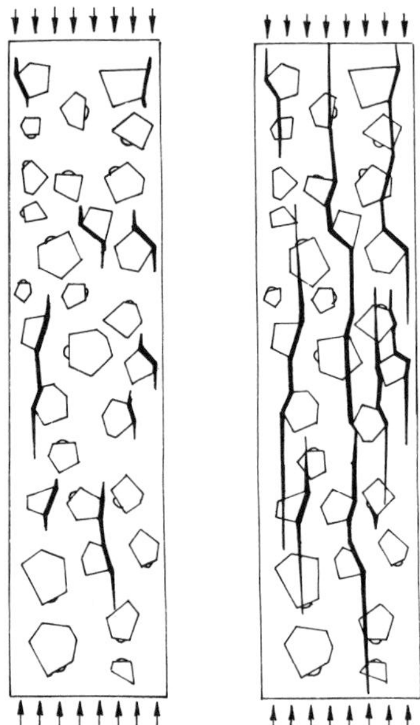

Figure 9.10 Crack patterns in high strength concrete under two levels of load, cracks run around or across the aggregate grains. (Reproduced from Zaitsev, Y.V. and Wittmann, F.H., Simulation of crack propagation and failure of concrete; *Materials and Structures*, **14**(83), pp. 357–65, RILEM, 1981.) [9.18]

different sets of input data, their ease of modification and the possibility of finding the best model for experimental results, represent the main advantages of computer modelling.

Two important factors determine the cracking and fracture of hardened cement composites [9.20]. The first is a clear relationship between porosity and strength. The regions with high porosity, where the rupture processes are initiated, are the weakest. This relation is expressed by the law of mixtures – the pores as weak components decrease the composite's strength. The second factor is that for the same total porosity the bigger pores affect the strength to the greatest degree. It confirms the Griffith's failure criterion and justifies the fracture mechanics approach.

9.6 Consequences of cracking

The cracks diminish the material's strength and stiffness and may seriously influence various properties of the material during ageing and exploitation. In the first place, the durability of structural and non-structural elements may be seriously endangered because the system of interconnected capillary pores and cracks enables the transportation of gases and liquids through the concrete structure. The following processes may be mentioned here:

- permeation of water and water solutions, described by Darcy's law;
- permeation of gases;
- rise of water level by capillary suction;
- diffusion of water vapour.

Several aggressive substances may enter the material structure as a result of a combination of these processes. A unified measure of concrete durability was proposed in the form of an air permeability characteristic which could complete the standard strength in material characterization [9.21].

The decrease of strength in the presence of cracks may be described independently of their origin in the frame of fracture mechanics on the basis of the Griffith's approach, or by using damage analysis. The decrease of stiffness is exhibited for instance by a decrease of slope of the strain–stress curve.

The danger that cracks may adversely affect the durability of the material is proportional to their width, and depends on the environmental conditions. Also, the location of cracks and the function of the elements are of importance. In Table 9.1 are listed the values of the crack widths which are considered as the maximum permissible according to various national and regional standards or other regulations. These values are indicated as examples only and should be considered together with such aspects as the quality of execution and control, dimensions and importance of examined elements, their role as structural or non-structural ones, the minimum cover depth required for steel bars, etc.

The cracks in plain or reinforced elements, made of cement-based composites and subjected to tension, are unavoidable due to the difference in Young's moduli of hardened cement and steel. It is, however, the task of the designer to select appropriate structural dimensions and material properties to ensure impermeability for the material itself, or by additional coatings.

In principle cracking is an irrecoverable process, particularly in an advanced stage of crack propagation. After the discontinuity point, i.e. after the first

Table 9.1 Maximum permissible crack width in concrete structures

Kind of structure and environment conditions	Crack width (mm)
In-door structures dry air, impermeable coating provided	0.4–0.5
Out-door structures medium humidity, no corrosive agents	0.3–0.4
Out-door structures high humidity	0.2–0.3
High humidity corrosive agents (de-icing, sea water)	0.1–0.15
Reservoirs for fluids	0.10

variation of the slope of the strain–stress curve, which is considered as the first crack opening, the hypotheses of material continuity are no longer valid; thus the notion of stress is applicable only with serious restrictions. It should be mentioned here, that the question as to whether these hypotheses are applicable at all should also be formulated. In brittle matrix composites the system of cracks and local discontinuities exists from the outset at different levels, and may be detected easily using appropriate methods.

The 'healing' of a crack was observed in numerous tests and this is considered briefly in Section 9.7.

9.7 Healing of cracks

The phenomenon of self-regeneration of cracks in cement-based matrices is known, but only superficially recognized. Basic observations confirm that cracks caused by tensile stress exhibit certain healing provided that both surfaces are rejoined to ensure adherence. The specimens should be kept in high humidity or preferably in water.

Initial remarks on the self-healing of bond cracks in reinforced concrete elements were made by Abrams as early as 1913. The problem was considered again in 1956 [9.22] and [9.23] more recent work has shown that the healing of the interfacial bond is greater than that observed for cracks in plain mortar and concrete.

In lightweight concrete healing effects were observed in both the steel–paste interface and in the cracks in the cement matrix [9.24].

The self-healing process may also be studied using acoustic emission measurements [9.25]. The effects of healing were also observed in [9.26], where it was shown that in cracked specimens, the greater is the healing – the younger is the concrete. The tests were made on specimens subjected to tension up to the point of cracking and later cured in water under a slight pressure. Examples of the results achieved are presented in Figure 9.11.

A complete restoration of the fracture toughness and even an increase of strength was observed [9.27] in plain concrete beams subjected to cracking under pure bending and later cured in fog room conditions over a 2 years period. The crack width at the notch was initially equal to 0.3 mm or more. Similar results were also obtained for steel fibre-reinforced elements, [9.28]. The elements were stored in natural environmental conditions and only the regain of the bearing capacity was measured.

The healing of cracks is related to prolonged hydration of cement grains when cracked elements are maintained in sufficient humidity. In such conditions new crystallization products partly recover the strength over the cracks. It has been observed that the healing is inversely proportional to the crack width, represented for instance by the values for the Crack Opening Displacement (COD). The question as to whether crack healing may be considered as a

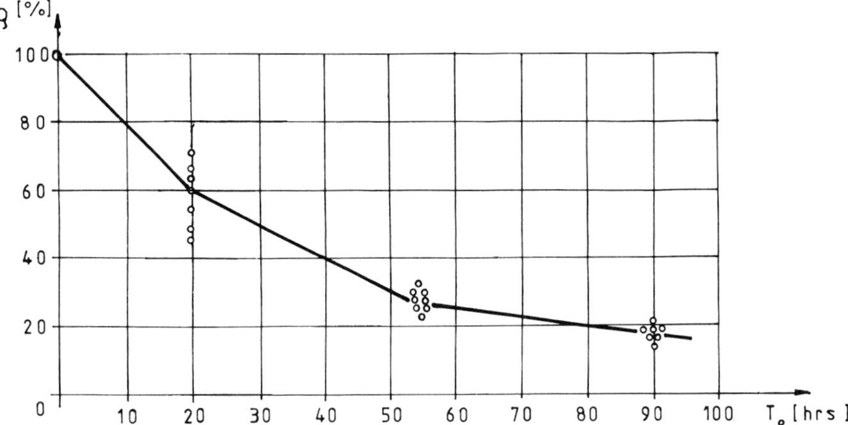

Figure 9.11 Strength restoration as a function of age of concrete at cracking. (Reproduced with permission from Zamorowski, W., The phenomena of self-regeneration of concrete; *International Journal of Cement Comp. and Lightweight Concrete*, **7**(2), pp. 199–201, published by Elsevier Science Publishers, 1985.) [9.26]

phenomenon of appreciable importance for the durability of concrete elements cannot as yet be answered and the possibilities of crack healing are not accounted for in the design of concrete elements.

References

9.1. Broek, D. (1986) *Elementary Engineering Fracture Mechanics*, 4th edn, Martinus Nijhoff, Dordrecht.

9.2. Kaplan, M.F. (1961) Crack propagation and the fracture of concrete. *J. of the American Concrete Institute*, **58**, 591–610.

9.3. Kawamura, M. (1978) Internal stresses and microcrack formation caused by drying in hardened cement pastes. *J. of the American Ceramic Society*, **61**(7–8), 281–3.

9.4. Malmberg, B. and Skarendahl, Å. (1978) Method of studying the cracking of fibre concrete under restrained shrinkage, in Proc. RILEM Symp. '*Testing and Test Methods of Fibre Cement Composites*', (ed. R.N. Swamy), The Construction Press Lancaster, England, 173–9.

9.5. Dahl, P.A. (1986) Influence of fibre-reinforcement on plastic shrinkage and cracking, in Proc. Int. Symp. '*Brittle Matrix Composites 1*', Jabłonna 1985, (eds A.M. Brandt and I.H. Marshall), Elsevier Applied Science, London and New York, 435–41.

9.6. Debicki, G. and Clastres, C. (1989) A shrinkage cracking test of a cement paste reinforced by synthetic fibres, Institut National des Sciences Appliquées, Lyon, unpublished.

9.7. Lusche, M. (1974) The fracture mechanism of ordinary and lightweight concrete under uniaxial compression, in Proc. Conf. '*Mechanical Properties and Structure of Composite Materials*', (ed. A.M. Brandt), Jabłonna, 18–23 November 1974, Ossolineum, Wrocław, 423–40.

9.8. Diamond, S. and Bentur, A. (1985) On the cracking in concrete and fiber-reinforced cements, Proc. NATO ARW '*Application of Fracture Mechanics to Cementitious Composites*', (ed. S.P. Shah), Martinus Nijhoff Publ., Dordrecht, 87–140.
9.9. Roy, C., Allard, J., Maslouhi, A. and Piasta, Z. (1991) Pattern recognition characterization of microfailures in composites via analytical quantitative acoustic emission, in Proc. Int. Coll. '*Durability of Polymer Based Composite Systems for Structural Applications*', (eds A.H. Cardon and G. Verchery), Elsevier Applied Science, London and New York, 312–24.
9.10. Mandelbrot, B.B. (1983) *The Fractal Geometry of Nature*, W.H. Freeman, New York.
9.11. Winslow, D.N. (1985) The fractal nature of the surface of cement paste, *Cement and Concrete Research*, **15**, 817–24.
9.12. Brandt, A.M., Stroeven, P., Dalhuisen, D.H. and Donker, L. (1989) Fracture mechanics tests of reference concrete beams in pure bending. Rep. 21.1.89-7/C4, Tech. Univ. Delft, pp. 57.
9.13. Brandt, A.M. and Stroeven, P. (1991) Fracture energy in notched steel-fibre-reinforced concrete beams, in Proc. Int. Symp. '*Brittle Matrix Composite 3*', (eds A.M. Brandt and I.H. Marshall), Applied Science Publishers, London and New York.
9.14. Brandt, A.M. and Glinicki, M.A. (1992) Flexural behaviour of concrete elements reinforced with carbon fibres, in Proc. RILEM/ACI Workshop '*High Performance Fiber Reinforced Cement Composites*', (eds H.W. Reinhardt and A.E. Naaman), Mainz 1991, Chapman and Hall/Spon, London, 288–99.
9.15. Aveston, J., Cooper, G.A. and Kelly, A. (1971) Single and multiple fracture, in Proc. Conf. '*The Properties of Fibre Composites*', National Physical Laboratory, IPC Science and Technology Press, Paper 2, Teddington, England, 15–24.
9.16. Hannant, D.J. (1978) *Fibre Cements and Fibre Concretes*, John Wiley & Sons, Chichester.
9.17. Bentur, A. and Mindess, S. (1990) *Fibre Reinforced Cementitious Composites*, Elsevier Applied Science, London.
9.18. Zaitsev, Y.V. and Wittmann, F.H. (1981) Simulation of crack propagation and failure of concrete. *Materials and Structures*, **14**(83), 357–65.
9.19. Petersson, P.E. (1981) Crack growth and formation of fracture zones in plain concrete and similar materials, Rep. TVBM-1006, Div. of Build. Mat., Lund Inst. of Techn., Lund, Sweden.
9.20. Mindess, S. (1983) Mechanical performance of cementitious systems, in *Structure and Performance of Cements*, (ed. P. Barnes), Applied Science Publishers, London and New York, 319–63.
9.21. Hilsdorf, H.K. (1989) Durability of concrete – a measurable quantity? Proc. of IABSE Symp. '*Durability of Structures*', Lisbon, 6–8 September, **1**, 111–23.
9.22. Lauer, K.R. and Slate, F.O. (1956) Autogenous healing of cement paste. *ACI Journal*, **27**(10), 1083–98.
9.23. Gray, R.J. (1984) Autogenous healing of fibre/matrix interfacial bond in fibre-reinforced mortar. *Cem. and Concr. Res.*, **14**, 315–17.
9.24. Mor, A., Monteiro, P.J.M. and Hetsre, W.T. (1989) Observations of healing of cracks in high-strength lightweight concrete. *Cement, Concrete and Aggregates*, CCAGDP, **12**(2), 121–5.
9.25. Flaga, K.J. and Moczko, A.T. (1991) Evaluation of the ability of microcracked concrete to self healing in *Proc. of 8th Biennial European Conf. on Fracture* (*ECF8*).

ECF and Fracture Behaviour and Design of Materials and Structures, Eng. Mat. Advisory Services Ltd, Warley, UK, 773–9.

9.26. Zamorowski, W. (1985) The phenomenon of self-regeneration of concrete. *The Int. Journ. of Cem. Comp. and Lightweight Concrete*, **7**(3), 199–201.

9.27. Kasperkiewicz, J. and Stroeven, P. (1991) Observations on crack healing in concrete, as [9.13], 164–73.

9.28. Hannant, D.J. and Edgington, J. (1975) Durability of steel fibre concrete, in Proc. RILEM Symp. '*Fibre Reinforced Cement and Concrete*', Construction Press, Lancaster, 159–69.

10 Fracture and failure in materials structures

10.1 Application of fracture mechanics to cement matrices

10.1.1 PRINCIPLES OF LINEAR ELASTIC FRACTURE MECHANICS (LEFM)

Fracture mechanics was first used by Griffith, as an approach to the analysis and evaluation of a material's behaviour, [10.1] and [10.2]. For the basic principles of fracture mechanics and their development, the reader is referred to one of the available books and manuals, e.g. [10.3]. It is sufficient here, to note a few of the most important notions necessary for considerations of the brittle matrix composites.

The Griffith's theory was based on two assumptions. The first one concerned the considerable difference between observed and calculated tensile strength of materials. Effective strength is lower by at least one order of magnitude than the theoretical one calculated on the basis of the interatomic bonds. That difference was attributed to stress concentrations at microcracks and defects existing in every solid body before application of any external load. In materials which exhibit plastic deformations these stress concentrations disappear without appreciable reduction of material strength. In brittle materials, in contrast, a stress concentration initiates microcracks and their propagation, thus leading to fracture.

The second assumption is related to the condition of an energetic equilibrium at the crack tip when a crack may start to propagate. The relation between the strain energy release rate $\partial U/\partial c$ considered as the crack extension force and the rate of energy $\partial S/\partial c$ necessary to create a new crack surface decides whether the crack is stable or is rapidly propagating. The strain energy is denoted by U and specific surface energy by S. The initial crack length is equal to $2c$. When:

$$\partial U/\partial c < \partial S/\partial c \tag{10.1}$$

the crack driving force is too low and the initial crack remains stable. If the load is increased over the equilibrium state,

$$\partial U/\partial c \geqslant \partial S/\partial c, \tag{10.2}$$

then the crack propagates. The strain energy is transformed into the surface energy. This means that the crack propagation up to the critical state is defined by equation 10.1 and is conditioned by an energy input exceeding the energy required for the creation of new surfaces.

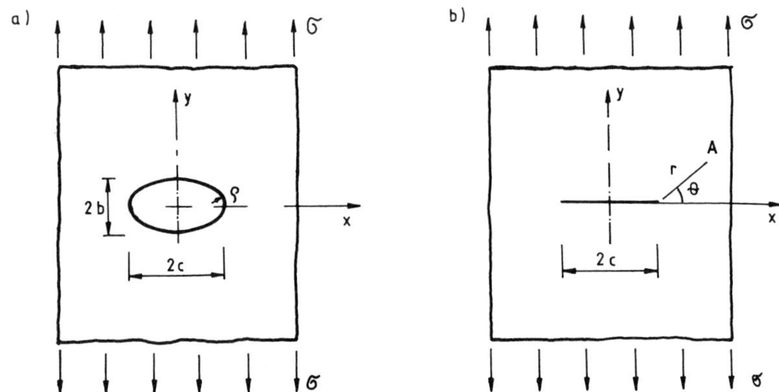

Figure 10.1 Schemes of an infinite plate subjected to tension; a) with an elliptical hole; b) with a penny-shape crack. (Reproduced with permission from Griffith, A.A., The phenomenon of rupture and flow in solids; *Phil. Trans. Roy. Society*, A221, pp. 163–98, Royal Society of London, 1921.) [10.1]

In an ideally elastic and brittle material further crack propagation does not require additional energy and a rapid crack propagation follows which results in final fracture.

On that basis the theoretical value for tensile strength was derived by Griffith in the following form,

$$\sigma_f = \left(\frac{2E\gamma_f}{\pi c}\right)^{1/2} \tag{10.3}$$

for a plate of infinite dimensions subjected to tensile stress σ and having an elliptical crack (Figure 10.1a) where γ_f is the fracture surface energy, considered as a kind of material property. However, the tests on real materials did not confirm the values of σ_f obtained from equation 10.3 because of stress concentrations at the tips of the microcracks. The value of the stress at the crack tip may be expressed by the relation:

$$\sigma_{\text{con}} = \sigma 2\left(\frac{c}{\rho}\right)^{1/2}, \tag{10.4}$$

where ρ is the curvature radius at the crack tip. When the crack is becoming sharper, it means with $\rho = 0$, the effect of concentration considered as ratio $\sigma_{\text{con}}/\sigma$ is increasing.

The concept of stress concentration at the crack tip is represented in Figure 10.2. Theoretical stress concentration for a very sharp crack (penny-shape crack, Figure 10.1b) in a elastic material leads to an infinite stress value, Figure 10.2a, which cannot be realized. If a local plastic zone appears around the crack tip, the value of the stress corresponds to the yield stress σ_y, which characterizes the material's behaviour (Figure 10.2b). In the concrete-like materials around

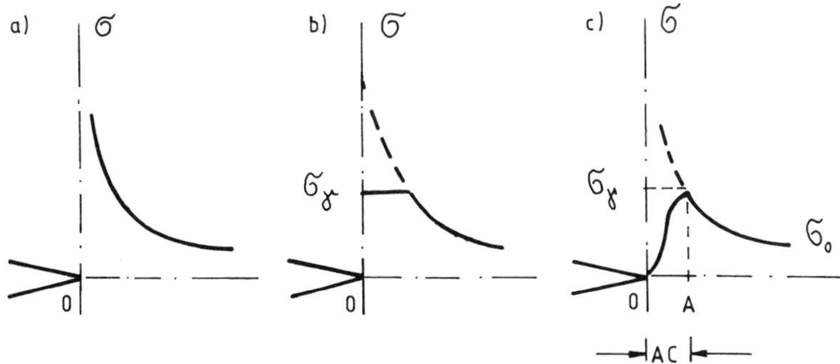

Figure 10.2 Stress concentrations at the crack tip.

crack tips zones of microcracking appear and the corresponding stress distribution is supposed as shown in Figure 10.2c.

In real materials much energy is used, not only to create new crack surfaces but the energy is also dispersed in zones of plastified or microcracked material. Therefore, outside the region where the threshold value of σ is reached (Figure 10.2) rapid crack propagation without an energy input does not occur at all, or is preceded by slow crack propagation which requires new energy to overcome obstacles in material structure and in material inelasticity.

The propagation of an initial crack may be divided into three independent modes which are most often studied separately before being considered as a mixed mode. These modes are shown schematically in Figure 10.3 but here only Mode I is described in more detail for two reasons – it is more suitable to analyse crack propagation at the macro-level and in most cases other modes are often neglected with respect to Mode I, unless the load is applied in a special

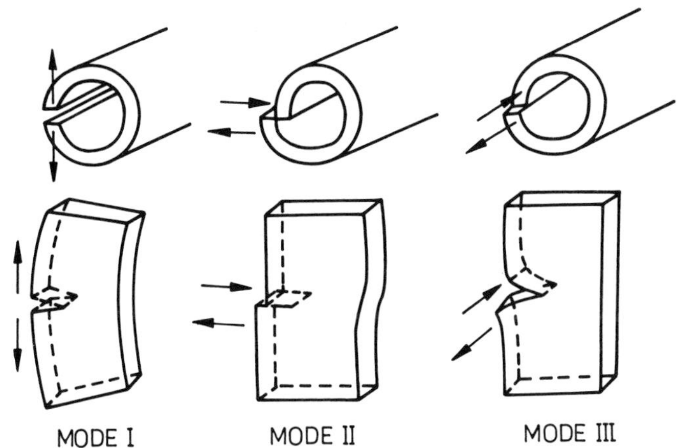

Figure 10.3 Three modes of propagation of a crack.

way, producing just Mode II or Mode III. Additional remarks on other modes and on their simultaneous action are given in Section 10.4.

Kaplan initiated the application of fracture mechanics to cement-based materials [10.4]. His works were continued by many others [10.5] and [10.6]. A very comprehensive review of these works and problems related to the introduction of fracture mechanics to these materials was published in [10.7] and [10.8] and also by other authors in [10.9] and [10.10].

The fracture mechanics derived by Griffith after his tests on glass specimens directly concerns the brittle behaviour of materials and is certainly better justified for hardened cement paste than for any other cement-based composite. The general application of fracture mechanics is therefore associated with the additional assumptions that plastic or quasi-plastic effects are negligible, or with appropriate modifications of the linear formulae in LEFM. In that context the linear and non-linear fracture mechanics approach should be distinguished.

In LEFM the material is considered as homogeneous, isotropic and following the principles of linear elasticity. The derived formulae do not reflect correctly the behaviour of real materials which present inhomogeneities, anisotropy and local plasticity.

In LEFM Mode I two main notions are specified.

K_I [$\mathrm{MNm}^{-3/2}$] is the stress intensity factor which describes the intensity of the elastic stress field in the neighbourhood of the crack tip. It is expressed by a simple relation for an infinite element loaded by stress σ:

$$K_I = \sigma(\pi c)^{1/2} \tag{10.5}$$

and for elements with finite dimensions,

$$K_I = \sigma(\pi c)^{1/2}\, Y(a/c) \tag{10.6}$$

where $Y(a/c)$ is a function expressing the influence of the shape of element, crack configuration and kind of loading. For several sets of such conditions the function $Y(a/c)$ is calculated and published, e.g. in [10.11], in the form of polynomials with respect to (a/c), where a is the characteristic dimension of the element and c is half length of the crack.

$G_I[kNm^{-1}]$ is the elastic stress energy release rate, it means that it describes the rate at which the energy for crack propagation is supplied. G_I as equal to $\partial U/\partial c$ is called also the crack extension force and is related to elastic properties of the material and element and to the applied load system.

For the simplest case of an infinite plate under tensile stress σ the strain energy release rate is given by relation,

$$G_I = \pi c \frac{\sigma^2}{E}. \tag{10.7}$$

In such a way there are two approaches to apply fracture mechanics – using a stress intensity concept or an energy one. Both are equivalent and give identical results in the case of an ideal brittle material and they are related as follows:

$$\text{for plane stress,} \quad K_I^2 = EG_I$$

$$\text{for plane strain,} \quad K_I^2 = EG_I \frac{1}{1 - v^2} \tag{10.8}$$

where v is the Poisson's coefficient. Because its value is approximately equal to 0.2 for various concretes, then the difference between the plane stress and plane strain values may be neglected in most of the practical problems in which precision of other parameters is often lower.

The notion of plane stress and plain strain are related to the geometrical stress distribution around the crack tip. For derivation of these relations the reader is again referred to the fracture mechanics manuals. It may be useful to mention here, that plane stress configuration corresponds to a relatively thin plate loaded in its plane, and plane strain to a thick element where strain components perpendicular to its plane may be neglected.

G_I and K_I characterize the situation around the crack tip at the stable state described by equation 10.1 in which further increase of loading does not produce crack instability. When, due to the load increase, the threshold (equation 10.2) is reached and the sign of the inequality is changed, then the onset of crack propagation is observed which corresponds to critical values G_{Ic} and K_{Ic}. These values form a kind of fracture criterion, completed by relation,

$$G_{Ic} = 2\gamma_f \tag{10.9}$$

derived from equation 10.3 and equation 10.7.

The values of G_{Ic} and K_{Ic} may be calculated from equation 10.5 and equation 10.6 when critical values of stress σ_{cr}, corresponding to observed onset of crack propagation, are introduced.

The application of the stress intensity factor K is preferable [10.12], because:

- K is a linear function of the load;
- K describes the stress field around the crack tip without attempting to represent the entire specimen or element;
- values of K due to different states of loading may be summed up.

Application of G_{Ic} and K_{Ic} as material constants to cement-based composites proved to be useful, however, there are several questions and limitations which should be considered.

Both these parameters have been derived for an ideal material and for particular conditions for crack dimensions and load application. Neither of these conditions is exactly satisfied, and calculated values may be considered as approximate ones only. Even if the geometrical conditions of element and loading are taken into account by appropriate determination of function $Y(a/c)$ as in equation 10.6, the behaviour of every material around the crack tip shows more, or less important, non-elastic effects in the form of local plastic deformations or microcracking.

Furthermore, for heterogeneous materials with internal structure composed of aggregate grains or fibres the fracture surface energy is considerably increased and crack propagation is more or less controlled in such a way that slow crack growth is observed and it is difficult to select an appropriate value for critical stress in equation 10.5, equation 10.6 or equation 10.7. Also the phenomenon of multiple cracking cannot be directly considered within the frame of LEFM.

It has been shown by several authors, e.g. [10.13] and [10.14], that taking into account normal concrete inhomogeneities due to aggregate grains, the application of LEFM requires large specimens, for example beams or cubes with characteristic dimensions larger than 1.0 metre, because the fracture toughness increases with the decrease of specimen size which, however, should be kept sensibly larger than the plastic zone around the crack tip. Tests become expensive and series composed of large specimens necessarily introduce other sources of errors which may disturb the results considerably.

In the situation described above it is necessary either to verify that the non-elastic effects are small and negligible or to try to consider them by appropriate modification of the formulae. For practical applications it will be useful to standardize the specimens and to compare only those with similar dimensions. It is also possible to use other parameters based mostly on experimental data in which the assumptions of an ideal elastic behaviour are not needed. All these ways of using fracture mechanics for cement-based composites are developed by several authors, cf. Section 10.2 and 10.1.3.

10.1.2 ROLE OF DISPERSED REINFORCEMENT AFTER CRACKING OF THE MATRIX

The influence of fibres on brittle matrix behaviour may be reduced to two points – the control of crack propagation and the increase of the ultimate strain. In the 1960s and early 1970s there were two theories which explained the behaviour of a brittle matrix reinforced with dispersed fibres. One of these theories was proposed in papers by Romualdi and Batson [10.15] and by Romualdi and Mandel [10.16]; that theory was called RBM. Another was published by Aveston, in Cooper and Kelly [10.17] and [10.18]; this was the ACK theory. Notwithstanding apparent differences, both approaches are rather close to each other and lead to similar conclusions.

The main difference between these two theories consists in that in RBM the main role of dispersed fibres is to control crack propagation by providing the forces which keep together the material ahead of the crack tip. In the ACK theory the fibres limit the maximum opening displacement of the crack.

In the RBM approach the propagation of a single crack is considered in a matrix reinforced with a system of parallel fibres. The material of the matrix follows linear elasticity and crack propagation is initiated from an existing intrinsic flaw when stress in the direction perpendicular to that flaw attains the tensile strength σ. If the flaw has a form of a penny-shape crack of length $2c$

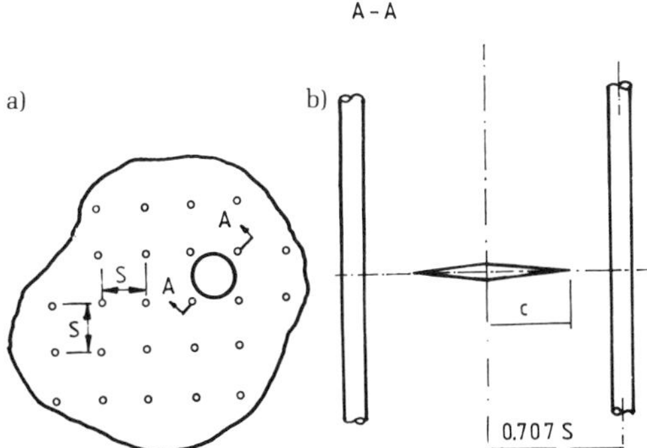

Figure 10.4 Assumed action of fibres in crack propagation control according to RBM theory; a) cross-section with a penny-shape crack and square array of fibres; b) two parallel fibres and a crack. (Reproduced with permission from Romualdi, J.P. and Batson, G.B., Mechanics of crack arrest in concrete; *J. Engng. Mech. Div.*, ASCE Proc. **89**(EM3), pp. 147–68, ASCE, 1963.) [10.15]

as it is considered in LEFM, cf. Section 10.1.1, then the critical value of the stress intensity factor is attained:

$$K_\sigma = 2\frac{\sqrt{c}}{\pi}\sigma. \tag{10.10}$$

The system of aligned fibres arranged according to a square array is shown schematically in Figure 10.4. Before the application of load, the matrix and fibre strains are equal but at crack opening the assumed inextensible fibres present a certain resistance against matrix displacements due to a perfect fibre–matrix bond. Therefore, the fibres provide a stress p which acts on the matrix in an opposite direction to its virtual cracking. Finally the expression for the stress intensity factor is:

$$K_T = 2\frac{\sqrt{c}}{\pi}(\sigma - p). \tag{10.11}$$

The value of stress p is unknown but may be determined taking into account the fibre spacing and the force imposed by a single fibre. The calculation was proposed in [10.15] from a system of linear equations which expressed the equilibrium between displacements of non-reinforced matrix in the cracked state and displacements due to the action of concentrated forces from fibres. The calculated examples for various spacing s derived from the fibres volume fraction V_f (cf. Section 8.4) indicated the increase of modulus of rupture caused by the fibre reinforcement. The comparison of calculated curve and experimental data is shown in Figure 10.5 and a general confirmation may be observed. Further development of the RBM theory in which the critical value G_c of elastic energy release rate was related to parameters of fibre reinforcement is presented in

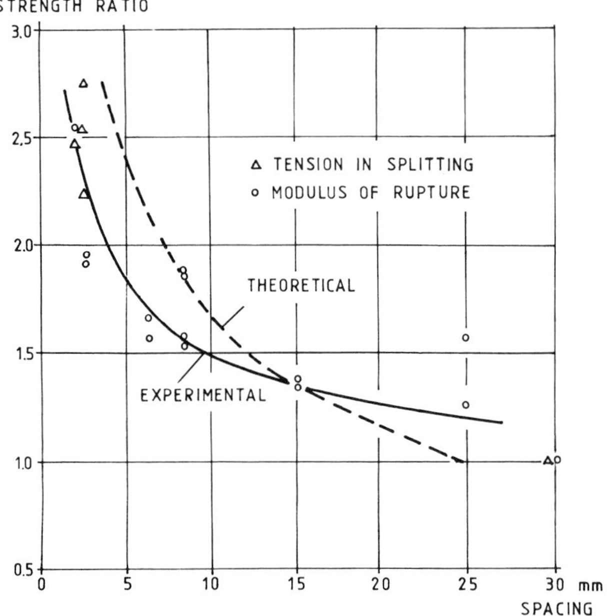

Figure 10.5 Calculated and experimental results of relation between fibre spacing s and matrix reinforcement for modulus of rupture and tensile strength in splitting. (Reproduced with permission from Romualdi, J.P. and Mandel, J.A., Tensile strength of concrete affected by uniformly distributed and closely spaced short lengths of wire reinforcement; *J. of Amer. Concr. Inst.*, **61**, pp. 651–71, 1964.) [10.16]

[10.19]. These considerations are not developed here in detail because its general utility for material design and strength verification is limited and the agreement with experimental results is inadequate.

The theory proposed by Aveston, Cooper and Kelly in its general form covers elastic and non-elastic effects in fibres and matrix. Therefore the entire ascending branch of the stress–strain curve may be described. For that purpose two cases are considered:

1. the fibres may be debonded from the matrix and the pull-out of fibres appears;
2. the fibres are bonded to the matrix and additional stresses are transformed from the fibres to the matrix.

In a composite element subjected to tension and reinforced with aligned fibres the stress–strain relation is initially linear. Its slope is given by elastic modulus determined by the law of mixtures, $E_c = E_f V_f + E_m V_m = E_f V_f(1 + a)$.

The cracking strain in the matrix may be expressed by the formula derived from known properties and volume of the matrix (E_m, V_m), of the fibres (E_f, V_f), the matrix surface work of fracture γ_m and fibre–matrix bond strength τ:

$$\varepsilon_{mc} = \left[\mathrm{A} \frac{24\gamma_m \tau E_f V_f^2}{E_m^3 V_m^2 d} \right]^{1/3}, \tag{10.12}$$

here constant A = 1 to 3 expresses unknown values characterizing the fibre debonding processes and creation of new surfaces. The form of relation (equation 10.12) was proposed in [10.20] on the basis of the ACK theory.

The matrix cracks when the critical strain for an unreinforced matrix ε_{um} or that for composite material ε_{uc} is reached, whichever is greater.

In an example of steel-fibre-reinforced cement-based matrix with $E_f = 210\,\mathrm{GPa}$, $E_m = 35\,\mathrm{GPa}$, $V_f = 0.03$, $\tau = 4\,\mathrm{MPa}$, $d = 0.4$, $\gamma_m = 10\,\mathrm{N/m}$ the result is, $\varepsilon_{uc} = (224$ to $323)10^{-6}$, and this value should be compared with ε_{um} which is usually equal to about $(150$ to $200)10^{-6}$. That example shows that in a very densely reinforced matrix with $V_f = 0.03$, which is difficult to realize in normal technology, a slight increase of critical strain of a composite material with respect to plain matrix may be expected.

Similar results may be obtained when the critical volume fraction of fibres V_{fcr} is considered. It may be easily defined for aligned long or even continuous fibres in an element subjected to tension parallel to the fibre direction. This reinforcement may carry on the load after cracking of the matrix. Therefore, the value of V_{fcr} is derived from the simple equivalence of forces carried on by a composite element of cross-section area A and by the fibres, $A_c E_c \varepsilon_{mu} = A_c V_{fcr} \sigma_{fu}$, $V_{fcr} = E_c \varepsilon_{mu} / \sigma_{fu}$, here the product $E_c \varepsilon_{mu}$ represents the cracking tensile stress in the matrix and σ_{fu} is the ultimate tensile stress in the fibres.

For example, for a high quality matrix with $E_c = 40\,\mathrm{GPa}$ and $\varepsilon_{mu} = 100.10^{-6}$ and fibres made of mild steel with $\sigma_{fu} = 200\,\mathrm{MPa}$ the critical volume fraction is equal to 0.02. In ordinary steel-fibre-reinforced concrete elements usually short and randomly dispersed fibres are used. Because of considerably lower efficiency of such reinforcement, in normal technical conditions the achievement of V_{fcr} is nearly impossible. If other methods of concreting are applied, like SIFCON, or fibres with increased bond and linearization are used, then the efficiency of reinforcement is sensibly improved.

These conclusions may be generalized for elements subjected to bending, provided that the difference in loading states is taken into account and are confirmed by tests of steel-fibre-reinforced cement elements.

The crack spacing may be calculated from another formula derived from the ACK theory giving the distance x of the load transfer from matrix to fibres:

$$x = \frac{E_m(1 - V_f)}{V_f} \frac{\varepsilon_{um} d}{4\tau}, \tag{10.13}$$

if for steel-fibre-reinforced concrete $V_f = 0.02$, $E_m \varepsilon_m = f_{mu} = 5\,\mathrm{MPa}$, and $\tau = 2.0\,\mathrm{MPa}$, then $x = 12.25\,\mathrm{mm}$.

The actual crack spacing is between x and $2x$ and its most probable value may be estimated as equal to $(1.364 \pm 0.002)x$.

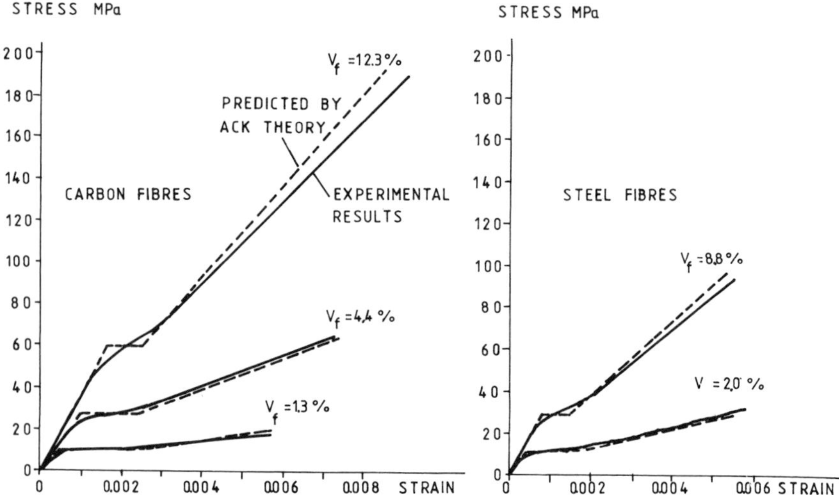

Figure 10.6 Tensile stress–strain diagrams for continuous carbon and steel wire reinforced cements. (Reproduced from Aveston, J. *et al.*, Fibre-reinforced cements – specific foundations for specifications; published by IPC Science and Technology Press, 1974.) [10.22]

The ACK theory also covers other orientations of fibres and in the paper [10.21] two formulae are given for 2D and 3D fibre distribution, $x'_{2D} = \pi x/2$, $x''_{3D} = 2x$.

After cracking the composite Young's modulus is depending on the fibre reinforcement, $E_c = E_f V_f$.

The experimental verification of ACK theory is presented in [10.22] and the approximation obtained may be considered as quite satisfactory (Figure 10.6). However, it should be mentioned that specimens produced for these verifications were made with different materials than those used in normal practice.

Results of other verification have been published in [10.23] following tests on cement paste specimens reinforced with continuous and aligned glassfibres of various volume fractions (Figure 10.7). The tensile strain at fracture of the plain paste was not given, anyway the influence of fibres is clearly visible and in general confirms the ACK theory predictions, if an increase of strength with increase of reinforcement may be estimated as sufficient verification.

Both theories presented lead to similar conclusions as concerns the cracking strain of reinforced matrices; however, both exaggerate the influence of fibres. After crack opening, the ACK theory may be used to calculate the probable crack spacing and the composite's Young's modulus. Furthermore, in that theory a few of the parameters used are taken from the testing of relevant composite elements and therefore it is to some extent more appropriate for verification and calibration than other proposed theories for fibre-reinforced composites.

The theories called RBM and ACK have two important limitations concerning their application to cement-based composites. The descending branch of the

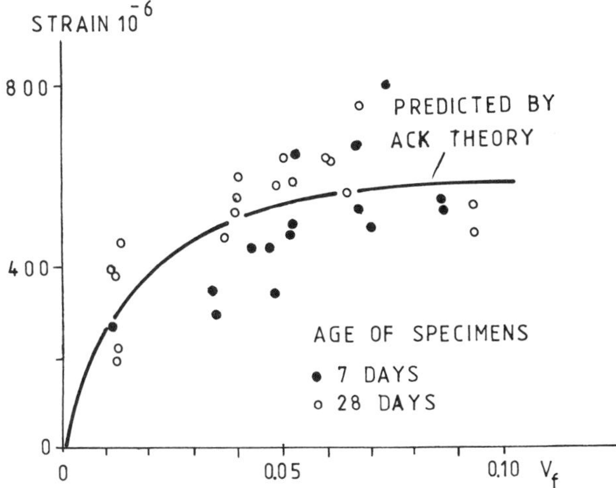

Figure 10.7 Matrix failure strain of glass-fibre reinforced cement paste. (Reproduced from Laws, V., On increase of tensile failure of Portland cement reinforced with glass-fibre bundles; published by IPC Science and Technology Press, 1974.) [10.23]

stress–strain curve is not covered, it means that the behaviour of composite materials after cracking is not described. Bearing in mind that the main purpose of fibres is to control cracking, and that their influence on that part of cement composites behaviour is the most meaningful, that limitation is important.

Furthermore, both theories better describe the stress–strain or load–displacement diagrams the higher is the fibre volume fraction. Or, in practical applications for many reasons, described elsewhere, low volume fractions of fibre reinforcement are used.

There is another notion derived for fibre-reinforced matrix and related to the post-cracking behaviour. It is the critical value of fibre volume fraction V_f which corresponds to the increase of the bearing capacity. For insufficient reinforcement $V_f < V_{f\text{crit}}$, after cracking of the matrix the load decreases. The role of fibres is limited to the crack control, but its efficiency is not sufficient for any load increase beyond the level of the first crack in the matrix. The expression for $V_{f\text{crit}}$ is derived in [10.24] on the basis of several simplifying assumptions for composites reinforced with short chopped fibres. The numerical examples show that the values calculated in that way are much lower than the results obtained from tests.

It appears from comparison of theoretical and experimental results that detailed calculations of fibre-reinforced concrete behaviour do not allow reliable data to be obtained without taking into account all influences and factors, like a precisely determined efficiency coefficient, space effects, etc.

The notion of $V_{f\text{crit}}$ may be generalized for all kinds of reinforcement and used to estimate their efficiency.

10.1.3 APPLICATION OF FRACTURE MECHANICS TO ELASTO-PLASTIC MATERIALS

The development of fracture mechanics aimed at consideration of non-elastic and non-linear effects is of particular importance for applications in composite materials in which the internal structure is actually designed to control cracking and to increase the effective fracture surface energy. A few non-linear fracture approaches are described below.

The J-integral has been defined in [10.25] initially for non-linear elastic materials as a linear integral on a closed contour Γ_i:

$$J_\Gamma = \int_{\Gamma_i} \left(W dy - T \frac{\partial u}{\partial x} \right) ds \tag{10.14}$$

where x, y are rectilinear coordinates with y-axis perpendicular to the plane of the crack propagation, W is the strain energy density, T is the vector of traction which is perpendicular to Γ_i, u is the displacement vector and ds is a section of the curve Γ_i.

The Rice integral (equation 10.14) is independent on the path, it means that $J_{\Gamma_1} = J_{\Gamma_2}$ (Figure 10.8) and the proof is given in [10.25]. The J-integral is proposed as a fracture criterion for materials characterized by nonlinear stress–strain relations and its critical value denoted J_c corresponds to rapid crack propagation. In linear elastic materials:

$$J_{Ic} = G_{Ic}. \tag{10.15}$$

Several methods were published for calculation of the J-integral and for determination of its critical value, e.g. [10.26], [10.27] and [10.28]. The tests carried out by various authors in different conditions furnished rather coherent results for J_{Ic}. The authors of paper [10.26] have shown, that J_{Ic} is much more sensitive to the effects of fibre-reinforcement than for example K_{Ic}. However, the dispersion of test results and dependence on arbitrarily estimated parameters do not allow them to be used for practical applications.

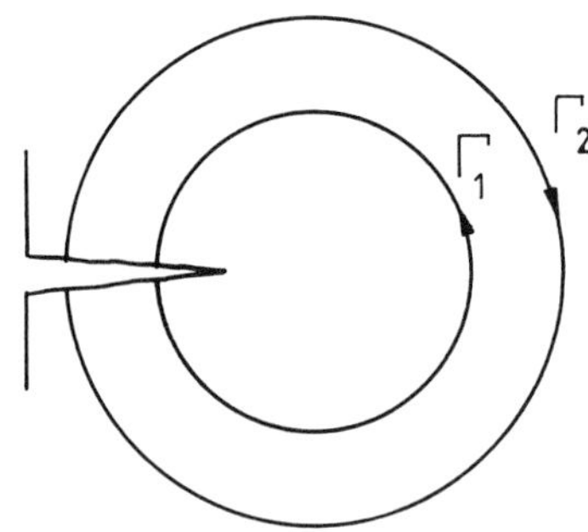

Figure 10.8 Integrating path for calculation of the J integral.

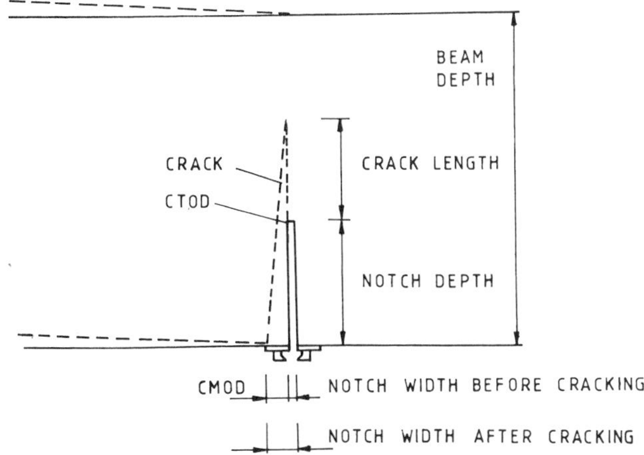

Figure 10.9 CTOD and CMOD in a notch after cracking.

Another method for characterizing the behaviour of composite elements under load is based on the crack opening displacement (COD). It consists of measurement of displacements at an initial notch subjected to Mode I of cracking; this was proposed initially in [10.29] for materials with high toughness. The characterization of cracking behaviour of materials by COD is possible in LEFM as well as beyond the linear relation [10.3] for slow crack propagation. The tests were undertaken in three or four point bending in displacement-controlled testing machines. However, the COD method does not allow the effective stress concentration to be calculated and may be used only as a valuable comparative measure.

In general, the experimental approach to problems of crack propagation in non-linear and non-elastic materials is based on the observation and recording of behaviour of specimens with initial notches.

COD measurements are developed by several authors. Velasco *et al.* determined CTOD (Crack Tip Opening Displacement) as a function of CMOD (Crack Mouth Opening Displacement) which was directly measured and recorded [10.30], according to ASTM [10.31] and BSI [10.32]; cf. Figure 10.9. In [10.33] double gauges were applied for CMOD measurement to establish the angle and centre point of rotation during bending. The shape of the curves obtained is shown in Figure 10.10. The critical value of CTOD designed as $CTOD_c$ was established in different ways – as corresponding to the maximum load, to a local maximum of load – CTOD curve or to a rapid decrease of load. This gives the possibility of using CTOD testing for various composite materials.

Theoretical formulations for COD measurements is related to the model of a crack proposed in [10.34] and was discussed further in [10.35].

The postulate that critical values of $CTOD_c$ are characteristic for material behaviour and independent from specimen dimensions and type of loading is

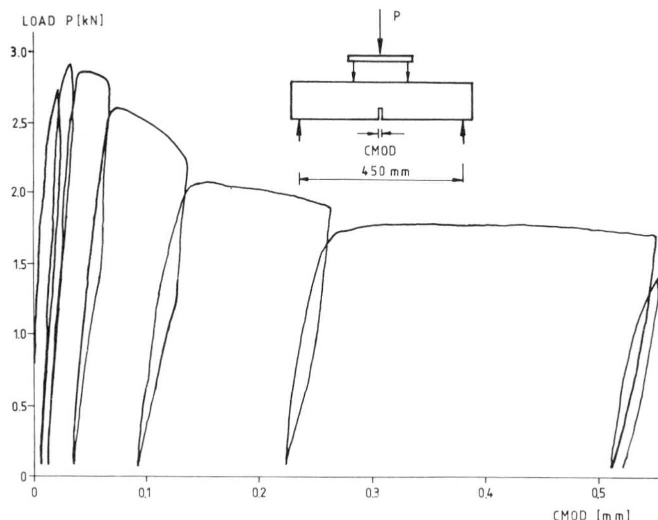

Figure 10.10 CMOD as a function of load for a fibre-reinforced concrete specimen subjected to bending. (Source: Brandt, A.M., *et al.*, Fracture mechanics tests of fibre-reinforced concrete beams in pure bending; published by Delft Univ. of Techn., 1989.) [10.33]

only partly satisfied, and may give only comparative indications on the material properties. However, the validity of $CTOD_c$ testing is extended beyond the elastic behaviour of materials, and that is its main value.

Fracture in the process zone before the crack tip in elements under direct tension, or in tensile zones of elements subjected to bending, was represented by different models. In these models transfer to stress across the process zone is related to displacement in the crack by a so called tension-softening diagram. The form of this diagram represents a constitution law, characteristic for the considered material.

One of the first published models was proposed in [10.36] in which a notion of a fictitious crack was applied. For stress variation, as shown in Figure 10.2c, it is assumed that between point O where effective crack ends and point A where value σ_y is reached the material is partly microcracked. This effect is assimilated by an additional crack length Δc. The partial destruction of the material ahead of the crack tip is confirmed experimentally by several tests and observations on cement matrix specimens. Discontinuous microcracks are clearly distinguishable in hydrated gel which consists of entangled crystalline needles and amorphous material. In this intermediary region between points O and A the tensile stress in only partly transferred and its value varies between zero and σ_y. Behind point A the stress is decreasing gradually to its mean value $\sigma = \sigma_0$.

The situation at the crack tip may be therefore described by two diagrams $\sigma(\varepsilon)$ and $\sigma(w)$, where w is the crack opening, Figure 10.11. The curve $\sigma(\varepsilon)$ is valid

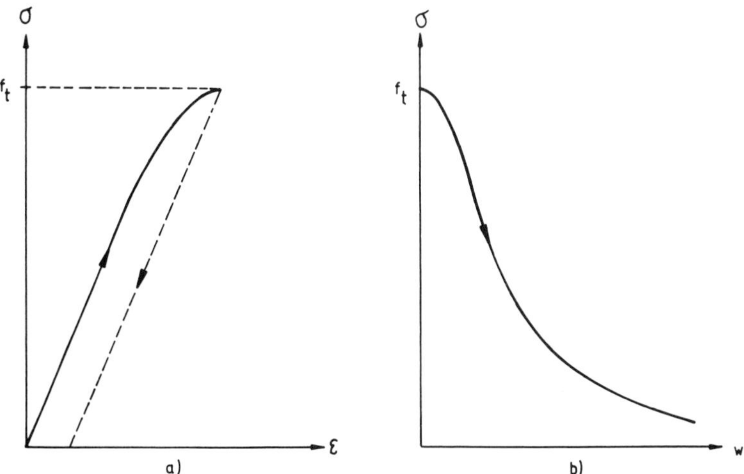

Figure 10.11 Curves $\sigma(\varepsilon)$ and $\sigma(w)$ for the Fictitious Crack Model (FCM) proposed by Hillerborg. (Reproduced with permission from Hillerborg, A., A model for fracture analysis; published by the Univ. of Lund, 1978.) [10.36]

for the zone where $\varepsilon < \varepsilon_y$ and for $\varepsilon > \varepsilon_y$ the notion of strain has no more sense because of the discontinuities of the material and stress σ transferred across the fictitious crack is related to the crack opening w.

At point O the critical value w_{cr} is reached and stress cannot be transferred – at that point an effective crack tip already exists.

The experimental and theoretical studies are completed by application of the Finite Element Method (FEM) for numerical analysis of fracture processes. By that approach the region surrounding the crack tip can be represented approximately by an equivalent system of discrete elements. One of the early works in that subject was [10.37] and it was followed by many others. A simple example shown in Figure 10.12 is partly based on work published in [10.38] as early as

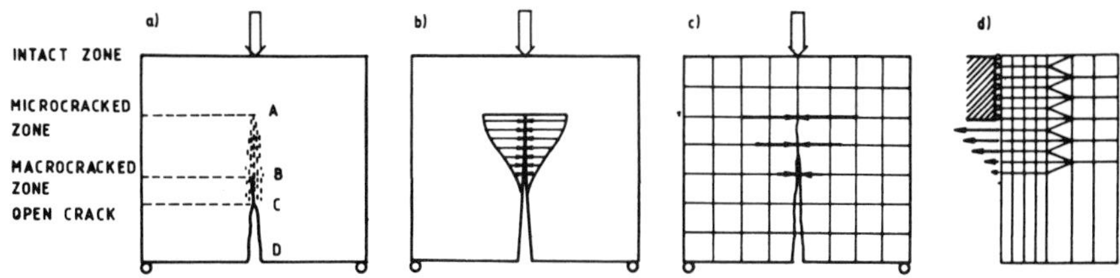

Figure 10.12 Application of FEM in the fictitious crack model; a) a crack with the fracture zone ahead of the crack tip; b) the fracture zone is replaced by a fictitious crack and appropriate stresses; c) and d) systems of finite elements and nodal forces which replace the stresses transferred across the crack. (Reproduced with permission from Petersson, P.E., Crack growth and development of fracture zone in plain concrete and similar materials; published by Lund Inst. of Techn., 1981.) [10.38]

1979. The density of the mesh for finite elements, their shape (e.g. triangles, rectangles, etc.) and forces at the nodes can be selected according to required accuracy of the calculations, possibilities of available computers and other circumstances. It is also possible to represent correctly though in an approximate way the material property as expressed by curves $\sigma(\varepsilon)$ and $\sigma(w)$.

Various methods of determination of the tension-softening diagrams which express the behaviour of different materials at fracture were proposed in [10.39], [10.40], [10.41], [10.42] and [10.43].

In the above-mentioned studies on the fracture processes there are several somewhat controversial assumptions and hypotheses. For the rather complicated structure of the composite materials on the micro-level, their homogeneity and isotropy is assumed on the macro-level. For materials with multiple crack systems, thorough studies on one single crack are presented. Modes I, II and III are considered separately, or certain modes are simply neglected, even though it is obvious that in real heterogeneous materials all three modes are mixed together in a more or less unknown way, cf. Section 10.4. On the basis of simplifying assumptions the structural and mathematical models are constructed to enable analytical and numerical treatment of cracking processes and to formulate problems which may be solved without much difficulty and expense:

- to obtain solutions expressed in stress and strain even if they are significantly different from the real materials behaviour;
- to predict material behaviour for different sets of parameters, like material properties, external actions, etc., with appropriate coefficients and correcting factors;
- to establish the influence of various selections of components, technologies, environmental conditions on the crack propagation.

When instead of one single crack the phenomenon of multiple cracking appears which is the case in advanced composites with internal structure (fibres or polymers), the fracture mechanics models are less effective for predicting the behaviour of the materials. Conditions for multiple cracking appear only when the energy required for unstable propagation of the first crack is greater than the energy required to form the next crack somewhere in the neighbourhood. That is the role of inclusions and fibres in brittle matrices.

10.2 Cement matrix composites under various states of loading

10.2.1 ROLE OF COMPONENTS

In this section a short description is given of how the elements and specimens made of composite materials behave under compression, tension, bending, shear and combined states of stress. Because of a very large number of different test results available in published papers and books it is not intended to summarize all of them here, but rather to show characteristic behaviour under static short-term loading, and to explain the role of reinforcement, leaving the reader to follow up particular aspects from the original test reports.

The composite's behaviour is the main aspect described here, i.e., how the heterogeneity of the materials and their purposefully designed structure influence their behaviour under external loads and other actions. It is not possible, on the other hand, to present the overall complexity of a material's behaviour and to pay full attention to the influence of the size of elements, rate of loading, stiffness of the loading machine and to many other important factors and conditions.

Inclusions of various types decrease the brittleness of the cement-based matrices. The aggregate grains add strength and hardness and these effects may be calculated approximately from the law of mixtures for the elastic region of stress–strain curves. The role of these inclusions is slightly different when first cracks appear – they are stopped at aggregate grains and the failure is less brittle, because additional energy input is necessary to break or to contour the grains.

The influence of fibres depends on their efficiency, this means that the fibres long enough, or provided with additional anchorages, and applied in sufficient volume, may slightly modify the composite's behaviour up to the point where the first crack opens. The increase of strength and of the Young's modulus is small, and related by the law of mixtures to the volume of fibres, which rarely and only with special technology may be larger than 3% per volume. In contrast, the behaviour after cracking is considerably modified. With efficient fibres the load bearing capacity may be substantially increased after the first crack has occurred and the fracture toughness as expressed by the area under the stress–strain or load–displacement curve is several times larger than that of the plain matrix.

The role of fibres depends on their volume, aspect ratio, strength and bond to the matrix. It has been shown on many tests how these fibre characteristics influence the composite's behaviour. In recent years, particular attention has been paid to the distribution of fibres – very small and well dispersed fibres may control the microcracks in the matrix from the very beginning of their opening, and particularly high deformability of the composite may be obtained.

The polymers added to the cement matrices influence the overall behaviour of the composite in various ways. By improving the matrix–aggregate bond the strength is increased which is accompanied by an increase in its brittleness. Larger amounts of polymers if they exhibit plastic behaviour may, on the contrary, enhance the deformability of the composite material.

Considerable possibilities for designing the material according to well specified requirements are opened up when a wide variety of modifications of the material structure and composition are considered and adequately applied.

More detailed information is given in subsequent chapters, according to different states of stress.

10.2.2 FRACTURE UNDER COMPRESSION

The influence of fibres on the stress and strain characteristics of compressed elements was examined by several authors and main common conclusions were proposed. Certain particularities observed may be attributed to different kinds of fibres, mix proportions and testing techniques applied.

The increase of strength due to dispersed steel-fibres is small and uncertain [10.44] and [10.45]). That observation may be explained by two controversial effects – steel-fibres are reinforcing but their introduction in to the fresh mix usually increases the porosity. Other authors even observed a certain decrease of strength, e.g. [10.46]. These discrepancies were explained [10.47] by the influence of fibre spacing and it was shown that only for a given spacing, actually in the tests equal to about 5 mm, did the strength of hardened composite increased by 10% as compared to the plain matrix. In other cases for smaller and larger spacing they have found a 10% decrease of compressive strength.

Other results were obtained [10.45] in which a slightly lower stress corresponding to the first crack was observed.

A 7% increase of strength was obtained when Duoform fibres were used [10.48], but other less efficient fibres gave no appreciable results. Polypropylene fibres decreased the matrix strength because of the lower Young's modulus. It may be concluded that fibres are not the best way to obtain high compressive strength. Even if certain increases may be expected, other measures like mix proportion modifications are more efficient by far. Also, the Young's modulus for the ascending branch of the stress–strain curve is of variable sensitivity with the introduction of fibres, [10.49].

There is, however, a general consensus that the descending branch of the stress–strain curve is considerably changed and at ductility and fracture

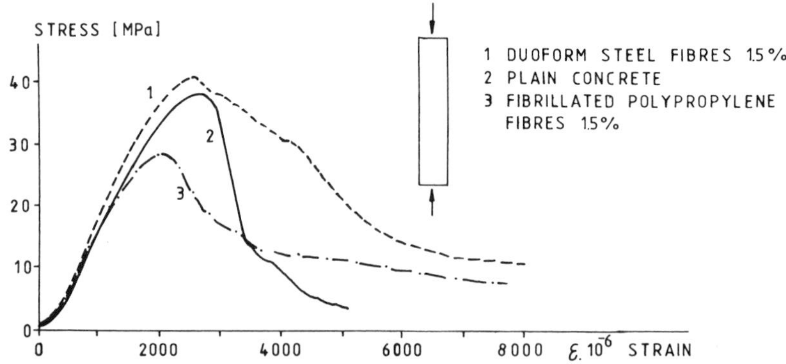

Figure 10.13 Compressive stress–strain curves for plain and fibre-reinforced concrete prisms 102 × 102 × 508 mm, $V = 1.5\%$. (Reprinted from *Cem. and Concr. Research*, **7**(2), Hughes, B.P. and Fattuhi, N.I., Stress–strain curves for fibre-reinforced concrete in compression, pp. 173–84, 1977, with permission from Pergamon Press Ltd, Headington Hill Hall, Oxford OX3 0BW, UK.)

toughness are increased because fibres control the opening and propagation of cracks. These effects are shown in Figure 10.13. Energy is dissipated for pull-out of the fibres and total energy absorption is considerably larger.

In an important test program [10.50], the limited but positive influence of steel-fibres on strength and post-cracking behaviour of specimens under compression has been proved. Using a high rigidity compression testing machine a clear image has been obtained of descending branches of stress–strain curves. In Figure 10.14 three groups of curves are shown for various aspect ratios (height/diameter) of tested prisms – 1, 2 and 3, and for various volume fractions of fibres – 0%, 0.75% and 1.5%. In all cases of the aspect ratio of prisms the influence of fibres is visible and unambiguous, however the relative difference due to fibre-reinforcement are rather small.

The application of any type of fibres in structural elements subjected to compression is rare, because the limited advantages do not counter balance increased cost and more complicated technology. However, by the addition of fibres to conventional reinforced concrete columns a moderate gain in strength and large increase of fracture energy were obtained, [10.51], which may be interesting for structures in seismic zones or in regions subjected to similar events due, for example, to mining exploitation.

The behaviour of polymer concretes under compression depends on the role and nature of the polymer component in the composite material, on the kind of polymer and on its amount (cf. Section 3.2). Therefore it is possible to design a composite material of more or less high strength and deformability. The stress–strain curves of specimens subjected to compression are shown in Figure 10.15 for different material compositions from high strength and low deformability to less strong and more deformable ones. The specimens were

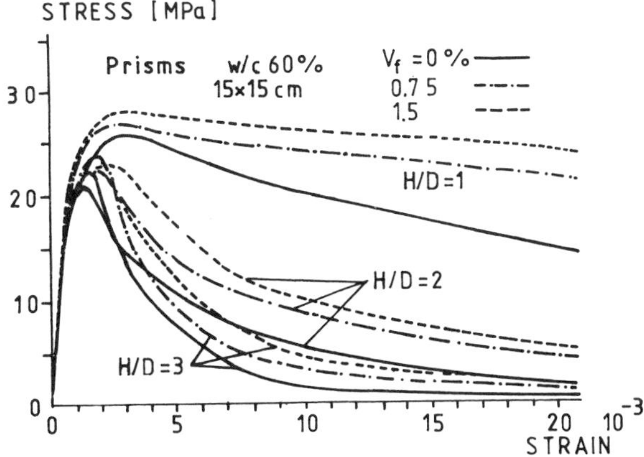

Figure 10.14 Stress–strain curves for steel fibre-reinforced prisms with various volume fraction of fibres and various height to width ratios. (Reproduced with permission from Tanigawa, Y. *et al.*, Stress–strain behaviour of steel fiber-reinforced concrete under compression; published by Japan Concrete Institute, 1980.) [10.50]

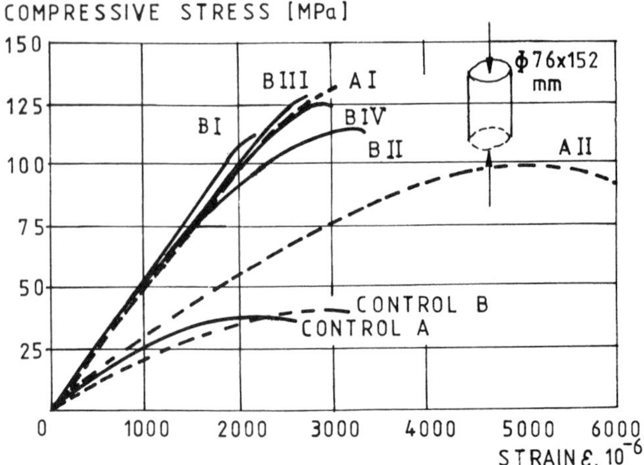

Figure 10.15 Compressive stress–strain curves for concrete impregnated with various compositions of MMA, BA and TMPTMA. (Reproduced from Dahl-Jorgensen, E. *et al.*, Polymer-impregnated concrete: laboratory studies; published by ASCE/EIC/RTAC, 1974.) [10.52]

Table 10.1 Polymer loading of specimens made of impregnated concrete

Identification	Combinations of monomers (%)	Average mass loading (%)
AI	100% MMA	4.8
AII	60% MMA + 40% BA	4.3
BI	90% MMA + 10% TMPTMA	5.2
BII	70% MMA + 20% BA + 10% TMPTMA	4.6
BIII	60% MMA + 30% BA + 10% TMPTMA	4.9
BIV	50% MMA + 40% BA + 10% TMPTMA	5.1

(Source: ACI, Design considerations for Steel Fibre Reinforced Concrete; *ACI Structural Journal*, September–October, pp. 565–80, 1988.) [10.53]

produced by impregnation of hardened Portland cement concrete [PIC] and corresponding data are given in Table 10.1. For impregnation the following monomers were used – methyl methacrylate (MMA), n-butyl acrylate (BA) and trimethylolpropane trimethacrylate (TMPTMA).

Other types of polymer concretes, i.e. PC (polymer concrete) and PPC (polymer cement concrete), also give various possibilities for adjusting mechanical properties to the required ones.

10.2.3 FRACTURE UNDER DIRECT TENSION

The behaviour of plain and fibre-reinforced concrete elements under tension is considerably affected by the testing techniques and it is difficult to eliminate all secondary effects. The specimen configuration and local stress concentrations, type of gripping system and testing machine stiffness are among the most important factors. To avoid all secondary effects or to reduce their importance and to obtain reliable results the tests should be well instrumented and carefully executed. Even with all precautions the test results may be influenced by certain material eccentricities due, for instance, to the heterogeneity of the fibres' distribution.

Local stress concentrations and accidental eccentricities may be decreased to some extent by special grips and the shape of specimens. A few examples of the tests of concrete are shown in [10.53], however, not all of them are appropriate for testing reinforced concrete.

The strain energy accumulated in grips and testing machine is released at the first crack and the specimen may be broken without any control. In that case it is impossible to obtain a descending branch of the stress–strain curve and even the maximum load is unknown, because after the first crack the element is rapidly ruptured. To avoid such accidents energy accumulation should be minimized and its release controlled by the application of testing machines with a closed-loop system and by sufficient stiffness of the grips and the machine itself.

In appropriately executed tests with direct tension the influence of different reinforcing may be clearly observed. The fibres improve strength and deformability provided that they are efficient enough. The influence of fibres is well presented

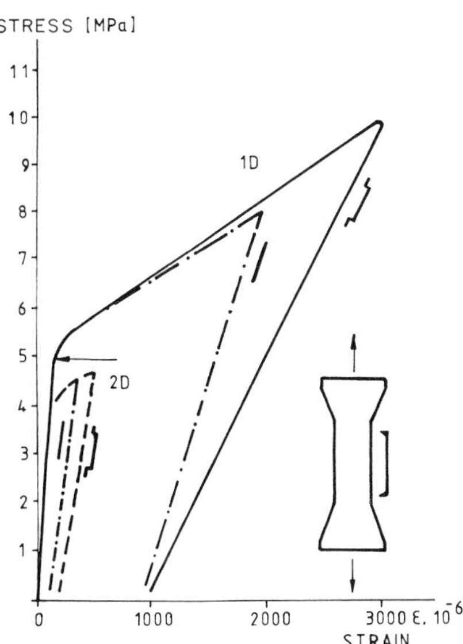

Figure 10.16 Average curves sigma–epsilon determined from direct tension tests. (Reproduced from Kasperkiewicz, J., Ultimate strength and strain of steel-fibre-reinforced concrete under tension; *Mech. Teoret. i Stos.*, **17**(1), pp. 19–34, 1979.)

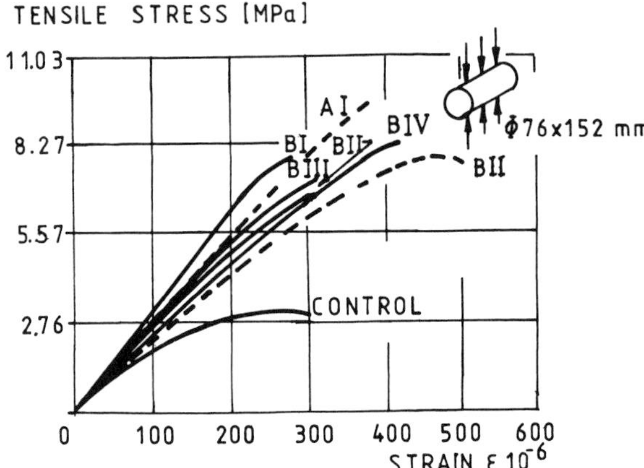

Figure 10.17 Tensile stress–strain curves for concrete impregnated with various compositions of MMA, BA and TMPTMA, (cf. Table 10.1). (Reproduced from Dahl-Jorgensen, E. *et al.*, Polymer-impregnated concrete: laboratory studies; published by ASCE/EIC/RTAC, 1974.) [10.52]

in the curves obtained in [10.54] and shown in Figure 10.16. It may be observed that the hooked fibres are more efficient than the straight ones. Next, the influence of the orientation of fibres is clear – only fibres aligned with the load direction increases both strength and deformability. The first crack appears sensibly at the same stress as in a plain matrix and this result confirms the law of mixtures up to that stress level. When the fibres are dispersed at random (2D), they slightly increase the deformability, but the first crack appears at a lower stress level due probably to increased porosity. The fracture energy calculated as proportional to the area under the curve is related closely to the fibre efficiency. Similar conclusions may be derived from [10.55], [10.56], [10.57] and others. Behaviour of glassfibre-reinforced cements was examined in [10.58].

The tensile strength may also be established after a splitting test, described among other FRC in [10.59] and [10.60]; also cf. Section 7.4.

The axial tensile tests of plain concrete specimens were also performed in [10.38] and [10.39]; the latter proposed a bi-linear model to represent the behaviour of concrete from the beginning up to the point of failure.

Examples of the behaviour of polymer impregnated concrete (PIC) elements subjected to tension by splitting are shown in Figure 10.17 for different compositions of impregnating agent.

10.2.4 FRACTURE UNDER BENDING

It has been shown on elements reinforced with fibres and subjected to bending how the role of the fibres is decisive for crack control.

The diagrams, as in Figure 10.18, are characteristic for a test when specimens

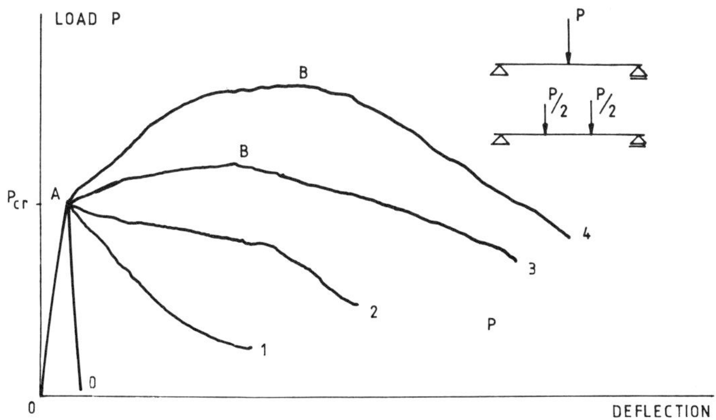

Figure 10.18 Schematic load–deflection curves for elements with various reinforcement, 0 – plain brittle matrix, 1, 2, 3 and 4 – increasing efficiency of reinforcement.

are loaded by one or two concentrated and symmetrical forces. These two cases are – four-point or third-point with two symmetrical loads and three-point or centre-point with one force in the middle of the span. The first system is considered as better reflecting the bending conditions in the central part of the element, where pure bending without shearing is created. The second system is simpler to execute but, in fact, the maximum effort is concentrated directly below the load and that small portion of the material is not necessarily representative for the tested element.

The curves shown in Figure 10.18 correspond to differing efficiency of the fibre-reinforcement. There are two characteristic points of each curve designed by A and B. Point A is the departure of the load–deformation (or load–deflection) curve from linearity and point B is the maximum load.

The curve 0 presents the brittle behaviour of a non-reinforced matrix. Specimens characterized by curves 1 and 2 were weakly reinforced and no increase of load is observed after first crack appearance but the cracking is controlled and brittle fracture is avoided. For curves 3 and 4 the maximum load is reached at point B after considerable cracking of the matrix. This effect is possible thanks to the reinforcement with high efficiency obtained by a combination of three factors – a relatively high volume fraction of fibres, a good bond to cement matrix and eventually an appropriate orientation of fibres with respect to the direction of the principal tensile stress.

Point A is often considered as corresponding to the first crack opening but that question should be treated with all due restrictions concerning the determination of the cracks in cement matrices. Point A is considered as a limit for the region of linear stress–strain relation and the corresponding load allows the Limit of Proportionality (LOP) for the material to be calculated.

The load at point B is used to calculate the Modulus of Rupture (MOR) – the

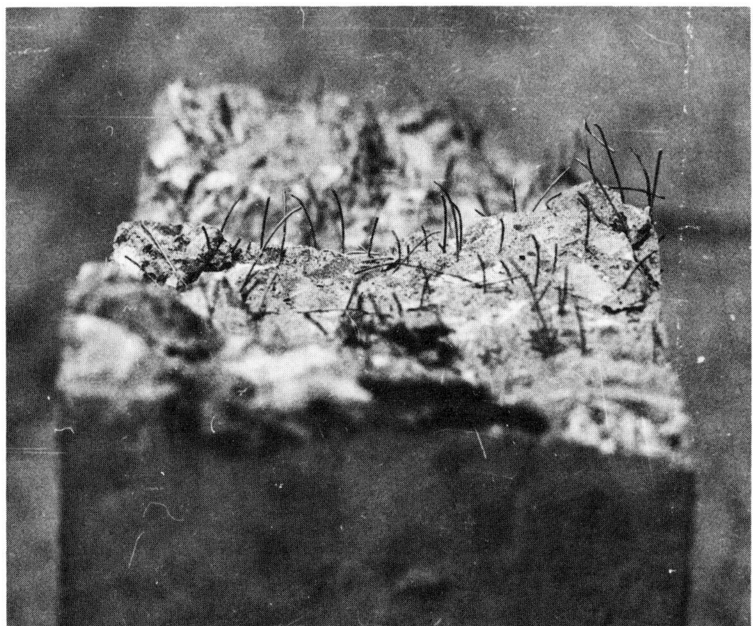

Figure 10.19 Steel fibres pulled-out of the matrix in a broken element.

stress due to bending of the cross-section assuming Hooke's law. MOR expresses in fact a fictitious value of the stress but it is a convenient measure to compare flexural behaviour of elements of different dimensions.

Up to point A the matrix is uncracked and its behaviour is linear. The influence of fibre-reinforcement on the angle between that section of the curve and the deflection axis is negligible. This means that Young's modulus depends only very slightly on the efficiency of the reinforcement.

After point A cracks appear and develop. Their opening and propagation is controlled by fibres which break or are pulled-out of the matrix, depending on which of these processes is actually prevailing. Both depend on the type of fibres, their aspect ratio, tensile strength and on the fibre–matrix bond. All these factors contribute to the efficiency of the fibres which determines the shape of the curves beyond point B. For steel fibres, in most cases the fibres do not break but are pulled-out of the matrix, as is shown in Figure 10.19.

The end point of the curve is sometimes difficult to establish, particularly when long fibres are pulled-out in the fracture process and the load is decreasing slowly with very large deflections. In such circumstances the end point may occur in considerably modified conditions of loading and support.

The behaviour of FRC elements under bending may also be characterized by strain measurements. The curves shown in Figure 10.20 give the strain measured at the bottom and top faces of a steel-fibre-reinforced element for

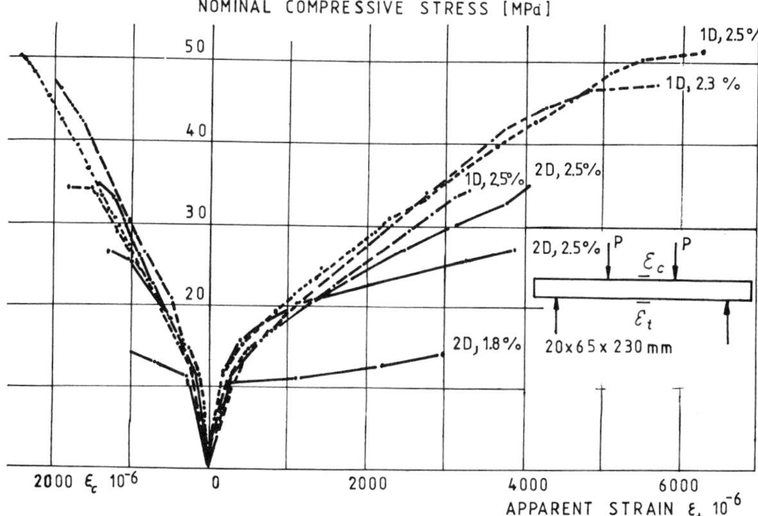

Figure 10.20 Nominal stress-apparent strain curves after measurements at the bottom and top faces of SFRC elements subjected to bending. The curves correspond to 1D and 2D fibre distributions and to various fibre volume content. (Source: Babut, R., Bearing capacity and deformability of SFRC elements subjected to bending; published by Ossolineum, 1983.)

various volume fractions and for fibre orientation 1D and 2D. After a short linear zone, the slope of curves changes in what corresponds to the onset of microcracking. Next, the gauges measured the apparent strain on the matrix with microcracks which developed under increasing load. Various curves corresponded to different efficiency of the fibre-reinforcement.

The variety of behaviours of cement-based elements under bending shows the large possibilities of material design. According to requirements, different properties of materials may be obtained by varying properties of the matrix, quality, amount and distribution of the fibres, etc.

An approach to the problem of how to apply linear elastic fracture mechanics (LEFM) parameters to concrete which neither behave as linear elastic bodies nor are isotrope, and to specimens of relatively small dimensions is proposed in [10.62] and [10.63]. In the first of them the method for determination of two fracture parameters K_{Ic} and CTOD_c is proposed after test results of a three-point notched beam.

In [10.63] a method is proposed to determine fracture energy and process zone size in concretes, using the same assumptions and executing tests on small beams of three different sizes.

Both methods were tested in different laboratories and are considered as valid for the characterization of concretes as to their resistance against crack propagation and fracture. That was an important step forward in the introduction of the methods of fracture mechanics to the design of brittle materials. Further tests are still needed to develop these methods.

When the above fracture characteristics are known, then the so called R-curves may be used in that problem. If in equations (equation 10.1 and equation 10.2) the rate of strain energy is denoted by G (cf. also equation 10.7), and the rate of change of energy necessary for crack propagation is denoted by R, then the state of the stabilization of the crack ends when the following condition is reached, $G = G_c = R$.

For highly brittle materials like glass or cement paste R characterizes the material and any crack propagation from the initial notch or flaw leads to a rapid failure of the element. The situation is different in materials with an internal structure which stops and may control crack propagation, i.e. in materials like mortar, concrete and fibre-reinforced concrete. The crack is propagating slowly until reaching the second condition, $d\frac{\partial G}{\partial c} = \frac{\partial R}{\partial c}$ and that condition corresponds to the critical crack length c_c. In these materials two values G_c and c_c characterize the state of fracture. The value c_c depends also upon the geometrical conditions, dimensions of the element and arrangement of the load, etc. In Figure 10.21 is shown how the stress–strain diagram corresponds to the cracking in an element reinforced with fibres. Along section OB of the curve only single cracks appear between the fibres. At point B a crack is crossing the

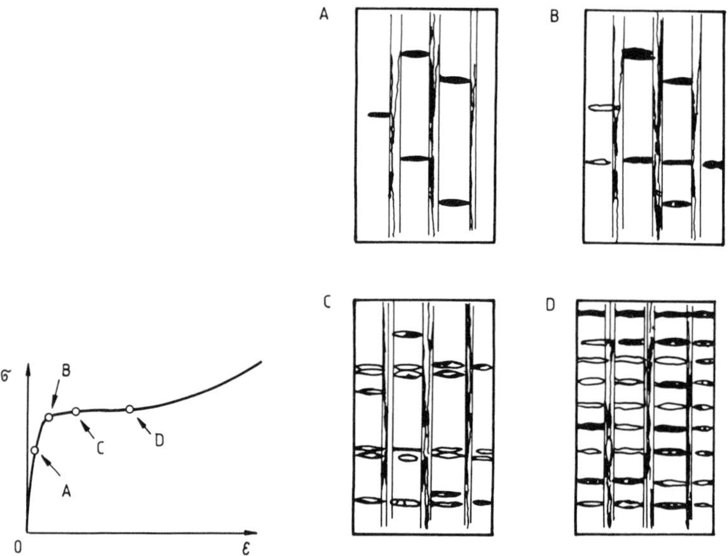

Figure 10.21 Stages of cracks in cement-based fibre-reinforced composites. (Source: Shah, S.P., Do fibers improve the tensile strength of concrete?; published by Universite Laval, 1991.) [10.64]

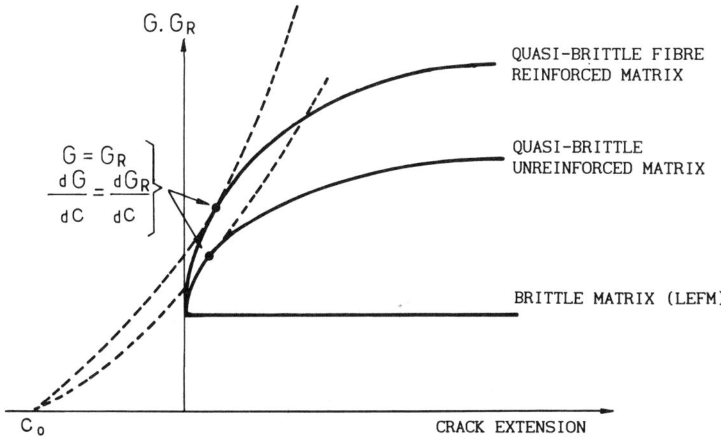

Figure 10.22 R-curves for different materials. (Source: Shah, S.P., Do fibers improve the tensile strength of concrete?; published by Université Laval, 1991.) [10.64]

element and that situation is reflected on the curve as a knee. At points C and D further cracking is controlled by the fibres and even the external load may be increasing until the final fracture when the crack length is equal to its critical value c_c. The images shown in Figure 10.21 of consecutive stages of cracking have been confirmed by microscopic observations of thin sections of tested elements. As is described elsewhere, according to the efficiency of the reinforcement, the stress–strain curves may have different form. In Figure 10.22 the R-curves correspond to more and less brittle materials. It has been shown among others, by Quyang *et al.* [10.65] that for quasi-brittle materials such as concrete composites the R-curves may be determined knowing K_{Ic}, E and $CTOD_c$, cf. [10.64]. When the R-curve is known, then the fracture behaviour for any geometry can be described. In such a way, using the R-curve approach, the crack control exercised by the fibres in brittle matrices may be simulated.

10.3 Fracture energy and fracture toughness

10.3.1 WORK OF FRACTURE

Work of fracture is the measure of the energy needed to break a material and is closely related to the kind of fracture – brittle or ductile. Brittle fracture is characteristic of amorphous materials like glass, and ductile fracture is usually related to crystalline materials like metals. Depending on conditions, the materials may behave in different ways, e.g. metals are brittle in low temperatures.

Cement-based composites are, characteristically, brittle and their fracture occurs usually along boundaries between inclusions and matrix; but cracks can pass also across both mortar and bulk matrix.

Ductile fracture is accompanied by large deformation. In metals, there are deformations along slip planes and in specimens under test which are subjected to tensile load it can be observed as necking and horizontal sections on stress–strain curves. It is also called plastic behaviour.

Brittle fracture appears in the planes perpendicular to the principal tension and is associated with small ultimate strain. Consequently, brittle fracture requires much less energy than ductile fracture, i.e. the work of fracture is much smaller.

The work of fracture regarded as the energy required to break the material is a magnitude characteristic for every material, its quality, etc. As a material characteristic it is, however, difficult to determine experimentally without ambiguity, because it strongly depends not only on the way of testing, but also on the presence and distribution of microcracks and other local defects at different scales. As there is no universally accepted definition of brittle and non-brittle behaviour, the description proposed in [10.66] may be used. Brittle solids break without large plastic flow so that the total work of fracture measured in a controlled notch bend test type is less than 0.1 k Nm/m^2 and the strain at failure is less than 1%.

Real structural material may be classified somewhere in between ideal brittle and ductile materials. Examples of fracture energies for a few solids are shown in Table 10.2 (after [10.67]).

Work of fracture is considerably increased when a brittle matrix is reinforced by a system of inclusions in the form of grains or fibres. An internal structure created purposefully transforms a brittle behaviour into a quasi-ductile one, characterized by large deformations and high fracture toughness. This transformation into a composite material is described here on many occasions.

Work of fracture is also related to bond strength in fibre-reinforced composites. A certain bond is necessary to ensure the composite's behaviour and thus to

Table 10.2 Fracture energy of some solids

Material	Fracture energy (kNm/m^2)
Steel	300–500
Aluminium alloys	10–50
Vulcanized rubber	10.0
Polymethyl methacrylate	0.6
Resins (epoxy, polyester)	0.1
Graphite	0.05
Alumina	0.03
Firebrick	0.03
Glass	0.005

(Source: Parratt, N.J., *Fibre Reinforced Materials Technology*, published by Von Nostrand Reinhold Co., 1972.) [10.67]

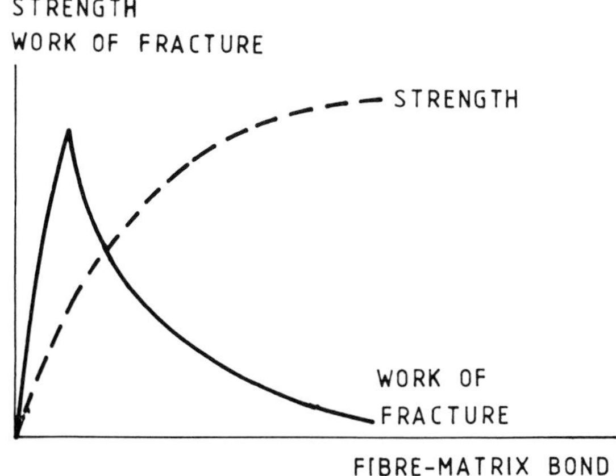

Figure 10.23 Schematic curves showing strength and work of fracture variation with the fibre–matrix bond strength. (Reproduced with permission from Mindess, S., Bonding in cementitious materials: how important is it?; published by Materials Research Society, 1988.) [10.68]

obtain an appreciable increase in the work of fracture and strength by the action of fibres. However, with further increase of the bond strength, there is a considerable decrease of the work of fracture and the composite's behaviour becomes brittle. This is shown schematically in Figure 10.23, proposed in [10.68].

An attempt to calculate the work of fracture in FRC elements at cracking was published in [10.69], [10.70] and [10.71] for elements under axial tension, and later extended to bending in [10.72]. The formulae were derived for calculation of the work in the fracture process in which fibres are pulled-out of the matrix across a crack. For that purpose the following assumptions were accepted:

- The fracture process may be split into a few independent mechanisms.
- The mechanisms may be described by relatively simple formulae from which the particular components of total work of fracture may be calculated.
- The energy due to creation of new surface in non-reinforced matrix and to elastic strain is considered as small with respect to the other energy components and may be neglected.

Total work of fracture was presented as a sum of five components W_i, $(i = 1, 2, \dots, 5)$:

W_1 – debonding of the fibres from the matrix;
W_2 – pulling-out of fibres against friction at fibre–matrix interface;
W_3 – plastic deformation of the fibres;
W_4 – yielding of the matrix under compression in the regions at the exits of fibres;
W_5 – additional friction at the interface due to local compression.

It is, consequently, also assumed that other possible effects induce only negligible amounts of fracture energy.

The formulae for calculation of particular components W_i were derived in the above-mentioned papers for different situations – short or continuous fibres, fibre distribution 1D, 2D or 3D, axial tension or bending. These formulae were also applied in optimization problems, cf. Chapter 13. A simple case of 1D fibres in an element subjected to tension with a crack of a given limit width is described in more detail below in accordance with [10.71].

An element of steel-fibre-reinforced concrete is considered as shown in Figure 10.24. The reinforcement is composed of a single system of parallel short fibres and ϑ is its angle with respect to the direction of tensile loading. It is assumed, for simplification, that in a neighbouring layer the respective angle is $-\vartheta$. In the case of symmetric reinforcement a single form of rupture is to be considered – a crack perpendicular to the direction of principal tension. The calculation of fracture energy is executed for a single crack of width equal to v_o and multiple cracking should be examined separately. The crack width is arbitrarily selected and may be related to a certain structural or functional requirement.

The following formulae are proposed for all five energy components, Figures 10.25, 10.26 and 10.27.

$$W_1 = N_o \cos^2 \vartheta \frac{l\pi D}{8} \tau_{\max} v_e, \tag{10.16}$$

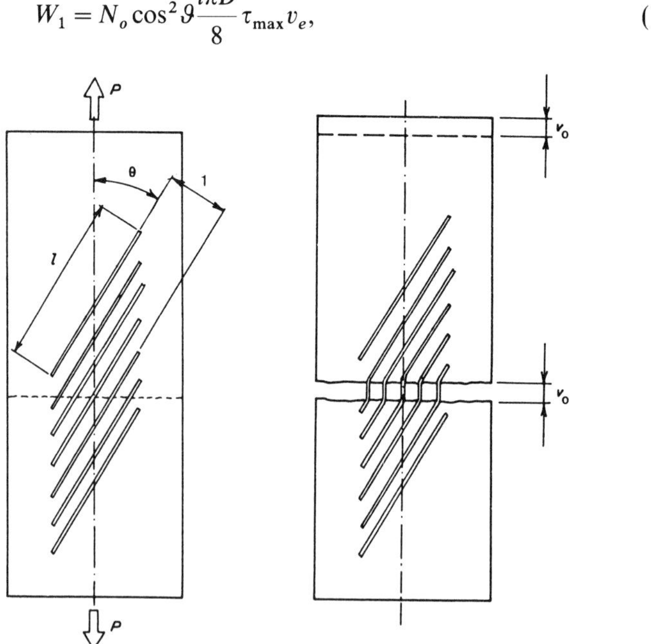

Figure 10.24 Fibre-reinforced element under axial tension before and after the crack opening. (Source: Brandt, A.M. On the optimal direction of short metal fibres in brittle matrix composites; *J. of Materials Science*, **20**, 1985.) [10.71]

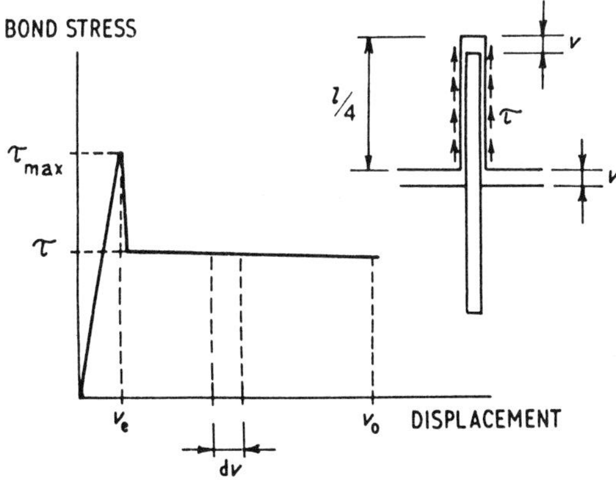

Figure 10.25 Bond stress as function of displacement in a pull-out test. (Source: Brandt, A.M., On the optimal direction of short metal fibres in brittle matrix composites; *J. of Materials Science*, **20**, 1985.) [10.71]

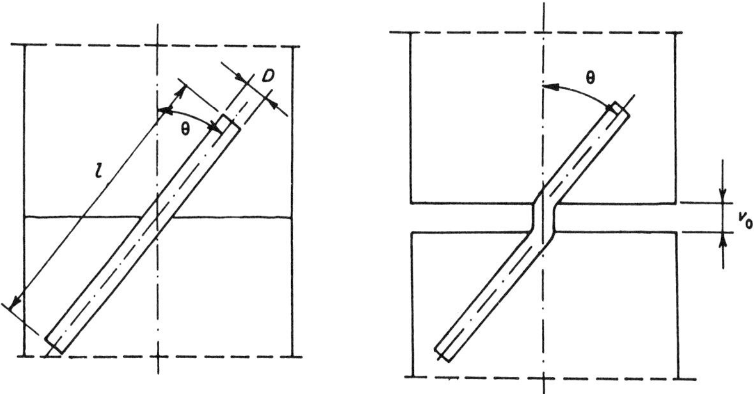

Figure 10.26 Plastic deformation of a fibre passing across a crack at an angle ϑ. (Source: Brandt, A.M., On the optimal direction of short metal fibres in brittle matrix composites; *J. of Materials Science*, **20**, 1985.) [10.71]

$$W_2 = N_o \cos^2\vartheta D\pi\tau\left[\frac{l}{4}(v_o - v_e) - \frac{1}{2}(v_o^2 - v_e^2)\right], \tag{10.17}$$

$$W_3 = N_o \cos\vartheta \frac{\pi D^2}{4} \vartheta v_o \tau_f, \tag{10.18}$$

$$W_4 = N_o\left(\alpha\frac{f_f}{f_m}\right)^2 \eta f_m D^2\left(\cos^2\vartheta - \vartheta\frac{\cos\vartheta^2}{\sin\vartheta}\right), \tag{10.19}$$

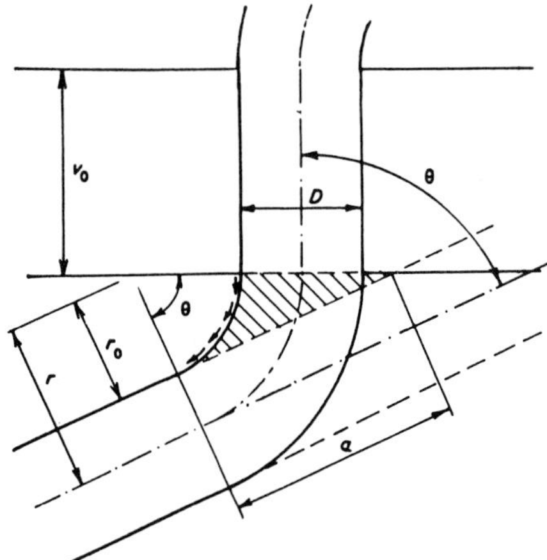

Figure 10.27 Yielding of the matrix due to local compression at the fibre bend. (Source: Brandt, A.M., On the optimal direction of short metal-fibres in brittle matrix composites; *J. of Materials Science*, **20**, 1985.) [10.71]

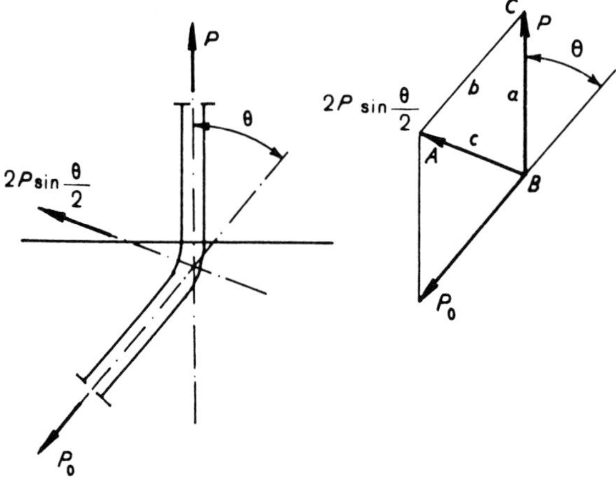

Figure 10.28 Additional force increasing friction at the fibre bend. (Source: Brandt, A.M., On the optimal direction of short metal-fibres in brittle matrix composites; *J. of Materials Science*, **20**, 1985.) [10.71]

$$W_5 = N_o \pi l \tau D \phi v_o \sin\frac{\vartheta}{2}\cos\vartheta. \qquad (10.20)$$

Here the symbols denote, l and D – length and diameter of a fibre; α and η – coefficients; τ_f – shear yield stress of fibres; f_f and f_m – tensile strength of fibres and compressive strength of the matrix; ϕ – friction coefficient between fibre and matrix; $N_o = \frac{4\beta}{\pi D^2}$ number of fibres; β – volume fibre content; cf. Section 6.6.2, and equation 6.10. Other symbols are shown in Figures 10.24–10.28.

The energy calculated from above formulae as a sum:

$$W = \sum_{i=1}^{i=5} W_i \tag{10.21}$$

was verified experimentally and results were published in [10.72]. The formulae were used in optimization of fibre orientation [10.71] and in other calculations in which the influence of fibre orientation was analysed [10.73] and [10.74]. In these papers energy was also calculated in elements with continuous fibres and fibres randomly distributed (2D and 3D). In [10.75] the formulae were used, together with experimental data, to analyse the behaviour of steel-fibres of different shapes and materials. The optimization problem based on the above adopted method of energy calculation and on equation 10.16–10.21 is presented and solved in Section 13.5.

The proposed formulae are precise enough to enable the analysis of different cases of steel-fibre-reinforced elements; however, their simplified form and assumed hypothesis leave scope for further development and improvement.

10.3.2 QUANTITATIVE DESCRIPTION OF FRACTURE TOUGHNESS

The most important material property of brittle matrix composites is their ability to absorb energy during the loading process, before final fracture. This property may be expressed quantitatively by that energy calculated as the amount of work of external forces, and it is called fracture energy. Fracture energy is defined in various ways related to the definition of the fracture, which sometimes is ambiguous and requires conventional assumptions. In brittle materials the fracture is immediate, after the opening of the first crack and the corresponding load is close to the maximum one. In composite materials with internal structure the fracture may also be defined in the same way, but then it corresponds to the final stage of a long process of cracking. It is therefore often necessary to define the fracture as a given limit of deflection, deformation or crack width. In such cases the notion of fracture energy also has a rather conventional meaning as it concerns a certain degree of rupture of the element.

The ability to absorb fracture energy is called fracture toughness and this term is used in various meanings, without any universally accepted definition. According to a published review [10.76] three main groups of meanings of the term, fracture toughness, may be distinguished.

The absolute description was proposed by the Japan Concrete Institute, RILEM and ASTM. In this approach energy absorption is measured on prescribed specimens, also loaded in a well-defined way and the energy calculated is considered to be the area under the load–deflection curve. In most recommendations specimens subjected to bending under four point loading are proposed, therefore the resulting magnitude which is established is called flexural toughness or just flexural energy absorption.

The second group of proposals, also made among others by ASTM, is based on relative values, i.e. without specifying the dimensions of tested specimens, the ratio of the total area under the curve to that limited by the first crack opening is considered. Such a ratio is called the fracture index with some additional specifications.

In the third group of toughness descriptions various authors proposed to consider particular specimen dimensions and certain parts of the stress–strain or load–deflection curve.

The term fracture toughness is also used by certain authors for the critical value of the stress intensity factor K_{Ic}.

For further details of various fracture toughness descriptions the reader is referred to [10.59]. Only a few proposals are presented below which seem to have both physical meaning and practical importance and gained more universal acceptance than the others.

Probably, the proposal to use a dimensionless magnitude called the fracture index as a possible material characteristic was first published in [10.77]. The test beam standardized by ASTM was used of cross-section 102 × 102 mm and of 305 mm span, which was loaded in its centre up to the total deflection of 1.9 mm. The toughness index (TI) was calculated as the ratio of area A + B to area A as is shown in Figure 10.29. For plain concrete or mortar the value of TI is 1.0 or a little more, and for strongly reinforced fibre composite it may reach values of 30 or even 46, as is reported in [10.78].

A similar method unrelated to any particular beam dimensions but presented in the form of flexural toughness indices was proposed by ASTM and is

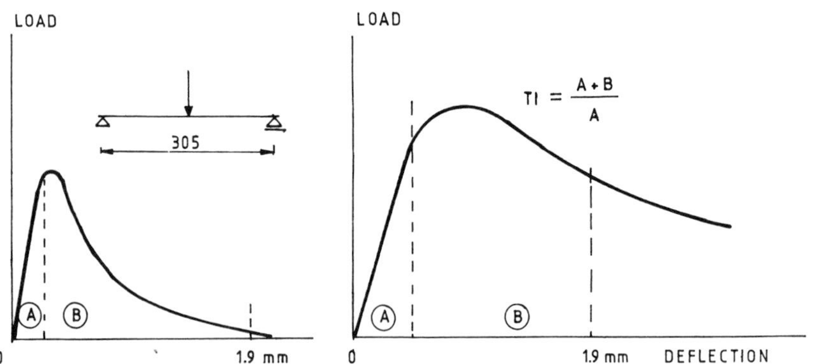

Figure 10.29 Schematic load–deflection curves for element under bending in calculation of the flexural toughness. (Reproduced with permission from Henager, C.H., A toughness index of fibre concrete; published by The Construction Press Ltd, 1978.) [10.77]

commented on in [10.79]. That concept is shown in Figure 10.30 as a load–deflection curve obtained for a third-point loading system. The deflection δ corresponding to the first crack is measured from point 0 and related to linear elastic behaviour. The indices are obtained by dividing the area under the load–deflecton curve by the area under that curve up to the first crack. The calculated values of flexural toughness indices are independent of the dimensions and rigidity of the tested element.

Index I_5 is determined at a deflection 3δ, I_{10} is determined at 5.5δ and I_{30} at 15.5δ. These values for an ideal elastic-plastic material are equal to 5, 10 and 30, respectively. For an ideal elastic-brittle material all indexes are equal to 1.0 because in that case the total deflection is limited to δ.

The proposed ASTM method has been largely accepted also by ACI Committee 544 according to the report [10.80]. The bending test is recommended for establishing the toughness of the material, understood as the capacity for energy absorption under static load.

The system of indices reflects the toughening effect of the fibres and their values allow researchers to compare quantitatively the energy absorbed by the element simultaneously with both ideal limit cases mentioned above. The indices are used to evaluate the influence of all possible modifications introduced in the design of material or in the technology that is applied.

The suitability of fracture toughness to represent the quality of the cement-based composite materials is proved by its multiple applications both as absolute values of the fracture energy and in the form of dimensionless indices. It is, however, to be stressed that a fracture toughness index cannot be considered as a definite and universal characteristic of material toughness in the sense of its resistance to crack propagation and its post-cracking behaviour. One of the

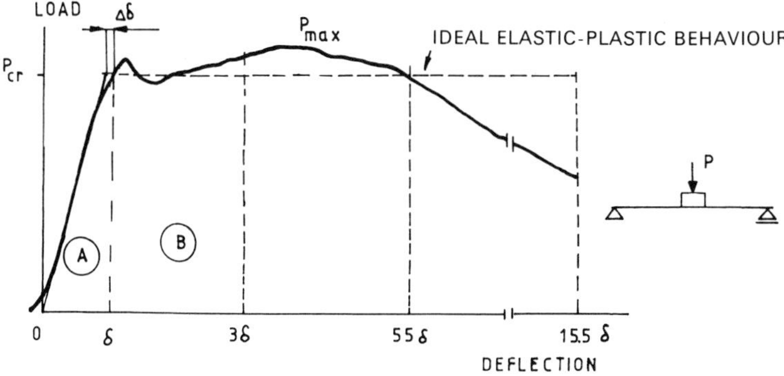

Figure 10.30 Schematic curve for determination of the flexural toughness indexes according to ASTM C 1018. (Reproduced with permission from ASTM, Standard C 1018-15: Standard test method for flexural toughness and first crack–crack strength of fiber-reinforced concrete (using beam with third-point loading); *Journal of Testing and Evaluation*, 1985.) [10.78]

weak sides of fracture toughness determination as it is recognized by ASTM in [10.78] is the difficulty of identification of the first crack occurrence. In strongly reinforced SFRC elements, for example, this fact is often impossible to recognize without some ambiguity. Observation of the specimen surface where cracks are expected is difficult and its results depend considerably upon the methods of crack recording. A characteristic offset of the curve and rapid change of its slope are also difficult to specify. As a result, the position of this point on the load–deflection curve is determined in an arbitrary way within relatively large limits. Consequently, area A (Figure 10.30) is susceptible to being determined with a large error, resulting in a final error of the toughness index.

Another disadvantage of toughness index determination is that the same values may be obtained for different load–deflection curves, e.g. a short ascending branch or a long descending branch after 3δ may give the same result. Furthermore, early cracking and a low value of A will give higher values of the index than similar curves with only slightly later cracking.

Those features of flexural toughness determination are related to the following two characteristics of fracture behaviour of brittle composites:

1. The first crack load and the susceptibility of the matrix to crack depend on its properties and not on the eventual reinforcement and its efficiency.
2. The postcracking behaviour and the area under the descending branch is related mostly to the reinforcement.

Examples of load–deflection curves in Figure 10.31 show the possible deficiencies of this type. Curve a describes a small strain hardening while curve a′ represents a rapid decrease of load after cracking and both are characterized by the same toughness index I_5. Similarly, for curves b and b′ the index I_{10} is the same and only index I_5 shows a small difference, while the material's behaviour is completely different. Also, for curves c and c′ only I_5 and I_{10} are different while the values of I_{20} are the same. These examples prove that the

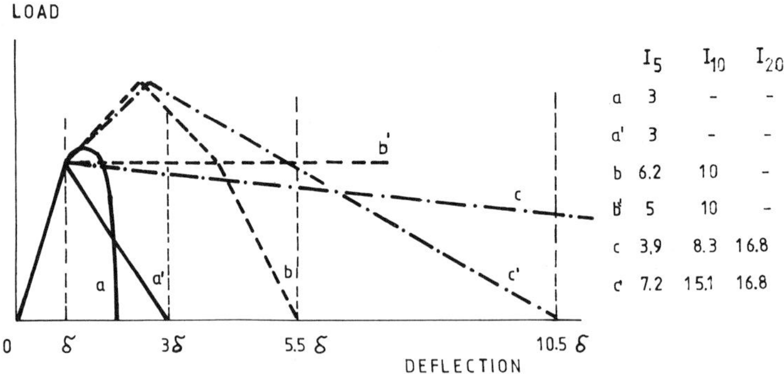

Figure 10.31 Examples of load–deflection curves with corresponding values of flexural toughness indices.

determination of the toughness index is a useful method of comparison for the behaviour of an effective material with that of an idealized linear elastic-plastic material. However, it cannot be considered as a perfect material characteristic.

Further research aimed at the characterization of the ability of a material to absorb fracture energy, and of post-cracking behaviour, have been continued by many authors. Examples of the calculation of work of fracture and toughness indices of tested elements are shown in Figures 10.32 and 10.33 where relevant curves are presented as functions of volume fractions of carbon fibres, [10.81]. The data obtained from tests of cement mortar elements, subjected to bending and following magnitudes are shown:

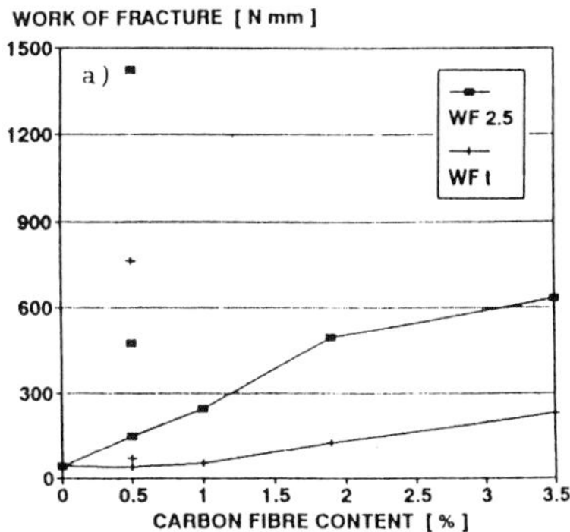

Figure 10.32 Values of the works of fracture WF2.5 and WF*t* plotted as functions of the volume fraction of fibre-reinforcement. (Source: Brandt, A.M. and Glinicki, M.A., Flexural behaviour of concrete elements reinforced with carbon fibres; Chapman & Hall/Spon, 1992.) [10.81]

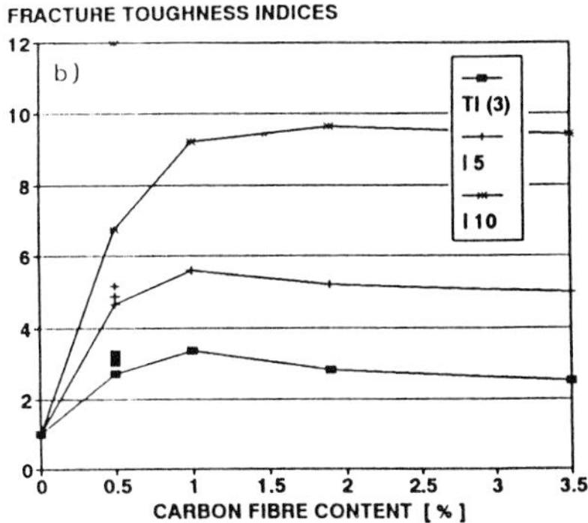

Figure 10.33 Values of the fracture indices TI(3), I_5 and I_{10} plotted as functions of the volume fraction of fibre reinforcement. (Source: Brandt, A.M. and Glinicki, M.A., Flexural behaviour of concrete elements reinforced with carbon fibres; Chapman & Hall/Spon, 1992.) [10.81]

1. WFt – total area under the load–deflection curve calculated up to the maximum load and δ_{max};
2. WF2.5 – total area under the load–deflection curve calculated up to the deflection equal to 2.5 mm;
3. TI(3) – toughness index calculated as ratio of respective areas up to deflection $3\delta_{max}$ and δ_{max};
4. I_5 and I_{10} – toughness indices calculated according to ASTM Standard C 1018–85.

It may be concluded from these tests that all applied measures of the efficiency of reinforcement gave similar results, namely the consistent increase of fracture toughness with an increase of fibre volume fraction up to 1%. Further increase of fibre volume induced a slight decrease of I_5 and TI(3) and negligible increase of I_{10}. In contrast, work of fracture increased up to the maximum fibre volume fraction. It appears from these tests that all applied measures may be of some use in particular cases as they furnish slightly different information about the behaviour of tested material.

10.3.3 INFLUENCE OF TESTING CONDITIONS

The energy absorption and overall behaviour of the composite elements subjected to external load is, to a large extent related to the conditions of loading and of testing in general. The following should be mentioned among several factors which influence specimen strength and the fracture processes:

- rate of loading;
- size of specimens and elements;
- stiffness of the loading system.

Normal tests are executed with such slow loading that the effects of loading speed are neglected. The results obtained in such tests are not relevant either for high rates of loading or for impacts and dynamic actions. On the other hand, the speed of loading must be limited if the introduction of rheological effects and fatigue are to be avoided. There are no test results related to the influence of the rate of loading on fracture toughness. It has been established only that, with an increase of the loading rate, then the strength of certain kinds of brittle matrix composites may be improved. The various rates of loading applied in laboratory experiments are intended to simulate, and more or less closely represent, the natural situation in different kinds of structures, cf. Section 11.2.

The size of element has a certain influence on strength and on fracture processes. If the material characteristics are looked for, then the results of testing should be independent of the element size. It is therefore advisable to always test a series of elements of different dimensions and to establish within what limits the size influence may be considered as sufficiently small and negligible.

Moreover, it is not only the size of the tested element itself that is of importance, but also the ratio of the element to the stiffness of the testing system. In general, it has been shown that when the dimensions of tested elements are increased, then the resulting brittleness is also increased. The relationship between the dimensions of the element and the corresponding toughness indices has not been established experimentally up to now. Several authors proposed to determine the fracture toughness parameters for concretes on very large elements. That viewpoint is based on the observed relations of these parameters and dimensions of elements. However, the testing of very large elements is difficult, expensive and loaded by other sources of errors, e.g. heterogeneity of material in a specimen and differences between the specimens belonging to the same series, different curing conditions, etc.

The stiffness of the loading equipment is another factor which influences the toughness of tested elements. In a stiff testing machine, i.e. with sufficient stiffness compared to the tested specimen, the elastic energy accumulated in the machine is not released after the first crack in the specimen. The test may be continued and a descending branch of the load–deflection (or stress–strain) curve may be established. In contrast, when the same element is tested on a less rigid machine, then after the first crack all the elastic energy accumulated is rapidly released and brittle fracture occurs at the maximum load, cf. Section 8.2.

The descending part of the characteristic curves may be established even better in special testing machines, in which the position of the loading head is automatically adjusted in such a way that the rate of change of a certain magnitude, e.g. deflection or deformation, is kept constant. The results obtained in such a way cannot be directly compared with those obtained from ordinary equipment more commonly used for material control in production units.

10.3.4 MATERIAL BRITTLENESS

In 1979 Nicholls stressed, with good reason, that all structures should be designed to avoid brittle fracture of any kind and that under particular conditions such fracture may occur practically in all materials [10.82]. If for metals or plastics, brittle fracture is conditioned by low temperature, fatigue, rate of loading, etc., it is a natural and common way of fracture for several kinds of matrices used in building and civil engineering materials. Matrices based on various cements and all kinds of ceramic materials are considered as brittle. Brittleness is the principal disadvantage which should be controlled in all structural and even non-structural applications of these materials.

The brittleness of the matrices as inverse to the toughness is not defined in any universally accepted way. One possible definition was proposed in [10.83] as follows, 'The essence of fast fracture is that it is a failure mechanism which involves the unstable propagation of a crack in a structure. In other words, once the crack has started to move, the loading system is such that it produces accelerating growth, a brittle fracture, one in which the onset of unstable crack propagation is produced by an applied stress less than the general yield stress of the uncracked ligament remaining when instability occurs'.

A slightly different description of material brittleness was proposed in [10.66], cf. Section 10.3.1. According to other proposals the strain of 0.04 or 0.05 at failure may be considered as a limit of the brittle behaviour. Normally, the maximum strain of cement-based matrices does not reach 200.10^{-6}, i.e. a few orders of magnitude lower. It is, therefore, universally admitted to consider cement-based materials as brittle though for concretes and mortars the brittleness is reduced by their internal structure of grain inclusions.

A quantitative description of the brittleness was proposed in [10.38] and [10.84] in the form of the characteristic length l_{ch} also called ductility, $l_{ch} = G_f/E/f_t^2$ [mm] where G_f is the fracture energy and f_t is the tensile strength. The brittleness is then defined as, $1/l_{ch} = f_t^2/EG_f$.

The application of l_{ch} for characterization of different materials is justified only when their σ–ε curves are of similar shape. The higher values of l_{ch} mean lower brittleness and higher toughness. The average values of l_{ch} for cement-based materials are:

Portland cement paste	5–15 mm
Mortar	100–200 mm
Ordinary plain concrete	200–400 mm

The brittleness of cement-based composites increases with their compressive strength. It may be observed that in recent years the strength of conventional concrete has increased, thanks to improved technology and material composition. Also, the extended use of micro-fillers like silica fume is the main reason that strength has increased considerably. However, the increase of E and G_f is quite moderate, and consequently l_{ch} tends to lower values. In the design of highperformance concretes, their brittleness is of special concern, cf. Section 14.5.5.

Other measures for brittleness have been proposed [10.85] such as the brittleness index BI determined as shown in Figure 10.34. It is defined as the ratio of elastic strain energy to irreversible strain energy, corresponding to the peak point of the σ–ε curve obtained in a compression test, for ideal elastic and brittle material BI = 0; for ideal elastic and ductile materials BI = ∞.

Brittleness depends not only on a material's properties and external conditions, but also on the size of the element [10.86]; therefore, this aspect should be considered in both material and structural design. Large elements exhibit more brittle behaviour than small ones when all other conditions are the same. In paper [10.86] a few indications are proposed as to how to accommodate the increased brittleness of modern cement-based composites in structural elements:

- the geometry should be simple, without sharp corners and potential notches;
- smaller elements are less exposed to brittle fracture;
- eventual damage should concern parts of structure only;

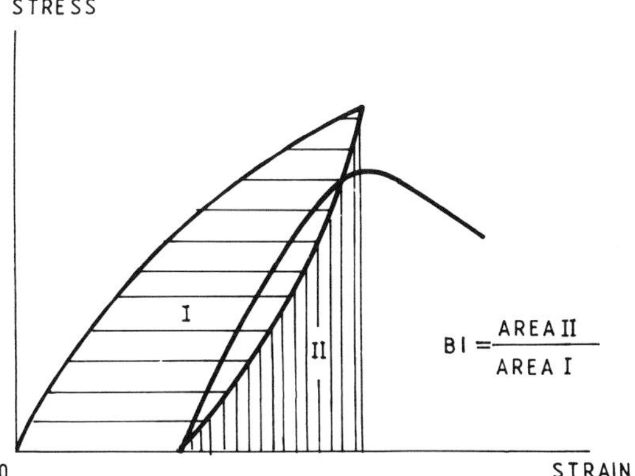

Figure 10.34 Complete σ–ε curve and brittleness index for a concrete specimen. (Reproduced with permission from Wu Keru and Zhou Jianhua, The influence of matrix–aggregate bond in the strength and brittleness of concrete; published by Materials Research Society, 1988.) [10.85]

- initial cracks and local stress concentrations should be prevented;
- for calculation of cracking and failure the theory of elasticity or LEFM is appropriate, however gives comparative results only;
- carrying capacity may be determined by the weakest link statistics.

To these precautions may be added a recommendation for the application of dispersed reinforcement or other measures of crack control. This may lead to a high volume of reinforcement, e.g. SIFCON, where a high strength and very brittle matrix is transformed into a crack resistant and elastic material. In paper [10.86] examples of structural elements combining ceramic strength and metallic toughness are given for the future development of FRC.

10.4 Modes of fracture

10.4.1 MIXED-MODE FRACTURE

There are three main types of failure by crack propagation, shown in Figure 10.3: I (opening), II (sliding) and III (tearing). The question of how these modes are represented in real composite structures subjected to external load is not yet completely solved. The models proposed at present seem to be still dependent on the scale – if in macro-scale, the tests executed according to these three modes are possible, the results obtained seem to characterize only the effects in the same scale with mean values of parameters. On a lower scale probably all modes appear simultaneously or at least Modes I and II act conjointly. The mixed-mode fracture parameters may be calculated for linear elastic materials within the frames of LEFM, but their direct application to cement-based composites is questioned. The considerations below are partly based on the paper, [10.87].

In a mixed-mode loading, when not only axial loading but also shearing is applied, it is assumed that fracture occurs when a total energy release rate G is larger than an energy consumption rate, R, and the fracture condition is given by $G \geqslant R$. The total energy release rate G for a linear elastic material is the following sum:

$$G = G_{\mathrm{I}} + G_{\mathrm{II}} + G_{\mathrm{III}} = \frac{(1 - v^2)}{E}\left(K_{\mathrm{I}}^2 + K_{\mathrm{II}}^2 + \frac{K_{\mathrm{III}}^2}{(1 - v)}\right). \tag{10.22}$$

For I–II mixed-mode loading, which may be adopted for the plane strain state, it is assumed that $K_{\mathrm{III}} = 0$. This situation occurs in most cases when the dimensions of a loaded element admit plane strain state. Therefore:

$$G = \frac{(1 - v^2)}{E}(K_{\mathrm{I}}^2 + K_{\mathrm{II}}^2) \tag{10.23}$$

here E – Young's modulus and v – Poisson's ratio.

Several authors do not accept the existence of Mode II and III failure in concrete composites, because such composites fail easily in Mode I at local stress concentrations, and then cracks tend to follow the path of principal tensile strain, [10.88]. In such a case the above formula might be simplified to the form:

$$G = \frac{(1 - v^2)}{E}K_{\mathrm{I}}^2 \tag{10.24}$$

as in nearly all published studies, it means that one of the following assumptions is accepted:

1. the material under consideration is characterized by $K_{\mathrm{II}} = 0$; or
2. the Mode II of fracture does not exist at all in the examined fracture process.

Assumption 1) cannot be proved for any structural material, independently of whether its behaviour is considered as linear and elastic or non-linear and plastic, the fluids and gels being here excluded from the considerations.

Assumption 2) may be adopted for ideally homogeneous materials subjected to tensile loading. Its application to concrete-like materials seems inappropriate because of the high level of inhomogeneity. Even in the case of an external loading applied in a way to produce ideally Mode I (opening), the local effects between grains and voids produce all three modes of fracture. The assumption that Mode III may be neglected in a plane–strain state seems to be more admissible.

Comprehensive reviews of mixed-mode fracture of two-dimensional models in LEFM have been published, [10.89] and [10.90]. They classified the models into two categories – fracture mechanics oriented and failure theories oriented.

In the first group the stress field at the crack tip is expressed using K_I and K_{II} and total stress intensity factor K_c^2 as shown below in equation 10.25. The second approach is based on two critical values which characterize the material by equation 10.26 or on determination of the effective stress intensity factor which is obtained from the principal stress and not from the tensile stress component. That second category comprises classical failure theories based on maximum tangential stress or strain, minimum strain energy density, Mohr–Coulomb stress theory, etc.

Other authors propose to determine Mode II failure according to the maximum energy release rate rather than to the principal stress, [10.91].

10.4.2 QUANTITATIVE DETERMINATION OF MIXED-MODE FRACTURE

In the following considerations paper [10.87] is again quoted.

Various experimental studies have shown that the cracks start from a mortar–aggregate grain interface, even if the external load is applied as an ideal axial tension. Regarding these crack patterns, as well as their model representation, it is difficult to admit that the crack propagation is limited to Mode I, e.g. [10.92].

Two examples of possible Mode II fracture in local situations around initial cracks or regions with different rigidity are shown in Figure 10.35 in the form of an initial crack or flaw (Figure 10.35a) in the matrix or a bond crack along the surface of an aggregate grain (Figure 10.35b). The nature of the external load – tension or compression – does not modify these possibilities. The deformations along lines a–a and b–b are different in such a way that the in-plane shearing appears at the tips of initial notches and the Mode II fracture begins.

A few series of tests aimed at examination of Mode II failure in cement-based composites were executed and published, e.g. [10.93]–[10.95] using a simple arrangement for testing elements under bending to create various combinations of Modes I and II, shown in Figure 10.36. A series of simply supported beams are provided with notches of different depth and location. The mode of cracking depends on the depth a of the notch and on its location defined by factor γ. The value of $\gamma = 0$ corresponds to pure Mode I and the

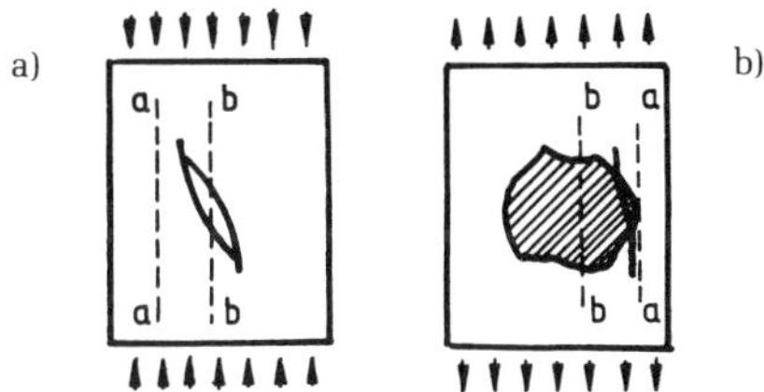

Figure 10.35 Local non-homogeneities as source of Mode II fracture. (Source: Brandt, A.M. and Prokopski, G., Critical values of stress intensity factor in Mode II fracture of cementitious composites; *J. of Materials Science*, **25**, 1990.) [10.87]

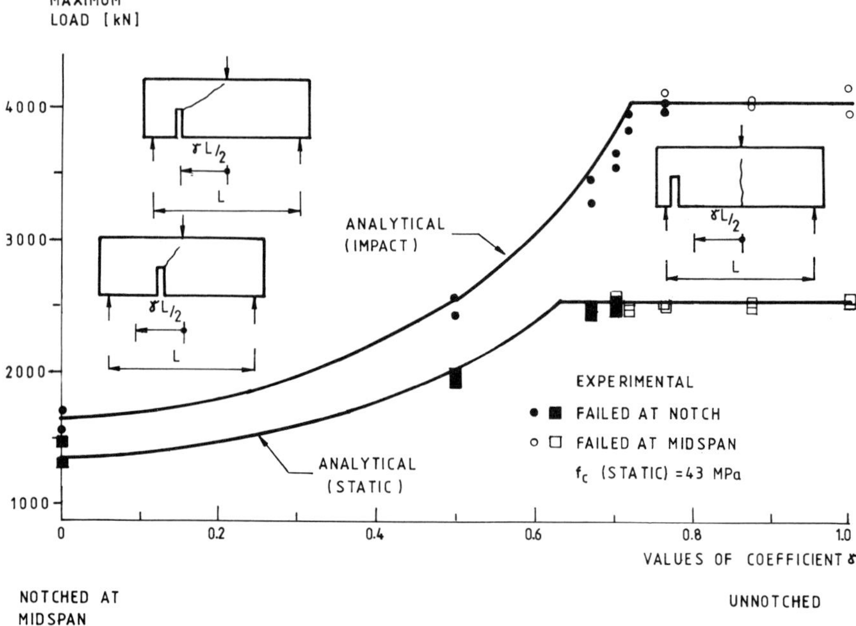

Figure 10.36 Influence of location of notch on maximum load and on mode of failure. (Reproduced with permission from John, R. and Shah, S.P., Mixed mode fracture of concrete subjected to impact loading; *J. Energy Mech. Div.*, **116** (EM3), published by ASCE, 1990.) [10.94]

other values of γ induce either a mixed mode at the notch tip or again pure Mode I when tension failure occurs at the midspan. Which of these possibilities is actually realized depends on both values, γ and a. The results obtained were compared with calculations by finite element method assuming LEFM solutions for Modes I and II. The tests were executed under static and impact loading and the test and calculation results are shown in Figure 10.36. As the notch was moved away from the centre of the span, the maximum load increased. When $\gamma \geqslant \gamma_{cr}$, the beam failed at the centre, unnotched cross-section according to the pure Mode I. Similar behaviour was observed under impact loading but for a different value of γ_{cr}. The tests furnished interesting results, however, strongly related to shape dimensions of specimens. Attempts at numerical modelling of the specimens using FEM were published in [10.88] and [10.91].

There is rather limited information about Mode III failure and only some experimental data, [10.96]. Also, in this subject, practical recommendations for material design and verification are still needed.

Interesting results for the mixed mode fracture were observed in [10.97] from the tests of transversally orthotropic fibre-reinforced mortar cylinders 80 × 160 mm, subjected to axial compression. The compressive force P was applied at different angles θ with respect to the casting direction 1–1 (Figure 10.37). Two different criteria have been used for different regions of angle, and excellent confirmation has been obtained by experimental results. For angle θ between 0° and 45° and between 75° and 90°, the splitting of the cylinder under compression was decisive. For angle θ between 45° and 75°, the shearing mode appeared because of the weaker resistance against tangent stresses along layers perpendicular to the casting direction.

Combined loading which produced the mixed mode of cracking was considered in [10.3] and two examples of fracture criteria were proposed:

$$K_{Ic}^2 + K_{IIc}^2 = K_c^2, \tag{10.25}$$

here it is assumed that $K_{Ic} = K_{IIc}$, and

$$\left(\frac{K_I}{K_{Ic}}\right)^2 + \left(\frac{K_{II}}{K_{IIc}}\right)^2 = 1, \quad \text{where} \quad K_{Ic} \neq K_{IIc}. \tag{10.26}$$

For the second of these criteria, it was assumed that the crack was propagated in a self-same manner and remained in the plane of the original crack. In experiments it is usually observed that the crack extends along an angle with respect to its original direction.

In strongly heterogeneous and anisotropic materials like concretes, the problem should be considered in a different but more complicated way. It is not a single crack subjected simultaneously to tension and in-plane shearing which produces a mixed mode of fracture, but a spectrum of loading conditions

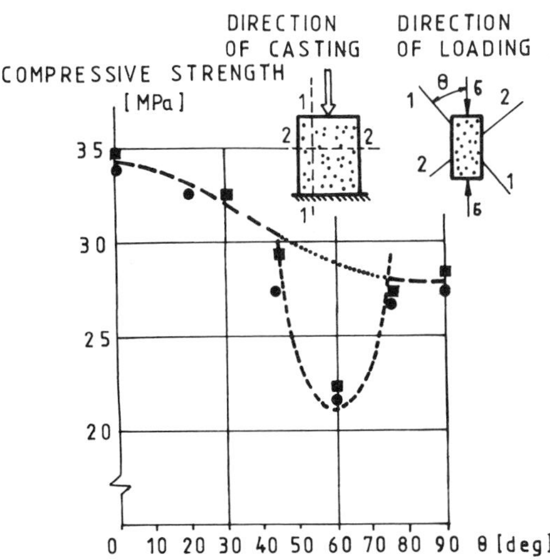

Figure 10.37 Results of compression tests: strength versus angle θ. Experimental results compared with calculation according to two strength criteria. (Source: Debicki, G., Doctorate Thesis; Institut National des Science Appliquées, 1988.) [10.97]

which produce various mixed modes of fracture. In that spectrum, Modes I and II are only limiting cases, all the others are different combinations of both of them.

A model may be therefore proposed in which critical values of K_{Ic} and K_{IIc} both determine a critical value of an overall factor K_c being a measure for the material crack resistance. It was written by [10.98] and [10.99] as a function describing the critical state:

$$f(K_{Ic}, K_{IIc}) = f_c, \tag{10.27}$$

without defining any particular form of that function.

One of the possible ways to find out an acceptable form of the function, equation 10.27, is to execute a series of experiments in which materials of known K_{Ic} and K_{IIc} will be combined. Different proportions of both materials and carefully arranged macro-regions in a tested element may help to determine the practically reliable function $f(K_{Ic}, K_{IIc})$. The high degree of indeterminacy of the system which represents a concrete specimen may cause such a problem and is quite difficult to deal with.

Tests in which the values of K_{IIc} were measured are not very numerous and the few available data are shown in Table 10.3. They concern concretes with different composition and internal structure. The data from different authors are not very dispersed, which may be explained by the similar way of testing adopted by all authors. In most cases the higher values of K_{IIc} correspond to the materials for which higher strength and better aggregate–matrix bond was also observed, or may be supposed if the appropriate data are not given. This is expected, and reflects to some extent the material's resistance against shearing crack propagation.

In the test results reported in Table 10.3, neither data for K_{Ic} nor information on the material's strength and internal structure are available. Therefore an analysis of the data is limited. In such a situation a new series of tests was executed in which more complex data were looked for. These tests are described below and based on [10.87].

The specimens for determining separately the fracture properties for both Modes I and II are shown in Figures 10.38 and 10.39 together with examples of load–deflection curves. The specimens were cast with ordinary Portland cement, a fine aggregate of a local deposit and river gravel with a maximum grain size of 10 mm.

The critical values of stress intensity factors in Modes I and II were determined according to [10.108] in the formulae:

$$\begin{aligned} K_{Ic} &= \frac{P_{cr}}{B\sqrt{W}} Y\left(\frac{a}{W}\right), \\ K_{IIc} &= 5.11 \frac{P_{cr}}{2Bb} \sqrt{\pi a}, \end{aligned} \tag{10.28}$$

Table 10.3 Values of K_{IIc}

Authors	Materials	Specimen characteristics	K_{IIc} ($MNm^{-3/2}$)
Watkins (1983) [10.100]	soil-cement	a/W = 0.3	0.42
		a/W = 0.4	0.41
		a/W = 0.5	0.43
Davies, Morgan, Yim (1985) [10.101]	soil-cement	a/W = 0.3	0.42–0.43
		a/W = 0.4	0.41–0.42
		a/W = 0.5	0.43–0.44
Liu, Barr, Watkins (1985) [10.102]	concrete with polypropylene fibres		0.48–0.55
	concrete with steel-fibres		0.44–0.60
Davies, So (1986) [10.103]	mortar 1:3	w/c = 0.45	
		a = 35 mm	1.76
		a = 40 mm	1.85
Davies (1987) [10.104]	mortar 1:3	w/c = 0.45	
		a/W = 0.30	1.86
		a/W = 0.35	1.75
		a/W = 0.40	1.78
		a/W = 0.45	1.78
Bochenek, Prokopski (1987) [10.10)]	gravel concrete 1:2.43:3.43:0.54 max. grain	a/W = 0.4	
	2–4		1.82
	4–6.3		4.14
	6.3–8		3.56
	8–10		4.24
	10–12		3.85
	12–16		4.24
Bochenek, Prokopski (1988) [10.106]	gravel concrete	a/W = 0.4	
	1:2.45:3.74:0.55		3.20
	:0.60		2.99
	:0.65		2.86
	:0.70		2.85
	:0.75		2.29
	:0.80		2.82
	:0.85		2.11
	:0.90		2.15
Bochenek, Prokopski (1989) [10.107]	basalt concrete	a/W = 0.4	
	1:2.31:4.06:0.55		4.45
	gravel concrete 1:2.29:3.87:0.55		3.97
	granite concrete 1:2.26:4.13:0.55		5.14
	burned shale concrete 1:0.96:1.45:0.55		3.54

(Source: Brandt, A.M. and Prokopski, G., Critical values of stress intensity factor in Mode II fracture of cementitious composites; *J. of Materials Science*, **25**, pp. 3505–10, 1990.) [10.87]

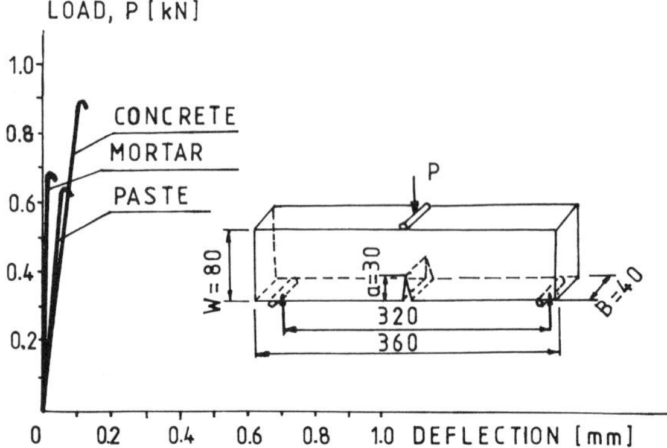

Figure 10.38 Examples of test results for K and dimensions of a notched beam subjected to bending. (Source: Brandt, A.M. and Prokopski, G., Critical values of stress intensity factor in Mode II fracture of cementitious composites; *J. of Materials Science*, **25**, 1990.) [10.87]

where P_{cr} is the value of the critical load P which initiated the crack propagation, W is specimen depth, b is ligament depth, a is notch depth and B is specimen width. That value of P_{cr} is identified on the curves (Figures 10.38 and 10.39) as a slight inflection for Mode II curves or as the maximum value for Mode I curves.

The above formulae were proposed by [10.108] and are used here following [10.100] and others, although they were initially intended for application for metallic specimens. Therefore, the numerical results obtained may be considered as only approximate. The question of the applicability of Linear Elastic Fracture Mechanics (LEFM) to relatively small specimens is discussed elsewhere.

The values calculated from formulae in equation (10.28) are presented in Table 10.4. The dispersion of obtained results is particularly high for K_{IIc} and is probably related to the high influence of local crack resistance of the specimens. The highest values of the variation coefficient were observed for cement paste in both types of specimens. This result may be attributed to the relative homogeneity of that material's structure and its brittleness. The cracks were not blocked by any inclusion and critical load was primarily related to random local defects at the crack path.

On the load–displacement plots for concrete and mortar specimens, a slight quasi-plastic effect in the form of inflections appeared (Figure 10.39). This phenomenon may be related to rearrangement of the aggregate grains, after which an additional energy supply was required for further crack propagation. It was not observed on the curves for paste specimens.

The transgranular path of the cracks and their changes of direction when passing around the grains also required additional amounts of energy to be supplied by the external load. This was probably the reason why higher values

Table 10.4 Test results

Parameters	Types of material		
	paste	mortar	concrete
Compressive strength (MPa)	56.9	30.5	35.3
Coefficient of variation (%)	2.2	5.3	3.4
Number of specimens	3	3	3
Critical value of stress intensity factor K_{Ic} (M Nm$^{-3/2}$)	0.472	0.557	0.935
Coefficient of variation (%)	13.2	7.5	4.3
Number of specimens	9	9	9
Critical value of stress intensity factor K_{IIc} (M Nm$^{-3/2}$)	1.480	2.430	3.648
Coefficient of variation (%)	23.0	9.5	8.5
Number of specimens	7	7	7

(Source: Brandt, A.M. and Prokopski, G., Critical values of stress intensity factor in Mode II fracture of cementitious composites; *J. of Materials Science*, **25**, pp. 3505–10, 1990.) [10.87]

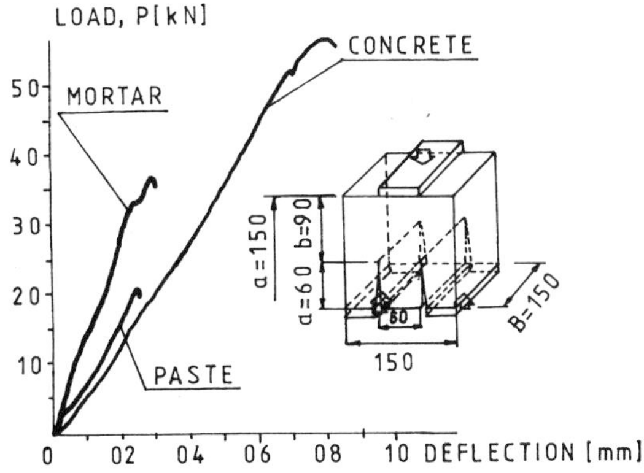

Figure 10.39 Examples of test results for K and dimensions of a punch-through shear specimen. (Source; Brandt, A.M. and Prokopski, G. Critical values of stress intensity factor in Mode II fracture of cementitious composites; *J. of Materials Science*, **25**, 1990.) [10.87]

of fracture loads were necessary for concrete and mortar specimens than for paste ones.

It may be concluded that the results obtained in paper [10.87] confirm the data published previously by other authors. The values of K_{Ic} and K_{IIc} for the same materials may be used in establishing a criterion for mixed-mode fracture in concretes which is still lacking.

10.5 Relationship between fracture toughness and fractal dimension in concretes

The irregular shape of cracks and fracture surfaces of cement-based composites is at the origin of the question as to whether they may be considered as fractal objects. The application of fractal analysis should be aimed at a better understanding of the fracture mechanics of these materials, by possible quantification of the fracture surface roughness, length and surface of cracks and all other irregular elements which may characterize the materials and their behaviour. These problems are presented below and based on paper [10.109].

The development of the fractal characterization of irregular lines and surfaces was initiated by Mandelbrot, who introduced in [10.110] and [10.111] the fractal concept to many fields of science.

Man-made objects have in most cases linear or curvilinear contours and surfaces, corresponding to Euclidean geometry in which points, lines, surfaces and volumes have topological dimensions represented by integers – 0, 1, 2 and 3, respectively. However, natural objects like coastlines, clouds and rock surfaces are irregular and composed of 'mountains' and 'valleys'. It is easy to observe that at higher magnification further families of 'mountains' and 'valleys' appear. The effective length of such an irregular line and the effective area of an irregular surface seem to be related to the magnification, and therefore cannot be determined in an objective way. At the discontinuities these curves and surfaces are non-differentiable.

The word 'fractal' was proposed in [10.110] together with fractal dimension D which characterizes the irregularity of the fractal objects. The lines have non-integer values of D between 1 and 2. The irregularity of surfaces is expressed by their fractal dimension, varying between 2 and 3. The more irregular is the object, the higher is its fractal dimension. The fractal dimension exceeds the Euclidean one.

The fractal dimension is defined by the relation corresponding to a segment of a line from which fractal line is generated,

$$D = \frac{\ln N}{\ln 1/r} \quad \text{or} \quad N = (1/r)^D,$$

here N is the number of subparts for which the initial segment of unit length is divided at each step and $1/r$ is the scalling factor, r being the length of each subpart. The generation of two simple fractal lines is shown in Figure 10.40.

The generation of a fractal line may be repeated indefinitely and the total length of the line is expressed as function of r and D

$$L = L_o r^{-(D-1)}, \tag{10.29}$$

here L_o is the length of initial straight segment. The total length increases

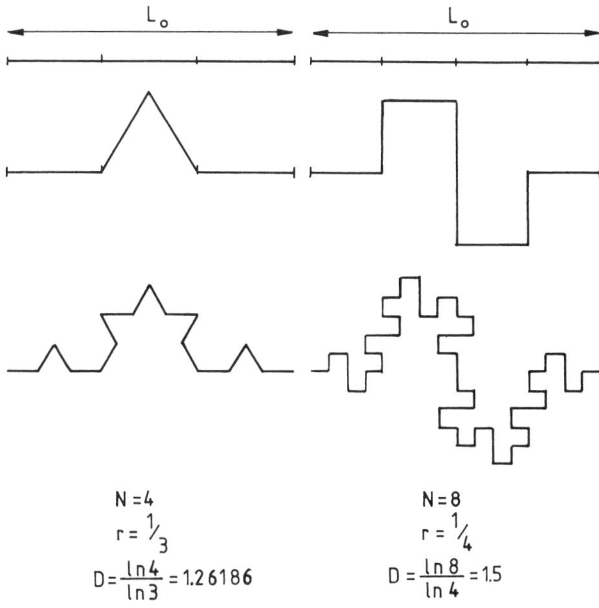

Figure 10.40 Generation of two examples of simple fractal lines.

indefinitely with decreasing r, e.g. for $D = 1.5$ it is:

r	1	0.5	0.1	0.01	0.001	0.0001
L	1	1.41	3.16	10.00	31.62	100.00

More general relation for lines and surfaces has the following form:

$$L = L_o E^{-(D_f - D)} \tag{10.30}$$

here L and L_o are the total and initial length and area, respectively, E is scale of measurement, D_f and D are fractal and topological dimensions.

The natural lines and surfaces with apparent irregularities are not always the fractal objects with given fractal dimension. The necessary requirement is self-similarity, i.e. within certain limits of magnification a larger region of the object should appear exactly or approximately similar to a smaller region observed with appropriate magnification. In natural objects the self-similarity is not extended over all ranges of magnification – below and above certain levels the object has no fractal character. The reasons are different, e.g. the structure of the object may be significantly different at different levels.

The fractal dimension as a quantitative measure of the irregularity of the objects may be applied in various fields of materials science. It has been shown [10.112] that the self-similarity over two orders of magnitude occurs for fracture surfaces of tempered steel and alumina. A linear relation between the fractal dimension and fracture toughness for these materials was also proposed.

There are many other papers in which correlations between mechanical properties of solids and fractal dimensions of fractured surfaces were investigated within different orders of magnitude of scale. In [10.113] fracture surfaces of cement paste were examined and their fractal character shown, indicating its limits. Also a relation between the water/cement ratio and the roughness of surfaces of fractured specimens was observed. Concrete specimens with different maximum aggregate grain size from 20 to 75 mm have been studied [10.114], representing concretes used for the construction of dams. The authors of [10.114] also observed the fractal character of examined concretes without there being significant differences in fractal dimension for different aggregates. This last conclusion was attributed to the identical origin of all aggregates used in tested specimens.

The roughness of a fracture surface is studied along a system of profiles. Their orientation is of great importance. In the investigations reported in [10.114] measurements were made with a specially designed profilometer which was displaced over the fracture surface along two families of orthogonal lines. Another technique is based on the production of a polymer replica of the fracture surface. The replica is then sawn into slices by parallel sections. The contours obtained are called fracture profiles and are subjected to close examination and analysis – the length of each fracture profile is measured with varying step r and the results are plotted in the logarithmic system of coordinates using equation 10.29 in the form, $\log L = \log L + (1 - D)\log r$.

If the result obtained is approximately a straight line, it means that the fractal dimension equal to its slope which is constant over certain levels of magnification. This is called the vertical section method. Another approach called slit-island method is explained in [10.115] and was used for the analysis of fracture surfaces of metallic specimens.

To obtain statistically reliable results from the analysis of a fracture surface by the vertical section method, a large number of sections should be examined. The parallel sections executed, for example, along rectangular coordinates may give information about possible orthotrope properties of the fracture surface. In most cases random sections oriented at different angles should be studied.

The characterization of the fracture surface after the analysis of fracture profiles is based on an assumption that having determined the profile roughness parameter,

$$R_L = \frac{L}{L_o},$$

it is possible to define the fracture surface roughness parameter,

$$R_S = \frac{S}{S_o},$$

here L_o and S_o are apparent projected length and area, respectively, and projection was on the mean or average topographic direction or plane, (Figure 10.41). Therefore, a relation of the following type is needed

$$R_S = \overline{R_L \Psi}, \tag{10.31}$$

here $\overline{R_L \Psi}$ is an expected or average value of the product and Ψ is the profile structure factor which expresses the position and orientation of each elementary segment of the analysed fracture profile.

The relation (equation 10.31) is general and is not based on any assumption concerning the nature of the examined surface. The values of R_L and Ψ are independent and should be obtained in a number of vertical sectioning planes oriented differently to ensure the statistical representativity of the product, in [10.116] an efficient sampling procedure is proposed for estimation of fracture surface roughness from the measurements. The profile roughness parameter R_L should not be correlated to fracture toughness and any correlations observed may be misleading [10.117]. The approximate formula proposed in [10.118] has the form:

$$R_S = 4/\pi(R_L - 1) + 1 \tag{10.32}$$

and provides, according to these authors, the best fit to experimental data. When comparing equation 10.31 and equation 10.32 the following remarks should be made:

- R_S is an important quantity in respect to its possible relation to the fracture properties of the materials, but it is inaccessible by simple experimental measurements;
- R_L is easy to be determined experimentally, but its relation to the surface roughness as given by equation 10.31 is not so simple;
- equation 10.32 has been proposed and discussed for metallic specimens and its application to cement-based materials has not yet been verified.

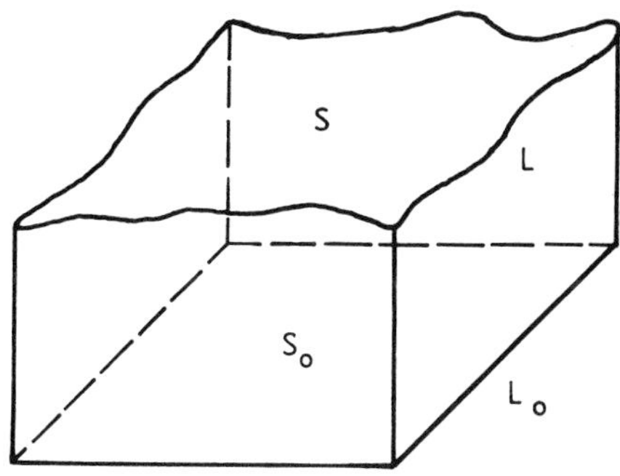

Figure 10.41 Symbols for irregular lines and surfaces with respect to their projections.

It should be also observed that R_L does not characterize completely and without ambiguity a profile – different profiles may have identical values of R_L, e.g. Figure 10.42. Also, two fracture surfaces with the same value of R_S are not necessarily similar.

The calculation of the fractal dimension D as well as of the fracture surface roughness parameter R_S is a valuable attempt to quantify the irregularities of natural fracture surfaces. Its application in the fracture mechanics of cement-based composites is promising. However, the quantitative conclusions from such calculations have only relative importance and should be limited to the materials of the same kind. For example, the roughness of the fracture surfaces of a series of mortar specimens with variable water/cement ratio, age or grading curves may reflect correctly their fracture toughness. In contrast, any comparison between fractal dimensions of cement pastes and concretes may give misleading results because of the different nature of these materials.

The question as to whether there is a general and reliable relationship between the fractal dimension of a surface and the fracture toughness of the material is considered by a number of authors and is examined below.

The results for concrete elements fractured under combined compression and internal pressure [10.114] are compared in Table 10.5 with those obtained for other materials. The results show a relation between fractal dimensions of the fractured surfaces and the critical values of the stress intensity factors K_{Ic} determined experimentally. The observed relation may be expressed as follows – in a group of similar materials those with higher values of K_{Ic} have a higher fractal dimension for their fracture surfaces. It may be considered as an indication that fractal dimensions of materials reflect their fracture toughness. The results in Table 10.5 are incomplete and do not allow for more detailed discussion.

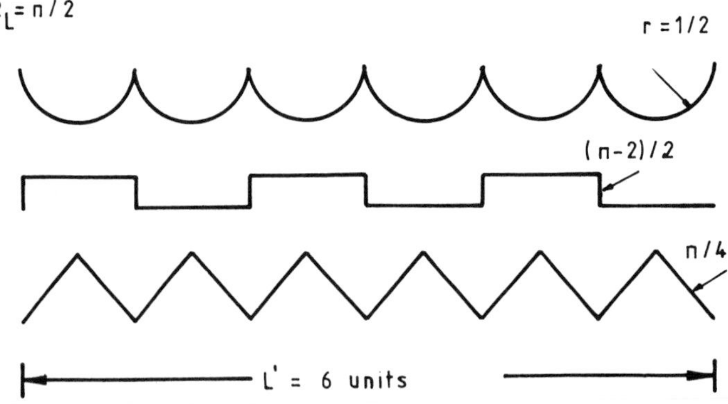

Figure 10.42 Three different profiles having identical values of the profile roughness parameter $R_L = 10.119/2$. (Reproduced with permission from Banerji, K., Quantitative fractography: a modern perspective; *Metallurgical Transactions A*, vol. **19A**, April 1988, 961–971.) [10.119]

Table 10.5 Mechanical properties and fractal dimensions D for different materials

Authors Material Test	Material specification	D	K_{Ic} ($MNm^{-3/2}$)	γ (J/m^2)	Temperature (°C)
Underwood and		1.085	–	–	200
Banerji [10.120]		1.091	–	–	300
		1.090	–	–	400
Steel	AISI 4030	1.072	–	–	500
Bending		1.084	–	–	600
		1.079	–	–	700
Mecholsky *et al.* [10.121]					
Alumina	UCC	1.15	2.5	–	–
Bending	Lucalox	1.31	4.0	20	–
Anstis *et al.* [10.122]					
Alumina	AD 90	1.21	2.9	11	
Tension	AD 999	1.31	3.9	19	
Neilson [10.123]					
Alumino-silicate					
Bending	GA Tech	1.18	2.2	–	
Hellmann [10.124]					
Alumina	WESGO (A1500)	1.20	3.6	23	
Tension	GEND	1.23	3.9	27	
Mecholsky	zinc-silicate 1	1.05	1.6	22	
[10.125]	zinc-silicate 2	1.09	1.8	22	
	zinc-silicate 3	1.11	2.2	27	
Glass-ceramics	lithia boro-	1.18	2.7	40.5	
Tension	silicate				
Mecholsky and		1.32	1.55	–	20
Mackin [10.126]		1.26	1.46	–	300
Ocala chert		1.24	1.25	–	400
Bending		1.15	1.05	–	500
Saouma *et al.* [10.114]					
Concrete		1.07–1.12			
Compression					

(Source: Brandt, A.M. and Prokopski, G., On the fractal dimension of fracture surfaces of concrete elements; *J. of Materials Science*, 28, 4762–6, 1993.) [10.109]

As mentioned above, it is incorrect to compare mechanical data and fractal dimension for different materials, e.g. no conclusion may be formulated from the fact that alumina and Ocala chert have similar values of D and different values of K_{Ic}. In [10.127] there is an indication that the correlation between the fracture toughness and fractal dimension may be either positive or negative and some additional specifications as to compared materials are necessary before formulation of useful conclusions. In concrete specimens with an important pore system the negative correlation might be expected, and positive correlation for a system of dispersed hard grains. The second possibility is typical for ordinary structural concretes.

The tests of concrete specimens subjected to Mode II fracture were aimed at a further investigation of relations between fractal dimension and roughness of the fracture surface after Mode II crack propagation.

The specimens were cast with concretes made with three kinds of coarse aggregate – crushed basalt, river gravel and crushed limestone. Other specimens were prepared with cement mortar and paste. The specimens were subjected to shearing as shown in Figure 10.39.

The values of K_{IIc} were calculated according to the formula proposed in [10.128]:

$$K_{IIc} = \frac{5.11P_{cr}}{2Bb}(\pi a)^{1/2} \tag{10.33}$$

here P_{cr} is the value of the critical load P which initiated the crack propagation, b is the ligament depth, a is the notch depth and B is the specimen width, Figure 10.39.

The fractured surfaces were used to prepare replicas with acrylic resin. The replicas were sawn into slices as shown in Figure 10.43. Then, the profile lines of each replica were subjected to the computer image analyser, Magiscan (Joyce–Loebl) and the length of each profile line was measured with varying steps equal to 0.45, 0.30, 0.15, 0.075, 0.05 and 0.0375 mm. The image of a profile line was transferred on a monitor and covered with a system of orthogonal lines 512 × 512 pixels. The modification of the scale of the profile lines caused a modification of the steps. To measure the length of the profile lines an erosion function has been applied of unit width equal to 1 pixel.

Mean values from 4 measurements of profile lines were used to calculate the fractal dimension from equation 10.29. Specimens of dolomite and gravel

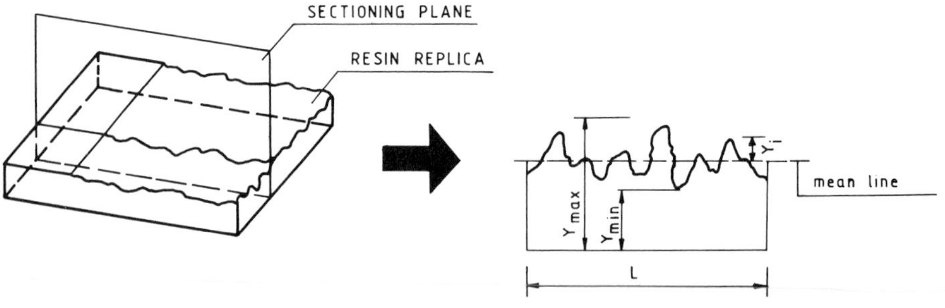

Figure 10.43 Preparation of replicas for analysis of profile lines. (Source: Brandt, A.M. and Prokopski, G., On the fractal dimension of fracture surfaces of concrete elements; *J. of Materials Science*, 28, 4762–6, 1993.) [10.109]

concretes were selected for fractal analysis from specimens with different values of K_{IIc}.

The results of tests are presented in Figure 10.44 and in Table 10.6. The following conclusions may be proposed after the tests.

The fracture surfaces are fractal objects within the scope of analysed scales and are characterized by fractal dimensions. The coefficients of the exponential correlation for lines in Figure 10.44 are close to 0.99.

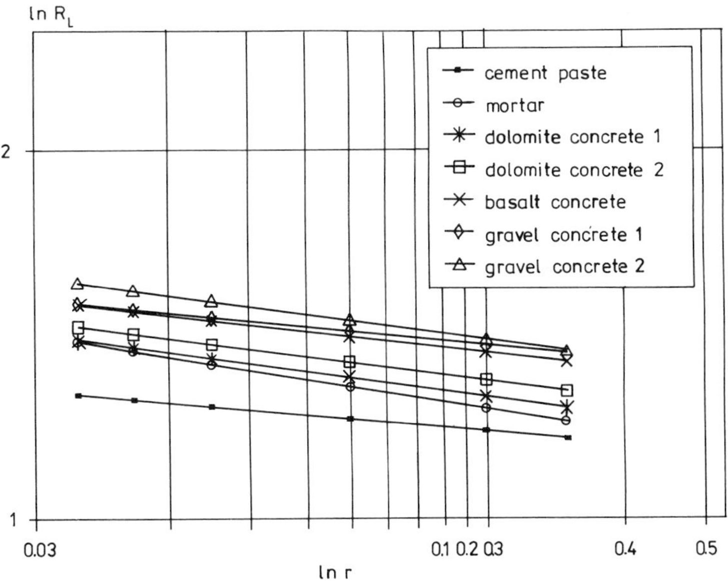

Figure 10.44 Fractal plots for profiles of specimens with different materials. (Source: Brandt, A.M. and Prokopski, G., On the fractal dimension of fracture surfaces of concrete elements; *J. of Materials Science*, 28, 4762–6, 1993.) [10.109]

Table 10.6 Fractal dimensions and fracture toughness of cement-based composites

Material	D	K_{IIc} (MNm$^{-3/2}$)
Cement paste	1.033	1.60
Cement mortar	1.060	3.37
Dolomite concrete 1	1.050	3.90
Dolomite concrete 2	1.054	4.36
Gravel concrete 1	1.038	2.74
Gravel concrete 2	1.051	3.40
Basalt concrete	1.043	5.16

(Source: Brandt, A.M. and Prokopski, G., On the fractal dimension of fracture surfaces of concrete elements; *J. of Materials Science*, 28, 4762–6, 1993.) [10.109]

In this analysis it has been assumed that the profile lines analysis allows the fracture surface roughness to be deduced. It is therefore expected that the approximate relation from equation 10.32 may be used as characteristic for the comparison of surfaces of different materials, belonging to the same group.

The relations between values of D and K_{Ic} confirm the previously mentioned conclusion. For Mode II fracture in cements-based composite materials it has been observed that higher fracture toughness is accompanied by higher values of fractal dimension of the fracture surfaces.

The differences in fractal dimensions for concrete, mortar and paste specimens may be explained by the influence of the smallest grains of sand and cement which have a completely different nature than the composite materials.

The results obtained do not furnish any quantitative relations for practical applications and it is not yet possible to design cement-based composites with given fractal dimension for required fracture toughness. It seems, however, that new evidence is being obtained to support the hypothesis that the fracture surfaces of concrete-like composites are fractal objects. It is expected that this hypothesis may be of some practical importance in the future after further tests.

References

10.1. Griffith, A.A. (1921) The phenomenon of rupture and flow in solids. *Phil. Trans. Roy. Society*, A221, 163–98.

10.2. Griffith, A.A. (1926) The theory of rupture. *Proc. 1st Int. Congress of Appl. Mech.*, Delft 1924, Waltman, 55–63.

10.3. Broek, D. (1983) *Elementary Engineering Fracture Mechanics*, 4th ed., Martinus Nijhoff Publishers, Dordrecht.

10.4. Kaplan, M.F. (1961) Crack propagation and the fracture of concrete. *J. of the American Concrete Institute*, **58**, 591–610.

10.5. Glücklich, J. (1968) The effect of microcracking on time-dependent deformations and the long-term strength of concrete. Proc. Int. Conf. *The Structure of Concrete*, September 1965, London, Cement and Concrete Association, London, 176–89.

10.6. Neville, A.M. (1959) Some aspects of the strength of concrete. *Civil Engineering*, **54**, Part 1: 1153–6, Part 2: 1308–11, Part 3: 1435–9.

10.7. Mindess, S. (1983) The application of fracture mechanics to cement and concrete: A historical review, in [10.9], 1–30.

10.8. Mindess, S. (1986) The cracking and fracture of concrete: an annotated bibliography 1982–5, in [10.10], 629–99.

10.9. Wittmann, F.H. (ed.) (1983) *Fracture Mechanics of Concrete*, Elsevier, Amsterdam.

10.10. Wittmann, F.H. (ed.) (1986) *Fracture Toughness and Fracture Energy of Concrete*, Elsevier Science Publishers, Amsterdam.

10.11. Brown, W.F. and Srawley, J.E. (eds) (1966) Plane strain crack toughness of high strength metallic materials. *ASTM Special Technical Publication*, No. 410, ASTM, Philadelphia.

10.12. Swamy, R.N. (1979) Fracture mechanics applied to concrete, in *Developments in Concrete Technology – 1*, F.D. Lydon (ed.), Applied Science Publishers, London 221–81.

10.13. Walsh, P.F. (1972) Fracture of plain concrete. *Indian Concrete Journal*, **46**, 469–76.

10.14. Bazant, Z.P. (1980) Material behaviour under various types of loading, in Proc. Workshop *High Strength Concrete*, 1979, S.P. Shah (ed.), Univ. of Illinois at Chicago Circle, University of Chicago Press, Chicago, 79–92.

10.15. Romualdi, J.P. and Batson, G.B. (1963) Mechanics of crack arrest in concrete. *Journal of Engineering Mech. Div.*, Proc. ASCE, **89**(EM3), 147–68.

10.16. Romualdi, J.P. and Mandel, J.A. (1964) Tensile strength of concrete affected by uniformly distributed and closely spaced short lengths of wire reinforcement. *Journal of the Amer. Concr. Inst.*, **61**, 657–71.

10.17. Aveston, J., Cooper, G.A. and Kelly, A. (1971) Single and multiple fracture. Proc. Nat. Phys. Lab. Conf. *The Properties of Fibre Composites*, IPC Science and Technology Press Ltd., Teddington, England 15–24.

10.18. Kelly, A. (1974) Some scientific points concerning the mechanics of fibrous composites, in Proc. Nat. Phys. Lab. Conf. *Composites – Standards, Testing and Design*, IPC Science and Technology Press Ltd., Teddington, 9–16.

10.19. Romualdi, J.P. (1968) The static cracking stress and fatigue strength of concrete reinforced with short pieces of thin steel wire. Proc. Int. Conf. *The Structure of Concrete*, September 1965, London, Cement and Concrete Association, London 190–201, 204–206.

10.20. Kasperkiewicz, J. (1983) Internal structure and fracture processes in brittle matrix composites (in Polish), *IFTR Reports*, nr. 39, IFTR, Warsaw.

10.21. Aveston, J. and Kelly, A. (1973) Theory of multiple fracture of fibrous composites. *Journal of Materials Science*, **8**(3), 352–62.

10.22. Aveston, J., Mercer, R.A. and Sillwood, J.M. (1974) Fibre-reinforced cements – scientific foundations for specifications, as [10.18], 93–102.

10.23. Laws, V. (1974) On increase of tensile failure strain of Portland cement reinforced with glassfibre bundles, Disc. Proc. Nat. Phys. Lab. Conf. *Composites – Standards, Testing and Design*, IPC Science and Technology Press Ltd., Teddington 102–3.

10.24. Hannant, D.J. (1978) *Fibre cements and fibre concretes*, J. Wiley and Sons, Chichester.

10.25. Rice, J.R. (1968) A path independent integral and the approximate analysis of strain concentration by notches and cracks. *Journal of Appl. Mech.*, Trans. ASME, **35**, 379–86.

10.26. Mindess, S., Lawrence, F.K. and Kesler, C.E. (1977) The J-Integral as a fracture criterion for fiber reinforced concrete. *Cem. and Concrete Research*, **7**, 731–42.

10.27. Östensson, B. (1974) Some information from load deflection curves, useful in fracture toughness testing. *Engineering Fracture Mechanics*, **6**(3), 473–82.

10.28. Brandt, A.M. (1980) Crack propagation energy in steel-fibre-reinforced concrete. *Int. Journal of Cement Composites*, **2**(3), 35–42.

10.29. Wells, A.A. (1963) Application of fracture mechanics at and beyond general yielding, *British Welding Res. Ass. Report*, **10**(11) 563–70.

10.30. Velasco, G., Visalvanich, K. and Shah, S.P. (1980) Fracture behaviour and analysis of fiber-reinforced concrete beams. *Cement and Concrete Research*, **10**, 41–51.

10.31. ASTM (1974) Standard Method of Test for Plane–Strain Fracture Toughness of Metallic Materials. *ASTM Designation E399–74*, part 10, ASTM Annual Standard, Philadelphia.

10.32. BSI (1972) *Methods for crack opening displacement (COD) testing.* British Standards Institution, 3D19, London.

10.33. Brandt, A.M., Stroeven, P., Dalhuisen, D. and Donker, L. (1989) *Fracture mechanics tests of fibre-reinforced concrete beams in pure bending.* Report 25.1–89–7/C4, July, Faculty of Civil Eng., Delft University of Technology, Delft.

10.34. Dugdale, D.S. (1960) Yielding of steel sheets containing slits, *Journal of the Mechanics and Physics of Solids*, **8**, 100–4.

10.35. Rolfe, S.T. and Barsom, J.M. (1977) *Fracture and fatigue control in structures.* Prentice-Hall, Englewood Cliffs, New Jersey.

10.36. Hillerborg, A. (1978) A model for fracture analysis. Report TVBM–4005, Div. of Build. Mat., Univ. of Lund, Lund.

10.37. Modeer, M. (1979) A fracture mechanics approach to failure analyses of concrete materials, Report TVBM–1001, Div. of Build. Mat. Univ. of Lund, Lund.

10.38. Petersson, P.E. (1981) Crack growth and development of fracture zone in plain concrete and similar materials. Rep. TVEM–1001, Div. of Build. Mat., Lund Inst. of Techn., Lund 1981.

10.39. Cornellissen, H.A.W., Hordijk, D.A. and Reinhardt, H.W. (1986) Experiments and theory for application of fracture mechanics of normal and lightweight concrete, in *Fracture Toughness and Fracture Energy of Concrete*, (ed. F.H. Wittmann), Elsevier, Amsterdam, 565–75.

10.40. Roelfstra, P.E. and Wittmann, F.H. (1986) Numerical method to link strain softening with failure of concrete, as [10.39], 163–75.

10.41. Li, V.C., Chan, C.M. and Leung, C.K.Y. (1987) Experimental determination of the tension softening relations for cementitious composites, *Cem. and Concr. Res.*, **17**, 441–52.

10.42. Hu, X.Z. and Wittmann, F.H. (1989) Fracture process zone and K_r-curve of hardened cement paste and mortar, in *Fracture of Concrete and Rock*, (eds S.P. Shah, S.E., Swartz, B. Barr), Elsevier Applied Science, London and New York, 307–16.

10.43. Rokugo, K., Iwasa, M., Seko, S. and Koyanagi, W. (1989) Tension softening diagrams for steel-fiber-reinforced concrete, as [10.42], 513–22.

10.44. Edgington, J., Hannant, D.J. and Williams, R.I.T. (1974) Steel-fibre-reinforced concrete, BRE Current Paper CP 69/74, BRE, Garston, England.

10.45. Morris, A.D. and Garrett, G.G. (1981) A comparative study of the static and fatigue behaviour of plain and steel-fibre-reinforced mortar in compression and direct tension. *Int. J. of Cement Composites and Lightweight Concrete*, **3**(2), 73–91.

10.46. Mangat, P.S. and Motamedi Azari, M. (1984) Influence of steel-fibre-reinforcement on the fracture behaviour of concrete in compression. *Int. J. of Cement Composites and Lightweight Concrete*, **6**(4), 219–32.

10.47. Swamy, R.N. and Mangat, P.S. (1974) Influence of fibre geometry on the properties of steel-fibre-reinforced concrete. *Cement and Concrete Research*, **4**(3), 451–65.

10.48. Hughes, B.P. and Fattuhi, N.I. (1977) Stress–strain curves for fibre-reinforced concrete in compression. *Cement and Concrete Research*, **7**(2), 173–84.

10.49. Ramakrishnan, V. (1987) Materials and properties of fibre-reinforced concrete. Proc. Int. Symp. on *Fibre Reinforced Concrete*, Madras, December 16–19, 1987, Oxford & IBH Publ. Co., New Delhi, 2.3–2.23.

10.50. Tanigawa, Y., Hatanaka, S. and Mori, H. (1980) Stress–strain behaviour of steel-fiber-reinforced concrete under compression. *Trans. of the Japan Concr. Inst.*, **2**, 187–94.

10.51. Craig, R.J., McConnell, J., Germann, H. *et al.* (1984) Behaviour of reinforced fibrous concrete columns, in Proc. Int. Symp. *Fiber Reinforced Concrete*, (ed. G.C. Hoff), 1982, ACI Committee 544, SP81, Detroit.

10.52. Dahl-Jorgensen, E., Chen, W.F., Manson, J.A., *et al.* (1974) Polymer-impregnated concrete: Laboratory studies. ASCE/EIC/RTAC Joint Transportation Engineering Meeting, Montreal, July 14–19, ASCE, New York.

10.53. ACI (1988) Design Considerations for Steel Fiber Reinforced Concrete, ACI 544 Committee Report, *ACI Structural Journal*, September–October, 565–80.

10.54. Kasperkiewicz, J. (1979) Ultimate strength and strain of steel-fibre-reinforced concrete under tension (in Polish), *Mech. Teoret. i Stos.*, **17**(1), 19–34.

10.55. Johnston, C.D. and Gray, R.J. (1978) Uniaxial tensile testing of steel-fibre-reinforced cementitious composites, in *Testing and Test Methods of Fibre Cement Composites*, (ed. R.N. Swamy), RILEM Symp. Sheffield, The Construction Press Ltd., Lancaster, 451–61.

10.56. Hughes, B.P. (1981) Experimental test results for flexure and direct tension of fibre cement composites. *Int. J. of Cement Composites and Lightweight Concrete*, **3**(1), 13–18.

10.57. Shah, S.P., Stroeven, P., Dalhuisen, D. and van Stekeleburg, P. (1978) Complete stress–strain curves for steel-fibre-reinforced concrete in uniaxial tension and compression, in Proc. Int. RILEM Symp. *Testing and Test Methods of Fibre Cement Composites*, (ed. R.N. Swamy), Sheffield, The Construction Press Ltd., Lancaster, 399–408.

10.58. Oakley, D.R. and Proctor, B.A. (1975) Tensile stress–strain behaviour of glass-fibre-reinforced cement composites, in RILEM Symp. on Fibre-Reinforced Cement and Concrete, (ed. A.M. Neville), London, 347–59.

10.59. Bentur, A. and Mindess, S. (1990) *Fibre Reinforced Cementitious Composites*, Elsevier Applied Science, London.

10.60. Potrzebowski, J. (1983) The splitting test applied to steel-fibre-reinforced concrete, *Int. J. of Cement Composites and Lightweight Concrete*, **5**(1), 49–53.

10.61. Babut, R. (1983) Bearing capacity and deformability of SFRC elements subjected to bending (in Polish) in Proc. Conf. *Mechanics of concrete-like composites*, (ed. J. Kasperkiewicz), 3–8 December 1979, Jabłonna, Ossolineum.

10.62. RILEM (1990) Determination of fracture parameters (K^s_{Ic} and $CTOD_c$) of plain concrete using three-point bend tests, RILEM Draft Recommendation, TC89-FMT Fracture Mechanics of Concrete – Test Methods, *Materials and Structures*, **23**, 457–60.

10.63. RILEM (1990) Size-effect method for determining fracture energy and process zone size of concrete, as [10.62], 461–65.

10.64. Shah, S.P. (1991) Do fibers improve the tensile strength of concrete? Proc. of First Canadian University–Industry Workshop on Fiber Reinforced Concrete, Université Laval, Quebec, 1–30.

10.65. Quyang, C., Mobasher, B. and Shah, S.P. (1990) An R-curve approach for fracture of quasi-brittle materials, *Engineering Fracture Mechanics*, **37**, 901–16.

10.66. Hannant, D.J., Hughes, D.C. and Kelly, A. (1983) Toughening of cement and other brittle solids with fibres, *Phil. Trans. Roy. Soc.*, A310, London, 175–90.

10.67. Parratt, N.J. (1972) *Fibre Reinforced Materials Technology*, Van Nostrand Reinhold Co., London.

10.68. Mindess, S. (1988) Bonding in cementitious materials: how important is it? in Proc. Symp. *Bonding in Cementitious Composites*, Boston 1987, (eds S. Mindess and S.P. Shah), Mater. Res. Society, Pittsburgh, 3–10.

10.69. Brandt, A.M. (1982) On the calculation of fracture energy in SFRC elements subjected to bending, in Proc. Int. Conf. *Bond in Concrete*, Paisley, June 1982, (ed. P. Bartos), Applied Science Publishers, London, 73–81.

10.70. Brandt, A.M. (1985) On the optimization of fibre orientation in the brittle matrix composite materials, Report of Stevin Laboratory, August 1985, Dept. of Civ. Eng., Delft Univ. of Techn., Delft.

10.71. Brandt, A.M. (1985) On the optimal direction of short metal fibres in brittle matrix composites. *J. of Materials Science*, **20**, 3831–41.

10.72. Brandt, A.M. (1986) Influence of the fibre orientation on the energy absorption at fracture of SFRC specimens, in Proc. Int. Symp. *Brittle Matrix Composites 1*, (eds A.M. Brandt and I.H. Marshall), Elsevier Applied Sci. Publ. London, 403–20.

10.73. Brandt, A.M. (1987) Influence of the fibre orientation on the mechanical properties of fibre-reinforced cement (RFC) specimens, in Proc. *1st Int. Congress RILEM*, **2**, Versailles, 1987, Chapman & Hall, London, 651–58.

10.74. Brandt, A.M. (1991) Influence of fibre orientation on the cracking and fracture energy in brittle matrix composites, in Proc. Euromech. Coll. 269 *Mechanical Identification of Composites*, (eds A. Vautrin and H. Sol), Elsevier Applied Science, London and New York, 327–34.

10.75. Brandt, A.M. and Stroeven, P. (1991) Fracture energy in notched steel-fibre-reinforced concrete beams, in Proc. Int. Symp. *Brittle Matrix Composites 3*, (eds A.M. Brandt and I.H. Marshall), Elsevier Applied Sci. Publ., London and New York, 72–82.

10.76. Kasperkiewicz, J. and Skarendahl, A. (1990) Toughness estimation in FRC composites, CBI Report 4:90, CBI, Stockholm.

10.77. Henager, C.H. (1978) A toughness index of fibre concrete, as [10.57], 79–86.

10.78. ASTM (1985) ASTM Standard C 1018–85, Standard test method for flexural toughness and first crack – crack strength of fiber-reinforced concrete (using beam with third-point loading). *Journal of Testing and Evaluation*, Philadelphia, 637–44.

10.79. Johnston, C.D. and Gray, R.J. (1986) Flexural toughness and first crack strength of fibre-reinforced concrete, using ASTM Standard C1018, in Proc. RILEM Symp. *Developments in Fibre Reinforced Cement and Concrete*, (eds R.N. Swamy, R.L. Wagstaffee and D.R. Oakley), Sheffield 1986, paper 5.1, Univ. of Sheffield, Sheffield.

10.80. ACI (1988) ACI Committee 544, Measurement of properties of fibre-reinforced concrete. *ACI Materials Journal*, Nov–Dec, 583–93.

10.81. Brandt, A.M. and Glinicki, M.A. (1992) Flexural behaviour of concrete elements reinforced with carbon fibres, in Proc. Int. RILEM/ACI Workshop *High Performance Fiber Reinforced Cement Composites*, (eds H.W. Reinhardt and A.E. Naaman), Mainz, 1991, Chapman and Hall/Spon, 288–99.

10.82. Nicholls, F.A. (1979) How brittle is brittle fracture? *Engineering Fracture Mechanics*, **12**, 307–16.

10.83. Knott, J.F. (1973) *Fundamentals of Fracture Mechanics*, part 7, Wiley, New York.

10.84. Hillerborg, A. (1985) Determination and significance of the fracture toughness of steel-fibre concrete, in Proc. of US-Sweden Joint Seminar *Steel Fiber Concrete*, (eds S.P. Shah and A. Skarendahl), CBI, Stockholm, 257–71.

10.85. Wu Keru and Zhou Jianhua (1988) The influence of the matrix–aggregate bond in the strength and brittleness of concrete, as [10.68], 29–34.

10.86. Bache, H.H. (1989) Fracture mechanisms in integrated design of new ultra-strong materials and structures, in Fracture Mechanics of Concrete Structures. From Theory to Application. Report of TC90 of RILEM, (ed. L. Elfgren), Chapman and Hall, London, 382–98.

10.87. Brandt, A.M. and Prokopski, G. (1990) Critical values of stress intensity factor in Mode II fracture of cementitious composites. *J. of Materials Science*, **25**, 3505–10.

10.88. Arrea, M. and Ingraffea, A.R. (1982) Mixed-mode crack propagation in mortar and concrete, Dept. of Struct. Eng., Rep. 81–13, Cornell Univ., Ithaca.

10.89. Carpinteri, A. (1987) Interaction between tensile strength failure and mixed mode crack propagation in concrete, Rep. Subcomm. C., RILEM TC89-FMT, Dept. of Struct. Eng., Politecnico di Torino, Italy.

10.90. Taha, N. and Swartz, S. (1989) Crack propagation models for mixed-mode loading, in *Fracture of Concrete and Rock*, (eds S.P. Shah, S.E. Swartz and B. Barr), Cardiff, 20–22 September 1989, Elsevier Applied Science, London and New York.

10.91. Bazant, Z.P. and Pfeiffer, P.A. (1986) Shear fracture tests of concrete. *Materials and Structures* RILEM, **19**(110), 111–21.

10.92. Zaitsev, Yu.V., Ashrabov, A.A. and Kazatski, M.B. (1986) Simulation of crack propagation in various concrete structures, in: *Brittle Matrix Composites 1*, (eds A.M. Brandt and I.H. Marshall), Elsevier Appl. Sc. Publ., London, 549–57.

10.93. Jenq, Y.S. and Shah, S.P. (1988) Mixed mode fracture of concrete. *Int. J. of Fracture*, **38**, 123–42.

10.94. John, R. and Shah, S.P. (1990) Mixed mode fracture of concrete subjected to impact loading. *J. of Structural Engineering*, **116**(3) ASCE, January, 585–602.

10.95. Shah, S.P. (1989) On the fundamental issues of mixed mode crack propagation in concrete, as [10.86], 27–38.

10.96. Bazant, Z.P. and Prat, P.C. (1988) Measurement of Mode III fracture energy of concrete. *Nuclear Energy Eng. and Design*, **106**, 1–8.

10.97. Debicki, G. (1988) Contribution à l'étude du rôle de fibres dispersées anisotropiquement dans le mortier de ciment sur les lois de comportément, les critères de résistance et la fissuration du matériau. Thèse de docteur d'état. Institut National des Sciences Appliquées, Lyon.

10.98. Sih, G.C., Paris, P.C. and Irwin, G.R. (1985) On cracks in rectilinearly anisotropic bodies. *Int. J. of Fracture Mech.* **1**, 189–203.

10.99. Sih, G.C. and Chen, E.P. (1973) Fracture analysis of unidirectional composites. *J. of Comp. Mater.*, **7**, 230–44.

10.100. Watkins, J. (1983) Fracture toughness test for soil–cement samples in Mode II. *Int. J. of Fracture*, **23**, R135–8.

10.101. Davies, J., Morgan, T.G. and Yim, A.W. (1985) The finite element analysis of a punch-through shear specimen in Mode II. *Int. J. of Fracture*, **28**, R3–10.

10.102. Liu, K., Barr, B.I.G. and Watkins, J. (1985) Mode II fracture of fibre-reinforced concrete materials. *Int. J. of Cement Composites and Lightweight Concrete*, **7**(2), 93–101.

10.103. Davies, J. and So, K.W. (1986) Further development of fracture test in Mode II. *Int. J. of Fracture*, **31**, R19–21.

10.104. Davies, J. (1987) Fracture behaviour of mortar in shear-compression field. *J. of Materials Science Letters*, **6**, 879–81.

10.105. Bochenek, A. and Prokopski, G. (1987) Investigations of the aggregate grain size influence on the fracture toughness of concrete (in Polish). *Archives of Civil Engineering*, **33**(3), 359–71.

10.106. Bochenek, A. and Prokopski, G. (1988) Investigations of water–cement ratio influence on micro-cracking of ordinary concrete (in Polish). *Archives of Civil Engineering*, **34**(2), 261–70.

10.107. Bochenek, A. and Prokopski, G. (1989) On the influence of the kind of coarse aggregate on the fracture toughness of concrete (in Polish). *Archives of Civil Engineering*, **35**(1), 49–61.

10.108. ANSI/ASTM (1978) Standard Test Method in Plane Strain Fracture Toughness of Metallic Materials, ANSI/ASTM, Philadelphia, E 399–78.

10.109. Brandt, A.M. and Prokopski, G. (1993) On the fractal dimension of fracture surfaces of concrete elements. *J. of Materials Science*, **28**, 4762–6.

10.110. Mandelbrot, B.B. (1977) *Fractals: Forms, Chance and Dimension*, W.H. Freeman, San Francisco.

10.111. Mandelbrot, B.B. (1983) *The Fractal Geometry of Nature*, W.H. Freeman, San Francisco.

10.112. Mandelbrot, B.B., Passoja, D.E. and Paullay, A. (1984) Fractal character of fracture surfaces of metals. *Nature*, **308**, 721–2.

10.113. Winslow, D.N. (1985) The fractal nature of the surface of cement paste, *Cement and Concrete Research*, **15**(5), 817–24.

10.114. Saouma, V.E., Barton, C.C. and Gamaleldin, N.A. (1990) Fractal characterization of fracture surfaces in concrete. *Engineering Fracture Mechanics*, **35**(1/2/3), 47–53.

10.115. Pande, C.S., Richards, L.E., Louat, N., *et al.* (1987) Fractal characterization of fractured surfaces. *Acta Metall.*, **35**(9), 1633–7.

10.116. Gokhale, A.M. and Drury, W.J. (1990) A general method for estimation of fracture surfaces roughness: Part II. Practical considerations. *Metallurgical Transactions A*, **21A**, 1201–7.

10.117. Gokhale, A.M. and Underwood, E.E. (1990) A general method for estimation of fracture surface roughness: Part I. Theoretical aspects. *Metallurgical Transactions A*, **21A**, 1193–9.

10.118. Underwood, E.E. and Banerji, K. (1983) Statistical analysis of facet characteristics in a computer simulated fracture surface, in Proc. 6th Int. Congr. for Stereology. *Acta Stereol.*, **2**, suppl. 1, 75–80.

10.119. Banerji, K. (1988) Quantitative fractography: A modern perspective. *Metallurgical Transactions A*, **19A**, 961–71.

10.120. Underwood, E.E. and Banerji, K. (1986) Fractals in fractography. *Mater. Sci. and Engng.*, **80**, 1–14.

10.121. Mecholsky, J.J., Passoja, D.E. and Feinberg-Ringel, K.S. (1983) Quantitative analysis of brittle fracture surfaces using fractal geometry. *J. Amer. Ceram. Soc.*, **72**(1), 60–5.

10.122. Anstis, G.R., Chantikul, P., Lawn, B.R. and Marshall, D.B. (1981) A critical evaluation of indentation techniques for measuring fracture toughness, I. Direct crack measurements. *J. Amer. Ceram. Soc.*, **64**(9), 533–8.

10.123. Neilson, C.L.A. (1981) Investigation of high temperature increase of alumino-silicate refractories, M.Sc. Thesis, Georgia Institute of Technology, Atlanta, Ga.

10.124. Hellmann, J.K. (1986) Alumina processing and properties characterization workshop. SAND–86–1224, Sandia National Laboratory, Albuquerque, New Mexico.

10.125. Mecholsky, J.J. (1982) Fracture mechanics analysis of glass ceramics, in *Advances in Ceramics*, **4**, Nucleation and crystallization in glasses, (eds J.H. Simmons, D.R. Uhlmann, G.H. Beall), Amer. Ceram. Soc., Columbus, Ohio.

10.126. Mecholsky, J.J. and Mackin, T.J. (1988) Fractal analysis of fracture in Ocala chert. *J. Mater. Sci. Lett.*, **7**, 1145–7.

10.127. Duxbury, P.M. (1990) Breakdown of diluted and hierarchical systems, in *Statistical Models for the Fracture of Disordered Media*, (eds H.J. Herrmann and S. Roux), Elsevier Science Publisher B.V. (North–Holland), 189–228.

10.128. Watkins, J. (1983) Fracture toughness test for soil-cement samples in Mode II. *Int. J. of Fracture*, **23**, R. 135–8.

11 Behaviour of cement matrix composites in various service conditions

11.1 Loads and actions

The elements and structures made of brittle matrix composites, in most cases based on cement matrices, are subjected to loads and actions of various origins and natures. Internal forces, i.e. axial and shearing stresses and bending moments are due to dead weight, service loads and imposed deformations. Besides, external actions of chemical (corrosion) and physical (low and high temperatures) are to be foreseen. Various combinations of these actions are possible and should be considered in both structural and material design and in execution.

Ordinary concrete elements have to support their own weight at a relatively early age, together with the dead weight of other parts of the structure and of non-structural elements. Usually, demoulding in a precast factory is planned as soon as possible for technological and economical reasons. Also, structures cast *in situ* have their forms and scaffoldings removed at an early date. Later the dead weight is combined with service loads and different other actions due to environmental conditions. Normally, structures are loaded slowly, and only a part of the stress for certain structures is caused by rapid actions, e.g. traffic on bridges or runways, which induce dynamic effects.

In normal conditions it is expected that loads and actions on structures are supported over a long time period, expressed in tens of years. This implies a requirement for long-term resistance of materials and durability of structures and their parts. At the other extreme there are situations in which loads are imposed very quickly.

The behaviour of cement-based materials is a result of a number of processes which develop simultaneously but are interrelated.

The process of hydration of Portland cement is relatively rapid in the first hours and its velocity gradually decreases over the next few days. It is supposed that in favourable conditions with adequate temperature and humidity the hydration of cement develops indefinitely with an appropriate increase of strength of the hardened material.

Permanent flow of heat and moisture between the material and the environment is characteristic for all composites based on Portland cement, cf. Section 11.7. Initially, these processes are of high intensity due to production of heat during Portland cement hydration. Later the exchange of heat and moisture with the environment is slow and goes in both directions from, and to, the hardened cement paste with a trend towards equilibrium with the environment. These flows are the sources of variations of the material's volume, e.g. shrinkage or swelling.

A system of microcracks already appears during the initial period of hardening of the cement paste. It is later subjected to action of external loads and imposed deformations which vary over time. Local stress concentrations contribute considerably to crack propagation, also under relatively low average stresses. In certain conditions the microcracks may exhibit healing, cf. Section 9.7. In most cases, however, they remain stable or develop into major cracks leading to disintegration of specimens and structural elements.

Several processes are caused by the action of detrimental agents from the environment. Corrosion of cement paste, leaching, excessive abrasion and cavitation, overloading and impacts, are all examples of degradation mechanisms acting simultaneously with normal wear from external loads.

All the above mentioned processes develop in such very heterogeneous and disordered materials as cement-based composites. The random distribution of all phases, complex situations at interfaces and the permanent flow of fluids and gases across pore systems in varying environmental conditions create the reasons for complex material behaviour. The coefficient of variation of the value of ultimate strength under a static loading of the simplest configuration may reach 15% for various kinds of brittle matrix composites. That dispersion of properties should be taken into account in both material and structural design.

In the following chapters the influence of high and low rates of loading, sustained load and different temperatures are considered.

11.2 Behaviour under dynamic loads

11.2.1 RATES OF LOADING

The influence of the rate of loading on the strength of cement-based materials was observed as early as 1917 [11.1]. Later, important test results were presented [11.2] and [11.3]. A comprehensive review of investigations was published [11.4] with an extensive list of references. The general conclusion is that the strength of cement matrix increases with an increase of the rate of loading. There are large variations of this effect for compressive and tensile strength, fracture toughness and Young's modulus. Also, the structure of the material and its composition are important factors influencing its sensitivity to the rate of loading.

The explanation of the increase of strength with the rate of loading is not yet complete and the proposed models for prediction of the material's behaviour are still imprecise. One of the main reasons proposed is that the slow crack growth which appears in cement-based composites already under about 50%

of short-term strength does not have enough time to develop and to decrease strength [11.5]. Deeper explanations are proposed on the basis of fracture mechanics and damage theory, e.g. [11.4]. The phenomenon is, however, important enough to be investigated and evaluated for practical purposes.

When the rate of loading is considered then usually high rates are understood, reducing to slow rates for normal quasi-static loading. Long-term loading and long-term effects such as basic creep combined with shrinkage are treated separately in Section 11.4.3. Here the influence of the high rates of load or strain as compared to quasi-static testing, i.e. without any dynamic effects, is considered.

High rates of stress or strain encountered in the cement-based materials are caused by impacts and other accidental situations or by a special way of exploitation. The influence of dynamic effects in concrete may be considered either in terms of rate of loading or strain rate. In the first case the rate is indicated in MPa/s and in the second, in sec^{-1}. The relation between these two groups of values is always approximate as the notion of the Young's modulus is not well defined. From the engineering viewpoint the loading rates are more meaningful because of their direct relation to situations of structures subjected to various kinds of external actions. In testing, however, the values of strain are measured directly and are related to observed variations of strength. The classifications are sometimes confusing, e.g. strain rates between 10^{-4} and 10^{-1}/sec are called quasi-static [11.6] while they have also been considered as dynamic and corresponding to the events like gas explosions and vehicle or ship impacts [11.7].

The spectrum of possible rates of stresses and strains in engineering structures are estimated approximately as shown in Table 11.1 where both measures are used. Tensile stress and strain are more carefully analysed because in brittle matrices these are the direct reasons for all kinds of destruction and fracture. The situations listed in Table 1 are related to impacts either during normal

Table 11.1 Ranges of rates of stresses and strains in different situations of concrete structures

Kinds of loading	Rates of tensile stress $\dot{\sigma}$ (MPa/s)	Rates of tensile strain $\dot{\varepsilon}$ (s^{-1})
Collision of a ship	10^{-1}–10^{0}	10^{-5}
Collisions in rail and road traffic	10^{0}–10^{1}	10^{-4}
Gas explosion	10^{0}–10^{1}	10^{-4}
Aircraft collision	10^{2}–10^{3}	10^{-2}
Earthquake	10^{2}–10^{5}	10^{-2}–10^{1}
Pile driving	10^{3}–10^{4}	10^{-2}–10^{0}

(Source: Reinhardt, W.H., Concrete under impact loading–tensile strength and bond; *Heron* **27**(3), 1982.) [11.7]

exploitation or due to accidental events. All these situations are considered in the design of structures having in mind the survival of people involved in the possible rupture of a structure (e.g. a column of a viaduct hit by a colliding car) or fulfilment of the function by a structure (e.g. a head of a pile driven by impacts from a hammer).

11.2.2 IMPACT STRENGTH AND INFLUENCE OF THE RATE OF LOADING

Impact strength is measured by the number of blows exerted on a tested specimen before it fails to exhibit rebound, i.e. becomes a composition of separate parts rather than a solid body. As there are neither standardized specimens nor universally agreed methods of testing, all published results have a relative and conventional value.

A few general conclusions have been established which form the present state of knowledge.

There are two groups of parameters which influence the impact strength:

1. internal structure of material (porosity, aggregate grading, possible dispersed reinforcement, etc.);
2. age of the cement matrix, conditions of curing and state of hydration.

The impact strength of concretes depends upon their static strength and also on the bond resistance in a matrix–aggregate interface.

The curves representing the relations between impact and static strength for ordinary concretes are shown in Figure 11.1 as tested on specimens cured in water. For air-cured specimens the impact strength curves are situated somewhere below this level. For the same reason of higher strength and for better bonding, fibre-reinforcement of all kinds increases considerably impact strength as compared with that of a plain matrix. Also, smaller aggregate grading improves the impact strength with all other conditions maintained the same.

It has been observed that the fracture processes are basically the same for various rates of loading. However, the differences are related to the progress of microcracks under loading, to the creep deformations in cement paste and to the relaxation of stress concentrations. All these phenomena develop with various rates – initially as slow and delayed processes, and later as very rapid ones. Consequently, the rate of loading is important. Namely, for static loading slow crack growth develops and this decreases gradually the strength of the cement matrix. Cracks in the matrix already propagate under mean stress equal to 50–60% of ultimate strength because of stress concentrations at the corners of hard aggregate grains or at the tips of microcracks. The local stress may reach very high values. These were the bases of Rüsch's conclusion proposed in [11.9] that under sustained load the strength is equal to 70–80% of ultimate strength under conventional short-time loading, cf. Section 11.4.3. In the other extreme case, for rapid loading, an increase of the strength is observed. Cracks

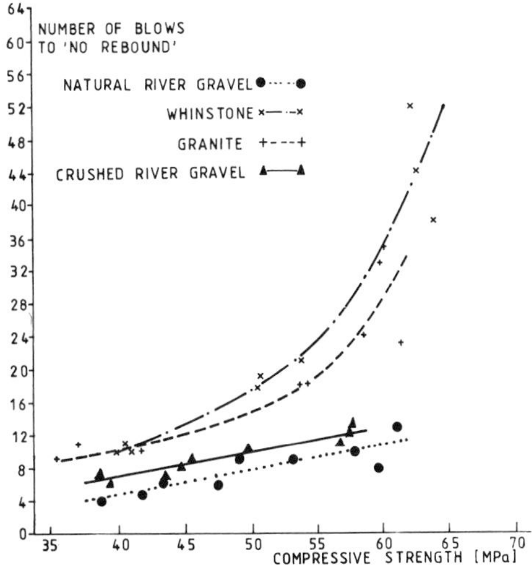

Figure 11.1 Relations between compressive strength and number of blows to 'no-rebound' for concretes made with different aggregates and stored in water. (Reproduced with permission from Green, H., Impact strength of concrete; *Proc. Inst. of Civ. Eng.*, **28**, July, pp. 383–96, published by Institute of Civil Engineers, London, 1964.) [11.8]

have no time for slow development and there is no possibility for creep and stress relaxation because the system of internal cracking is less developed. Cracks passing across hard aggregate grains are observed.

Simple phenomenological explanations based on the works by Rüsch and other contemporary authors seem insufficient for sound quantitative predictions, and a qualitative explanation based on fracture mechanics was proposed [11.10] which concludes that there are the same parameters for impact strength as for static strength. However, it seems that the state of initial cracking due to multiple desponding of aggregate grains and to shrinkage in the cement matrix are more detrimental for impact strength than for short-term static loading. It has been shown [11.11] that the work of fracture commonly used for characterization of the fracture toughness of specimens subjected to static or quasi-static loading is only weakly sensitive to the rate of loading. In contrast, it was proved that the fracture toughness expressed by K_c, namely $K_c = \sigma_c\sqrt{\pi a}$ increases with loading rate.

The rate theory and stochastic approach was proposed in [11.12] and was intended as a basis for quantitative prediction. However, none of these models give a satisfactory agreement with experimental results and further research is necessary.

The values of ultimate strain ε_u vary with the rate of loading according to the curve shown in Figure 11.2. The minimum is reached at rates corresponding approximately to the standard static tests.

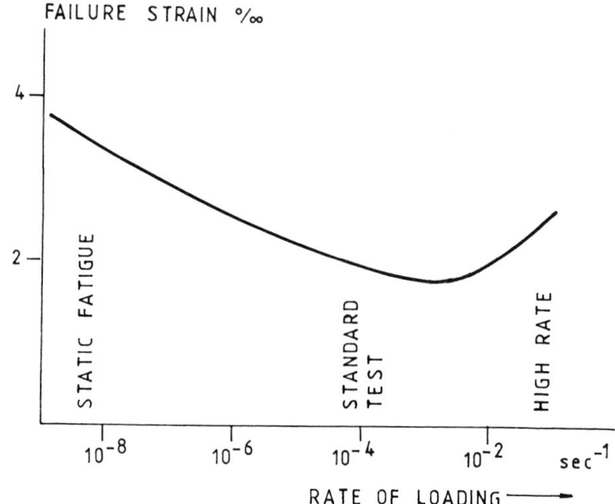

Figure 11.2 Failure strain as function of rate of loading. (Reproduced with permission from Wittmann, F.H., Influence of time on crack formation and failure of concrete; published by Kluwer–Martinus Nijhoff Pub., 1984.) [11.10]

The impact strength of cement-based composites is tested on relatively small specimens and the following methods are applied:

1. in hydraulic testing machines with rates up to 10^3 MPa/s;
2. in Hopkinson bar up to 4.10^6 MPa/s [11.13];
3. in Charpy hammer with special equipment allowing for tensile loading, up to 8.10^2 MPa/s [11.14];
4. by a falling weight (drop tests) up to 10^4 MPa/s, [11.15];
5. by a rotating hammer with impact velocity up to 30 m/s, [11.16].

Wave propagation events are somewhere beyond this scale.

The experimental results are collected in Figure 11.3, where the scale of the strain rate $\dot{\varepsilon}$ is added assuming a constant Young's modulus and of the same value for all compared tests. All test results show a consistent increase of strength with the rate of loading. The following approximate formulae was proposed [11.23] for tensile strength as a function of the rate of stress $\dot{\sigma}$; for concretes – $ln\,f_t = 1.51 + 0.042\,ln\,\dot{\sigma}$; for cement mortars – $ln\,f_t = 1.23 + 0.045\,ln\,\dot{\sigma}$.

An interesting series of tests were executed [11.17] on specimens made with materials characterized by the same tensile strength and having a different structure:

1. cement mortar (MR);
2. model concrete made with aggregate of discontinuous grading composed of sand $\leqslant 2.0$ mm and crushed grains 8–12.5 mm (CE);
3. cement mortar reinforced with Bekaert fibres $V_f = 1.2\%$ (BF);

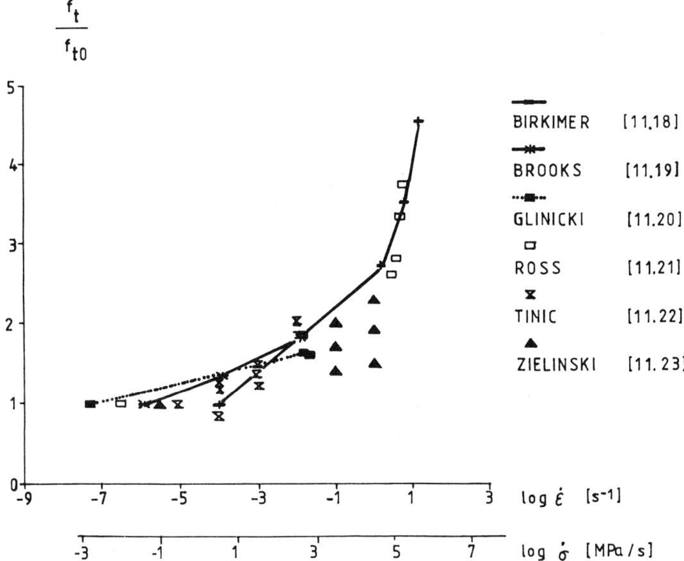

Figure 11.3 Concrete strength at axial tension as function of the rate of loading. (Reproduced from Glinicki, M.A., Influence of the rate of loading on the strength and deformation of cement matrix composites; Doctoral thesis, IFTR, Warsaw, 1991.) [11.17]

4. cement mortar reinforced with Harex fibres $V_f = 1.7\%$ (HF);
5. porous cement mortar with artificial pores 0.4–4.0 mm $V_p = 14.5\%$ (PM).

The differences intentionally introduced in the material structure are shown in Figure 11.4 where other possible combinations are also presented. The tests were realized on dog-bone specimens subjected to axial tensile loading in an Instron 1251 machine. The results in Figure 11.5 show a considerable increase of strength for different materials with their densities which are indicated on the right-hand side in the figure. The conclusion is that the relative increase of the strength is inversely proportional to the material density.

The explanation which may be suggested for the above found relation is based on existing system of microcracks in the cement paste. In more porous materials there is less stress concentrations at the crack tips and at higher loading rates the cracks have no possibility to propagate as it is at lower rates. That effect is less important for higher density materials.

The observed increase of strength was non-linear with respect to loading rate – it was larger for higher rates. It may be supposed after these tests, as well as after other authors' investigations, that for the loading rates above 10^3 MPa/s the observed increase of strength is even greater.

The porosity, or apparent density, of cement-based matrices is by far the most important single parameter as to the material's sensitivity to loading rate.

Under dynamic loadings the strength of fibre-reinforced cement-based materials

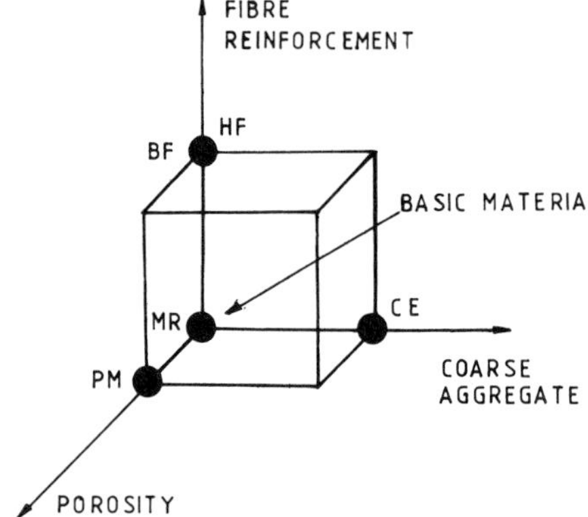

Figure 11.4 Schema of tested materials in the space of variables. (Reproduced from Glinicki, M.A., Influence of the rate of loading on the strength and deformation of cement matrix composites; Doctoral thesis, IFTR, Warsaw, 1991.) [11.17]

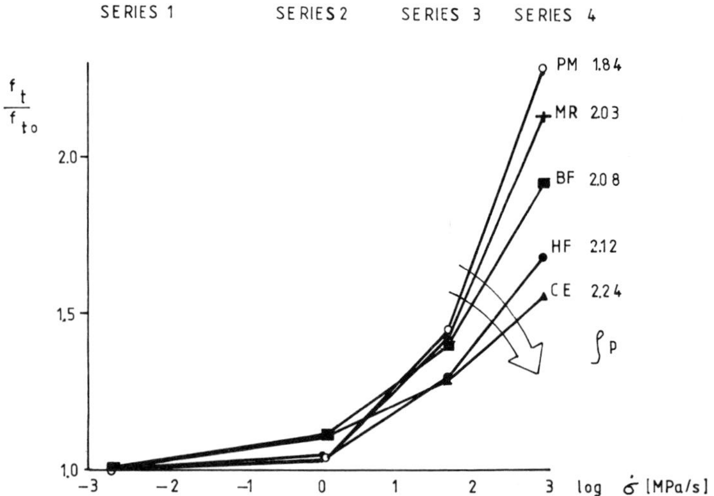

Figure 11.5 Relative increase of the tensile strength as function of the loading rate $\dot{\sigma}$ for materials with different apparent density. (Reproduced from Glinicki, M.A. Influence of the rate of loading on the strength and deformation of cement matrix composites; Doctoral thesis, IFTR, Warsaw, 1991.) [11.17]

is estimated as 3–10 times greater than that of plain matrix, [11.24] and [11.25]. Total energy under blows exerted on beams by different testing equipment is estimated to be 40 to 100 times greater.

Several experiments were performed on slabs and plates subjected to perforation by a projectile or falling weight. A review of results related to fibre-reinforced concretes is published in [11.26].

The increase of material strength with higher loading rates might be taken into account in design for the assessment of the structural integrity and safety in accidental situations. It is also of primary importance for such structures as concrete piles, foundations for machinery with dynamic actions, etc.

Another application of sound data on the strength increase with high loading rates may be for the analyses of accidental destructions of structures where an assessment of the causes and the sequence of events is looked for. For all these reasons further investigations are needed, because systematic test results based on a sufficient number of specimens or elements are not yet available.

Moreover, the present state of knowledge consists mostly of laboratory tests without adequate confirmation in natural scale by measurements from real structures. That is why the proposed models and formulae do not create a sufficient theoretical basis for prediction of a material's behaviour, or for design of structures taking into account the increase of strength under high rate loading. Critical reviews of the theoretical models are published in [11.4], [11.6] and [11.7].

11.3 Fatigue

11.3.1 FACTORS AND EFFECTS

Fatigue of a material is a progressive fracture which consists of the cumulation of damage resulting from sustained, long-term loading of a constant, variable or cyclic nature. Local modifications which appear in the material structure under load may lead to a kind of stabilization, for example, in the form of permanent deformation and stress or of elastic deformation. The word fatigue is used, however, for such situations where there is no stabilization but rather a gradual increase in damage.

In cement-based brittle materials cracks spread out from a system of initial microcracks and multiply under relatively low loads, cf. Chapter 9. The opening and propagation of microcracks determine the material's behaviour under sustained and cyclic loads.

The fatigue strength of materials means the maximum value of stress which may be supported indefinitely and is indicated in relation to the static strength under single, short-term, loading. Usually, and for practical applications, it is assumed that the maximum load supported during 10^6–2.10^6 cycles may be considered as the fatigue strength of the material in relation to cyclic loading. The strength under cyclic loads is always represented as decreasing with time, and it may be stated that the fatigue strength does not exist at all for concrete-like materials. It means that after a sufficiently high number of cycles failure occurs. That assumption is supported by the fact that permanent damage appears in heterogeneous brittle materials under quite low stress. To accommodate these apparently contradictory assumptions the application of the notion of probability is helpful. In that sense, the fatigue strength corresponds to a situation, and to a kind of loading, in which after approximately 2.10^6 cycles the probability of failure is high. For fibre-reinforced cement-based materials, however, it is believed that the fatigue strength does exist and is reached approximately at $1–2.10^6$ cycles. This means that if a specimen withstands such a fatigue, then it is highly probable that it will resist an infinite number of similar cycles.

The strength depends on the nature of the load (compression, tension or flexion, constant or cyclic, range between maximum and minimum stress in a cycle, etc.), on the temperature and humidity. In the case of a cyclic load its frequency may also have some importance. For long-term application of a load of either nature, a certain reduction of strength should be foreseen.

Fatigue strength under sustained loads and cyclic loads is an important material characteristic. In all structures the long-term stress should be maintained below the fatigue strength and only for rare and infrequent accidental situations may higher stress be allowed without serious risk of a failure. Also, in many structures, variable loads and their range between the maximum and minimum values determine their behaviour, e.g. bridge structures subjected to traffic loads and marine structures exposed to waves.

The present state of knowledge of the fatigue strength of brittle matrix composites under various kinds of loads is far from being satisfactory. The main reason is that the testing of elements under fatigue is particularly long and expensive and observation of the structures does not furnish all the information necessary for such an assessment. Basic phenomena in gradual degradation of the material structure are strongly related to the randomness of all the factors involved and until now only approximate predictions have been possible.

In this chapter only the main experimental data and proposed approximate estimates are presented.

11.3.2 FATIGUE UNDER CYCLIC LOADS

The fatigue processes in brittle matrix composites are entirely different from those in metals and ductile matrices of high strength composites. In a highly brittle matrix like glass and ceramics the cracks appear at very low tensile strain and stable crack growth is nearly non-existent. Therefore, the first crack strength is very close or practically the same as fatigue strength, [11.27]. In cement-based composites, however, the cracks are controlled by such elements of their internal structure as aggregate grains and reinforcing fibres. Microcracks of various dimensions exist from the very beginning. They propagate and multiple cracks appear caused by an additional input of the external energy. The load is supported initially by the matrix and later by reinforcement, if it exists. Usually, the stress at local concentrations (tips of initial cracks, inclusions) exceeds the tensile matrix strength. That is the reason why the cracks propagate at each load cycle even if the mean stress values in a cross-section are relatively low. By this accumulation of damage, the strength and stiffness of the composite material decreases. The transfer of load from matrix to fibres is assured by the bond and friction in the process called pull-out, in which gradual damage and fatigue is also observed, cf. Section 8.5. The fatigue consists of a decrease of strength and stiffness resulting from different phenomena during the load cycles.

The strain necessary for initiation of multiple cracking and crack propagation is lower for a cyclic load than for a static and constant load. The process of fatigue in fibre-reinforced cement composites is similar to static increase of load in the sense that debonding and pull-out also occur gradually. The fibres used as reinforcement for cement matrices usually do not show fatigue at all because the stress in the fibres is maintained at quite a low level as related to their strength, e.g. steel or carbon fibres.

Various approaches have been proposed with moderate success for predicting the fatigue strength of, so called, advanced composite materials, [11.27], from continuum mechanics characterization of damage, through application of fracture mechanics to fatigue reliability. The studies of fatigue behaviour of cement-based composites are limited to tests of specimens and to the formulation of practical conclusions for prediction of fatigue strength.

The damage to the material is also recognized under cyclic load as a set of permanent micro-structural modifications caused in a material by physical or chemical actions. These changes in the material's structure may have various forms, e.g.:

- matrix cracks;
- fibre breaks;
- fibre–matrix or inclusion–matrix debondings, etc.

The micro-structural damages may be randomly distributed and oriented in the material or may have their preferred orientation and position. Debonding is situated along the fibre–matrix interface and cracks occur mostly at the tips of initial cracks and at stress concentrations around hard inclusions. In the first stage, non-interacting cracks develop in the brittle cement matrix. In the next stages either a kind of stabilization occurs in which strength and stiffness do not decrease with consecutive load cycles, or on the contrary, cracks interact and join each other to form major cracks, leading to a rupture. The stabilization mentioned corresponds to such a slow rate of decrease of strength that safety is assured up to approximately the standard number $N = 2.10^6$ cycles.

The cycles of loading are defined either by the range of the cycle stress, i.e. by $\sigma_{max}-\sigma_{min}$ or by the ratio of the stress $\rho = \sigma_{min}/\sigma_{max}$. For brittle materials it has been observed that the sign of ρ is important, it means that the existence of compression and tension in one cycle may adversely affect the fatigue strength.

According to approximate estimations based on experimental results represented on the so-called Goodman diagram as shown in Figure 11.6, for N cycles the fatigue strength under cyclic loading is inversely proportional to the amplitude between maximum and minimum stress related to the concrete strength, σ_{max}/f_c, σ_{min}/f_c. The diagram allows, for example, σ_{max} to be determined for given σ_{min}

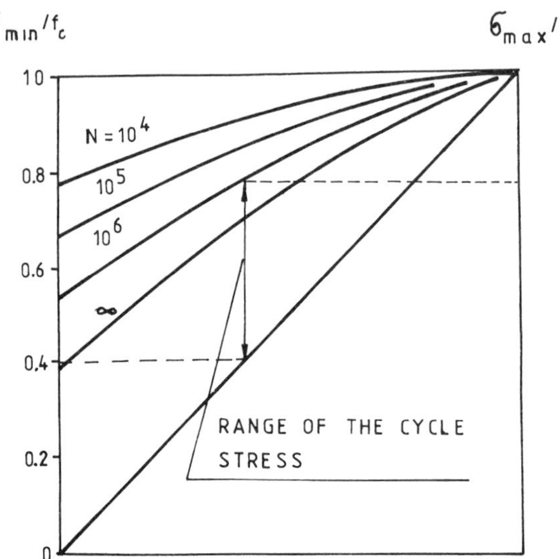

Figure 11.6 Modified Goodman diagram for fatigue strength of concrete subjected to compression with 2.10^6 cycles. (Reproduced with permission from Neville, A.M., *Properties of Concrete*; published by Pitman Publishing, London, 1973.) [11.28]

and for the required number of cycles N which concrete can withstand. The curves for different values of N are non-linear which indicates that for higher values of stress the admissible range is rapidly decreasing. In a similar diagram shown in [11.29] slight differences may be observed which confirm the approximate character of that kind or representation. According to other estimations the fatigue strength is established after 10^6 cycles and is equal to approximately 50% of static short-term strength. The frequency of cycles has a smaller influence than the range of stress but the fatigue strength of steel-fibre-reinforced concretes also depends upon the loading rate which confirms the general observations made in that respect [11.30]. The relevant tests were performed on specimens reinforced up to 3.3% vol. with melt-extracted stainless steel-fibres, 0.5 × 25 mm.

The considerable influence of the range and nature of loading on fatigue strength was observed [11.31] in tests of beams reinforced with approximately 3% vol. of steel-fibres. The fatigue strength of 74% and 83% of first crack static flexural strength at 2.10^6 cycles for complete reversal and non-reversal cycles of loading were obtained, respectively. The beams failed by pulling-out of the fibres. The fatigue strength of only 50% of the static strength was determined at 10.10^6 cycles.

Physically the fatigue accumulation in cement matrices is based on the gradual progress of cracks after each cycle of loading in which stress concentrations occur. Crack propagation has immediate consequences – decrease of strength and toughness, together with decrease of stiffness and of Young's modulus. The

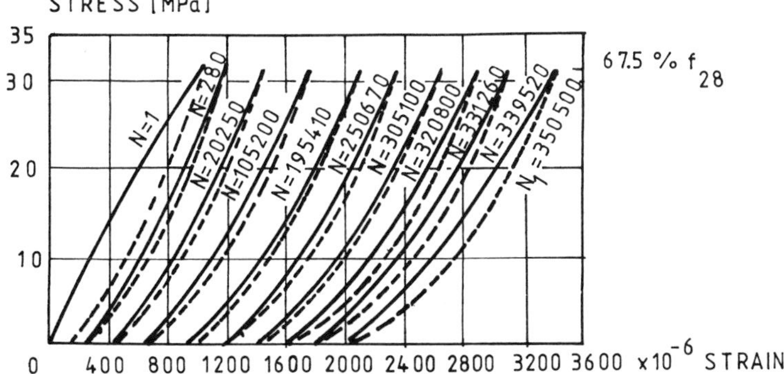

Figure 11.7 Gradual modification of the stress–strain curves of concrete elements subjected to compression and decrease of their Young's modulus. (Reproduced with permission from Bennet, E.W. and Raju, N.K., Cumulative fatigue damage of plain concrete in compression; Proc. of the Southampton 1969 Civil Engineering Materials Conference, (ed. M. Te'eni), published by John Wiley & Sons, Ltd, 1971.) [11.32]

evolution of Young's modulus with increasing fatigue of concrete under compression is shown in Figure 11.7.

Fatigue strength depends considerably upon the material's structure and its sensitivity to the cumulation of damage in successive cycles. The existence of an initial system of microcracks and their propagation in cycles of loading is a self-stimulating factor in this cumulative fatigue. When a material's structure is provided with mechanisms which control the propagation of cracks, then the fatigue strength is considerably increased.

According to [11.28] and [11.33] the slow and stable crack growth at the interface of the aggregate grains is the most important process which determines fatigue and the characteristic endurance limit of the composite. That the debonding processes at sand particles are decisive factors was identified more precisely in [11.32].

The fatigue of concretes made with lightweight aggregate is basically the same as for ordinary concretes.

The fibre-reinforced concretes exhibit higher fatigue strength if compared with plain concrete elements. This general statement was confirmed experimentally in the 1970s [11.31] and [11.34]. The conclusions may be summarized as follows:

- in flexion the fatigue strength may reach 70–80% of the static strength;
- the steel-fibres do not break but are pulled-out as in the static tests.

Important results have been obtained [11.33] which examined concrete specimens subjected to flexure and reinforced with four types of fibres – straight, corrugated and hooked steel-fibres and polypropylene fibres up to 1% vol. The relations between number of cycles N and maximum fatigue stress $f_{f\max}$ divided par the modulus of rupture f_r are shown in Figure 11.8 as estimated regression

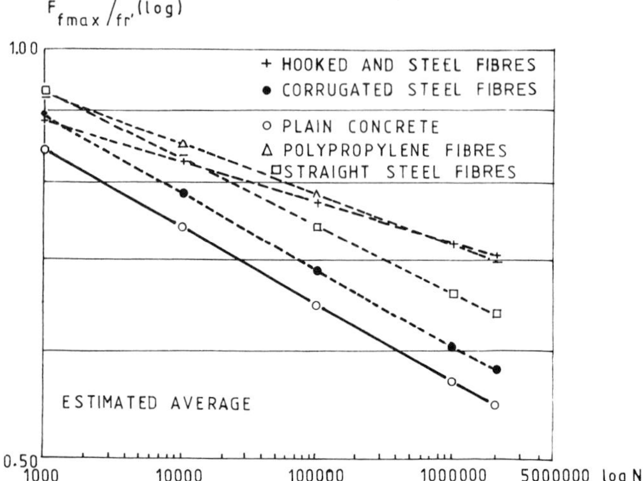

Figure 11.8 Flexural fatigue strength of concrete reinforced with 1% vol of different fibres. (Reproduced with permission from Ramakrishnan, V. and Lokvik, B.J., Flexural fatigue strength of fiber reinforced concretes; published by Spon/Chapman & Hall, 1992.) [11.33]

lines for different kinds of fibres. The proposed formula for prediction of the fatigue behaviour is the following:

$$f_{f\max}/f_r = C_o N^{C_1} \tag{11.1}$$

where C_o and C_1 are two coefficients to be determined experimentally. These tests have also indicated that polypropylene fibres improved considerably the fatigue strength even if added in a small volume of 0.5%, while the same low modulus fibres do not improve appreciably the static short-term strength of the cement matrix.

An interesting series of tests were presented in [11.35], in which the fatigue strength of plain concrete was compared to that of steel fibre-reinforced concrete.

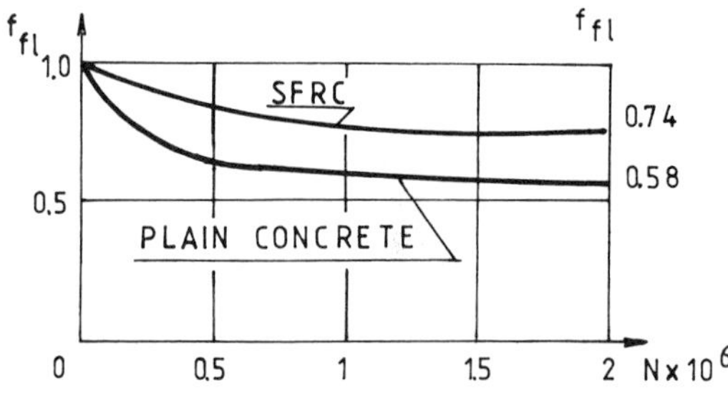

Figure 11.9 Decrease of the fatigue flexural strength with number of cycles. (Reproduced from Radomski, W., *Fibre Reinforced Concrete*; Kanazawa University, 1991.) [11.26]

The fatigue strength was determined for 2.10^6 cycles. The decrease of fatigue strength with the number of cycles in flexion after the tests is shown in Figure 11.9. The main results may be summarized in the form of relations between fatigue strength f_F and static strength f_{st};

For specimens under flexion:
- Plain concrete $f_F = 0.575\, f_{st}$
- Fibre concrete $f_F = 0.714\, f_{st}$

For specimens under compression:
- Plain concrete $f_F = 0.54\, f_{st}$
- Fibre concrete $f_F = 0.62\, f_{st}$

It has been also concluded that the fatigue strength of fibre concrete was dependent on two conditions:

1. that the reinforcement is efficient, i.e. at least 1.3–1.5% vol. is necessary;
2. that the fibres are distributed in a uniform way, because local regions without fibres decrease considerably the composite material strength.

The influence of the nature of aggregate was observed in [11.36] where specimens were tested under bending at 2.10^6 cycles with the ratio of the stress cycles $\rho = 0.2$. It appeared that the concrete with limestone aggregate had a fatigue strength equal to $0.49\, f_{st}$ and with granite aggregate to $0.63\, f_{st}$; such a difference is meaningful for special applications.

Fibre orientation seems to be an important factor influencing fatigue strength. Such tests were performed, for composites with ductile matrices [11.27]. The comparison of fatigue limiting strain ε_f as a function of the off-axis angle is shown in Figure 11.10 for two different composite materials with glassfibres and epoxy matrix:

1. unidirectional composite, [11.37],
2. symmetric angle-plied laminate, [11.38].

Both curves give similar results for angles $\geqslant 60°$ when the fatigue limit corresponds to debonding of fibres. For smaller angles $< 60°$ the situation is different – the symmetrical fibres in laminates control the cracking perfectly with angles between 0 and 40°, and in composite's reinforced with parallel fibres their influence for angles above 10° is negligible. Similar experimental or theoretical results are not yet available for cement-based brittle composites and the diagrams in Figure 11.10 are only qualitative illustrations of that possible influence.

The increased fatigue strength of fibre concretes was confirmed by applications in structural elements subjected to cyclic loads. Also fibres added to ordinary reinforced concrete elements increase the fatigue strength by providing better control of the development of microcracks. The structures of cement-based composites to be exposed to cyclic loading are designed using rare experimental data of fatigue strength and large safety factors are necessary, as no reliable mathematical models have been developed, based on thorough studies of the processes in all their complexity.

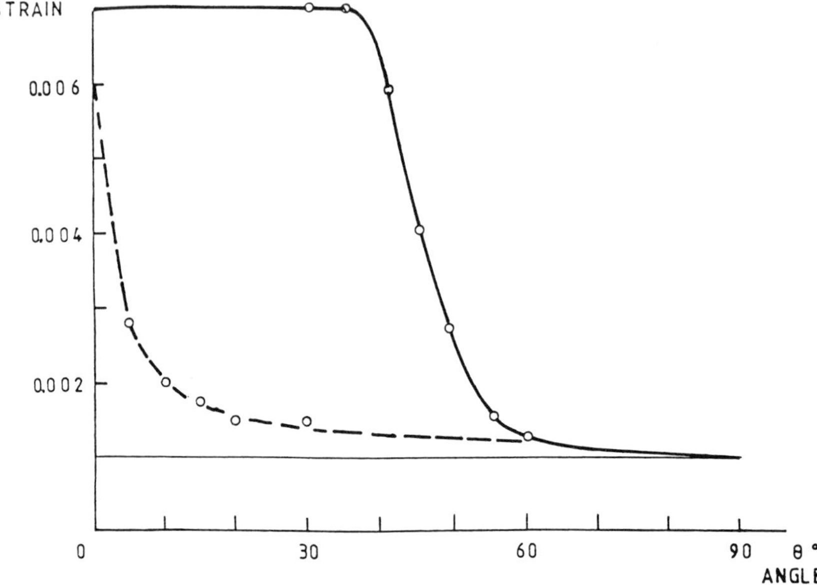

Figure 11.10 Variation of the fatigue limit strain with fibre angle in symmetric angle-plied laminates (continuous line) and in unidirectionally reinforced laminates (dotted line). (Reproduced from Talreja, R., *Fatigue of Composite Materials*; published by Technom. Publ. Co., Lancaster, 1987.) [11.27]

The safety factor should also allow for a particularly large scatter of fatigue properties as tested on specimens, [11.33]. A high coefficient of variation as compared with that for plain concrete materials is believed to result from non-uniform distribution and orientation of fibres and of their variable bonding properties.

The particular effect of cycle loading which has been experimentally proved [11.39] consists of an increase in the flexural strength of fibre concrete elements, exhibited after being subjected to cyclic loading. This effect is more important the lower the level of stress which is imposed during fatigue loading. In a certain sense cyclic loading has a kind of strengthening effect on the material. No reliable explanation is offered for these effects.

11.4 Long-term behaviour and ageing

11.4.1 GENERAL REMARKS

The behaviour of cement-based materials under sustained loads and actions depends on several factors and conditions and may be considered as a result of the following processes:

- development of damage due to local stress concentrations under permanent and service loads;
- slow hydration of cement grains which is believed to continue indefinitely if there is sufficient moisture and heat for chemical reactions;
- shrinkage and creep of cement matrix depending on moisture and loading conditions, respectively;
- possible degradation due to detrimental action of external agents, e.g. carbonation, chemical attack, etc.

The strength and Young's modulus of a cement matrix are expected to be increased in time provided that favourable conditions are maintained. The rate of hardening of the Portland cement is decreasing with time and it is considered that the final level is practically attained after 90 days. The delayed hydration of Portland cement is becoming very slow for two main reasons – the amount of available cement grains is decreasing and the transfer of free water is reduced by the hydration products which fill the capillary pores, cf. Section 6.3. The nonhydrated grains increase the composite strength of the matrix as hard inclusions.

All these processes are developing simultaneously and are interrelated, even as, for reasons of simplicity, they are often tested and analysed separately. The results of these processes may be considered in terms of strength, cracking and durability, but also in further economic analysis the outward aspect, safety and serviceability should be taken into account. The final results depend in every case upon the quantitative importance of each particular process. The results are not only related to the behaviour of the material itself, but in a large measure also to structural constraints. Free movements do not cause stresses but they do not exist in real structures, where constraints occur at various levels.

11.4.2 SHRINKAGE AND CREEP

According to a generally accepted hypothesis shrinkage and creep are independent and additive. It means that shrinkage is related exclusively to the loss of water, and creep to the stress state and its intensity. Consequently, it is possible, by suitable arrangement of testing procedures, to specify each phenomenon separately and to measure relevant strain – shrinkage on specimens free from any stress, and creep on specimens without loss of humidity. Even if this assumption is not perfectly valid, it is, nevertheless, very useful.

(a) Shrinkage

Shrinkage of the cement-based matrix is the change in its volume caused by the loss of water during and after the hydration process. In the cement-based composites the cement paste is the source of shrinkage while other components are inert and may only control deformations due to shrinkage.

Three basic phenomena have been mentioned as being responsible for shrinkage in cement paste – capillary stress, disjoining pressure and changes in surface free energy [11.29]. Without entering into detailed analysis, the following kinds of shrinkage of cement paste may be distinguished:

- Autogenous shrinkage occurs when drying is due to hydration and water is used for chemical processes, but all loss of water to environment is excluded.
- Drying shrinkage corresponds to the loss of water of hardened cement matrix.
- Plastic shrinkage is observed in fresh cement paste and it is increased with cement content and decreased with amount of aggregate.
- Carbonation shrinkage occurs in hardened concretes exposed on the influence of carbon dioxide from atmosphere.

Certain kinds of shrinkage may occur simultaneously. Their separate analysis is only possible in special laboratory conditions or based on simplified assumptions.

Autogenous shrinkage is due to the loss of water used for hydration even if no drying to the environment occurs. It is more important in high performance concretes than in ordinary ones. The proposed explanation is based on the fact that the water is maintained in fine capillaries in which high capillary forces appear when this water is used for hydration, [11.40]. Usually autogenous and plastic shrinkage develop simultaneously and are not distinguishable.

Drying shrinkage is by far the most important. It is believed that its origin lies in the increase of capillary forces caused by loss of water. The forces are supported by the hardened cement skeleton. Detailed analysis of the shrinkage in Portland cement paste was studied by many authors and comprehensive reports were presented, among others, [11.41] and [11.29]. These descriptions are formulated in a slightly different way and justified by a multitude of conditions, methods of testing and kinds of cements, but the main conclusions are the same.

Drying shrinkage may be controlled to a large extent by appropriate curing of fresh cement-based material. It is accompanied by carbonation shrinkage, which may also start much later according to circumstances, i.e. to the presence of CO_2 in the atmosphere.

Total drying shrinkage in high performance concretes is considerably smaller than in ordinary concretes (approx. 50%), but it develops more rapidly, [11.40]. This different behaviour should be considered in structural design in order to avoid cracking of fresh concrete.

The strain due to shrinkage is partly irreversible because it is developed during the hardening process. Other parts may be recovered when humidity of the environment is increased. It is generally assumed that the final value of shrinkage depends upon:

- total cement content in the mix composition;

- water/cement ratio and amount of water loss during hydration and hardening;
- conditions of curing at early age of cement hydration;
- environmental conditions in service life;
- internal structure of material in which inert inclusions reduce the volume changes and control the deformations.

Final values of strain due to shrinkage may be predicted from various empirical formulae, some of them based on different assumptions and simplifications. The equations shown below should be considered as examples. Guyon proposed the following formula [11.42]:

$$\varepsilon_{sh} = \frac{1300\, V_w}{E V_s} \log \vartheta, \tag{11.2}$$

where V_w and V_s are volumes of water and solid part, respectively, in the concrete composition, ϑ is atmospheric relative humidity (RH) and E is Young's modulus.

Three different formulae were proposed by L'Hermite, each related to other measurable quantities [11.43]:

$$\varepsilon_{sh} = \frac{\varepsilon_{cp}}{\dfrac{2800}{V_c} - 1.3} \tag{11.3}$$

where ε_{cp} is shrinkage of neat cement paste and V_c is the cement content:

$$\varepsilon_{sh} = \varepsilon_{cp} \frac{V_c}{V_c + [1 - (V_c + V_w + V_p + V_d)]a_{sh}} \tag{11.4}$$

here V_w, V_p and V_d are contents of water, pores and smallest particles, respectively, and a_{sh} is a coefficient depending on the quality of aggregate – its value is smaller the more compressible is the aggregate. For siliceous aggregate and continuous sieve curve a_{sh} is between 0.8 and 1.0.

The last relation was obtained from the preceding one for medium Portland cement content V_c between 300 and 400 kgs/m^3:

$$\varepsilon_{sh} = b_{sh}(V_c + V_w + V_p + V_d)^{1.5} \tag{11.5}$$

here b_{sh} is another empirical coefficient and for exponent different authors proposed values from 1.32 up to 1.52.

The ACI Committee 209 indicated only lower and upper limits for strain [11.44] namely, $\varepsilon_{sh} = 415 - 1070.10^{-6}$, and actual values should be selected according to a material's properties and the curing conditions. Also, in many other national and regional recommendations the final values of shrinkage are given for specified material composition and conditions of curing.

The development of shrinkage over time depends on the duration of moisture retention during curing, humidity of the environment and on the dimensions of the particular element. In an element of small dimensions the rate of loss of

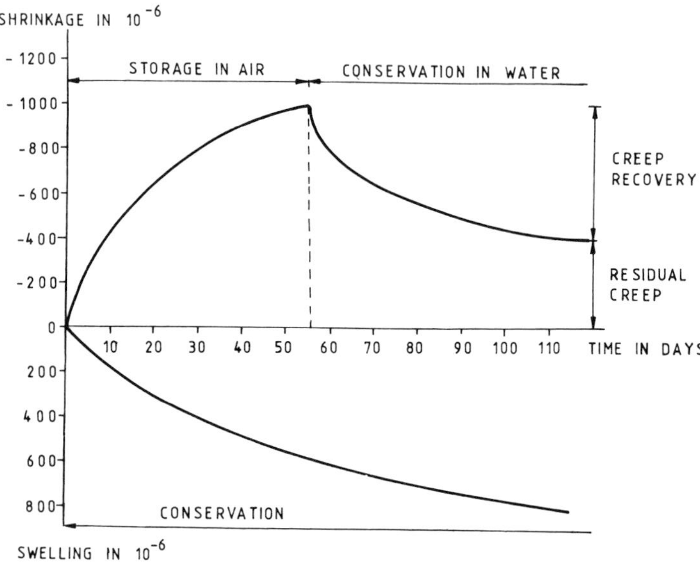

Figure 11.11 Characteristic development of shrinkage and swelling of concrete elements in average conditions.

water is quicker, yet in the large ones it may last for years. The respective curves of deformation over time have the general form shown in Figure 11.11. Swelling may be expected in fully saturated air with RH = 100% or when specimens are in water. The rate of shrinkage is the main factor which determines the importance of possible cracking and other destructive processes in concrete structures, because it is developing simultaneously with hardening – early shrinkage cannot be supported by fresh concrete with low tensile strength.

Typical values of shrinkage of a neat cement paste as indicated by [11.28] are -1300.10^{-6} after 100 days (env. 3 months); 2000.10^{-6} after 1000 days (env. 3 years); 2200.10^{-6} after 2000 days (env. 6 years).

Corresponding values for concrete are 10 to 20 times smaller because of the introduction of aggregate as an inert component and the inclusions of stiffeners. Also, curing in high humidity is a way of decreasing the final values of shrinkage because the cement paste may reach a further stage of hardening.

These data are in agreement with the general indication on percentage development of shrinkage given in [11.42] – 33% after ten days; 50% after one month; 90% after one year, and 100% after two or three years.

In recent years extensive tests were executed on the shrinkage of high performance concretes, when these kinds of concretes were studied in several countries, cf. Section 14.5. The research programmes were closely related to the application of concretes in outstanding structures where delayed deformations were of great importance. In high performance concretes (HPC) with

$f_{c28} \geqslant 60$ MPa and very high performance concretes (VHPC) with $f_{c28} \geqslant 100$ MPa, the final values of shrinkage are smaller than in ordinary concretes. Also, cracking in the external layers is reduced due to smaller amounts of free water. However, a higher rate of shrinkage may occur, e.g. for HPC concrete with SF as admixture and $f_{c28} = 80$ MPa already 70% of shrinkage may be expected after ten days. This explains why extensive curing in high moisture is even more important than for ordinary concretes, [11.45], [11.40] and [11.46].

The reinforcement of a cement-based matrix with different kinds of fibres may modify the shrinkage of the composite material, but the extent of modification depends on many conditions. Experimental results are not entirely concordant as to the importance of these modifications. It was found that fibres decrease the shrinkage by 10–20% with respect to that of plain mortar or concrete [11.47]. A decrease of only 10% was observed in mortar and concrete specimens reinforced with glass and polypropylene fibres [11.48]. Also a considerable reduction of drying shrinkage was found when steel-fibres were applied with a high volume content of 2% [11.49]. On the other hand, other researchers [11.50] have not observed any influence of steel-fibres of 2–4% vol. on shrinkage. Also, only a negligible decrease of shrinkage was found using 0.5% vol. of Bekaert fibres [11.51].

The tests published in [11.52] on high–early strength lightweight aggregate concrete reinforced with AR glassfibres showed no conclusive results. According to one report, [11.53] the shrinkage of glass fibre-reinforced composite was decreased with the use of a higher content of fine aggregate.

These different conclusions based on experimental results may be explained by the complicated influence of fibres on the matrix – increase of tensile strength combined with an increase of porosity and modification of workability. Therefore, all comparisons are difficult in the sense that they concern slightly different materials even if authors have tried to maintain the same composition and conditions. It is, however, certain that dispersed fibres are an effective reinforcement against cracking caused by shrinkage. This was known many years, and indeed, centuries ago. Generally accepted test methods of specimens cast around stiff steel rings permitted researchers to measure the crack width of mixes with different reinforcement when subjected to shrinkage. The authors of the above mentioned reports obtained clear conclusions concerning the effects of dispersed reinforcement in controlling cracking due to shrinkage.

The influence of polyacrylonitride fibres on early shrinkage cracking was tested on similar specimens. A rather low fibre content, equal to 0.45% vol, was sufficient to prevent early shrinkage cracking, [11.54]. For some types of polypropylene fibres even 0.067% vol. was sufficient. Various kinds of polymeric fibres are used to control cracking, cf. Section 5.6.

Tensile stress caused by the shrinkage of cement-based matrix is related to existing constraints which preclude free deformations. Obviously free shrinkage does not produce any stress but it hardly ever appears in real structural or even non-structural elements. The difference in deformations of neighbouring elements or layers due to different types of shrinkage induce tensile stress which may exceed local strength. This occurs, for example, between the external layer and internal core of every cast concrete element, because the conditions of loss of water are different, if careful humidification is not assured during curing. The phenomenon called differential shrinkage also occurs when a layer of fresh cement-based mix is put on old concrete elements during repair. There are a number of methods to help decrease any dangerous influence of shrinkage:

- by reducing the shrinkage itself of Portland cement paste (lower amount of cement, special brands of low-shrinkage cements with appropriate amount of gypsum, etc.);
- by adequate design of material structure with correctly selected aggregate and introduction of fibres or polymers;
- by intensive cure in high humidity during long periods, at least a few days after casting;
- by correct structural design allowing for free displacements of particular elements without much constraint.

(b) Creep

In a micro-structure of hydrated cement paste as described in Section 6.3 the crystalline phase is interconnected with hard particles, capillary pores and smaller gel pores. A system of discontinuous capillaries is partly filled with water which participates in load bearing. The creep of the hardened cement matrices is explained by the gradual transfer of external load, from the solid skeleton and the water in capillaries, to the skeleton alone – due to evacuation of water. By definition, creep of a material occurs when the deformations are increasing under constant stress. The strain due to creep and designed ε_{cr} are represented as additional to that which appears immediately after loading and which is called instantaneous strain ε_i. The opposite situation, when the stress is decreasing with no strain, is defined as relaxation; it is in fact another form of creep when constraints on displacements and deformations do exist.

Extensive reviews on possible sources of creep and their respective relations are given by [11.29] and [11.55].

Tests and observations executed by several authors have led to the following general conclusions concerning the magnitude of creep in cement-based composites:

1. creep depends directly upon the imposed stress but for stress above 50% of the material strength the relation is highly nonlinear;
2. creep is influenced by external humidity and is higher in dry cured specimens – a part of creep is called drying creep and is probably caused by the loss of water so that its separation of shrinkage is doubtful;
3. quality and nature of concrete and its components also have an influence on creep;

4. values of strain ε_{cr} are comparable to ε_i and under high stress may be equal to $3\varepsilon_i$.

It should be added that the age of concrete when the load is applied is of great importance, particularly for young concretes when it determines the degree of their hardening.

The phenomenon of creep has different consequences in structural design. The following may be mentioned as examples:

- creep of concrete is one of the sources of decrease of the prestressing force in post-tensioned elements;
- creep may help to decrease importance of local stress concentrations.

That last case may be illustrated by curves in Figure 11.12, where the development of tensile concrete strength and tension due to shrinkage in a restrained ring is shown. Without creep a crack may be expected to develop after time t_1; and due to creep not before time t_2, [11.28].

Creep is lower when various kinds of lightweight aggregate are used which maintain humidity, [11.56]. When the amount of aggregate is increased then lower creep of mortar and concrete may be expected, but nature of aggregate is also relevant – concretes made with sandstone aggregate exhibit higher creep than those with limestone. For compositions with ordinary Portland cement, creep is higher than for high alumina cement and rapid hardening cement. Also, the application of air-entraining agents and plasticizers may increase creep.

The typical development of creep in concrete specimens is represented by curves in Figure 11.13 where different possibilities are indicated and delayed deformations are combined with instantaneous ones on an example of a plain

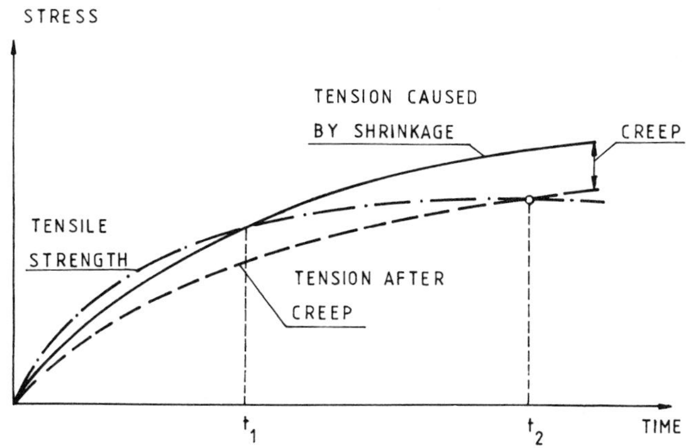

Figure 11.12 Curves representing tensile strength and stress due to restrained shrinkage in a concrete ring with and without creep. (Reproduced with permission from Neville, A.M., *Properties of Concrete*; published by Pitman Publishing, London, 1973.) [11.28]

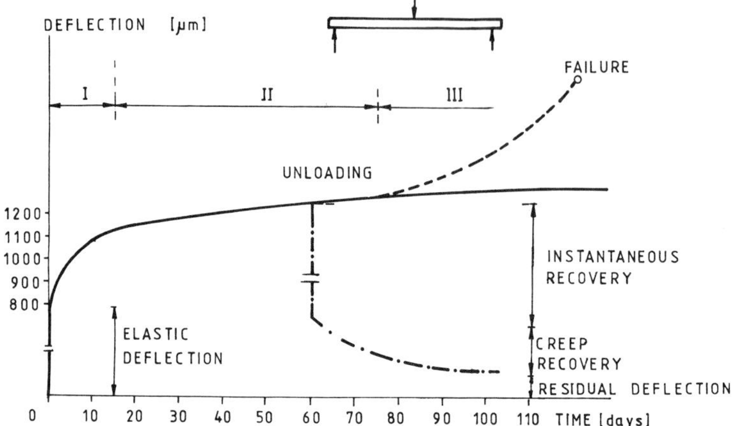

Figure 11.13 Creep of plain concrete beam in flexure as example of creep development in time. Consecutive stages and characteristic features are specified.

concrete beam subjected to flexure, [11.57]. After instantaneous deflection, stage I of creep is observed in which deflection rose at a decreasing rate. Next, deflections were also slowly increasing in stage II of quasi-stabilization. Then, two possibilities are demonstrated – either an effective stabilization to a certain constant value of deflection is achieved or in stage III a rapid increase of deflection occurs leading to a failure. The unloading at a specific age caused instantaneous recovery and creep recovery with specific residual deflection. More complex behaviour may also be hypothesized with modifications of environmental conditions and with various sequences of loading and unloading, but according to adopted assumptions the final results may be deduced from the principle of superposition of effects caused by different actions. In this research a step-wise curve was obtained at an early stage after loading (Figure 11.14), which can be interpreted as a result of crack and slippages in the material structure.

There are several published expressions for creep $\varepsilon_{cr}(t, T)$ as a function of time t since loading and age T of cement paste at the loading. The creep $\varepsilon_{cr}(t, T)$ may be also related to the final value of creep $\varepsilon_{cr}(\infty, T)$, based on an assumption that the creep rate is in a certain way proportional to a creep value still to be developed. In that approach the decreasing creep rate was taken into account. One of the expressions proposed in [11.58], [11.59] and [11.60] maintains its validity even after many years and has the following form:

$$\varepsilon_{cr}(t, T) = \varepsilon_{cr}(\infty, T)[1 - e^{-(k_1 \log((T+t)/T) + k_2 t)}] \tag{11.6}$$

where after [11.58] $k_1 = 0.62$, $k_2 = 0.30$ and after [11.60] $k_1 = 0.75$, $k_2 = 0.28$. Similar formulae were later published in [11.61], [11.62] and [11.63]:

$$\varepsilon_{cr}(t, T) = \varepsilon_{cr}(\infty, T)[1 - e^{-A(t-T)}]^{B}, \tag{11.7}$$

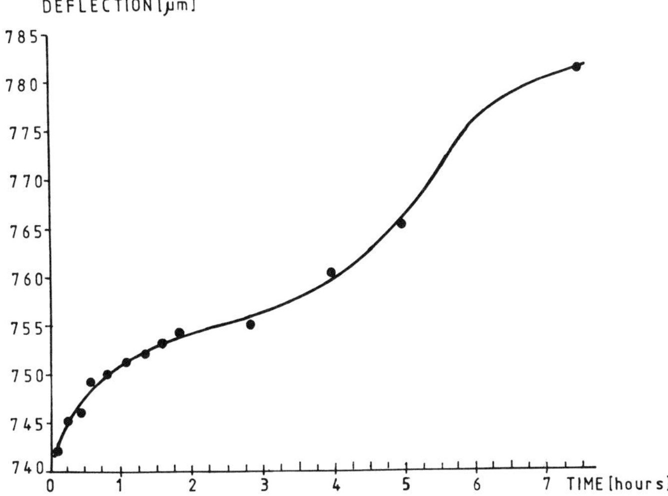

Figure 11.14 Step-wise curve reflecting the flexural creep immediately after loading. (Source: Brandt, A.M., Testing of concrete creep in non-reinforced beam subjected to bending; *Archives of Civ. Eng.*, **11**, pp. 87–93, 1965.) [11.57]

here again A and B are constants to be determined after experimental data. Age of concrete is not considered here in a direct way.

A completely different form of function was indicated in the French recommendations for prestressed and ordinary reinforced concretes BPEL and BAEL for creep deformation, mentioned in [11.45]:

$$\varepsilon_{cr} = \varepsilon_i K_{cr}(T) f(t - T), \tag{11.8}$$

where K_{cr} is the creep coefficient understood as ratio of creep to instantaneous strain $\varepsilon_i = \sigma_i / E$, and

$$f(t - T) = \frac{(t - t_o)^{1/2}}{\mathrm{B} + (t - t_o)^{1/2}}. \tag{11.9}$$

A different expression was proposed in [11.44] and a so called creep coefficient was used:

$$\frac{\varepsilon_{cr}}{\varepsilon_i} = A \frac{(t - T)^{\mathrm{D}}}{\mathrm{B} + (t - T)^{\mathrm{D}}} \tag{11.10}$$

where B and D are constants and A is the ultimate creep coefficient,

$$A = \frac{\varepsilon_{cr}(\infty, T)}{\varepsilon_i} \tag{11.11}$$

A logarithmic expression was recommended by [11.64]:

$$\varepsilon_{cr} = F(T) \log[(t - T) + 1], \tag{11.12}$$

here $F(T)$ is an experimental coefficient. Also power-type expressions were proposed in the following form:

$$\varepsilon_{cr} = A(t - T)^B, \qquad (11.13)$$

by which curves fitting closely with the experimental results may be easily determined.

The test results and models adopted for shrinkage and creep were verified again when new kinds of cement-based composites were introduced. It appeared that in fibre-reinforced concretes and in high performance concretes both the final values and development over time were different.

After [11.56] creep coefficient K_{cr} in (equation 11.8) varies from 1.05 up to 1.67 for high performance concrete specimens sealed to avoid drying and from 1.96 up 2.96 for non-protected specimens. In the case of ordinary concretes the standard value of K_{cr} is close to 1.0 and between 3.0 and 4.0, respectively. The coefficient B was varying from 1.7 to 11 for high performance concretes and is equal to 10 for ordinary concretes.

Polymer cement concretes (PCC) usually exhibit higher creep which may even be increased in higher temperatures. This is not the case for polymer impregnated concretes (PIC) in which a hardened skeleton does not allow for increased creep, particularly when a low volume of polymer is used for impregnation, [11.55].

Apparently, dispersed fibre-reinforcement does not appreciably modify the behaviour of cement-based elements subjected to creep. There have been few experimental studies of this problem and the results obtained are inconclusive. As mentioned above for shrinkage, modification of the internal structure of composite materials causes quite complex results and comparisons are difficult. In the tests made by [11.50] and [11.53] a similar behaviour of plain and fibre-reinforced elements was observed under creep conditions, both qualitatively and quantitatively. Extensive studies executed by [11.65], however, proved that various fibre-reinforcement decreased creep considerably. Similar conclusions were formulated by [11.66] where tested elements were under eccentric compression over long periods of time. The creep was small for higher reinforced specimens. The most important factor relating to the final creep values was the level of load with respect to the material's strength and that factor was also influenced by the volume of fibre-reinforcement. That was the reason why creep recovery measurements did not furnish consistent results.

Creep tests performed on gypsum specimens reinforced with glassfibres [11.67] have shown similar behaviour to that of cement-based concretes.

A prediction of the final values shrinkage and creep is needed, i.e., after a precise state of stabilization is achieved. Perfect stabilization is, however, possible only in artificial conditions created in a laboratory, because in the natural environment hygrothermal conditions vary and a flow of heat and moisture to and from hardened cement paste is continued indefinitely. Predictions may also concern the development over time and the rate of both processes.

Various sets of data may be considered as bases for prediction – mix composition, conditions of cure and during service life, values characterizing shrinkage and creep as measured over a short period of time, etc. All sets of data are not always available. Furthermore, most of the data are subject to stochastic distribution and should be considered as random variables.

Detailed reviews of relevant relations for shrinkage and creep in Portland cement mortars and concretes are published in [11.55], [11.29]. In this chapter only a few remarks are given relating specifically to polymer and fibre-reinforced composites. It is worth mentioning, however, that reliable formulae and extensive test results for these materials are scarce. Simple relations for the prediction for shrinkage and creep of ordinary concretes are given in [11.68] which may be used for most practical calculations. These formulae are provided with coefficients to allow for actual conditions.

Differences between recommended formulae for shrinkage and creep predictions and experimental data are caused by a multiplicity of parameters which lead to considerable under- and over-estimation of results. Reasons for these discrepancies are discussed in [11.66] and [11.69].

Further studies of shrinkage and creep are necessary in relation to high performance concretes with silica fume and superplasticizers. Some interesting remarks based on experimental research are published in [11.45]. According to that research, a considerable reduction of final values of shrinkage and creep may be expected in general, together with their higher rates. No conclusive results are available, mainly because of the great variety of admixtures on the market which may have different effects, either when used together with the various kinds of Portland cement and aggregate.

11.4.3 STRENGTH UNDER SUSTAINED LOAD

The notions of sustained load and of strength under sustained load are of great importance for obvious reasons – in all structural applications cement-based composites are subjected to long-term states of loading. As is mentioned in Section 11.3 the phenomenon of fatigue occurs not only under cyclic loading but a sustained load may also cause failure under an average stress below the short time static strength of the material.

Rüsch in 1960 [11.9] published his results, based also on earlier tests [11.3], showing the influence of duration of loading on strain–stress curve and strain development over time. In Figure 11.15 a few curves represent the results of axial compression imposed by constant strain rate on concrete specimens. For slow loading the influence of creep and propagation of microcracks is important, while for higher loading rates strength is apparently increased, cf. Section 11.2.1.

In Figure 11.16 curves for different values of ratio σ_c/f_c show the development of strain over time for compressed specimens. It appears that for maximum load when $\sigma_c/f_c = 1$ failure was obtained in about 20 minutes, for $\sigma_c/f_c = 0.8$ after a few days and for lower values of this ratio the increase of strain was

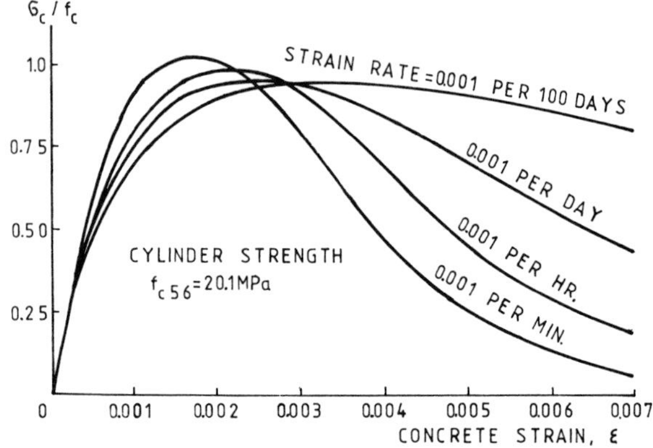

Figure 11.15 Strain–stress curves for various strain rates of axial compression of concrete specimens at an age of 56 days. (Reproduced with permission from Rüsch, H., Researches toward a general flexural theory for structural concrete; *J. of the American Concrete Institute*, **57**, pp. 1–28, 1960.) [11.9]

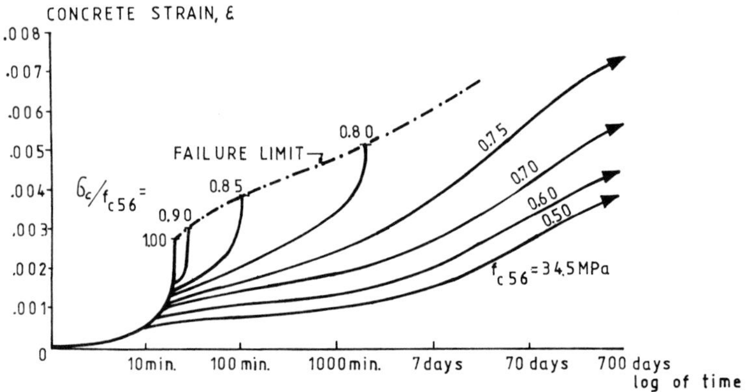

Figure 11.16 Development of strain in time under sustained compression of concrete specimens with different ratio of σ_c/f_c. (Reproduced with permission from Rüsch, H., Researches toward a general flexural theory for structural concrete; *J. of the American Concrete Institute*, **57**, pp. 1–28, 1960.) [11.9]

stabilized and no failure was observed. The same test results are presented in Figure 11.17 in a slightly different way.

In [11.68] an average value for strength under a sustained load of 78% with respect to 28-days' strength is indicated. Similar limits for tensile strength may be suggested, but no reliable test results are available and in a case of important structures experimental verification is recommended in local conditions and with actual materials.

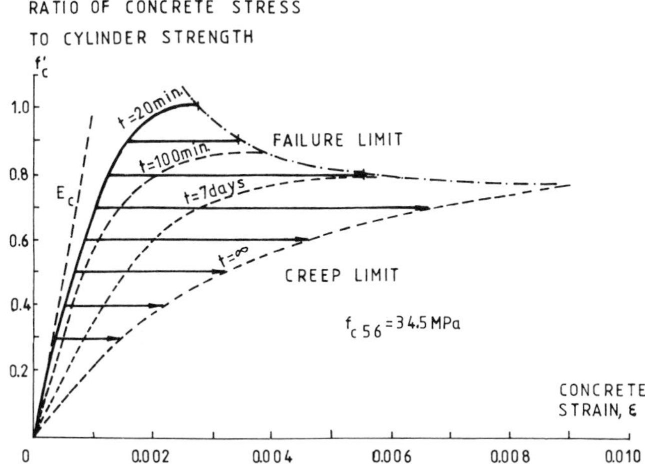

Figure 11.17 Influence of ratio σ_c/f_c and duration of load on concrete strain under compression. (Reproduced with permission from Rüsch, H., Researches toward a general flexural theory for structural concrete; *J. of the American Concrete Institute*, **57**, pp. 1–28, 1960.) [11.9]

In high performance concretes (HPC) with the addition of silica fume and other admixtures behaviour under sustained load should be verified. As the long-term strength is a result of two processes – increase in strength of Portland cement paste due to hydration of cement grains and accumulation of local damage due to the slow growth of microcracks, both develop differently than in ordinary concretes. In fact, the relative increase of strength after 28 days is smaller in HPC because of its higher loading rate from the beginning. It is reasonable to expect that strength under long-term loading is equal to 78% of 28-days strength, even if certain experimental results seem to allow higher values for HPC, [11.70 and [11.71].

The process of increase of strength with age is closely related to hygrothermal conditions during hydration and hardening which cannot be predicted precisely during the design of structures. The enhancement of hydration and of healing of cracks under compression has been observed [11.72] but reversal phenomenon and decrease of strength after unloading have been fixed elsewhere [11.73].

The application of dispersed fibres and polymers to create a more complex internal structure and control the cracking process may increase relative long-term strength. For carbon fibre-reinforced cement mortar elements the fatigue due to sustained load and a reduction of strength of 30% was observed after 7 months [11.74]. The static fatigue of glassfibre was also determined [11.75]. There is, however, not enough experimental evidence to propose general indicators. In all cases where needed, special tests of representative specimens are recommended.

11.5 Durability

11.5.1 DEFINITION AND IMPORTANCE OF DURABILITY

Durability is defined as 'the safe performance of a structure or a portion of a structure for the designed life expectancy', [11.76], or as 'the ability of a building and its parts to perform its required function over a period of time and under the influence of agents (that cause deterioration)', [11.77]. This definition can also be presented in several different ways, but the main elements in which maintenance of safety and serviceability are essential are always included.

The period of time in which durability is ensured is more or less consciously related to the lifetime of the structure, which is not always precisely defined for buildings and civil engineering structures, as is often the case for example for structural elements of aircraft and ships, cf. [11.78].

If the lifetime and requirements are likely to be foreseeable for the structures, it is not the case for the materials. The same materials may be used for a variety of purposes and their expected lifetime will be different. Therefore, their durability will be estimated according to different criteria. It is perhaps more correct to talk about the long-term behaviour of materials and keep the term durability for elements or structures. The material's behaviour may be considered in various service conditions and compared with the actual requirements imposed on structures. Durability of materials is, however, a universally accepted term which is understood correctly, through analogy, to the above mentioned definitions of the durability of structures. That is why the term durability, even if not perfectly correct, is also used here to describe a material's properties. In this chapter durability is limited rather to the behaviour of materials and as far as possible any relations to structures are avoided.

Durability is a very important feature of the general performance of materials. For both technical and economical reasons durability, in the full meaning of the term, should be taken into account in design, selection and execution of brittle matrix composites as materials for building and civil engineering structures [11.82].

Durability is always examined in situations when certain destructive processes are to be foreseen as unavoidable due to environmental influences and as a result of exploitation. However, one particular aspect of all damage and destruction processes should be examined carefully for every practical problem – this is their rate. The rate of a destruction process decides whether the effects are or are not dangerous during the lifetime of the structure. Consequently, the decision should be taken as to what measures are appropriate to prevent appreciable negative results and to ensure safety and serviceability of the structure.

Analytical, experimental and simulative methods are applied to solve the problem of how to predict the performance of a structure in given conditions. In those methods the interaction of damage modes should be considered properly and incorporated in predictions.

All processes involved in the behaviour of materials and in their durability are random, and have uncertain causes and effects. Not only the composition of a material and its initial properties such as physical values are subjected to random variations, but the occurrence and intensity of exposure of the structure and of all external actions are also random. There is only a limited amount of data from experience and tests concerning the ageing of materials, actions on structures, etc. Finally, the extent of simplifications in description and modelling of the various phenomena and of the cause–effect relationships is unknown. These are the reasons why an exact analysis of durability of composite materials, taking into account their stochastic nature, is in most cases impossible and all attempts in that direction are based on several simplifications. Durability is considered in a deterministic way by the application of appropriate safety coefficients in practical calculations in order to allow for unfavourable values for certain random parameters.

Selected groups of general problems related to durability and the long-term behaviour of concrete-like composites are examined below. Particular questions concerning the durability of glassfibres in Portland cement matrix and with alkali–aggregate reactions (AAR) are described in Sections 4.2.2 and 5.3, respectively.

The main conditions for high durability of cement-based composites may be summarized as high impermeability and density of the matrix, good workability of the fresh mix, internal structures which control microcracks and chemical compatibility of the material components.

11.5.2 PERFORMANCE OF A STRUCTURE AND ITS VARIATION WITH TIME

Performance is the behaviour of a product related to its use. The user formulates the requirements, expressed in terms of quantities and properties relevant in the use of the product, usually without imposing particular restrictions on the components, technological methods, etc. The durability of structures and materials is included in such a formulation of performance.

However, for appropriate design and execution of structures and materials, performance is expressed in the form of various properties and processes which are subjected to regulations, standards and various restrictions.

Cement-based materials exhibit complicated processes over time during their ageing and exploitation, which influence their properties. Hydration and the hardening of cement paste continue over long periods of time. They continue to progress but at a decreasing rate during the entire lifetime of a structure, and in favourable conditions it is believed that the strength of the cement matrix is continuously increasing. All other processes in materials during their ageing tend to be somewhat detrimental and are caused by various kinds of external actions of a mechanical, chemical, biological and hygrothermal nature, related to exploitation and the environmental conditions. All these actions have a negative influence on a material's durability, particularly if their intensities are increasing beyond certain limits. The following may be mentioned as examples:

- fatigue due to long-term or repetitive application of excessive loads and other actions;
- abrasion and wear due to normal exploitation;
- freezing and thawing, heating and cooling, soaking and drying cycles which cause excessive internal forces in a heterogeneous material structure and in constrained elements;
- penetration of CO_2, Cl ions and various corrosive fluids and gases which cause destructive processes in matrix or reinforcement, also UV radiation for certain materials;
- leaching, cavitation, and erosion, related to the kind of water and to the intensity of flow;
- processes which are caused by incompatibility of materials like shrinkage and swelling of the matrix, chemical reactions with aggregates (AAR) or corrosion of reinforcement, etc.

It should be mentioned that all detrimental effects usually increase the rate of further destruction in the form of a feedback, e.g. local cracks or spallings open the way to accelerated corrosion of reinforcement and cracking of the matrix. Here also, various cases which qualify as misuse are to be considered – overloading, local accidental impact, etc.

Maintenance comprises more or less continuous execution of small repairs and discrete major repairs which probably take a large part of the financial resources allocated by the owner. The following groups of maintenance operations may be defined and scheduled during the ageing of the structure and its decreasing performance:

- corrective maintenance (occasional repairs, cleaning and replacements);
- scheduled maintenance (periodic inspections and repairs);
- rehabilitation (restoration of initial performance);
- upgrading (improvement of initial performance).

The initial cost of a structure, the cost of exploitation and maintenance together with eventual cost of demolition and dismantling of the structure are all components of the total cost. How to properly split the total cost into particular allocations is an economic problem rather than a technical one. It is obvious that with a higher initial cost spent for rational improvements of materials and structures, cheaper maintenance may be expected.

The performance of a structure which is varying over time is represented in a schematic form in Figure 11.18. A necessary minimum level of performance is considered as constant throughout the life cycle and all repairs are supposed to ensure reconstruction back to that level. The intervals between consecutive repairs are indicated as decreasing with time and in this way the influence of negative ageing processes are taken into account. A decision as to when a repair

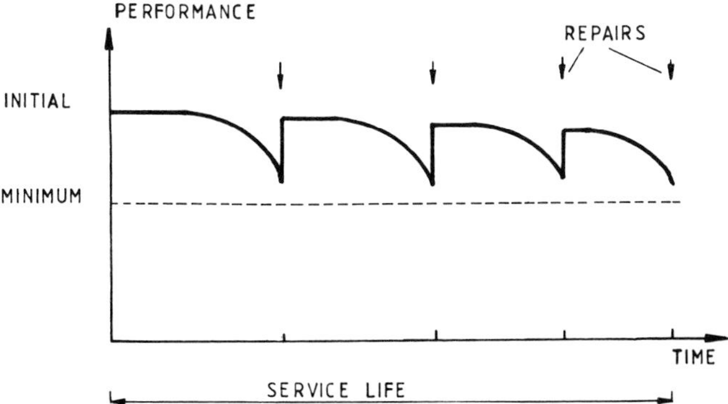

Figure 11.18 Variation of performance of a structure with time.

is necessary and what should be its extent is taken up after having considered technical and economical arguments to ensure the reliability of the structure in an optimum way.

The performance as understood for Figure 11.18 is a function of several variables which could be measured, like strength or stiffness. There are also, however, other properties like the aspect of the structure or the comfort of the traffic on a road which are not directly measurable. In such cases conventional methods for their quantification should be established, e.g. the aspect may be estimated separately by a group of specialists who, taking into account several fuzzy parameters or so called linguistic variables, establish their final though subjective decision.

The end of the service life of a structure is not necessarily related to the durability of that structure or of the materials used. Many structures do not achieve the end of their durability because of various situations that occur at an earlier date, like major accidental destruction or some important modification of functional requirements. In practical situations the 'lifetime' is ill defined as many factors are beyond the designer's control.

The durability of concrete and concrete structures is related not only to solution of chemical and physical problems, but also to economical aspects. Some comments on this subject are given in Sections 14.5.7 and 15.3.

Several problems concerning durability of cement-based materials are examined in the following sections.

11.5.3 DURABILITY IN FREEZE–THAW CYCLES

Cement-based matrices are exposed to destructive processes when subjected to variations of temperature below zero and to the freezing of water in the pore system. An increase in the volume of ice of about 9% produces important internal stresses which may induce cracks and spallings. This is particularly dangerous in the following situations:

1. when due to large value of water/cement ratio the matrix has a high volume of capillary pores in which free water is accumulated and is subjected to freezing;
2. the outdoor structures like bridges, roads and jetties are directly exposed to environmental moisture due to rain, sprinkling by sea water or steam condensation. This may concern structural and also nonstructural elements like external loadings and decorations;
3. in the large geographical zones of Central Europe, North America and Japan, etc. temperature variations across 0 °C are frequent in winter and also occur in spring and autumn, so that the number of dangerous freezing and thawing cycles is of the order of a hundred in a year;
4. de-icing agents are used on roads and runways which increase the corrosive influence on concrete and dangerous influence by enhancing the corrosion of steel-reinforcement;
5. in ordinary concretes the tensile strength of the matrix is not sufficient to support local tensions due to freezing, particularly at early ages.

The resistance of the matrix to freezing is related to the intensity of internal forces which appear when pore water is frozen, and to the tensile strength of the matrix.

The distribution of diameters of capillary pores in a cement matrix is essential for the intensity of internal stress due to freezing. The distribution is characterized by so-called spacing factor L according to [11.79]. It is equal to the average maximum distance of any point on the matrix to the nearest pore, i.e. to half the distance between neighbouring pores. Larger pores with larger spacing factor are dangerous, because tensile stress at freezing cannot be balanced by the tensile strength of the matrix, and microcracks are unavoidable. The critical value L_{cr} is its maximum, yet corresponding to the safe supporting of the tensile stress produced in the matrix by transformation of water into ice, cf. Section 6.5. The spacing factor is the most important parameter characterizing the resistance of cement-based materials to freeze–thaw cycles.

It has been established that in ordinary cement matrix the spacing factor L is equal to 600–1000 μm approximately and the critical value is usually below 200 μm for mortars and below 300 μm for concretes. Therefore, in ordinary concretes special air-entraining agents are added (cf. Section 4.3.6) to produce an artificial system of pores with a spacing factor of about 200 μm. The diameters of pores vary between 50 and 1200 μm with a majority of them below 250 μm. The most dangerous pores are of a diameter of between 0.1 and 1.0 μm.

The air-entrainment effects are related to the workability of the fresh mix – with higher slump the value of air is increased, but for too high slump ($\geqslant$150–175 mm) the mix is too fluid to retain the air bubbles before hardening. The proper amount and nature of an air-entraining admixture is needed to obtain the required effects and this is usually established by testing with a given mix. The effects have the form of a system of spherical air bubbles uniformly distributed in the hardened matrix. The main aim is to obtain $L \leqslant 200\,\mu m$ approximately and to keep the total air volume low, as it influences the strength of hardened material, [11.80], [11.83] and [11.84].

The total volume of air voids is not the most important parameter, but it does give certain indications as to the freeze–thaw resistance. It is measured in a fresh mix or in hardened material, but between these two measures large differences may occur. When the total air volume is between 5 and 8%, both volumes are close enough and the conclusions from any one of them are reliable. A volume below 5% may indicate that there is not enough air and probably $L > L_{cr}$. If the air volume is greater than 7%, then with appropriate air bubbles distribution a satisfactory situation may be expected, i.e. $L \leqslant L_{cr}$.

The critical value of a spacing factor depends on the tensile strength of the matrix, but for ordinary concretes that relationship is of secondary importance.

However, it has been proved [11.81] that for high performance concretes with a low water/cement ratio approaching 0.25 the critical value L_{cr} is close to 750 μm and no air-entrainment is needed. This is an important advantage for high performance concretes because pores produced by air-entraining agents decrease strength, and the application of air-entraining admixtures increases the final cost of the composite material.

Entrained pores are quasi-closed and even in a completely saturated matrix are not filled with water, but they are available for expansion when water is freezing. This is the reason why entrained pores decrease all detrimental results of frost–thaw cycles in laboratory testing by 5–10 times. It has been proved that air-entraining admixtures can also decrease the danger for structures exposed to out-door conditions by similar proportions.

The freezing of water in capillary pores depends on their dimensions. As is shown in Figure 11.19 the freezing point decreases with pore diameter and it has been found that a temperature of about −15 °C is required for nearly 100% of the water to be frozen; but water in pores which are smaller than 20 nm freezes in temperatures below −43 °C. The freezing process is complicated by diffusion of water from smaller pores to larger ones and by simultaneous water evaporation and capillary suction, the latter being of a considerably higher rate. Moreover, in the natural conditions of outdoor structures, external temperature is varying, e.g. the water freezing process during the night may be interrupted by higher temperature periods occurring in the day. The rate of cooling and frequency of freezing–thawing cycles are of primary importance.

The danger of water freezing is related to pore saturation. In completely saturated pores freezing produces high tensile stress, while for the pores which are partly filled these stresses may be negligible, cf. Figure 11.20.

In difficult climatic conditions, i.e. frequent freezing in the nights, de-icing agents are used on roads and bridges to facilitate road traffic movement and safety. As a result, water freezes in nearly the same range of temperatures in pores of all diameters. Therefore, the possibility of water distribution during these processes is strongly reduced and for temperatures below −20 °C the

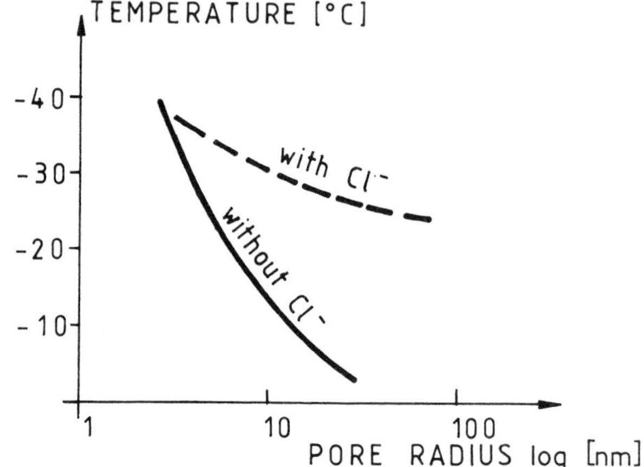

Figure 11.19 Freezing of water in capillary pores as function of their diameter. (Reproduced with permission from CEB (Comité Euro-International du Béton) Bulletin No. 182, *Durable Concrete Structures – CEB Design Guide*; 2nd Edition, Lausanne, June, 1989.) [11.82]

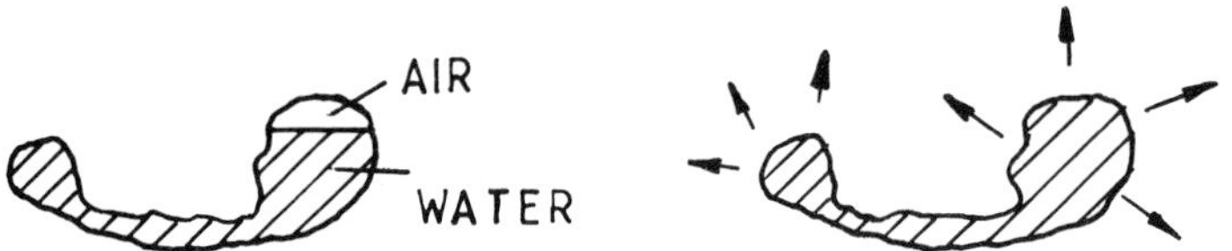

Figure 11.20 Partly and completely water saturated pores.

damage to cement matrix may be more serious than without de-icing agents. Moreover, the de-icing agents based on salt 5 NaCl $CaCl_2$ increase the corrosion of steel-reinforcement.

The resistance of concrete-like composites to freezing is verified by standard freezing–thawing cycles in a form of accelerated tests. According to Swedish Standard SS 137244 the material lost from a tested specimen should not exceed 1 kg/m^2 after 56 cycles. In the Polish Standard cycles $\pm 18\,°C \pm 2\,°C$ are required and lost material should be less than 2% with decrease of the compressive strength below 20% [11.85]. The number N of cycles is determined as a function of the requested resistance against freezing, i.e. – the design lifetime. For concrete bridges $N = 150$ is usually accepted, as corresponding to zero crossings a year, taking into account that in the standard tests the imposed conditions (rates, temperature) are more stringent than during normal exposure to environmental influences.

To ASTM Recommendations C 666 and C 672 are relevant for the two methods of testing, respectively:

1. 'Resistance to rapid freezing and thawing' – cycles in water;

2. 'Scalling resistance of concrete exposed to de-icing chemicals' – resistance against surface spalling in exposure to freezing with de-icing agents.

It may be concluded that all these standard procedures of testing give only approximate indication as to the actual frost resistance. The main value is that testing different concretes' comparative results may be obtained and thus the best material may be selected for the purpose.

11.5.4 DURABILITY WITH RESPECT TO CARBONATION

Carbonation is a process in which calcium oxide CaO and calcium hydroxide $CaO \cdot 2H_2O$ in hardened cement paste are converted to calcium carbonate by carbon dioxide CO_2 penetrating by diffusion from the atmosphere into the system of pores and microcracks. In this reaction the alkaline hydrates take part which contain Ca, NaOH and KOH, producing additional micro-crystals of calcium carbonate. The carbonation products fill the matrix structure, reduce the porosity and the specific surface area. Finally, there are two effects of carbonation:

1. density of cement paste is increasing as well as its strength;
2. passivity of intercrystalline water is decreasing considerably, sometimes from $pH \geqslant 12.5$ down to $pH \leqslant 9.0$.

If the first effect can be considered as beneficial for the durability of the matrix itself, the second one increases the danger of accelerated corrosion of steel-reinforcement. The final effects of carbonation are strongly dependent on the quality of Portland cement and on the permeability of the hardened cement paste. Cements with small amount of alkalis are less exposed to carbonation and the same concerns cements blended with fly ash and blast furnace slag.

Large capillary pores and microcracks increase the carbonation rate particularly in open air and with humidity between 50 and 70% RH. Moreover, it has been observed that cyclic soaking and drying with exposure to an atmosphere with high CO_2 content produce quicker carbonation than do less variable conditions. It is therefore concluded that with a low water/cement ratio, e.g. below 0.25 as for high performance concretes, the carbonation is very slow and does not decrease appreciably the durability of reinforced concrete structures. The long curing of fresh concretes in high humidity increases the density of the hardened material and slow carbonation may also be expected. For low quality concretes with a water/cement ratio > 0.5 the carbonation can be harmful [11.86]. Specimens made with the high performance concrete of compressive strength equal to 65 MPa or more and a water/cement ratio $\leqslant 0.35$ do not exhibit any measurable carbonation after accelerated tests equivalent to several years of natural exposure [11.86]. Specimens made of the same components, having the same workability expressed by slump test but having a higher water/cement ratio $= 0.5$ and lower strength of an order of 40 MPa, when subjected to the same testing procedure have shown 13 and 23 mm of carbonation depth after moisture and dry curing, respectively.

An interesting relation between the advance of carbonation and the compressive strength of concretes f_c was published in [11.87]. The tests were performed on various concretes of different quality subjected to the open air during a three-year period. The results obtained in that investigation are summarized in Figure 11.21 and confirmed earlier established relations [11.88] in the form of straight lines for various water/cement ratios representing carbonation depth as a function of time (Figure 11.22). Carbonation is a process with a decreasing

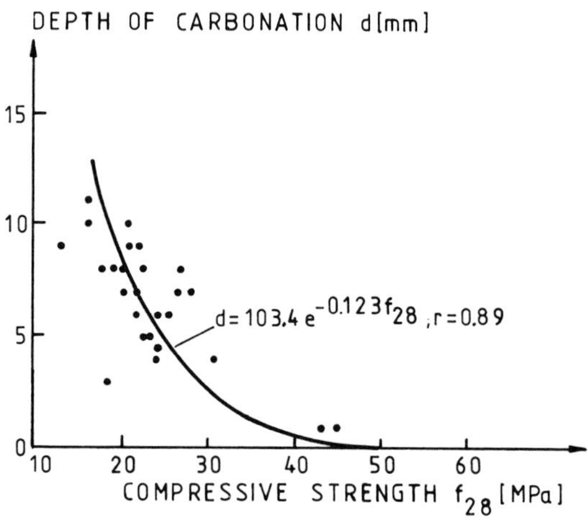

Figure 11.21 Influence of compressive strength f_c on carbonation depth after open air exposure over three years. (Reproduced with permission from Nischer, P., Influence of concrete quality and environment on carbonation; published by RILEM, 1984.) [11.87]

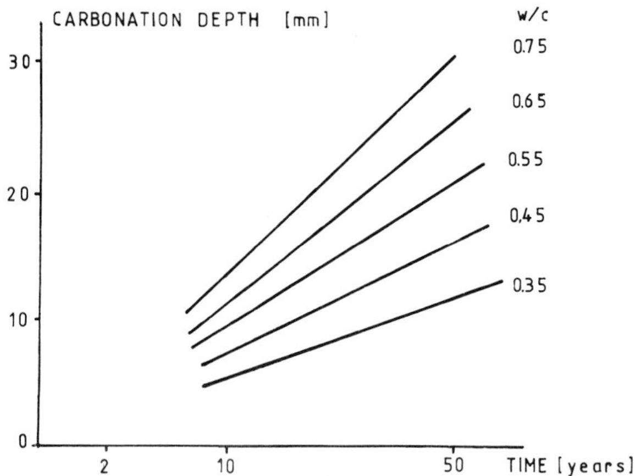

Figure 11.22 Carbonation rate as function of w/c ratio. (Reproduced with permission from Schiessel, P., Durability of concrete structures; published by CEB/RILEM, 1983.) [11.88]

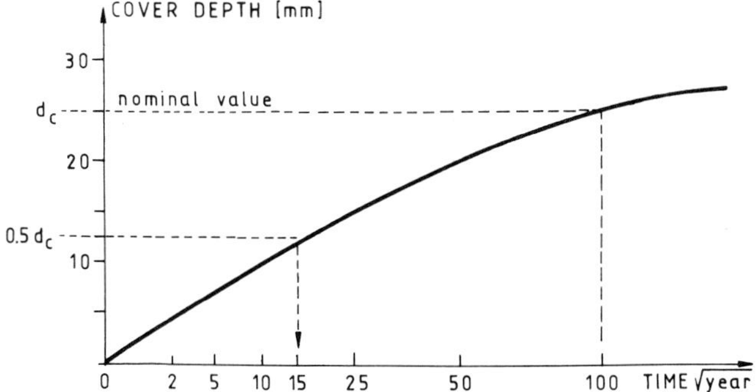

Figure 11.23 Rate of carbonation or chloride penetration depth in cement mortar. (Reproduced with permission from CEB Bulletin No. 182, *Durable Concrete Structure – CEB Design Guide*; 2nd Edition, Lausanne, June, 1989.) [11.82]

rate of change, because the density of external layers is increasing with carbonation products, [11.89].

The rate of carbonation in ordinary concretes is schematically shown in Figure 11.23. It is assumed that the depth of cover d of steel-reinforcement should be bigger than the depth of carbonation d_c estimated after a hundred years to ensure the safety of reinforcement, [11.82]. In normal conditions half of that depth can be reached already in 15 years. A simplified formula proposed for the carbonation rate is, $d_c = 10b\sqrt{t}$; here d_c is in mm and t in years; b is a numerical coefficient which characterizes the quality of concrete, for example for a very good quality concrete $b = 0.15$.

The predictions for d_c are based on accelerated tests and on experience gained after examination of old structures. These predictions are expressed in the form

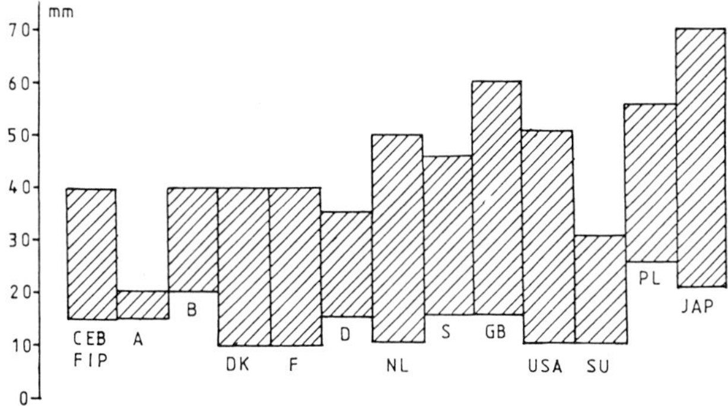

Figure 11.24 Lower and upper values required for reinforcement cover depth in different countries and in CEB–FIP Recommendations. (Reproduced with permission from Lambotte, H., Survey of rules intended to guarantee durability; published by RILEM, 1984.) [11.90]

of standardized requirements for depth of reinforcement cover in concrete structures. In Figure 11.24 the examples of the depth of standard cover imposed in a few countries and recommended by specialized international organizations are shown. Lower and upper values correspond to extremes of favourable and unfavourable situations, respectively, taking into account environmental humidity, air pollution, consequences of corrosion, etc. It may be concluded that the large scatter between the different recommended depth of reinforcement cover is not always justified by objective arguments, while the appropriate depth of cover is the simplest method to improve durability of several kinds of concrete structure.

11.5.5 DURABILITY WITH RESPECT TO OTHER EXTERNAL ACTIONS

In hot and dry climates the vulnerability of cement-based composites to deterioration by excessive cracking due to accelerated shrinkage and thermal effects is increased. At early ages elements are particularly exposed, because of the high shrinkage rate and relatively low tensile resistance. Hot weather also accelerates processes of corrosion of steel-reinforcement in the presence of aggressive salts in the air, [11.91].

The sensitivity of concrete structures to sulphate attack is strongly related to the exposure conditions. Structures in an environment of high sulphate content in the air or in water, e.g. sewage tunnels, are particularly vulnerable. After sulphate ions penetrate the pore system of cement paste complex reactions start with C_3A, leading principally to two kinds of processes – gypsum corrosion and sulphoaluminate corrosion [11.29]. The products of sulphate reactions with cement expand and can cause cracking and destruction. The permeability of the material's structure and the quality of cement decide upon the rate of these processes. Special Portland cements as well as high alumina cements may be used for elements exposed on sulphates, cf. Section 4.1.

Acid attacks from air or water may produce the conversion of calcium in Portland cement paste into soluble salts. As a result the binding capacity of hardened mortars and concretes is reduced.

Chloride ions Cl^- in concrete materials act as a catalyst for processes of corrosion of steel-reinforcement. Their influence on cement paste itself is less important. A thin oxide passivation film around reinforcing bars provides electrochemical protection to the steel. When it is destructed by chloride ions the corrosion may be rapidly enhanced.

Chloride ions may be introduced to the fresh mix from mixing water, marine aggregate, or admixtures with chloride components. The chloride ions also penetrate from air to the hardened concrete materials through pores, bleed-water channels, entrapped-air voids and cracks. The density of the material and its impermeability is decisive at this stage of chloride ions penetration and its intensity is considered as proportional to the value of the water/cement ratio. It has been observed that curing of the concrete at $+50\,^{\circ}\mathrm{C}$ increased the penetration of chloride ions from marine water is compared with concretes which were cured at environmental temperature, [11.92].

High chloride content in the air combined with soaking and drying cycles create the dangerous conditions which may appear for example in industrial or marine environments in hot climates. Concrete structures in harbours and sea fronts at seaside localities are strongly exposed, but the wind direction may extend the danger zone far in land. When melamine based superplasticizers are applied, then the risk of corrosion of steel resulting from chloride penetration is reduced, especially when Portland cement which is sulphate-resistant and low in C_3A is used.

The rate of penetration of chloride ions and the depth of destroyed material are similar or even greater than those which are characteristic of carbonation.

The durability of organic fibres as reinforcement may be endangered by the destructive action of alkaline pore solutions. In unfavourable conditions, i.e. high alkalinity of cement, high environmental moisture and inadequate impermeability of cement matrix, the result will simply be the disappearance of fibres and of their reinforcing effects. A certain number of failures of roofs made of cement sheets reinforced with vegetable fibres of local origin occurred during the 1980s, [11.93]. Additional precautions may sometimes be difficult but they are necessary, and natural fibres cannot be used as a simple replacement for asbestos fibres which have excellent durability in alkaline environment, cf. Section 5.2.

Steel-fibres do not corrode in a cement-based matrix provided it is of adequate density. However, when fibres are partly exposed to external influences they corrode quickly and may spoil the appearance of concrete surfaces with reddish dots.

All kinds of chemical agents which attack hardened concrete-like materials are dangerous if they are allowed to penetrate into a material's structure and if there is enough moisture for chemical reactions. Impermeability of the matrix stops the penetration of chemicals and migration of water to such an extent that the reaction becomes slow with respect to the structure's lifetime and the material has improved durability. As is mentioned elsewhere, high performance materials with a low water/cement ratio, low capillary porosity and high density are durable in conditions in which ordinary materials may exhibit sensitivity to destructive agents.

The application of fibres and polymeric admixtures, in general, improve durability in the same measure as for impermeability and the control of cracking.

11.6 Behaviour in high and low temperatures

11.6.1 LIMITS OF TEMPERATURES

The limits for normal exploitation of concrete-like composites in temperate climates are from $+50\,^{\circ}C$ to $-30\,^{\circ}C$. The upper limit corresponds, for example, to a bridge deck or building cladding exposed to solar radiation in summer time and the lower limit – to an outdoor structure in winter. Both limits may be extended for polar and tropical regions by 10–20 degrees, approximately.

For special applications and for accidental conditions the above limits are extended considerably. For refractory elements a temperature of +300 °C is admitted as normal. In the case of a fire in a building the temperature of elements may exceed +1000 °C. In the reservoirs for liquefied gases the temperature of a concrete element may reach due to an accident a level as low as −165 °C. This is the range of temperatures to which cement-based composites may be exposed either in a form of cyclic actions or in rare situations.

Beside temperature, other conditions are also of importance – rate of temperature variation, number of heating/cooling cycles and material humidity. Furthermore, there is no linear relationship between the temperature variation and its influence on a material's properties because there are several factors acting with different intensity and in opposite directions.

The behaviour of cement-based composites in high and low temperatures is mainly considered with respect to two different processes:

1. local cracking and fracture of the matrix due to internal pressure caused by expansion of contraction of a material's components;
2. basic modification of a material's components due to elevated temperature.

The influence of temperatures in cold and hot climates on the curing of concretes and special measures to avoid damage at an early age due to cement hydration and hardening are described in full detail in a number of manuals on concrete technology, e.g. [11.28], and are not considered here. Only the influence of extreme temperatures is examined below.

11.6.2 CEMENT-BASED MATERIALS IN ELEVATED TEMPERATURES

According to [11.94] there is the following sequences of processes when cement-based materials are exposed to elevated temperatures:

1. evaporation of water, over +100 °C;
2. destruction of cement gel due to dehydration, at +180 °C;
3. decomposition of Portland cement clinker, at +500 °C;
4. transformation of quartzite at +570 °C;
5. decomposition of CSH, at +700 °C;
6. decarbonization of limestone aggregate, over +800 °C;
7. melting of concrete components begins at +1150 °C;
8. complete destruction occurs at approximately +1300 °C.

This schematic list does not contain all the accompanying processes in cement paste and aggregates which may occur simultaneously, often as consequences of the above.

At elevated temperatures over +100 °C the cement paste exhibits a moderate

Table 11.2 Coefficients α of thermal expansion of rocks for temperatures +20– +100 °C

Types of rocks	Values of α
Granites, rhyolites	$8 \pm 3 \times 10^{-6}$
Andesites, diorites	7 ± 2
Basalts, gabbros, diobases	5 ± 1
Sandstones	10 ± 2
Quartzites	11 ± 1
Limestones	8 ± 4
Marbles	7 ± 2
Slates	9 ± 1

(Source: Skinner, B.J., Thermal expansion; *Handbook of Physical Constants*, published by Geol. Soc. of America, 1966.) [11.95]

expansion up to +150 °C and then some contraction up to +600 °C. At temperatures over +600 °C again expansion was observed.

Internal pressure is caused by the restrained expansion of various of the material's components which form heterogeneous materials such as cement-based composites. Linear coefficients of thermal expansion of aggregate vary according to their mineralogical origin from 5 to 11×10^{-6} per °C and their approximate values are shown in Table 11.2. For example, the expansion of basalts below +200 °C is approximately half of that of sandstones and quartzites. The values of the thermal expansion coefficient for plain cement paste vary between 10.8 and 21.6×10^{-6} according to [11.95]. While these incompatibilities of expansions do not cause microcracks in the interface layers when the temperature is maintained below +100 °C, significant destruction is produced in the elevated temperatures during fire. Over +400 °C the differential expansions of aggregate grain decide upon the point of material destruction.

For steel the values of coefficient α are given by equations [11.96], $\alpha = 0.4 \times 10^{-8} \times T^2 + 1.2 \times 10^{-5} \times T - 3 \times 10^{-4}$, or in a simplified form; $\alpha = 1.4 \times 10^{-5}$/°C, where T is temperature in °C. It means that the usually admitted constant value of α is an approximation which may not be acceptable in extreme temperatures.

The value of α coefficient for a composite material results from values characterizing all components, taking into account their respective fractions. For example, the value of α coefficient for a concrete may be calculated from the relation proposed in [11.97]; $(\alpha_c - \alpha_a) = (\alpha_p - \alpha_a)(1 - g)^n$, where α_a, α_c and α_p are coefficients for aggregate, concrete and cement paste, respectively, g is the volume fraction of aggregate and n is a numerical coefficient, which is determined experimentally.

Furthermore, the expansion coefficient for cement paste varies with its

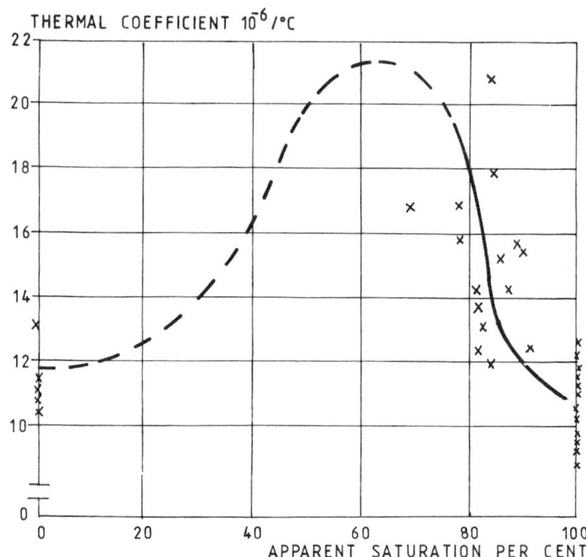

Figure 11.25 Thermal coefficient for plain cement paste as a function of its moisture content. (Reproduced from Mitchell, L.J., Thermal expansion tests on aggregate, neat cements and concretes; Copyright ASTM. Reprinted with permission.) [11.98]

moisture content as is shown in Figure 11.25, namely it exhibits the maximum for both extreme cases – very dry and completely saturated material. Both these processes – heating or cooling of elements and variation of their moisture content due to drying or humidifying are superimposed. Their gradients are related to external conditions and to moisture and thermal conductivity. As a result the thermal expansion of concrete composites and induced stresses may be greater than might otherwise be anticipated, [11.99], and [11.100].

The resulting internal pressures may cause cracking if they exceed the tensile strength of the material. As is described elsewhere, the tensile strength of these materials is relatively low, unless additional internal structures of fibres or polymer links are created. Therefore, at elevated temperatures extensive cracking has to be foreseen if not reduced by other measures.

It is assumed according to [11.101] that at temperatures between +250 and +300 °C low quality concretes practically lose their strength. That limit is moved up to +600 °C for high performance concretes.

The decrease in the compressive strength of concrete was observed on many tests and characteristic curves are shown in Figure 11.26. The ratio of compressive strength f_{ct} of cylinders (after exposure to high temperature) to initial compressive strength f_c at normal temperature is presented as function of temperature of exposure. The decrease of tensile strength with temperature is slightly more important – at +800° the tensile strength reaches 20% of its value

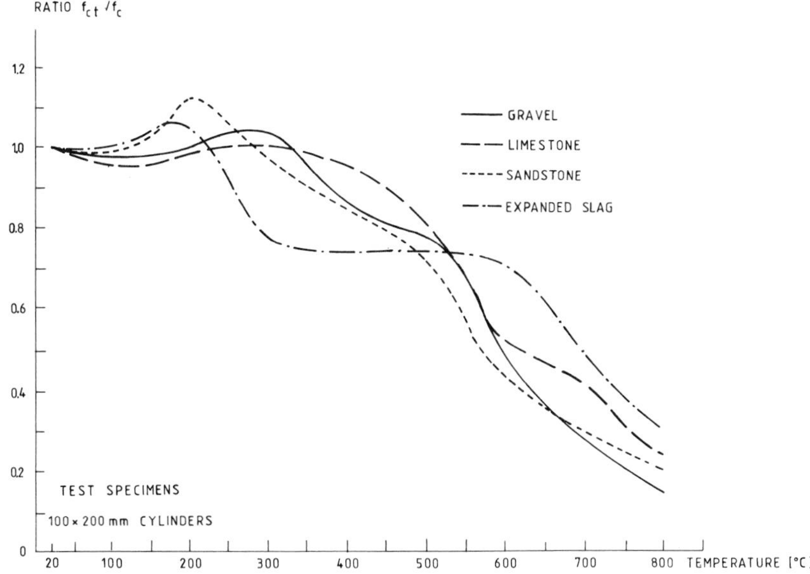

Figure 11.26 Relations of the ratio between compressive strength at temperature T to that at +20°C for concretes with various kinds of aggregate. (Reproduced from Zoldner, N.G., Effect of high temperatures on concrete incorporating different aggregates; Copyright ASTM. Reprinted with permission.) [11.102]

at +20 °C. It has been also observed that Young's modulus decreases rapidly, down to 5% of its initial value.

Only a few investigations on fibre composites' behaviour in elevated temperatures were published up to now.

The behaviour in high temperatures of concretes reinforced with steel-fibres was studied in [11.103]–[11.106]. Thermal expansion was measured on specimens reinforced up to 2.5% vol. and subjected to up to +800 °C. The influence of plain fibres was rather limited, however, up to +300 °C thermal strain was reduced by fibres and that reduction was proportional to fibre volume. At higher temperatures between +300 and +800 °C thermal expansion was apparently bigger than for comparable plain concrete specimens. The fibres may participate in the distribution of heat, the interaction between fibres and matrix at high temperatures is fairly complex and no explanation was furnished for observed relations, [11.103].

The influence of brass coated, crimped and plain steel-fibres on the compressive strength of cement composites at high temperatures was presented in [11.104]. As is shown in Figure 11.27, up to +400 °C the fibres efficiently controlled cracking and reinforced the matrix against a decrease of strength. In contrast, their influence at higher temperatures between +400 and +800 °C was quite

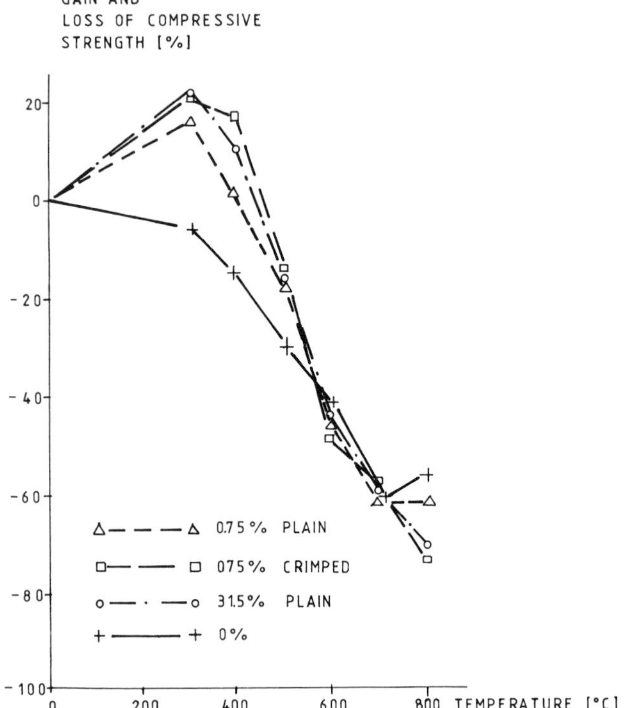

Figure 11.27 Variation of gains and losses of compressive strength of specimens tested in different temperatures. (Reproduced with permission from Purkiss, J.A., Steel-fibre reinforced concrete at elevated temperatures; *International Journal of Cement Comp. and Lightweight Concrete*, **6**, pp. 179–84, published by Elsevier Science Publishers, 1984.) [11.104]

negligible and the strength of reinforced specimens was equal to that of plain concrete ones. Similar results were obtained for specimens under flexure.

The influence of fibres on fracture toughness was studied in,[11.105] where several toughness indices were calculated and discussed on the basis of experimental tests. The general conclusion was that cement composites reinforced with steel-fibres are more resistant to moderately high temperatures than non-reinforced materials, without any particular differentiation as to the type, shape and volume of the fibres. It is, however, believed that stainless steel-fibres are better than fibres made of ordinary steel.

Reinforcement with glassfibres used up to 1.5% vol. did not modify the behaviour of the cement matrix in high temperatures, [11.106].

All kinds of polymeric fibres are rather sensitive to elevated temperatures. For example, polypropylene fibres exhibit a considerable decrease of strength at 100–120 °C and their melting point is approximately 160 °C.

11.6.3 CEMENT-BASED MATERIALS IN VERY LOW TEMPERATURES

Concrete has been used since the early 1950s as a structural material for liquefied gas storage at atmospheric pressure and cryogenic temperatures, and also for other applications. An extensive study of the related problems was published, [11.107].

Deep freezing of concrete causes multiple processes in its structure related to the contraction of the solid skeleton and expansion of ice in the pores. The pores are not completely filled with water, which freezes at different temperatures in different sized pores. The expansion of the ice is not linear with decreasing temperature. In real situations water filtration and diffusion are continuous with temperature variations. Formation of ice may disrupt certain parts of the concrete structure but larger voids filled with ice also represent hard inclusions which may increase the strength of the composite material. All these phenomena cause relatively complex behaviour in cement-based composites at very low temperatures, and conclusions from experimental investigations are not entirely convergent.

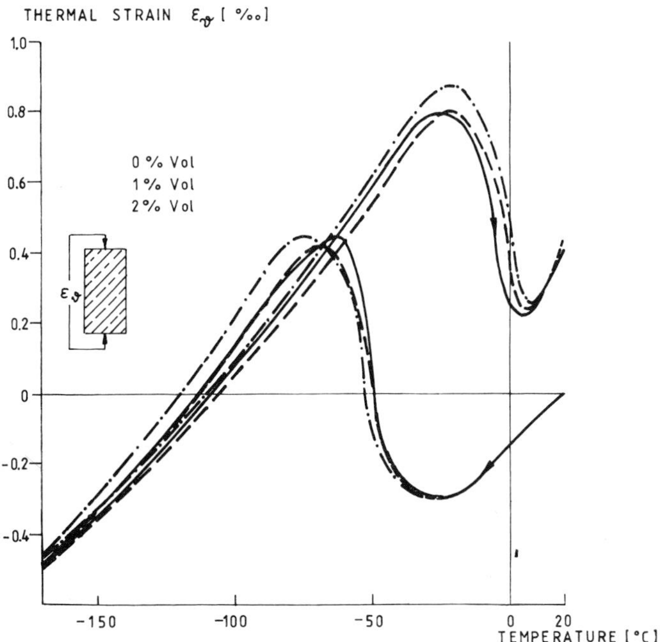

Figure 11.28 Thermal strain curves of specimens made of plain concrete and SFRC with blended Portland and blast furnace slag cement. (Reproduced with permission from Rostasy, F.S. and Sprenger, K.H., Strength and deformation of steel-fibre-reinforced concrete at very low temperatures; *International Journal of Cement Comp. and Lightweight Concrete*, **6**, pp. 47–51, published by Elsevier Science Publishers, 1984.) [11.110]

It is generally believed that the compressive strength of plain concretes increases at cryogenic temperatures and that increase is proportional to the moisture content, [11.108]. However, thermal cycling may cause damage to a material's structure leading to an appreciable decrease of strength.

Extensive testing of specimens made of structural lightweight concrete subjected to cycles of temperature between +20 °C and −85 °C was performed in [11.109]. It has been found that lightweight concretes of f_{c28} between 50 and 60 MPa behaved similarly to ordinary concretes, i.e. their sensibility to cooling cycles was related to their degree of water saturation – the higher the saturation the

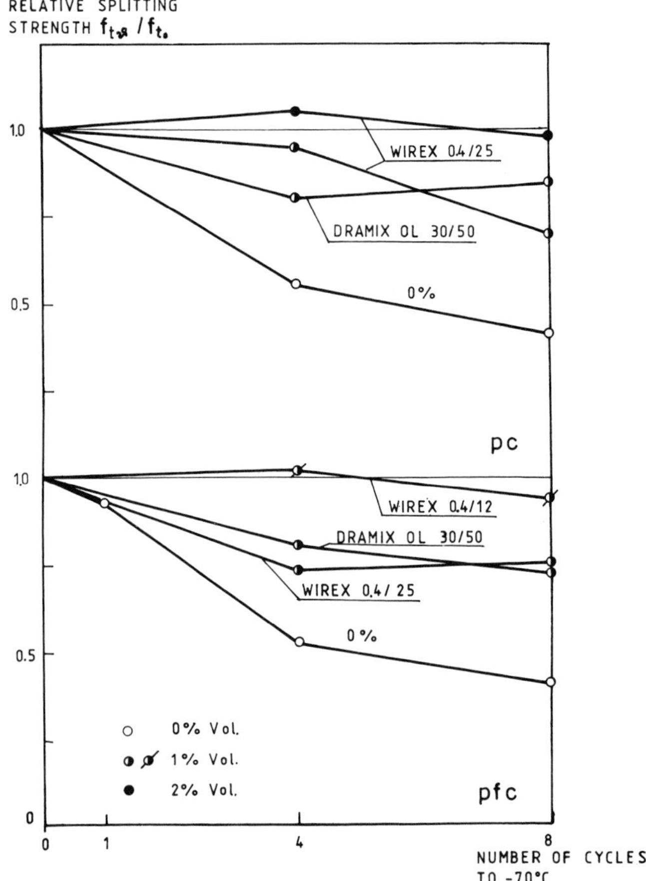

Figure 11.29 Relative splitting strength of specimens made of plain concrete and of SFRC after low temperature cycles, pc – Portland cement, pfc – blast furnace slag cement. (Reproduced with permission from Rostasy, F.S. and Sprenger, K.H., Strength and deformation of steel fibre-reinforced concrete at very low temperatures; *International Journal of Cement Comp. and Lightweight Concrete*, **6**, pp. 47–51, published by Elsevier Science Publishers, 1984.) [11.110]

more damage was observed to the material's structure. But in these kinds of material, evaporable and freezable water is stored in pores in the aggregate grains and the strength after cooling may be considerably diminished proportionally to the total moisture content.

Investigations with fibre-reinforcement were executed [11.110] in view of its application in the construction of the outer containment for liquefied natural gas (LNG). The specimens were tested at temperatures of $-170\,^{\circ}C$ and cycles between $+20$ and $-70\,^{\circ}C$ were also imposed. The influence of various volume fractions of Wirex fibre was examined together with applications of two kinds of cement – Portland cement and cement blended with blast furnace slag (up to 70%). No appreciable influence of fibre-reinforcement on thermal strain was observed, as shown in Figure 11.28; however, only one cooling cycle was applied. In tests under compression at different temperatures from $+20$ down to $-170\,^{\circ}C$ only a slight increase of strength and ultimate strain was observed for specimens

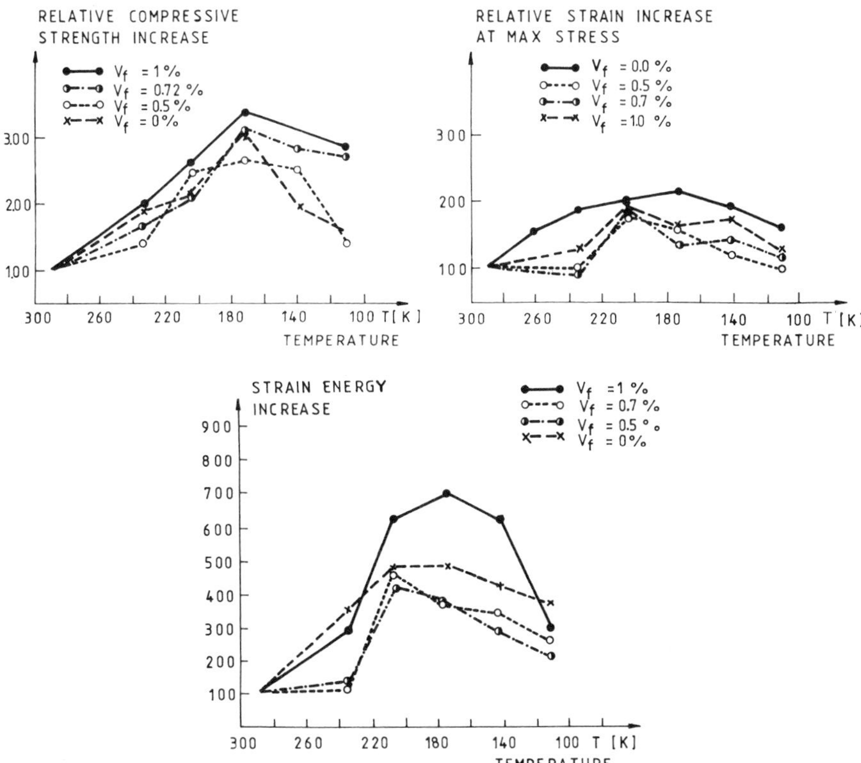

Figure 11.30 Relationships between test temperature and mechanical properties. a) compressive strength; b) strain at maximum stress; c) strain energy. (Reproduced from Burakiewicz, A. and Marshall, A.L., Compressive strength and the test methods for concrete at cryogenic temperatures; *Arch. of Civ. Eng.*, **33**(1), 1987.) [11.108]

reinforced with fibres. More important results of fibre-reinforcement were obtained in specimens subjected to several (up to eight) cycles of cooling prior to loading. As is presented in Figure 11.29 the specimens without fibres exhibited a clear decrease of tensile strength due to cooling cycles. Fibres used at 1% and 2% vol. reduced that decrease considerably. Also, in specimens subjected to axial compression an appreciable influence of fibre-reinforcement was observed.

In the investigation published in [11.108] specimens of plain and fibre concretes were subjected to compression at different temperatures down to −165 °C. The consistent method of testing specimens at very low temperatures was established and applied. The strength, strain at maximum stress and strain energy were recorded and analysed, Figure 11.30. It has been established that the effect of fibres is appreciable only if at least 0.7% vol. of fibres is added. However, a considerable decrease of all three mechanical parameters was observed at temperatures approaching −165 °C.

The above test results are a bit dispersed and concern particular cases of low temperature and test methods. Further research is needed before consistent conclusions and design recommendations may be formulated.

11.7 Transportation of liquids and gases in hardened composites

In hardened cement-based composites the transportation of liquids and gases through pore and microcrack systems plays a very important role in many processes like hydration of Portland cement, pozzolane effects of microfillers, corrosion of cement paste and reinforcement due to reaction with external factors, shrinkage and creep, etc. These processes are partly described in respective sections, cf. 4.1, 4.3, 6.5, 11.5. Only basic information is reiterated below concerning permeation and diffusion and liquids and gases based on [11.68] and other sources.

Permeation or pressure flow is due to external pressure which causes a flow of fluids or gases through systems of pores and microcracks. In the case of water permeability it may be described by Darcy's law as volume $V[\mathrm{m}^3]$ which passes in time $t[\mathrm{s}]$ through area $A[\mathrm{m}^2]$

$$V = K_w \frac{\Delta H}{l} At \qquad (11.14)$$

here: $\Delta H/l$ is hydraulic gradient [m/m] and K_w is coefficient of permeability [m/s], which may be related to concrete strength f_{c28},

$K_w = 10^{-(f_{c28}/9+8)}$, or to the water/cement ratio, $K_w = 10^{(-18+10(w/c))}$ for $0.4 < \mathrm{w/c} < 0.7$.

For practical calculations the permeability of concrete is considered as equal to that of hardened paste. In that assumption, the existence of microcracks and aggregate grains in concrete compensate each other for water flow. For higher concrete strength and low water/cement ratio the coefficient K_w and permeability itself decrease considerably. A further decrease may be expected for high and very high performance concretes with low values of water/cement ratio and with the extensive use of microfillers.

In the case of gas permeability equation 11.14 becomes:

$$V = K_g \frac{A}{l} \frac{(p_1 - p_2)}{\eta} \frac{p_m}{p} t \tag{11.15}$$

here: $(p_1 - p_2)$ – difference of pressures [N/m^2], p_m and p – mean and local pressure, η – gas viscosity [Ns/m^2]. For air and oxygen, $0.02 \cdot 10^{-16} < K < 2 \cdot 10^{-16}$ [m^2].

Diffusion when the motion of particles is caused by a difference of concentration is represented by Fick's first law. The respective formula proposed in [11.68] is derived in the following form for the amount of transported mass Q as function of difference of concentration $(c_1 - c_2)$

$$Q = D \frac{c_1 - c_2}{l} At \quad [g] \tag{11.16}$$

Here D may be calculated as function of f_{c28} and gas properties. For oxygen and carbon dioxide values of D are between 0.5×10^{-8} and 6×10^{-8} [m^2/s]. For chloride ions, D is between 1×10^{-12} and 10^{-12} [m^2/s] in Portland cement paste, and between 0.3×10^{-12} and 5×10^{-12} in blast furnace slag cement.

Capillary flow is described by Washburn's law [11.99]:

$V = \frac{r\gamma_L}{4d\mu} At \cos \vartheta$, here V is volume of fluid, r – capillary radius, γ_L – surface tension, d – depth of penetration, μ – viscosity of the fluid and ϑ – contact angle. Both γ_L and μ depend on temperature, for example the viscosity μ at +30 °C is about half of that at +5 °C. Also, the purity of the fluid is important and pore water is less fluid than distilled water, but admixtures may have some influence.

The above relations cannot be applied directly in calculations of the volume of gases or fluids which may pass through the element of composite material under consideration even if it was the intention of the authors to provide practical formulae for designers, cf. [11.69]. The formulae may only indicate parameters which enhance or reduce the transportation of a gas or fluid. In general, this depends on several parameters characterizing the transported medium, on pore and microcrack systems of material and on external conditions like concentration, pressure and temperature. For example, by decreasing the

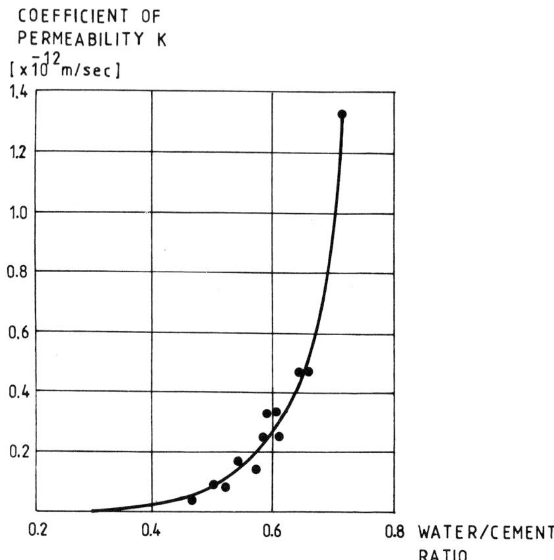

Figure 11.31 The effect of water/cement ratio on the permeability of mature cement paste. (Reproduced from Browne, R.D. and Baker, A.F., The performance of concrete in a marine environment; Applied Science Publishers, 1978.) [11.111]

water/cement ratio, considerable decrease of the coefficient of water permeability of Portland cement paste may obviously be expected, as is shown in Figure 11.31. Other measures enhancing the impermeability of a composite material would be the better cure of fresh mix to decrease capillaries and the application of micro-fillers.

Reinforcement with fibres may have different results with regard to permeability. Obviously, the control of cracking is better and transport through a system of cracks and microcracks may be reduced. In contrast, the introduction of fibres to the fresh mix usually increases its porosity.

A few remarks are needed as a reminder that all the processes considered develop in highly disordered media. High porosity does not necessarily mean high permeability, because only interconnected pores represent channels for the possible flow of gases and fluids. The relationships governing the flow are linear only within narrow limits and more often high non-linearity should be expected. A pore system may be considered as a system of objects which are not completely connected and a flow of a gas or a fluid is a process of percolation in which a clear threshold exists. This creates a separation between two situations – whether the system is permeable or not. The threshold is expressed by a certain percentage of open capillary pores. For further information on percolation processes in strongly disordered media the reader is referred to specialized papers and books, e.g. [11.112] or [11.113]

11.8 Accelerated testing

Methods for testing cement-based composites are examined in several sections together with other problems related to a material's composition and properties. Only questions concerning accelerated test methods are considered below.

The long-term behaviour of materials and their durability with respect to certain required performance levels for structures and buildings are forecast after experience, tests and observation over shorter periods of time. Results of observations in 50 or 100 years of exploitation are not available for modern composite materials. Even observations of a limited number of traditional materials like brick, wood and stone are partly irrelevant because present environmental and exploitation conditions did not exist before.

Three main kinds of tests of concrete-like composites are carried out:

1. real time observations of composite elements exposed to natural conditions with variation of particular factors according to climatic changes or exploitation cycles and with their synergetic effects;
2. real time tests in laboratory conditions where particular factors may act separately and their intensity corresponds to natural situations;
3. accelerated tests of specimens or elements subjected to special conditions in which after a shorter time the results obtained are considered to be equivalent to natural long-term exposure.

The traditionally accepted basic test for concrete after 28 days is often not sufficient because of rapidity of execution of modern structures, and the accelerated methods are aimed at quicker methods to evaluate this standard value and to estimate long-term behaviour.

Real time tests are necessary to understand long-term behaviour, but appreciable results of ageing cannot be expected for a few years. However, research programmes lasting ten or more years are rare for organizational and economic reasons. That is why accelerated tests are useful. They are composed of different actions or cycles of actions which should produce measurable and appreciable effects after a certain number of hours, days or months. Typically, accelerated tests do not exceed a few months of steady action or a certain number of cycles is imposed.

According to standard recommendations [11.114] three methods are applied to concretes:

1. in the warm water method the concrete specimens are cured in water at $35 \pm 3\,°C$ and tested at age of 24 hours;
2. in the boiling water method the specimens after a curing over 23 hours in moisture at $21 \pm 6\,°C$ are put to boiling water for another 3.5 hours and tested at age of 28.5 hours;
3. in the autogenous method the specimens are subjected to heat due to the hydration of cement in a completely insulated environment over 48 hours.

Various kinds of actions are applied in accelerated tests of cement-based composites, [11.115]:

- freezing and thawing cycles in clear water or in water with a de-icing agent which simulates day and night temperature variations in winter for bridges and road overlays;
- soak and dry cycles with sea water or other aggressive water solutions corresponding to real conditions of exploitation while drying can simulate periods of exposure to sunshine;
- warm and cool cycles with higher temperatures imitating natural exposure, e.g. of refractory materials;
- exposure to highly concentrated gases or liquids, e.g. pure CO_2 in accelerated carbonation tests, immersion in hot water, etc.

The sequence of the various treatments in consecutive cycles should in principle simulate natural exposure whilst accelerating its effects in a standardized way.

No single accelerated test can fully simulate the full range of ageing processes and therefore a series of tests is usually executed of a different character, after identification of the main ageing mechanism which may be accelerated considerably in that way.

It is difficult to determine a relationship between accelerated tests and the duration of natural exposure. The interpretation of accelerated tests to determine both 24 hour strength and long-term strength is difficult. However, many attempts are published in which a safe life cycle is estimated from the results of accelerated tests. For example, it has been proposed that exposure to pure CO_2 with a ratio of concentration equal to 3 000 may give the same ratio of acceleration, so that exposure during 36 days is equivalent to 300 years, [11.86].

Because the simulation of natural processes is far from perfect and all these forecasts are uncertain, it is essential to combine accelerated tests with real time observations. Real test results even after a relatively short time may help considerably when calibrating a forecast based on accelerated tests.

Standardized accelerated tests are useful for carrying-out comparative tests of different materials. It is easier to determine which material is better than to forecast its effective durability. For example, it is believed that freeze–thaw tests as imposed by ASTM (cf. Section 11.5.3) could ensure good durability of cement-based materials in natural conditions during their lifetime in the climate of North America and Central Europe even as the validity of simulation of natural conditions is doubtful.

Particular tests for durability of fibre-reinforced composites are not yet available, [11.117]. Basic requirements may be tested in the same way as for plain concretes; however, for example, questions concerning compatibility of fibres and matrices should be tested by special methods [11.117].

High and Very High Performance Concretes (HPC and VHPC) should be tested according to special methods. For these materials, it is particularly important to know, well in advance, their strength and other properties at a given age. On many occasions, structural elements are subjected to partial loading at a very early stage, e.g. after three or seven days. Different formulae should be used in the accelerated methods than for ordinary concretes, because the development of strength, Young's modulus and other properties is different over time. Such methods are not yet fully operational; however, several proposals are already published, for example in [11.118].

References

11.1. Abrams, D.A. (1917) Effects of rate of application of load on the compressive strength of concrete, *Amer. Soc. for Testing of Materials*, Proc. 17, part II, 364–77.

11.2. Watstein, D. (1953) Effect of straining rate on the compressive strength and elastic properties of concrete. *J. of the ACI*, **49**, 729–44.

11.3. Rasch, C. (1958) Stress–strain diagrams of concrete obtained by constant rates of strain, in Proc. *RILEM Symp. on the Influence of Time on the Strength and Deformation of Concrete*, Munich.

11.4. Mindess, S. (1985) Rate of loading effects on the fracture of cementitious materials, in *Application of Fracture Mechanics to Cementitious Composites*, NATO Adv. Res. Workshop, (ed. S.P. Shah), Northwestern Univ., 1984, Martinus Nijhoff, Dordrecht, 617–36.

11.5. Newman, K. (1964) Concrete control tests as measures of the properties of concrete, in Proc. *Symp. on Concrete Quality*, Cem. and Concr. Ass., London, 120–38.

11.6. Sierakowski, R.L. (1984) Dynamic effect in concrete materials, as [11.4], 535–57.

11.7. Reinhardt, W.H. (1982) Concrete under impact loading. Tensile strength and bond, *Heron*, **27**(3), pp. 48.

11.8. Green, H. (1964) Impact strength of concrete. *Proc. Inst. Civ. Eng.*, **28**, July, London, 383–96.

11.9. Rüsch, H. (1960) Researches toward a general flexural theory for structural concrete. *Journ. of the ACI*, **57**, 1–28.

11.10. Wittmann, F.H. (1984) Influence of time on crack formation and failure of concrete, as [11.4], 593–615.

11.11. Suaris, W. and Shah, S.P. (1983) Properties of concrete subjected to impact. *J. of Structural Engineering*, **109**, 1727–41.

11.12. Mihashi, H. and Izumi, M. (1977) A stochastic theory for concrete fracture, Cem. and Concrete Research, **7**, 411–22.

11.13. Ross, C.A., Thompson, P.Y. and Tedesco, J.W. (1989) Split–Hopkinson pressure-bar tests on concrete and mortar in tension and compression. *ACI Materials Journal*, **86**(5), 475–89.

11.14. Ansari, F. and Yang, S.X. (1988) Computer assisted instrumented impact testing of reinforced concrete. *Experimental Techniques*, **12**(11), 18–21.

11.15. Bentur, A., Mindess, S. and Banthia, N. (1986) The behaviour of concrete under impact loading: experimental procedures and method of analysis. *Materials and Structures*, **19**, 371–8.

11.16. Radomski, W. (1981) Application of the rotating impact machine for testing fibre-reinforced concrete. *Int. Journ. of Cem. Comp. and Lightwt. Concr.*, **3**(1), 3–12.

11.17. Glinicki, M.A. (1992) Influence of the rate of loading on the strength and deformation of cement matrix composites (in Polish), Doctoral Thesis, IFTR Report 1/1992 Warsaw.

11.18. Birkimer, D.L. and Lindemann, R. (1971) Dynamic tensile strength of concrete materials. *J. of ACI*, January, 47–9.

11.19. Brooks, J.J. and Samariae, N.H. (1989) Influence of rate of stressing on tensile stress–strain behaviour of concrete, in *Fracture of Concrete and Rock*, (eds S.P. Shah, S.E. Swartz, B. Barr), Elsevier Applied Science, London, 397–408.

11.20. Glinicki, M.A. (1989) Loading rate sensitivity of concrete-like composites under tensile loading, in *Brittle Matrix Composites 2*, (eds A.M. Brandt and I.H. Marshall), Elsevier Applied Science, London, 559–67.

11.21. Ross, C.A. (1990) Fracture of concrete at high strain-rate, in *NATO Advanced Research Workshop on Toughening Mechanisms in Quasi-Brittle Materials*, (ed. S.P. Shah), NSF, Northwestern University, Evanston, USA, 571–89.

11.22. Tinic, C. and Brühweiler, E. (1985) Effect of compressive loads on the tensile strength of concrete at high strain rates. *Int. Journ. of Cem Comp. and Lightwt. Concr.*, **7**(2), 103–8.

11.23. Zielinski, A.J. (1982) *Fracture of concrete and mortar under uniaxial impact tensile loading*, Delft Univ. Press, Delft.

11.24. Suaris, W. and Shah, S.P. (1984) Test method for impact resistance of fiber reinforced concrete, in Proc. Int. Symp. *Fiber Reinforced Concrete*, SP81, ACI Detroit, 247–60.

11.25. Robins, P. J. and Calderwood, R.W. (1978) Explosive testing of fibre-reinforced concrete. *Concrete*, **12**(1), 26–8.

11.26. Radomski, W. (1991) *Fibre Reinforced Concrete*, Kanazawa University, Kanazawa.

11.27. Talreja, R. (1987) *Fatigue of Composite Materials*, Technom. Publ. Co., Lancaster.

11.28. Neville, A.M. (1973) *Properties of Concrete*, Pitman Publishing, London.

11.29. Mindess, S. and Young, J.F. (1981) *Concrete*, Prentice-Hall, Englewood Cliffs, New Jersey.

11.30. Butler, J.F. (1989) The performance of concrete containing high proportions of steel-fibers with particular reference to rapid flexural and fatigue loadings, in *Fiber Reinforced Cements and Concretes, Recent Developments*, (eds R.N. Swamy and B. Barr), Elsevier Science Publ., London, 544–52.

11.31. Batson, G., Ball, C., Bailey, L. *et al.* (1972) Flexural fatigue strength of steel-fiber reinforced concrete beams. *J. of the ACI*, **69**(11), 673–7.

11.32. Bennett, E.W. and Raju, N.K. (1971) Cumulative fatigue damage of plain concrete in compression, in Proc. of the Southampton 1969 Civil Engineering Materials Conference, (ed. M. Te'eni), Wiley, Chichester, 1089–102.

11.33. Ramakrishnan, V. and Lokvik, B.J. (1992) Flexural fatigue strength of fiber-reinforced concretes, in Proc. Int. RILEM/ACI Workshop *High Performance Fiber Reinforced Cement Composites*, Mainz 1991, (eds W.H. Reinhardt and A.E. Naaman), Spon/Chapman and Hall, London, 217–87.

11.34. Romualdi, J.P. (1968) The static cracking stress and fatigue strength of concrete reinforced with short pieces of thin steel wire, in Proc. of Int. Conf. *The Structure of Concrete*, 1965, disc 204–6, Cem. and Concrete Assoc., London, 190–201.

11.35. Sąsiadek, S. (1980) Fatigue strength of concrete with small aggregate grains and steel-fibre-reinforcement (in Polish), PhD Thesis, Cracow Techn. Univ., Cracow.

11.36. Sąsiadek, S. (1991) Fatigue strength of concrete with limestone aggregate, in Proc. Int. Symp. *Brittle Matrix Composites 3*, (eds A.M. Brandt and I.H. Marshall), Elsevier Applied Science, London, 148–53.

11.37. Hashin, Z. and Rotem, A. (1973) A fatigue failure criterion for fiber-reinforced materials. *J. of Comp. Mat.*, **47**, 448–64.

11.38. Rotem, A. and Hashin, Z. (1976) Fatigue failure of angle ply laminates. *AIAA J.*, **14**(7), 868–72.

11.39. Wu, G.Y., Shivaraj, S.K. and Ramakrishnan, V. (1989) Flexural fatigue strength, endurance limits and impact strength of fiber-reinforced refractory concretes, in *Fiber Reinforced Cements and Concretes, Recent Developments*, (eds R.N. Swamy and B. Barr), Elsevier Science Publishers, London, 261–73.

11.40. de Larrard, F. and Malier, Y. (1990) Propriétés constructives des bétons à très hautes performances: de la micro à la macrostructure, in *Les Bétons à Hautes Performances*, (ed. Y. Malier), Presses de LCPC, Paris, 107–38.

11.41. L'Hermite, R. (1957) Que savons-nous de la déformation plastique et du fluage du béton?, *Ann. ITBTP*, **10**(117), 777–810.

11.42. Guyon, Y. (1958) *Béton précontraint*, 3rd ed., Eyrolles, Paris.

11.43. L'Hermite, R. (1955) *Idées actuelles sur la technologie du béton.* Docum. Tech. Bât. Trav. Publ., Paris.

11.44. ACI (1991) Com. 209 – Designing for Effects of Creep, Shrinkage. Temperature in Concrete Structures. *American Concrete Institute SP 27*, Detroit, 51–93.

11.45. Auperin, M., de Larrard, F., Richard, P. and Acker, P. (1989) Retrait et fluage de bétons à hautes performances. Influence de l'âge au chargement. *Ann. de l'ITBTP*, no. 474, May, 49–75.

11.46. Cadoret, G. and Courtel, C. Reprise en sous-oeuvre en B.H.P. la Grande Mosquée Hassan II, as [11.40], 371–387.

11.47. Malmberg, B. and Skarendahl, Å. (1978) Method of studying the cracking of fibre concrete under restrained shrinkage, in Proc. RILEM Symp. *Testing and Test Methods of Fibre Cement Composites*, Constr. Press, London, 173–9.

11.48. Swamy, R.N. and Theodorakopoulos, D.D. (1979) Flexural creep behaviour of fibre-reinforced cement composites. *Int. J. of Cement Composites*, **1**(1), May, 37–48.

11.49. Fukuchi, T., Ohama, Y., Nishimura, T. and Suguhara, T. (1980) Effects of steel-fiber-reinforcement on drying shrinkage of mortar. *Trans. Jap. Concr. Inst.*, **2**, 195–202.

11.50. Edgington, J., Hannant, D.J. and Williams, R.I.T. (1974) Steel-fibre-reinforced concrete. Build. Res. Establ., CP 69, Garston, England, pp. 17.

11.51. Balaguru, P. and Ramakrishnan, V. (1980) Properties of fibre-reinforced concrete: workability, behaviour under long-term loading and air-void characteristics. *ACI Materials Journ.*, May–June, 189–96.

11.52. Gunasekaran, M., Ichikawa, Y. and Dunlap, A.B. (1974) On the properties and behaviour of high early strength lightweight polymer impregnated concrete reinforced with alkali resistant glassfibres, Fibre Reinforced Concrete. *ACI SP No. 44*, Detroit, 265–85.

11.53. Building Research Establishment (1976) A study of the properties of Cem-FIL/OPC composites. Current Paper, CP 38. Garston, pp. 14.

11.54. Wörner, J.D. and Müller, M. (1992) Design and application of polyacrylonitride fibre concrete, as [11.33], 115–26.

11.55. Neville, A.M., Dilger, W.H. and Brooks, J.J. (1983) *Creep of Plain and Structural Concrete*, Construction Press, Lancaster.

11.56. Acker, P. and de Larrard, F. (1990) Fluage des bétons à hautes et à très hautes performances, as [11.40], 139–50.

11.57. Brandt, A.M. (1965) Testing of concrete creep in non-reinforced beam subjected to bending (in Polish). *Archives of Civ. Eng.*, **11**(1), Warsaw, 87–93.

11.58. Glanville, W.H. (1933) Creep of concrete under load. *The Structural Engineer*, **11**(2), 57–73.

11.59. Davis, R.E., Davis, H.E. and Brown, E.H. (1937) Plastic flow and volume changes of concrete. *Proc. ASTM*, **37**(II), 317–30.

11.60. Le Camus, B. (1947) Recherche expérimentale sur la déformation du béton et du béton armé, *Ann. ITBTP*, no. 32, 33, 34.

11.61. McHenry, D. (1943) A new aspect of creep in concrete and its application to design. *Proc. ASTM*, **43**, 1069–84.

11.62. Arutyunian, N.K. (1966) *Some Problems in the Theory of Creep in Concrete*. Pergamon Press, London.

11.63. L'Hermite, R. (1960) Volume changes of concrete. Proc. 4th Int. Symp. on the *Chemistry of Cement*, part I, Washington DC, 659–94.

11.64. US Bureau of Reclamation (1956) Creep of concrete under high intensity loading, Concrete Lab. Report No. C-820, Denver, Co.

11.65. Swamy, R.N., Theodorakopoulos, D.D. and Stavrides, H. (1977) Shrinkage and creep characteristics of glassfibre reinforced cement composites. Proc. Int Congress on *Glassfibre Reinforced Cement*, Brighton, 75–96.

11.66. Brandt, A.M. and Hebda, L. (1989) Creep in SFRC element under long-term eccentric compressive loading, in Proc. Int. Conf. *Composite Structures*, (ed. I.H. Marshall), Elsevier Applied Science, London, 743–54.

11.67. Bijen, J. and van den Plas, C. (1992) Polymer modified glassfibre reinforced gypsum, as [11.33], 100–14.

11.68. FIP–CEB (1990) Model Code 1990, Comité Euro-International du Béton, March, Lausanne.

11.69. Gardner, N.J. and Zhao, J.W. (1991) Mechanical properties of concrete for calculating longterm deformations, in Proc. Second Canadian Symp. on *Cement and Concrete*, (ed. S. Mindess), Vancouver, Univ. of British Columbia, 150–9.

11.70. Fouré, B. (1985) Étude expérimentale de la résistance du béton sous contrainte soutenue, Ann. de l'ITBTP, 435, June, 1–21.

11.71. Fouré, B. (1990) Quelques propriétés mécaniques. as [11.40], 93–105.

11.72. Coutinho, A.S. (1977) A contribution to the mechanism of concrete creep. *Materials and Structures*, **10**(55), 3–16.

11.73. Cook, D.J. and Chindaprasirt, P. (1980) Influence of loading history upon compressive properties of concrete. *Mag. of Concr. Res.*, **32**(111), 89–100.

11.74. Briggs, A., Bowen, D.H. and Kollek, J. (1974) Mechanical properties and durability of carbon-fibre reinforced cement composites, in Proc. Int. Conf. *Carbon Fibres, their Place in Modern Technology*, The Plastic Institute, London.

11.75. Proctor, B.A. (1971) Sources of weakness in reinforcing fibres. *Composites*, **2**(2), 85–92.

11.76. ASTM Recommended Practice for Increasing Durability of Building Construction Against Water-Induced Damage, ASTM E241–90.

11.77. BSI (1992) British Standard: Guide to Durability of buildings and building elements, products and components, BS 7543: 1992.

11.78. Roper, H. (1989) Durability aspects in maintenance, repair and rehabilitation, in Proc. IABSE Symp. *Durability of Structures*, 57/2, Lisbon, IABSE, 651–62.

11.79. ASTM (1982) Standard Practice for Microscopical Determination of Air-Void Content and Parameters of the Air-Void System in Hardened Concrete. ASTM C457–82a.

11.80. Saucier, F., Pigeon, M. and Cameron, G. (1991) Air-void stability, Part IV: Temperature, general analysis and performance index. *ACI Materials Journal*, **88**(1), 25–36.

11.81. Gagné, R., Pigeon, M. and Aïtcin, P.C. (1990) Durabilité au gel des bétons de haute performances mécaniques. *Materials and Structures*, **23**(134), 103–9.

11.82. CEB (1989) (1992) Durable Concrete Structures. Design Guide. Bulletin d'Information CEB No. 182 and No. 183, May, Th. Telford, London.

11.83. Pigeon, M. (1989) La durabilité au gel du béton. *Materials and Structures*, **22**(127), 3–14.

11.84. Pigeon, M., Gagné, R. and Foy, C. (1987) Critical air void spacing factor for low water-cement ratio concretes with and without condensed silica fume. *Cement and Concrete Research*, **17**(6), 896–906.

11.85. Polish Standard (1989) Ordinary Concrete, PN-88/B-06250.

11.86. Lévy, Ch. (1990) A propos de la carbonation accélérée des bétons: comparaison béton ordinaire – béton hautes performances du pont de Joigny, as [11.40], 203–10.

11.87. Nischer, P. (1984) Influence of concrete quality and environment on carbonation, in Proc. of RILEM Sem. *Durability of Concrete Structures under Normal Outdoor Exposure*, Hannover, 26–29 March, Univ. of Hannover, Hannover, 231–8.

11.88. Schiessl, P. (1983) in Proc. CEB–RILEM Int. Workshop *Durability of Concrete Structures*, May, Copenhagen, Bull. d'Information CEB, no. 152, Lausanne.

11.89. Hilsdorf, H.K., Kropp, J. and Günter, M. (1984) Carbonation, pore structure and durability, as [11.87], 182–96.

11.90. Lambotte, H. (1984) Survey of rules intended to guarantee durability, as [11.87], 4–8.

11.91. Soroka, I. and Jaegerman, C. (1984) Deterioration and durability of concrete in hot climate, as [11.87], 52–60.

11.92. Detwiler, R.J., Kjellsen, K.O. and Gjørv, O.E. (1991) Resistance to chloride intrusion of concrete cured at different temperatures. *ACI Materials Journal*, **88**(1), 19–24.

11.93. Gram, H.E., Persson, H. and Skarendahl, Å. (1984) Natural Fibre Concrete, SAREC Report, Stockholm, pp. 139.

11.94. Schneider, M. (1982) *Verhalten von Beton bei hohen Temperaturen*. Deutscher Auschuss für Stahlbeton, h. 337, Berlin.

11.95. Skinner, B.J. (1966) Thermal expansion, *Handbook of Physical Constants*, sec. 6, Geol. Soc. of America, **97**, 75–96.

11.96. Kosiorek, M., Pogorzelski, J.A., Laskowska, Z. and Pilich, K. (1988) *Fire Resistance of Building Structures* (in Polish), Arkady, Warsaw.

11.97. Dougill, J.W. (1968) Some effects of thermal volume changes on the properties and behaviour of concrete, in Proc. Int. Conf. *Structure of Concrete*, Cement and Concr. Ass., London.

11.98. Mitchell, L.J. (1953) Thermal expansion tests on aggregate, neat cements and concretes. *Proc. ASTM*, **53**, 963–77.

11.99. Marshall, A.L. (1990) *Marine Concrete*, Blackie, Glasgow and London.
11.100. Neville, A.M. and Brooks, J.J (1987) *Concrete technology*, Longman Scientific & Technical, New York.
11.101. Kordina, K. and Meyer-Ottens, C. (1979) *Beton Brandschutz Handbuch*, Beton-Verlag, Düsseldorf.
11.102. Zoldner, N.G. (1960) Effect of high temperatures on concrete incorporating different aggregates. *Proc. ASTM*, **60**, 1087–108.
11.103. Purkiss, J.A. (1987) Thermal expansion of steel-fibre-reinforced concrete up to 800 °C, in Proc. 4th Int. Conf. on *Composite Structures*, Paisley College, (ed. I.H. Marshall), Elsevier Applied Science, London and New York, 404–15.
11.104. Purkiss, J.A. (1984) Steel-fibre-reinforced concrete at elevated temperatures. *Int. J. Cement Composites and Lightweight Concrete*, **6**(3), 179–84.
11.105. Purkiss, J.A. (1988) Toughness measurements on steel-fibre concrete at elevated temperatures. *Int. J. Cement Composites and Lightweight Concrete*, **10**, 39–47.
11.106. Purkiss, J.A. (1985) Some mechanical properties of glass reinforced concrete at elevated temperatures, in Proc. 3rd Int. Conf. on *Composite Structures*, Paisley College, (ed. I.H. Marshall), Elsevier Applied Science, London and New York, 230–41.
11.107. Marshall, A.L. (1982) Cryogenic concrete. *Cryogenics*, **21**(11), 555–65.
11.108. Burakiewicz, A. and Marshall, A.L. (1987) Compressive strength and the test methods for concrete at cryogenic temperatures. *Archives of Civil Engineering*, **33**(1), Warsaw, 9–22.
11.109. Rostasy, F.R. and Pusch, U. (1987) Strength and deformation of lightweight concrete of variable moisture content at very low temperatures. *Int. J. Cement Composites and Lightweight Concrete*, **9**(1), 3–17.
11.110. Rostasy, F.S. and Sprenger, K.H. (1984) Strength and deformation of steel-fibre-reinforced concrete at very low temperature. *Int. J. Cement Composites and Lightweight Concrete*, **6**(1), 47–51.
11.111. Browne, R.D. and Baker, A.F. (1978) The performance of concrete in a marine environment, in *Developments in Concrete Technology 1*, (ed. F.D. Lydon), Appl. Sc. Publ. London.
11.112. Guyon, E. and Roux, S. (1987) Les matériaux hétérogènes. *La Recherche*, **18**(191), 1050–58.
11.113. Mandelbrot, B.B. (1982) *The fractal geometry of nature*, Freeman, San Francisco.
11.114. ASTM (Philadelphia) Accelerated curing and testing of concrete, ASTM C684.
11.115. RILEM (1985) Durability of Fibre Reinforced Cement Composites, Seminar of RILEM TC 49-TFR, Sheffield, April, (unpublished contributions).
11.116. Johnston, C.D. (1991) Testing fibre-reinforced concretes, in Proc. 1st Canadian University-Industry Workshop on *Fibre Reinforced Concrete*, Univ. Laval, Quebec, 31–43.
11.117. Bentur, A. and Mindess, S. (1990) *Fibre Reinforced Cementitious Composites*, Elsevier Applied Science, London and New York.
11.118. Y. Malier (ed.) (1990) Proc. Sem. *Les Bétons à Hautes Performances*, Cachan Juin, Presses de l'ENPC, Paris.

12 Design of cement-based composites

12.1 Requirements imposed by the conditions of execution

The main requirement formulated in a material's design beside its final properties is appropriate workability for all necessary operations during the preparation and placing of the fresh mix. In the initial stage all cement-based composites behave as more or less viscous fluids and this stage lasts usually for up to approximately 2 hours. During that time as a result of hydration processes the fresh mix is continually transformed into a solid. The properties in the liquid state are essential for easy mixing, handling and proper placing of the fresh mix. The general term workability is translated into other terms describing particular requirements – flowability, placeability, pumpability, finishability, etc. The workability may also be defined by the amount of energy necessary for complete compaction of the fresh mix.

The material's behaviour in the fresh stage may be represented by different rheological models in which shear stress and displacements are related. Two of these models are described below.

According to the Newton model shear stress τ is related to the coefficient of viscosity η and to the rate of shear γ by the following equation, $\tau = \eta\dot{\gamma}$.

This is the model of an ideal fluid and even fresh cement paste behaves in a different way than that, due to many factors, e.g. attraction between cement particles in a relatively dense suspension.

The Bingham model allows for an initial shear stress τ_o which represents a threshold before any displacement may occur, $\tau = \tau_o + \mu\dot{\gamma}$.

Two constants τ_o – yield value and μ – plastic viscosity, characterize the viscous fluid considered. The Bingham model is used to describe cement matrix behaviour with satisfactory results. It is combined with thixotropic effects in which the apparent viscosity is decreasing with shear stress application. Both the Newton and Bingham models are presented in Figure 12.1. Several more complicated models exist in which other factors are considered.

The selection of an appropriate model is made, not only according to its ability to represent experimental results, but also to its simplicity. The properties of cement paste are not the only factors determining the behaviour of cement-based composites – concretes, mortars, fibre concretes, etc. Other components of the fresh mix, their volume fractions and properties are also important. That is why for practical consideration it is not necessary to use very complicated

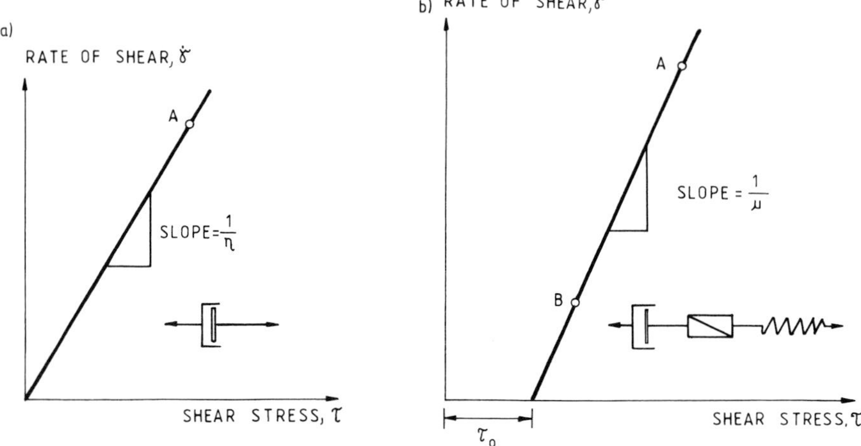

Figure 12.1 Two simple rheological models used for fresh cement paste. a) Newton model; b) Bingham model.

models for the cement paste. For the most detailed description of linear and non-linear rheological models the reader is referred to specialized manuals, e.g. [12.1], [12.2] and to the classic treatise [12.3].

The appropriate behaviour of the fresh mix is obtained in the material's design by selection of its composition (cf. Section 12.3) and particularly by application of admixtures (cf. Section 4.3). Then, the workability of the fresh mix is controlled and possibly corrected on site.

Workability is considered in the mix design by also taking into account methods of execution – concrete may be batched and mixed on site or in a precast plant, may be delivered on site from a plant as a ready-mixed concrete and may be mixed during transportation in special trucks.

As measures of workability of the fresh mix several different tests are proposed but each of them gives a certain indication which is not comparable with the others. The slump test and the Vebe test only give single values by which the mix is characterized, in millimetres and seconds, respectively. Therefore, nothing more complicated than the Newton model may be used. More serious tests are carried out on various types of coaxial cylinder viscometers, which are basically composed of two cylinders. The space between them is filled with the liquid under examination (Figure 12.2). The external cylinder is rotated and the movement is transferred through the liquid to the internal cylinder, where the torque is measured. The analysis of the results allows both constants in the Bingham equation to be determined. Detailed descriptions of similar tests are available in every manual for concrete technology and are not therefore given here. It is sufficient to mention that there are serious shortcomings for every test of that kind related to any form of simplification and limits of

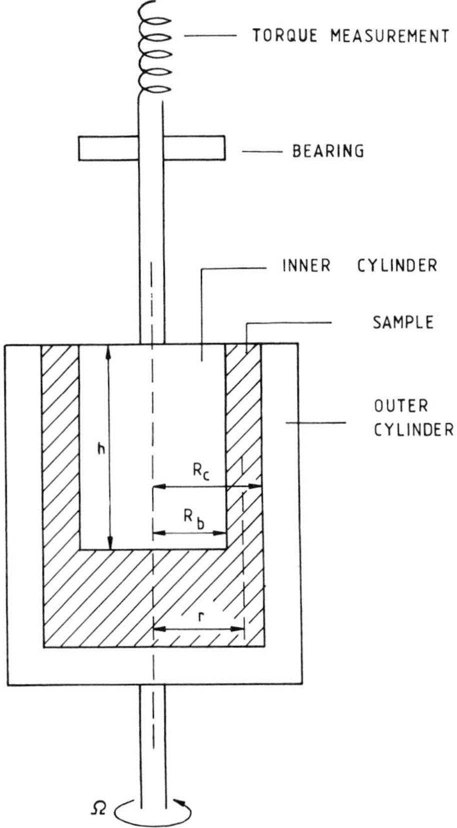

Figure 12.2 Scheme of a coaxial cylinders rheometer. (Reproduced with permission from Tattersall, G.H. and Banfill, P.F.G., *The Rheology of Fresh Concrete*; Published by Pitman, 1983.) [12.1]

applicability. For example, very fluid and very stiff mixes cannot be tested and compared with valid results. On the other hand, complex tests are more suitable for advanced laboratories and even in that case only simplified results may be expected. Both the Abrams cone, Vebe test and other similar tests are therefore used frequently, mainly for their simplicity and repeatability of results. The required workability is expressed as minimum slump, maximum Vebe time, or any other measure.

The slump test is one of the most popular, but its applicability to very liquid mixes with superplasticizers is doubtful. Special measures of workability may be necessary when pumpability, finishability, improved resistance to segregation or other features are required. Estimation 'by eye' given by an experienced practitioner may be also valid.

In the case of fibre-reinforced composites a special measure of workability was proposed by [12.4] called inverted slump cone. A standard Abrams cone is suspended upside down and filled with test material without any compaction. The internal vibrator is activated and the bottom cover of the cone is removed. Then the time of out flow of the material is recorded which is usually between 10 and 30 seconds. This method is still in use; however, it is subjected to some criticisms. Another method dealing with the flowability of the fresh mix with dispersed fibres is proposed by Laboratoire des Ponts et Chaussées in France, cf. Section 12.4.

It has been observed that with high fibre content both τ_o and μ are increased, while the length of the fibres only influences the plastic viscosity μ, [12.1]. The main factor however is the amount of dispersed fibres (cf. Chapter 5) when ordinary technology is applied. For higher fibre content non-conventional methods of placing the fresh mix in the forms like SIFCON are necessary, cf. Section 14.2.4.

Appropriate workability should ensure easy and correct placing of the fresh mix in the forms, without excessive bleeding and segregation. The workability should be maintained over certain time, e.g. one hour, which is needed for necessary transportation and operations on the site.

All mix components contribute to final workability. Large grains reduce the volume of voids and consumption of the cement paste and consequently improve the economy of the mix's composition. In many cases the continuous sieve curve is the best solution, [12.5], but the standard regulations may also be satisfied with a step sieve curve, i.e. one composed only of a few selected fractions of coarse aggregate and without others.

The voids between coarse aggregate grains are reduced by the spherical shape of grains which are also more easily compacted. The general condition imposed on the aggregate grading is the minimum of voids, i.e. the maximum density. The small particles in the aggregate composition fill the voids but increase cement and water consumption. The smallest particles of microfillers like silica fume or fly ash have a different influence, as described in Section 4.3.

The simplest way to improve workability, by the addition of water, causes considerable loss of strength. The excess of water precludes high strength and high performance in general. It is therefore necessary to maintain the amount of water as low as possible, and there is sometimes a conflict between the amount of water which should be kept as prescribed for the required strength and the spontaneous trend on the site to add water for easier placing. The designed composition must be maintained and controlled.

The behaviour of the fresh mix is improved by application of air-entraining agents and water-reducing admixtures, the latter exist and have been known in consecutive generations as plasticizers or superplasticizers. The mechanisms of increasing the flow of the fresh mix are based on the formation of a kind of double layer around each cement particle which facilitates reciprocal displacements for which less water is needed. A similar role has interparticle attraction forces decreasing. There are new superplasticizers containing reactive polymers which allow the slump of the fresh mix to be maintained at the range of approximately 200 mm over a 60 minute period. Here, not only are the properties of the cement paste of importance, but also the amount of paste. The effects obtained may be enhanced in a classic way by mechanical vibration, but flowing concrete is also used, e.g. for self-levelling of slabs.

Considering the behaviour of the fresh mix in the context of the Bingham model it should be mentioned that the superplasticizers mostly decrease the yield value τ_o and air-entrainers decrease the plastic viscosity μ.

A very important condition to be satisfied in the mix design is the maximum size of aggregate grains which must be related to the dimensions of elements to be cast and to the density of reinforcement.

12.2 Requirements imposed on hardened material

The requirements imposed by structural applications and relating to the properties of the hardened material concern basically compressive and tensile strength, frost resistance, impact strength, etc. The mechanical properties determine the dimensions of the structural elements and also a conflict may be specified between the requirement of high strength and the difficulties of obtaining it with given components and in given conditions *in situ* or in a precast factory. It should be mentioned that the requirement of high strength should be accompanied by a system of frequent controls at different stages – quality of components, composition of the mix, methods of placing and compaction, cure and properties of hardened material.

The strength at an early age is often specified for reasons of serviceability or economy. Special requirements formulated for high performance materials are described in more detail in Section 14.5.

Replacement of Portland cement by natural or artificial pozzolans reduces the heat of hydration and also the unit price of concrete. However, it slows down the process of hardening and the early strength of the material is sometimes lower.

Durability is another requirement which is imposed on the hardened material. This means that its behaviour during its known service life and in given conditions should satisfy imposed limits. Durability is reduced to the maintenance cost and for many structural applications it is as important as the strength; both requirements often can be satisfied simultaneously, cf. Section 11.5. In the design of the mix the need for durability means a requirement for high density and impermeability of the hardened composite and of a high resistance against cracking.

The compressive strength which is considered in this chapter and presents a basis for mechanical characterization is the so-called characteristic strength. In the structural design another notion is applied known as design strength which is calculated from the characteristic strength taking into account assumptions concerning the general format of structural design. For all problems related to the design strength the reader is referred to manuals for structural design and verification of reliability.

12.3 Other requirements and methodology of design

Economic conditions, understood as design requirements, concern the specific cost of the components and labour, all foreseeable maintenance costs, as well as the possible cost of destruction. The technical requirements should be satisfied in an economical way and this condition should be understood in a general sense. It is, therefore, necessary to take into account that better quality of components and higher level of execution will increase the specific cost of the material, but probably also the quality of the product, i.e. the strength and durability of the structure will be also higher. The cost of the components is certainly the easiest to calculate and there is often a trend towards making economies on the consumption of the most expensive component – it may be the Portland cement or the fibres. In a correct calculation of the total cost it appears that the expenses for maintenance of the structure in its life time may be of similar importance.

Other more complex requirements like the outward aspect of the structure or resistance against particular external factors may be derived from these basic ones and are taken into account in a direct way, e.g. by an imposed method of finishing of the external surfaces.

Several above requirements are conflicting. For obvious reasons high strength and improved durability may increase certain components of the cost. Materials for outstanding structures or for elements in particularly corrosive environments may be more expensive. Therefore, in the material's design a kind of compromise is always looked for in order to accommodate contradictory conditions, either by trial and error or by the solution of an optimization problem.

The restrictions as to the mix's composition of the concrete-like composites are given by standards and recommendations in various countries and regions. In some cases they are imposed in the form of laws which have to be applied, in others – as regulations which may also be compulsory for other reasons, e.g. the insurance of buildings. Standard requirements may concern the lowest admissible qualities of cement for certain categories of structures, recommended sieve distribution of aggregate grains and also the minimum and maximum contents of cement may be imposed. These restrictions limit the freedom of the designer and present a kind of constraint in the design process; but on the other hand they are intended to ensure that the minimum acceptable quality of the product is maintained.

Two basic principles are accepted for nearly all methods of mix design:

1. relation between water/cement ratio and compressive strength of hardened material in the form of an equation as proposed by Féret, Abrams or Bolomey, cf. Chapter 8;
2. aggregate grading assuring the best packing, i.e. leaving minimum voids to be filled by cement paste, cf. Section 4.2.5.

The first principle may be modified when admixtures, improving strength or reinforcement with dispersed fibres, are used. It gives, however, a basic relationship which is generally valid for all cement-based materials after adjustments allowing for local conditions and for experimental results which have been obtained. It is assumed that plasticizers and superplasticizers do not influence the strength and other mechanical parameters of the hardened material – they only increase workability during the initial time necessary for placing. In other words, their role is to make low values of water/cement ratio acceptable from the viewpoint of the workability of the fresh mix. It should be taken into account, however, that certain admixtures like air-entraining agents influence both the fresh mix and the hardened composite. In fact, high quality superplasticizers improve final strength, often as much as by 15–20%, due to better packing of the particles. This is a supplementary increase beside that due to lower w/c ratio.

The second principle was initially presented in the form of an optimum grading curve according to Fuller and Thompson and translated into grading limits, imposed by various standards and recommendations, cf. Section 4.2. Such an ideal or optimal aggregate grading is usually impossible to apply for various reasons:

- for good workability more fine particles are needed;
- ideal grading is rare in natural aggregate resources and in normal production and it would be very expensive to modify the available aggregate to obtain the optimum grading.

It is, however, believed that excessive differences with grading would be impractical and uneconomical and some compromise between an optimal grading and that obtained from the quarry is necessary. Moreover, the great range of sizes of aggregate fractions may increase the cost of stockpiling.

When more fine aggregate is used, it means a lower fineness modulus of the aggregate is accepted, then lower values of Young's modulus may be expected, with all other parameters constant. Also, increased cement content may be necessary in that case to maintain the required strength, and higher shrinkage is very probable. However, these disadvantages may be balanced by the lower cost of the aggregate.

The selection and design of a material is quite similar to the design of a structure or any other product. Both are more or less iterative processes, in which, by successive trials and verifications, an acceptable design is obtained and which lead to a very defined aim – all design parameters should be specified to enable execution in an unambiguous way. There is, however, a difference between designing structures and the designing of cement-based materials – the material's design is executed with numerous uncertainties in relation to the properties of components, their effective volume fractions, conditions of execution and cure, etc. The result is subjected to random variations of all properties. That is why corrections and adjustments of composition, of selection of components and of technologies are necessary before the final result is obtained and then the accepted design of a material is again verified in local conditions. The personal experience and intuition of the designer are valued in that process. The verifications are executed by calculation, tests or by a combination of both. In the design of structures the randomness of the dimensions of elements and of mechanical properties of materials are covered by a system of safety coefficients. Trial assembling, to allow for corrections of dimensions, is rare and limited to very special structures. Also, acceptance tests of structures are not necessarily followed by corrective measures. Interesting general remarks on the design methodology are given in [12.6].

The design may be accompanied and preceded by an optimization approach, described in more detail in Chapter 13.

Variability of the components and their properties is important and leads to a situation in which by using the same nominal technologies and components the final results are always somewhat different. Uncertainty of the final material's properties and its behaviour in service conditions is also related to the variability of the conditions of execution, curing and ageing. All these data are assessed quantitatively bearing in mind that the random distribution of final results is unavoidable. As full information about the statistical distribution of all parameters is not available, experimental verification and appropriate safety coefficients are therefore necessary.

The strength and all other properties of the material are considered as random variables. The statistical distribution of strength is particularly important; and not only its mean value, because randomly distributed weak regions in a structure determine its safety. One of the objectives of the design of the mix and the execution of the technology for concrete-like composites is therefore to achieve the smallest possible scatter of strength and other properties.

The design methodology is presented in a schematic form in Figure 12.3.

The preliminary selection of materials is the first step. Here the decision is based on initial input data – functions, requirements, environmental conditions, etc., which are used in a somewhat vague and intuitive way with personal experience and the rational belief of the designer. This decision is based upon apparently obvious considerations which include basic mechanical properties, service requirements and specific cost. In certain cases, however, serious consideration may be given to materials belonging to different classes. If the cement-based composite materials are selected, then the material's design is initiated which is the subject considered here.

In the second step data about components and possible technologies are collected, together with requirements on strength, durability, etc.

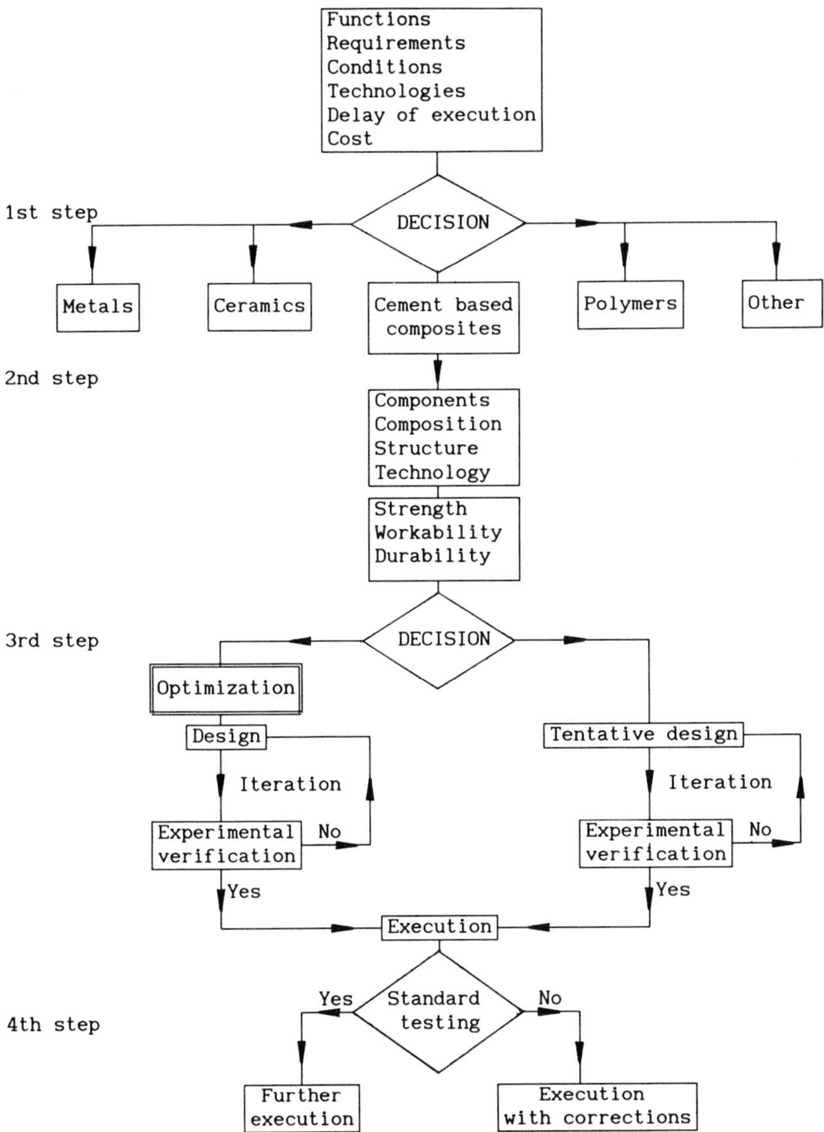

Figure 12.3 Scheme of the methodology of design of the cement-based materials.

The third step is again preceded by a decision – is the design of the mix to be performed with or without application of an optimization approach. In both cases iterative procedure is necessary. It is, however, believed that the left hand path is shorter and leads to better results, because objective indications from the optimization approach are used. The tentative design may be started in many cases from a very distant solution compared with the final one.

The fourth step corresponds to permanent checking on the site during execution and with regard to possible corrections.

In this chapter standard mix design methods for concretes are only briefly described as they are presented in detail in many manuals, e.g. [12.5], [12.7] and [12.8]. There are also computer programs available for the design of concrete. More attention is given in Chapter 13 to the application of the optimization approach to the design of brittle matrix composites.

12.4 Review of concrete mix design methods

There are many methods of concrete mix design and a few of them are briefly described below. They are much better developed for ordinary concretes than for High Performance Concretes which have only recently been studied, [12.9]. Design methods for fibre-reinforced materials do not exist in the exact meaning of that term. Instead, there are several general indications and examples which should always be carefully verified before application, [12.10].

The review is based on a variety of books [12.7], [12.8], [12.11] and papers [12.12], [12.13], [12.14] and [12.15]. The designations of methods 'French' or 'Polish' have no general meaning and are used here only to indicate the origin of their written presentations. It is obvious that in various countries different methods are used and are currently modified according to new components, requirements and applications. If properly used, all methods lead to good results even if they are developed from slightly different assumptions. A large input of experimental data is a factor which ensures convergent results even when starting points are different.

The methods discussed here are called 'analytical' as they are based on certain analytical relations, which are, however, derived from practical observations and experience. It is also assumed that the results obtained are verified experimentally and some corrections are introduced on the site. Other methods which are basically experimental are not considered here.

(a) American Concrete Institute method

The ACI method was published in [12.16] and is largely used in North America. The design is based on a set of tables where basic assumptions are presented in the form of simple values for application. First, the maximum aggregate size and the workability expressed by slump should be selected according to the type of structure. Then, for that data the necessary amount of water is estimated for two cases – air-entrained and non-air-entrained concretes. In the same table the approximate volume of air is given – air which is entrapped during mixing and also air-entrained if it is provided, according to exposure to freeze–thaw cycles. The water/cement ratio for the required compressive strength is selected from the next table, which is based on the Abrams formula, cf. Section 8.2. Here, not only the required strength but also durability should be considered – for concretes exposed to detrimental conditions less water is proposed in the form of the maximum water/cement ratio to be imposed. This enables the amount of cement to be calculated from water/cement ratio. The volume of coarse aggregate is again given in a table according to two parameters – maximum grain diameter and the fineness modulus of sand. The last component – sand – is determined as the difference between one cubic meter and the sum of the volumes of all other components – cement, water, coarse aggregate and air.

The ACI method is based entirely on experience over a long period of time and its application, with the tables, is easy. The results should be corrected according to particular requirements and local conditions concerning workability, strength, durability, aggregate moisture, etc. Also, when any kind of admixture is used, an appropriate modification should be introduced to the procedure described above.

For a detailed description of the method the reader is referred to [12.16] and to the above-mentioned manuals.

(b) United Kingdom method

The method was presented in [12.17] and developed further at a later date.

At the beginning of the design procedure the grading of the aggregate is determined and it should be within the imposed limit curves. The minimum amount of cement is imposed as a function of the kind of concrete structure (plain, reinforced or prestressed) and aggressiveness of environment. For a given aggregate and water/cement ratio = 0.5 the compressive strength at after 28 days is found from a table. These two values determine a point which is placed between a set of curves based on Abrams' formula. Then, an appropriate curve is interpolated as belonging to the same family, passing through the point mentioned above. It is used to determine the water/cement ratio for the required strength, cf. Figure 12.4. The water content for a given quality of coarse aggregate and for required slump is taken from another table, and therefore the amount of cement may be easily calculated. The total amount of aggregate is established from tables for four different workabilities. The amount of sand is established again using a series of tables for various values of slump, maximum aggregate grain size and aggregate grains texture.

The mix design is in fact reduced to ensure the appropriate exploitation of previous results, arranged in a form of tables. The composition determined is then checked experimentally and corrected for actual conditions.

(c) Baron–Lessage (French) method

The method was provided by [12.13] and later developed among others by [12.14]. It is based on two traditional approaches. One known after the names

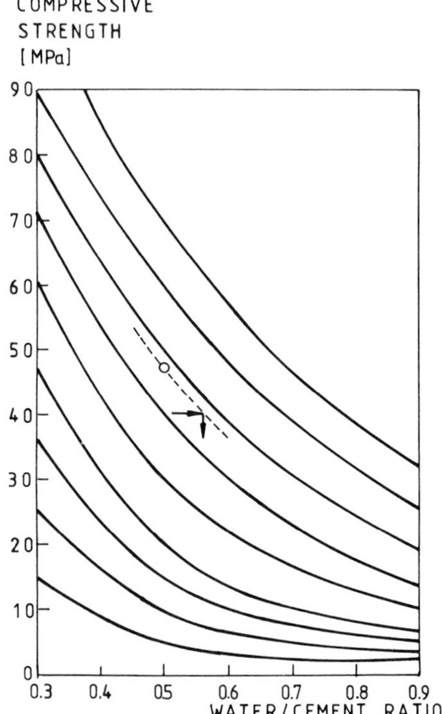

Figure 12.4 Set of curves representing relation between compressive strength and water/cement ratio for the UK mix design method. (Reproduced with permission from Teychenne, D.C. *et al.*, Design of normal concrete mixes; published by Building Research Establishment, 1975.) [12.17]

of Faury and Joisel was derived from an assumption that the amount of water needed is related to the volume of the voids between solid grains. In the other method proposed by Vallette the amount of water is assumed to be proportional to the surface of the grains. Both methods together with a third one called the Dreux method are still in use in France. The authors of the Baron–Lesage method proposed to start with a selection of the ratios between fine and coarse aggregate to obtain the best workability, which is the most important criterion of the mix quality. The workability for that method is determined on a special LCL Workabilimeter shown in Figure 12.5, on which a result is expressed as flow time. The Workabilimeter was constructed in the Laboratoire Central des Ponts et Chaussées (LCPC) in Paris and it has two advantages over slump measured on the Abrams cone or on the Vebe time scale:

1. the amount of fresh mix is five times greater than that for the Abrams cone and therefore the results are more representative;

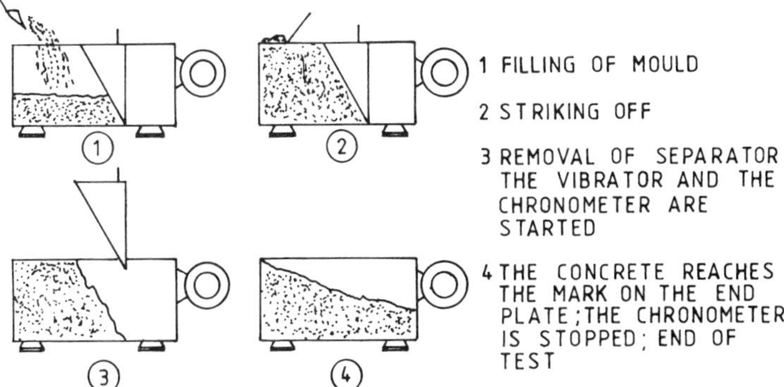

Figure 12.5 Determination of the flow time in the LCL Workabilimeter. (Reproduced from Rossi, P. *et al.*, Method for optimizing the composition of metal fibre-reinforced concrete; published by Elsevier Applied Science, 1989.) [12.18]

2. the flow of fresh mix in the box as shown in Figure 12.5 is more dynamic and simulates better the behaviour of the fresh mix in a mould.

The design is started by selecting the water/cement ratio and the amount of cement which follow the general indications for the kind of work intended. The initial data selected do not have much importance for the final result and should only ensure that the flow time is contained within the limits of 15 and 40 seconds. Then the experimental relationship is established between the fine to coarse aggregates ratio s/g and the flow time as shown in Figure 12.6. The minimum flow time gives the optimum value for that ratio. Usually, not more

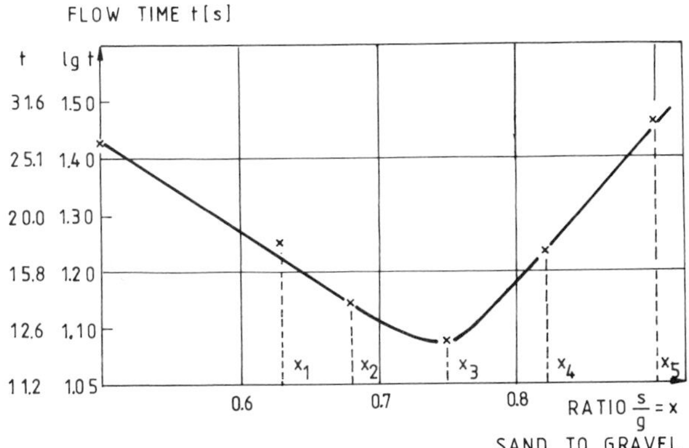

Figure 12.6 Determination of the best workability and the appropriate s/g ratio. (Reproduced with permission from Baron, J. and Lesage, R., La composition du béton hydraulic du laboratoire au chantier; published by LCPC, 1976.) [12.13]

than 5 experimental mixes are needed to obtain such a curve and it depends on how many different sizes of aggregate are distinguished for design purposes – only two as in Figure 12.6, i.e. sand and gravel, or more, e.g. two or three sizes of coarse aggregate. In a more or less complicated way the optimum aggregate size distribution is determined for the minimum of the flow time. It is assumed, and it has been checked, that this aggregate composition does not depend upon the quality and amount of cement paste.

The next stage of the design is to establish the actual w/c ratio as a function of the required flow time and related to the kind of structural elements to be cast, difficulty of placing and vibrating, etc. For that aim a special table is available with recommendations. Again, a few mixes are needed with only one variable – volume of water. Line 1 in Figure 12.7 shows how the volume of water influences the flow time, where all local conditions are taken into account in experimental mixes.

In the case of the application of a water reducing agent (plasticizer or superplasticizer), then another line is traced experimentally – line 2 in Figure 12.7. The last step of design is the calculation of the composition of the mix for 1 m^3 and the final verification together with possible corrections for all the additional factors and effects which were not considered in the design procedure. The verification is accomplished again by trial mixes.

In the Baron–Lesage method the application of superplasticizers only varies the flow time. When fibres are added, then the amount of coarse aggregate should be decreased to compensate their influence on the flow time accordingly, [12.18].

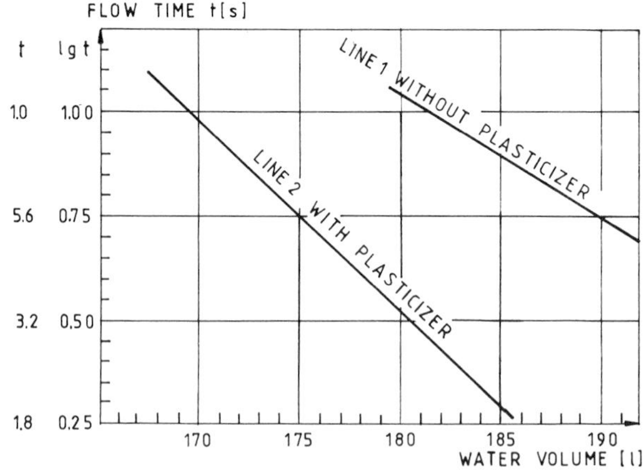

Figure 12.7 Example of variations of the flow time as function of the volume of water, line 1 – without plasticizer, line 2 – with a plasticizer. (Reproduced from Baron, J. and Lesage, R., La composition du béton hydraulique du laboratoire au chantier; Rapp. de Recherche No. 64, published by Laboratoire Centrale des Ponts et Chaussées, 1976.) [12.13]

(d) Polish method

The method used in Poland was published in many local manuals and the most complete presentation is in [12.19]. It is based on the solution of three linear equations, which express strength, density and water requirements of particular fractions of aggregate.

The compressive strength is calculated after the so-called Bolomey's formula (cf. Chapter 8) from the equations of following form:

$$f_{28} = A_1\left(\frac{1}{w/c} - 0.5\right) \quad \text{for } w/c > 0.4 \qquad (12.1)$$

$$f_{28} = A_2\left(\frac{1}{w/c} + 0.5\right) \quad \text{for } w/c \leqslant 0.4 \qquad (12.2)$$

Both constants are dependent on quality of cement and aggregate.

The equations expressing density reflects the fact that the sum of the volumes of all components is equal to 1 cubic metre, and has the following form:

$$\frac{C}{\rho_c} + \frac{K}{\rho_k} + W = 1.0 \quad [\mathrm{m}^3] \qquad (12.3)$$

here C and K are masses of cement and aggregate and ρ_c and ρ_k are specific densities of cement and aggregate, respectively.

The third equation expresses the amount of water required for cement and for aggregate:

$$W = Cw_c + Kw_k \qquad (12.4)$$

where w_k may be calculated for each fraction of aggregate separately according to formulae given by Bolomey and Stern:

$$w_{\mathrm{Bol}} = \frac{\mathrm{N_b}}{\sqrt[3]{d_1 d_2}}, \quad w_{\mathrm{Stern}} = \mathrm{N_s}\left[\frac{1}{0.5(\log d_1 + \log d_2)}\right] \qquad (12.5)$$

here d_1 and d_2 determine the fraction for which the calculation is executed, and $\mathrm{N_b}$ and $\mathrm{N_s}$ are constants depending upon quality of aggregate. According to Bolomey, $w_c = 0.23$ and according to Stern, w_c may take values from 0.23 up to 0.27 for concretes of low and high workability, respectively.

In these three equations the unknown values are: w/c, C and K. As in other methods the minimum amounts of cement and aggregate grading are imposed by standard regulations.

In all four methods presented above it is assumed that after calculation of the masses of all components a trial batch should be made and further corrections may be necessary to adjust the standard coefficients and data from the tables to local conditions and actual components.

More recent results concerning special composite materials like high performance concretes, fibre-reinforced concretes or polymer concretes are not covered by the classic methods of design. That remark also concerns the application of different admixtures and additives. In that subject the reader is referred to published papers widely mentioned in other chapters of this book.

The design methods for ordinary concretes are presented by many authors and firms, and are also available in the form of user friendly computer programs which provide quick anwers to basic problems concerning the design of a mix for required properties. The programs are based an available analytical formulae and by using important collections of available experimental results. The computer-aided-design of materials is aimed at the easy exploitation of all previous experience in that field. Moreover, the final results are less dependent upon the personal ability of the designer. That is valid for most ordinary problems where requirements and compounds correspond to normal practice. These programs, as well as the above mentioned design methods do not cover the full variety of admixtures and types of dispersed reinforcement which are available to designers for special concretes – high or very high performance, with increased resistance against corrosion, improved permeability, etc. Again, in such cases a method of trial and error is to be applied.

The design of HPC and VHPC is basically similar, but because of the high specifications a few special measures are advised:

- selection of the best quality of raw materials (aggregate, cement, admixtures);
- previous verification as to whether there is any incompatibility between different components (cement and admixtures, aggregate and cement, cement and fibres, etc.);
- verification of the mix composition in the actual technology of mixing, transportation, placing, vibration, etc.

In all cases of a material's design an iterative process is used, by which the possible differences between nominal and actual component properties and conditions of execution may be corrected, cf. Figure 12.3.

12.5 Recommendations for the design of fibre reinforced and polymer cement composites

Until now the general procedures for design of cement-based materials other than plain concrete and mortar have not been available. They do not exist or they may not have been published, being restricted for internal application and consultation by firms and procedures of fibre reinforced composites. An example of the 'designer' approach to steel fibre reinforced elements subjected to bending is described in Section 8.4. Many recommendations for the design of fibre reinforced materials exist together with examples of compositions applied on various occasions. A few general recommendations and specified examples are examined and discussed below.

The first question to be answered is what type of fibres should be selected, i.e. what material, dimensions and shape.

The objective of fibre reinforcement should be clearly specified and the following cases may be considered:

- Fibres are added to improve tensile strength and therefore to increase the load corresponding to the first crack in elements subjected to bending or tension, and also when increased impermeability of hardened composite material is required.
- Fibres have to increase the ductility of the element and the fracture toughness of the material by control of the cracking process; this ability may be checked by one of available fracture indices. The control of microcracks caused by restrained shrinkage or thermal strain is of particular importance.
- Fibres are expected to improve particular mechanical parameters like abrasion resistance, and are added for better durability or for any other reason.

Similar reasoning is needed for the design of polymer modified concretes. The high cost of polymer admixtures in PCC or of impregnation in the case of PIC should be justified by clearly established goals, e.g.:

- impermeability of containers for gases or liquids or in the case of a corrosive environment;
- improved durability of elements subjected to abrasion;
- high strength and toughness of elements, e.g. exposed to impacts.

There is no way that fibre-reinforcement can replace classic steel-reinforcement in the form of steel bars which are situated in the correct places in structural elements in order to carry the principal tensions. Fibres may be used in parallel with steel bars to improve bonding, to carry a part of the shearing stresses, to control local cracking, etc. In contrast, different types of fibres (steel, glass, polypropylene) are used as the main reinforcement in non-structural elements, like claddings and tiles. Fibres are also applied in elements in which reinforcement is introduced for temporary loads during transportation or against shrinkage cracking. For obvious reasons the design of reinforcement in non-structural elements is mostly based on the designer's experience, and on standard requirements on experimental verifications.

In particularly complex problems of heavily loaded elements the application of hybrid reinforcement composed of two or more kinds of different fibres may be considered. In the selection of reinforcement the specific price and purpose of application of particular types of fibres should also be taken into account, cf. Chapter 5. The volume of fibres is usually limited by their cost and by the workability of the fresh mix. Also, the efficiency of fibres decrease when a high percentage is applied. It is rare in practical cases that the volume fraction of steel fibres higher than 2.5% is used and composites with reinforcement lower than 1% are very often applied. This remark does not concern particular cases where higher volume fractions of fibres are purposefully used and where other technologies of placing are applied, e.g. SIFCON, cf. Section 14.2.4. The application of polymer admixtures with fibres may also be foreseen, if the exploitation requirements cannot be satisfied in a less expensive way.

In most cases the random distribution of the fibres is considered in the material's design. If for any reason any other distribution of fibres is envisaged, for example linearized fibres 1D or 2D or continuous fibres in the form of mats or meshes, then the design of the material's composition should be modified. For that purpose experience from other applications or a trial and error method have to be employed.

As an example, the design considerations proposed by [12.12] may be mentioned. To obtain an appreciable increase of fracture toughness long fibres ($\geqslant$ 20 mm) and a low volume fraction ($\leqslant$ 3%) are used. For better control of microcracking and increase of the first crack load short fibres ($\leqslant$ 5 mm) should be selected with a high volume fraction ($\geqslant$ 10%), but such a situation rarely occurs. For a more detailed consideration of the different types of fibres the reader is referred to Chapter 5.

It has been observed in many cases that the addition of fibres to a given composition of the matrix is not a correct procedure. The fibres completely transform the behaviour of the fresh mix and also change considerably the properties of the hardened material. It is then necessary to design the composite material from the beginning, either as a plain matrix, i.e. no-fibre composite, or as a composite material with dispersed reinforcement. The addition of fibres modifies the workability of the fresh mix in a similar way as coarse aggregate does. It is therefore possible to counterbalance the addition of fibre by increasing the fine to coarse aggregate ratio, [12.18]. The influence of steel fibres on the workability of the fresh mix was studied by [12.20] and it is shown in Figure 12.8. The mix compositions are therefore characterized by higher cement contents and by higher values of the fine–coarse aggregate ratio in order to increase the amount of cement paste. The paste itself exhibits higher porosity than in non-reinforced materials because of the air entrapped with the fibres. The steel fibres are used in compositions with smaller aggregate grains – the maximum size is usually about 10 mm. The workability of the fresh mix with fibres is usually improved by superplasticizers.

The steel fibre contents applied in concrete mixes are shown in Table 12.1 according to recommendations [12.21]. To establish these values different arguments are taken into account – mechanical efficiency, workability and economy. It should be reminded here, that in the cement-based composite materials the fibres are by far the most expensive component which considerably influences the total cost of the material. That aspect is considered also in Section 15.1.

The general conclusion is that while there are many established procedures to design ordinary concretes, there is no such method for high performance

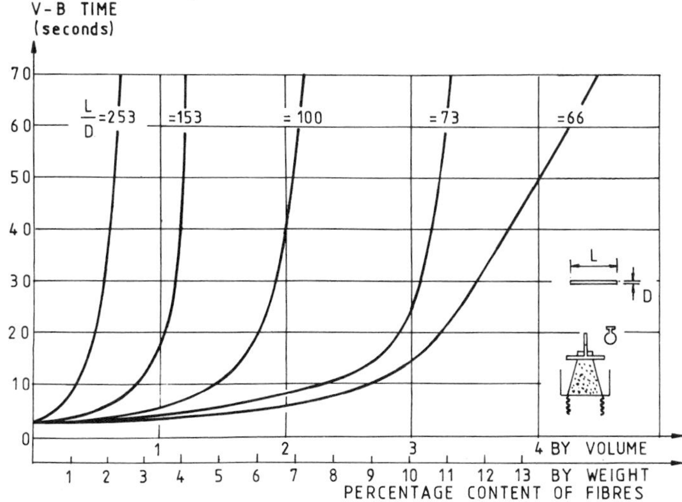

Figure 12.8 Influence of steel fibre volume fraction on the workability of cement-based materials for different fibre aspect ratio l/d. (Reproduced with permission from Edgington, J. *et al.*, Steel fibre reinforced concrete; published by Building Research Establishment, 1974.) [12.20]

Table 12.1 Mix proportions for ordinary fibre reinforced materials

Description of the mix	Mortar	Concrete of max. aggreg. size 9.5 (mm)	19.0 (mm)
Cement (kgs/m^3)	415–710	355–590	300–535
Water/cement ratio	0.30–0.45	0.35–0.45	0.40–0.50
Fine aggregate (%)	100	45–60	45–55
Entrained air (%)	7–10	4–7	4–6
Fibre volume content (%):			
– deformed steel fibres	0.5–1.0	0.4–0.9	0.3–0.8
– smooth steel fibres	1.0–2.0	0.9–1.8	0.8–1.6
– glassfibres	2.0–5.0	0.3–1.2	–

(Source: ACI, State-of-the-Art Report and Fibre Reinforced Concrete; *Concrete International*, May, 9–30, 1982.) [12.21]

materials, polymer modified concretes, composites with different types of admixtures and reinforcement, etc. Also, for fibres other than short steel ones (glass, polypropylene, long steel-fibres, etc.) there are few general recommendations. It is clearly stated in [12.22] '... it is not possible at present to rationally predict ultimate strength of fiber-reinforced concrete'. In each case only previous experience in the form of approximate formulae and the application of general recommendations are available to help in the design process, which has to be completed by trial mixes and tests on hardened material.

References

12.1. Tattersall, G.H. and Banfill, P.F.G. (1983) *The Rheology of Fresh Concrete*, Pitman, Boston, London, Melbourne.
12.2. Nowacki, W. (1963) *Théorie du fluage*, Eyrolles/Arkady, Paris.
12.3. Reiner, M. (1949) *Twelve lectures on theoretical rheology*, North Holland Publ. Co., Amsterdam.
12.4. ACI (1978) ACI Committee 544, Measurement of properties of fiber-reinforced concrete. *Proc. ACI*, **75**, 283–89.
12.5. Nicholls, R. (1976) *Composite Construction Material Handbook*, Prentice-Hall Inc., New Jersey.
12.6. Ashby, M.F. and Jones, D.R.H. (1986) *Engineering Materials 2*, Pergamon Press, Oxford.
12.7. Mindess, S. and Young, J.F. (1981) *Concrete*, Prentice-Hall, Englewood Cliffs, New Jersey.
12.8. Neville, A.M. and Brooks, J.J. (1981) *Concrete Technology*, Longman Scientific & Technical, New York.
12.9. Malier, Y. (ed.) (1990) *Les Bétons à Hautes Performances*, Presses de LCPC, Paris, 139–50.
12.10. Fernandez, A.V. (1981) Fibre-reinforced concrete and shotcrete technology: fact, myth or magic? in Proc. 1st Canadian University–Industry Workshop on Fibre Reinforced Concrete, Univ. Laval, Quebec, 140–54.
12.11. Neville, A.M. (1981) *Properties of Concrete*, 3rd ed. Pitman, London.
12.12. Rossi, P. (1991) Formulation et comportement mécanique des bétons de fibres métalliques (BFM), *Ann. de l'ITBTP*, **492**, Mars–Avril, 90–107.
12.13. Lesage, R. (1974) Etude expérimentale de la mise en place du béton frais. Rapp. Tech. 37, LCPC, Paris.
12.14. Baron, J. and Lesage, R. (1976) La composition de béton hydraulique du laboratoire au chantier. Rapp. Tech. 64, LCPC, Paris.
12.15. Kasperkiewicz, J. (1992) Private communication.
12.16. ACI (1977) Recommended Practice for Selecting Proportions for Normal and Heavyweight Concrete, ACI 211.1–77, American Concrete Institute, Detroit.
12.17. Teychenne, D.C., Franklin, R.E. and Erntroy, H.C. (1975) Design of normal concrete mixes, Building Research Establishment, Garston.
12.18. Rossi, P., Harrouche, N. and de Larrard, F. (1989) Method for optimizing the composition of metal-fibre-reinforced-concrete, in Proc. Int. Conf. *Fibre Reinforced Cements and Concretes: Recent Developments*, Cardiff, (eds. R.N. Swamy and B. Barr), Elsevier Applied Science, London, 3–10.
12.19. Bukowski, B., Bastian, S., Braun, K., *et al.* (1972) *Concrete Technology* (in Polish), part. 2, Arkady, Warsaw.
12.20. Edgington, J., Hannant, D.J. and Williams, R.I.T. (1974) Steel-fibre-reinforced concrete. CP 69/74, Building Research Establishment, Garston.
12.21. ACI (1982) State-of-the-Art Report on Fiber Reinforced Concrete, ACI Committee 544, 1R–82, *ACI Concrete International*, May, Detroit, 9–30.
12.22. ACI (1988) Design Considerations for Steel Fiber Reinforced Concrete, ACI Committee 544, 85–S52. *ACI Struct. Journal*, Sept.–Oct. 563–80.

13 Optimization of cement-based composites

13.1 Optimization approach in the design of materials

The optimization approach to any activity in technology, economics or other fields is aimed at finding methods of determining the best solutions in an objective way. In particular, the optimization of composite materials deals with problems of selecting the values of several variables which determine composition and internal structure. Other variables which describe the conditions of mixing, vibration, placing and curing may also be included.

This chapter is limited to the application of methods of mathematical optimization to materials with cement-based matrices, like ordinary plain concretes, fibre-reinforced concretes, etc. Other methods of improving the design of materials by separate consideration of particular aspects and criteria or by comparison of a number of designs in order to select the best one are mentioned only briefly.

Optimization methods are aimed at furnishing certain inputs of rational indicators for design procedures. It is considered useful, and in many cases even essential, to support traditional design methods by an objective approach. This seems particularly helpful in the design of composite materials where, due to a large number of design criteria and variables, any intuitive approach to design is difficult. The review of the optimization methods applied to the design of materials is given below based on [13.1]. For design methods of cement-based composites, where optimization is looked for in a somewhat indirect way, the reader is referred to Chapter 12.

The optimization of structures was studied by Galileo in 1634 and since then thousands of valuable papers have been published in this field, some of which include [13.2], [13.3], [13.4] and [13.5]. The optimization of materials was started not that long ago and the results obtained are not numerous. A short list of papers on optimization of composite materials is given and commented upon in papers [13.6] and [13.7]. A review of papers published in the former USSR was given [13.8]. In [13.9] it was shown how important optimization of composite materials is with regard to fracture processes. The inapplicability of intuitive determination of the optimum filament orientation along the direction of principal stress for many composite materials and the need for failure criteria to be taken into account has been proved in [13.10].

Interesting remarks on optimization of concretes were published in [13.11]–[11.13], which indicated the applicability of relatively simple methods and procedures, leading to the best solutions from the economic standpoint.

In papers [13.1], [13.6] and [13.14] it was shown that the determination of the maximum fracture energy of fibre reinforced cement-based composites as a function of the direction of fibres is not simply a problem of the alignment of fibres along the direction of principal tensions. Because of cracking, certain components of fracture energy increase when the fibres are inclined with respect to the cracks, cf. Example 13.1 below. The results of calculations were developed later in [13.15] and [13.16], where experimental verifications were presented. The problem of optimal orientation of fibres was also studied in [13.17] and [13.18].

A series of valuable works on the optimization approach to fibre-reinforced cement composites was published in [13.19] and [13.20]. Particular factors were considered from the viewpoint of an optimal solution. Maximum fracture energy was looked for in [13.19], by considering fibre pull-out as the major mechanism contributing to the accumulation of fracture energy. The conclusions concerned the selection of fibre length, distribution and band to the matrix. Also, in paper [13.20] the problem of the optimization of FRC has been considered and the main criteria were specified together with their limitations. In [13.21] the optimization of a material's structure is realized by selection of the aggregate sizes needed to achieve maximum workability, cf. also Chapter 12. In all these papers the problems examined are not accompanied by any formulation of criteria, variables and constraints for optimization, but it is shown how particular aspects of designed materials may be improved with respect to a previous design. Their value is based on the demonstration of the range of possible solutions and on an indication of how, by consecutive steps, better solutions may be determined.

A simple method was proposed in paper [13.22] for optimization of a concrete mix with the minimum cost of components where the relations between variables, constraints and criterion are linear. In that paper a commercially available spreadsheet, incorporating an optimization procedure, was applied. The paper is an interesting proposal and may serve as a starting point for the development of methods which also deal with non-linear problems in which the main conditions, constraints and criteria appearing in practical design problems will be considered.

Basic concepts and examples are presented below of how to optimize cement-based composites using methods and solutions taken from three well advanced fields – concrete technology, mechanics of composites and mathematical optimization.

13.2 Basic concepts of material optimization

The general formulation of the problem of optimization of a material is the same as in structural optimization, cf. [13.4] and [13.5].

An optimal material is described by a set of decisive variables x_i $(i = 1, 2, \ldots, n)$ which minimize or maximize an optimization criterion.

Variables x_i are considered as independent and together with arbitrary selected parameters they determine completely the object of optimization – a structure or a material. These are material variables.

In the problems of structural optimization the variables determine the shape of the structure, distribution in space of its elements, shape and dimensions of cross-sections, etc. The physical properties of the construction materials may also be considered as variables.

In the case of material optimization, the variables are – volume fractions, kinds and qualities of components, their distribution in space, their reciprocal relations like adherence, etc. The variables may be defined as continuous or discontinuous (discrete) ones. Quantities (e.g. volume contents) of particular components may be considered as continuous variables. A few discrete kinds of components represent discontinuous variables, e.g. different types of Portland cement and different kinds of fibres may be used in the composition. Methods of production may also be considered as discrete variables provided that they determine the final or transitory properties of the material.

The decisive variables should belong to a feasible set. This means that their values, beyond imposed limits, cannot be accepted in the problem for constructional, functional or other reasons. The constraints may have the form of equalities or inequalities

$$\begin{aligned} g_p(x_i) &= 0, \quad p = 1, 2, \ldots, r \\ h_s(x_i) &\leqslant 0, \quad s = 1, 2, \ldots, t \end{aligned} \tag{13.1}$$

or simply limit values may be imposed, $\underline{x} \leqslant x_i \leqslant \bar{x}_i$, $i = 1, 2, \ldots, n$, where the lower and upper bars indicate imposed lower and upper limit values, respectively. For example, the variables which describe the components are limited to available materials (cement, sand, gravel, etc.) and their possible properties. All constraints determine the feasible domain.

The volume fractions and properties of the components, as well as their effective distribution in a composite material, are random variables. Their final values and their nominal values, determined by testing, are subjected to unavoidable scatter. When in an optimization problem only design and nominal values are considered, then that is a deterministic approach. In an opposite case, when the distribution functions are taken into account, the stochastic problem of optimization may be formulated.

Optimization criteria describe the basic properties of materials. They are also called objective functions. In structural optimization we choose factors such as – minimum volume or weight, maximum bearing capacity or strength, maximum stiffness, minimum cost, etc. as optimization criteria. In material optimization the objective functions describe selected properties which are considered as important and decisive for the material's quality and applicability. The solution consists of the determination of those values of the design variables which extremize these properties. All physical, chemical and other properties may be considered as material properties. For engineering materials of particular importance are mechanical properties like strength, Young's modulus, specific fracture energy, durability and also specific cost.

When a set of independent variables x_i, $(i = 1, 2, \ldots, n)$ is considered the optimization criterion is expressed by those variables as a function $F(x_i)$ subject to constraints of different kinds and forms, e.g. the limited volume of material may be presented as an integral.

If the problem is formulated with one single criterion $F(x_i)$ with the constraints (equation 13.1), then the necessary conditions for a maximum are derived from the Kuhn–Tucker theorem [13.23] and have the following form:

$$x_i \frac{\partial F^*}{\partial x_i} = 0; \quad \frac{\partial F^*}{\partial x_i} \leqslant 0; \quad \frac{\partial F^*}{\partial \mu_p} = 0;$$

$$\mu_s \frac{\partial F^*}{\partial \mu_s} = 0; \quad \frac{\partial F^*}{\partial \mu_s} \leqslant 0;$$

$$x_i \geqslant 0, \quad i = 1, 2, \ldots, n \tag{13.2}$$

here $\mu_s \geqslant 0, s = 1, 2, \ldots, t$, and $\mu_p, p = 1, 2, \ldots, r$ are so called Lagrange multipliers, and

$$F^*(x_i, \mu_p, \mu_s) = F(x_i) + \sum_{p=1}^{r} \mu_p g_p(x_i) + \sum_{s=1}^{t} \mu_s h_s(x_i) \tag{13.3}$$

In structural and material optimization problems there are several common features. These problems are correctly formulated when criteria, constraints and variables are defined. Sometimes the design variants are imprecisely called 'optimal solutions'. Calculation of a few cases and selection of the best one is not an optimization approach. There is no optimal solution without a clear determination of – in what sense and within what feasible region if it is achieved.

It should be also emphasized that the optimization problem is solved not on a real structure or material, but on their approximate models. The results of an optimization procedure are dependent on assumptions and approximations admitted for those models, e.g. elastic and homogeneous materials.

Material optimization does not entirely replace the material's design, because it may not cover certain aspects and requirements, which make up the complete material. The omission of some secondary aspects is justified by the necessary simplification of the optimization problem. In the next step of the material's design, in contrast, all conditions and requirements concerning safety, serviceability, economy, etc. should be satisfied and necessary modifications should be introduced to the material's composition and structure. That is why the material's optimization, like structural optimization, does not replace design but is that part of it in which some intuitive procedures are replaced by objective calculations.

The sensitivity of the objective function with respect to variables is a separate problem. When the objective function does not really depend on the decisive variables, then probably the variables are incorrectly selected.

Determination of constraints and objective functions is important in the formulation of the problem – it is based on given conditions, but sometimes an objective function may be replaced by a constraint or vice versa. It sometimes also occurs that a small modification of a constraint may influence considerably the objective function. In such a case the resignation of preliminary assumptions concerning constraints may be justified.

In rare problems it is admissible to limit the optimization to one single criterion, e.g. a structure of minimum cost or a material of maximum strength may be considered as an appropriate solution. In general, such a formulation has a somewhat academic character and may only be used as a simplified example for preliminary explanation of the problem. In most cases the existence and necessity of several criteria is obvious, though often they are considered in an indirect way, i.e. by appropriate constraints. Multi-objective or multi-criteria optimization is the next step, presented below, in which several criteria are directly considered.

13.3 Multi-criteria optimization of materials

Let us consider the n-dimensional space of variables x_i in which objective functions $F_j(x_i)$, $j = 1, 2, \ldots, k$ are determined, here k is the number of objective functions or functionals. It means that a solution of the problem should satisfy k objective functions and the problem may be formulated as follows:

> determine n-dimensional vector in the space of decisive functions which satisfies all constraints and ensures that the functions F_j have their extrema.

The decisive functions are the components of the vector $\mathbf{X}^N$ in the n-dimensional space. Every point of that space indicates one particular material defined by n decisive variables. The feasible region Q is a part of the n-dimensional space and is defined by the constraints (equation 13.1).

The space of the objective functions R^K has k dimensions. Every point of that space corresponds to one vector of the objective function $F_j(x_i)$. In that space the feasible region Q is represented by a region $F(Q)$. Without entering into all the mathematical formulations which may be found in manuals [13.23]–[13.25], it may be proved that the points of feasible region Q are represented by the points in the region $F(Q)$. An example of regions Q and $F(Q)$ are shown in Figure 13.1 in the case of $k = 2$ and two-dimensional region.

The optimization problem formulated in this way may have several solutions and the solution appropriate for given conditions should be selected using other arguments. To present that procedure a few definitions are necessary.

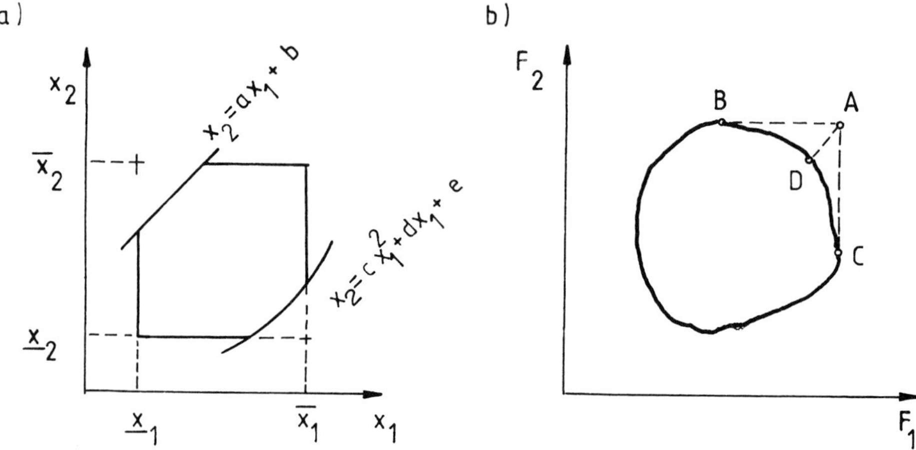

Figure 13.1 Feasible regions. a) in variables space; b) in objective functions space. (Source: Brandt, A.M. (ed.), *Foundations of Optimum Design in Civil Engineering*; published by Martinus Nijhoff, 1989.) [13.5]

The ideal solution is an extremum for all objective functions. Because a characteristic feature in multi-objective optimization is that the criteria are in conflict, then the ideal solution is outside the feasible region. That is indicated by point A in Figure 13.1, in which both objective functions F_1 and F_2 have their maximal values but which are outside region $F(Q)$.

The solutions of the problem are situated on section BDC of the boundary of the feasible region. These are called nondominated solutions, Pareto ideal solutions or the compromise set, i.e. no one objective function can be increased without causing the simultaneous decrease of at least one other function. In effect, the difficulty is that there are a great number of Pareto solutions. It is necessary therefore to apply other procedures for the selection of one solution, called the preferred solution.

The compromise set may be determined from the Kuhn–Tucker theorem (equation 13.2) in which function F from equation 13.3 is expressed by:

$$F = \sum_{j=1}^{k} \lambda_j F_j, \quad \text{where} \quad \sum_{j=1}^{k} \lambda_j = 1, \quad \lambda_j \geqslant 0. \tag{13.4}$$

For different λ_j the particular points belonging to the compromise set may be found from equations (equation 13.2).

The compromise set is a rigorous and strict solution to the problem, but the next step, i.e. selection of the preferable solution is based on a subjective decision. It may be found by using different assumptions and methods. For example, when strength and cost are two conflicting objective functions, then the compromise set contains all possible solutions. For one application the cheapest solution may be selected, and for the other – the strongest one. In general, a system of arbitrary weights may be assumed for each objective function, i.e. some functions are considered as more important than others. Further development of that method is by the creation of a utility function, by which the weights of various criteria are introduced.

Another method is based on the selection of a point on the curve of Pareto solutions which is closest to the ideal solution in the space of normalized functions. That second method is applied in the examples below, cf. also Section 13.6. For an explanation of other methods the reader is referred to manuals on mathematical optimization, e.g. [13.24]–[13.27].

13.4 Application of multi-criteria optimization to the design of cement composites

The application of the optimization approach to cement-based composite materials requires the selection of appropriate decisive functions and objective functions. Effective solutions to such problems are possible only when the relations between those functions can be presented in an analytical form. Those relations should be based either on verified models of materials or on experimental results, presented in the form of approximate functions.

The decisive functions (variables) and objective functions (criteria) may be presented in the form of a table (Table 13.1). Table 13.1 is shown here as a general indication of how the problems may be formulated – what are the possible criteria (objective functions) and variables (decisive functions). Their representation in Table 13.1 is not exhaustive – many others may be selected according to the particular conditions of a problem under consideration, i.e. of a material to be designed. It is not possible to present all of them, even if it does not seem necessary; only a few criteria and variables are shown. It is also possible to imagine a three-dimensional set of optimization problems when different constraints would be considered as a third dimension of such a table. The subsequent numerical examples are selected in such a way that they show simple optimization problems of concrete-like composite materials and the relevant parts of Table 13.1 are represented in Tables 13.2–13.4.

13.5 Examples of material optimization

EXAMPLE 13.1

In this example a simple optimization problem is considered in which there is only one variable and one objective function. The problem has been solved in papers [13.1], [13.4], [13.14] (also partly presented in Section 10.3.1) and is only briefly described here.

Table 13.1 Examples of criteria (objective functions) and design variables in optimization of cement-based composites

Criteria Objective functions	Design variables												
	Basic components				Dispersed reinforcement (fibres)				Admixtures				Other
	cement	water	sand	aggregate	steel	glass	polymeric	other	plastic	air entr.	polymers	other	
Strength Compressive Tensile Elastic modulus Other													
Energy Tough. index I5 Tough. index I10 Impact Fracture energy Other													
Economy Specific cost Exec. cost Energy Other													
Other													

Table 13.2 Example 13.1 criteria and design variables

Criteria Objective functions	Design variables					
	–	steel fibres (1D)				–
		diameter D	length l	angle θ	other	
–						
Energy Tough. ind. I5 Tough. ind. I10 Impact Fract. energy Other						
Economy Spec. cost Exec. cost Energy Other						
–						

Table 13.3 Example 13.2 criteria and design variables

Criteria Objective functions	Design variables					
	–	steel fibres (1D)				–
		diameter D	length l	angle θ	other	
–						
Energy Tough. ind. I5 Tough. ind. I10 Impact Fract. energy Other						
Economy Spec. cost Exec. cost Energy Other						
–						

Table 13.4 Example 13.3 criteria and design variables

Criteria Objective functions	Design variables					
		steel fibres (1D)				
	–	diameter D	length l	angle θ	other	–
–						
Strength Compressive Tensile El. modulus Other						
Energy Tough. ind. I5 Tough. ind. I10 Impact Fract. energy Other						
Economy Spec. cost						

A composite element shown in Figure 10.24 is subjected to direct tension. The only variable is angle ϑ which determines the direction of parallel fibres (1D) reinforcing the considered element. The objective function is the fracture energy W accumulated in the element at limit state, which is formulated as corresponding to the appearance of a crack of given width v_o. The energy W is expressed as a function of variable ϑ and of several parameters characterizing the mechanical properties of the matrix and fibres and the matrix–fibre bond

$$W^{1D} = W^{1D}(\vartheta)$$

The analytical function W was derived from a complex model in paper [13.14] and has the following form:

$$\begin{aligned} W^{1D}(\vartheta) = {} & N_o D l v_e \frac{\pi}{8} \tau_{\max} \cos^2 \vartheta + N_o D \pi \tau \left[\frac{l}{4}(v_o - v_e) - \frac{1}{2}(v_0^2 - v_e^2) \right] \cos^2 \vartheta \\ & + N_o D^2 v_o \tau_f \frac{\pi}{4} \vartheta \cos \vartheta + N_o D^3 f_m \left(\alpha \frac{f_f}{f_m} \right)^2 \left(\cos^2 \vartheta - \vartheta \frac{\cos^3 \vartheta}{\sin \vartheta} \right) \\ & + N_o D l \tau v_o \pi \phi \sin \frac{\vartheta}{2} \cos \vartheta \end{aligned} \qquad (13.5)$$

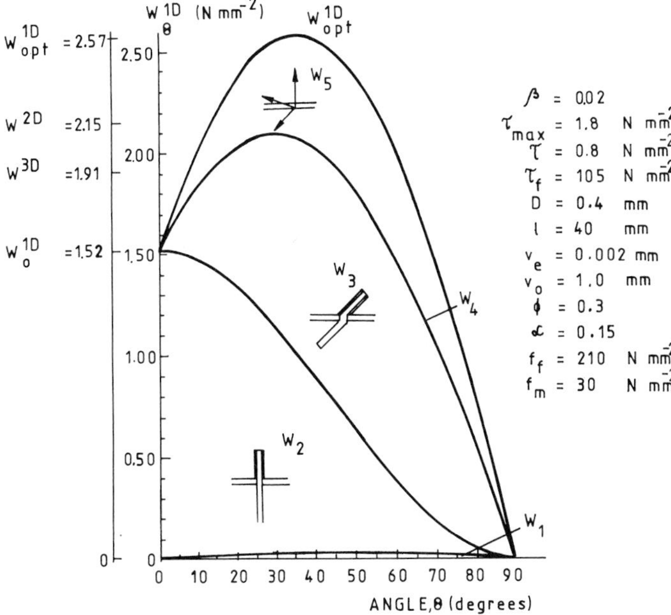

Figure 13.2 Diagram of the fracture energy W^{1D} as a function of the angle ϑ, here $W_1, W_2, \ldots$ are energy components, Example 13.1. (Source: Brandt, A.M., On the optimal direction of short metal fibres in brittle matrix composites; *J. of Materials Science*, **20**, 1985.) [13.14]

and the solution was obtained from equation, $\dfrac{dW}{d\vartheta} = 0$ in the region $0° \leqslant \vartheta \leqslant 90°$.

Here the following symbols are used: N_o – number of fibres; D and l – diameter and length of a single fibre; v_e and v_o – elastic and limit displacement of a fibre determined in a pull-out test; τ_{max} and τ – maximum and mean value of bond stress between matrix and fibre also determined experimentally; τ_f – ultimate shearing stress in the fibres; f_f and f_m – strength of fibres and matrix; α – numerical coefficient; ϕ – friction coefficient between fibres and matrix. The values of the parameters specify the matrix, the fibres and the fibre–matrix bond, and they are determined from the experiments. The particular members of equation 13.5 express various components of the fracture energy, caused by debonding of the fibres, their pull-out of the matrix, fibres plastification at the crack, etc. They are explained in full detail in Section 10.3.1.

In Table 13.2, a part of Table 13.1 is shown where the problem as formulated here is indicated. In Figure 13.2 the solution is shown in the case of a cement-based matrix and steel fibres and it may be observed that the optimal value of angle ϑ is equal to 36° approximately for given set of parameters describing the used materials and $W_{opt} = 2.57\,\text{Nmm}^{-2}$.

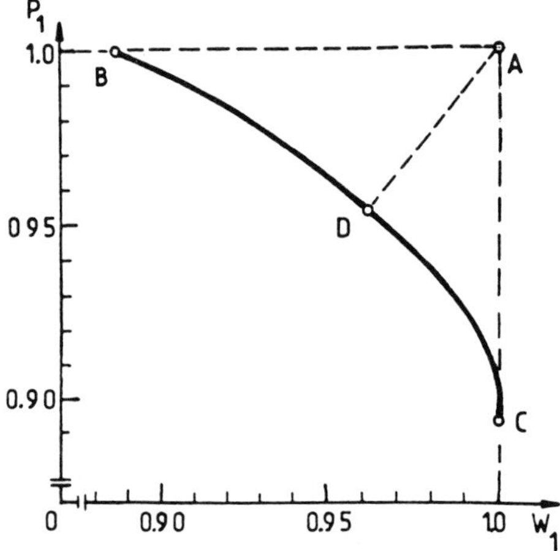

Figure 13.3 Compromise set BC and preferred solution D for Example 13.3; A is ideal solution, (Source: Brandt, A.M. and Marks, M., Examples of the multicriteria optimization of cement-based composites. *Composite Structures*, **25**, 1993, 51–60.) [13.7]

EXAMPLE 13.2

Here the same problem dealt with in Example 13.1 is considered in a more general way. Namely, with the same objective function two other variables are introduced – the length of a single fibre l and its diameter D. In Table 13.3 another part of the general Table 13.1 is shown which corresponds to this problem, presented here and based on paper [13.5].

The constraints for the variables are, $0 \leqslant \vartheta \leqslant \frac{\pi}{2}$; $\underline{l} \leqslant l \leqslant \bar{l}$; $\underline{D} \leqslant D \leqslant \bar{D}$.

To solve the problem an auxiliary function is constructed:

$$F^* = W - \mu_1 \vartheta + \mu_2\left(\vartheta - \frac{\pi}{2}\right) + \mu_3(\underline{l} - l) + \mu_4(l - \bar{l}) + \mu_5(\underline{D} - D) + \mu_6(D - \bar{D}), \tag{13.6}$$

and the necessary conditions are derived from the Kuhn–Tucker theorem (equation 13.2)

$$\frac{\partial F^*}{\partial \vartheta} = 0, \quad \frac{\partial F^*}{\partial l} = 0, \quad \frac{\partial F^*}{\partial D} = 0, \quad \mu_i \frac{\partial F^*}{\partial \mu_i} = 0, \quad \text{here } i = 1, 2, \ldots, 6, \tag{13.7}$$

and

$$\frac{\partial F^*}{\partial \vartheta} \leqslant 0, \quad \frac{\partial F^*}{\partial l} \leqslant 0, \quad \frac{\partial F^*}{\partial D} \leqslant 0, \quad \mu_i \frac{\partial F^*}{\partial \mu_i} \geqslant 0, \quad \text{here } i = 1, 2, \ldots, 6,$$

$$\vartheta \geqslant 0, \quad l \geqslant 0, \quad D \geqslant 0, \quad \mu_i \geqslant 0. \tag{13.8}$$

Introducing here all the numerical values of the parameters as in Example 13.1 and assuming following limit values $\underline{l} = 10$ mm, $\underline{D} = 0.1$ mm, $\bar{l} = 100$ mm, $\bar{D} = 1.00$ mm, the solutions for decisive functions are $\vartheta \cong 19°5'$, $l = 100$ mm, $D = 0.1$ mm, and $W_{opt} = 17.68$ Nmm^{-2}.

It appears that one variable has its maximal value and the other its minimal value on the boundaries of the feasible region. Angle ϑ is much smaller than in Example 13.1. The value of the objective function is much higher because other more effective fibres are used.

EXAMPLE 13.3

Example 13.2 is further complicated with a second objective function which expresses the loading capacity of the element $P = P(\vartheta)$, cf. [13.7]. The function $P(\vartheta)$ is based on experimental results and it is assumed that it does not depend on the other two variables.

The function $P(\vartheta)$ is presented in the form of a polynomial

$$P(\vartheta) = 28 - 8.941585\vartheta - 0.318293\vartheta^2 + 0.445299\vartheta^3. \tag{13.9}$$

The constraints imposed on variables ϑ, l and D are the same as in Example 13.2.

That is the problem of multi-criteria optimization and for the determination of the compromise set auxiliary normalized functions are constructed:

$$W_1(\vartheta, l, D) = \frac{W(\vartheta, l, D)}{W_{id}}; \quad P_1(\vartheta) = \frac{P(\vartheta)}{P_{id}},$$

here $W(\vartheta, l, D)$ and $P(\vartheta)$ mean functions (equation 13.5 and equation 13.9), respectively, and W_{id} and P_{id} are maximum values of these functions. The combined objective function according to equation 13.3 and equation 13.8 has the form: $F^* = \lambda W + (1-\lambda)P_1 - \mu_1\vartheta + \mu_2(\vartheta - \pi/2) + \mu_3(\underline{l} - l) + \mu_4(l - \bar{l}) + \mu_5(\underline{D} - D) + \mu_6(\bar{D} - D)$; here $0 \leqslant \lambda \leqslant 1$.

The necessary conditions for solution are of the same form as equation 13.7 and equation 13.8 in Example 13.2. With the numerical values of parameters as in previous calculations, the compromise set has the form as shown in Figure 13.3. The preferred solution with $W_1 = 0.9625$, $P_1 = 0.9544$ corresponds to the following values of variables: $\vartheta = 8°9'$, $l = 100$ mm, $D = 0.1$ mm.

Objective functions take values: $W = 0.9625 \times 17.68 = 17.02$ N mm^{-2}; $P = 0.9544 \times 28 = 26.72$ kN.

The values obtained for the two objective functions are found to be corresponding to that point of the compromise set which is closest to the ideal solution, according to the method previously adopted. It can be observed, that due to the introduction of the second objective function into the problem, the value determined for angle ϑ is much smaller than in both previous Examples because the second criterion of maximum P is also satisfied here. For obvious reasons

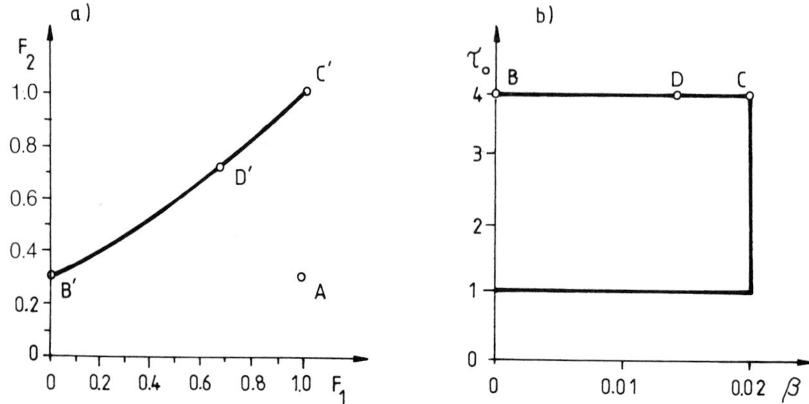

Figure 13.4 a) Compromise set BC with ideal solution A and preferred solution D in variables space for example 13.4; b) in objective functions space feasible region and point E which indicates preferred solution. (Source: Brandt, A.M. and Marks, M., Optimization of cement based composites; published by The Plan and Budget Org., 1992.) [13.28]

maximum strength is related to these fibres closely oriented to the direction of principal tensile stress. The variables and criteria are shown in Table 13.4.

EXAMPLE 13.4

This Example is taken from paper [13.28] and is based on a modification of the problem in Example 13.1. Two objective functions are introduced – the maximum fracture energy in an element subjected to tension and minimum cost of that element, which is made of brittle matrix composite and is reinforced with parallel fibres 1D with angle $\vartheta = 0°$. There are two variables – volume fraction of fibres β and factor τ_o determining the quality of fibres:

$$\tau_o = \frac{\tau_{\max}}{\underline{\tau}_{\max}},$$

here $\tau_{\max}$ is the actual characteristic value of the pull-out test for selected fibres and $\underline{\tau}_{\max}$ is the characteristic value for fibres which are least effective for fibre–matrix bonding, here a bar below symbol τ indicates its lower bound. The values of β and τ_o may be selected from the ranges $\underline{\beta} \leqslant \beta \leqslant \bar{\beta}$ and $\underline{\tau}_o \leqslant \tau_o \leqslant \bar{\tau}_o$, respectively. As the quality of the bond is reflected by two parameters, it is assumed that $\tau = 0.5\tau_{\max}$. The equation (equation 13.5) from Example 13.1 is transformed here into the following form:

$$W^{1D} = \frac{1}{D}\left(\frac{1}{2}lv_e + 2\left(\frac{l}{4}(v_o - v_e) - \frac{1}{2}(v_o^2 - v_e^2)\right)\right)\beta\underline{\tau}_{\max}\tau_o \tag{13.10}$$

This function has its maximum for $\beta = \bar{\beta}$ and $\tau_o = \bar{\tau}_o$. Therefore the normalized objective function is:

$$F_1(\beta, \tau_o) = \frac{W^{1D}(\beta, \tau_o)}{W^{1D}(\bar{\beta}, \bar{\tau}_o)} = C\beta\tau_o \tag{13.11}$$

here C is constant which accounts for all values of the parameters as in Example 13.1 and is C = 12.5.

The cost of the composite material is expressed in the following form, $K(\beta, \tau_o) = k_c V_c + k_f[\underline{\tau}_o + (\tau_o - \underline{\tau}_o)0.25]V_f + g(\beta)V_f$, here k_c, k_f, V_c and V_f are unit costs of concrete matrix and of fibres and their volumes, respectively. The function $g(\beta) = b_1\beta^2 + b_2\beta$ is proposed to account for the increased cost of material technology related to the application of fibres. This function is assumed as non-linear, because the increased volume of fibres introduced to the matrix causes an additional complication of the production of the composite material. Here b_1 and b_2 are constant which are selected according to local conditions of production.

The function $K(\beta, \tau_o)$ has its maximum for $\beta = \bar{\beta}$ and $\tau_o = \bar{\tau}_o$ and the second objective function has the following form,

$$F_2(\beta, \tau_o) = 1/K_o\{(1 - \beta)k_c + k_f[\underline{\tau}_o + (\tau_o - \underline{\tau}_o)0.25]\beta + (b_1\beta^2 + b_2\beta)\beta\}$$

here $K_o = (1 - \bar{\beta})k_c + k_f[\underline{\tau}_o + (\bar{\tau}_o - \underline{\tau}_o)0.25]\bar{\beta} + (b_1\bar{\beta}^2 + b_2\bar{\beta})\bar{\beta}$.

To solve the problem and to determine the compromise set, the maximum of the auxiliary objective function according to equation 13.3 and equation 13.4 should be determined, namely, $F^* = \lambda F_1 - (1 - \lambda)F_2 + \mu_1(\bar{\beta} - \beta) + \mu_2(\tau_o - \underline{\tau}_o) + \mu_3(\bar{\tau}_o - \tau_o)$, $\underline{\beta} = 0$. From the Kuhn–Tucker theorem the necessary conditions of the solution are:

$$\frac{\partial F^*}{\partial \tau_o} = 0, \quad \beta\frac{\partial F^*}{\partial \beta} = 0, \quad \mu_i\frac{\partial F^*}{\partial \mu_i} = 0 \quad i = 1, 2, 3. \tag{13.12}$$

The solutions of the problem should satisfy the necessary conditions of inequality for the maximum of function F:

$$\frac{\partial F^*}{\partial \tau_o} \leqslant 0, \quad \frac{\partial F^*}{\partial \beta} \leqslant 0, \quad \frac{\partial F^*}{\partial \mu_i} \geqslant 0 \quad i = 1, 2, 3. \tag{13.13}$$

$$\tau_o \geqslant 0, \qquad \beta \geqslant 0, \qquad \mu_i \geqslant 0.$$

In the problem under consideration the numerical values of the parameters are as in Example 13.1 and the following constraints are assumed: $\underline{\beta} = 0$, $\bar{\beta} = 0.02$, $\underline{\tau}_o = 1$, $\bar{\tau}_o = 4$.

The cost of the components is characterized by the values, $k_c = 8 \times 10^5$, $k_f = 36.57 \times 10^6$, $b_1 = 4 \times 10^{10}$, $b_2 = 6 \times 10^8$, taking into account particular unit costs.

The feasible region is determined from equation 13.12 and is presented in Figure 13.4b. In the space of decisive variables the solution is represented by corresponding section BC in Figure 13.4a. The ideal point A is determined by

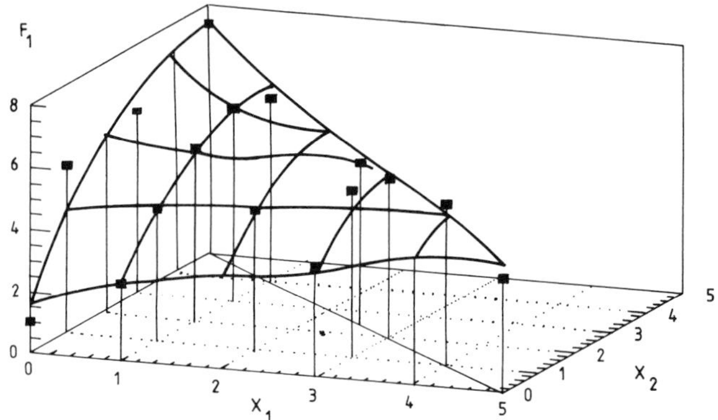

Figure 13.5 Function $F_1(x_1, x_2)$, from equation (13.19) in Example 13.5. (Source: Brandt, A.M. *et al.*, Optimization of cement based composites reinforced with carbon-fibres; published by Pluralis, 1992.) [13.29]

its coordinates (1.0, 0.30488). A point is proposed as the preferred solution which is closest to the ideal solution A in the space of normalized functions. Its coordinates are determined from the relation:

$$T(\beta, \tau_o) = [F_1(\beta, \tau_o) - 1]^2 + [F_2(\beta, \tau_o) - 0.30488]^2. \tag{13.14}$$

Here the preferred solution is obtained in point D with coordinates, $F_1 = 0.6819$ and $F_2 = 0.7145$ (Figure 13.4a). In the space of the variables the solution is obtained in point E in Figure 13.4b for $\beta = 0.014$ and $\tau_o = 4$. This means that in the preferred solution the volume fraction of the fibres is $\beta = 1.4\%$ and for the best possible fibres $\tau_o = 4$ should be applied.

EXAMPLE 13.5

Example 13.5 has been published in [13.29]. Let us consider the cement-based matrix with hybrid reinforcement composed of steel and carbon fibres. Elements made of this composite material are subjected to bending. In the problem there are the following three objective functions:

1. The ratio of the fracture energy of the composite material to that energy for the plain matrix. The ratio should be the maximum, i.e. the best effect of the reinforcement is looked for:

$$F_1(x_i) = \frac{G_f(x_i)}{G_f(x_i = 0)} = \max F_1. \tag{13.15}$$

2. The ratio of the first crack composite stress to that stress for the plain matrix should be maximum. Again the maximum effect of the reinforcement is expected:

$$F_2(x_i) = \frac{\sigma_c(x_i)}{\sigma_c(x_i = 0)} = \max F_2. \tag{13.16}$$

3. The total cost of fibre-reinforcement should reach its minimum:

$$F_3(x_i) = k_1 x_1 + k_2 x_2 = \min F_3. \tag{13.17}$$

Here x_1 and x_2 are volume fractions of carbon and steel fibres, respectively, and these are the only variables, k_1 and k_2 being specific costs of these fibres. The additional conditions:

$$x_1 + x_2 \leqslant c, \quad x_i > 0, \quad i = 1,2 \tag{13.18}$$

mean that the total volume fraction of both kinds of fibres is limited by the good workability of the fresh mix which is required, and the fact that these volumes are expressed by non-negative values. In the solution of the problem, volume fractions of both kinds of fibres should be determined in such a way, that the effects of reinforcement, in the sense of the fracture energy and first crack strength, are the maximum and the cost of reinforcement is the minimum. In this problem there are several simplifying assumptions, among others:

1. the matrix does not depend on the kind of reinforcement;
2. the cost of both kinds of reinforcement may be expressed as proportional to their volume fractions.

The functions $F_1(x_i)$ and $F_2(x_i)$, $i = 1,2$, are determined from the test results published in [13.30] and shown in Figures 13.5 and 13.6. These experimental data are represented by two polynomials:

$$F_1(x_i) = \alpha_0 + \alpha_1 x_1 + \alpha_2 x_2 + \alpha_3 x_1 x_2 + \alpha_4 x_1^2 + \alpha_5 x_2^2, \tag{13.19}$$

$$F_2(x_i) = \beta_0 + \beta_1 x_1 + \beta_2 x_2 + \beta_3 x_1 x_2 + \beta_4 x_1^2 + \beta_5 x_2^2. \tag{13.20}$$

in which coefficients α_j and β_j are determined by the least squares method. The results of approximations are given in Table 13.5.

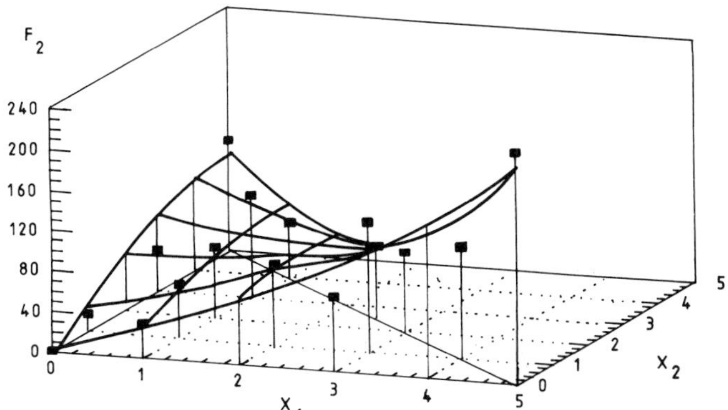

Figure 13.6 Function $F_2(x_1, x_2)$, from equation (13.20) in Example 13.5. (Source: Brandt, A.M. *et al.*, Optimization of cement-based composites reinforced with carbon fibres; published by Pluralis, 1992.) [13.29]

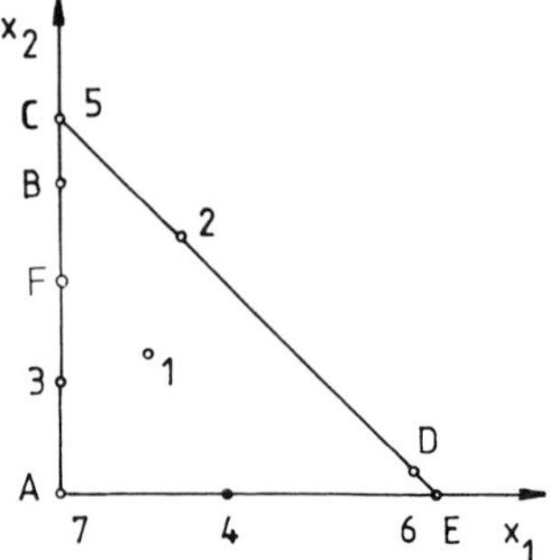

Figure 13.7 Feasible region in Example 13.5. (Source: Brandt, A.M. *et al.*, Optimization of cement based composites reinforced with carbon fibres; published by Pluralis, 1992.) [13.29]

Table 13.5 Values of coefficients α_j and β_j

j	α_j	β_j
0	1.658	−4.02
1	0.946	33.02
2	2.647	32.22
3	−0.425	−13.33
4	−0.089	1.90
5	−0.323	−2.30

The feasible region for design variables is shown in Figure 13.7. The maxima of normalized functions F_1 and F_2 from equation 13.15 and equation 13.16 with constraints in equation 13.18 are determined after the Kuhn–Tucker theorem, equation 13.2, in which, $F_i^* = F_i + \mu(x_1 + x_2 - c)$. For the function F_i^* in equation 13.2 have the following form:

$$\begin{aligned} x_1(\alpha_1 + \alpha_3 x_2 + 2\alpha_4 x_1) + \mu &= 0, \\ x_2(\alpha_2 + \alpha_3 x_1 + 2\alpha_5 x_2) + \mu &= 0, \\ \lambda(x_1 + x_2 - c) &= 0. \end{aligned} \tag{13.21}$$

Equation 13.21 has seven solutions which are shown as points in Figure 13.7. These are the solutions inside the feasible region in point 1, on the constraints in points 2, 3, 4 and in points A′, C′ and E′. The maximum of function F_1 is obtained only from that solution which satisfies the inequality conditions in equation 13.2. The solutions for the function F_2 is analogous. The function F_3 is linear with respect to variables x_1 and x_2 and has its minimum in point ($x_1 = 0$, $x_2 = 0$).

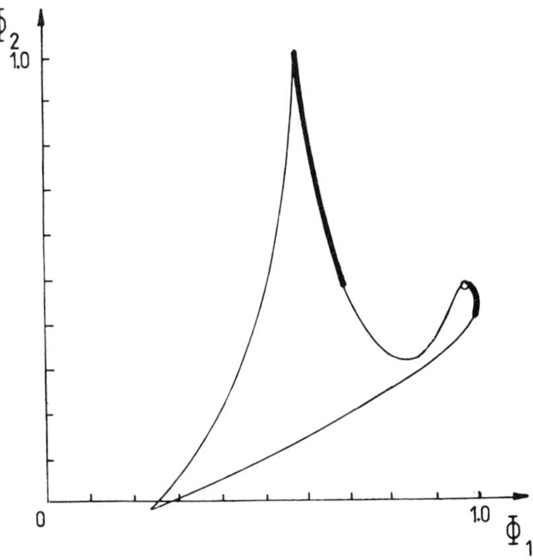

Figure 13.8 Compromise set for functions ϕ_1 and ϕ_2 and preferred solution in Example 13.5. (Source: Brandt, A.M. *et al.*, Optimization of cement based composites reinforced with carbon fibres; published by Pluralis, 1992.) [13.29]

The solution of the optimization problem for the three criteria is the compromise set, the ideal solution and the preferred solution may be identified. For that aim let us determine the ideal solution –

$$F_1(\hat{x}_1, \hat{x}_2) = \max F_1(x_1, x_2) = \bar{F}_1; \quad F_2(\hat{x}_1, \hat{x}_2) = \max F_2(x_1, x_2) = \bar{F}_2;$$
$$F_3(\hat{x}_1, \hat{x}_2) = \min F_3(x_1, x_2) = 0;$$

and the non-dimensional normalized objective functions are introduced –

$$\phi_1 = F_1(x_i)/\bar{F}_1; \quad \phi_2 = F_2(x_i)/\bar{F}_2; \quad \phi_3 = F_3(x_i)/k_1 c; \quad i = 1, 2.$$

In the dimensionless space of objective functions the ideal solution is in the point (1.0, 1.0, 0.0).

In the problem considered for imposed $c = 5\%$ and $k_1/k_2 = 10$, the maximum of function Φ_1 is obtained for $x_1 = 0$ and $x_2 = 4.0975$ (point B in Figure 13.7). The maximum of function Φ_2 is for $x_1 = 5$ and $x_2 = 0$ (point E). The minimum of function Φ_3 is for $x_1 = 0$ and $x_2 = 0$.

The set of compromises may be determined using one of the methods proposed in manuals of multi-criteria optimization, e.g. [13.24]–[13.27]. In Figures 13.8–13.10 the compromise sets $\phi_1\phi_2, \phi_1\phi_3 i \phi_2\phi_3$ are presented. The total compromise set is a surface in space ϕ_1, ϕ_2, ϕ_3 described on the curves which are the two-criteria compromise sets. In that problem the two-criteria compromise sets are determined using weighted coefficients and taking into account that the parts of the boundaries of the feasible regions are represented in the objective space as the boundary points of the objective region. These points are the compromise sets.

The preferred solution is determined as the point nearest to the ideal solution. Its coordinates satisfy the following condition:

$$\phi(x_i) = [\phi_1(x_i) - 1]^2 + [\phi_2(x_i) - 1]^2 + \phi_3^2 = \phi_{\min}$$

and are: $\phi_{1pr} = 0.9629$, $\phi_{2pr} = 0.4774$, $\phi_{3pr} = 0.10$. This point is projected on planes $\phi_3 = 0$, $\phi_2 = 0$ and $\phi_1 = 0$ presented in Figures 13.8–13.10. In the space of the design variables point C with coordinates $x_1 = 0$, $x_2 = 5$ (Figure 13.7) corresponds to the preferred solution.

It may be concluded that the solution is a composite material with a volume fraction of steel-fibres equal to 5% and without the carbon fibres which are considered to be 10 times more expensive. If the conditions of the problem are modified in such a way that the difference between the cost of fibres will be neglected and $k_1/k_2 = 1$, then the solution is 2.37% of steel-fibres and in this case also without carbon fibres (point F′ in Figure 13.7). In another case when the cost of fibres is completely neglected in the problem, then from both other criteria the solution will be: 4.83% of carbon fibres and 0.17% of steel-fibres, (point D in Figure 13.7). It is interesting to compare all three cases of the same problem but solved using different conditions for the cost of fibres. Its influence is the determining factor for the solution. In such a way by an appropriate formulation of the optimization problems, it is possible to take into account the importance of the cost of components for the final solution.

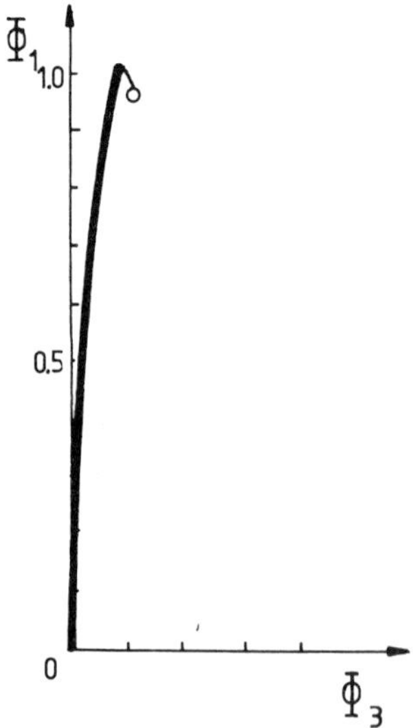

Figure 13.9 Compromise set for functions ϕ_1 and ϕ_3 and preferred solution in Example 13.5. (Source: Brandt, A.M. *et al.*, Optimization of cement-based composites reinforced with carbon fibres; published by Pluralis, 1992.) [13.29]

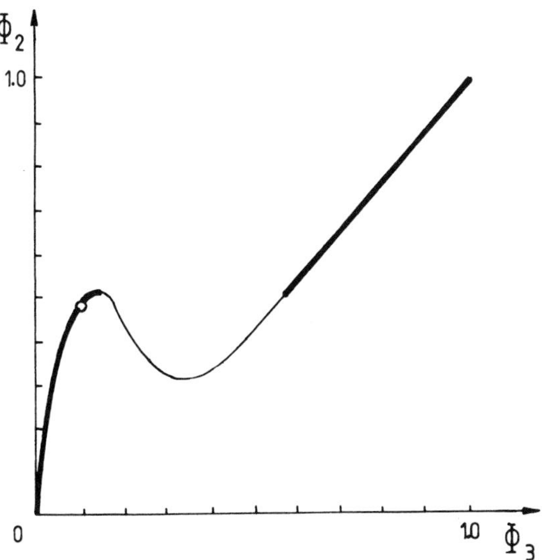

Figure 13.10 Compromise set for functions ϕ_2 and ϕ_3 and preferred solution in Example 13.5. (Source: Brandt, A.M. *et al.*, Optimization of cement-based composites reinforced with carbon fibres; published by Pluralis, 1992.) [13.29]

EXAMPLE 13.6

In this Example the optimization problem has been formulated on the basis of data obtained from testing concrete used for constructing piers of a highway bridge across the Vistula near Zakroczym. The text which follows is based on [13.31].

Two criteria were used – maximum compressive strength and minimum specific cost. Five independent variables were selected, namely, p – mass fractions of sand (0–2 mm); z – gravel (2–8 mm); g – crushed stone (8–16 mm); c – mass fractions of cement and w – water.

Using experimental data approximated by the least squares method and a set of curves from a design method used in the UK the compressive strength was presented as function of the five independent variables.

The compressive strength at 28 days was expressed as follows:

$$\begin{aligned} f_c(c, p, g, w, z) = & -4605.637 + 2.85641\, c - 0.000385989\, c^2 + 3.29077\, g + \\ & - 0.00093803\, c\, g - 0.000603422\, g^2 + 7.13967\, p + \\ & - 0.00208529\, c\, p - 0.00251967\, g\, p - 0.00199952\, p^2 + \\ & - 6.6717\, w + 0.00191048\, c\, w + 0.00231208\, g\, w + \\ & - 0.0012573\, p\, w + 0.0105818\, w^2 + 4.89951\, z + \\ & - 0.0014249\, c\, z - 0.00173254\, g\, z - 0.00323852\, p\, z + \\ & + 0.00111604\, w\, z - 0.00119418\, z^2. \end{aligned}$$

Specific cost was proposed as a sum of costs of particular components (water was excluded) multiplied by a nonlinear coefficient α related to the content of cement and representing the increased cost of high strength concrete. The cost function has the following form: $F(c, p, g, z) = \alpha(540c + 12p + 20z + 40g)$ where numerical coefficients are the approximate cost of components in PLZ per 1 kg and the coefficient was proposed as,

$$\alpha = \frac{9.025.10^{-3}c^{-2} - 2.28c + 423.75}{1.425c + 52.5}.$$

The following inequalities represent constraints imposed for decision variables:

$$320 \leqslant c \leqslant 450$$
$$190 \leqslant p \leqslant 600$$
$$430 \leqslant z \leqslant 1480$$
$$290 \leqslant g \leqslant 910$$
$$160 \leqslant w \leqslant 210$$

The constraints were taken from effective mixes used on site, where approximately the same workability was maintained for technological conditions.

Using similar mathematical methods as in previous examples, the solution obtained is shown in Figure 13.11 where points C and B represent solutions

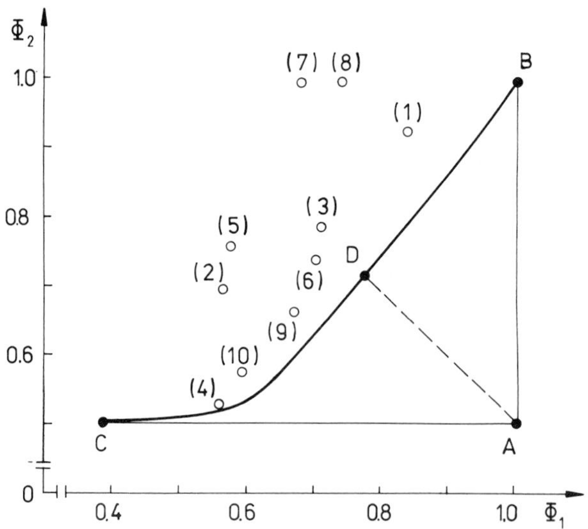

Figure 13.11 Compromise set, ideal solution and preferred solution. Points 1–10 correspond to particular mixes listed in Table 13.6. (Source: Marks, W. and Potrzebowski, J. Multicriteria optimization of structural concrete mix; *Civ. Eng. Arch.*, 1992.) [13.31]

for maximum compressive strength and minimum cost, respectively, and

$$\Phi_1 = \frac{f_c}{\bar{f}_c}, \quad \Phi_2 = \frac{F}{F(\bar{f}_c)}.$$

All characteristics of the preferred solution in point D are presented in Table 13.6. That solution gives less strong concrete than the solution for the maximum of f_c and more expensive than that for the minimum of F, but was selected as the closest one to the ideal solution in the space of normalized functions Φ_1 and Φ_2. Points with numbers indicate realized mixes as listed in Table 13.6.

It is interesting to note that the compressive strength of optimum concrete appeared to be 9 MPa higher than the average taken from 10 samples of actual mixes. At the same time the specific cost turned out to be 6% lower than the actual figure on the construction site. The closest to the theoretical best solution was the actual mix number 6, but it was less strong.

The results of this Example show that useful information may be obtained from the solution of an optimization problem even though a rather simplified model was adopted as a basis for calculations.

Table 13.6 Compositions of 10 mixes as compared to the optimum solution

No. of mix	Components (kgs/m^3) cement c	sand p	gravel z	crushed stone g	water w	w/c	Compressive strength (MPa) f_c	Cost (PLZ) F
Executed mixes								
1	423	430	633	905	161	0.38	63.12	
2	365	484	620	909	163	0.45	42.50	
3	387	465	606	887	176	0.45	53.21	
4	320	213	1 468	307	160	0.50	42.66	
5	362	197	1 403	293	181	0.50	42.59	
6	376	585	488	909	171	0.45	52.33	
7	443	563	444	828	201	0.45	50.85	
8	445	522	491	909	171	0.38	55.37	
9	363	414	1 190	320	171	0.47	49.92	
10	337	446	1 186	320	168	0.50	44.00	
Calculated mix for f_c maximum								
	450	600	987	290	160	0.36	74.99	497 250
Calculated mix for F minimum								
	320	578	966	318	209	0.65	29.14	257 500
Optimum mix corresponding to preferred solution D								
	379	579	965	407	160	0.42	58.80	356 290

(Source: Marks, W. and Potrzebowski, J., Multicriteria optimization of structural concrete mix; *Civ. Eng. Arch.* **31**(4), 1992.) [13.31]

13.6 General remarks

After the basic formulae, a few examples of the application of the methods and notions of optimization to the design of concrete-like composites have been presented. The solved examples are selected to provide fairly simple explanations of the proposed procedures. In all cases only one method of selection of the preferred solution from the Pareto compromise set was applied – in the space of normalized objective functions a point closest to the ideal solution was found as representing the preferred solution. It is possible to determine the preferred solution in many other ways, e.g. using numerical factors as weights which represent the importance of each particular objective function. By that method a so called utility function may be created which represents all objective functions with their weights in the form, $\Phi = \Phi_1 k_1 + \Phi_2 k_2 + \Phi_3 k_3 + \cdots$ where Φ_i are objective functions and k_i are their weights.

The principal difficulty in the problems of material optimization is in establishing their correct formulation, from which effective and useful solutions may be derived. Here the sensitivity of the objective functions with respect to the variables is a separate question which is related to the quality of the general formulation of a given problem.

The next difficulty is the determination of the analytical relationship between the objective functions and the variables. Such relations may be established from various test results available from publications. It seems unnecessary to carry out experimental research in each case when an optimization problem is formulated. Often, however, the relations between all the variables and objective functions are not given explicitly and special methods should be applied to obtain approximate solutions from incomplete test results.

The last difficulty in these problems is the effective solution of the equations obtained.

All values characterizing the properties of the material's components are subject to random and systematic variations. The same concerns their effective volume fractions and distribution in space. That is why experimental verification with actual materials and in local conditions of implementation is necessary to test the final result, and in most cases to introduce certain modifications into the set of values of the design variables as established in the optimization procedure. The requirement for tests before any full scale application is also accepted in simple mix design methods for ordinary concretes. It is also compulsory when optimization is applied, and is even more important in the case of high performance concretes, cf. Chapter 14.

Further development of the optimization approach for cement-based composites should be directed at various realistic objective functions and variables and at better expressions for objective functions. The generalization for random variables and the improvement of mechanical models may also be introduced to the optimization approach. Optimization for the least cost seems to be of particular importance as is shown in an approximate way in Examples 13.4, 13.5 and 13.6.

References

13.1. Brandt, A.M. (1985) On the optimization of fibre orientation in the brittle matrix composite materials. Stevin Lab. Rep. Delft Univ. of Technol., Delft.

13.2. Prager, W. (1974) *Introduction to Structural Optimization*, Springer Verlag.

13.3. Rao, S.S. (1978) *Optimization, Theory and Application*, Wiley Eastern Ltd, New Delhi.

13.4. Brandt, A.M. (ed.) (1984) *Criteria and Methods of Structural Optimization*, Martinus Nijhoff, The Hague.

13.5. Brandt, A.M. (ed.) (1989) *Foundations of Optimum Design in Civil Engineering*, Martinus Nijhoff, The Hague.

13.6. Brandt, A.M. (1984) On the optimization of the fiber orientation in cement-based composite materials, Proc. Int. Symp. *Fiber Reinforced Concrete*, Detroit 1982, (ed. G.C. Hoff), ACI, Detroit, 267–85.

13.7. Brandt, A.M. and Marks, M. (1993) Examples of the multicriteria optimization of cement-based composites. *Composite Structures*, **25**, 51–60.

13.8. Teters, G.A., Kregers, A.F. and Rikards, R.B. (1981) Models of a composite material in the optimization problems (in Russian), *Mechanics of Composite Materials*, Academy of Sciences of Latvian SSR, Riga, **5**, 807–14.

13.9. Mullin, J.V. and Mazzio, V.F. (1972) Optimizing composite properties. Society for the Advancement of Materials and Processes Engineering [SAMPE] quarterly, **3**(2), 22–7.

13.10. Brandmeier, H.E. (1970) Optimum filament orientation criteria. *Journal of Composite Materials*, **4**, July, 422–5.

13.11. Popovics, S. (1982) Production schedule of concretes for maximum profit. *Materials and Structures RILEM*, **15**(87), 199–204.

13.12. Popovics, S. (1982) Graphical method of optimization: A short cut. *ASCE Proc.*, **108**(CO2), June, 211–18.

13.13. Popovics, S. (1982) *Fundamentals of Portland Cement Concrete: A Quantitative Approach*, **1** ch. 7, J. Wiley, New York, 235–325.

13.14. Brandt, A.M. (1985) On the optimal direction of short metal fibres in brittle matrix composites. *J. of Materials Science*, **20**, 3831–41.

13.15. Brandt, A.M. (1986) Influence of the fibre orientation on the energy absorption at fracture of SFRC specimens, in Proc. Int. Symp. *Brittle Matrix Composites* 1, (ed. A.M. Brandt and I.H. Marshall), Elsevier Applied Sci. Publ. London, 403–20.

13.16. Brandt, A.M. (1987) Influence of the fibre orientation on the mechanical properties of fibre-reinforced cement (FRC) specimens, in *Proc. Int. Congress RILEM*, 2, Versailles, 651–8.

13.17. Marks, M. (1989) Optimal fibre orientation in concrete like composites, in Proc. Int. Symp. *Brittle Matrix Composites* **2**, (Eds A.M. Brandt and I.H. Marshall), Elsevier Applied Science, London, 54–64.

13.18. Marks, M. (1988) Composite elements of minimum deformability reinforced with two families of fibres (in Polish). *Engineering Transactions* (Rozpr. Inz.) **36**(3), 541–62.

13.19. Li, V.C., Wang, Y. and Backer, S. (1991) Fracture energy optimization in synthetic fiber reinforced cementitious composites, in *Proc. Mat. Res. Soc.* Boston, November 1990, **211**, 63–9.

13.20. Li, V.C., Maalej, M. and Hashida, T. (1992) Optimization of discontinuous fiber composites, in Proc. ASCE 9th Conf. *Engineering Mechanics*, (eds L.D. Luter and I.M. Niedzwecki), 1000–3.

13.21. Rossi, P., Harrouche, N., de Larrard, F. (1989) Method for optimizing the composition of metal-fibre-reinforced-concrete, in Proc. Int. Conf. *Fibre Reinforced Cements and Concretes. Recent Developments*. Cardiff, (eds R.N. Swamy and B. Barr), Elsevier Applied Science, London, 3–10.

13.22. Kasperkiewicz, J. (1992) Optimization of concrete mix using a spreadsheet package, (in print).

13.23. Kuhn, H.W. and Tucker, A.W. (1951) Nonlinear programming. Proc. of Second Berkeley Symposium on *Mathematical Statistics and Probability*, Univ. of California Press, Berkeley, Cal., 481–92.

13.24. Hwang, C.L. and Masud, A.S.M. (1979) Multiple objective decision making – methods and applications. A State-of-Art-Survey. *Lecture Notes in Economics and Mathematical Systems*, Springer-Verlag, Berlin.

13.25. Jendo, S., Marks, W. and Thierauf, G. (1985) Multicriteria optimization in optimum structural design, in *Large Scale System*, (ed. Sage A.P.), Elsevier Science Publishers, B.V. (North-Holland) 9, 141–50.

13.26. Borkowski, A. and Jendo, S. (1990) Structural Optimization, **2** *Mathematical Programming*, Plenum Press, New York and London.

13.27. Künzi, H.P. and Krelle, W. (1966) *Nichtlineare Programmierung*, Springer-Verlag, Heidelberg.

13.28. Brandt, A.M. and Marks, M. (1992) Optimization of cement-based composites, in Proc. Int. Conf. *Concrete 92*, The Plan and Budget Organization, Tehran.

13.29. Brandt, A.M., Glinicki, M.A. and Marks, W. (1992) Optimization of cement-based composites reinforced with carbon fibres, in Proc. 2nd Int. Symp. *Textile Composites in Building Construction*, part 1, Pluralis, Lyon, 17–28.

13.30. Banthia, N. and Sheng, J. (1991) Micro-reinforced cementitious materials, in *Fiber Reinforced Cementitious Materials*, (ed. S. Mindess and J. Skalny), Mat. Res. Soc. Symp. Proc., **211** MRS, Mat. Res. Soc., Pittsburgh, 25–32.

13.31. Marks, W. and Potrzebowski, J. (1992) Multicriteria optimization of structural concrete mix, *Civ. Eng. Arch.*, Warsaw **38** (4), 323–3.

14 Special kinds of cement-based composites

14.1 Soil cements

14.1.1 GENERAL INFORMATION

Soil cements are defined by the American Concrete Institute Committee 230 as 'a mixture of soil and measured amounts of Portland cement and water compacted to a high density' and the main differences with concrete is that 'individual particles are not completely coated with cement paste', [14.1]. Application of other binding materials like natural or artificial pozzolans is also possible, [14.2]. The main reason for their application is the relatively low cement content and lower cost compared with ordinary concretes.

Soil cement is used for creating layers under bituminous or concrete pavements in road structures. It is also used in the construction of slope protection, liners for channels or reservoirs and various kinds of stabilization layers under structural foundations. The application of soil cements for the construction of local roads in rural regions, particularly in developing countries, is spreading. In most cases the soil cement layers are maintained permanently in high moisture conditions during service.

Nearly all kinds of soils may be used as a component for soil cements; however, granular soils are considered to be better than clays. The volume fraction of organic materials should preferably be lower than 2%. Aggregate grains are restricted to 50 mm and fine fractions are limited because their excess may cause increased cement consumption. The best composition is closely related to local conditions and any requirements imposed on the final product – price, exposition to external actions, required durability, etc. For further technical details the reader is referred to manuals and recommendations, e.g. [14.1].

14.1.2 MECHANICAL PROPERTIES

The density of the soil cement is dependent on the moisture content and an example of that relationship is shown in Figure 14.1. Density increases with the cement content up to a certain optimum value and then it decreases.

The compressive strength of the soil cement f_c may be characterized by an increase in density compared to that of a wet soil without cement or any other binder f_{co} and that increase is represented by a coefficient a, $a = (f_c - f_{co})/f_{co}$

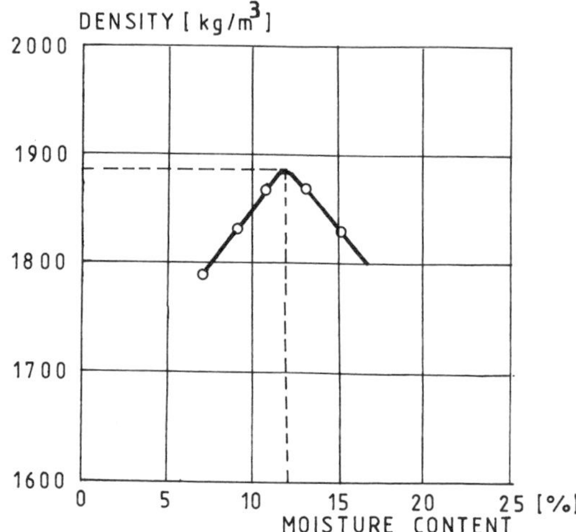

Figure 14.1 Typical moisture–density curve for soil cement. (Reproduced with permission from ACI, State-of-the-Art Report on Soil Cement; *American Concrete Institute Materials Journal*, **85**(4), pp. 395–417. 1990.) [14.1]

Based on [14.2] the coefficient a for Portland cement admixture of 8% per volume may vary from 4.5 after 7 days to 12.6 at 180 days. The improvement of strength depends considerably on the soil properties and ageing conditions and is increasing linearly with the Portland cement content up to 15%. According to [14.1] the strength after 28 days may reach 7 MPa.

The compressive strength of the product should be determined experimentally because any prediction is not reliable enough particularly as far as it concerns its increase over time, [14.3]. The flexural strength (modulus of rupture) may be calculated approximately from the formula proposed in [14.4], $f_r = 0.51 f_c^{0.88}$ (in psi) or $f_r = 0.27 f_c^{0.88}$ (in MPa). Experimental data are given in Figure 14.2 and it appears that values up to $f_c = 15$ MPa may be reached.

Among other mechanical properties, both water permeability and shrinkage are to be considered. Both depend on cement content, quality of the initial curing and at a later stage moisture conditions. High shrinkage should be avoided and reduced by moist curing and limited cement content. Permeability is considerably enhanced and the durability of the soil cement layers may be reduced as a result of shrinkage cracking.

14.1.3 GRANULAR SOIL WITH FIBRE REINFORCEMENT

This is a relatively new material composed of granular natural soil, i.e. sand, and thin continuous fibres distributed in the material volume with or without cement or any other binding agent. The polyester or polyamide fibres are very

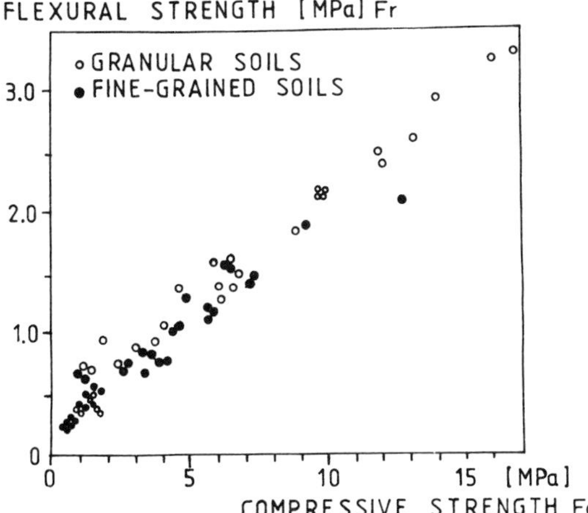

Figure 14.2 Relationship between compressive strength f_c and modulus of rupture f_r of soil cements. (Source: FHA, Soil Stabilization in Pavement Structures. A User's Manual; Federal Highway Administration, 1979.) [14.4]

thin and their volume fraction is low – between 0.1 and 0.3%. The fibres are distributed in a uniform and isotropic way (3D) or are parallel to a selected plane (2D).

The main influence of the reinforcement is the resultant cohesion of sand which is enhanced with the fibre content, while the angle of internal friction is constant.

The tests of the specimens under compressive load proved a considerable increase in bearing capacity. The descending branch of the load–deformation curve may be long and its shape is strongly related to the type of fibres. In the case of elastic fibres a quasi-linear behaviour is observed, but for ordinary polymeric fibres an elastic quasi-plastic behaviour should be expected.

Thanks to the artificial cohesion of the reinforced sand it was used for the construction of walls and slopes with steep gradients between 60 and 90°. The best known kind of reinforced sand called Texsol was tested in France in 1982, [14.5] and [14.6].

14.2 Composites with special reinforcement

14.2.1 ASBESTOS CEMENTS

Asbestos fibres have been used as reinforcement for cement matrices since the beginning of the century. The main products are pipes and tiles for roofs and floors. Among several production processes the most used was the Hatschek method in which a suspension of fibres in water is prepared. In the Magnani process the fibres are subjected to a sequence of vibration in water, suction and pressure. The Manville extrusion process is based on dry mixing of fibres with sand, cement and the necessary amount of water. More details on the production methods may be found [14.7] and [14.8].

The mechanical properties of asbestos fibre cements depend on the quality, amount and orientation of fibres. The data from different sources given in Table 14.1 should be considered as orientation only and have to be checked with relevant information from producers.

Asbestos fibre cements are considered as cheap and durable, with high corrosion and abrasion resistance and good performance in elevated temperatures. The application of asbestos fibres with coarse aggregate is not appropriate. Usually the volume fraction of asbestos fibres in composites is 6% and may be increased up to 20%. Asbestos fibres are also used extensively as reinforcement for resins and plastics, thereby improving considerably their mechanical and thermal properties; they may also be mixed with glassfibres, cf. Section 5.2.

The important strengthening effect of asbestos fibres is due to their high strength and Young's modulus and to the excellent bonding to cement paste. The fibres control cracks in the brittle matrix and any rupture of the composite is accompanied by the pull-out of fibres. Linear elastic behaviour is observed at almost maximum load and then the shape of the descending branch is determined by the efficiency of the fibres, cf. Figure 14.3.

The pull-out mechanism was examined in [14.10] and it appears that the load–displacement curve is similar to that for steel-fibres (Figure 14.4). An appreciable difference of shear strength at the interface was observed for two main kinds of asbestos fibres, namely – for chrysotile fibres $\tau_{max} = 1.8$ MPa; and for crocidolite fibres $\tau_{max} = 3.1$ MPa. Chrysotile fibres are flexible and crocidolite fibres are stiff. The results obtained cannot be explained solely by that difference and further reasons should be looked for in the inter-fibre bond within the fibre bundles. In the manufacturing process of composite elements the crocidolite fibres are subjected to more damage than chrysotile ones. The mechanical

Table 14.1 Mechanical properties of asbestos cement composites

Properties	Values	Units
Density	1.800–2.100	(kg/m^3)
Young's modulus	24	(GPa)
Tensile strength	12–25	(MPa)
Tensile strength under bending	30–60	(MPa)
Compressive strength	50–200	(MPa)

(Source: Hannant, D.J., *Fibre Cements and Fibre Concretes*, published by John Wiley & Sons, London, 1978.) [14.7]

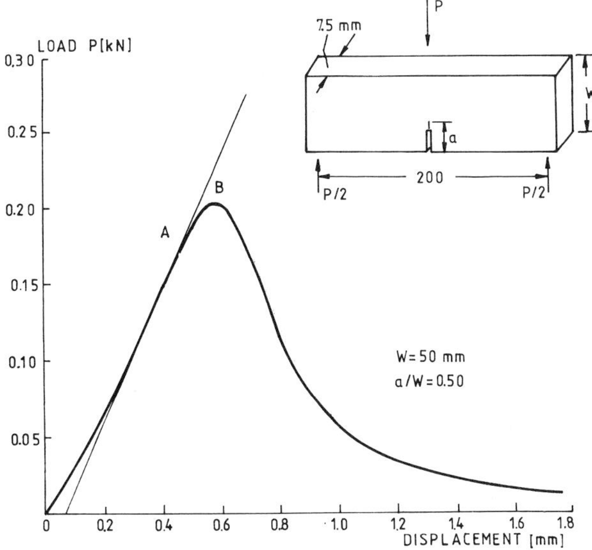

Figure 14.3 Characteristic load–displacement curve for the notched specimen made of asbestos cement. (Reproduced with permission from Mai, Y.W. *et al.*, Size effects and scalling laws of fracture in asbestos cement; *International Journal of Cement Composites* **2**(1), pp. 23–33, published by Elsevier Science Publishers, 1980.) [14.9]

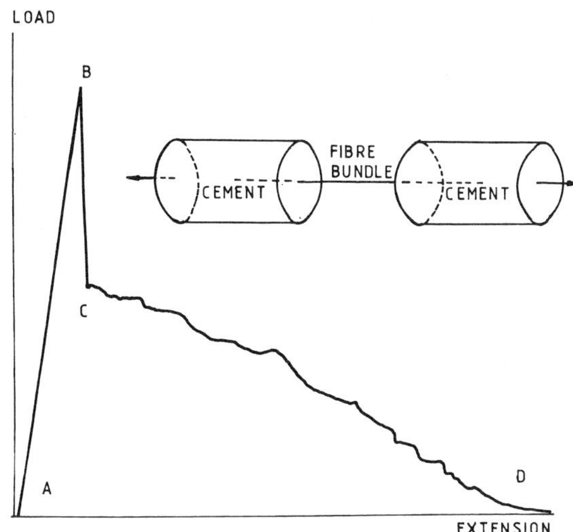

Figure 14.4 Characteristic load–extension curve for pull-out test of an asbestos fibre from cement matrix. (Reproduced with permission from Akers, S.A.S. and Garrett, G.G., The relevance of simple fibre models to the industrial behaviour of asbestos cement composites; *International Journal of Cement Comp. and Lightweight Concrete*, **5**(3), pp. 173–9, Elsevier, 1983.) [14.10]

behaviour of asbestos cement elements cannot be directly related to the results of the pull-out tests of single fibres or their bundles which, however, is considered to be a highly relevant test.

The mechanical properties of asbestos fibre cements may be calculated from the law of mixtures [14.11] or by using the fracture mechanics formulae from which the specific work of fracture and R-curve were determined in [14.12] and compared with experimental results from specimens of different sizes. The observations made in [14.9] also indicated that crack initiation was close to the bending strength which was itself related to a quasi elastic and brittle behaviour. For specimens with depth greater than 50 mm the size effect on mechanical behaviour was negligible. For smaller specimens the pull-out of fibres across cracks could not be developed before quick crack propagation took place followed by the failure of the specimen.

Recent studies of asbestos fibre cements were mostly performed with a view to replacement by other kinds of fibres, [14.9]. These interesting investigations have shown, among others features, that for hybrid asbestos–cellulose fibre-reinforcement the modified law of mixtures also provided good agreement with experimental results and that linear elastic fracture mechanics formulae may be applied to these composites. Even with fibres of relatively short length the aspect ratio l/d is high enough so that the fracture energy is provided by the fibre pull-out processes in 95%. Extensive lists of references on asbestos fibres applications and the fracture behaviour of asbestos cement elements are given in the above-mentioned papers.

The application of asbestos fibres in shotcrete was subjected to an extensive study [14.13], and excellent mechanical properties and resistance against freeze–thaw cycles were recorded for mixes with fine and coarse aggregate. It has also been observed that, with fibres premixed with cement paste in a 'wet-mix' process, there was no danger for workers' health.

Because of the dangerous effects of asbestos fibres on people's health the application of asbestos cements has decreased considerably in recent years and other kinds of fibres are now used as replacement, cf. Section 5.2.

14.2.2 FERROCEMENTS

(a) Components and applications

A rather broad definition proposed by the American Concrete Institute Committee 549 for ferrocement is – 'A type of thin wall reinforced concrete constructed of hydraulic cement mortar reinforced with closely spaced layers of continuous and relatively small wire diameter mesh. The mesh may be made of metallic or other suitable materials', [14.14].

In the above definition all kinds of non-metallic meshes are included, but in this chapter only ferrocement with metallic reinforcement is considered. Other types of meshes, fabrics and mats made with non-metallic fibres are treated as textile reinforcement and are examined in Sections 5.9 and 14.2.2.

The matrix for ferrocement consists of hydrated Portland cement paste with a filling material like sand or micro-aggregate, similar to those used for FRC. An adequate penetration of the mesh by the fresh cement mix is required and its fluidity should be adjusted by modification of the water/cement ratio and by using appropriate admixtures.

The concreting is executed by various methods from well instrumented automatic shotcreting to hand plastering and patching. Concreting with or without one side mould is possible, depending on the position and density of reinforcement. The construction methods can be adapted to the equipment available locally and to the more or less complicated shape of the final product. Particular advantages of ferrocement are obtained when large and curvilinear structures are built with reduced forms and scaffoldings.

The reinforcement of the ferrocement is composed usually of several layers of mesh of various shapes and structure. The following examples may be mentioned:

- woven and interlocking mesh;
- welded mesh of rectangular, diagonal or more often square pattern;
- expanded metal lath;
- punched or perforated metal lath;
- continuous filament irregularly assembled into two-dimensional mat;
- rarely used tri-dimensional structure of wires.

Examples of types of mesh for ferrocement are shown in Figure 14.5.

The wires for making the reinforcements are used as received, but may be galvanically coated or covered with polymer coating to increase wire–matrix bonding and to reduce the danger of eventual corrosion. Expanded metal lath and welded meshes perform better than woven ones because the latter causes discontinuities at nodes which act as stress concentrators.

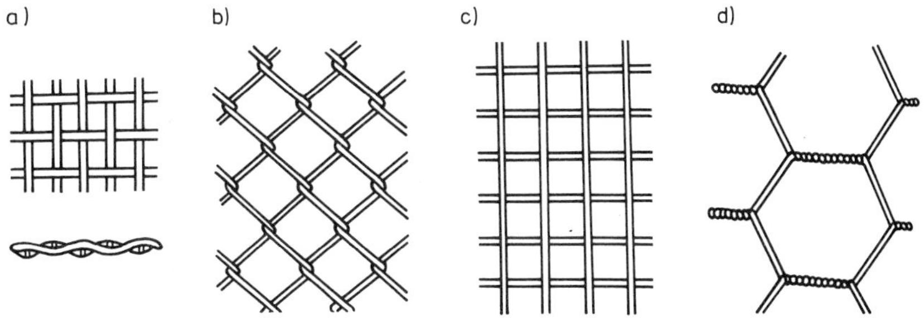

Figure 14.5 Examples of mesh for ferrocement. a) woven; b) plaited; c) welded; d) twisted. (Source: Brandt, A.M. *et al.*, Bases for application of concrete-like composites; published by COIB, Warsaw, 1983.) [14.15]

The cement-based matrices for ferrocement may be subjected to modifications, e.g. by admixtures of polymers and resins to the fresh mix or by impregnation of hardened ferrocement. The modifications are aimed at particular improvements of the final product like an increase of strength or impermeability, (cf. Sections 3.2.8 and 14.2.2).

(b) Mechanical properties

The mechanical properties of ferrocement depend on the volume fraction and type of reinforcement as well as on the properties of the matrix. In particular:

- the ultimate tensile strength under static load depends on the efficiency of the reinforcement;
- the cracking resistance and so-called first crack load is depending mostly on the matrix properties which may be considerably improved provided that a relatively high volume fraction of reinforcement is used;
- the compressive strength is only infrequently determined for ferrocements, because local compressions are usually supported directly by the matrix.

The volume fraction of the reinforcement is rarely lower than 5–6% which corresponds to 400–500 kg/m^3. This may be considered as a relatively high reinforcement, compared with ordinary concrete structures. The spacing of the wires is then varied from 5 to 10 mm and a specific area of reinforcement S_R should satisfy the condition, $S_R = 4\,V_f/d > 0.08\,[\text{mm}^{-1}]$.

In meshes with a rectangular pattern the reinforcement area S_R is divided into transverse and longitudinal directions, $S_R = S_{RT} + S_{RL}$.

The ultimate matrix strain ε_{mu} is difficult to determine because it is related to the definition of a crack. It is generally admitted that for a non-reinforced matrix $\varepsilon_{mu} = 100\text{–}200 \cdot 10^{-6}$. The first deviation from linear behaviour as observed on the stress–strain or load–deformation curves for ferrocement elements corresponds to $\varepsilon_{cu} = 900\text{–}1500 \cdot 10^{-6}$, but these values are strongly influenced by the volume and type of reinforcement. It has been proved that thinner wires, densely distributed, perform better than thicker ones.

The spacing between layers of reinforcement is ensured by special links; usually it is uniform across the depth, but for elements subjected to bending it may be smaller in the tensioned zone in order to increase the efficiency of the reinforcement and the bearing capacity of the element. An approximate formula proposed for the number of layers N is $N > 0.16t$, where t is total depth in mm. This means that a spacing of between 4 and 6 mm is commonly used for ferrocement plates or walls up to 10 mm depth.

The load is transferred from matrix to wires not only by the bond but also by nodes and transverse wires. That is the reason why the crack pattern visible on ferrocement elements is often a reflection of the distribution of the wires and nodes.

The elastic modulus of ferrocement after matrix cracking depends on that of the reinforcement and is denoted by E_R. It is lower than E_s for steel because the wires are not usually straight and, particularly in woven meshes, they stretch when subjected to tensile load. Only for rectangular welded mesh is $E_R = E_s$. Diagonal wire systems are also characterized by decreased stiffness and reinforcing efficiency, e.g. for wires oriented at 45° the efficiency is estimated between 65 and 80%. The mechanical properties of ferrocement elements were examined by many authors, e.g. [14.16] in which extensive tests have been published on specimens under bending and a formula was proposed for determining the moment–curvature and load–deflection curves based on the mechanical properties of both wires and matrix.

In [14.17] some interesting data are given on the influence of the orientation of wires on the ultimate bending moment (Figure 14.6) and the relevant calculation procedure is put forward.

The fatigue strength of the ferrocement depends on the efficiency and type of reinforcement. It is higher for woven than for welded meshes. It has been established [14.18] that the failure as a result of fatigue is always caused by failure of the external steel mesh due to tensile fatigue. The authors of [14.18] proposed relations to predict the deflection and crack width of ferrocement elements under bending as functions of the number of cycles.

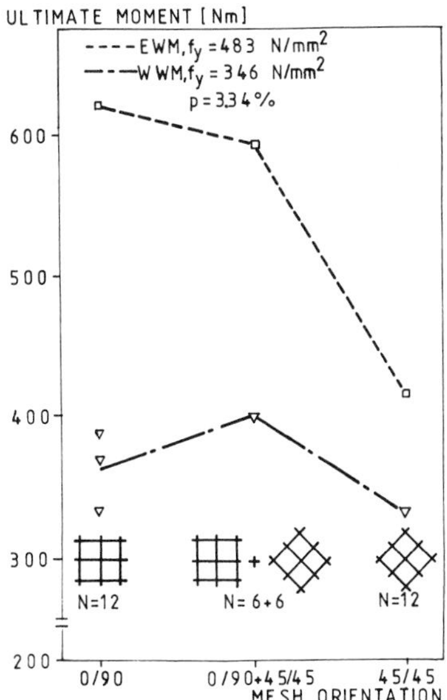

Figure 14.6 Influence of orientation on ultimate bending moment for ferrocement elements with welded and woven meshes, here EXM – expanded metal with steel elements on a 31 mm × 13 mm diamond shaped grid; EWM – electro-welded-wire (galvanized) on a 13 mm grid. (Reproduced with permission from Johnston, C.D. and Mowat, D.N., Ferrocement – material behaviour inflexure; *Proc. ASCE*, **100**(ST10), pp. 2053–69, 1974.) [14.17]

Durability of the ferrocement elements is a function of cover depth and cracking characteristics. When improved durability in a corrosive environment is required, then a small diameter reinforcement with high specific surface should be used and impermeability of the matrix should be ensured by additional measures. In such a case, for liquid retaining structures the admissible crack width is limited up to 0.02–0.05 mm, while for ordinary structures and in ordinary conditions 0.10 mm is considered to be acceptable for the ferrocement.

Impact strength of the ferrocement is essential for such applications as boat hulls, container walls and ballistic panels. It was tested by several authors, e.g. [14.19], with drop hammers, Charpy hammers and air gun projectiles. The results of comparative tests are expressed in crater depth or perforation characteristics and failure energy. The failure energy increases linearly with the wall depth and specific surface of the reinforcement. In Figure 14.7 tensile strength and Charpy impact strength are compared as functions of the specific surface S_R of reinforcement.

Basic recommendations for the design of ferrocement elements are also given in [14.14].

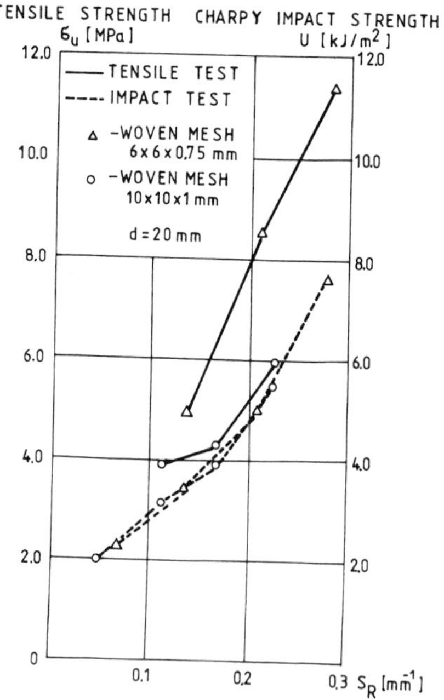

Figure 14.7 Tensile strength and Charpy impact strength versus specific surface of reinforcement. (Reproduced from Grabowski, J., Ferrocement under impact loads; *Journal of Ferrocement*, **15**(4), pp. 331–41.) [14.19]

(c) Ferrocement with reinforced matrices

Crack control and resistance against local loads in ferrocement is improved considerably by the addition of fibres and polymers into the matrix composition. Various kinds of fibres – steel, glass, low modulus carbon, vinylon and polypropylene are used with different volume contents, usually similar to that for fibre concretes. Polymers are also used to modify a matrix, both as liquid resins as for PCC, or by using an impregnation technique as for PIC. The main reinforcement is based on a classic steel mesh or on a hybrid combination of steel wire fabric and crimped wire cloth, as tested in [14.20]. As a result, increased first crack and maximum loads were observed due to a significant improvement of matrix quality. Also, deflections at the ultimate stage were increased thanks to improved bonding. The improved resistance of such composites against impact permitted their use for shields and protective layers in industrial and military structures.

14.2.3 CEMENT COMPOSITES WITH TEXTILE REINFORCEMENT

Composite elements with Portland cement matrices and textile reinforcement have been used for some time as thin roof plates, partition walls, cladding, etc. A few remarks on textile reinforcement are given in Section 5.9. As well as systems of plane fabrics, 3D reinforcement is also manufactured and tests of elements with 3D carbon fibre-reinforcement were reported in [14.21].

The reinforcement of cement matrices with textiles has certain advantages, namely:

- better mechanical properties due to more regular distribution of wires than in the case of short chopped fibres;
- the possibility of more efficient orientation of wires if the direction of principal strain components due to loading is known;
- the elimination of accidental regions of weak reinforcement;
- increased durability by application of non-corroding fibres and by ensuring at least the minimum depth of cover for all wires;
- the possibility of the application of advanced industrial techniques (e.g. lamination) and simple production of complicated shapes with plane sheets laminated as sandwiches and folded before hardening;
- the possibility of application of very simple technologies, e.g. hand-patching or laying mats and fabrics while spraying them with cement slurry and low pressure rolling.

The mechanical properties of hardened materials are similar to those of ordinary fibre-reinforced composites. They are determined by the quality of the matrix, reinforcement and interface layer between these two. Particularly interesting are the improved resistance and toughness against impact loading.

For a review of the test results of elements with textile reinforcement the reader is referred to [14.22] and [14.23]. Interesting remarks on the design of structural elements are published in [14.24].

14.2.4 SLURRY INFILTRATED FIBRE CONCRETE (SIFCON)

SIFCON is composed of a high percentage of fibres in a cement-based matrix. Fibres are pre-placed in a mould and the fibre system obtained is infiltrated by a cement-based slurry. In most cases steel fibres are used which have a fibre volume fraction between 7 and 12%, but sometimes reinforcement up to 27% is reported. Steel-fibres are straight and plain, often bigger than in ordinary FRC materials; hooked fibres also are used. Polypropylene fibres are sometimes used in the form of mats and fabrics.

The cement slurry may be filled with fine sand, micro-aggregate and special additives like fly ash and silica fume. The mass proportions of the components are – Portland cement: fly ash: sand from 9 : 1 : 0 up to 3 : 2 : 5 with the water/cement ratio varying from 0.20 up to 0.45, depending on the use of superplasticizers, [14.25].

The high fluidity (low viscosity) of the slurry is necessary for adequate penetration of the dense fibre system in the mould. By the addition of fly ash and fine sand, the Portland cement content may be diminished and possible shrinkage cracking reduced. Vibration of pre-placed fibres before and after pouring of cement slurry is often advisable in order to improve the density and distribution of reinforcement.

Research into the properties and the technology of SIFCON is in progress in several laboratories. One of the first published reports was [14.26]. A comprehensive review of mechanical properties is presented by [14.27]. The optimum design of SIFCON composition was considered by [14.28]. Mechanical properties under shearing were tested in [14.29] and [14.30].

The behaviour of SIFCON elements under compression and bending as compared with classic fibre-reinforced mortar is presented in Figures 14.8 and 14.9. It can be observed that SIFCON elements exhibited a considerable increase in strength and ductility. The fracture toughness, calculated as proportional to the area under the load–deflection curves, was also increased and the curves were characterized by a post-peak plateau. After these tests it was concluded that the quality of the matrix itself contributed significantly to the overall behaviour of the composite material. That effect was studied further in [14.31] which showed an increased strain and strength capacity for a matrix subjected to tension. Therefore, these results confirmed earlier achievements in SIFCON technology and also supported theoretical predictions which had been formulated [14.32]. It has also been shown that the matrix properties are improved only when fibre volume exceeds a certain threshold – below that value the crack opening load is unaffected by reinforcement, and that has been established for ordinary fibre-reinforced mortars and concretes. Beyond that threshold the

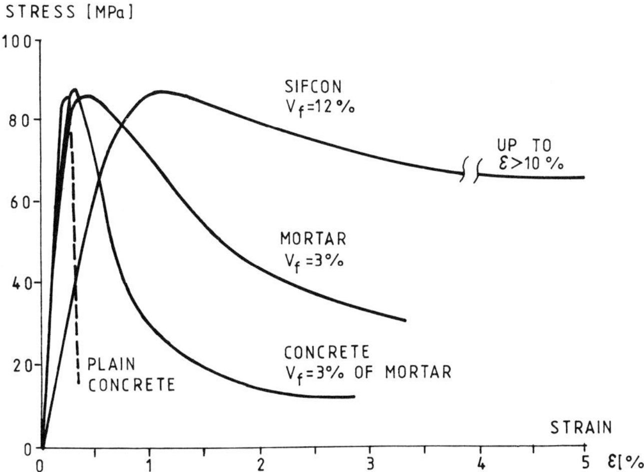

Figure 14.8 Stress–strain curves in compression of various composites as compared with SIFCON. (Reproduced with permission from Naaman, A.E., SIFCON: tailored properties for structural performance; published by Chapman & Hall/Spon, 1992.) [14.27]

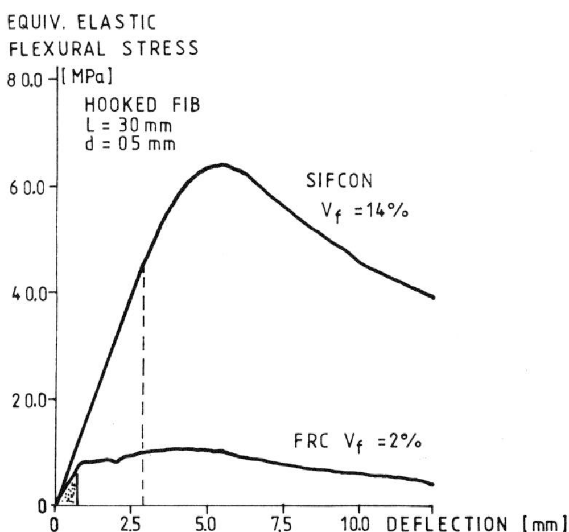

Figure 14.9 Stress–deflection curves in bending of SIFCON and FRC elements. (Reproduced with permission from Naaman, A.E., SIFCON: tailored properties for structural performance; published by Chapman & Hall/Spon, 1992.) [14.27]

tensile strength and fracture energy vary linearly with fibre content, at least within the scope of the fibre volumes used for SIFCON.

Multiple cracking under direct tension contributed to higher strength and increased energy absorption as compared with FRC. The excellent ductility of SIFCON was also observed under cyclic compressive loads. Other mechanical properties such as Young's modulus and bond strength to the matrix are also increased in SIFCON.

The majority of fibres are situated in approximately horizontal planes; therefore, the in-plane and out-of-plane properties are different and SIFCON clearly exhibits some orthotropic properties.

The considerably improved mechanical properties of SIFCON can be exploited in various structures or in their particular regions, where locally improved properties may modify overall structural behaviour. The following may be mentioned as examples – radiation shields, repair of outdoor structures, joints in structures exposed to seismic actions or possible explosions, precast impact resistant panels, etc. Up to now the practical applications of SIFCON have not been numerous, mostly because of the lack of precise information and of simple guides, necessary for both designers and contractors. Also, the question as to whether the high additional costs of materials and construction are balanced by the performance of the product should be answered in every case.

A special type of this material is called SIFCA – Slurry Infiltrated Fiber-Reinforced Castable. This is a composite material ceramic matrix with calcium aluminate cement and with aggregate made of aluminium oxide, mullite, zircon and calcined fireclay. The matrix is reinforced with stainless-steel fibres. SIFCA is used to make precast elements for refractory structures, where temperatures can rise to 1100 °C. Heat curing is often used during the precasting, [14.33].

14.3 Polymer concretes

Synthetic materials used in cement composites should satisfy to a larger or smaller extent the following conditions:

- low viscosity and high wetting ability for aggregate grains;
- good bond to aggregate and reinforcement;
- controlled hardening allowing to cast the mix in prepared forms;
- low toxicity, particularly after hardening;
- appropriate durability in humid environment and, as far as it is possible, resistance in elevated temperatures.

Viscosity is the internal resistance to flow exhibited by a fluid depending also on suspended particles – their size, volume content, etc. Low viscosity is one of the main characteristics required for monomers used in cement-based composites.

There are three main groups of polymer concretes – PC, PCC and PIC according to definitions adopted by the American Concrete Institute, cf. Section 3.2, and basic information is presented on applied monomers in Section 4.1. Those materials with their pore systems are presented in a schematic way in Figure 14.10 together with ordinary concrete, designated OC. In the small designs capillary pores and matrix are shown. In OC the capillary pores are filled with water or air. In PCC pores are filled in a similar way, but dispersed polymer

	I	II	III	IV
	OC	PCC	PIC	PC
POLYMER LOADING % wt.	0	≤30	3-8	6-20
POLYMER/BINDER RATIO % wt	0	0.15-50	5-15	100
POROSITY OF BINDER (paste) % vol.	12-16	10-20	3-5	≤5
POLYMER PHASE	DOES NOT EXIST	DISPERSED	SEMI-CONTINUOUS	CONTINUOUS

Figure 14.10 Scheme of pore structure in hardened paste in materials based on ordinary Portland cement (OC, PCC, PIC) and in PC. Black areas represent polymer, cross-hatched areas – partially polymer filled areas. (Reproduced with permission from Czarnecki, L., The status of polymer concrete; *ACI Concrete International*, September, 1991.) [14.34]

particles are shown in the matrix. In PIC capillary pores are nearly completely filled with polymer particles. In PC there are practically no pores and only the polymer matrix represents the continuous phase without cement. These materials are not covered by the general term 'cement-based composites'. That is why they are only mentioned briefly below.

The role of polymers in PCC, PIC and PC is entirely different mainly because of the fact that additive and synergetic mechanisms are different. Additive mechanisms depend on the properties of the components and on their fractional volumes. The rule of mixtures is decisive on the macro-structural level and it determines the final properties of the composite. The synergetic mechanisms depend rather on the phenomena occurring in the micro-structure of the interfacial layers on the surface of the components, and certain small quantities of admixture may play a considerable role in final behaviour of the composite.

In PC both groups of resins – those hardened by polymerization and polycondensation – are applied. Polymers are more expensive but there are no additional products emitted during hardening. Polycondensates are cheaper and support elevated temperatures better during exploitation, but water from the condensation process increases the porosity of the final composite and consequently reduce strength, frost resistance and impermeability. Large modifications to a material may be obtained simply by using different kinds of polymers. Polymers and resins are 5–40 times more expensive than Portland cement and the optimum design of a material's composition is of particular importance because in that way the minimum consumption of polymers is often looked for, [14.34].

The application of PC has developed quickly since the 1950s when it was used initially to produce synthetic marble. Since the 1970s PC has been widely known as a material for the repair of reinforced concrete structures, mainly highway overlays and bridges, but also for the production of machine bases, building panels and utility boxes. Because of both its excellent bonding to ordinary concrete and its high mechanical properties, PC is used for overlays on bridges when a short time for execution and a low dead load, thanks to thin layers (about 13 mm), are valued. The quality of overlays made of PC has been verified over almost 20 years of service on several structures and it has still proved to be in a good state of serviceability. Other applications of PC are in precast elements – lining of steel pipes, skins for lightweight sandwich panels for buildings, ballistic panels, etc., but high materials' costs and sensitivity to elevated temperatures present certain limitations. PC may also be reinforced with steel or glassfibres and steel bars, [14.35].

In polymer cement concretes (PCC) natural and synthetic caoutchouc, polyvinyl acetate, acrylics, vinyls and others are added to Portland cement mixes mostly in the form of latexes, i.e. as colloidal suspensions in water. Latexes were used as modifying admixtures for concretes as early as the 1920s, [14.36].

In PCC synthetic materials are added to the Portland cement or to water before mixing and eventually all components are mixed together. The selection of the best technology is essential in each particular case to obtain an appropriate distribution of the polymer, in the form of a film, around all the particles and pores. The processes of polymerization and cement hydration are, however, conflicting. Polymerization may be disturbed by the presence of water in the cement slurry. Free water from polymerization also modifies, in a negative sense, the water/cement ratio which determines the strength of the hardened cement and other properties. These difficulties and limited successes resulting from the various investigations in the field of PCC led to the situation in which pre-mixed polymerized materials including latexes and polymer solutions were used, [14.37]. Polymer dispersions (latexes) can be added to mortars and concretes during mixing. The processes of hardening of the cement and polymerization of monomers should develop in such a way that latex particles concentrate in the void spaces of cement hydrates. Because of the size of latex particles – usually above 100 nm – not all capillary pores are filled.

Workability of PCC depends not only on the composition but also on the temperature, and it should be assessed 'by eye' and experience because there are no standard methods and the slump test is not appropriate.

The final product has improved mechanical properties, bond strength to concrete substrates, resistance under flexure and impact, impermeability, frost resistance, etc. The resultant properties of the PCC elements depend to a considerable extent upon the quality of latex and of additional ingredients, and on the appropriate construction procedures as well as on the later curing process.

Polymer composition has a major influence on the final properties of the hardened composites and also on the workability of the fresh mix. Admixtures are often added to improve:

- protection against bacteria;
- resistance against ageing and the influence of sunlight, durability in freeze–thaw cycles;
- compressive and tensile strength.

Styrene–butadiene latex is used as an admixture for cement-based mixes used for repair of concrete structures, for protective overlays and for industrial floors, [14.38]. A typical application would be for the repair of bridge decks subjected to de-icing agents and to freeze–thaw cycles. The PCC is also applied for special purposes like protective spray-on coatings for various kinds of structures. The latex is added as between 5 and 20% of cement mass during mixing. If the latex content is below 5% of cement mass the term Polymer Modified Concrete (PMC) is used instead of PCC, [14.39].

If compared with a basic material without latex admixture the following improvements are observed:

- several times (5–10) increased bond to concrete surface;
- diminished water absorption;
- considerably decreased carbonation depth and chloride ions penetration.

Also the creep strain and creep coefficient are considerably smaller than for unmodified concretes, and special expansive additives are used to reduce drying shrinkage, [14.40]. The bond of PMC to ordinary concretes was examined in [14.41] and excellent performance was observed over long periods of time. That property is of considerable importance for repair work to concrete structures.

Latex modified concretes should not be placed underwater and exposure to highly concentrated chemicals is not permitted. A temperature above +10 °C is recommended for placing in outdoor structures. Because of the large variety of products commercially available for use in PC it is impossible to show here a complete image of their mechanical properties and applications. The results of tests executed in [14.42] are presented in Figure 14.11 as an example. The

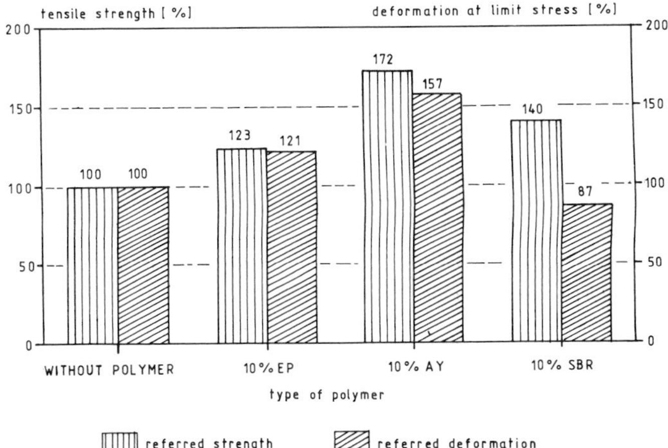

Figure 14.11 Influence of the polymer type on the mechanical properties under tensile stress. EP – epoxy; AY – acrylate; SBR – styrene-butadiene. (Reproduced from Krüger, T., Mechanical behaviour of polymer modified cement mortar under complex stress states; published by University of Bochum, 1991) [14.42]

improvement of mechanical properties was different for the three kinds of admixture examined but tensile strength was increased for all of them. The influence of polymers did not give such a clear image for compression. When certain polymers are applied, e.g. an acrylic latex emulsion, the increase of creep strain was also observed, [14.43].

After many years of research and numerous successful applications there are still a few concerns beside the above-mentioned incompatibilities, namely:

- Usually only the large pores in PCC are filled by polymer and disappear, while smaller ones may become even larger.
- It is believed that to obtain the real effect of polymer admixtures a minimum amount of 15% of Portland cement mass is needed and only with that amount can a kind of continuous film around solid particles in the mix be expected.
- High alkalinity of Portland cement paste may degrade some kinds of monomers, like MMA and styrenes.
- The execution of PCC is more difficult than that of ordinary concretes and rigorous procedures should be applied for mixing and curing.

It appears from many studies that the experimental verification is advisable at each application of a new composition of PCC.

In polymer impregnated concretes (PIC) the system of pores in hardened cement is filled by liquid monomers. The effects are multifold:

- decrease of porosity;
- formation of a reinforcing system in the porous hardened matrix;
- increase of matrix–aggregate and matrix–reinforcement bond;
- modification of the internal stress state by decreasing the stress concentrations.

The examples of monomers used in impregnation are shown in Chapter 4 (Table 4.4). The composite properties may be tailored to suit imposed conditions by the application of different monomers. Hardened polymers increase considerably the strength, toughness and durability of the final products. The best results are obtained with methyl methacrylate (MMA) combined with (trimethylolpropane trimethacrylate (TMPTMA) as a cross-linking agent which builds a polymer structure; both components are used in various proportions according to requirements for strength and other mechanical properties. Examples of test results of PIC specimens under compression and tension are presented in Section 10.2 and they prove how behaviour and strength may be modified by proper materials' design. The composition is usually completed by addition of inhibitors, catalysts and promoters in small volume fractions. Efficient in processing systems were designed and best rates of impregnation and polymerization were obtained. Also, performance of the final product – pore sealing, mechanical properties and durability were found to be satisfactory by several authors and were recommended in [14.44]. The tightness of the concrete is increased considerably by penetration of a small percentage of synthetic materials and that improvement was also observed for relatively high quality concretes with a water/cement ratio < 0.5.

Notwithstanding the extensive research programs carried out in the 1960s and 1970s the full-depth PIC is only slowly becoming a commercially applied material because of technological difficulties *in situ*. Its use is limited mostly to partial-depth impregnation and to relatively small elements produced in precast plants. Examples are power transformers made of PIC thanks to its low dielectric constant and low creep. Fibre-reinforcement is also used [14.45].

Polymers in cement-based materials may degrade more quickly than the products of Portland cement hydration due to the action of time, temperature, light and other factors. That aspect should be taken into account when different compositions of materials of that kind are being considered.

14.4 High strength matrices

Very high compressive strength of cement matrices was already obtained over seventy years ago. In the laboratory of the Lone Star Cement Corporation in USA in 1930, under direction of D.A. Abrams, the compressive strength of cement paste equal to 276 MPa was achieved after 28 days [14.46]. The paste was of a very low water/cement ratio equal to 0.08. This record achieved in a laboratory had no particular influence on contemporary practice and up to the 1970s the strength of concretes rarely exceeded 30 or 40 MPa.

The high strength of cement-based materials is directly related to low porosity and closed capillary pores in the matrix which may be achieved in various ways – low water content, dense packing of particles and addition of micro-fillers, improved mixing (e.g. Omnimixers) and compressing of the fresh mix, compacting by efficient vibration, increasing density by long and complete hydration of the cement and additional impregnation of pore and void systems. All these methods are used and simultaneously combined to decrease total porosity and to control pore dimension distribution.

Low water content and low values of w/c ratio were always considered in formulae for concrete strength. A few of the well known and traditional formulae for compressive strength based on the classical law [14.47] proposed by Féret are given in Section 8.2. The excess of water creates additional capillary pores which decreases the matrix strength considerably (cf. Section 6.5):

- as the weakest component in the hardened composite material, (cf. law of mixtures);
- as initiators of cracking due to local stress concentrations.

That is why mix compositions of high strength contain as small an amount of water as possible for hydration. The workability of the fresh mix is ensured by admixtures – application of plasticizers and superplasticizers (cf. Section 4.3) leads to appropriate fluidity and workability of the fresh mix with a low w/c down to 0.22, which is considered the minimum necessary for the hydration of Portland cement. It is generally required that the slump, as a measure of workability, is between 120 and 200 mm corresponding to the technology that is applied. Such workability should be maintained for about one hour which is usually sufficient for transportation and casting of the fresh mix.

Further improvement of packing is achieved by micro-fillers and the application of condensed silica fume for high performance matrices is considered where necessary. The properties of microsilica are described in Section 4.2.4 and its role in up-grading the matrix is shown in Figure 14.12.

A special procedure for the introduction of small particles has been known since 1981 as DSP – Densified with Small Particles [14.49]. The ratio of 1:30 is considered as the optimum between smaller and bigger particle dimensions [14.50] and [14.51]. The smallest particles are not available in the natural sand composition and should be admixed with fly ash or silica fume. Silica fume particles (from 5 nm to 0.5 μm) enter into interstitial spaces between Portland cement grains (30 to 100 μm) and satisfy the above-mentioned ratio. The second effect of microsilica particles is their pozzolanity, i.e. ability to react with $Ca(OH)_2$ during the hardening of the material. The products of the reaction fill the pores and increase toughness and strength (cf. Section 4.2.4). The percentage of non-hydrated cement grains is relatively high because of the low water content in the fresh mix, and hard cement grains also strengthen the microstructure. DSP are characterized by a high compressive strength up to 250 MPa but relatively low tensile strength and increased brittleness.

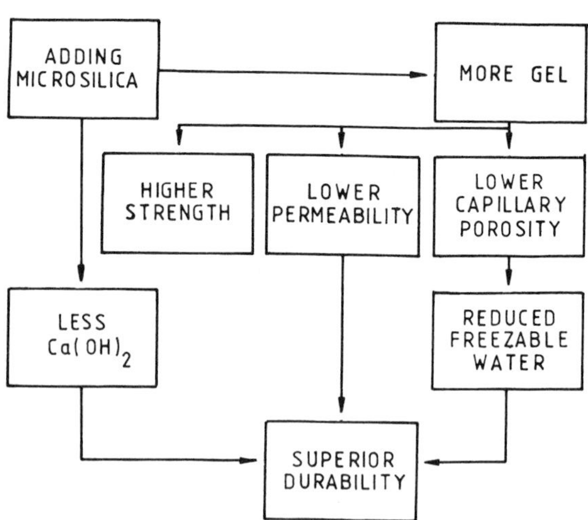

Figure 14.12 Flow chart presentation of microsilica action in up-grading concrete. (Reproduced with permission from Radjy, F.K. and Loeland, K.E., Microsilica concrete: A technological breakthrough commercialized; published by Materials Research Society, 1985.) [14.48]

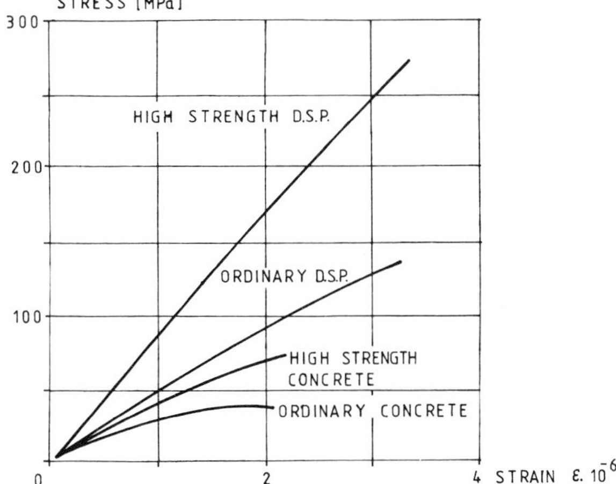

Figure 14.13 Stress–strain curves for concretes and DSP matrices. (Reproduced with permission from Hjorth, L., Development and application of high density cement-based materials; *Phil. Trans. Royal Society*, A310, pp. 167–73, 1983.) [14.52]

To improve toughness the fibre-reinforcement is applied which may be to better effect than in ordinary FRC due to the higher strength of the matrix. The difference in behaviour of concretes and DSP matrices is presented in Figure 14.13.

The application of DSP materials extends beyond building construction to application such as heavy duty industrial floors and mechanical parts. The service life of elements subjected to heavy abrasion was five times longer than those made with steel or cast basalt, [14.52].

Another way to increase packing and to reduce the thickness of the interface is to push particles closer together by initial pressure exerted on the fresh mix. According to tests [14.51] and [15.53] a compaction pressure of 345 MPa enabled a very low porosity of 2% to be reached, along with improved tensile strength up to 64 MPa and compressive strength up to 655 MPa. That example is probably essentially a laboratory record and cannot be easily transferred into building practice for larger elements or structures.

It was discovered later, that a much lower pressure of about 5 MPa is sufficient if accompanied by the addition of a water soluble polymer, e.g. hydroxypropylmethyl cellulose or hydrolysed polyvinylacetate, and the application of high energy shear mixing. The mass proportions of cement, polymer and water are approximately 100:7:10. The addition of the polymer reduces interparticle friction and together with intensive mixing, enables cement particles to be rearranged and their closer packing obtained. Not only is porosity considerably lower and may reach 1%, but the microstructure is also significantly improved and appears more amorphe than for ordinary Portland cement pastes. The

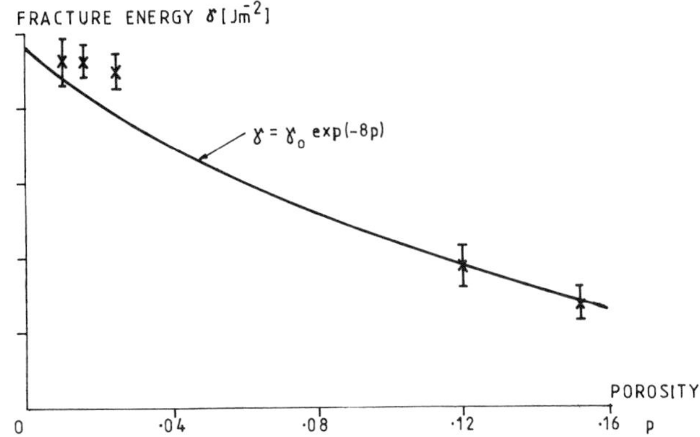

Figure 14.14 Fracture energy experimental results versus volume porosity to compare with curve R(p). (Reproduced with permission from Kendall, K. and Birchall, J.C., Porosity and its relationship is the strength of hydraulic of cement paste; published by Materials Research Society, 1985.) [14.54]

bond to aggregate is increased and transgranular fractures are observed. The material obtained in such a way is called Macro-Defect Free paste.

It has been shown [14.54] that, by decreasing porosity, very high values for fracture energy may be obtained. The tests were executed on MDF paste specimens without polymer admixture and the results are shown in Figure 14.14. Similar specimens made with polyvinylalcohol/acetate exhibited higher value–100 Jm^{-1} for $p = 0.01$ and 25 Jm^{-1} for $p = 0.2$. In these investigations the notch sensitivity of MDF paste was also tested on specimens, with different notches subjected to bending. The relation between modulus of rupture and notch depth for two different porosities is shown in Figure 14.15. The equation

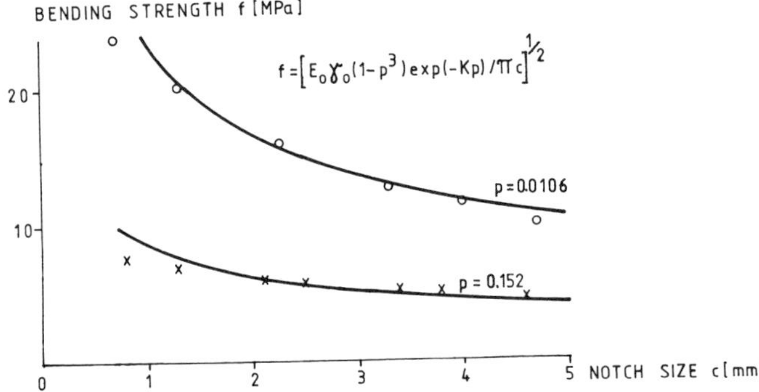

Figure 14.15 Bending strength for various notch length c and for two sample porosities p, here E_0 and γ_0 are Young's modulus and fracture energy for $p = 0$. (Reproduced with permission from Kendall, K., and Birchall, J.G., Porosity and its relationship to the strength of hydraulic cement paste; published by Materials Research Society, 1985.) [14.54]

proposed in [14.55] is verified and it is proved that brittle materials increase considerably their strength and fracture energy with decreasing porosity, cf. Section 6.5. However, they exhibit high notch sensitivity and this may be correctly determined from the fracture mechanics approach. The conclusion concerning high strength matrices is that the reduction of the volume of pores from 30% to zero may double the strength, while the reduction of microcrack length from 1 mm to 0.01 mm may increase the strength by a factor of 10. However, both procedures are applied with independent effects.

The MDF pastes are used to produce elements of complicated shapes by various technologies – press-moulding, extruding, roll-compacting, roll-milling, etc. The final product has no micro-pores, exhibits high compressive and also tensile strength and improved ductility, thanks to polymer component creating a film in the interface between the cement grains. The compressive strength may reach 400 MPa and the modulus of rupture up to 200 MPa. Also, Young's modulus of 40–50 GPa is considerably increased if compared with ordinary Portland cement concretes.

The MDF pastes are also filled with metallic powders, silicon carbide, fine sand and other kinds of hard materials to obtain particular properties, e.g. improved abrasion resistance. When polymers are not added, then the increase of compressive strength and low porosity are accompanied by high brittleness.

In MDF pastes with high alumina cements the process of conversion was never observed, certainly because of very low water content and water/cement ratio values.

Other combinations of special components and technologies were applied in [14.56] to obtain so called super-high-strength mortars characterized by a compressive strength of over 200 MPa. As fine aggregate, silica sand was used of two sizes – 0.05–0.21 mm and 0.70–1.70 mm, together with stainless steel particles of 0.40 and 0.80 mm. Two kinds of microfillers were added–high purity

Table 14.2 Compositions of super-high-strength mortars

Cementitious materials: fine aggregate ratio (by mass)	Water: cementitious materials	High-purity silica: cementitious materials	Silica fume: cementitious materials	Superplasticizer: cementitious materials
		0		
	0.17	0.10	0.10	
		0.20		
1:0.5		0.30		0.03
		0		
	0.15	0.10	0.20	
		0.20		

(Source: Ohama, Y., Development of superhigh-strength mortars; published by Ed. Concrete, Leura, NSW, Australia, 1990.) [14.56]

silica of sizes up to 4.4 μm and silica fume of 0.1–0.3 μm. High range superplasticizers of different kinds were tested on that occasion, but ordinary Portland cement was used. Examples of the mix proportions are given in Table 14.2.

The specimens were subjected to different kinds of cure – ordinary cure in water, 6-day cure in hot water, autoclave cure alone and combined with hot water. In Figure 14.16 compressive strength is shown as a function of the high purity silica content. A compressive strength of over 300 MPa was observed for compositions with steel particles.

The basic mechanical properties of the high performance materials are shown in Table 14.3, where two special materials are considered as well as cement paste and concrete.

High strength materials are also used as matrices for composites in which reinforcements by fibre structures increase their toughness. The application of fibres is the most efficient way to control the excessive brittleness of high strength pastes, mortars and concretes. The matrix–aggregate and matrix–fibre bond should be ensured by appropriate technology – intensive mixing, lamination of thin sheets, pressure exerted on the fresh mix and by various kinds of admixtures. A high quality matrix for FRC is even necessary to obtain the full effect from fibre reinforcement, [14.57]. The final effect is the toughening of the matrix and the transformation of single cracks into a multiple cracking process. Maximum crack width may be decreased by 20–50% in bending elements when appropriate fibre reinforcement is used, thus improving their durability considerably.

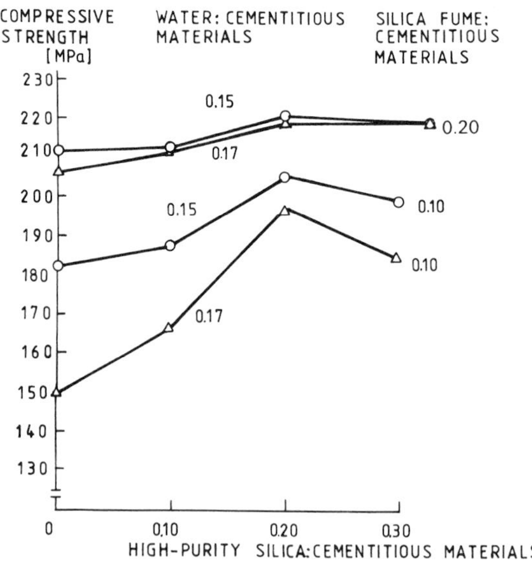

Figure 14.16 Compressive strength of superhigh-strength mortars as a function of the high-purity silica content. (Reproduced from Ohama, Y. *et al.*, Development of superhigh-strength mortars; published by Ed. Concrete, Leura, NSW, Australia, 1990.) [14.56]

Table 14.3 Mechanical properties of high strength cement based materials

Materials	Compressive strength f_c (MPa)	Tensile strength f_t (MPa)	f_{c/f_t}	Young's modulus E (GPa)	Stress intensity factor K_{Ic} (MPa/m$^{1/2}$)	Specific fracture energy γ (J/m^2)
Cement paste	150	6	25	18	0.2	15
Concrete	60–120	5–12	10–12	25	1.2	80
DSP	250	15–25	10–16	80	2	1.0
MDF	300	150	2	50	3	200
Steel	500	500–700	1.0–1.4			10^5
Sintered Alumina	3000	500	6			30

Impregnation of pore systems in hardened cement-based materials is achieved by various kinds of organic monomers (cf. Sections 3.2.5 and 10.5) which are later polymerized. An internal system of polymeric links increases the initial tensile strength of the matrix by several times, Young's modulus is also improved, and the compressive strength may be quadrupled, [14.58]. By appropriate composition of the impregnant, various mechanical properties may be obtained to satisfy imposed design conditions.

Interesting information on high strength materials are given by [14.59] and [14.60]. A review of micro-structural problems related to high performance concretes is also published in [14.61].

14.5 High performance concretes (HPC)

14.5.1 DEFINITIONS AND GENERAL INFORMATION

The terms 'high performance' and 'advanced' were applied mostly to such materials as carbon fibre-reinforced plastics and metal matrix composites, used in aircraft, rockets and satellites. These terms used for concrete-like materials have a similar meaning – these are materials with improved properties, designed and produced to fulfil special requirements.

The high performance concept if translated into technical terms for cement-based composites means:

- such a consistency in the fresh mix that its workability, flowability, mobility, compactability, pumpability and finishability ensure good results of execution without much effort from workers or an excessive expense of energy;
- excellent behaviour of materials in their hardened state, i.e. strength and deformations satisfying standard requirements imposed by the applications;

- relatively high strength at an early age;
- acceptable behaviour in the long-term, i.e. durability adequate to requirements during the forecast life of the structure, low maintenance costs and relative facility of repair works;
- good aspect of the structure during its service life, i.e. without visible cracks, voids and spallings, excessive deflections, etc.

Many other requirements may be imposed according to the character and destination of the structural or non-structural elements which are to be produced with these materials. Several attributes of HPC are listed in [14.62] which answer the main questions formulated by all parties involved in the construction process, [14.63]. Not all of them are equally important on all occasions. A set of conditions is established in each particular case and a high performance concrete is designed and executed to satisfy them in the most economical way.

The concepts of high strength and high performance concrete varied over time. Its evolution is presented in a simplified way in Table 14.4. The compressive strength of ordinary concrete increased from about 15 MPa in 1910 to 60 MPa in 1991 in the relevant recommendations of advanced countries. At present, high performance concretes (HPC) of $f_{28} \geqslant 60$ MPa and very high performance concretes (VHPC) with $f_{28} \geqslant 120$ MPa are conventionally distinguished. Other authors also propose 50 and 100 MPa as respective limits and consider them as mean or characteristic values.

In the performance approach to concretes the main questions which are formulated by all parties involved in the construction process are answered – the contractor who takes care of production, transportation, casting and curing of the fresh mix, the investor, the owner of the structure and the general public. All of them are interested in a low general cost for the structure, its long-term serviceability and safety. The users are less aware of various physical and chemical properties, but the overall performance is of primary importance. The scope of application of HPC and VHPC is determined by their improved properties with respect to ordinary concretes and by the technical and economic advantages which may be obtained as a result.

In this chapter, the basic characteristics of high performance mortars and concretes are described and discussed. Special composites with dispersed fibre

Table 14.4 Evolution of cement concrete compressive strength f_{28}

	Year					Remarks
	1850	1910	1950	1979	1991	
f_c (MPa)	8–10	12–15	30	$\leqslant 40$	$\leqslant 60$	ordinary concrete
				$\geqslant 40$	$\geqslant 60$	high performance concrete
					$\geqslant 120$	very high performance concrete

reinforcement or polymer admixtures and impregnation are not considered here, even though they are included in the general term of High Performance Concretes and the reader is referred to specialized publications, e.g. [14.64], [14.65].

14.5.2 COMPONENTS

HPC (that abbreviation covers also VHPC if these two groups of materials are not considered separately and a special remark is not added) are made with basically the same components as ordinary concretes but without the application of special technologies. As is shown in Figure 14.17, the composition of HPC is characterized with respect to ordinary concretes by:

- increased fractions of fine and very fine grains
- lower w/c ratio and use of superplasticizers (also known in this context as High-Range Water-Reducing Admixtures – HRWRA);
- smaller fraction of coarse aggregate and smaller maximum grain dimension.

In the design of HPC composition two main groups of problems need to be solved in a well coordinated way. The first one covers the chemical and physical properties of all components, their compatibility and synergisms, together with their particular roles in the material structures. The second group of problems concerns the feasibility of using the designed material in local conditions and at a reasonable cost. Usually, the required strength is also attained when these problems are solved.

The examples of the composition of HPC and VHPC presented in Table 14.5 show the features listed above.

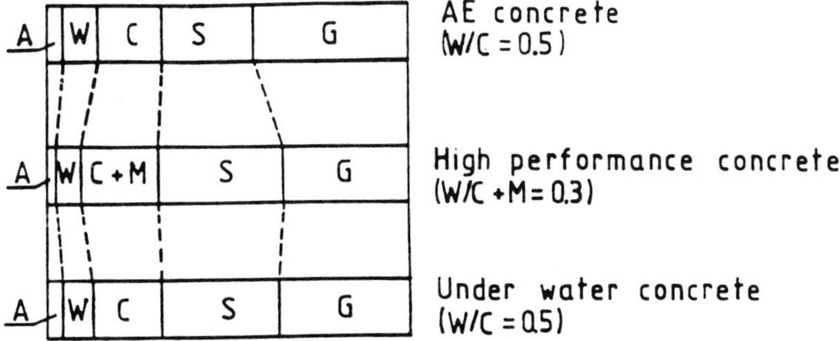

Figure 14.17 Comparison of mix proportions for different concretes: a) ordinary air-entrained concrete; b) HPC; c) under water concrete. (Reproduced from Ozawa, K. *et al.*, High performance concrete with high filling capacity; published by Chapman and Hall, 1990.) [14.66]

Table 14.5 Examples of high and very high performance concretes

High performance concretes						Very high performance concretes		
	(1) (kg)	Size	(2) (kg)	Size	(3) (kg)		(4) (kg)	(5) (kg)
Gravel 12.5/20	852	10/20	698	5/16	955			
Gravel 5/12.5	267	6/14	465	2.5/6.3	217	2.5/10	1075.6	1093.6
Sand 0/5	765	0.1/2.5	738	0/2.5	934	0/5	753.9	772.6
Cement	425		425		425	Cement	502.6	506.6
Water	150		160		160	Water	115.6	115.4
Superplast.	6.4		8.5		12.8	Superplast.	12.1	21.1
Retarder	1.7		1.7		1.7	Silica fume	50.2	50.7
Slump (mm)	180–250		110–190		200–210	Slump (mm)	230	230
	(MPa)		(MPa)		(MPa)		(MPa)	(MPa)
fc_1	17.8		36.2		57.7	fc_{28}	120.7	120.0
fc_7	60.6		68.3		57.7			
fc_{28}	74.0		75.9		67.2			
fc_{90}	82.5		81.5			d (kg/m^3)	2 510	2 560
ft_{28} (splitt.)	5.3		4.5			E (MPa)	49 751	50 314
w/c	0.35		0.38		0.38	w/c	0.21	0.21

(Sources: different papers published in [14.67] (Y. Malier (ed.) and other publications.)

(a) Admixtures and additives

Two main groups of admixtures are considered to be very important components of HPC – superplasticizers which improve the workability of the fresh mix with low values of water/cement ratio, and micro-fillers to increase the density of the hardened material, [14.68], and [14.61].

There are several kinds of superplasticizers available and every year many others appear on the market cf. Section 4.3.5. They belong to two main groups – sulphonated melamine-formaldehyde condensates and sulphonated naphthalene-formaldehyde condensates. Their action is explained by the absorption of polyanions on the surface of cement grains and by the generation of negative potential which eliminates the attraction and coagulation of the grains. As a result, a decrease of internal friction is obtained and the workability expressed for example by slump of 180–250 mm is ensured for 1–1.5 hours. The correct selection of a superplasticizer for other mix components is important. Usually superplasticizers are added as 2–4% of cement mass, according to the producers' prescription, [14.68], [14.69]. With higher dosages some delay may occur in hydration and hardening together with the apparent early setting of the fresh mix.

When Portland cement is partly replaced by fly ash or blast-furnace slag, then better flowability of the fresh mix is usually obtained and lower dosages of superplasticizers are possible. This is quite profitable from the economical

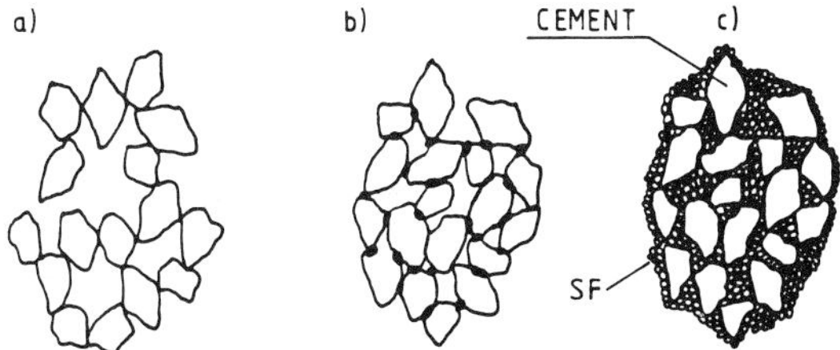

Figure 14.18 Packing of cement grains: a) in coagulated cement paste; b) in cement paste with superplasticizer; c) in cement paste with superplasticizer and silica fume. (Reproduced from Roy, M.D., New strong materials: chemically bonded ceramics; Science, **235**, pp. 651–8, 1987.) [14.73]

viewpoint: superplasticizer is an important part of cost of concrete components [14.70], [14.71].

The compatibility of superplasticizers with cement as well as their efficiency, duration of the fresh mix fluidity, sensitivity to ambient temperature and other factors should be verified by experiments executed in local conditions, [14.72].

Fly ash, silica fume and other silica products are used as micro-fillers. They are furnished as powders or slurry with grains of one or two orders smaller than Portland cement. They enter into the voids between the cement grains (Figure 14.18) and by acting as water-reductors enhance the efficiency of the superplasticizers. By their addition, the contacts between aggregate grains and cement paste are increased, the intergranular friction is reduced and hydration processes are modified. Fine spheroidal grains of micro-fillers improve material cohesion, and decrease the possibility of bleeding and segregation of the fresh mix during transportation and casting.

Silica fume is considered as the most efficient micro-filler for HPC. Its role is shown schematically in Figure 14.12 and its twofold effects are, according to [14.74]:

1. reduction of the w/c (or w/c + m – water/cement and microfiller) ratio when silica fume is used jointly with superplasticizers;
2. increase of the strength of hardened material with respect to a concrete with the same w/c ratio but without silica fume.

The pozzolanic properties of silica fume result in a slow hydration process and in more efficient gel development. Silica fume considerably improves the performance of the binder phase and increases its bonding action with the aggregate and reinforcement. The highly porous interface is the weakest element in the structure of an ordinary concrete and its strengthening is decisive for HPC. As is shown in Figure 14.19, the strength of cement paste is not improved by silica fume, but the concrete strength is greatly increased.

High quality silica fume is composed mostly of SiO_2 (up to 98%) and has very fine grains of 0.1–0.5 μm in diameter. It contains only small amounts of alkalis (Na_2O and K_2O) and is white due to low content of carbon, [14.76].

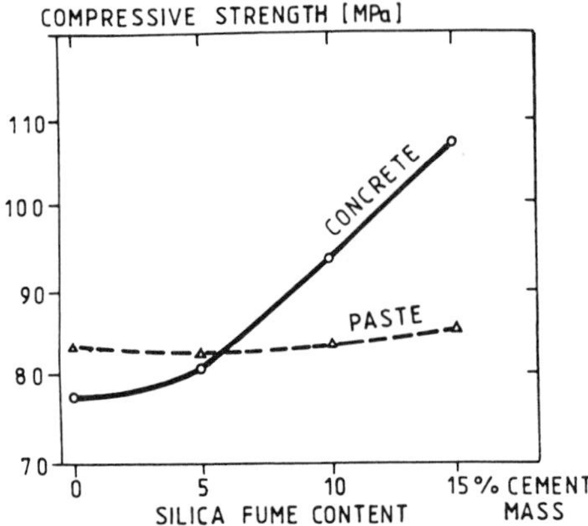

Figure 14.19 Effect of silica fume on the strength of 28 day old paste and concrete of the same w/c or w/c + sf ratio equal 0.33. (Reproduced from FIP/CEB Bulletin d'Information 197, 1990.) (14.75)

The application of silica fume is not necessary for concretes of compressive strength up to 60 MPa, cf. Table 14.5, but it is considered as a compulsory component of VHPC. However, in HPC and ordinary concretes silica fume also improves their density and durability.

According to [14.77] the optimum content of silica fume is 7–15% of cement mass. A higher dosage may increase brittleness and influence unfavourably the total cost of the final composite material.

Because of limited availability of silica fume on the world market and its gradually increasing price, it is difficult to predict its future application for HPC. It is probable that some kinds of fly ash, blast-furnace slag or metahaolinite may play a similar role in HPC composition, certainly after necessary verification of their quality and compatibility with other components.

The influence of fly ash and ground blast furnace slag on properties of HPC is positive according to many sources, e.g. [14.71]. As for ordinary concretes, these mix components act as microfillers, densifying the structure, and because of their pozzolanic properties they take part in hydration processes. Partial replacement of Portland cement by fly ash and ground slag enables a decrease in cost of materials, improves the workability and reduces the heat of hydration. However, in certain countries outdoor structures made in the 60s and 70s with blended cements containing fly ash and ground slag apparently showed lower durability. It is not quite clear whether only the addition of both these components was the reason for difficulties, or whether it was their inadequate properties and possible incompatibilities. This problem is subject to further research.

Other admixtures are used for HPC as for ordinary concretes. However, their necessity should be verified in terms of improved impermeability and early strength. It has been observed that air-entraining agents are not needed for

HPC in most cases and certainly not for VHPC, because pores are already well distributed and the total porosity is low. Furthermore, it can be difficult to produce an additional pore system in a dense and coherent fresh mix, [14.78]. This question is, however, still subject to tests and discussions.

(b) Portland cement

Ordinary Portland cement of good quality may be used for HPC. A high content of tricalcium silicate C_3S and bicalcium silicate C_2S (alite and belite) is favoured together with a low content of tricalcium aluminate C_3A. Because of the low values of water/cement ratio required, a relatively high amount of Portland cement is used – 400 kg/m^3 and more. The amount of cement may be reduced by blending with other micro-fillers like fly ash [14.66] or high purity silica with grains of about 4 μm in diameter [14.56].

A Portland cement of rather fine grains is preferred, but not too fine, so as to avoid excessive acceleration of all processes. The compatibility with other components should be verified as well as low shrinkage and heat from hydration.

(c) W/c ratio

As is mentioned in Section 14.4, the reduced amount of water and low value of the w/c ratio are necessary for the high strength and low porosity which characterize HPC. The excellent workability of fresh mix required is ensured by admixtures. When the w/c ratio is equal to 0.22, it means that the amount of water is limited to that necessary for cement hydration. In such a case, however, a complete hydration is impossible. On the other hand, any additional amount of water, it not bound to cement, may decrease the strength and increase the porosity of the hardened matrix.

Several authors propose the value of 0.22 as an optimum w/c ratio [14.69]. In many published compositions of VHPC, w/c ratio remains between 0.25 and 0.30 and between 0.30 and 0.35 for HPC, probably for higher percentage of hydration of Portland cement. Also, lower dosage of superplasticizer might be possible for required workability.

Because of the pozzolanic properties of microfillers, it is common to also calculate the water to cement and microfiller ratio: w/(c + m). In many published compositions both these ratios are exposed and discussed.

(c) Aggregate

The properties of aggregate are important and for HPC they should satisfy several different requirements. First of all, good workability must be ensured and for that reason continuous sieve distributions are preferred, [14.80].

Maximum grain diameter should be limited in order to improve workability and to reduce discontinuities and stress concentrations. According to [14.81]

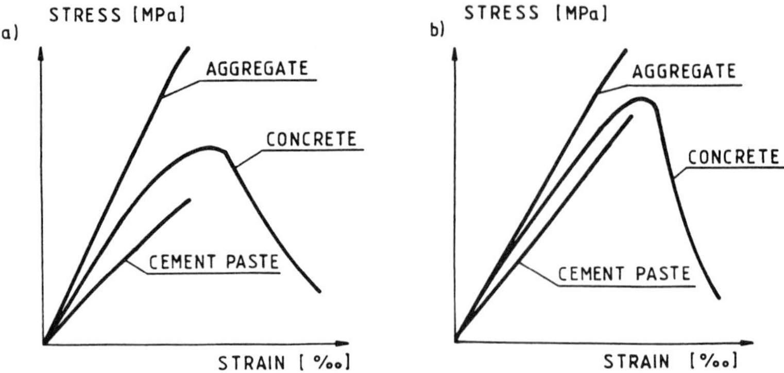

Figure 14.20 Stress–strain curves under compression for cement paste, aggregate and concrete in two cases: a) significant difference in rigidity between cement paste and aggregate; b) minor difference. (Reproduced from FIP/CEB Bulletin d'Information 97 [14.75]

the grains should not exceed 25 mm, in [14.75] 20 mm is indicated and certain authors even propose 10 mm as maximum grain diameter.

Grains of spheroidal shape are preferred and natural gravel is considered better than crushed aggregate for improved workability and lower water requirement. In terms of concrete strength, the following conditions are formulated:

- Young's modulus and strength should be close to those of hardened cement matrix to avoid stress concentrations;
- good bond to cement paste;
- water absorption below 3%.

As is shown in Figure 14.20, a low difference in strength and deformability of aggregate grains and cement matrix improves composite strength. The tests published in [14.80] showed that the strongest concrete was obtained with

Table 14.6 Mechanical properties of rocks compared with mortars and concretes at age of 91 days

	Quartzite			Limestone			Sandstone	
	rock	mortar	concrete	rock	mortar	concrete	rock	concrete
Compressive strength MPa	87	108	99	115	106	106	147	107
Young's modulus GPa	42	38	45	49	36	44	40	31
Porosity (%)	1.0			2.7			6.4	

(Source: Baalbaki, W. *et al.*, Influence of coarse aggregate on elastic properties of high performance concrete; *ACI Materials Journal*, **88**(5), 499–503, 1991.) [14.77]

coarse sandstone aggregate which was characterized by the highest strength and lowest Young's modulus, Table 14.6. The authors concluded that the better deformability of sandstone grains compared to quartzite and limestone ones contributed to reduce stress concentrations. The high porosity of sandstone improved its bond to cement paste. The σ–ε curves for three kinds of concretes are shown in Figure 14.21.

The appropriate sieve distribution and packing of aggregate grains, together with other particles, in the mix is the direct and classic way to ensure the high density of the hardened concrete, (Figure 14.22). In practice, the composition of grains obtained from quarries should be improved, but such modifications

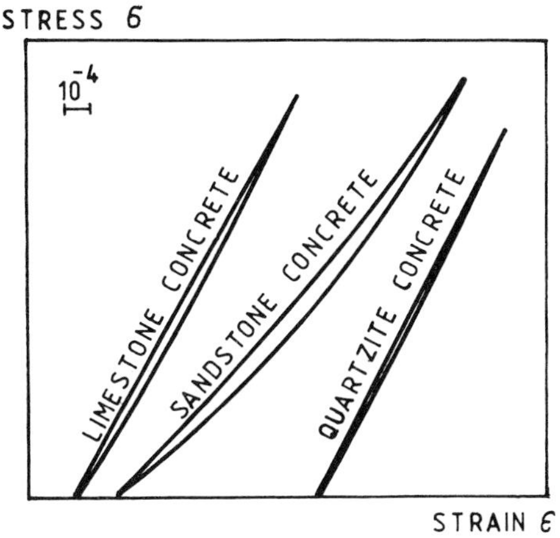

Figure 14.21 Comparison of hysteresis for concretes made with different coarse aggregates. (Reproduced with permission from Baalbaki, W. *et al.*, Influence of coarse aggregate on elastic properties of high performance concrete; *ACI Materials Journal*, **88**(5), pp. 499–503, 1991.) [14.80].

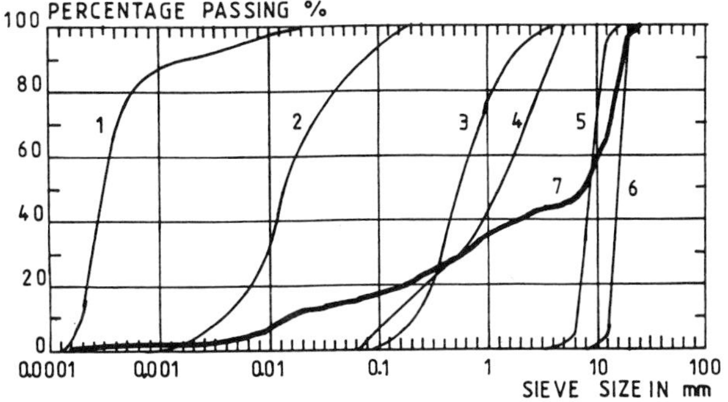

Figure 14.22 Grading of all components of a VHPC. (Reproduced from Lecomte, A. and Thomas, A., Caractère fractal des mélanges granulaires pour bétons de haute compacité; *RILEM Materials and Structures*, **25**(149), pp. 255–64, 1992.) [14.82]

can be expensive. In other situations, the correct proportions of grains of different diameter are furnished on request. In most instances, the production of HPC should be based on a local source of good aggregate, taking into consideration the economic side of its improvement and transportation.

The quality of sand seems to play a smaller role, and requirements as for ordinary concrete apply. Continuous sieve distribution is also favourable and mineralogical composition should be similar to that of the coarse aggregate.

14.5.3 MICRO-STRUCTURE

The micro-structure of HPC is characterized by the following features with respect to ordinary concretes:

- closer packing of grains of variable dimensions (aggregate, non-hydrated cement, micro-fillers), cf. Figure 14.22;
- different pore distribution in the sense that total porosity is smaller and larger pores are eliminated;
- better homogeneity by uniform distribution of hydration products;
- reduction of the least useful calcium hydroxide crystals.

The first feature is obtained by a lower water/cement ratio after complex action of superplasticizer and silica fume as is shown schematically in Figure 14.18. The second, is the simple consequence of the better packing of grains and of the pozzolanic reactions of the silica fume. The modification of the micro-structure is particularly important in the interface between aggregate grains and cement matrix in HPC. All differences between the interface and the bulk matrix are reduced considerably (Figure 14.23) when both superplasticizer and silica fume are used. Therefore, the interface is no longer the weakest zone in

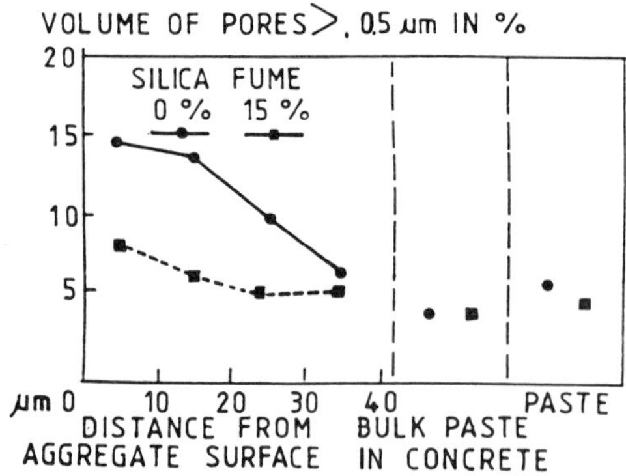

Figure 14.23 Relative volume of pores larger than 0.5 μm in the interface, in bulk cement paste in concrete and in neat cement paste at age of 180 days. (Reproduced from Scrivener, K.L. *et al.*, Quantitative characterization of the transition zone in high strength concretes; *Advances in Cement Research*, **1**(4), pp. 230–7, 1988.) [14.74]

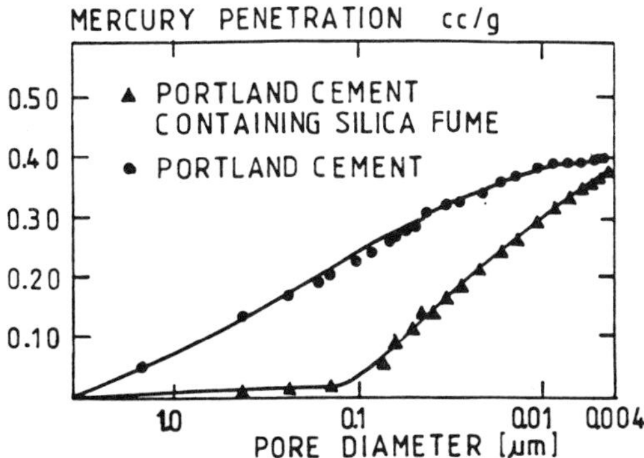

Figure 14.24 Pore distribution in cement pastes with and without silica fume. (Reproduced from Mehta, P.K. and Gjørv, O.E., Properties of Portland cement concrete containing fly ash and condensed silica fume; Cement and Concrete Research, **12**(5), pp. 587–95, 1982.) [14.83]

the composite material and that is why transgranular fracture is characteristic for HPC. For the same reasons the penetration of gases and fluids through the interface is decreased in HPC compared with ordinary concretes and hence the overall durability is improved.

The distribution of pores in cement paste, according to their diameter, is shown in Figure 14.24. It is clear that pores larger than 0.1 μm practically do not exist in pastes with silica fume.

14.5.4 TECHNOLOGY

The methods of production of HPC are basically the same as in the case of ordinary concretes. A high quality of components and their prescribed proportions should be maintained in the fresh mix. The quality of components and of the final product should be controlled at all stages of execution.

The main reason whereby HPC is accepted and fully supported by contractors and investors is the excellent workability of the fresh mix obtained by the appropriate application of superplasticizers which are either added to the water before mixing or, when the mix is transported over a longer distance, are added in two portions – before mixing; and after transportation, directly before casting. The facility to fill the moulds or forms by the fresh mix and its pumpability is ensured when sufficient slump of the Abrams cone and the coherence of the mix are maintained during the full amount of time required for both transportation and casting.

The slump of the Abrams cone is not the best measure of the consistency of HPC and other methods are available, [14.81]. However, these methods are not generally approved, and standardized and specialized equipment varies in different countries. That is why the Abrams cone is still used. It seems that the degree of compactability as indicated by the European Prestandard [14.84] is better adapted to HPC, and values close to 1.0 indicate high fluidity of the mix when the need for vibration is highly reduced. By that measure it is possible to determine slight differences between mixes of, apparently similar, high fluidity.

If vibration of the fresh mix is necessary, then the characteristics of the equipment used should be adapted with regard to its frequency and amplitude.

When a micro-filler is used for HPC, like silica fume or fly ash, the prescribed way of adding it to the mix, and the correct sequence of adding other components, should be carefully executed. The good dispersion of silica fume is particularly important because its effects result from combined physical and chemical mechanisms.

The cure of HPC after casting is different than in the case of ordinary concretes. There is no need to maintain high humidity over a long time period because of the high rate of increase of strength. In order to avoid microcracking on the surface, it is advised that any evaporation of water during the first few hours should be prevented, e.g. by perfect sealing. Furthermore, to prevent stress induction due to the characteristic ability of HPC for self-desiccation, curing in water is not advised, because non-uniform swelling may occur due to the low permeability of HPC. The absence of bleeding in HPC is the reason why the humidity of the fresh mix should be maintained immediately following casting. Sufficient curing should allow the chemical mechanism to develop its full effect.

The high rate of hardening and relatively high early strength after one, three or seven days enables the moulds and scaffolding to be removed earlier than in the case of ordinary concretes. That is an advantage which is used for quick re-use of moulds or for the reduction of traffic closures on structures being repaired. The fresh mix is also only exposed for a short time to possible adverse ambient factors.

In view of the large variety of possible compositions of HPC and of ambient conditions, the hardening process may develop differently depending on circumstances. That is why a detailed method of cure and the time delay for demoulding should be established following verification and observations *in situ*.

14.5.5 MECHANICAL PROPERTIES

Analysis of the mechanical properties of HPC is partly based on notions and methods developed not only for ordinary concretes but also for advanced composite materials. The results obtained from the application of fracture mechanics and general damage theory appeared to be effective for examining crack propagation and energy accumulation in concrete elements, and also for analysing their strength and deformability.

The mechanical properties of HPC are related to their composition and structure, characterized by a dense and strong matrix with good bonding to the aggregate grains and by an absence of excessive pores and other inhomo-

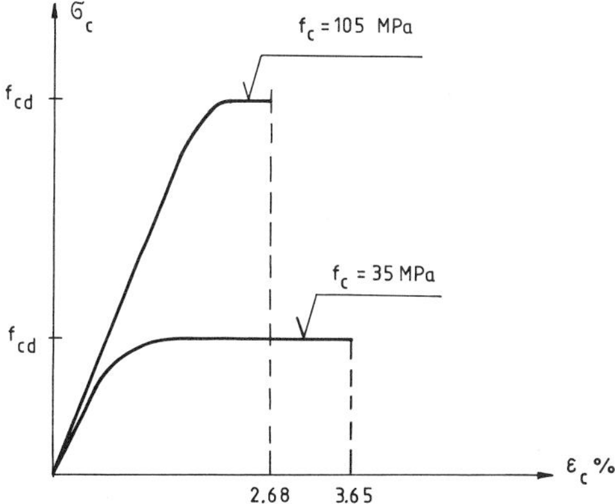

Figure 14.25 Stress–strain curves for ordinary and high performance concretes. (Reproduced from FIP, Concrete for the World; Norwegian Concrete Engineering NB, 1990.) [14.85]

geneities. In ordinary concretes with normal weight aggregate the following inequalities between strength of aggregate, mortar and concrete are satisfied, $f_{agg} > f_m > f_c$ which indicate that fracture is determined as much by the strength of the interface zone as by the weakest element, cf. Table 14.5.

In HPC thanks to the full transmission of stress between the mortar and aggregate grains their contribution to composite strength is increased and that effect may also be observed in Figure 14.21. The different behaviour of specimens made of ordinary concrete and of HPC is shown in Figure 14.25. The stress–strain curves for HPC show their linear and elastic part to be longer and plastic deformation smaller or even non-existent before rupture.

In a two-phase composite such as HPC both phases – hardened cement matrix and aggregate grains – behave as linear elastic bodies up to the point of highly brittle fracture. The overall behaviour of the composite material under load is non-linear and quasi-plastic due to microcracking. The difference in Young's moduli (cf. Figure 14.20 and Table 14.5) is the reason for stress concentrations in the interface where a system of microcracks appear under relatively low external load. These concentrations are reduced in HPC where high modulus matrix and low modulus aggregate are used. As a result, microcracks usually open in HPC under stress corresponding to 70–90% of strength, while in ordinary concretes this already occurs below 40–50%. There are two consequences – HPC may behave in a more brittle manner, and the application of linear elastic fracture mechanics (LEFM) corresponds better to their real behaviour than for ordinary concretes.

The results obtained both from calculations and measurements proved that fracture energy G_f and critical value of stress intensity factor K_{Ic} increase with compressive strength but at a reduced rate, cf. Figure 14.26. It means that, for example, when compressive strength f_c is increased by 2.5 times, the increase

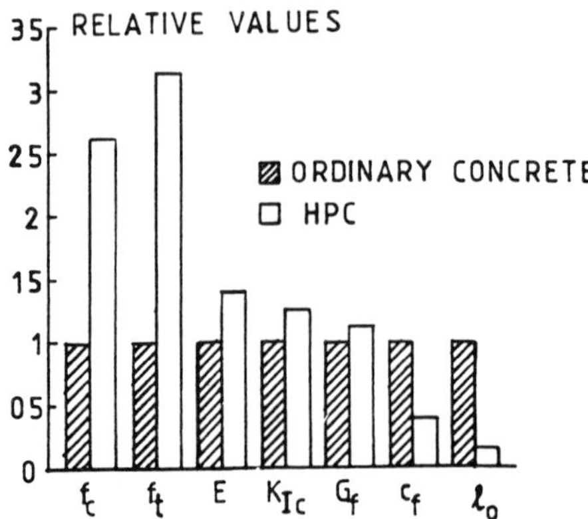

Figure 14.26 Comparison of mechanical properties of ordinary concrete and HPC (relative values). (Reproduced from Gettu, R. *et al.*, Fracture properties and brittleness of high-strength concrete; *ACI Materials Journal*, Nov–Dec, pp. 608–18, 1990.) [14.86]

of G_f and K_{Ic} is only 15 and 30%, respectively. The values of parameters c_f and l_o describing dimensions of a microcracked zone ahead of the tip of an advancing crack decrease for stronger concretes, and consequently crack propagation is relatively less controlled than in ordinary concretes.

The brittleness of HPC and VHPC deserves more attention. Experimental results obtained [14.81] on specimens made with three different concretes are given below as an example:

Compressive strength	$f_c =$	54	76	105	[Mpa]
Critical value of stress intensity factor	$K_{Ic} =$	2.16	2.55	2.85	[MPam$^{1/2}$]
Critical value of elastic energy release rate	$G_{Ic} =$	131	135	152	[J/m^2]

The smaller increase of fracture toughness than of compressive strength is related to the difference in values of tensile to compressive strength ratio f_t/f_c which varies between $\frac{1}{10}$ and $\frac{1}{12}$ for ordinary concretes and may be as low as $\frac{1}{20}$ for HPC. In all three concretes compared above the tensile strength f_t was the same and equal to 5 MPa if these relations applied. Therefore, even if higher compressive strength is admitted, there is no reason to expect that higher tensile stress may also be safely supported.

Critical strain also increases less than compressive strength and for HPC values of 200 and 350 μm were observed under high and low rates of loading, respectively.

An increase of strength and of fracture toughness is related to two phenomena – decrease of total porosity due to the application of superplasticizers and micro-fillers and reduction of microcracks and other discontinuities which enhance stress concentrations and crack propagation according to the basic relations proposed by Griffith. That second phenomenon was described among the others in [14.54].

The increased brittleness of HPC as compared to ordinary concretes may have no importance in structural applications. Cracks in concrete elements depend not only on the brittleness of the material and its tensile strength but mostly upon tensile efforts induced by loads and by constraints imposed on displacements. The main tensions are supported by adequate reinforcement systems and not by the concrete itself. Also, local tensions in external zones of concrete elements due to shrinkage and high rate of drying, thermal stresses and freeze–thaw cycles are reduced in HPC by decreased permeability and absorption. Therefore, there is no reason to fear that structures made of HPC may exhibit lower crack resistance or increased brittleness, [14.87].

The most important property of HPC is its improved durability thanks to the increased impermeability and homogeneity of the material's structure. Hydration products are in a higher degree amorphe than in ordinary concretes, and capillar pores of 0.1–1.0 μm are considerably reduced or eliminated, cf. Figure 14.23. Thus the material's resistance to different climatic actions and corrosive factors is enhanced. Increased capability to adopt alien (Cl^-, Na^+, K^+) and improved impermeability decrease the diffusion of chlorides [14.52], improve resistance against the long-term action of sulphates [14.68] and against alkali–aggregate reaction and related swelling [14.88].

The carbonation process in HPC is basically reduced because CO_2 cannot penetrate its dense structure. Accelerated tests executed in [14.89] showed practically no traces of carbonation. When silica fume is added as admixture, e.g. for VHPC, the pH of concrete may decrease thus creating conditions more favourable for corrosion of steel-reinforcement. However, in that case the electrical resistance of the concrete is enhanced and consequently it will slow down the corrosion process, [14.90] and [14.91].

The shrinkage of HPC develops differently than in ordinary concretes. A higher rate of autogenous shrinkage may induce additional stresses when free displacements are constrained at an early age. In contrast, drying shrinkage is less important because of the smaller amount of free water and the lower permeability of the matrix. The total strain due to shrinkage depends on the size of the elements and on the curing conditions; however, in most cases smaller values than for ordinary concretes were observed, [14.67] and [14.75].

So-called plastic shrinkage may cause cracks in external layers of elements which appear immediately after casting. Such effects are related to local desiccation because of the dense structure of HPC and the low w/c ratio pore water does not migrate from the internal core of elements and the phenomenon of bleeding is absent. The only remedy is abundant moisturing of HPC at a very young age. The phenomenon of plastic shrinkage in HPC requires further research, cf. Section 14.5.4.

The evolution of heat during hydration of HPC should be considered carefully. The amount of heat depends on cement content and on the degree and rate of its hydration. The admixture of silica fume and low water/cement ratio result in a smaller degree of hydration and lower heat evolution. It is expected, therefore, that a smaller amount of heat is produced in HPC. However, appropriate measures should be prepared if necessary, to lower the temperature of components, to evacuate heat, and to allow for possible displacements, etc. Furthermore, it should be borne in mind that for the appropriate action of silica fume lower temperatures are favourable. More research is needed in that area to quantify the effects of different material composition, methods of execution and ambient conditions.

Detailed descriptions of composition, technology and mechanical properties of HPC may be found in many sources, e.g. [14.70], [14.92] [14.93], [14.94]. Important reviews of particular investigations and applications in this field were published for two international conferences in Lillehammer [14.95] and in Dundee [14.96].

14.5.6 APPLICATION OF HPC AND VHPC

The increased demand for high performance materials in general, and for high performance cement-based composites in particular, is related to two groups of concerns:

1. developed needs for structures exposed to high loads and external actions of different kinds;
2. increased cost of maintenance of existing infrastructure, which exhibits insufficient durability.

In many countries several kinds of structures are built which require high performance materials. These include underwater tunnels, offshore platforms, tall buildings and towers, long span bridges, road and runway overlays, etc. These tasks cannot be rationally fulfilled without new and better building materials. Also, the maintenance of structures which were built 30–50 years ago requires a very high percentage of both national and regional budgets. These expenses are, at least, partly attributed to inadequate durability of the structures. There are reasons to expect that correctly executed structures made of high performance concretes will be durable.

The increased interest for HPC has been exhibited since the mid-1980s by the sponsoring of investigations in that direction. It appears that for large applications of high performance concretes the coordinated support of the various parties involved is required – research institutes and high schools, producers of Portland cement, producers of other components and of ready mixed concrete, constructors of outstanding structures, and governmental bodies at central and local levels. Successful projects in that field in France, Canada, USA and other countries are developed by such multi-party organisms, working for a common benefit.

The use of high performance concretes allows steel structures to be replaced by concrete ones in tall buildings over 250 m. The first case where concrete of mean characteristic strength $f_{c28} = 120$ MPa was used was the Two Union Square Building of 62-stories in Seattle (USA) built in 1988–9, [14.97]. The high quality concrete was produced with excellent syenite aggregate, low alkali cement, condensed silica fume (8% mass of cement) and superplasticizer. Many buildings of that type were subsequently built in North America including:

- One Wacker Place of 290 m in Chicago in 1990 with concrete of 80 MPa;
- Dain Bosworth Tower of 160 m in Minneapolis in 1991 with concrete of 97 MPa;
- Scotia Plaza building of 68 stories in Toronto with concrete of 70 MPa;
- Park Place building of 35 stories in Vancouver with concrete of 55 MPa.

Several other tall buildings were built with concrete of up to 131 MPa in USA, Canada and Japan. High performance concrete is used for reinforced frames and for composite concrete–steel frames. The high modulus of these concretes is specifically requested in seismic zones to increase stiffness and ensure comfort for inhabitants, [14.98]. A design for a building 600 m high is already prepared in USA for construction, scheduled for year 2000. The application of high strength concrete defined in North America as above 41 MPa is spreading, and has been accepted in the Uniform Building Code for Seismic Zones Three and Four. In [14.67] several outstanding structures are considered with regard to the application of high performance concretes, namely:

- a bridge in Denmark across the straits between the Baltic and the North seas;
- a tunnel for the rapid railway line, TGV Atlantique in France;
- a tunnel under English channel;
- the nuclear reactor vessels Civaux One and Two in France;
- the refrigerating towers for electric power stations from 900 to 1400 MW;
- the precast and post-tensioned concrete beams for industrial and public buildings;
- the offshore structures and bridges made of precast elements.

In all these cases the final selection was in favour of high performance concretes, taking into account not only materials and construction costs, but also the reduction of consumption of materials, lower weight of structural elements, etc. Improved durability as an additional and important factor in the economic analysis has not been taken directly into account. Thus, increased durability was gratis. Five examples of HPC and VHPC compositions and properties of materials used in France are presented in Table 14.4.

In the Norwegian Code by 1989 the compressive strength of normal weight concrete reached 105 MPa and for light-weight concrete, 85 MPa, [14.90]. High performance concrete is used for large precast girders for bridges and for giant offshore platforms. Both types of structures are used in particularly difficult climatic conditions and under heavy loads. Improved durability and reduction of dimensions due to high strength are therefore very important. Similar materials are foreseen for use in submerged tube bridges or tunnels which are likely to be scheduled for construction in the near future.

Also, in Norway, due to climatic conditions on the roads, the extensive application of steel studs on car tyres causes high requirements for abrasion resistant road surfaces. High performance concrete with carefully selected aggregate and compressive strength up to 135 MPa exhibited a level of abrasion resistance similar to massive granite. According to laboratory tests this concrete may last four times longer than traditional concrete of 55 MPa. The addition of small amount of steel and polypropylene fibres improves crack control in elements reinforced with traditional steel bars, e.g. in deep beams where steel-fibres partly replace stirrups. A considerable increase of steel–matrix bonding is brought about by fibre-reinforcement.

HPC is also used in special elements in which, rather than large dimensions, non-conventional requirements are decisive. As an example, the containers used for radioactive waste may be quoted, which should usually ensure:

- extensive durability expressed in hundreds of years, corresponding to periods of decaying of radioactive compounds;
- high strength against accidental loads of unpredictable character;
- high resistance against all possible corrosive agents.

In the case of such containers the specific cost of material is quite negligible because of its small volume. As an additional requirement, a project for accelerated testing should be proposed in relation to the design of the material's structure and composition. Such problems are often solved by a design of boxes made of fibre-reinforced resin concrete or other highly sophisticated composite.

Stainless steel-fibres are added to concrete refractory elements to provide better resistance against cracking and spalling due to thermal cycles and thermal shocks. A considerable increase in service life abundantly covers the additional costs paid for these fibres. Strongly reinforced cement-based elements are also applied as parts of machinery equipment, [14.64].

The development of high performance cement-based materials has another important advantage – the application of advanced methods in research, testing and design of materials attracts competent and highly motivated staff. That factor completely changed the image of cement-based materials which are also becoming 'hi-tech', [14.99]. It is not necessary to stress all the beneficial effects of such an upgrading for employment potential in the field of cement-based materials.

14.5.7 ECONOMIC CONSIDERATIONS AND FURTHER DEVELOPMENT OF HPC

The economic questions concerning the application of cement-based composites have considerable importance for their development in various building and civil engineering structures. The advanced components and products are relatively expensive and their application requires special equipment, highly qualified staff and assistance from research centres. Consequently, the specific cost of such composites may be higher when compared with medium strength, ordinary concretes.

It appears, however, that the cost of HPC is not particularly high. On the contrary, commercially available concrete of nearly 100 MPa costs significantly less that 3.5 times the price of ordinary 28 MPa concrete. Thus, more strength is obtained per unit cost and per unit mass, together with more stiffness per unit cost and lower specific creep, [14.98].

Furthermore, the specific cost of the material, calculated after the cost of components and execution, is only a small part of the total cost which also comprises maintenance costs of various kinds, including repairs, possible replacement, breaks in normal exploitation, etc. Using high performance materials, smaller dimensions of structures are necessary, and lower maintenance cost may be expected. By 1933 it was observed that high performance concrete elements may be subjected very early to partial service loadings [14.100]. All these factors decide upon the total cost of the entire structure.As a result, apparently expensive composite materials can turn out to be very interesting from an economic standpoint [14.67] and [14.91].

In the economic calculations the cost of increased control of all components and of high performance materials in subsequent stages of execution should be partly compensated by gains due to the lower mean values of their required properties. When variations of the material's properties are reduced, then lower mean values may be designed and that aspect again allows a decrease in cost. Methods to evaluate the increased durability and other advantages of HPC are needed. These should be based on rational provision of repair and maintenance expenses during the lifetime of the designed structure. Without such calculations the investor will not be convinced that in many situations the use of HPC is the optimum solution.

Research in the field of optimization of the structure and composition of materials [14.101] is also aimed at improving the economic advantages of HPC.

Questions of economy determine the fields of application of cement matrix composites and that is the reason why ordinary concretes are still used and will continue to be used in the future for traditional plain and reinforced structures where high strength and improved durability are not necessarily required. Advanced composite materials are needed for special outstanding structures or for their specific regions, sometimes called 'hot-points' like joints and nodes or for elements likely to be particularly exposed to destruction.

A new generation of advanced cement-based composites is developing quickly. Increased interest for HPC has been exhibited since the mid-1980s through the sponsorship of research and pilot construction projects.

Notwithstanding multiple applications of HPC and VHPC, there are several important problems which should be studied further and in order that solutions may be found. These are:

- optimization of mix composition for given requirements and conditions;
- new kinds of admixtures, microfillers and dispersed reinforcement;
- application of lightweight aggregate;
- thermal effects related to hydration of Portland cement;
- possibility of decreasing the content of Portland cement;
- mechanical behaviour in various conditions, etc.

An effort is needed to further develop both structural design with the application of HPC. Further work should be aimed at preparation of appropriate design codes and quantitative recommendations [14.102]. Without any doubt, the trend towards improving the performance of concrete-like composites will also be developed in the future, corresponding to new needs in building and civil engineering structures.

References

14.1. ACI (1990) State-of-the-Art Report on Soil Cement, American Concrete Institute Committee 230. *ACI Materials Journal*, **85**(4), 395–417.

14.2. Ambroise, J., Pera, J., Taibi, H. *et al.* (1987) Amélioration de la tenue à l'eau de la terre stabilisée par ajout d'une pouzzolane de synthèse, in Proc. 1st Int. Congress of RILEM, Versailles 1987, **2** *Combining Materials: Design, Production and Properties*, Chapman and Hall, London, 575–82.

14.3. Dupas, J.M. and Pecker, A. (1979) Static and dynamic properties of sand–cement. *Proc. ASCE*, **105**(GT3), March, 419–36.

14.4. FHA (1979) Soil Stabilization in Pavement Structures. A User's Manual, **2**, Report No. FHWA-IP-80-2, October, Fed. Highway Adm., Washington, DC.

14.5. Leflaive, E., Khay, M. and Blivet, J.C. (1983) Un nouveau matériau: le Texsol, *Bulletin de Liaison des Laboratoires des Ponts et Chaussées*, 125, May–June, 105–15.

14.6. Villard, P., Jouve, P. and Riou, Y. (1990) Modélisation du comportement mécanique du Texsol. *Bulletin de Liaison des Laboratoires des Ponts et Chaussées*, 168, July–August, 15–27.

14.7. Hannant, D.J. (1978) *Fibre Cements and Fibre Concretes*, J. Wiley & Sons, Chichester.

14.8. Bentur, A. and Mindess, S. (1990) *Fibre Reinforced Cementitious Composites*, Elsevier Applied Science, London and New York.

14.9. Mai, Y.W., Foote, R.M.L. and Cotterell, B. (1980) Size effects and scalling laws of fracture in asbestos cement. *Int. J. of Cem. Comp.*, **2**(1), 23–34.

14.10. Akers, S.A.S. and Garret, G.G. (1983) The relevance of simple fibre models to the industrial behaviour of asbestos cement composites. *Int. J. of Cement Comp. and Lightweight Concr.*, **5**(3), 173–9.

14.11. Allen, H.G. (1971) Tensile properties of seven asbestos cements. *Composites*. **2**, 98–103.

14.12. Mai, Y.W. (1979) Strength and fracture properties of asbestos–cement mortar composites. *J. of Mat. Science*, **14**, 2091–102.

14.13. Beaupré, D., Pigeon, M., Morgan, D.R. and McAskill, N. (1991) Le béton projeté renforce de fibres d'amiante, in Proc. *1st Canadian Univ.–Ind. Workshop on Fibre Reinforced Concrete*, (ed. N. Banthia), Univ. Laval, Quebec, 197–211.

14.14. ACI (1982) State-of-the-Art Report on Ferrocement, American Concrete Institute Committee 549. *Concrete International*, August, 13–18.

14.15. Brandt, A.M., Czarnecki, L., Kajfasz, S. and Kasperkiewicz, J. (1983) *Bases for application of concrete-like composites* (in Polish), COIB, Warsaw, pp. 91.

14.16. Balaguru, P.N., Naaman, A.E and Shah, S.P. (1977) Analysis and behaviour of ferrocement in flexure. *Proc. ASCE*, **103** (ST10), 1937–51.

14.17. Johnston, C.D. and Mowat, D.N. (1974) Ferrocement – material behaviour in flexure. *Proc. ASCE*, **100** (ST10), 2053–69.

14.18. Balaguru, P.N., Naaman, A.E. and Shah, S.P. (1979) Fatigue behaviour and design of ferrocement beams. *Proc. ASCE*, **105** (ST7) 1334–46.

14.19. Grabowski, J. (1985) Ferrocement under impact loads. *Journal of Ferrocement*, **15**(4), 331–41.

14.20. Ohama, Y. and Shirai, A. (1992) Development of polymer–ferrocement, in [14.64], 164–73.

14.21. Zia, P., Ahmad, S.H., Garg, R.K. and Hanes, K.M. (1992) Flexural and shear behaviour of concrete beams reinforced with 3-D continuous carbon fibres, in [14.64], 495–506.

14.22. Hamelin, P. and Verchery, G. (eds) (1990) *Textile Composites in Building Construction*, Proc. of Int. Symp. in Lyon, July 1990, Part 1, Pluralis, Paris.

14.23. Hamelin, P. and Verchery, G. (eds) (1992) *Textile Composites in Building Construction*, Proc. of Int. Symp. in Lyon, June 1992, Parts 1 and 2, Pluralis, Paris.

14.24. Hamelin, P. and Matray, P. (1991) Mechanical behaviour of cement-based composites, in Proc. Int. Symp. *Brittle Matrix Composites BMC3*, Warsaw, September 1991, (eds A.M. Brandt and I.H. Marshall), Elsevier Applied Science, London 335–43.

14.25. Schneider, B. (1992) Development of SIFCON through applications, in [14.64], 177–94.

14.26. Lankard, D.R. (1985) Preparation, properties and application of cement-based composites containing 5 to 20% steel-fibres, in *Steel Fiber Concrete*, US–Sweden Joint Seminar, (eds S.P. Shah and Å. Skarendahl), CBI, Stockholm, 189–217.

14.27. Naaman, A.E. (1992) SIFCON: tailored properties for structural performance, in [14.64], 18–38.

14.28. Reinhardt, H.W. and Fritz, C. (1989) Optimization of SIFCON mix, in *Fibre Reinforced Cements and Concretes–Recent Developments*, (eds R.N. Swamy and B. Barr), Elsevier Applied Science, London. 11–20.

14.29. Wang, M.L. and Maji, A.K. (1992) Shear properties of slurry infiltrated fiber concrete, in [14.64], 203–12.

14.30. Fritz, C. and Reinhardt, H.W. (1992) Influence of crack width on shear behaviour of SIFCON, in [14.64], 213–25.

14.31. Shah, S.P. (1991) Do fibres improve the tensile strength of concrete? in Proc. 1st Canadian Univ.–Ind. Workshop on *Fibre Reinforced Concrete*, Université Laval, 10–30.

14.32. Aveston, J., Cooper, G.A. and Kelly, A. (1971) Single and multiple fracture. Proc.

Nat. Phys. Lab. Conf. *The Properties of Fibre Composites*, IPC Science and Technology Press Ltd, Teddington, England, 15–24.

14.33. Lankard, D.R. (1992) Manufacture of SIFCA composite precast shapes, in [14.64], 195–202.

14.34. Czarnecki, L. (1985) The status of polymer concrete. *Concrete International ACI*, July, 47–53.

14.35. Fowler, D.W. (1980) Status of Concrete–Polymer Materials, in Proc. of the 6th Int. Congress on Polymers in Concrete, Beijing 1990, Int. Acad. Publ. Beijing, Int. Acad. Publ. Beijing, 10–27.

14.36. ACI (1989) State of the Art Report on Polymer Modified Concrete (PMC), Report of the American Concrete Institute, Committee 548A, (unpublished).

14.37. Steinberg, M. (1972) Concrete–Polymer Composite Materials Development, Informal Report, Brookhaven Laboratory, February, (unpublished).

14.38. Kuhlmann, L.A. (1990) Styrene-butadiene latex-modified concrete: the ideal concrete repair material? *Concr. Int.*, **12**(10), October, 59–65.

14.39. ACI (1992) State-of-the-Art Report on Polymer-Modified Concrete. ACI Comm. 548, Amer. Concr. Inst. 548. 3R–91, March, Detroit.

14.40. Ohama, Y. and Demura, K. (1991) Properties of polymer-modified mortars with expansive additives, Int. Symp. *Concrete Polymer Composites* (eds H. Schorn and M. Middel), Bochum, 12–14 March, University of Bochum, Germany, 19–26.

14.41. Ohama, Y. (1981) Adhesion durability of polymer-modified mortars, in Proc. 3rd Int. Congr. *Polymers in Concrete*, Koriyama, 13–15 May, 209–21.

14.42. Krüger, T. (1991) Mechanical behaviour of polymer modified cement mortars under complex stress states, as [14.40]. 135–46.

14.43. Mangat, P.S., Baggot, R. and Evans, D.A. (1981) Creep characteristics of polymer modified concrete under uniaxial compression, as [14.41], 193–208.

14.44. Manson, J.A. (1980) User's guide for polymers in concrete: Surface impregnation. Working Draft by ACI Committee 548, Lehigh University, February 1980 (unpublished).

14.45. Gunasekaran, M. (1991) PIC high-voltage insulation for large power transformers, as [14.40], 87–91.

14.46. Powers, T.C. (1947) A discussion of cement hydration in relation to the curing of concrete. *Proc. of Highway Research Board*, 27th Ann. Meeting, Washington Nat. Res. Council, Washington, 178–88.

14.47. Féret, R. (1892) Compacité des mortars hydrauliques. *Ann. des Ponts et Chaussées*, Paris.

14.48. Radjy, F.K. and Loeland, K.E. (1985) Microsilica concrete: A technological breakthrough commercialized, in Mat. Res. Soc. Symp. *Very High Strength Concrete-Based Materials*, **42**, Materials Research Society, Pittsburgh, 305–12.

14.49. Bache, H.H. (1981) Densified cement-ultrafine particle-base materials, in Proc. 2nd Int. Conf. on *Superplasticizers in Concrete*, Ottawa.

14.50. Jennings, H.M. (1992) Advanced cement-based matrices for composites. in [14.64], 3–17.

14.51. Tan, S.R., Howard, A.J. and Birchall, J.D. (1987) Advanced materials from hydraulic cements. *Phil. Trans. Roy. Soc.*, A322. London, 479–91.

14.52. Hjorth, B.L. (1983) Development and application of high-density cement-based materials. *Phil. Trans. Royal Soc.*, A310, London, 167–73.

14.53. Birchall, J.D., Howard, A.J. and Kendall, K. (1981) Flexural strength and porosity of cements, *Nature*, **289**, London, 388–9.

14.54. Kendall, K. and Birchall, J.G. (1985) Porosity and its relationship to the strength of hydraulic cement pastes, in Proc. of Met. Res. Soc. Symp. *Very High Strength Concrete-Based Materials*, **42**, Materials Research Society, Pittsburgh, 153–8.

14.55. Kendall, K., Howard, A.J. and Birchall, J.D. (1983) The relation between porosity, microstructure and strength, and the approach to advanced cement-based materials. *Phil. Trans. Roy. Soc.*, A310, London, 139–53.

14.56. Ohama, Y., Demura, K. and Lin, Z. (1990) Development of superhigh-strength mortars, in Proc. Int. Conf. *Concrete for the Nineties*, (eds W.B. Butler and I. Hinczak), Ed. Concrete, Leura, Australia, 1–12.

14.57. Krenchel, H. and Hansen, M.S. Low porosity cement for high performance concrete and FRC-materials, in [14.64], 65–83.

14.58. Regourd, M. (1985) Microstructure of high strength cement paste systems, as [14.54], 3–17.

14.59. Diamond, S. (1985) Very high strength cement-based materials – a prospective, in Proc. Mat. Res. Soc. Symp. *Very High Strength Concrete-Based Materials*, **42**, Materials Research Society, Pittsburgh, 233–43.

14.60. Mindess, S. (1985) Relationship between strength and microstructure for cement-based materials: an overview, in Proc. of Symp. *Very High Strength Concrete-Based Materials*, **42**, Materials Research Society Pittsburgh, 53–68.

14.61. Kucharska, L. (1992) Design of material structure of high performance concretes: role of additives and admixtures (in Polish). *Przegląd Budowlany*, **64**, (8/9), 351–4.

14.62. Carino, N.J. and Clifton, J.R. (1991) High-performance concrete: research needs to enhance its use, *Concrete International ACI*, Detroit, September, 70–6.

14.63. Bartos, P. (1992) Performance parameters of fibre-reinforced cement-based composites, in [14.64], 431–43.

14.64. Reinhardt, H.W. and Naaman, A.E. (eds) (1992) *High Performance fibre-reinforced cement composites*. Proc. Int. Workshop RILEM/ACI, 23–26 June 1991, Mainz, Chapman and Hall/Spon, London.

14.65. Schorn, H. and Middel, M., (eds) (1991) *Concrete Polymer Composites*, Proc. Int. Sym. in Bochum 12–14 March, University of Bochum, Germany.

14.66. Ozawa, K., Maekawa, K. and Okamura, H. (1990) High performance concrete with high filling capacity, in *Proc. Int. Symp. RILEM Admixtures for Concrete. Improvement of Properties*, (ed. E. Vásquez), Barcelona, 51–61.

14.67. Malier, Y. (ed.) (1990) *Les bétons hautes performances. Du matériau à l'ouvrage*, (1992) Caractérisation, durabilité, applications. Presses de l'ENPC, Paris.

14.68. Collepardi, M. (1990) Effects of chemical admixtures on concrete durability, as [14.66], 1–13.

14.69. ACI Committee 212 (1993) Guide for the Use of High-Range Water-Reducing Admixtures (Superplasticizers) in Concrete. *Concrete International*, Detroit, April, 40–7.

14.70. Aïtcin, P.-C. and Neville, A. (1993) High Performance Concrete Demystified. *Concrete International*, Detroit, February, 21–6.

14.71. ACI Committee 211 (1993) Guide for Selecting Proportions for High-Strength Concrete with Portland Cement and Fly Ash. *ACI Materials Journal*, May–June, 272–83.

14.72. Kucharska, L. and Moczko, M. (1993) Influence of cement chemical composition on its response to superplasticizer addition in the light of the rheological research, in Proc. Interuniv. Res. Sem., 18–20 November 1992, Tech. Univ. Eindhoven, Eindhoven, 135–43.

14.73. Roy, M.D. (1987) New strong materials: chemically bonded ceramics. *Science*. **235**, 651–8.

14.74. Scrivener, K.L., Bentur, A. and Pratt, P.L. (1988) Quantitative characterization of the transition zone in high strength concretes. *Advances in Cement Research*, **1**(4), 230–7.

14.75. FIP/CEB (1990) *High Strength Concrete*, State of the Art Report, FIP/CEB Bulletin d'Information 197.

14.76. de Larrard, F., Gorse, J.F., Puch, C. (1992). Comparative study of various silica fumes as additives in high-performance cementitious materials. *Materials and Structures* RILEM, **25**(149), 265–72.

14.77. Regourd, M. (1990) Microstructure des bétons à haute performance, in [14.67], 21–9.

14.78. Pigeon, M., Gagné, R. and Aïtcin, P.C. (1991) La durabilité au gel du béton à haute performance, in Proc. of the Second Canadian Symposium on *Cem. and Concr.*, (ed. S. Mindess), The Univ. of B.C., Vancouver, Canada, 160–71.

14.79. Luther, M.D. (1993) Silica fume (microsilica) concrete in bridges. *Concrete International*, April, 29–33.

14.80. Baalbaki, W., Benmokrane, B., Chaallal, O., and Åitcin, P.C. (1991) Influence of coarse aggregate on elastic properties of high performance concrete. *ACI Materials Journal*, **88**(5), 499–503.

14.81. de Larrard, F. and Malier, Y. (1990) Propriétés constructives des bétons à très hautes-performances: de la micro à la macrostructure, in [14.67], 107–38.

14.82. Lecomte, A. and Thomas, A. (1992) Caractère fractal des mélanges granulaires pour bétons de haute compacité. *Materials and Structures* RILEM, **25**(149), 255–64.

14.83. Mehta, P.K. and Gjørv, O.E. (1982) Properties of Portland cement concrete containing fly ash and condensed silica fume. *Cement and Concrete Research*, **12**(5), 587–95.

14.84. European Prestandard ENV 206 (1990) Concrete – Performance, production, placing and compliance criteria. European Committee for Standardization, Brussels, 33pp.

14.85. FIP (1990) Concrete for the World, Norwegian Concrete Engineering NB, FIP Congress, Norwegian Concr. Ass., Oslo.

14.86. Gettu, R., Bazant, Z.P., and Karr, M.E. (1990) Fracture properties and brittleness of high-strength concrete. *ACI Materials Journal*, Nov–Dec, 608–18.

14.87. Pliskin, L. (1990) Béton à hautes performances: aspects reglémentaires, in [14.67], 179–93.

14.88. Al-Hussaini, A. and Ramdane, K.E. (1992) Properties and creep of high strength concrete, in Proc. Int. Conf. on Concrete '92. Tehran, The Plan and Budget Org., Tehran, 762–79.

14.89. Lévy, C. (1990) A propos de la carbonatation accelérée de béton: comparaison béton ordinaire–béton hautes performances du pont de Joigny, in [14.67], 203–22.

14.90. FIP (1988) *Condensed Silica Fume Concrete*, FIP State-of-the-Art Report, Thomas Telford, London.

14.91. CEB (1989) *Durable Concrete Structures*, CEB Design Guide, Bulletin d'Information CEB 182, Lausanne.

14.92. ACI Committee 363 (1992), State-of-the-Art Report on High-Strength Concrete, ACI 363R-92, Detroit, 55 pp.

14.93. Kucharska, L. and Brandt, A.M. (1993) High Performance Concretes: composition, technology and mechanical properties (in Polish). *Inżynieria i Budownictwo*, **50**, (9), 356–60.

14.94. Brandt, A.M. and Kucharska, L. (1993) Mechanical properties and application of high performance concretes, in Proc. Int. Symp. on Innovative World of Concrete, **1**, August 30–Sept. 3, Bangalore, India, KN3–KN20.

14.95. Proc. Int. Symp. (1993) 'Utilization of High Strength Concrete' (eds I. Holand and E. Sellevold) Lillehammer, 20–3 June 1993, Norwegian Concrete Association, Oslo.

14.96. Proc. Int. Conf. (1993) Concrete 2000 University of Dundee, Scotland, UK, 7–9 Sept. eds R.K. Dhir and M.R. Jones, vol. 1 and 2, E & FN Spon, London, 1913 pp.

14.97. Aïtcin, P.C. (1990) Le développement des bétons à hautes performances en Amérique du Nord, in [14.67], 389–402.

14.98. Ghosh, S.K. (1991) High strength concrete in highly seismic regions, in The Second Canadian Symp. on Cem. and Concr., (ed. S. Mindess), The Univ. of B.C., Vancouver, 140–9.

14.99. RILEM (1992) Concrete Technology in the Future, RILEM Workshop, Espoo, 14–16. *Concrete Precasting Plant and Technology*, **11**, 44–53.

14.100. Eiger, A. (1933) High performance concrete (in Polish). *Cement*, **4**(1), 4–8.

14.101. Brandt, A.M. and Marks, M. (1993) Examples of the multicriteria optimization of cement-based composites. *Composite Structures*, **25**, 51–60.

14.102. Bickley, J.A. (1993) Prequalification requirements for the supply and testing of very high strength concrete. *Concrete International*, February, 62–64.

15 Application and development of cement-based composites

15.1 Conditions and main directions

15.1.1 IMPROVEMENT OF QUALITY

The great development of all kinds of cement-based materials was the result of their ability to satisfy new requirements in building and civil engineering structures. This chapter is devoted primarily to the consideration of new areas of application for advanced cement-based composites, traditional materials are not examined in full detail.

Improvement of quality of structural materials is a general trend which may be observed in our civilization. At different periods that trend has followed a steady continuous function or a step function. Advanced cement-based composites appeared a few years ago, and now represent a new generation of composite materials in building and civil engineering. Without doubt their application will be increased in many kinds of structures when special requirements are imposed. There are still, however, several problems which should be investigated to ensure further development.

15.1.2 PRINCIPAL DIRECTIONS OF APPLICATIONS

The main fields of present and future applications of cement-based composites besides ordinary concrete and reinforced concrete structures, are:

- heavy-duty pavements and industrial floors;
- airport overlays, runways, taxiways, etc.;
- nuclear energy reactor buildings;
- water and industrial waste-retaining structures;
- structures of tall buildings, particularly in seismic zones;
- long span bridges and other large structures;
- refractory elements;
- 'hot spots' in structures, e.g. hinges, free exits, etc.;
- different kinds of external claddings for buildings and tunnels;
- tunnels and slopes strengthening (shotcrete);
- repair of concrete structures in various situations.

15.1.3 MAIN PROPERTIES

Among the properties of cement composites, as compared with ordinary concretes, which decide upon the various applications mentioned above, are:

- improved resistance against cracking and fracture toughness;
- increased compressive and tensile strength;
- water and gas tightness and improved resistance against various types of corrosive agents;
- improved resistance against local spallings and destructions caused by excessive mechanical and thermal external actions;
- increased durability and longer lifecycle, related to all the above reasons;
- special features not related directly to high mechanical strength but required for special applications.

How properties of the advanced materials are presented to potential users and how these properties are obtained at full scale and in industrial production is also important.

15.1.4 CONDITIONS FOR FURTHER DEVELOPMENT

It may be foreseen that in the future the difference between ordinary materials and advanced cement composites like HPC (High Performance Concretes) and fibre-reinforced concretes will be increased. While the mass production of concretes of low and medium quality will be developed to achieve minimum cost through maximum use of industrialization and automation, special outstanding structures and elements will require higher performance materials. To satisfy that demand several conditions should be fulfilled [15.1]:

- transfer of information between research centre, design and building firms, producers of component materials, etc.;
- improvement of higher education by implementation of new methods and research results in educational programmes;
- improvement of the system of standards and approvals for new products and methods;
- improvement of life-costing of construction to take fully into account better performance and improvement durability.

Application of HPC and VHPC in building and civil engineering structures was the object of detailed reports containing descriptions of practical problems and proposed solutions, e.g. [15.2] and [15.3]; cf. also Section 14.5.6.

15.1.5 NEW COMPONENTS AND TECHNOLOGIES

In the mix composition of advanced cement-based materials, a few admixtures for improving their special properties in the fresh and in hardened state are normally included, cf. Section 4.3. In particular, different water reducers and fluidifiants are used in a large percentage of concrete production, [15.4], [15.5]. It is outside the scope of the book to describe them here in detail. Moreover, in different countries different products are available and are known under specific names.

It is worth mentioning that in the last few years much attention has been paid to the application of mineral admixtures like ground blast furnace slag, fly ash and various pozzolanic materials. That fact is probably justified by at least three reasons.

1. It appears that these admixtures, when carefully selected and correctly proportioned, impart considerable technical advantages to the resulting composites. Amongst these advantages better workability, lower heat exhaustion during hydration and improved resistance against chemical aggression may be included, cf. Section 4.3.9.
2. These are in most cases waste material, which is stored in large volumes in industrial regions and presents difficult problems for environmental protection in developed countries.
3. Partial replacement of Portland cement with mineral admixtures enables considerable savings, cf. Section 14.5.7.

Increasing application of these waste materials in advanced concretes requires further research aimed at standards and recommendations related to their quality and proper use. The reader is referred to specialized publications, e.g. [15.6], [15.7], [15.8].

New technologies should be considered from two viewpoints. The fresh mix may be prepared in different ways, improving final properties. In this respect special active mixing should be mentioned, e.g. by the use of so-called Omnimixers, as well as by the introduction of a superplasticizer to the mixing of the concrete in two or three portions in view of its prolonged action, cf. Section 14.5.4. On the other hand, in many cases special requirements are imposed, such as that of pumpability for longer distances or of self-levelling for industrial pavements. In such situations, selection of mix components and their proportions are conditioned by the methods of execution.

15.1.6 STANDARDS AND RECOMMENDATIONS

The application of advanced cement composites is still limited by lack of standards in many countries. For example, there are only few standards for concrete structures in which HPC is admitted with compressive strength after 28 days exceeding 50 to 60 MPa. In several published papers a request is expressed for design rules and materials provisions for high-strength concretes to be incorporated into national standards, e.g. in the USA [15.9]. In Norway a standard was adopted only in 1992 in which concrete strength up to 94 MPa was considered [15.10]. In France high strength of concretes is only partially introduced to standards BAEL 91 and BPEL 91 [15.11]. In other countries the lack of standards is a real difficulty for all applications, because designers should find and justify for their purposes all numerical data which are necessary for the design and detailing of structures.

A similar situation exists for special cement-based composites, like fibre-reinforced concretes or polymer concretes. Only a few examples of standards may be mentioned: in Japan [15.12], in France [15.13] and in Belgium [15.14].

In standards for advanced cement-based materials, a so-called performance format is needed. This means that the performance requirements define objectives in the form of properties in both the fresh and hardened state, durability, aspects and other features of quality without prescribing how these are to be obtained. On the other hand, the quality of advanced materials is a result of appropriate organization and control. The quality measures comprise a definition of requirements, organizational methods and control at every stage of material design, execution and curing. Here again specific standards should be developed, perhaps on the basis of ISO Standard [15.15]. According to John Ruskin 'Quality is never an accident. It is always the result of intelligent effort', and such an effort should be well organized.

The application of new methods of testing which are frequently used for advanced composites is often based on the recommendations of international organizations, because of lack of respective national documents. This is the case for two important documents prepared and published by RILEM for application of fracture mechanics to concrete elements and specimens [15.16], [15.17]. Both these draft recommendations are universally applied, even though they have no formal validity as standard documents.

Further development of national and international standards and recommendations is very important for future applications of advanced cement-based composites in building and civil engineering structures.

15.2 Non-structural applications

Several elements made of cement composites have no structural functions. It means that their mechanical role is either limited to supporting their own weight in service life and minor local loads, or that the structural role is important mostly during short periods of manufacturing, transportation and erection of structures. Non-structural elements made with cement-based composites represent a significant field of application in the construction industry and account for a large percent in mass and value. As examples various kinds of wall sandwich panels, claddings, industrial floors and architectural details may be mentioned.

Non-structural elements should satisfy several particular requirements and their rapid development is possible thanks to the use of large variety of special cements, fibres, admixtures and technologies.

15.2.1 ELEMENTS FOR LOW COST BUILDINGS

During the next 10–20 years ordinary concrete will remain the main construction material for low cost houses in developing countries [15.1]. The application of local raw materials and unqualified workers will be essential for solving the housing problem in large regions of the globe.

Low cost cement may be produced from the natural zeolite which is a rich resource and globally spread. As a soft mineral it requires less energy for milling. It may be used as replacement for the Portland cement for many applications where high strength is not required or as cement admixture.

The problems relating to safe and durable roofs for low cost houses are usually more difficult than those for walls and other elements of the house. For this reason various kinds of low cost fibre-reinforcement are used in regions where cellulose pulp (Nordic countries) and natural vegetable fibres (Tropical and Subtropical countries) are available [15.18], cf. also Sections 5.8 and 14.2.

15.2.2 LININGS OF TUNNELS

Lining of tunnels may be only partly considered as a non-structural element. The lining in coal mine tunnels was executed in Poland in the 60s by shotcreting with concrete with 1.5% volume of short steel-fibres [15.19]. Results are still excellent after over 20 years of service. Similar applications in coal mine tunnels in Canada was reported in [15.20] and [15.21]. In Norway, the lining for road and railway tunnels is also executed using a wet-process of shotcrete and steel-fibres as a dispersed reinforcement [15.22]. With a dosage of about 1–1.2% of Dramix or EE fibres the following results were achieved:

- a reduction of construction time from 3 weeks in the case of a cast lining to 3–4 days;
- a reduction of the costs by half;
- improved ductility of the lining, which was put directly on the rough surface of the rock.

The difference between standard shotcrete reinforcement and steel-fibre-reinforced shotcrete is that the mesh reinforcement should be fixed at a certain distance from the uneven surface of the rock, while the steel-fibre-reinforced shotcrete is put directly on the rock surface. Hence, additional fixing operations are avoided and there are no void spaces behind the shotcreted layer, cf. [15.20] and [15.23], where many applications are quoted: mines, road and railway tunnels, slope stabilization, repair and rehabilitation works and so on in Europe, North America, Southern Asia and Japan.

Thin claddings with or without fibre-reinforcement, also curved in the form of shells, are precast as:

- roofing sheets, panels and tiles for facades, etc.;
- certain walls made of fibre-reinforced cement and of ferrocement;
- wave absorbers and anti-ballistic panels;
- permanent forms.

Claddings and curtain walls reinforced with carbon fibres were used in Japan with good results: reduction of thickness was made possible because of higher strength, toughness and better fibre resistance [15.24].

Claddings reinforced with glassfibres are used for facades, and precast blocks for retaining walls. Cladding panels are usually produced by the spray-up process with dimensions up to a few metres and a depth 5–15 mm, [15.25]. Alkali-resistant glassfibres are used as a reinforcement even when their long-term durability is not perfectly assured. In many cases the reinforcement is needed only or mostly during execution, transportation and construction. Later, when fixed onto walls, these elements do not need to support loads and poor durability of ordinary glassfibres in the cement-based matrix may be sufficient as it does not determine the durability of all structures. Glassfibres are applied also as reinforcement for matrices other than Portland cement: gypsum, high alumina cement, etc.

Extensive efforts in research and technology led to positive results concerning the durability of glassfibre reinforced cement elements. A combination of modifications in the matrix composition and an improvement of the properties of the fibres enabled the use of these composites taking into account their long-term durability, [15.26], [15.27], cf. also Section 5.3. For example, glass-reinforced cement thin plates are used as elements of partition walls, which may be subjected to accidental impacts.

Polymeric low-modulus fibres are added for crack control during execution in claddings, tiles and decorations made of products known under various trade names like Caircrete and Faircrete in the United Kingdom [15.28]. The matrix with these fibres in the fresh state may be easily formed in various shapes. In several cases where the strength and toughness of cladding is required, the hybrid combinations of fibres (carbon + steel, carbon + polypropylene, etc.) are applied, for example for harbour facilities, channel linings or lining of oil-storage caverns. Polypropylene fibres are extensively used for control of microcracking due to thermal and shrinkage strain, cf. Section 5.6. Thus, the large variety of available fibres gives the possibility for tailoring the cement-based composites for different applications.

15.2.3 PERMANENT FORMWORKS

Cement-based composites are used to precast permanent formworks for construction of large scale bridges and industrial halls. Formwork in the form of plane or ribbed sheets is placed directly on to main girders and the slab may be cast directly onto it. The ribs in the slab may be formed by profiling the sheets or by the inclusion of polystyrene void formers [15.29]. Permanent formworks with glassfibre reinforcement are also used to produce precast concrete blocks for retaining walls. In all these cases long-term durability of glass fibres is not necessary.

15.3 Repair and rehabilitation of concrete structures

The concrete structures deteriorate by climatic, physical, chemical and mechanical actions of different kinds. The outdoor structures are particularly exposed.

The main reason for destruction of concrete structures is corrosion of reinforcement, due to increasing intensity of the detrimental influence of polluted air and water, extensive use of de-icing salts on roads, frequent errors in execution of concrete structures and so on. Cracking and spalling caused by internal pressure exerted by corrosion products are by far the most frequent reason of reconstruction of structures [15.30], [15.31]. It is essential that in repair all possible sources of steel corrosion are consequently stopped; these may be by depassivation of concrete cover by advanced carbonation, chloride attack, cracks with excessive width and so on. Long-term impermeability of repair material is the condition which may be satisfied by high quality repair materials, e.g. fibre-reinforced mortars and concretes, polymer modified concretes, etc.

Compatibility of repair materials and existing substrate is another important condition for a successful repair. Compatibility should be considered analytically and then experimentally verified both in the laboratory and *in situ* [15.32]. The interface between new and old material should ensure that all stresses are safely transferred which unavoidably appear due to mechanical and hygrothermal actions.

The problems related to repair and rehabilitation of structures are of great importance in many countries. For example, the highway infrastructure in the USA is in a state of severe deterioration and thousands of bridges require repair and rehabilitation because of climatic-induced stresses, corrosion of reinforcing steel and repeated overloading [15.33]. In Japan the high amount of salt in the air and frequent alkali–aggregate reactions are the main reasons for degradation of structures. In Poland, low quality of execution of bridges in the 50s and 60s, as well as difficult climatic conditions, characterized by a large number of freezing and thawing cycles in a year, are probably the most detrimental factors. Similar situations in all kinds of outdoor structures are observed in other countries, where different specific reasons occur. As a result, the repair and rehabilitation of concrete structures requires large funds from local and central budgets. The appropriate methods for repair which may assure high durability, together with technical and economical feasibility in various conditions are developed and improved in many research centres over the world.

Modified cement-based matrices of various kinds were tested in view of application for surface repair of concrete structures. Several compositions were used.

1. Latexes based on styrene–butadiene, acrylic and other co-polymers, with the amount of latex solids to cement mass from 5 to 20%.
2. Dry polymers such as vinyl acetate and vinyl versatic acid.
3. Microfillers, i.e. mainly silica fume (SF).
4. Alkaline-resistent glassfibre and polymeric low modulus fibres.

Layers of composite mortars with latexes and SF varied from 6 to 250 mm in depth and were applied by a wet shotcrete method on walls and on overhead shotcreted slabs. The following mechanical properties were obtained [15.34]:

- modulus of rupture 5–13 MPa
- compressive strength 35–55 MPa
- tensile strength 3.5–4.8 MPa.

Good resistance to freeze/thaw cycles and chemical attack due to high density and very low permeability was also obtained. Carbonation and chloride ions penetration are strongly decreased [15.35]. Layers of thickness over 12 mm exhibited sufficient strength and ductility to bridge and waterproof the substrate cracks. Increased adhesion to substrate material, i.e. old concrete, was excellent provided that the surface was cleaned and wetted. The adhesion was tested using tensile and shear bond specimens.

Application of Latex Modified Concretes (LMC) for repair of outdoor structures is developing and in the report [15.36] several successful case studies are presented. They concern following structures:

- bridge desk overlays,
- pavements and stadiums,
- thin coatings of swimming pools,
- liners for pipelines, etc.

LMC appeared to be easy to place using various methods related to local conditions and dimensions of the projects: from pumping to mobile mixers and drum mixers for small size works.

Rapid set cements of various kinds are applied for repair work in view of the decreasing of duration of works and inconvenience for the users. As examples, Regulated Set Portland Cement in the USA and Pyrament Cement in Canada may be quoted. Over 20 MPa of compressive strength is already assured after 3 hours of setting and over 40 MPa in 24 hours.

Steel-fibres are used for tunnelling, mining and concrete repair and glass-fibres as a reinforcement for cement mortar. Polymeric fibres are used mostly for control of the shrinkage cracking of external layers.

In Poland an extensive programme of research was initiated in 1990 to prepare a set of appropriate methods of repair for concrete bridges, including application of steel-fibre-reinforced composites, using traditional placing of the fresh mix, patching and shotcreting. The first applications confirmed the advantages of SFRC. The research also covers basic problems of the strength and durability of the old/new material interface, which is essential for the quality of the repair works [15.37] and [15.38].

Both main methods of shotcreting are used in repair works with additional modifications. Dry shotcrete is based on mixing components with water in the nozzle. It results in high rebound and heavy dusting, which is detrimental for the workers' health, particularly in closed spaces. Wet shotcrete is mixed with water before projecting. If used, overhead areas require high amount of set accelerator which in turn decreases the strength. A mortar modified with polymers and silica fume and reinforced with fibres is often applied by the wet process. The fibre-reinforced shotcrete is used extensively for different repair works, like tunnel and channel linings, water storage and treatment facilities, bridge decks, piers and abutments, retaining walls, etc.

In many cases the repair of a structure may be limited to casting a new external layer of highly impermeable material with properties carefully adjusted to those of the substrate. In other cases, however, it is essential that new material takes part in the load bearing. Then, active and durable connections are to be foreseen to ensure transfer of load on to new material. For example, increasing the load-carrying capacity of reinforced concrete beams may be realized by different methods:

1. bonding steel plates to the beam,
2. applying external post-tensioned tendons,
3. providing a jacket of reinforced concrete over the existing host member [15.39].

These problems exceed the scope of the book and the reader may consult specialized publications such as [15.40]. Interesting remarks on the economical and organizational sides of repair works, together with binding procedure and assurance of quality, are given amongst others in [15.41].

15.4 Development of research and testing methods

In the last few years rapid development of methods of testing and observation in the field of cement-based composites enables present knowledge about processes and influences of different parameters to be considerably extended. Certain methods are imported from the mechanics of high strength composites and ceramics. A few examples of these methods are used in various research centres[1].

Optical fluorescence microscopes are applied to observe specially prepared specimens subjected to tension. The specimens are vacuum impregnated with fluorescent dye resins and then thin sections are prepared. The images obtained are analysed and as a result quantitative measurements of systems of microcracks can be obtained.

Environmental Scanning Electron Microscope (ESEM) makes possible the observation of wet specimens. Thus, without drying the specimens the hydration processes in cement paste may be analysed and formation of the microcracks may be observed, cf. Figure 10.21.

Extensive application of computer image analysis to various kinds of images and diagrams obtained by different methods leads to quantitative results in several tests where until last year qualitative results were available only.

[1] e.g. The National Science Foundation Center for Science and Technology of Advanced Cement-Based Materials, USA, National Institute of Standards and Technology, Gaithersburg, MD, USA and the Laboratoire Central des Ponts et Chaussées, Paris, France.

Simulating models have been developed to represent various processes in the microstructure, among others the hydration of cement, intrusion of mercury into pore systems, etc. Two- and three-dimensional simulations allow not only quick and inexpensive verification of the influence of different conditions on examined processes but also demonstrate them to students in an extremely instructive way.

Acoustic emission source location and analysis enables us to distinguish the place and origin of recorded effects. Thus matrix cracking, fibre debonding and other mechanisms of material damage may be separated and analysed.

These few examples concern the observation of the microstructure of cement-based composites, which is considered essential for understanding basic processes determining the final properties of these materials, cf. Chapter 6. It is therefore possible to improve the microstructure, to obtain for example:

- segmentation of pores to avoid or at least to reduce permeability,
- densification of microstructure leading to higher strength,
- homogenization of interfacial zones which determine the overall properties of the material.

It is well understood thanks to these and other results of basic research that the microstructure may be modified by deflocculation of cement grains which can slide and move for better packing. In such a system the finest particles, like those of silica fume, may find their position around cement grains, cf. Figure 14.18. Deflocculation is possible with the application of high-range water-reducers (superplasticizers) which create negative electrostatic charges on cement grains thus causing high repulsion forces between them. It has been shown that the densifying effect of microfillers is probably more important for the final quality and strength of the composite material than the pozzolanic properties of certain microfillers (Goldman and Bentur [15.42]). By use of carbon blank particles which are chemically inactive instead of silica fume, the obtained effect in composite strength was practically the same. The possibility of replacing silica fume for HPC is of great importance because of the limited availability and rising price of this admixture, cf. Sections 14.4 and 14.5.

The importance of the interface between aggregate grains and cement paste is better understood. Because of the small distances between grains in the dense microstructure of high performance concretes, the interfacial zones extending approximately up to 50 μm from the grains in fact occupy the most of so-called bulk cement paste. The main effort in improving the overall composite properties by modification of the microstructure is therefore concentrated at the interfacial zones and this means the decrease of porosity, reduction of local agglomerations of ettringite and calcium hydroxide and avoidance of orientation of crystals parallel to contours of grains [15.43].

The large variety of new components, new methods of research and testing and advanced possibilities of modellization, together with improved methods of execution on site, create a real development of cement-based materials towards ceramics and high strength composites. That trend is expressed among others by joint symposia, e.g. BMC1 (1985), BMC2 (1988), BMC3 (1991) and BMC4 (1994) [15.44], organized together with specialists dealing with all kinds of brittle materials.

15.5 Research needs

Considerable effort in aim-oriented research is still needed to evaluate the applications of advanced cement-based materials. Notwithstanding recent achievements, many pressing questions are not yet solved.

Selection of components and their proportions are in most cases based on consecutive trials. There is room for considerable improvement of the material design by application of the optimization approach, in which objective indications are obtained, cf. Chapter 13. Also, the compatibility between particular components should be determined together *a priori* with their efficiency and not observed afterwards as a result of success or failure. This concerns cements, admixtures, microfillers and fibres which introduced together in a mix may cause positive or negative synergetic effects.

At present the design and execution methods of cement-based composites are strongly limited to a few given components and technological procedures. They are in fact reduced to certain generalization of test results with numerical coefficients obtained from curve fitting. The proposed formulae for the forecast of strength and toughness needs large test programs in which these coefficients can be determined. In big precasting factories and execution firms the design formulae are restricted for local conditions and internal use, and are not published. Such a situation reduces to some extent the spreading of design methods, their open discussion and further development. The proportioning of advanced and high performance materials cannot be entirely based on empiricism, because application of a large variety of cements, different admixtures, dispersed reinforcement and various technologies for mixing, compaction and other execution operations is not compatible with trial-and-error design methods. New methods based on expert systems, optimization approach and neural networks are developing [15.45].

In material testing a breakthrough is expected also. Generally adopted test methods and acceptance requirements should open possibilities for international exchange and cooperation in the design and execution of elements and structures of cement-based composites. The testing recommendations proposed by regional (ASTM, CEN) and world (RILEM, CEB, ISO) organizations cover only selected types of materials and are not universally recognized. New kinds of materials, like high performance concretes, require special methods and special equipment. For example, traditional types of hydraulic press, used in laboratories on site for control testing of concrete specimens, are often not sufficient for specimens made of high strength materials. Standardized interfacial layers (capping) between steel plates and tested concrete specimens subjected to compression should also have higher strength.

Important features such as material durability should be tested using accelerated methods to predict the effects of used components and technologies in given conditions.

The execution methods of cement–matrix composites were initially based exclusively on traditional operations developed for low and medium quality concretes. With the increasing variety of components and final products those methods proved to be insufficient and inappropriate. Hence, they should be continuously developed and improved. It is recognized that because of large volumes of produced materials, types of used components and conditions of production the methods should be relatively simple and as far as possible insensible to the technological variations of composition, quality of components and conditions of execution and care. Several particular composite materials like SIFCON and use of admixtures like condensed silica fume require special technologies. Well defined execution procedures are needed for materials which satisfy special requirements, e.g. air-entrained concretes with improved resistance against freezing and thawing cycles.

Special execution methods in which fresh mix is pumped at long distances or projected directly on to the substrate need specialized test methods to establish their efficiency and influence on properties of the final product. Problems of their economical validity and possible effects on the health of workers are also necessary.

The needed research directions are briefly summarized in Table 15.1. The present research programmes aimed at larger application of the cement-based composites are directed at following aims:

- low life-cycle cost of buildings, including all components of the cost,
- safety and serviceability of ordinary structures, ensuring full satisfaction of conditions imposed by users,
- large possibilities of upgrading and modification (increase of service load, change of functions and dimensions),
- fulfilment of non-conventional conditions and requirements (lunar concretes, structures exposed on severe climatic actions, elements serving in nuclear energy industry, etc.),
- low cost building for developing countries, where the application of local raw materials and non-qualified staffing is imposed,
- fulfilment of ecological requirements, concerning low energy consumption in construction and maintenance, use of waste materials and elimination of detrimental products.

These are probably the main challenges to which cement-based composites will furnish adequate solutions in the future.

The results of the RILEM Workshop [15.1] and of other gatherings of that kind organized in recent years indicate a special role in the future development played by HPC and VHPC. To make these advanced materials fully available

Table 15.1 Aim-oriented research in the cement-based materials

Research directions	Aims to be achieved
Materials science	New components
	Synergism of components
	Micro- and macro-structural effects
	Stress concentrations in interfaces
	Porosity
Design of materials	Objective methods of material design
	Computerization of material design
	Exploitation of statistical data
	Optimization approach
Design of structures	Quantitative data
	Long term behaviour
Execution and cure	Improved workability as one of main features
	Full application of available admixtures
	Low energy consumption
	Decrease of scatter of properties
Test methods	Standardization of test methods
	Relation between properties of specimens and of material in structure
	Testing of structures in natural scale
	Accelerated test methods and evaluation of durability
Economical methods	Evaluation of life-cycle cost
	Optimization of maintenance operations

in a few countries, large programmes of basic and applied research have been realized since the late 80s. Involvement of all parties and reliable financial support from the producers and governmental bodies was necessary. The aim was clearly formulated: to obtain standardized mixes and their properties from ready mix concrete plants or on the site.

All the above-mentioned problems should be solved for designers and builders and this means that realistic test conditions should be applied and quantitative answers are needed. Only such answers enable a designer to determine the dimensions of elements, to establish values of prestressing force, to calculate displacements and thus to prove serviceability and safety of the structure. Also precise instructions for execution and curing of HPC are required. Notwithstanding present achievements future research, oriented at applications, is still needed to support and develop the use of cement-based composites in building and civil engineering.

References

15.1. RILEM Workshop (1992) 'Concrete Technology in the Future', Espoo, 14–16 September 1992, *Concrete Precasting Plant and Technology*, **11**, 44–53.

15.2. Malier, Y. (ed.) (1990) *Les bétons à hautes performances. Du matériau à l'ouvrage.* Presses de l'ENPC, Paris.

15.3. Malier, Y. (ed.) (1992) *Les bétons à hautes performances. Caractérisation, durabilité, application.* Presses de l'ENPC, Paris.

15.4. *Chemical Admixtures for Concrete* (1991) ACI Committee Report 212.3R-91, American Concrete Institute, Detroit, 31 pp.

15.5. Guide for the use of high-range water-reducing admixtures (superplasticizers) in concrete (1993) ACI Committee Report 212.4R. *Concrete International*, April, 40–7.

15.6. Guide for selecting proportions for high-strength concretes with Portland cement and fly ash (1991) ACI Committee Report 211.4R. ACI *Materials Journal*, May/June 272–83.

15.7. Swamy, R.N. (1993) Fly ash and slag: standards and specifications – help or hindrance? *Materials and Structures*, RILEM, **26**, 600–13.

15.8. Massazza, F. (1993) Pozzolanic cements. *Cement & Concrete Composites*, **15**(4), 185–14.

15.9. Lane, S.N. and Podolny, W., Jr. (1993) The federal outlook for high strength concrete bridges. *PCI Journal*, **38**(3), 20–33.

15.10. NS 3473E (1992) Concrete Structures. Design Rules. Norges Standardiserings-forbund, 4th ed. Oslo, November 1992, 78 pp.

15.11. Pliskin, L. (1992) Béton à hautes performances: aspects réglementaires, in [15.3], 243–52.

15.12. Recommendation for Design and Construction of Steel Fiber Reinforced Concrete (1983) Concrete Library, no. 50, Jap. Soc. of Civ. Eng., Tokyo, March.

15.13. (1993) Béton avec fibres métalliques. Essai de flexion. AFNOR, Paris, 18–409.

15.14. (1992) Essais des bétons renforcés de fibres. Essai de flexion sur éprouvettes prismatiques, NBN B 15-238, IBN, Bruxelles.

15.15. ISO Standard 9000 (1987) Quality management and quality assurance. Guidelines for selection and use. International Organization for Standardization, Geneva.

15.16. Determination of fracture parameters (K_{Ic}^{s} and $CTOD_c$) of plain concrete using three-point bend test (1990) RILEM Draft Recommendation, TC 89-FMT Fracture Mechanics of Concrete – Test Methods. *Materials and Structures*, RILEM, **23**, 457–60.

15.17. Size-effect method for determining fracture energy and process zone size of concrete (1990) RILEM Draft Recommendation, TC 89-FMT Fracture Mechanics of Concrete – Test Methods. *Materials and Structures*, RILEM, **23**, 461–5.

15.18. Gram, H.E., Persson, H. and Skarendahl, Å. (1984) *Natural fibre concrete.* Swedish Agency for Research Cooperation with Developing Countries, Stockholm.

15.19. Sikorski, C. (1961) Steel-fibre-reinforced concrete (in Polish), Patent Nr. 58128, kl. 80a, 51.

15.20. Morgan, D.R. (1991) Use of steel-fibre-reinforced shotcrete in Canada, in: *Proc. 1st Canadian University-Industry Workshop on Fibre Reinforced Concrete*, Univ. Laval, Quebec, 164–82.

15.21. Wood, D.F. (1991) Application of fibre-reinforced shotcrete in tunnelling, as [15.20], 183–96.

15.22. Concrete for the World (1990) FIP-NB, Norwegian Concrete Engineering, Oslo.

15.23. Dramix (1990) Information publication by NV Bekaert International Trade SA Zwevegen, Belgium.

15.24. Ohama, Y., Amano, M. and Endo, M. (1983) Properties of carbon fiber-reinforced cement with silica fume. *Concrete International*, **7**(3), 58–62.

15.25. Hannant, D.J. (1978) *Fibre Cements and Fibre Concretes*, John Wiley & Sons, Chichester.

15.26. Majumdar, A.J. and Laws, V. (1991) *Glass fibre-reinforced cement*. Oxford BSP Professional Books, London.

15.27. Glinicki, M.A., Vautrin, A., Soukatchoff, P. and François-Brazier, J. (1983) Impact performance of glassfibre reinforced cement plates subjected to accelerated ageing, in: Proc. 9th Biennial Congress of the Glassfibre Reinforced Cement Association, Copenhagen, Denmark 13–17 June 1993, London.

15.28. Brandt, A.M. (ed.) (1974) *Mechanical Properties and Structure of Concrete-like Composites* (in Polish), Proc. of Study Session in Jabłonna, November, Ossolineum, Wrocław, 18–23.

15.29. Raithby, K.D., Galloway, J.W. and Williams, R.I.T. (1981) Polypropylene reinforced cement composites for surface reinforcement of concrete structures. *The Int. J. of Chem. Comp. and Lightweight Concr.*, **3**(4), 237–46.

15.30. Vaysburd, A.M. (1993) Some durability considerations for evaluating and repairing concrete structures. *Concrete International*, March, 29–35.

15.31. Hime, W.G. (1993) Corrosion of steel – random thoughts and wishful thinking. *Concrete International*, **15**(10), October, 54–7.

15.32. Emmons, P.H., Vaysburd, A.M. and McDonald, J.E. (1993) A rational approach to durable concrete repairs. *Concrete International*, September, 40–5.

15.33. Kelsey, R.A. (1991) Traffic ready concrete in 3 hours with regulated set Portland cement, in *Proc. of. The Second Canadian Symp. on Cement and Concrete*, S. Mindess (ed.), The Univ. of Brit. Columbia, Vancouver, 32–5.

15.34. Razl, I. (1991) Novel materials for concrete restoration, in *Proc. 1st Canadian University-Industry Workshop on Fibre Reinforced Concrete*, Univ. Laval, Quebec, 118–28.

15.35. Ohama, Y., Moriwaki, T. and Shiroishida, K. (1984) Weatherability of polymer-modified mortars through ten-year outdoor exposure, in *Proc. Int. Congr. of Polymers in Concrete*, September, Darmstadt.

15.36. State-of-the-Art Report on Polymer-Modified Concrete (1991), Amer. Concr. Inst. Comm. 548, Report 3R-91, Detroit.

15.37. Brandt, A.M., Burakiewicz, A., Potrzebowski, J. and Skawinski, M. (1992) Application of steel-fibre-reinforced mortars for repairs (in Polish), Proc. Conf. *Modern Methods of Reconstruction and Strengthening of Bridges*, Poznan (not published).

15.38. Brandt, A.M. and Potrzebowski, J. (1992) Premature deterioration of concrete in bridges and other outdoor structures and methods of repair, in Proc. Int. Conf. '*Concrete 92*', Tehran University, 667–81.

15.39. Liew, S.C. and Cheong, H.K. (1991) Flexural behaviour of jacketed RC beams. *Concrete International*, **13**(12), 43–7.

15.40. Nanni, A. and Dolan, C.W. (eds) (1993) Fiber-reinforced-plastic reinforcement for concrete structures, Int. Symp. March 28–31, 1993, Vancouver, American Concrete Institute SP-138, Detroit, 997 pp.

15.41. Dikeou, J.T. and Schrader, E.K. (1981) Polymer modified glassfiber reinforced mortar coatings protect navigation lock walls, in *Proc. 3rd Int. Congr. on Polymers in Concrete*, **1**, Koriyama, 331–46.

15.42. Goldman, A. and Bentur, A. (1993) The influence of microfiller on enhancement of concrete strength. *Cement and Concrete Research*, **23**(4), 962–72.

15.43. Mehta, P.K. and Monteiro, P.J.M. (1993) Concrete: Structure, Properties and Materials, 2nd ed., Prentice-Hall, Inc., Englewood Cliffs, N.J., 548 pp.

15.44. Brandt, A.M. and Marshall, I.H., (eds) Proc. of Int. Symp. Brittle Matrix Composites 1 (1985), 2 (1988), 3 (1991), Elsevier Applied Science, London 4 (1994), Woodhead and IKE, Cambridge and Warsaw.

15.45. Brandt, A.M. (1993) RILEM 3C Workshop 'Optimization of Concrete Mix Design, Warsaw, 17–18 May 1993. *Materials and Structures*, RILEM, **26**, 441–2.

Author index

Authors' names are given when they appear in the text, in the figure subscripts and legends. The names of authors and editors in the reference lists are also included.

Subject index

Subjects in the main text, tables, subscripts and figures are given by page number. Entries repeated on consecutive pages are only given by the first page.